How to Do *Everything* with Adobe® Acrobat® 8

Doug Sahlin

Mc Graw Hill

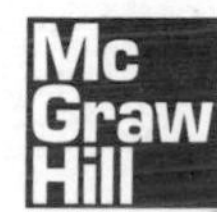

New York Chicago San Francisco L
London Madrid Mexico City Milan N
San Juan Seoul Singapore Sydne

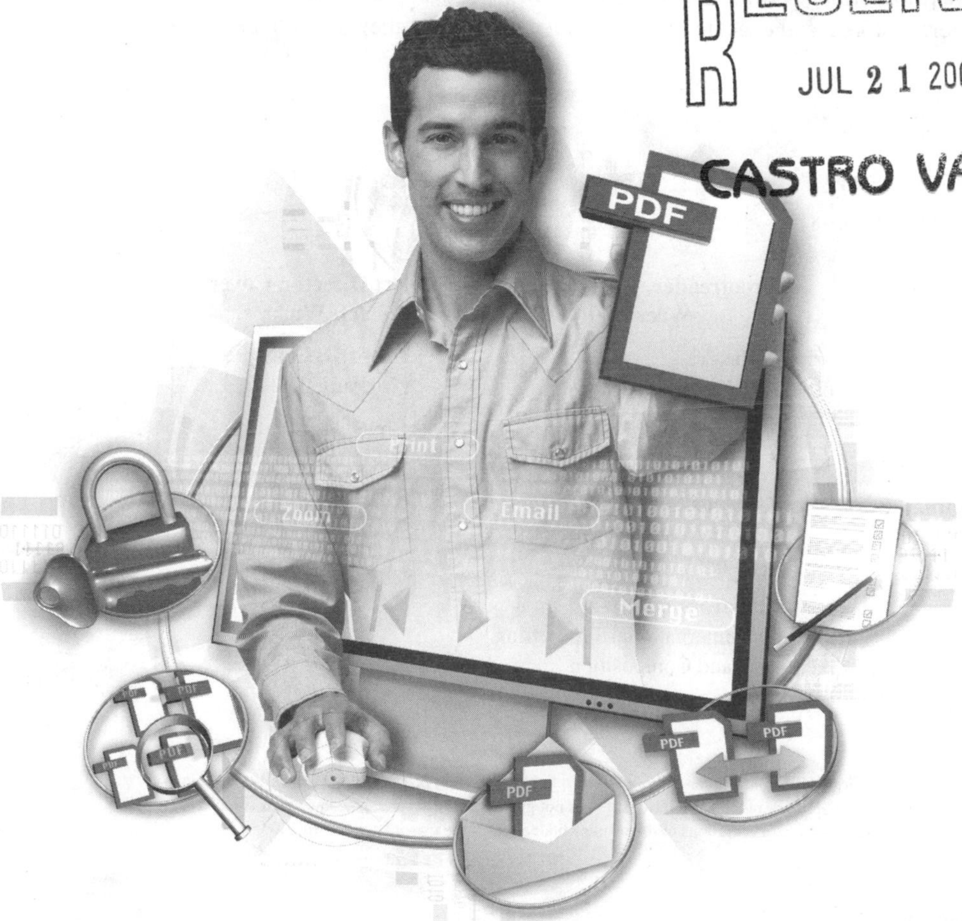

The McGraw-Hill Companies

Cataloging-in-Publication Data is on file with the Library of Congress

McGraw-Hill books are available at special quantity discounts to use as premiums and sales promotions, or for use in corporate training programs. For more information, please write to the Director of Special Sales, Professional Publishing, McGraw-Hill, Two Penn Plaza, New York, NY 10121-2298. Or contact your local bookstore.

How to Do Everything with Adobe® Acrobat® 8

1234567890 FGR FGR 01987

ISBN-13: 978-0-07-226393-0
ISBN-10: 0-07-226393-8

Sponsoring Editor
Roger Stewart

Editorial Supervisor
Patty Mon

Project Manager
Vasundhara Sawhney

Acquisitions Coordinator
Carly Stapleton

Technical Editor
Dave Wraight

Copy Editor
Marcia Baker

Proofreader
Bev Wiler

Indexer
Kevin Broccoli

Production Supervisor
George Anderson

Composition
International Typesetting and Composition

Illustration
International Typesetting and Composition

Art Director, Cover
Jeff Weeks

Cover Designer
Pattie Lee

Cover Illustration
Jacey

Dedicated to the memory of Barry Murphy and Susan Polito, good friends who left this mortal plane way too early.

About the Author

Doug Sahlin is an author and Acrobat instructor living in Lakeland, Florida. He has written 16 books on computer applications and digital photography, including the popular *How to Do Everything with Adobe Acrobat 7.0*. Doug is also a professional photographer and the author of *Digital Photography QuickSteps*. In addition, he has written and co-written books on video-editing and image-editing applications. Sahlin has taught businesses and government organizations how to create paperless offices with Adobe Acrobat.

Contents

Acknowledgments

Even though a single name appears on this book cover, this book would not be possible without a large supporting cast. Many thanks to Roger Stewart for making this project possible. Thanks to Carly Stapleton for making sure the chapters and accompanying illustrations were delivered to the proper parties at the right time. Thanks to Patty Mon for spearheading this project and making sure that the words you read are squeaky clean. Thanks to Dave Wraight, the tech editor from down under. Congratulations to Adobe for releasing another stellar version of Acrobat with significant new features and enhancements. Thanks to Margot Maley Hutchison for handling the fine print and being a super agent.

Thanks to fellow authors, Bonnie Blake, Joyce Evans and Ken Milburn for being sources of inspiration, good friends and stellar citizens of this planet. Special thanks to my friends, mentors and family members, especially you Ted and Karen.

Introduction

Welcome to *How to Do Everything with Adobe Acrobat 8*. Acrobat continues to be the premier solution for electronic publishing. Acrobat makes it possible for you to convert documents to PDF (Portable Document Format) files that retain the look and feel of the original document. PDF files can be viewed with the full version of Acrobat, or the free Adobe Reader.

Acrobat 8.0 comes in two flavors: Standard and Professional. This book covers both versions. When a section pertains to the Professional version only, this will be noted with a parenthetical reference. This book is divided into four parts. The first part of this book is an introduction to Acrobat, where you'll also find information about the exciting new features in this release and information about the workspace. The second section of this book gives you the nuts and bolts that you need to convert documents into the PDF format as well as how to convert web pages to the PDF format. In this third part of this book you'll find information on editing and reviewing PDF document as well as how to add security to PDF documents. The fourth part of this book contains information that pertains to the Professional version of Acrobat. Here you'll find information on how to create sophisticated forms, how to incorporate multimedia elements into PDF files, and much more. In the appendixes, you'll find all of the Acrobat keyboard shortcuts and Acrobat internet resources.

Part I

Welcome to Adobe Acrobat 8.0

Chapter 1

Get to Know Adobe Acrobat 8.0

How to...

- Utilize the power of Acrobat
- Create PDF documents
- Create PDF documents for the Web
- Capture web sites as PDF documents
- Optimize PDF documents

Most computer users are familiar with Acrobat in some form or another. People who've never experienced the full power of Acrobat think it's the application that pops up when they double-click a file with the .pdf (Portable Document Format) extension. That little gem is some iteration of the Adobe Reader. But there's much more to Acrobat than the Reader. Major corporations, software manufacturers, and businesses use the full version of Acrobat to create and publish documents for electronic distribution. Forms are another important feature of Acrobat. Interactive forms can be created in Acrobat Professional or Adobe LiveCycle Designer (Windows only) and distributed online. Forms can be filled in with Acrobat Professional, Acrobat Standard, and Adobe Reader 6.0 or newer (provided the author has enabled form fill in using the Adobe Reader). The fact that you're reading this book probably means you either own the full version of Acrobat 8.0 Standard or Acrobat 8.0 Professional, or will soon purchase either program to create interactive PDF documents that retain the appearance of the original document.

If you've used Acrobat before, you know it's chock-full of features—so many features that it takes a while to learn them all. If you're brand new to Acrobat, the prospect of publishing sophisticated electronic documents might seem a bit daunting. As you read this book, though, you learn to harness the power of whichever version of Acrobat you own to create and publish electronic documents you never thought possible. Whether you need to create a simple electronic memo, an employee manual, an indexed electronic catalog, or a sophisticated form, Acrobat is the tool for you.

In this chapter, you also learn about the different components that come with Acrobat and the many uses for the software. If you just upgraded from Acrobat 7.0, you likely already noticed many changes to the software. If you're an experienced Acrobat user, you may be tempted to skip this chapter. However, even if you're an Acrobat publishing veteran, I suggest you browse through this chapter, especially when you consider the numerous new features, new tools, additional menu commands, enhanced features, and so on. As you read this chapter, you may discover an application for the program that you never knew existed. As you learn about the new features and enhanced functionality of Acrobat 8.0, you may develop ideas of how to best utilize Acrobat 8.0 for your publishing needs.

About Adobe Acrobat

Adobe Acrobat has been around for some time now. Adobe created the product for individuals and corporations that needed to publish documents for distribution in electronic format (which became known as *ePaper* after Acrobat had been out for a while). The original goal was to create a paperless office.

The application made it possible for authors to distribute electronic documents that had the look and feel of the original document. A PDF file can be viewed by anyone, on any computer, with the only required software being the Adobe Reader. Adobe accomplished this goal, and then some.

Early versions of Acrobat found great favor with software manufacturers who used Acrobat to create electronic manuals for their products. The manuals could easily be bundled on program installation disks with a free copy of what is now known as Adobe Reader. Many software manufacturers opted to publish program manuals only in PDF format. Software companies selling applications with manuals published in this manner saved on packaging and shipping costs, enabling them to price their software more competitively. Help manuals published in PDF format are easy to navigate and read. Figure 1-1 shows a brochure that was created using Adobe InDesign and exported as a PDF file, as viewed in Acrobat Professional.

As Acrobat grew in popularity, Adobe added more features to the product. Newer versions of the software featured enhanced usability, the addition of document security, and the capability

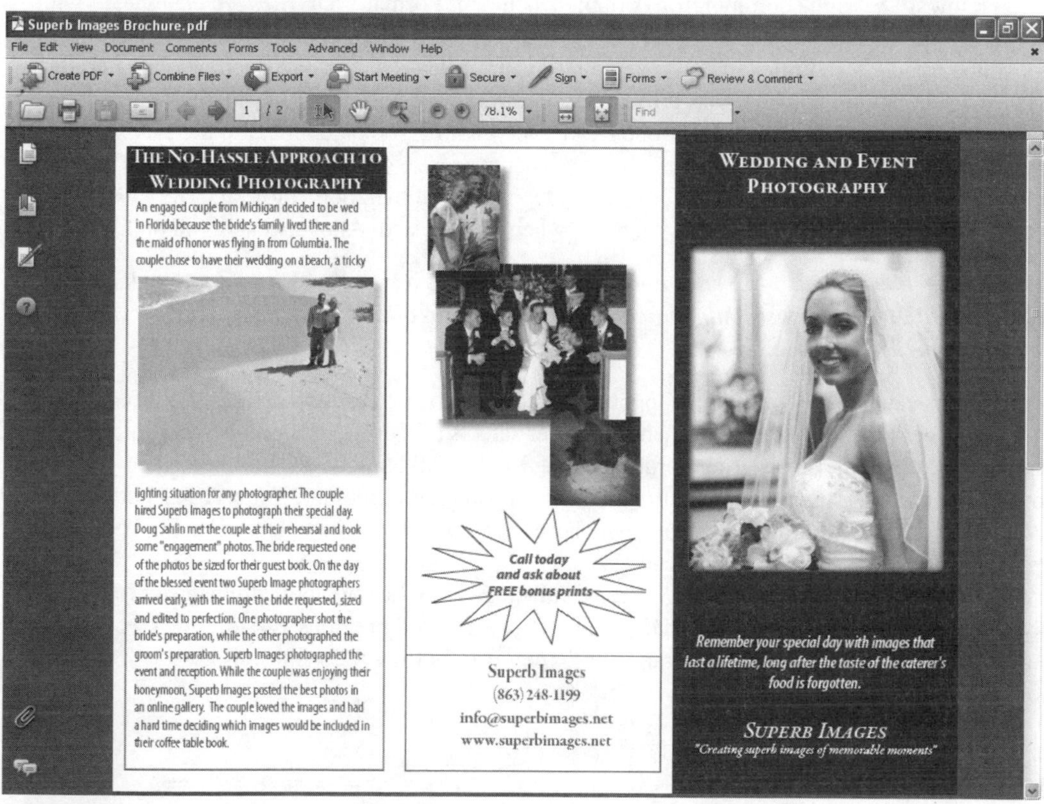

FIGURE 1-1 PDF documents can be viewed in Acrobat Standard, Acrobat Professional, or the Adobe Reader.

to create a searchable index of multiple PDF documents. Users of the software found new applications for PDF documents; the documents soon appeared as corporate memos, portable product catalogs, and multimedia presentations for salespeople. Most popular browsers support the Adobe Reader plug-in, so many companies post PDF documents on their web sites. The PDF acronym aptly describes the published file, as it is truly a portable document, viewable by anybody with Adobe Reader 6.0, Adobe Reader 7.0, Adobe Reader 8.0, or earlier versions of the Acrobat Reader installed on their computers. The Adobe Reader used to be called Acrobat. However, too many users confused the Acrobat utility used to read PDF documents with the full version of Acrobat that's used to author PDF documents. To end the confusion, Adobe changed the name to Adobe Reader.

About the PDF Format

If you've used computers for any length of time, you're probably familiar with the PDF format. As you know, PDF is the acronym for Portable Document Format. PDF files are designated with the .pdf file extension, and are, indeed, portable. You can view them on any computer with the free Adobe Reader 8.0. For example, if someone sends you a PDF file of a document created on a Macintosh computer using Adobe InDesign, you can view it on a Windows PC that has Adobe Reader 8.0. The file you view with Adobe Reader 8.0 on a PC looks identical to the PDF file published on the Macintosh computer. All the elements used to create the file on the Mac are saved when the author exports, prints, or saves (depending on the application) the file to PDF format, which is the reason it appears identical when viewed with Adobe Reader 8.0 on a PC.

PDF files can also be viewed on portable devices, such as the Palm Pilot, in which case the PDF creator uses Adobe Reader for Palm OS to optimize the document for viewing on the Palm Pilot.

PDF files can also be viewed in supported web browsers, where Adobe Reader 8.0 functions as a plug-in or helper application. Whenever a user selects a PDF file posted on a web site, Acrobat Professional, Acrobat Standard, or Adobe Reader 8.0 launches in the user's web browser, depending on which application the user has on their computer. If a user has both the Adobe Reader and a version of Acrobat, whichever application was installed last is the default application used to read PDF documents.

Acrobat 8.0 Professional and Standard are full-fledged authoring applications used for publishing electronic documents in PDF format. If you've used previous versions of Acrobat, you're already familiar with the program's basic premise. In the sections to follow, you learn about the new features and uses for Acrobat 8.0.

Adobe Acrobat 8.0

With the introduction of Acrobat 6.0, Adobe created two versions: Acrobat Standard, for the small business or individual needing to convert existing files to the PDF format, and Acrobat Professional, for task-oriented professionals needing to publish PDF files with objects such as form fields and multimedia elements. Acrobat 8.0 is also distributed in both Professional and Standard versions. Acrobat Professional has several features for the "power user." The general capabilities of each version are listed in the following sections.

Acrobat Standard

With Acrobat Standard, you can easily create a PDF document from any number of sources. You can create PDF documents from within authoring applications, such as Microsoft Word, which uses PDFMaker, Acrobat's Adobe PDF plug-in to convert Word documents to PDF files (see Chapter 5). You can also use a single file, multiple files, a web page, or a document in your scanner (as outlined in Chapter 6) to create a PDF document from within Acrobat Standard. Acrobat Standard enables you to send PDF documents for review and to track the review process. You can also mark up a PDF document with notes, text, or graphic elements. In addition, you can initiate browser-based reviews. Reviewing and marking up PDF documents is covered in detail in Chapter 10.

Adobe has yet another tool to create PDF documents: Acrobat Elements. Large organizations can use Acrobat 8.0 Elements to convert Microsoft Office documents to PDF documents. Acrobat 8.0 Elements is a product you can license through Adobe. For more information, visit the Acrobat 8.0 Elements web page at http://www.adobe.com/products/acrobatel/main.html.

Acrobat Professional

Acrobat Professional has the same feature set as Acrobat Standard, but with some powerful additions. With Acrobat Professional, you can create PDF documents from within AutoCAD, Microsoft Project, and Microsoft Visio. Acrobat Professional also features additional commenting tools, enhanced multimedia support, and much more. Acrobat 7.0 Windows featured the addition of the *Adobe LiveCycle Designer,* which enables you to create interactive PDF forms either by using preset templates or from scratch. An enhanced version of Adobe LiveCycle Designer is included with the Windows version of Acrobat Professional 8.0 (Part IV of this book covers the features unique to Acrobat Professional). Some features don't fall within the context of these chapters, however, and these are covered in earlier chapters. When a feature is only available for Acrobat Professional, it is designated by the parenthetical reference (Professional Only) in the section heading.

As mentioned previously, Acrobat 8.0 comes in two versions: Standard and Professional. The Acrobat CD-ROM ships with the following components.

Adobe Acrobat

This is the core application. You use Acrobat to publish and edit PDF documents. In future chapters, you will learn how to use the program features to create and publish PDF files for a variety of destinations. You can also use Acrobat to capture web pages and save them as PDF files, as well as scan printed documents into Acrobat and save them as PDF files.

Adobe Reader 8.0

This application is used to read published PDF documents. You don't need to install the Reader; PDF documents can be read within the Acrobat application. Adobe includes Adobe Reader 8.0 with the application CD-ROM, so you can bundle it with applications you create for distribution on CD-ROM. You can distribute Adobe Reader 8.0 without paying a licensing fee, as long as you comply with the Adobe distribution policy. This policy requires you to distribute the End User License Agreement (EULA) and information included with the installation utility.

Acrobat Catalog (Professional Only)

This application is used to create indexes of PDF documents. When you create a PDF index, you create a searchable index of several—or several hundred—PDF documents. After you create a PDF index, you can use the Advanced Search Options in the Acrobat Search dialog box to search the indexed documents for specific information.

Adobe LiveCycle Designer 8.0 (Professional and Windows Only)

Adobe LiveCycle Designer 8.0 is installed with the Windows version of Acrobat Professional. This application, which can be launched from within Acrobat, gives you the power to create interactive PDF forms either from scratch or by using one of the many preset templates that ship with the application. In addition, you can edit existing PDF forms in Adobe LiveCycle Designer 8.0. You can launch Adobe LiveCycle Designer 8.0 from within Acrobat 8.0 Professional or as a stand-alone application. You will find detailed information on Adobe LiveCycle Designer 8.0 in Chapter 15.

Acrobat Distiller 8.0

Acrobat Distiller 8.0 is used to create PDF documents from PostScript files in Encapsulated PostScript (EPS) or PostScript (PS) format. The *Distiller Conversion Settings* help you to optimize the document for its intended destination. Although Acrobat Distiller 8.0 is a separate application, you can launch it from within Acrobat.

What's New in Adobe Acrobat 8.0

Acrobat 8.0 consists of two separate entities named Acrobat and Acrobat Distiller 8.0. If you're an Acrobat Professional user, Adobe Catalog has been a plug-in within the core application since Acrobat 6.0. As described above Catalog is used to create a searchable index of PDF files.

Acrobat 8.0 has many new features that enhance usability when creating files within a network environment. You can easily share your PDF documents within a team. Individual team members can review PDF documents using Acrobat 8.0's enhanced commenting tools to create annotations, add audio and written comments, and much more. For example, if you use Acrobat Professional to create PDF documents, you can easily create interactive forms to gather information from within a corporate environment. These forms can be filled in and printed out, they can be filled in and submitted on a corporate intranet, or they can be filled in and submitted via e-mail. If you use Acrobat Professional on a Windows machine, you can use Adobe LiveCycle Designer to create enhanced PDF forms either from a template or from scratch.

Recipients of your form can use Acrobat Standard or Professional to fill in the form. You also have the option of enabling users of the Adobe Reader to fill in a form, to sign an existing signature field, and to save comments and form data. In the sections that follow, you learn about the exciting new features at your disposal in Acrobat 8.0. And, you'll be happy to know that the new features don't add any overhead to Acrobat—in fact, Acrobat 8.0 loads quicker than its predecessors.

Enhanced Adobe PDF Performance in Microsoft Office Applications

If you use Microsoft Office applications, you know that when you install Acrobat, the application adds Adobe PDF icons to each Office program, enabling you to create PDFs of files you are currently authoring in Office applications, such as Word, Excel, or PowerPoint. If you install Office applications after installing Acrobat, the Adobe PDF icons will also be added (except to Microsoft InfoPath). Acrobat 8.0 boasts enhanced performance in all Microsoft Office applications. For example, from within Microsoft Word, you can now convert Mail Merge documents to PDFs and send them via e-mail.

Acrobat also adds Adobe PDF icons to Microsoft Outlook. This enables you to archive e-mail messages pertaining to a project, client, or business transaction into a single PDF document. You can append the document as new e-mail messages are received and use Acrobat's powerful Edit | Search command to search for specific information in the PDF.

Getting to Know Adobe LiveCycle Designer 8.0 (Professional and Windows Only)

With Adobe LiveCycle Designer 8.0, you can create PDF forms from scratch or from preset templates. The application creates XML code as you add form elements, such as text, text fields, check boxes, lists boxes, and so on. You can also add graphic elements, such as images and logos, and size the graphic elements to suit your design. The resulting form is published as a PDF document.

Start a Meeting

When Adobe acquired Macromedia, it was obvious that Adobe would become a powerhouse with all manner of interactive software. The first evidence of this in Acrobat is the capability to launch a meeting from within Acrobat using a new feature called Acrobat Connect. This feature uses a watered-down version of Macromedia Breeze to get the job done. With Acrobat Connect, you can create a meeting and share documents with other attendees. The colleagues you invite to your meeting don't need to download any special software. Acrobat comes with a free 30-day trail for Acrobat Connect.

Create a Blank Document

If you've ever wished that you could use Adobe Acrobat like a word processor, you now have that option. With Acrobat 8.0 Standard and Professional, you can now create a blank document and start typing. You can specify the font type, size, style, and so on.

Redaction

Have you ever seen a government document where portions of the document have black ink over sensitive parts of the document? You can do the same thing within Acrobat. The feature, which removes content specified by the document author is known as *redaction.* You use this feature when you need to send a document with sensitive information, but you don't want prying eyes to see the information. With the new Redaction toolbar, you can mark text or objects for redaction, apply redaction, set properties for the Redaction tool, and search for text to which you want to apply redaction.

Create PDF Documents with Adobe PDF

If you haven't upgraded since Acrobat 4.0, you'll notice the PDFWriter is missing. In older versions of Acrobat, the PDFWriter was added as a system printer, which enabled you to print a file in PDF format from within another application. When you install Acrobat 8.0, Adobe PDF is added as a system printer. Adobe PDF is actually Acrobat Distiller with a different name. You can create a PDF file by choosing Adobe PDF as a printer when using an authoring application's Print command, or you can use a command from the Create PDF menu group or task button from within Acrobat to convert supported files to PDF documents. Another Acrobat 8.0 benefit is this: the commands in the Create PDF menu group can create a PDF document from a single file or multiple files of different formats supported by Acrobat. You can also create PDF document using Web Capture, by scanning a document into Acrobat or using an image previously pasted to the system clipboard with the Snapshot tool. Another major enhancement in Acrobat 8.0 is the File | Combine Files command. This is an enhancement of the File | Create PDF | From Multiple Files command. In fact, the old command is still there, but it summons the Combine Files dialog box. The new command gives you the option of creating a PDF by including a set of files from previously combined files or by including a subset of a document, an option that enables you to choose which pages or sheets from a document to combine. You can also specify the quality of the resulting PDF, which enables you to trim the document to a file size for Internet use, or create a high-resolution version of the document. Combine files also specify allows you to a cover sheet to use for the document.

Archive Microsoft Outlook E-Mail Messages

If you use Microsoft Outlook to manage your e-mail, you can archive selected e-mails or entire folders from Outlook as PDF files. When you archive an e-mail message with attachments, the attachments are saved within the PDF document. You can view the attached files by selecting them from within the Attachments tab, and then opening them in the native application. When you open an archived e-mail message, you can respond to the sender or any of the other recipients from within Acrobat.

User-Friendly Header and Footer Interface

If you need headers and footers on your PDF documents, you'll appreciate the enhanced header/footer user interface. With Acrobat 8.0, you can quickly format a header or footer for your PDF documents. The *Add Headers & Footers dialog box* for this task enables you to add a footer and header to your document in one fell swoop. This enhanced usability also applies to watermarks and backgrounds. You can create a watermark from text or graphic objects and specify the rotation of the watermark, as well as the opacity. New to Acrobat 8.0 is the capability to remove headers and footers applied by Acrobat, Microsoft Word, or Microsoft Excel. You can also set font color, underline text, and shrink the document to avoid overwriting the document's text or graphics with the header/footer.

Improved Document Commenting and Review

If you work on a PDF project with multiple authors, you and your team members can review and add comments to a PDF file from within a web browser via the Internet or a corporate intranet. When you open a PDF file for review within your web browser, every Acrobat commenting tool is at your disposal. You can freely annotate the PDF file, and then save it, or share your comments with other authors through protocols such as Web Distributed Authoring and Versioning (WebDAV). If your team is working on a corporate intranet, you can create a shared data repository by setting up a shared network folder, using Open Database Connectivity (ODBC) to connect to such databases as MDB (Microsoft Access) or SQL Server databases, or Microsoft Office Server Extensions. Prior to Acrobat 7.0, participating in browser-based reviews was a Windows-only option. Now, Macintosh Safari users can also participate in a browser-based review. If you own Acrobat 8.0 Professional, you have the option to include Adobe Reader users in a document review. Document reviews initiated in Acrobat 8.0 Professional can also enable Adobe Reader reviewers to add comments to the document being reviewed. A major enhancement in Acrobat 8.0 is the Wizard, which enables Acrobat Standard and Acrobat Professional users to easily initiate a shared review. The Wizard has an option that enables you to include Acrobat Reader 8.0 users in the review.

Enhanced Security and Review Features

With Acrobat 8.0, you can apply enhanced security features to the documents you create. Available since Acrobat 7.0, 128-bit AES encryption makes it possible for you to distribute confidential documents with complete peace of mind. If you author a confidential PDF document, you can limit access to the document by assigning a password to the file. You can also certify a document. When you certify a document, you attest to its contents by adding your digital signature to the document. When you certify a document, you can prevent tampering, by specifying what changes can and cannot be made. A *digital signature* is like an electronic fingerprint: it identifies which member of the team worked with the document and when. Acrobat 8.0 Professional now gives you the option for Reader 7.0 and 8.0 users to digitally sign documents.

Print Booklets

Adobe Acrobat 8.0 has new printing options which enable you to print booklets from a PDF document. You can print a *2-up saddle-stitched booklet,* where two side-by-side pages, printed on both sides are folded once and fastened along the fold. The new print option prints the pages in the proper configuration, so the booklet has the correct pagination.

New User Interface

Acrobat 6.0 had a myriad of menu commands arranged below the menu bar. Tool choice could often be confusing, because some of the tools were buried deep in submenus. Acrobat 7.0 launched with a vastly improved interface. You'll be glad to know the Acrobat 8.0 interface is even more user-friendly. One of the first things you notice when you launch Acrobat is the Getting Started page, as shown in Figure 1-2. Click a button to reveal a new dialog box with options related to the task designated on the button.

After you open a document, or create a new document, you'll see the menu commands are easier to locate. If you own Acrobat 8.0 Professional, you'll find extra tools, such as Measuring and Print Production. With the latest revision, the most commonly used tool groups are neatly

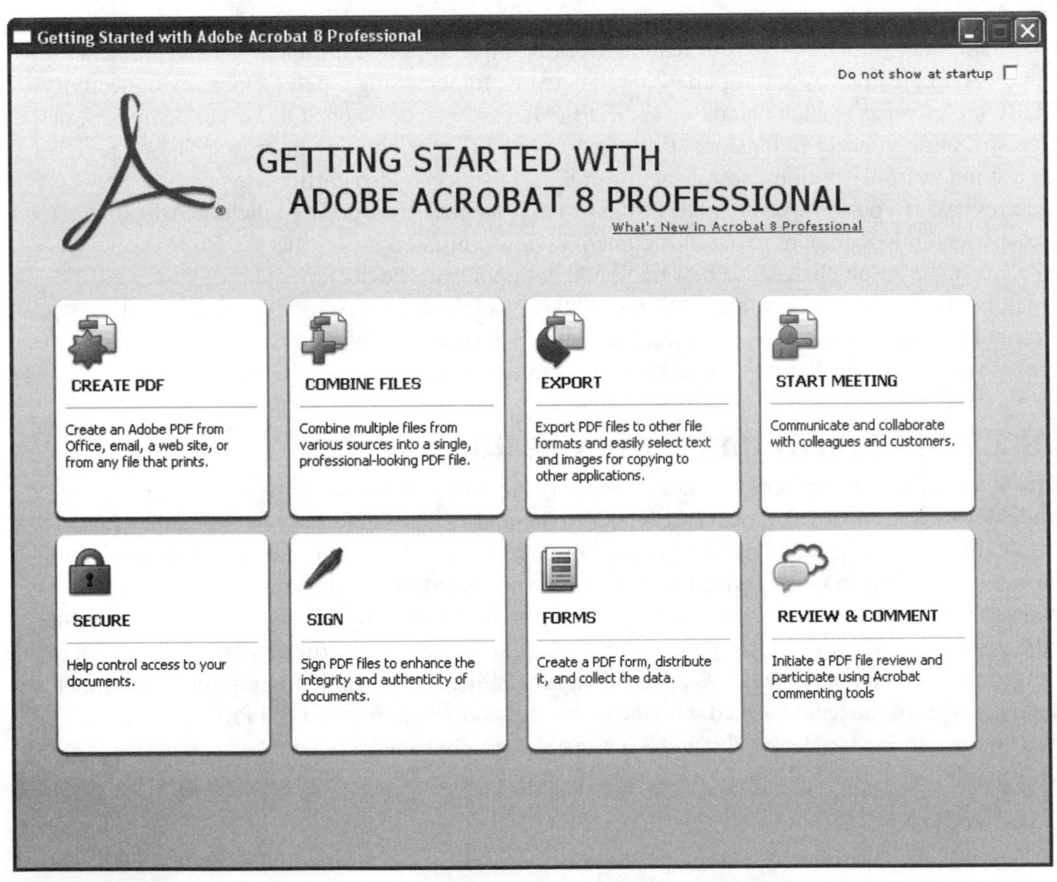

FIGURE 1-2 You can perform a myriad of tasks from within the Getting Started page.

arranged as task buttons below the menu bar, as shown in Figure 1-3. Click a task button and you have access to all tools within that group. When you need to access toolbars, such as the Forms toolbar that aren't listed below the menu bar, you open the toolbar using a command from the Tools menu. The selected toolbar floats in the workspace and can be moved as desired. You can also dock the toolbar below the menu bar.

Another significant change is the left side of the workspace. The tabs that appeared on the left side of the interface in previous versions of Acrobat have been replaced by graphic icons. Each icon has a *tooltip,* which tells the user what they can do after clicking the icon. When an icon is clicked, the left side of the interface expands to show items such as pages, bookmarks, digital signatures, and so on. Figure 1-3, shows the interface when the Pages icon is clicked. The How-To tab, which previously opened in the right side of the interface, now appears in the left side of the interface, when the icon with the question mark is clicked.

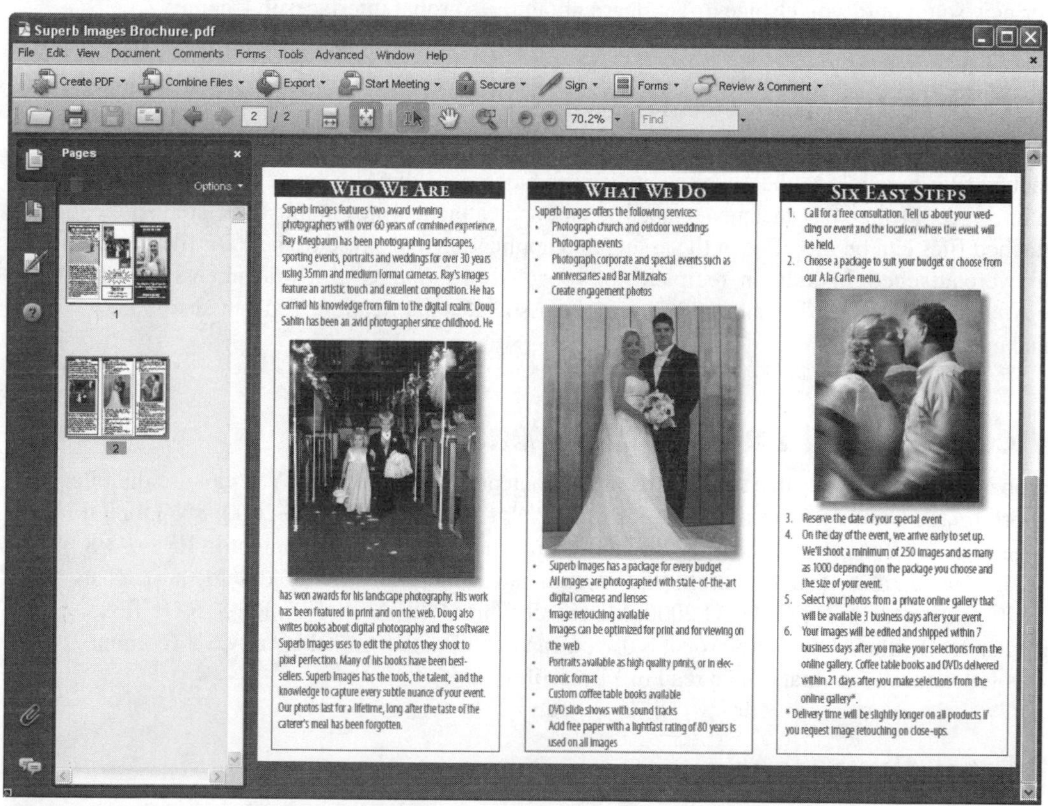

FIGURE 1-3 The Acrobat workspace enables you to quickly select the desired tool.

In Acrobat 7.0, the Search dialog box appeared in a pane on the right side of the workspace. In Acrobat 8.0, the Search dialog box appears in a separate window on the left side of the interface. The main Acrobat window decreases in size to make room for the Search dialog box. There is an option to arrange windows, which either shows the Search window and the main window side-by-side, or the main window maximized with the Search window floating on top. The Search window can also be maximized, if desired. The new design devotes more area to the PDF document itself, making it easier to navigate, read, and edit the document.

Customize the Workspace

The Tasks toolbar that appears below the main menu can be moved or floated in the workspace. Toolbars accessed from the Tools menu are fully customizable. You can float them in the workspace or add them to the toolbar.

When you arrive at an optimum setup to suit your working preference, Acrobat preserves your new setup until you change it. You learn about the Acrobat interfaces in Chapter 2.

Manage Document Attachments

With Acrobat 8.0, you can easily add files as attachments to any PDF document. You manage attached files by clicking the Attachments icon, which opens the Attachment tab at the bottom of the interface. From the Attachments tab, you can open attached files in the associated application. Attached files can be modified in the associated application and saved to the PDF file to which they were attached. In addition, recipients of your PDF documents with attachments can use the Attachments tab to view attached files in the associated application. You can also include attached files in a search.

Enhanced Export and Import Features

Acrobat 8.0 makes it possible to repurpose PDF content for other formats. You can use the File | Export| Image command to extract images from PDF files in JPEG, JPEG 2000, PNG, or TIFF image formats. You can use the File | Save As command to export PDF content in EPS or PS format. You can also save the current PDF document as an optimized PDF document or as an HTML (3.2 or 4.01), JPEG, JPEG 2000, Microsoft Word, PDF/A, PDF/X, PNG, RTF, Text, TIFF, or XML file. And, with Acrobat 8.0, you can export data from tables as CSV (comma separated values) data that can be read in Microsoft Excel.

New Menu Commands

In Acrobat 8.0, you have new menu commands available to help you streamline workflow and increase productivity. In upcoming chapters, you can find in-depth information about the following new command and menu groups:

- **Forms menu (Professional Only)** The new Forms menu enables you to create a new form using Adobe Live Cycle Designer 8.0 (Windows Only), or edit an existing form in Acrobat. Another powerful feature on the forms menu is the capability to recognize a form field in a scanned form (Windows only). Other commands in this new menu enable you to distribute forms, compile returned forms, manage form data, and more.
- **Redaction submenu (Professional Only)** The new Redaction submenu commands give you the power to remove sensitive information in a document. From this menu, you select the Redaction tool, which you use to mark text and graphics to be redacted. There are also commands to set properties for the Redaction tool, search for text strings you want to redact, and apply redaction to items selected with the Redaction tool.
- **Print Production** The Print Production menu, which formerly resided as a submenu of the Tools menu, now resides on the Advanced menu. The command to launch Acrobat Distiller is now also part of this menu.

Create a PDF Document

The flexible tools in Acrobat give you several options for creating and publishing documents for electronic distribution in PDF format. You create PDF files from within Acrobat by importing documents authored in other applications, or by saving documents created in authoring applications, such as Adobe Photoshop, or using the Acrobat PDFMaker to convert a Microsoft Office document. Several third-party plug-ins are available for working with PDF files in previous versions of Acrobat, a trend that is bound to continue with Acrobat 8.0. Many scanning utilities, such as ScanSoft's OmniPage Pro 15, feature PDF output as an option. Third-party Acrobat plug-ins also have been tailor-made to suit specific industries.

After you convert a supported file type into a PDF document or open a PDF filecreated by another author, you can add interactive elements, such as text hyperlinks, image hyperlinks, and, with Acrobat Professional, multimedia elements, such as QuickTime movies, Flash SWF movies, and sound files. The only caveat to the previous sentence is security. If another author has protected the document with security, you need the password before you can edit the document. You can append an existing PDF file by inserting other documents, deleting pages, inserting pages, or replacing pages. You can also do other housekeeping chores, such as extract graphic elements from a PDF file, crop the physical size of a page, or each page in the document to delete unwanted elements. You can also modify a PDF document by removing unnecessary pages. Acrobat has a set of TouchUp tools that let you make minor modifications to graphic and text elements in the document. New for Acrobat Professional 8.0 is the capability to see and change the color space of a selected object, or to rotate and clip the object with the Touchup Object tool.

A published PDF document retains the look and feel of the original. All the fonts and images you used in the original document are carried over to the PDF document. Figure 1-4 shows a document in Microsoft Word; Figure 1-5 shows the same document after being converted to a PDF file. Other than the different interfaces, the documents look identical.

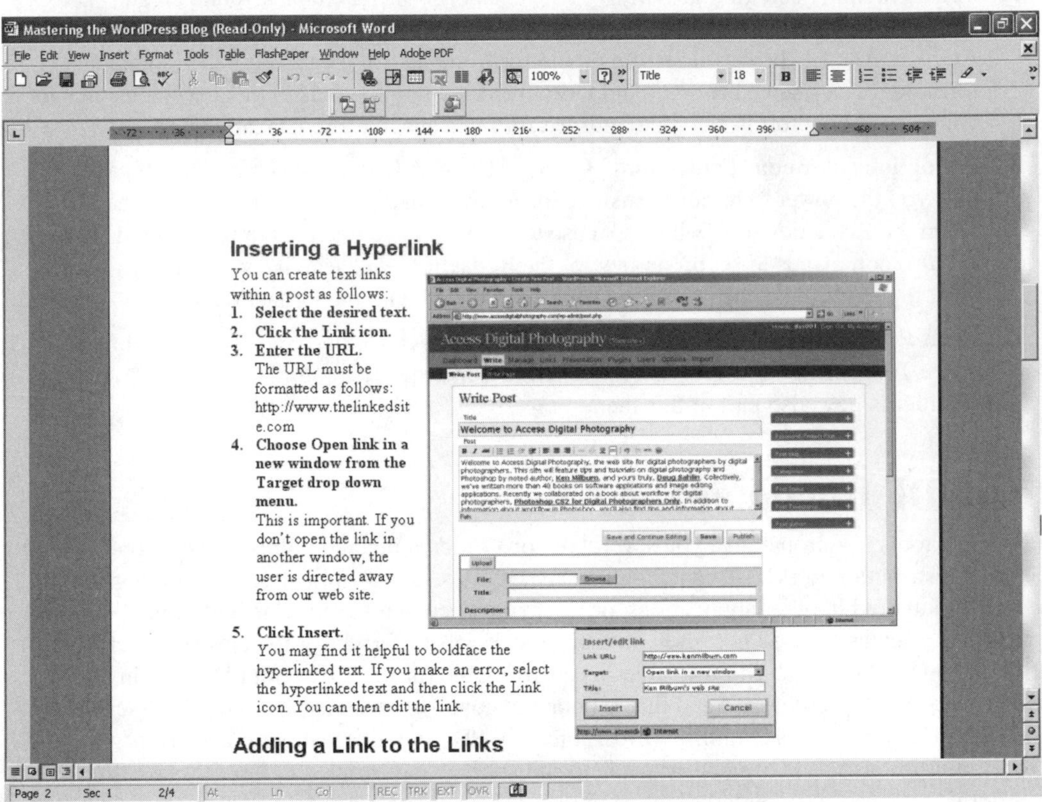

FIGURE 1-4 You can convert Microsoft Word files, such as this, into PDF documents.

Create PDF Documents from Authoring Applications

The easiest way to create a PDF document is to create a file in an authoring application, and then convert it to a PDF file. You can create PDF files from any of these popular Microsoft programs (Microsoft Office 97 or newer):

- **Microsoft Word** *Microsoft Word* is a word processing application. Within limits, you can add graphic elements to the content of a Word document.
- **Microsoft Excel** *Microsoft Excel* is a spreadsheet program. Excel also has limited support for graphic elements.
- **Microsoft Outlook** *Microsoft Outlook* is an application used to manage contacts, appointments, and e-mail. You can archive selected e-mail messages or complete folders as PDF documents. All message attachments are archived as well, and are available through the Attachments tab.

- **Microsoft PowerPoint** *Microsoft PowerPoint* is software used to create presentations. A PowerPoint presentation is similar to a slideshow. You can add graphic elements to your presentation, and then convert it to a PDF file. Many slideshow transitions and other effects are preserved in the resulting PDF document.
- **AutoCAD (Professional Only)** *AutoCAD* is 2-D and 3-D drafting software used to design products. The software can be used to create, view, and share design drawings.
- **Microsoft Project (Professional Only)** *Microsoft Project* is project management software. With this software, you can track schedules and project resources, as well as communicate and report the project status to others.
- **Microsoft Visio (Professional Only)** *Microsoft Visio* is used to create floor plans, flowcharts, software diagrams, and more. This software dovetails seamlessly with Microsoft Project to create project schedules.

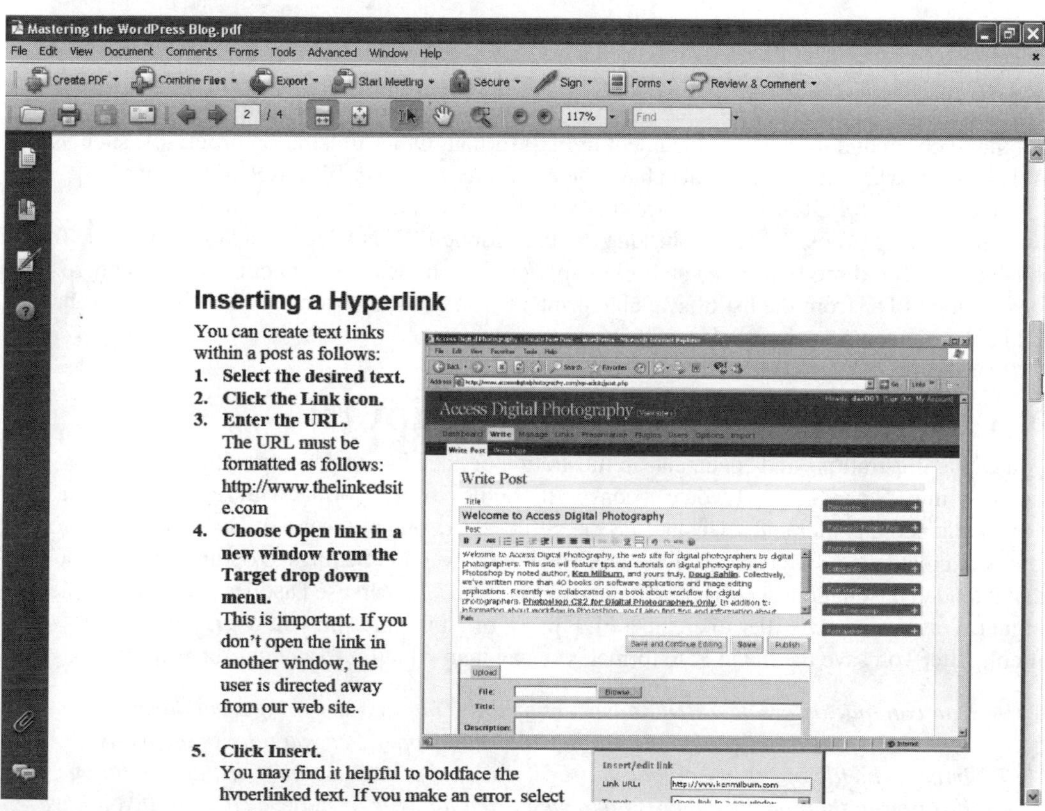

FIGURE 1-5 The PDF version of a converted Word document retains the look and feel of the original.

When you install Acrobat 8.0, the installer adds the Adobe PDFMaker plug-in to any Microsoft Office application (with the exception of InfoPath) and Internet Explorer. After installing Acrobat, you see the Adobe PDF shortcuts on your menu bar. The icon on the left converts the current document to a PDF file. The icon in the middle converts it to a PDF file and launches your default e-mail program, enabling you to send the PDF file as an e-mail attachment. The icon on the right converts the document to a PDF file and sends the file for review. Acrobat also adds an Adobe PDF menu to the Microsoft Office application, as the following illustration shows. This menu gives you two additional commands: the capability to change conversion settings, and the capability to start a meeting using Acrobat Connect. You learn how to convert Microsoft Office documents to PDF documents in Chapter 5.

If you own certain Adobe products, such as InDesign, Illustrator, or Photoshop, you can use a menu command to export a document in PDF format. Other illustration programs, such as CorelDraw, Quark, and Freehand, also have the capability to export files in PDF format.

You can publish PDF files from any other application you use to generate images, illustrations, or text files. When you install Acrobat, Adobe PDF is added as a system printer. To publish a PDF file directly from an authoring application, choose the Print command, and then choose Adobe PDF from the list of available printers. You can then open the PDF file in Acrobat to add enhancements, such as links and form fields.

Create PDF Documents from PostScript Files

If you create illustrations and documents in illustration or page layout programs and publish the documents in EPS or PS format, you can convert these files to PDF format with Acrobat Distiller. After you launch Distiller and select an EPS or PS file, select one of the preset Distiller Conversion Settings or create your own conversion setting. You use Conversion Settings to optimize a PDF file for an intended destination, such as print, screen, or the Web. You can use Distiller to create complete designer, you can use Distiller to create a PDF proof of an illustration you're creating for a client. After you save the file in PDF format, you can then e-mail it to a client for approval.

TIP *You can quickly create a PDF document by dragging-and-dropping a supported file icon from your desktop onto the Acrobat shortcut icon. After you release the mouse button, the file opens in Acrobat. If the file isn't supported, Acrobat displays a dialog box noting that the file either is not a supported file type or may be corrupt. If you have the Distiller shortcut on your desktop, you can create a PDF document by dragging-and-dropping an EPS or PS file onto the Distiller icon.*

Create PDF Documents for the Internet

If you design web sites, you can use PDF documents in a variety of effective ways. For example, you can create a product catalog, create interactive PDF tutorials, create PDF forms, or publish a manual, all in PDF format. The web site visitor can choose to view the document in the web browser or download the complete file for future viewing. Most popular web browsers support Adobe Acrobat and Adobe Reader 8.0 as plug-ins or helper applications. Figure 1-6 shows a published document as displayed in Internet Explorer. Note, the figure shows a document displayed in the plug-in version of Acrobat Professional, not Adobe Reader 8.0.

Capture Web Pages as PDF Documents

If you do a lot of research on the Internet, you can capture web pages for future reference. When you capture a web page, Acrobat downloads the text and graphic elements from the web page,

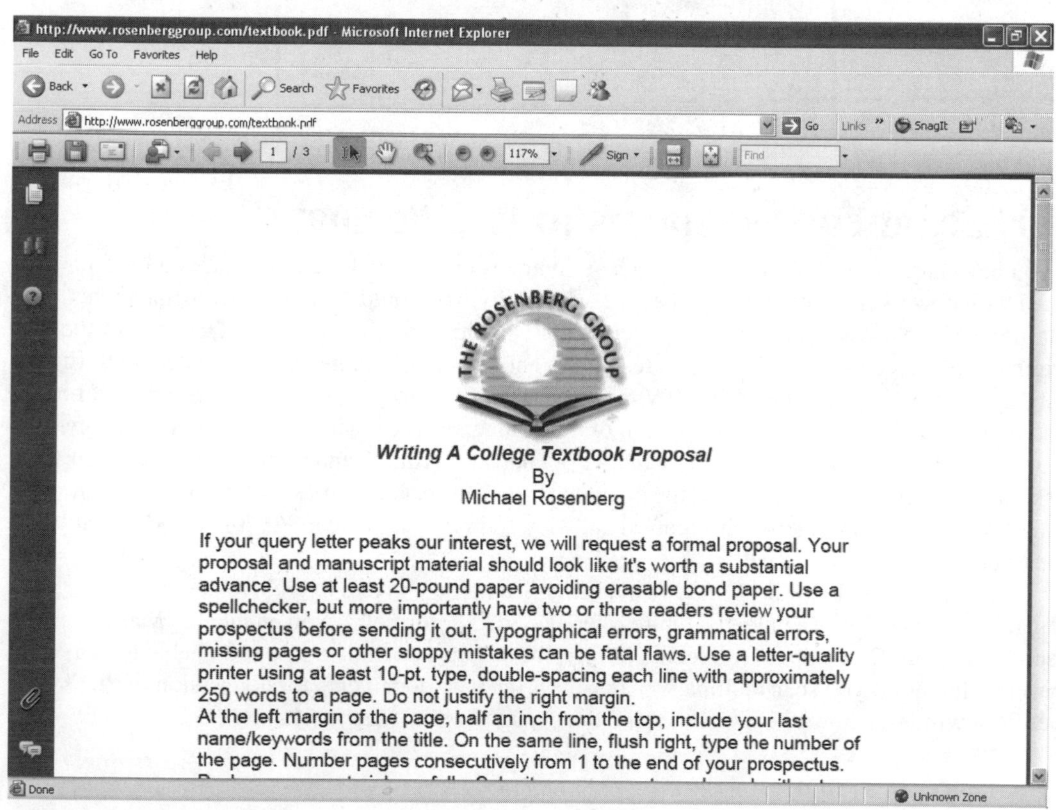

FIGURE 1-6 Acrobat also serves as an Internet Explorer plug-in that enables you to view PDFs from web sites.

complete with hyperlinks. If you want to add additional pages from the same site to the PDF file, simply click the desired hyperlink in the captured page and Acrobat will append the document by downloading the linked page. You can use the Acrobat File | Create PDF | From Web Page command to download complex tutorials from the Internet and save them as PDF files for easy reference. If you download numerous web pages for reference and own Acrobat Professional, you can create a searchable index of your reference files with the Advanced | Document Processing | Full Text Index with Catalog command. The following illustration shows the dialog box that appears when you use the File | Create PDF | From Web Capture command to download a web page. You will learn how to capture web pages in Chapter 6.

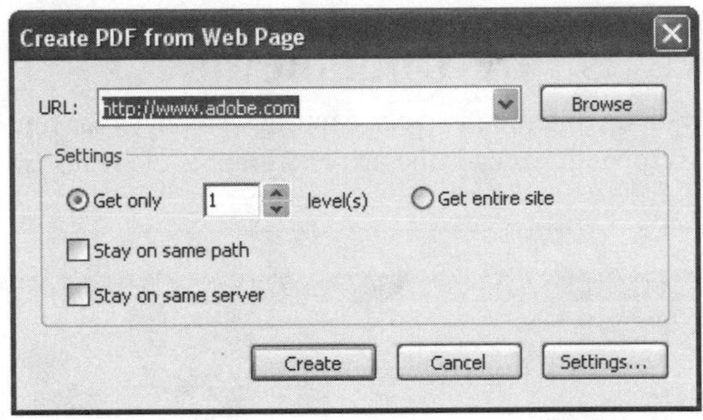

Convert Scanned Documents to PDF Format

If you have hard copies of documents, such as contracts or product brochures that you need to share with coworkers or clients, Acrobat is user-friendly. You could send the documents by fax, but in most cases, what your recipient receives isn't anything near a reasonable facsimile of the original. To overcome the difference in resolution and quality of fax machines, create a PDF file for the document you want to share. If you have a scanner hooked up to your system, the Acrobat install utility adds the TWAIN information of the scanner as a scanner in the Create PDF From Scanner dialog box. Then, it's simply a matter of choosing From Scanner from the Create PDF task button or menu. After you scan the document into Acrobat, save it as a PDF file, and then e-mail it. When your document is received and viewed in Adobe Reader 8.0, it looks identical to what you scanned into Acrobat.

You can also use the File | Create PDF | From Scanner command to archive dog-eared magazine articles, for example, for future reference in PDF format. If you enable the Make Searchable (Run OCR) option, Acrobat converts the scanned document into searchable text, a powerful feature if you scan multipage magazine articles or documents for conversion to PDF files. You will learn how to convert scanned documents to PDF files in Chapter 6.

Create PDF Documents for Print

You also benefit from using Acrobat when you create PDF documents for print. Thanks to the available formatting and conversion setting options, both versions of Acrobat, as well as the Adobe Reader 8.0 software, make sure your published documents always print as you intended regardless of limitations imposed by the recipient's software or printer.

After you optimize a file for print, Acrobat 8.0 gives you options for sending the file to the output device. The Print dialog box in Acrobat 8.0 has an Advanced button. When you click the Advanced button, a separate dialog box opens, enabling you to specify print resolution and output options. If you own Acrobat Professional, you can specify options, such as trim marks, transparency levels, and the capability of omitting images when printing a proof of the PDF file. Acrobat Professional also enables you to print a PDF as a booklet. If you use Acrobat Professional, viewing and printing separations are only two of the many options available when creating a PDF to be used by a printing service. You can find more options for creating a PDF for a printing service under the Print Production menu group, which is a submenu of the Advanced menu.

Create Interactive PDF Documents

When some Acrobat users create PDF documents for the first time, they tend to think the document will be read in linear fashion. However, you can use the Acrobat Link tool to create documents that can be navigated like web pages. You can use the Link tool to change static text or images into hyperlinks. When you create a link in a PDF document, it serves many purposes. You can use the link to open another PDF document, to navigate to a specific page in the current PDF document, to link to a URL on the Web, and much more. A link in a PDF document functions identically to a link in an HTML page. When you position your mouse over the link, the cursor changes to a pointing hand. Interactive navigation for PDF documents is covered in Chapters 7 and 8.

Create PDF Documents for Multimedia Presentations (Professional Only)

The age of electronic education is very much upon us. Fluctuating demands in the workplace make lifelong learning a necessity. People in all stages of life need to increase their knowledge base. Most lifelong learners don't have time for formal classroom education and, instead, they use online education to learn at their own pace. Online learners can log on and take a lesson according to their schedule. Other lifelong learners purchase interactive CD-ROMs and play the discs in their spare time to educate themselves. PDF documents are an excellent way to educate online, as they can contain multimedia content and are viewable in the student's web browser.

If, on the other hand, you're authoring a PDF document for an online or CD-ROM presentation, you can accomplish the task with Acrobat Professional. When you create a PDF document for an online or CD-ROM presentation, Acrobat Professional gives you the necessary tools to elevate your presentation to the next level. *Multimedia* is the current buzzword for online education, educational CD-ROMs, and business presentations. With Acrobat Professional, you can create PDF documents with multimedia elements, such as movie clips, music, and the spoken word. You can use the Sound tool in Acrobat Professional, or the Record Audio Comment tool in Acrobat Professional and Acrobat Standard, to record an audio clip or add a prerecorded sound clip to a document. After you add interaction, you can create links within the document to play multimedia clips or have them play when a document page is opened. In Chapter 17, you learn to create PDF files with multimedia elements.

Create PDF Documents for Internal Distribution

Many modern companies realize the futility of using paper to distribute information. Paper is bulky, it takes up room, and it's an expensive way to distribute written information with a short life span. If the company is a multi-location operation, there's also the cost of transporting published documents between locations. A PDF document is a much better solution for disseminating information efficiently over the corporate intranet, sent via e-mail, or distributed on disk. An employee manual in print form might take up hundreds of pages, plus a hefty portion of the employee's workspace. The same document can be created in PDF format and distributed to employees on a floppy disk or CD-ROM. A PDF employee manual uses fewer resources, is easier to distribute, and is easier to use. An employee looking for specific information can use the Search dialog box (as shown in Figure 1-7) to find specific information in a PDF document.

You can also use PDF documents to distribute memos. If you author a confidential memo, you can password-protect the document and add other Acrobat security measures to prevent editing or viewing by unauthorized personnel. If you need to edit a confidential document, you can always change the security settings to allow editing, and then disable editing after you make the changes.

When you create a document for internal distribution, recipients can sign off on the document using the Digital Signature feature. Digital signatures and document security are discussed in Chapter 11.

Create a PDF Form

Acrobat 8.0 Professional has advanced tools you can use to create forms to accumulate data. You can create forms complete with text boxes for collecting data, radio buttons, and check boxes for selecting form options, and buttons for navigating the form or submitting the form data to a web server. You can even create a drop-down list of form choices. You can use Common Gateway Interface (CGI) scripting options to route data from a form submitted over the Web to a server, or opt to have the completed document printed as hard copy and submitted internally. You will learn how to create PDF forms in Chapter 14.

If you use Acrobat Professional on a Windows machine, Adobe LiveCycle Designer 8.0 (Windows Only) was installed when you installed Acrobat. You can access Adobe LiveCycle Designer from within Acrobat Professional, or launch it as a stand-alone application. With Adobe LiveCycle Designer, you can create interactive forms using one of the preset templates, or create a custom form from scratch.

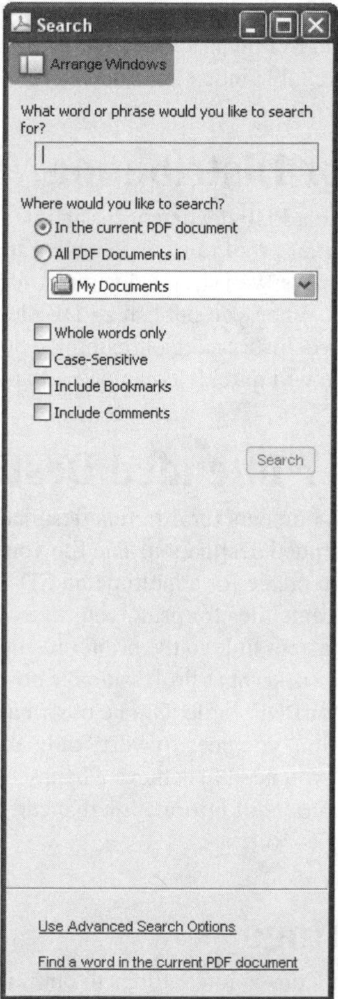

FIGURE 1-7 The Search command makes it possible to locate specific information in a multipage document.

Create an Acrobat Catalog (Professional Only)

If you create PDF documents in a corporate environment, you might end up publishing a large collection of related PDF documents. For example, if you create documents for your Human Resources department, you could end up with a collection of varied memos concerning employee procedures, benefits packages, and the like. When employees need to find specific information, they will end up using the Edit | Search command on numerous documents to find the data. The solution to this problem is to use Acrobat Professional's Advanced | Document Processing | Full Text Index with Catalog command to create a searchable index of PDF files. After you create an index, use the Edit | Search command to find specific documents that contain data related to a query. You will learn to create a searchable index in Chapter 18.

Optimize Documents for Distribution

Acrobat also enables you to optimize a PDF document for an intended destination, whether it be a CD-ROM presentation, a customer proof (a PDF document that serves as an example of a design in progress, such as a brochure or web site), a document for a web site, or a document that will be printed by a printing service. When you publish a PDF file optimized for a web site and the web site's hosting service supports *byteserving* (streaming a document into the viewer's web browser), you can be assured the file will quickly download into the viewer's web browser.

Optimize Documents for Intended Destinations

If you've ever created images and documents for different destinations, you know a file needs to be formatted correctly for the intended destination. The file you create for print, the file you create for a web site, and the file you create for a multimedia CD-ROM presentation all have different requirements. When you create files for print, you need to optimize them for the output device, matching the file as closely as possible to the printer resolution. If the file is destined for a commercial printing service, you use Acrobat Professional's powerful Print Production options and save the document as a PDF/X or PDF/A file. On the other hand, when you create a PDF file for a multimedia CD-ROM application, you need to worry only about screen resolution. When you create a document for the Web, you need to achieve a happy medium between image quality and bandwidth. (*Bandwidth* is the amount of information that can be downloaded per second at a given connection speed—for example, 56 Kbps.)

Modify Conversion Settings

Acrobat Distiller comes with preset Conversion Settings to optimize a document for an intended destination. If you create a PDF file from a Microsoft Office application, the Adobe PDF plug-in has several options available in the Adobe PDF | Change Conversion Settings command. If none of the presets suits the document you're publishing, you can modify a preset to create and save the parameters as a custom Adobe PDF Settings File with the .joboptions extension. Chapter 12 is devoted to optimizing PDF documents.

View PDF Documents

When you use different applications to publish documents for electronic distribution, the documents can be read only if the recipients have a copy of the authoring software installed on their computers. If you work for a large corporation and need to electronically distribute documents to a large number of coworkers, your employer ends up spending a fortune in software licensing fees. But if you publish the documents in PDF format, any coworker can read them as long as a copy of Adobe Reader 8.0 is installed on their computer. Adobe doesn't charge licensing fees when you distribute copies of Adobe Reader 8.0. Therefore, sending documents in PDF format is a cost-effective way to distribute documents within large organizations. PDF documents created using Acrobat 8.0 format (PDF 1.7) can only be read with the latest version of Acrobat or the Adobe Reader, and certain features may not be supported by earlier versions of Acrobat or the Adobe Reader. To make the document compatible with earlier versions of the software, you have to optimize the document for the version of the software or reader used by your intended audience.

If your published PDF documents are included on a web site, most popular web browsers support Adobe Acrobat or the Adobe Reader, which enables viewers to display PDF files within their browsers. The plug-in used to view PDF documents in a web browser is installed when Adobe Acrobat or the Adobe Reader is installed on a user's computer. To facilitate any visitors to your web site who don't have Adobe Reader 8.0 or an earlier version installed, you can add a direct link from your web site to the Adobe web site so these visitors can easily download the Reader free.

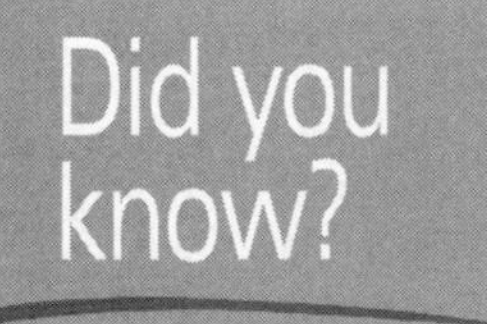

How Streaming Works

Many file formats viewed over the Internet are streamed into the user's browser. When a file is streamed into a browser, it doesn't have to download completely before the viewer can begin to see the file. The first part of the file (or *frame*, if the file is a Flash movie or a streaming movie) is displayed as soon as enough data has been downloaded. When a viewer opens a PDF document in a web browser, if the author has saved the document properly, the document downloads a page at a time, which is known as byteserving and is similar to *streaming*. As soon as enough data has downloaded, the first page of the document appears in the user's browser. After the first page has loaded, a user can elect to advance to a later page, which is then byteserved into the user's browser. While the user is viewing the desired page, the rest of the document is streamed in the background until it is loaded in the user's browser cache.

Adobe Reader 8.0 is available for free at the following URL: http://www.adobe.com/products/acrobat/readstep.html.

Another benefit you have as a PDF author is cross-platform compatibility. Any graphics you use are embedded in the published PDF document, and fonts can be embedded as well. When your published PDF documents are viewed with Adobe Reader 8.0, they display as you created them, regardless of resources available on the viewer's operating system. If fonts aren't embedded in the document, and the viewer's machine doesn't have a font used in the PDF, Acrobat automatically uses a Multiple Master font to produce a reasonable facsimile of the font used in the original document. Embedding fonts is covered in Chapter 12.

Certain limitations are present: Generally speaking san serif and serif fonts are reproducible using the MM fonts. Fonts such as Wingdings or Handwriting fonts, however, aren't reproducible.

Use Acrobat as a Publishing Solution

If you read this chapter from the start, you're beginning to realize the power and diversity of Acrobat. You can use Acrobat as a publishing solution within a large corporation, to distribute documents over the Internet, to share documents with clients who don't own the software you used to create the original document, and to review documents. Acrobat can be used to create a simple electronic interoffice memo, a form for collecting data, or a complex presentation with interactive navigation and multimedia elements. Acrobat makes it possible for you to create a single document in an authoring program, such as Microsoft Excel, and publish the file as different PDF documents optimized for different destinations. If you own Acrobat Professional, you can publish interactive PDF forms and PDF documents with multimedia elements, such as full-motion video and sound files.

Summary

In this chapter, you learned about the powerful new features in Acrobat 8.0 and how you can utilize the software as a paperless publishing solution. You also learned the difference between Acrobat Standard and Acrobat Professional. In Chapter 2, you get a look at the nuts and bolts that make it possible for you to create a wide variety of PDF documents. You learn how to navigate the Acrobat interface, and how to customize the tools and tabs to suit your working preferences.

Chapter 2

Navigate the Acrobat Workspace

How to...

- Navigate the Acrobat workspace
- Customize the Acrobat interface
- Select Acrobat tools
- Set Acrobat preferences

In this chapter, you will discover what you can accomplish with the wide variety of tools on the Acrobat toolbar. As an author of PDF documents, you spend a good deal of time working in Acrobat. In this regard, you'll find it useful to know the layout of the Acrobat workspace like the back of your hand. When you begin working with Acrobat, you'll see that the navigation pane and task buttons are logically arranged for productive workflow. Knowing that no two people work alike, Adobe has designed Acrobat so you can easily rearrange the layout of the toolbars to suit your working preference. You can also change the settings in Acrobat's Preferences dialog box to suit your workflow.

But before we get started touring the Acrobat interface, here's something to keep in mind regarding the Adobe Reader. As an author of PDF documents, you may not feel learning how to use Adobe Reader 8.0 is imperative. After all, you'll do most of your work in the full version of Acrobat Standard or Acrobat Professional. The people who receive and view your PDF documents, however, may have only the Adobe Reader. Also, you will be sending PDF documents to people with varying levels of computer savvy. Occasionally, the recipients of your documents may require assistance with the Adobe Reader, so you should take some time to familiarize yourself with the Adobe Reader 8.0 menu commands and tool groups. This is especially important, if you plan to include Adobe Reader 8.0 users in a document review cycle and enable them to fill in forms. The Adobe Reader has an interface similar to Acrobat Standard and Professional, except for the robust toolset and menu commands used to author a PDF document, add security, and so on.

Navigate the Acrobat Interface

Acrobat Standard and Acrobat Professional share a similar interface. When you open a document in either application, the workspace consists of two panes, several task buttons, and a menu bar, as shown in Figure 2-1. The icons on the left side of the interface take the place of the tabs that appeared in previous versions of Acrobat. The end result, though, is the same: when you click an icon, the applicable panel opens in the Navigation pane.

The additional features in Acrobat Professional aren't readily apparent until you start exploring the available commands when you click a task button, explore the Tools menu, or investigate the menu groups. The majority of the features and tools unique to Acrobat Professional are covered in the last part of this book. In the following sections, you can find a brief overview of each tool group and the various menu commands for both versions of Acrobat. You can find concise information on how to use each tool in the subsequent chapters of this book. The tools unique to Acrobat Professional are parenthetically referred to as follows: (Professional only).

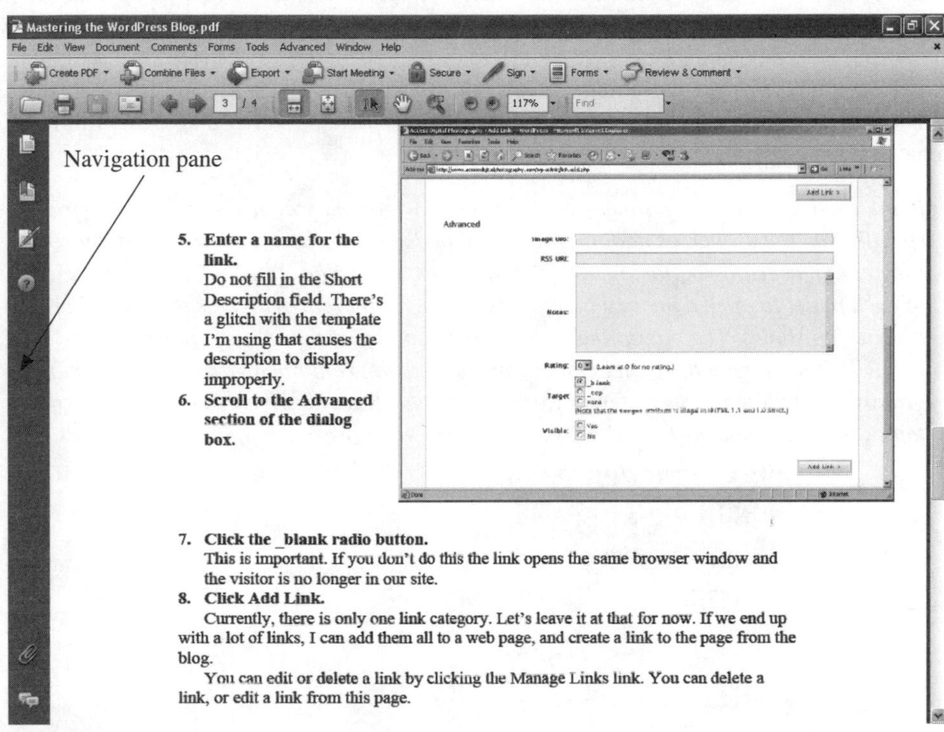

FIGURE 2-1 The Acrobat working space consists of two panes, a menu command bar, task buttons, and several toolbars.

Use the Navigation Pane

The Acrobat Navigation pane has seven icons you can click to navigate to specific items in a document.

- **Bookmarks** Displays a list of the bookmarks in the document.
- **Pages** Provides thumbnail images of each page in the document.
- **Signatures** Lists the digital signatures applied to the document.
- **Comments** Lists all comments added to the document and the names of people who authored them.
- **How To** Opens the How To pane, which contains numerous links that show how to do specific tasks in Acrobat such as securing a PDF document.
- **Attachments** Enables you to manage any files attached to the PDF document.
- **Layers** Lists the layers in the document. This panel enables you to toggle whether layers are visible or not. as well whether to flatten or merge, layers.

The first six icons appear by default in the Navigation pane. The Layers panel appears only when you're working on a PDF document with layers. Figure 2-1 shows the icons in their default docked position, but you can undock them and float the panels in the workspace. You will learn to float interface objects in the upcoming section "Customize the Workspace." Click an icon to open the Navigation pane to that particular panel, and then click an icon or text area within the panel to navigate to a specific point in the document.

TIP *In addition to using these panels for document navigation, you also use them to perform specific functions, such as adding or deleting bookmarks; changing the size of thumbnails; extracting, inserting, replacing, or deleting pages; and so on. You click the Options icon of each panel to open a menu with options that pertain to the panel, as the following illustration shows. The operations you can perform differ, depending on the selected panel. You will find many of the panel Options menu commands duplicated in menu command groups. You will learn the different ways you can achieve the same result when specific topics, such as bookmarks and digital signatures, are covered in upcoming chapters.*

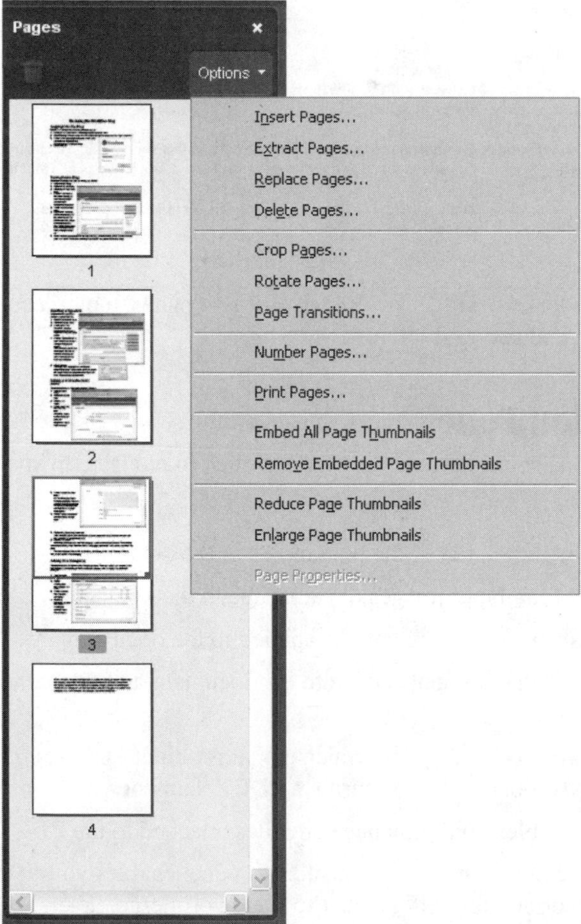

In addition to the Options menu, other icons vary in accordance with the tab you selected. The universally recognized garbage-can icon is used to delete selected items from the tab. In the upper-right corner of each panel's window, you'll find an *X*, which you can click to close the Navigation pane.

About the Document Pane

You use the Document pane (the large window to the right of the Navigation pane, previously shown in Figure 2-1) to edit a PDF document, as well as to read it. At the top of the Document pane is a toolbar that contains tools you can use to navigate to a specific page or pan to a specific place in the document. You use a new command when you read a document, which hides all toolbars and the navigation pane, to maximize your screen real estate. You can unhide the tools and panels with a keyboard shortcut or menu command. In Chapter 3, you learn how to use this new feature and all the other Acrobat tools.

About the How To Window

You can summon Acrobat's How To window, as shown in Figure 2-2, by clicking the icon with the question mark. The How To window contains task-oriented information for specific topics. To reveal information for a topic, click the Help task button, and then click the desired topic's name. For example, when you click the Comment & Markup title, you find a list of topics that pertain to reviewing a document and adding comments to it.

Use the Acrobat Menu Commands

You find the Acrobat menu commands at the top of the interface, grouped by command type. Acrobat has ten command groups, described in the following list, in order from left to right on the menu bar. In upcoming chapters, you will learn to use the commands from these menus to unlock the powerful features of Acrobat, such as capturing web pages. Individual menu commands are presented in detail when they pertain to the topic of discussion.

- **File** The commands in the *File* group are used to create PDF files, and to open, close, and save documents. There are also additional commands used to e-mail PDF files, export a document in different file formats, view document information, and start a meeting. In addition, you can find the powerful Organizer submenu in this menu group, which enables you to quickly locate and open PDF documents you previously viewed. You can also use the Organizer to create a collection of PDF documents.
- **Edit** As the name implies, the commands in the *Edit* group are used to perform edits to the current PDF document. There are also commands to search for items in the current document, search for words or phrases in PDF documents stored in folders on your computer, find words or phrases in a document, and set Acrobat preferences. You will learn how to set Acrobat preferences in the upcoming section "Set Preferences."

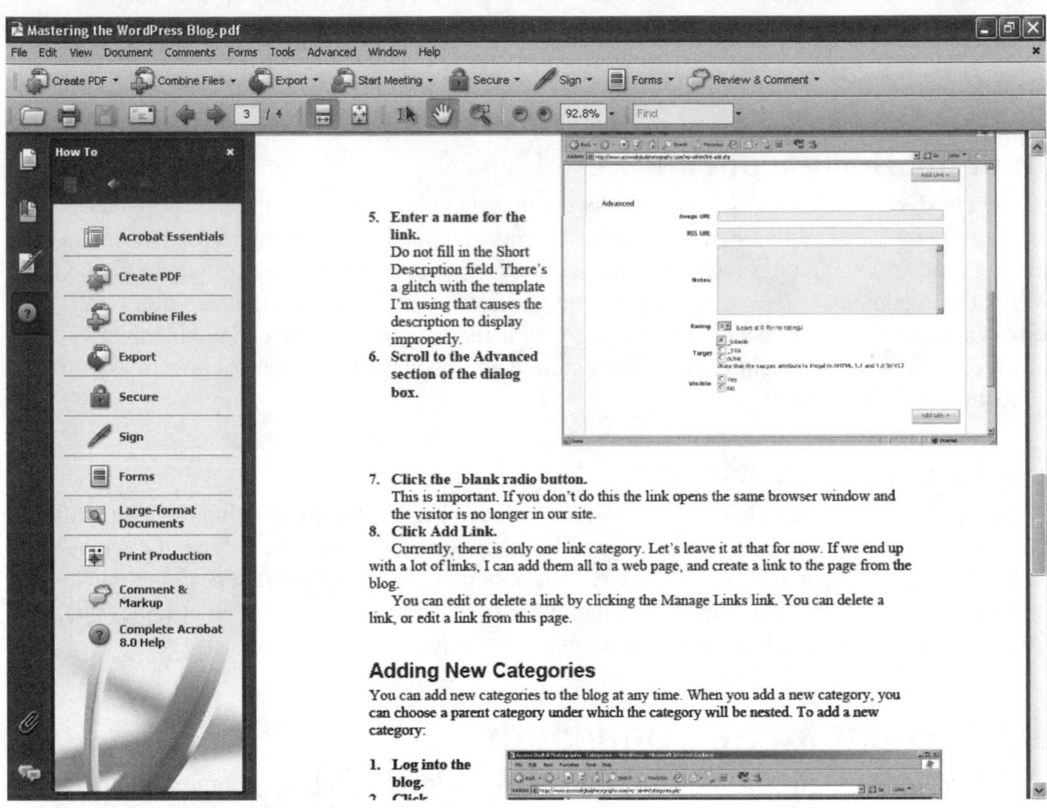

FIGURE 2-2 You can summon help whenever you need it.

- **View** The commands in the *View* group are used to change your view of the document. You use menu commands in this group to navigate to a specific page in the document, zoom in or out, change the manner in which the page is displayed, rotate the view, and so on. You will also find commands in this group to access Navigation panels and the toolbars.
- **Document** In the *Document* group, there are commands to add a header, footer, or watermark to a document. In addition, you use commands in this group insert, extract, replace, delete, and crop pages. If you have paper documents you want to convert to PDFs, complete with OCR recognition, you can find the applicable commands in this group.
- **Comments** In the *Comments* group, you find commands to add comments and mark up a PDF document, send a document for review, manage comments within a document, and manage reviews.

- **Forms (Windows Professional Only)** In the Forms group, you find commands to create new forms using Adobe Live Cycle Designer 8.0, recognize form fields from forms scanned into Acrobat, distribute forms, and manage distributed forms.
- **Tools** In the *Tools* group, you can choose tools to perform specific tasks. Similar tools are stored in submenus. For example, the tools used to create forms are found on the Forms submenu. You can also display a toolbar by using the Show command from the tool group submenu.
- **Advanced** The commands in the *Advanced* group are used to access the enhanced features of Acrobat, such as security, redaction, print production, document processing, web capture, and accessibility. You can also launch Acrobat Distiller, manage Digital IDs, optimize a PDF document, and perform advanced web capture commands using commands in this group.
- **Window** The commands in the *Window* group are used to select documents you currently have open, as well as arrange the view of multiple documents. You can also view a document in Full Screen mode by accessing a command from this menu. Another command enables you to open the active document in a new window.
- **Help** In the *Help* command group, you can find access to the How To window, complete program help, links to online help and program updates, as well as a feature you can use to repair the Acrobat installation if you feel something has gone awry. If you use Acrobat to read eBooks, you can manage digital editions from the Help command group.

Use Acrobat Toolbars

The tools you most often use to unleash the full power of Acrobat are conveniently grouped and laid out as task buttons and tool groups on a toolbar. You can access the rest of the Acrobat tools by choosing View | Toolbars, and then selecting the desired toolbar. You can also select individual tools from the submenus in the Tools menu. And, here, you can find the option to display a tool group's toolbar. Acrobat 8.0 toolbars are similar to those you've come to know in Acrobat 7.0. In version 8.0, you find subtle enhancements that speed your workflow. For example, you can customize toolbars to remove tools you don't use, or add tools not currently displayed on the toolbar. In the default display of toolbars, you can find task buttons that perform operations related to an Acrobat feature, such as commenting and marking up a document, creating a PDF file, and so on. In the other toolbars, you find related tools to edit, view, and navigate documents, and to perform many other operations.

Many of the toolbars have drop-down menus containing other options. The page magnification options are a perfect example: the display and magnification options appear when the down-pointing arrow to the right of the current display option is clicked.

TIP *You can click the Show command at the bottom of each toolbar submenu to display it as a floating toolbar, as outlined in the upcoming section "Float Toolbars."*

You can do most of your work in Acrobat using the toolbars, but most of the tools have equivalent menu commands. Most Acrobat users find it convenient to work with a combination of menu commands, tools, context menus, and shortcuts. For a list of popular Acrobat shortcuts, refer to Appendix A. Figure 2-3 shows the default display of Acrobat Professional toolbars.

The following sections describe the default Acrobat display of task buttons and toolbars as they appear below the menu bar. In each toolbar section, individual tools are listed with a brief description of the task for which they are used. In future chapters, you find detailed information about using a specific tool in conjunction with a related task. To clearly designate individual toolbars, illustrations show the toolbars as they appear when undocked.

Acrobat Professional has additional toolbars you can use to access the program's enhanced features. These toolbars are designated by the parenthetical reference (Professional only).

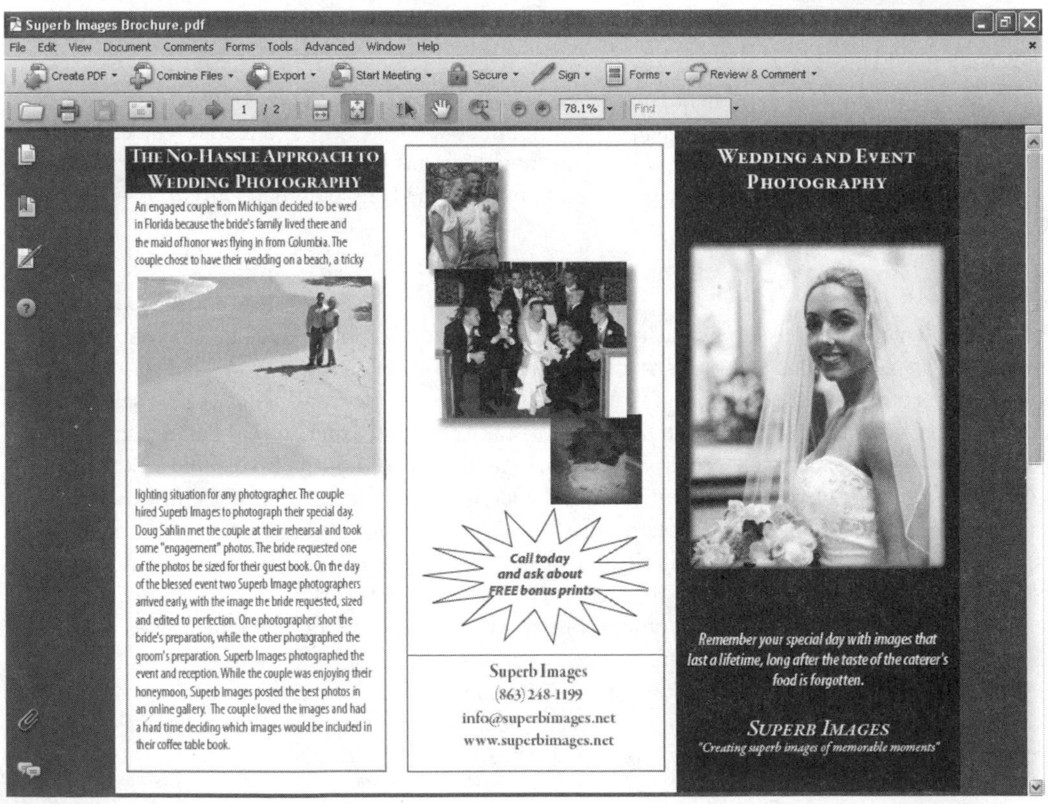

FIGURE 2-3 You use Acrobat task buttons and toolbars to create, edit, and navigate PDF documents.

The Tasks Toolbar

The default display of the *Professional Tasks toolbar* has eight task buttons you use to create PDF documents, combine files to create a PDF document, export PDF documents in other file formats, start a meeting, secure a document, digitally sign a document, create and track forms (Professional only), and review and comment PDF documents. The upcoming sections give you a brief overview of what you can accomplish with the commands you access when you click a task button. In addition to the commands used to perform tasks, each task button menu contains a Getting Started With... command, which, in essence, is a task-oriented dialog box that shows you how to get up and running quickly with the task button commands. The following illustration shows the Tasks toolbar.

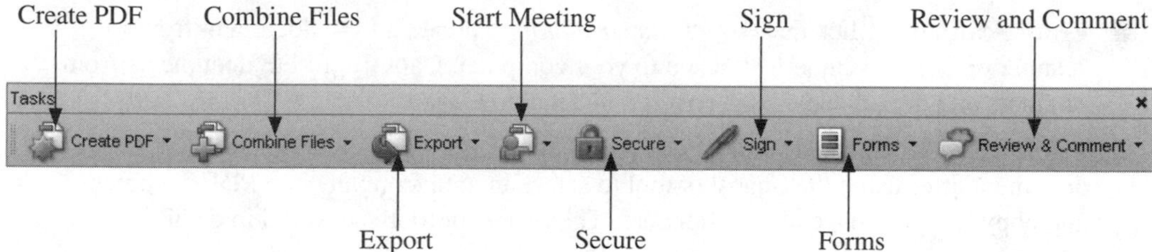

The Create PDF Task Button

The *Create PDF task button* accesses commands used to create a PDF document. When you click this button, a drop-down menu appears with all the commands you need to create PDF documents from files stored on your computer, from web pages, from documents you scan into the Document pane, and from images you've copied to the system clipboard. The Create PDF task button shown here, opens a menu with commands, which the following list describes:

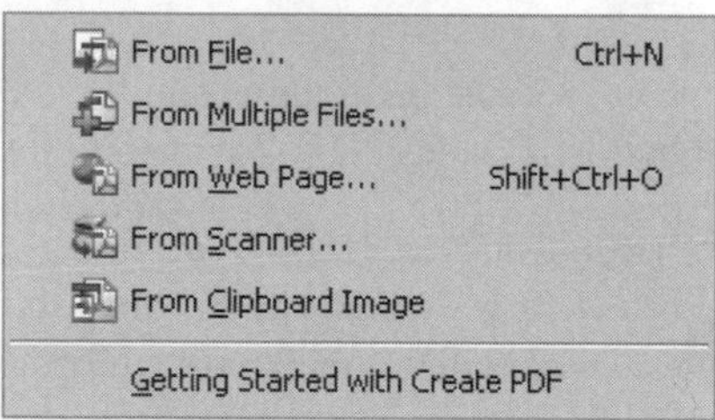

- **From File** Click the *From File button* to navigate to a file on your computer and convert it to a PDF document. Creating PDF documents from supported files is covered in detail in Chapter 4.
- **From Multiple Files** Click the *From Multiple Files button* to select several files and combine them as a single PDF document. The files you select can be different formats. For example, you can select a combination of Microsoft Word documents, PostScript files,

and image files, and then convert them to a multipage PDF document. After you select the files, you can arrange the order in which they appear in the PDF document, add additional files, and remove files. You also have the option of specifying the quality and resulting files' size of the PDF document. And, you can select an individual file and specify which pages of the file you want included in the finished PDF document. Creating PDF documents from multiple files is covered in Chapter 4.

- **From Web Page** Click the *From Web Page button* and a dialog box appears in which you enter the URL of the web page you want to convert to a PDF document. After converting the web page, you can modify it by choosing Advanced | Web Capture, and then choosing the desired command from the submenu. Capturing web pages is covered in Chapter 6.
- **From Scanner** Click the *From Scanner button* to create a PDF document from a scanner or a digital camera attached to your computer. Capturing PDF documents from scanners and digital cameras is covered in detail in Chapter 6.
- **From Clipboard Image** Click the *From Clipboard Image button* to create a PDF document after using the Snapshot tool to select an area from an open PDF document and copy it as an image to the clipboard. The Snapshot tool is covered in detail in Chapter 3.

The Combine Files Task Button

You click the *Combine Files task button* to open the menu shown in the following illustration.

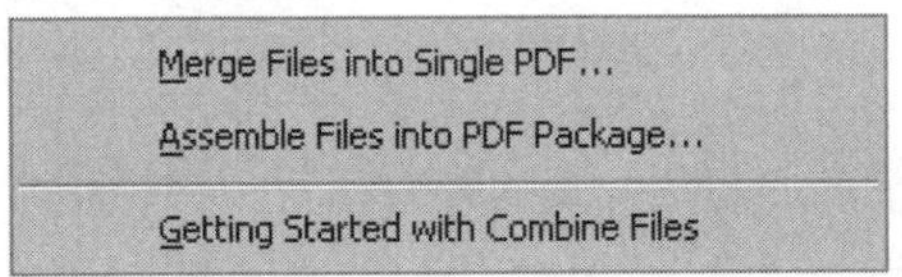

When you combine files, you can combine them into a single PDF document or create a PDF Package. The Combine Files task button includes the following commands:

- **Merge Files into Single PDF** Click the *Merge Files into Single PDF button* to open the Combine Files dialog box, which enables you to select individual files or a folder of files to combine to a single PDF. The files can be mixed formats supported by Acrobat. In addition, you can specify which pages of each document are combined into the resulting PDF.
- **Assemble Files into PDF Package** The *Assemble Files into PDF Package button* also opens the Combine Files dialog box. Instead of creating a single PDF document, though, each file is converted to a PDF document. When opened, the first PDF document appears in the document pane. Additional PDFs in the package can be opened by clicking the corresponding bookmark in the Bookmark tab.

The Export Task Button

You click the *Export task button* to open the menu shown next, which has commands to repurpose a PDF document into other file formats.

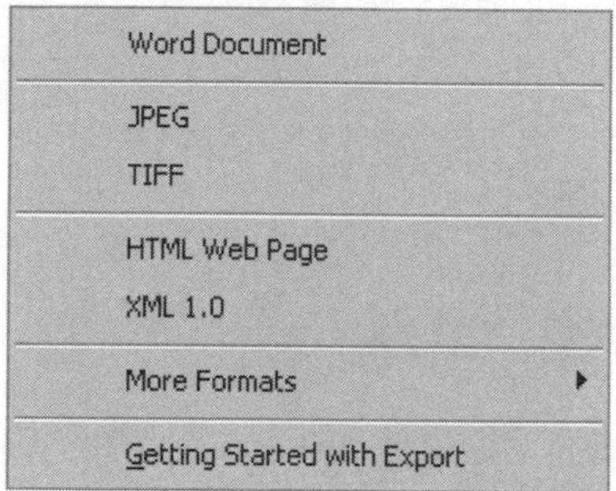

You have the following options from the Export task button menu:

- **Word Document** Click this button to export the document as a Microsoft Word document.
- **JPEG** Click this button to export the document as a JPEG image file.
- **TIFF** Click this button to export the document as a TIFF image file.
- **HTML Web Page** Click this button to export the document as a web page. Each page of the document is exported as an image file embedded in an HTML document (HTML 4.01 with CSS 1.0).
- **XML** Click this button to export the document as an XML file.
- **More Formats** Click this button for additional commands to export a PDF document in the following formats: Encapsulated Postscript (EPS), HTML 3.2, PNG, PostScript (PS), Rich Text Format (RTF), Text (Accessible), or Text (Plain).

The Start Meeting Task Button

You click the *Start Meeting task button* to reveal the menu shown next.

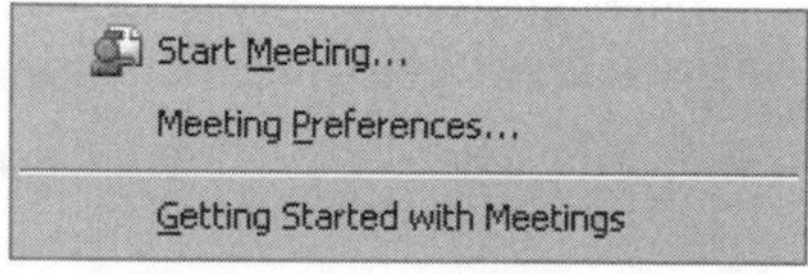

This new Acrobat feature enables you to start an online meeting using Acrobat Connect, a derivative of Macromedia Breeze. The Start Meeting task button has the following commands:

- **Start Meeting** Click this button to open a dialog box, which enables you to start a meeting using Acrobat Connect. When you first open this dialog box, you have an option to sign up for a free trial of the service.
- **Meeting Preferences** Click this button to open the Meeting section of the Preferences dialog box.

The Secure Task Button

With the commands available via the *Secure task button*, you can restrict access to a document, create an encrypted document, or display the security and restrictions applied to the currently selected document. When you click the Secure task button, you can choose from the following commands:

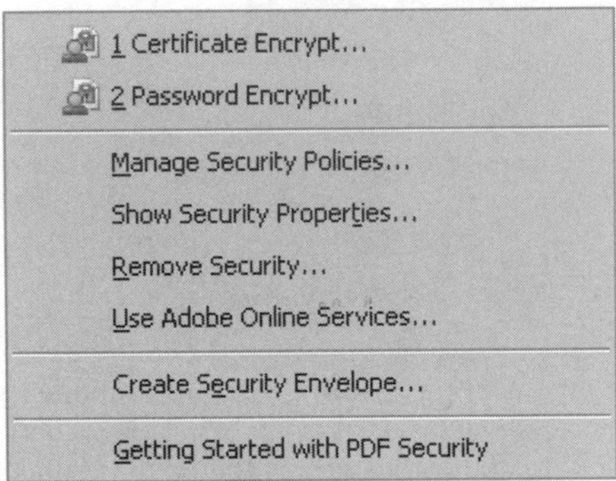

- **Certificate Encrypt** With this command, you certify the contents of the document and encrypt them as well.
- **Password Encrypt** With this command, you password-protect and encrypt the document contents. You can apply security, so a password is needed to open the document. If you need to take security one step further, you can apply a second password to restrict editing of the document.
- **Manage Security Policies** This command opens the Manage Security Policies dialog box, which enables you to edit a security policy you've already applied to the current document, create a new security policy, copy a security policy, view a security policy, edit a security policy, delete a security policy, and designate a security policy as your favorite.
- **Show Security Policies** This command opens the Document Properties dialog box with the Security tab selected. After viewing the security policies applied to the document, you can modify them and apply them to the document.
- **Remove Security** This command opens a dialog box that enables you to remove all security from the document with the click of a button.
- **Use Adobe Online Services** This command opens the Secure Using Adobe Online Service dialog box. You must be a registered user of Adobe Online Services to secure a document in this manner.

- **Create Security Envelope** This command opens the Create Security Envelope dialog box, which enables you to secure files already open in Acrobat, and/or files you select from folders on your computer or network. The files can be any file format supported by Acrobat. After deciding which files to secure, you select a template, select the security policy, add your identity, and select the method by which the secured files will be delivered. The method of security is designed for file attachments to be sent via e-mail.

The Sign Task Button

You can use the commands available via the *Sign task button* to digitally sign a document and verify any signatures applied to the document. When you click this button, you have access to the following commands:

- **Place Signature** You use this command to apply your digital signature to a document.
- **Sign This Document** You use this command to apply your digital signature to a document being reviewed.
- **Certify with Visible Signature** You use this command to certify the contents of a document with your digital signature. A blue seal in the upper-left corner of the signature signifies that the owner of the digital signature has certified the contents.
- **Certify Without Visible Signature** You use this command to certify the contents of a document, without placing a visible signature inside the document. When the certified document is opened, a blue seal appears at the top of the navigation pane.
- **Validate All Signatures** You use this command to validate all digital signatures that have been applied to the document. A signature is validated if it is part of your Trusted Identities list.

The Forms Task Button (Professional and Windows Only)

If you need to create interactive PDF forms, Acrobat Professional gives you all the tools you need to accomplish the task. You can create forms using existing PDF documents or, if you use Acrobat Professional on a Windows machine, you can create forms from scratch with an application known as Adobe LiveCycle Designer 8.0. When you click the Forms Task button, the following commands are available, as described in the following list:

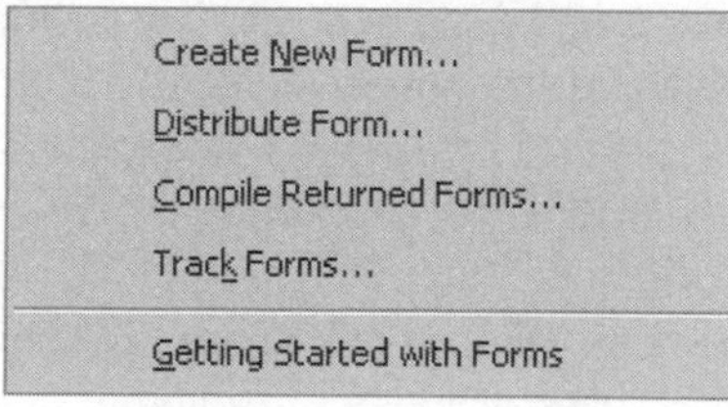

- **Create New Form** You use this command to open the Create a New Form dialog box, which gives you several options for creating an interactive form in Adobe LiveCycle Designer 8.0.
- **Distribute Form** You use this command to open a dialog box that enables you to distribute a PDF form via e-mail.
- **Compile Returned Forms** You use this command to compile data collected from distributed forms that have been returned. The returned data is saved as a PDF data set, which can be exported as CSV (comma delimited data) that can be used in a spreadsheet application.
- **Track Forms** This command opens the Forms Tracker, which enables you to manage forms you have distributed, and forms you've received from other authors.

The Review & Comment Task Button

You click the *Review & Comment task button* to open the menu shown next, which has commands you use to add comments (called *annotations* in early versions of Acrobat) to a PDF document.

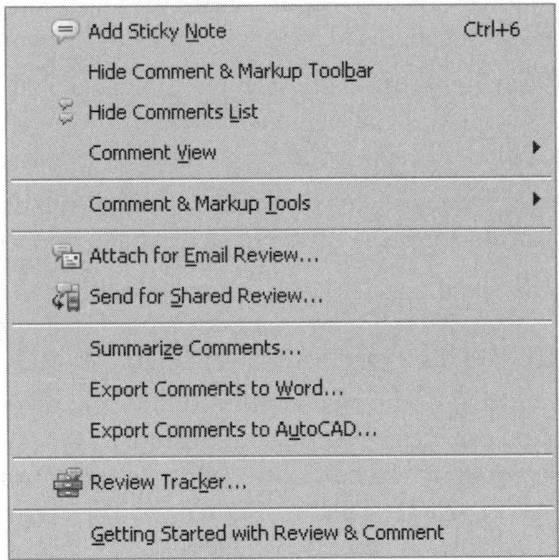

Your comments can be in the form of sticky notes, free-form text, file attachments, and sound files. The Comment & Markup task button menu also includes two toolbars:

- **Add Sticky Note** You use this command to add a blank Sticky Note to a document. This is the equivalent of the Note tool in previous versions of Acrobat.
- **Show Comment & Markup Toolbar** You use this command to display the Comment & Markup toolbar in the workspace. After displaying the toolbar, this command becomes Hide Comment & Markup Toolbar.

- **Show Comments List** You use this command to open the Comments panel, which enables you to manage all comments within the document.
- **Comment View** This command displays a submenu of options that enable you to specify which comments are displayed in the document and Comments panel.
- **Comment & Markup Tools** This command displays a submenu of all Comment & Markup Tools.
- **Attach for Email Review** This command opens the Send by Email for Review dialog box, which enables you to choose reviewers, and then send the document to the intended recipients.
- **Send for Shared Review** This command opens the Send PDF for Shared Review dialog box, which enables you to specify the repository where the comments are stored, and the recipients of the shared review.
- **Summarize Comments** This command opens the Summarize Options dialog box. After choosing your options, you can create a PDF that contains a summary of all comments.
- **Export Comments to Word** This command exports all comments in the PDF to a Word document. This command only works with Word 2002 and newer.
- **Export Comments to AutoCAD** This command exports all comments in the document to AutoCAD if installed on the host system.
- **Review Tracker** This command opens the Review Tracker, which enables you to create and manage reviews.

The File Toolbar

The File toolbar, as the next illustration shows, consists of four tools you use to open, print, save, and e-mail PDF documents.

Here are the tools on the File toolbar:

- **Open** Click this button to navigate to and open an existing PDF file stored on your computer or network.
- **Print** This tool is used to print a document with a system printer.

- **Save** This tool is used to save the current PDF document. This command is dimmed out (unavailable) if you open an existing document and do not edit it, or if you open an existing document that cannot be edited because of restrictions applied by the document's author.
- **Email** Click this button to send a PDF document as an e-mail attachment using your default e-mail application. If you're logged onto the Internet, and your e-mail application supports automatic mailing, the message and attachment is sent. Otherwise, the message and attachment appear in the out basket of your e-mail application. Information on sending PDF documents as e-mail attachments is presented in detail in Chapters 5 and 13.

The Page Navigation Toolbar

The *Page Navigation toolbar* is comprised of the tools you use to navigate from one page to the next. The Page Navigation toolbar, shown next, has a forward and back button, which you use to go to the next or previous page. You can also navigate to a page by entering its number in the text box.

The Page Display Toolbar

The *Page Display toolbar,* shown next, has two buttons by default. You use these buttons to control your view of the page.

The buttons on the Page Display toolbar are:

- **Continuous** This page display option conforms the width of the page to fit within the width of the Document pane.
- **Single Page** This page display option displays a single page. You can use the Hand tool to pan within the page, and use the navigation tools to navigate to different pages.

The Select and Zoom Toolbar

The tools in this toolbar (as the following illustration shows) are used to select objects, manually navigate to different parts of a document, and activate links in the document. The enhanced features of these tools are discussed in Chapter 3. Selecting text and graphics for use in other applications is also discussed in detail in Chapter 3.

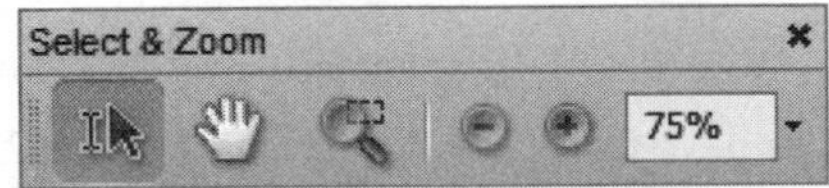

- **Select** This tool enables you to select text, tables, or images in a PDF document. You can then copy selected objects to the clipboard for use in other applications.

- **Hand** This aptly named tool is used to manually navigate through the pages of a PDF document. First, click the tool to select it; then, when you click inside the Document pane to navigate with this tool, your cursor becomes a closed fist. To navigate from the top to the bottom of a page and vice versa, select the Hand tool, move the tool over the document, and then click-and-drag. Release the left mouse button to stop scrolling the page. The Hand tool is also used to find and activate links within the document. When you pass your cursor over a document link or a bookmark in the Bookmark tab, the cursor becomes a pointing finger. Click the link or bookmark to navigate to the specified destination within the document.
- **Marquee Zoom** This tool is used to zoom to a specific part of the document. After selecting the tool, click-and-drag diagonally within the document to zoom to that part of the document.
- **Zoom Out** Click this tool to zoom out to the next lowest level of magnification.
- **Zoom In** Click this tool to zoom in to the next highest level of magnification.
- **Magnification Window** Acrobat displays the current percentage level of magnification in this window. You can click the triangle to the right of the window and select a magnification percentage from the drop-down menu, or you can enter the desired level of magnification directly into the window, and then press ENTER or RETURN to apply. You can also specify a magnification level by choosing View | Zoom To, and then entering a value between 1 percent and 6400 percent in the Zoom To dialog box (the available range of magnification in Acrobat). Note, the lowest magnification level available from the Magnification drop-down list is 10 percent, but you can enter a value of 1 if desired.

TIP *If you use the zoom tools frequently, you can float the Zoom toolbar (the Acrobat Standard Zoom toolbar is shown in the previous illustration) by clicking the triangle to the right of the currently selected zoom tool, and then choosing Show Zoom Toolbar.*

Use the Find Window

The Find window was reintroduced in Acrobat 7.0. You use the *Find window* to search for words or phrases within a document. To search for a word or phrase, type it in the window, and then press ENTER or RETURN. The Find window, has a drop-down menu that enables you to fine-tune a query or use the powerful Search command.

NOTE Find *is for current document only searching, whereas* Search *can be used for multiple documents or index-based searching.*

Use the Other Acrobat Toolbars

In previous sections, you learned about the task buttons and toolbars displayed by default. The designers of Acrobat have uncluttered the interface by hiding infrequently used toolbars. You can, however, display these toolbars as needed by choosing the proper command from the View menu. The sections that follow describe one additional task button and the other toolbars.

The Acrobat Standard Advanced Editing Toolbar

The *Advanced Editing toolbar* provides the tools you need to add interactivity to your PDF documents. On this toolbar, you find tools to add links, crop pages, touch up text, and more. To access the Acrobat Standard Advanced Editing toolbar, choose View | Toolbars | Advanced Editing. After choosing the toolbar, you can modify a PDF document using the following tools:

- **Select Object** This tool is used to select objects in a PDF document. Click the page to show all links, fields, and objects. Double-click an object to edit it.
- **Article** This tool is used to select a portion of a PDF document and give it a name, known in Acrobat as an *article* or *article thread.* An article can be a single block of text or several blocks of related text dispersed throughout the document. When readers view your document, they can follow the thread of the article using the Articles panel.
- **Crop** This tool is used to reduce the size of a page by cropping to a smaller area than the original page. This tool can be used to crop out elements, such as unwanted graphics and extraneous text, from a PDF document page. If you have used cropping tools in image-editing programs, you'll find this tool performs in a similar manner.
- **Link** This tool is used to add interactivity to your documents. You can create visible or invisible links. You can use document links for navigation or to trigger an event, such as opening a file or opening a web page. Acrobat calls these events *actions*, and you have a wide variety of actions from which you can choose. Detailed uses for this tool are discussed in Chapter 7.
- **Digital Signature Field** This tool is used to add a blank digital signature field to documents, which can be digitally signed by document recipients. You can specify whether signing the document is required, whether a border is displayed, whether an action occurs when the field is signed, and so on.
- **TouchUp Text** This tool is used to make minor corrections to text objects in a PDF document. After selecting this tool, you can replace text, add text, and change text color, font, size, or style.
- **TouchUp Object** This tool is used to make minor corrections to graphic elements in a PDF document. After selecting an object with the tool, you can resize the object. Right-click (Windows) or CTRL-click (Macintosh) an object with the tool to access other options from the context menu.

The Acrobat Professional Advanced Editing Toolbar

If you own Acrobat Professional, you have additional tools on the Advanced Editing toolbar, as shown in the following illustration. You may notice the Digital Signature tool is missing from the Professional Advanced Editing toolbar. The tool is still available, but in the Professional version, it's on the Forms toolbar (see the upcoming section, "The Forms Tools").

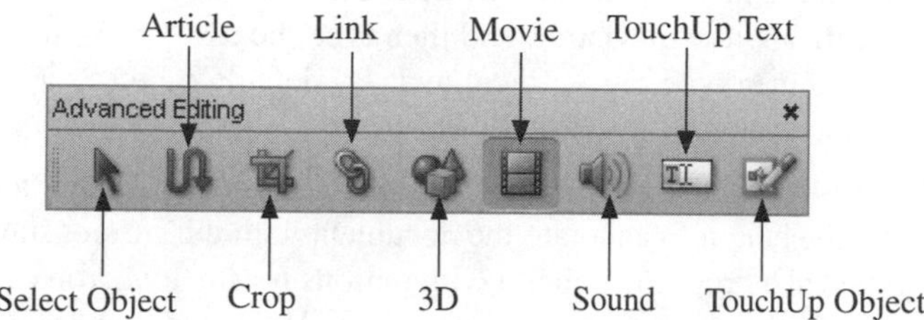

- **3D** You use the 3D tool to add 3D content in the form of *U3D files to a document. This tool works similarly to the Movie tool in that you specify what appears in the document.
- **Movie** This tool is used to add supported video files and Flash SWF movies to your PDF files. You specify the location where the movie will play in the document and the trigger used to begin the movie. You can choose to display the first frame of the movie, which, when clicked, will begin playing, or choose to leave the movie invisible until a button is clicked or a page action executes to begin play.
- **Sound** This tool is used to add sound clips to a PDF document. You specify the location where the sound will play in the document and the trigger used to begin playing the sound.

The Comment & Markup Toolbar

The *Comment & Markup toolbar* is used quite frequently during a review cycle. You access this toolbar by choosing View | Toolbars | Comment & Markup. The tasks you perform with the commenting and markup tools are discussed in detail in Chapter 10. The Comment & Markup toolbar, shown in the following illustration, includes the following tools:

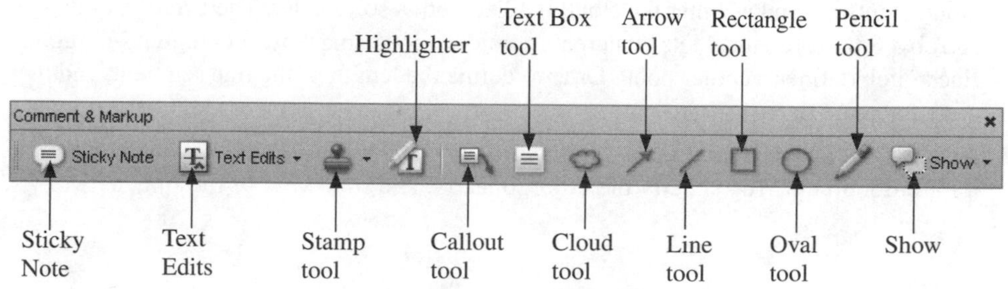

- **Sticky Note** Click this button to add a note to a document, which is the PDF equivalent of a Post-it Note. When you annotate a PDF document with a note, you can leave the note open or display it in the document as an icon that, when clicked, displays the note.
- **Text Edits** Click this button to display a list of commands you can use to select text that needs to be edited in a document. You can select text and mark it for deletion. You can also create an insertion caret, and then type the text you want to add, or select a block of text, and then type replacement text. By default, a note is added to the selected text.
- **Stamp Tool** This tool is used to add your stamp of approval (or other annotations) to a document. Click the button to annotate the document with the current stamp, or click the down arrow to reveal a drop-down menu with options for the tool. You can choose a stamp from three major categories: Dynamic, Sign Here, and Standard Business. Each category is subdivided into a wide array of presets, such as Approved, Reviewed, and Confidential. You can also find menu commands to create a custom stamp, manage stamps, and show the Stamps Palette.
- **Highlighter** To the right of the Stamp tool, you find the Highlighter tool. This is the electronic equivalent of the highlighter you buy in your office supply store. You know, the one you keep forgetting to cap after use. Fortunately, this Highlighter tool never dries up. Use it to add a yellow highlight to text in a PDF document.
- **Callout Tool** This tool is used to add a text callout that points toward a particular object in a PDF document. The text box is a fixed size, which changes when you add enough text to wrap to another line. You can edit the callout after adding it to a document.
- **Text Box** Use this tool to add freeform text notes to a PDF document. When you annotate a document with this tool, you can specify the color, opacity, and thickness of the text box border, as well as the text box fill color (or lack thereof, if you so choose). If desired, you can use the Properties bar to change the font type, size, and style of selected text within a text box.
- **Cloud Tool (Professional Only)** This tool is used to annotate a PDF document with shapes that look like clouds. You specify the color, opacity, style, and thickness of the cloud's outline, and whether the cloud is filled with a solid color. The *Cloud tool* in Acrobat 8.0 Professional lets you create a unique cloud shape by clicking-and-dragging. Each click defines a corner point. Drag to define the length of the line segment, and then click to create the next point.
- **Arrow Tool (Professional only)** This tool is used to add lines with arrowheads to a PDF document. You specify the color, opacity, and thickness of the line, as well

as the shape of the arrowhead, and whether one end of the line (or both) has an arrowhead.

- **Line** This tool is used to add straight lines to a PDF document. You specify the color and width of the line. You can even modify the appearance of the line by adding a shape, such as a diamond, to either end of the line.
- **Rectangle** This tool is used to add a square or rectangle to a PDF file. You can specify the thickness and color of the border, and whether the shape is filled with color.
- **Oval** This tool is used to create circles and ovals. You can specify the thickness and color of the border, and whether the shape is filled with color.
- **Pencil** This tool is used to add a freeform line to a PDF file. You can modify the color and thickness of lines you draw. Acrobat smoothes the line after you create it, but your drawing skill with a mouse determines the final appearance of the line.
- **Show** Click this button to choose from a list of commands that enable you to manage comments within the document. You can display the Comments list and determine whether connector lines and comment pop-ups are displayed.

The Edit Toolbar

If you prefer the convenience of toolbars when editing a document, the Edit toolbar is right up your alley. You can undo and redo commands with the *Edit toolbar*, copy selcted items to the clipboard, and spell check comments and form fields. To float the Edit toolbar in the workspace, choose View | Toolbars | Edit. The Edit toolbar, as shown next, contains the tools described in the following list:

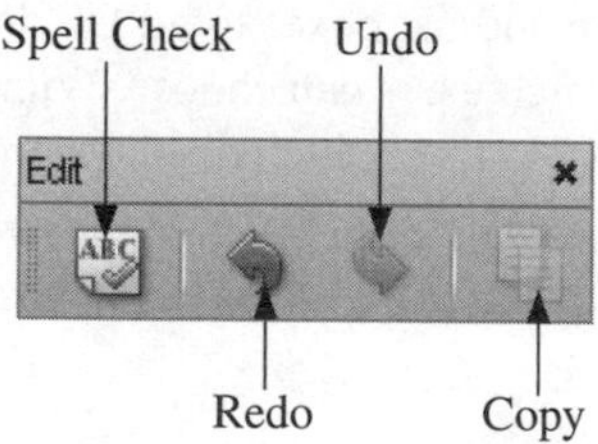

- **Spell Check** This tool is used to spell check comments and form fields.
- **Undo** This tool undoes the last command you performed.
- **Redo** This tool redoes the last command you performed.
- **Copy** This tool copies selected objects to the clipboard.

The Forms Toolbar

When you're creating or editing forms with Acrobat Professional, you'll find it handy to display the Forms toolbar by choosing View | Toolbars | Forms. The Forms toolbar, shown next, contains the following tools:

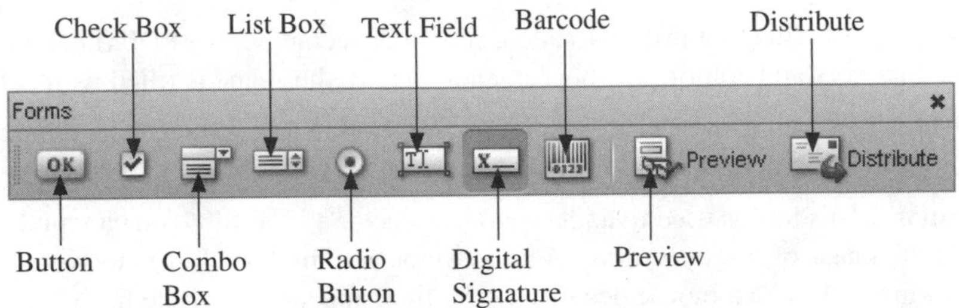

- **Button** This tool is used to add interactive buttons to a PDF document. The buttons work like buttons in an HTML document.
- **Check Box** This tool is used to add check boxes to a PDF document. Check boxes can be used as items in a PDF form that you use to gather information. You can create a series of check boxes when you want viewers to be able to select more than one item from a list of choices, for example, a viewer survey asking why a certain product is used.
- **Combo Box** This tool is used to add combo boxes to a PDF document. A combo box displays a single item from a pop-up menu. Viewers of the PDF document click a button to reveal the entire list.
- **List Box** This tool is used to add list boxes to a PDF document. A *list box* is used to display a list of items from which users can choose. With a list box, the entire list is displayed, as opposed to a *combo box*, which displays only one item from the list.
- **Radio Button** This tool is used to add radio buttons to a document. *Radio buttons* are used when you want viewers to choose only one item from a list—for example, the type of credit card they intend to use.
- **Text Field** This tool is used when you want to add a text field to a PDF document. Text fields can be used to gather information from viewers of a PDF document or display read-only information.
- **Digital Signature** This tool is used to add a placeholder for a digital signature.
- **Barcode** This tool is used to add a field to encode data that users enter into a fillable PDF form. This field is used for forms that will be converted to paper and processed using Adobe's Barcoded Paper Forms Solution, which requires a separate license.
- **Preview** This enables you to preview and test the form. After clicking this button, its name changes to Edit Layout, which, when clicked, enables you to edit the document and form fields.
- **Distribute** This tool opens the Distribute Form dialog box, which enables you to distribute the form to the desired recipients via e-mail.

The Measuring Toolbar (Professional Only)

The *Measuring toolbar* gives you a set of tools with which you can accurately measure the distance between objects. After using this tool, an annotation appears in the form of a single line (Distance tool) or multiple lines (Perimeter and Area tool). The measurements appear in the tool's dialog box, and also appear in the form of a tooltip, which appears when a user hovers a mouse over the tool's annotation. This toolset is especially useful if you're working with PDF documents that were created from AutoCAD documents. To access the Measuring toolbar, shown in the following illustration, choose View | Toolbars | Measuring.

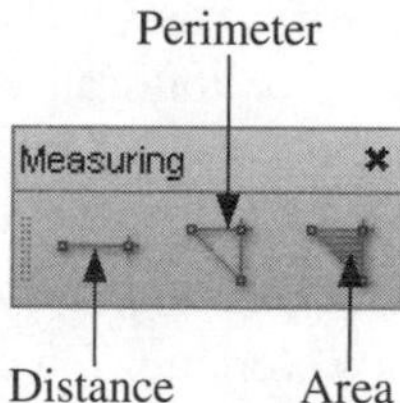

The following are the three tools on the Measuring toolbar:

- **Distance** This tool is used to measure the distance between two points.
- **Perimeter** This tool is used to measure the distance between multiple points.
- **Area** This tool is used to measure the area within points that you create with the tool.

The Object Data Toolbar

This toolbar has one tool, the *Object Data Tool*, which is used to view object metadata. If you open a PDF document with Visio object data, the Object Data Tool automatically appears in the Status Bar. To access the Object Data toolbar shown next, choose View | Toolbars | Object Data.

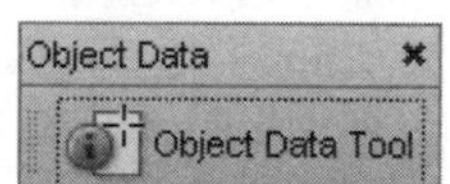

The Print Production Toolbar (Professional Only)

The tools on the *Print Production toolbar* are used to prepare a document for high-resolution, full-color output on a commercial printer. The tools are used in conjunction with two menu commands to provide you with a complete workflow for print production. The following list describes tools that are available on the Print Production toolbar, which is shown next:

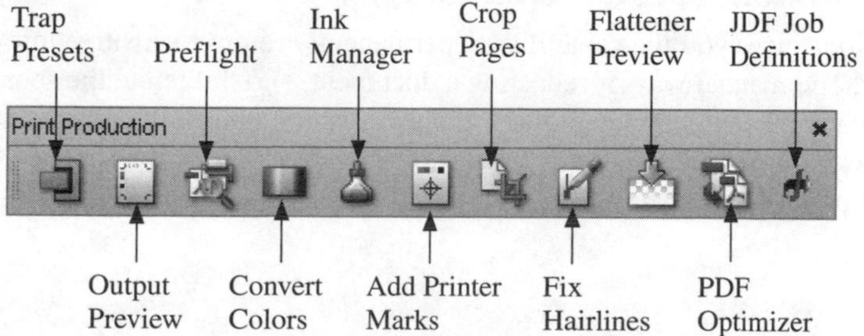

- **Trap Presets** With this tool, you can create and apply trap settings for later use on an Adobe PostScript 3 RIP that licenses Adobe In-RIP trapping.
- **Output Preview** This tool opens the Output Preview dialog box, which enables you to view a separation preview, soft proofing, and so on. You can also access the Ink Manager from within this dialog box.
- **Preflight** This tool enables you to perform over 400 predefined checks for output errors commonly associated with a designer's file. You can also check a document for PDF-A compliance, PDF-X compliance, and more.
- **Convert Colors** With this tool, you can convert CMYK (**C**yan, **M**agenta, **Y**ellow, and Blac**K**), RGB (**R**ed, **G**reen, and **B**lue), or grayscale colors to the target CMYK color space. The tool also enables you to embed an ICC (International Color Consortium) color profile in the document.
- **Ink Manager** With this tool, you can modify the way inks are treated in the PDF document on which you are currently working. You use the Ink Manager to determine how inks are viewed in the Output Preview dialog box, and how inks print when printing separations.
- **Add Printer Marks** With this tool, you can add printer marks to the PDF document on which you are working. Printer marks are embedded as content as they were in Acrobat 6.0.
- **Crop Pages** This tool launches the Crop Pages dialog box, which enables you to specify the size of the crop, trim, bleed, art, and media boxes on a PDF document.
- **Fix Hairlines** This tool opens the Fix Hairlines dialog box, which enables you to replace thin lines that may not be printable with lines of a heavier weight.
- **Flattener Preview** With this tool, you can detect transparent objects and objects that will be affected by transparency flattening.
- **PDF Optimizer** This tool opens the PDF Optimizer dialog box, which enables you to optimize the document for the intended destination, as well as embed fonts if desired.
- **JDF Job Definitions** This tool enables you to create a JDF (Job Definition Format) job definition, a document that provides your printer with information such as the number of copies to be printed, the product name, client information, and so on.

The Redaction Toolbar (Professional Only)

The *Redaction toolbar* gives you the capability to permanently remove sensitive information within a document. The manual way of redacting a document is to obliterate the sensitive information with black ink, and then copy the document. Virtual redaction works in the same way; the recipient cannot decipher the redacted information. The Redaction toolbar, shown next, features the following tools:

- **Mark for Redaction** This tool gives you the capability to mark text or objects for redaction.
- **Apply Redactions** This tool applies redaction to text and objects previously marked for redaction.
- **Redaction Properties** This tool opens the Redaction Tool Properties dialog box where you specify the fill color for redaction objects, apply overlay text if desired, and more.
- **Search and Redact** This tool opens the Search dialog box with the default Search button relabeled Search and Redact. You enter the text you want to redact, and then click the Search and Redact button.

The Typewriter Toolbar

With the *Typewriter tool*, you can type inside a PDF document provided it hasn't been locked for editing. The Typewriter toolbar, shown in the following illustration, has additional tools to change text you've typed with the tool.

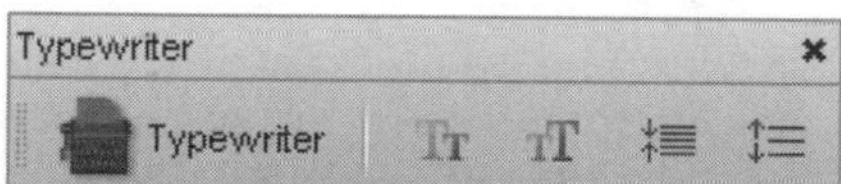

The Typewriter toolbar has the following tools:

- **Typewriter** This tool gives you the capability to type within a PDF document.
- **Smaller Text** This tool becomes available when you click the Typewriter tool in a block of text created with the tool. Click the tool to decrease the size of the text to the next lowest size. You can click the tool repeatedly to further decrease text size.
- **Larger Text** This tool becomes available when you click the Typewriter tool in a block of text created with the tool. Click the tool to increase the size of the text to the next largest size. You can click the tool repeatedly to further increase text size.
- **Decrease Line Spacing** This tool becomes available when you click the Typewriter tool in a block of text created with the tool. Click the tool to decrease the line spacing. You can click the tool repeatedly to further decrease line spacing.
- **Increase Line Spacing** This tool becomes available when you click the Typewriter tool in a block of text created with the tool. Click the tool to increase the line spacing. You can click the tool repeatedly to further increase line spacing.

The Properties Bar

If you've used Acrobat previously, you know that objects such as comments, links, and form fields have properties you can edit. You can right-click (Windows) or CTRL-click (Macintosh) and open the Properties dialog box from the context menu to edit the object. If you are going to edit the properties of several objects, however, you can choose View | Toolbars | Properties Bar to display the Properties bar, shown in the following illustration. After displaying the Properties bar, select an object to reveal and edit the object's properties. The title in the Properties bar changes, depending on the type of object you selected.

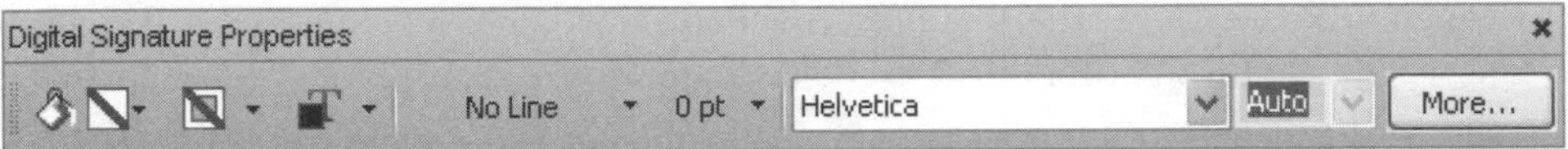

Customize the Workspace

As you become more comfortable with Acrobat, you'll find you use certain tools more often than others. Adobe has engineered flexibility into the program, making it possible for you to customize the workspace to suit your working preference. You can customize the workspace by floating toolbars and tabs, as well as by expanding toolbars you frequently use.

Float Toolbars

When you edit PDF documents and perform the same task numerous times, reaching up to select a tool from the command bar can be distracting. If this is the case, or if you prefer working with a certain toolbar in a different position, you can float any toolbar to a different position. To float a toolbar displayed on the command bar, click the vertical line at the left edge of the toolbar and drag it into the Document window. Release the mouse button when the toolbar is where you want it. To float a toolbar that isn't displayed, choose View | Toolbars, and then select the toolbar you want to float in the workspace. To move a floating toolbar, click its title bar, drag it to a new position, and release the mouse button. Figure 2-4 shows several floating toolbars in the Document pane.

To dock a floating toolbar to the command bar, click the toolbar title, and then drag-and-drop it on the command bar. When you close a floating toolbar, it does not redock itself. When you open the toolbar again, it floats in the last position you left it.

Float Navigation Pane Panels

You can float any panel in the Navigation pane by clicking its icon and dragging it out of the Navigation pane. Release the mouse button when the panel is in the desired position. After you float a panel, you can change its height by clicking-and-dragging the horizontal bar at the base

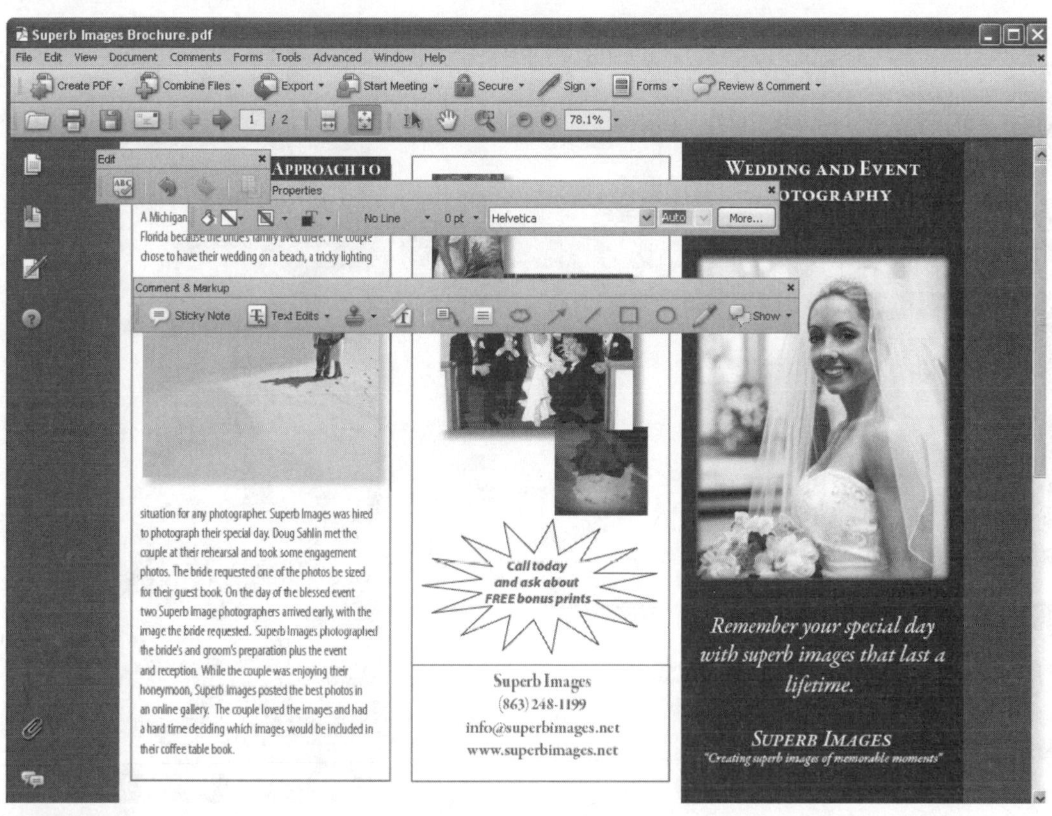

FIGURE 2-4 You can rearrange the workspace by floating toolbars.

of the panel. You change the width of a floating panel by clicking-and-dragging the vertical bar on the left or right side of the panel. Figure 2-5 shows two floating panels in the Document pane. The panel on the right has been resized.

To redock a panel in the Navigation pane, click its name, and then drag-and-drop it into the pane. Note, when you redock a panel, it appears at the bottom of the pane, but above the Comments and Attachment panels, regardless of its original position. If you float, and then redock the Comments or Attachments panels, they resume a default position at the bottom of the Navigation pane.

TIP *To reset the panels to their default positions, choose View | Navigation Panels | Reset Panels.*

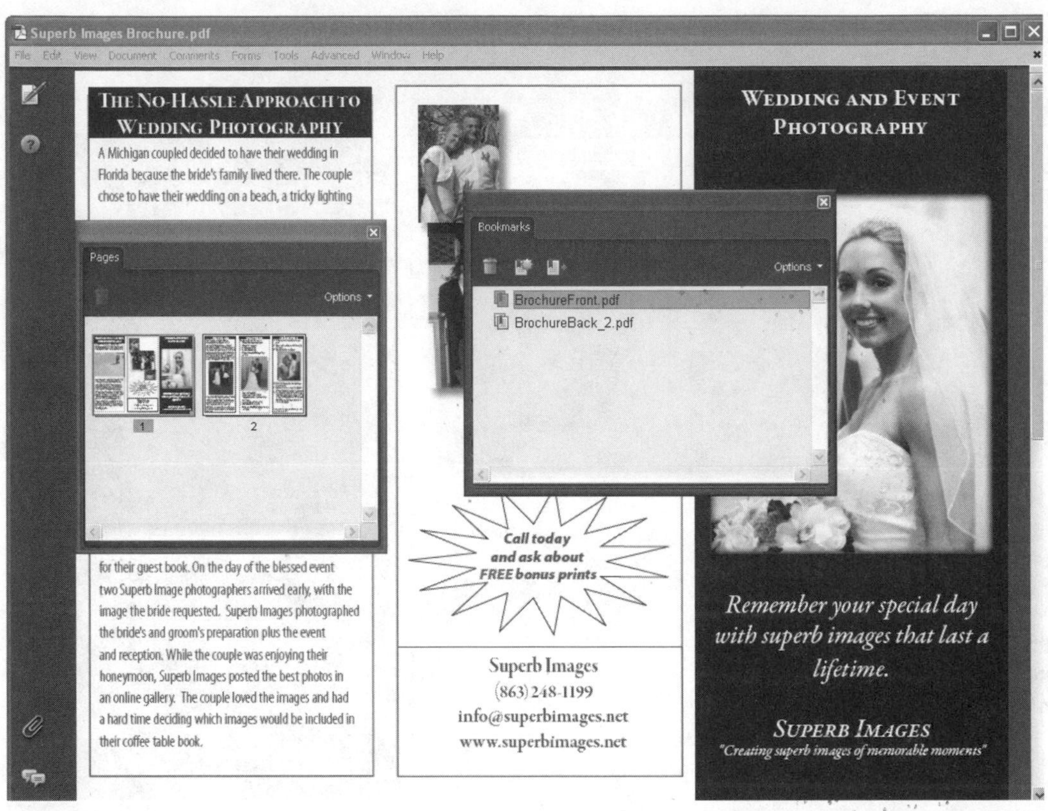

FIGURE 2-5 You can float and resize panels to suit your working preference.

Group Panels

When you have more than one panel floating in the Document pane, you can group them to conserve monitor space. To create a panel group, click the name of a floating panel and drag it into another floating panel. As you drag the panel, a bounding box shows you the current location of the panel. When the bounding box locks on the target group, release the mouse button to add the panel to the existing group. You can group as many panels as needed. To access an individual panel in a group, click its name. Note, you can combine Navigation pane panels with panels opened from menu commands, such as the Destinations and Articles panels. In Figure 2-6, you see a custom panel group consisting of panels accessed from the View menu.

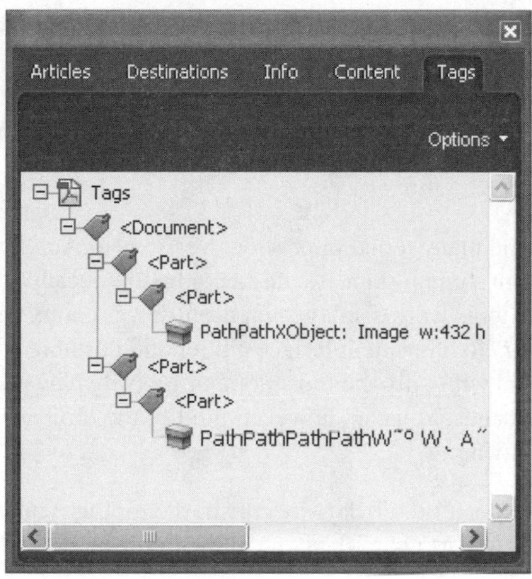

FIGURE 2-6 You can create a panel group by dragging-and-dropping one panel into another.

How to ... Save Time with Context Menus

Acrobat Standard and Acrobat Professional have context menus that can streamline your production and speed your workflow. Context menu options vary depending on the tool you use and the pane in which you work. For example, if you access a context menu in Acrobat after selecting a block of text with the Select tool, you have a list of several options or commands you can perform on the selected block of text. If you open the context menu in Acrobat while in the Signatures panel, you have a different set of options that pertain to digital signatures within the document and their properties. Individual panel context menu commands and options are discussed in detail in later chapters of this book. To open a context menu associated with a panel, position your cursor within the panel, and then right-click (Windows) or CTRL-click (Macintosh). To open a context menu specific to an object, select the object, and then right-click (Windows) or CTRL-click (Macintosh).

If you frequently use panels (like the Destinations and Articles panels), you can dock them within the Navigation pane or leave them floating in the Document pane. To dock a panel to the Navigation pane, choose the desired panel from the View menu. After the panel appears in the Document pane, click its name and drag it into the Navigation pane. The next time you launch Acrobat, the panel will be in its new home.

Access More Tools

Acrobat has many features, and many tools. In previous versions of Acrobat, the tools were all displayed on toolbars, which in some instances caused confusion because the tools had similar icons. In other instances, like tools were displayed on drop-down menus with the last used tool being displayed on the toolbar. To alleviate interface clutter and possible confusion, the designers of Acrobat 8.0 created toolbars with only the most popular tools displayed. The other tools can be accessed from menu commands. You can, however, modify the toolbars by displaying more or fewer tools by doing the following:

1. Right-click (Windows) or CTRL-click (Macintosh) the toolbar you want to modify to display the options for the toolbar. The context menu for the Page Navigation toolbar is shown next.

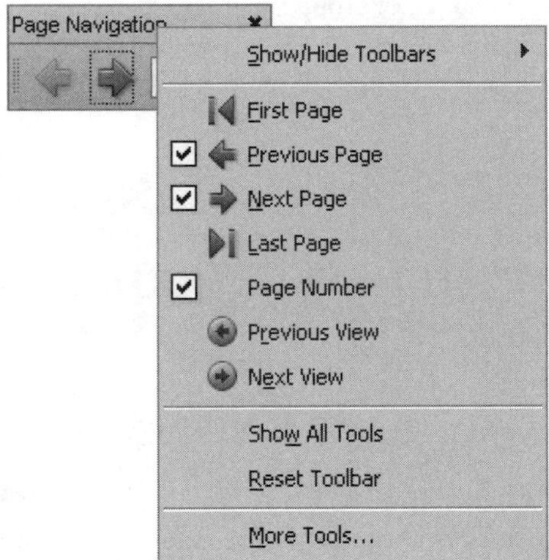

2. Click the area to the left of the tool you want to add to the toolbar. Or, you can choose Show All Tools to display all the available tools for the toolbar. The image shown next is the Page Navigation toolbar with all tools displayed.

To reset a toolbar, right-click (Windows) or CTRL-click (Macintosh) it and choose Reset Toolbar from the context menu. To reset all toolbars to their default states, choose View | Toolbars | Reset Toolbars.

Get Complete Acrobat 8.0 Help

This book covers every major aspect of Acrobat. However, if you need more information about a specific topic, you can search the Acrobat 8.0 Help document or choose another topic from the Acrobat Help menu. To open the complete Acrobat 8.0 Help document in the Adobe Help Viewer, choose Help | Complete Acrobat 8.0 Help.

Set Preferences

Many people find the Acrobat configuration easy to work with on installation. However, you can change many Acrobat defaults by selecting the appropriate title in the Preferences dialog box. A preference setting exists for virtually every Acrobat task you can perform. Unfortunately, the sheer volume of parameters you can change is beyond the scope of this book. When preference options are important to an individual task, the options are covered in that section of the book. Many of the preference settings are easily understood even by casual computer users and, therefore, they won't be covered. If you need more information on an individual setting, however, choose Help | Complete Acrobat 8.0 Professional (or standard if you use that version of the application) Help. After the Acrobat Help file opens, click the Search link and enter the key word or phrase for the specific information you need. To open the Preferences dialog box, shown in the following illustration, choose Edit | Preferences, and then select the desired preference category from the left-hand column.

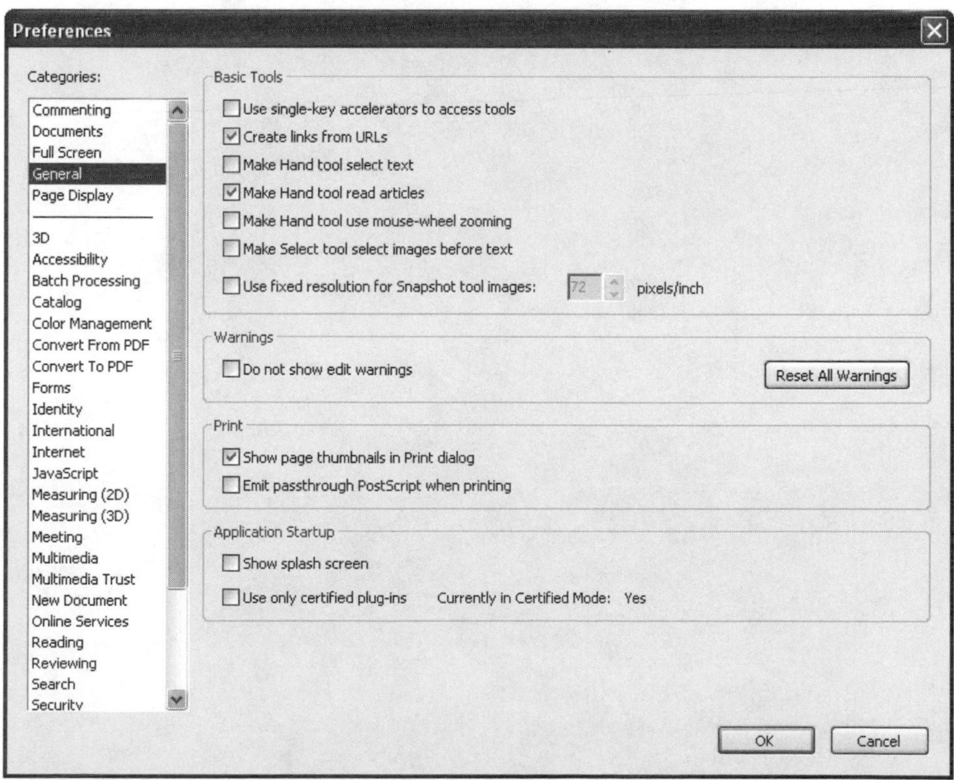

Summary

In this chapter, you learned to navigate the Acrobat workspace. You were also introduced to the toolbars and task buttons you'll use to edit and add interactivity to PDF documents. You were shown the differences between the Acrobat Standard and Acrobat Professional toolsets, and you learned how to customize the workspace to suit your working preferences. In the next chapter, you learn how to read PDF documents with Acrobat, as well as how to extract text and graphic elements from PDF files.

Chapter 3

Read PDF Documents with Adobe Acrobat 8.0

How to...

- Open and navigate documents
- Change document view
- View multiple documents
- Search PDF documents
- Search a PDF index
- Use the Organizer

You purchased Acrobat—and for that matter, this book—to create and distribute electronic documents. Many people will read your PDF documents in linear fashion—from start to finish—which is fine for a one-or two-page document, but cumbersome when reading a large document. When you publish PDF documents with several hundred pages, your readers can choose which parts of the document they view. Acrobat and Adobe Reader 8.0 can be used to read PDF files. Both programs have the tools you need to navigate to specific parts of a document, or to find and navigate to keywords or phrases. You can also use the Acrobat and Adobe Reader 8.0 Search feature to search a single document, a folder of documents, or an index of several PDF documents. In this chapter, you learn how to use Acrobat and Adobe Reader 8.0 to view a document.

NOTE *In this chapter, "Acrobat" is used generically refer to both versions of Acrobat and Adobe Reader 8.0.*

Open a PDF Document

Authors of PDF documents can specify what viewers will see when they open a PDF document. A PDF document can be set to open to a certain page and at either a certain magnification or in Full Screen mode.

TIP *If the document opens in Full Screen mode, the toolbar, command bar, and other navigation aids are not visible. If you prefer, you can exit Full Screen mode by pressing ESC or by pressing CTRL-L (Windows) or COMMAND-L (Macintosh). To change how you view documents in Full Screen mode, choose Edit | Preferences, select Full Screen in the Categories list of the Preferences dialog box, and then select the desired viewing options.*

To open a PDF file, choose File | Open and use the Open dialog box to navigate to the PDF file you want to view. Select the file(s) you want to view, and then click Open. To select multiple files from a folder, hold down SHIFT and click the files you want to select.

TIP *You can quickly open a recently viewed document by choosing File, and then clicking the document filename. The last five documents you viewed appear at the bottom of the menu. You can modify the number of documents shown on this menu by choosing Edit | Preferences and, in the Documents section, specifying the desired number of files to display in the Recently Opened Documents lists.*

If you prefer, you can access the Open dialog box by clicking the Open tool, as shown here. Or, you can launch Acrobat and open a file by double-clicking a PDF file icon on your desktop, or by double-clicking a document with a PDF extension within any file folder you navigate to using Explorer (Windows) or Finder (Macintosh).

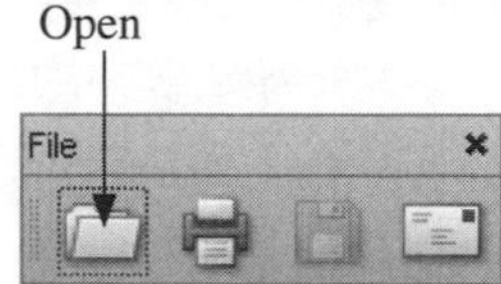

3

Navigate the Document

After you open a PDF document, you can begin viewing the first page, or you can use the Acrobat viewing tools to navigate to specific parts of a document. If you're viewing an e-book or similar document, you may find the author has added a menu or index you can use to navigate to specific pages. If this isn't the case, you can use the Navigation pane panels for navigation. Adobe Reader 8.0 has four navigation panels—Bookmarks, Layers, Pages, Comments and Attachments—while Acrobat has an additional panel: Signatures. The Comments panel is covered in Chapter 10 and the Signatures panel is covered in Chapter 11.

If you initiate an e-mail-based review in Acrobat Professional 8.0 and enable Adobe Reader 8.0 users to participate, they have a Signatures panel available, as well as the commenting and markup tools.

Navigate to a Bookmark

A *bookmark* is a link to a specific point in a document. A bookmark can be a link to a full page or to a portion of a page. When a magnified version of a page is opened, it is known as a *view.* To navigate to a bookmark, open the Bookmarks panel, click the desired bookmark icon (it looks like a document with blue bookmarker), and Acrobat displays the bookmarked page or view.

You use the *Bookmarks panel* to navigate to bookmarks within the document. Bookmarks are similar to chapters and section headings in a book. In other words, a bookmark is a specific place in a document. Bookmarks give a document structure and make it easier for you to find specific information. The number of bookmarks is determined by the method used to create the document. When Acrobat PDFMaker converts a document to PDF format, it uses features from the original document to create bookmarks. For example, if a PDF author uses the Adobe PDFMaker plug-in to convert a Word document to PDF format, a bookmark is created wherever a Word Heading style is used. If you use the application's Print command and choose Adobe PDF as the printing device, no bookmarks are created. When you open a PDF document, click the Bookmark icon to open the Bookmarks panel. Or, choose View | Navigation Panels | Bookmarks. A typical Bookmarks panel is shown in Figure 3-1.

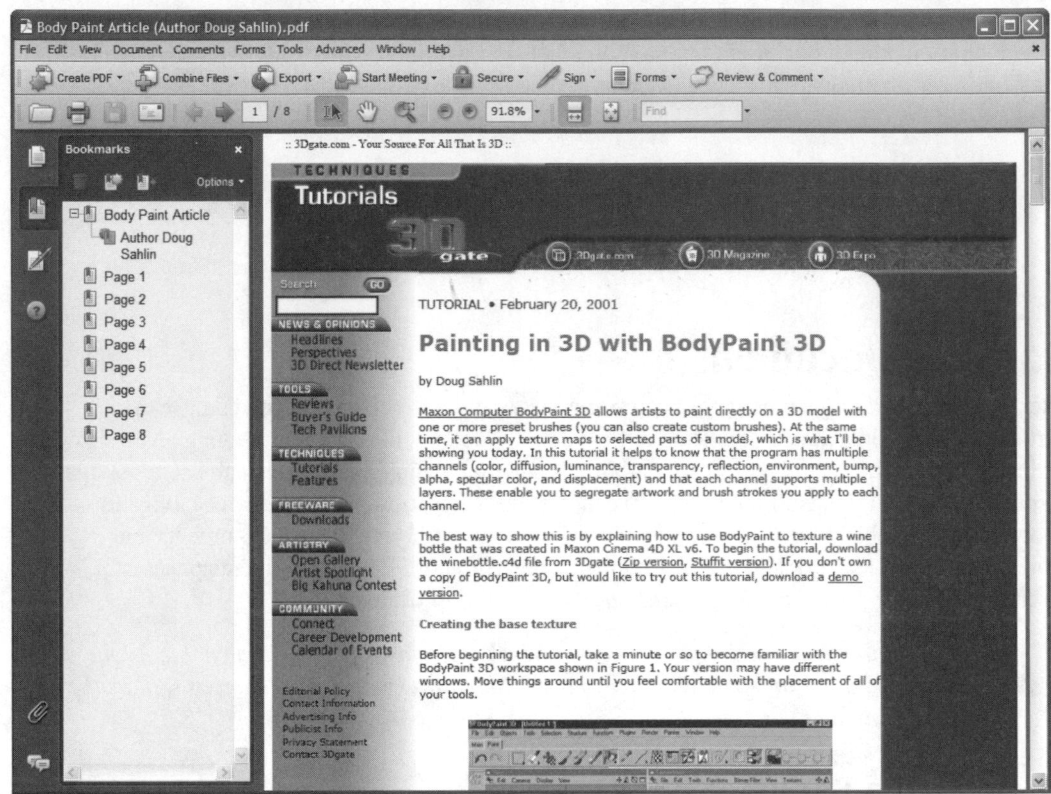

FIGURE 3-1 You use bookmarks to navigate to a specific page in a PDF document.

Expand a Bookmark

Many PDF documents you view have bookmarks with a plus sign (+) beside them. This designates that the bookmark can be expanded to show more bookmarks nested within the parent bookmark. To expand a bookmark, click the plus sign, and Acrobat displays the bookmarks related to the subject heading. If you're viewing a complex document with several heading levels, the expanded bookmark may include bookmarks with additional subheadings, which are also signified with a plus sign. To view the additional subheadings, click the section heading plus sign. The following illustration shows a few nested bookmarks that have been expanded:

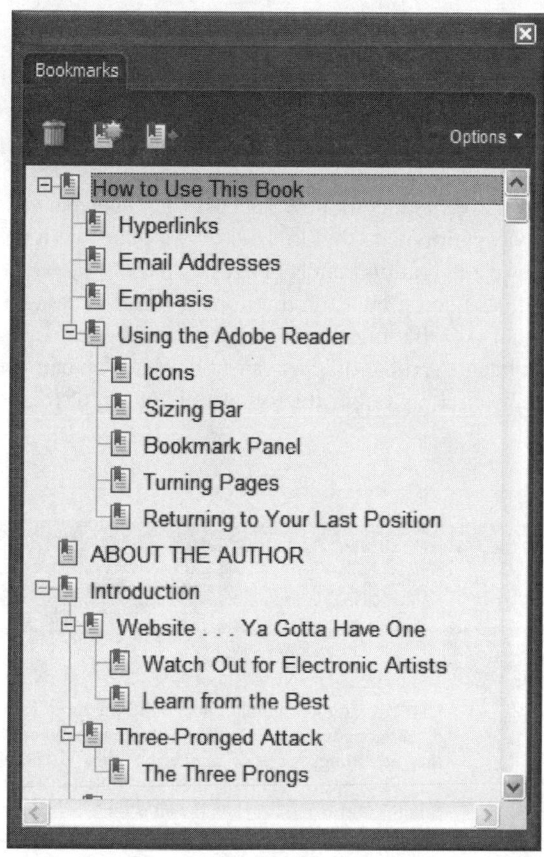

Collapse a Bookmark

When you view a complex document with several heading levels and expand the bookmarks, you end up with an indented treelike structure that displays all the document bookmarks. When you expand several bookmarks, the Bookmark panel becomes quite cluttered, making it difficult to find a specific bookmark. You can easily simplify the view by clicking the minus sign (–) to the left of each bookmark to *collapse* it, so that you again see only the parent bookmark with its corresponding plus sign.

Use the Bookmarks Options Menu

You can also expand and collapse selected bookmarks, as well as make additional bookmarks from document structure by choosing commands from the Bookmarks Options menu. To open the Bookmarks Options menu, click the Options icon at the top of the Bookmarks panel.

TIP *You can quickly collapse all top-level bookmarks by opening the Bookmarks panel, and then choosing Collapse Top-Level Bookmarks from the Options menu.*

Use Page Thumbnails

When you open a PDF document created within the full version of Acrobat or the Acrobat Reader, a thumbnail is created for each document page. A *thumbnail* looks like a miniature snapshot of a full-size PDF page. You find document thumbnails in the Pages panel of the Navigation pane, but unless the author of the document has specified otherwise, the Navigation pane doesn't appear when you open a document. To access the Pages panel, shown in Figure 3-2, click the Pages icon in the Navigation pane that looks like two pages with the corner folder on the top page. Or, choose View | Navigation Panels | Pages.

Notice the page number is listed below each thumbnail. You can navigate to a specific page by clicking its thumbnail. Acrobat highlights the page number, as shown in the following illustration. *Within* the thumbnail, Acrobat displays a red border. You can use this to scroll the page in the Document pane by clicking either the top or the bottom of the red border

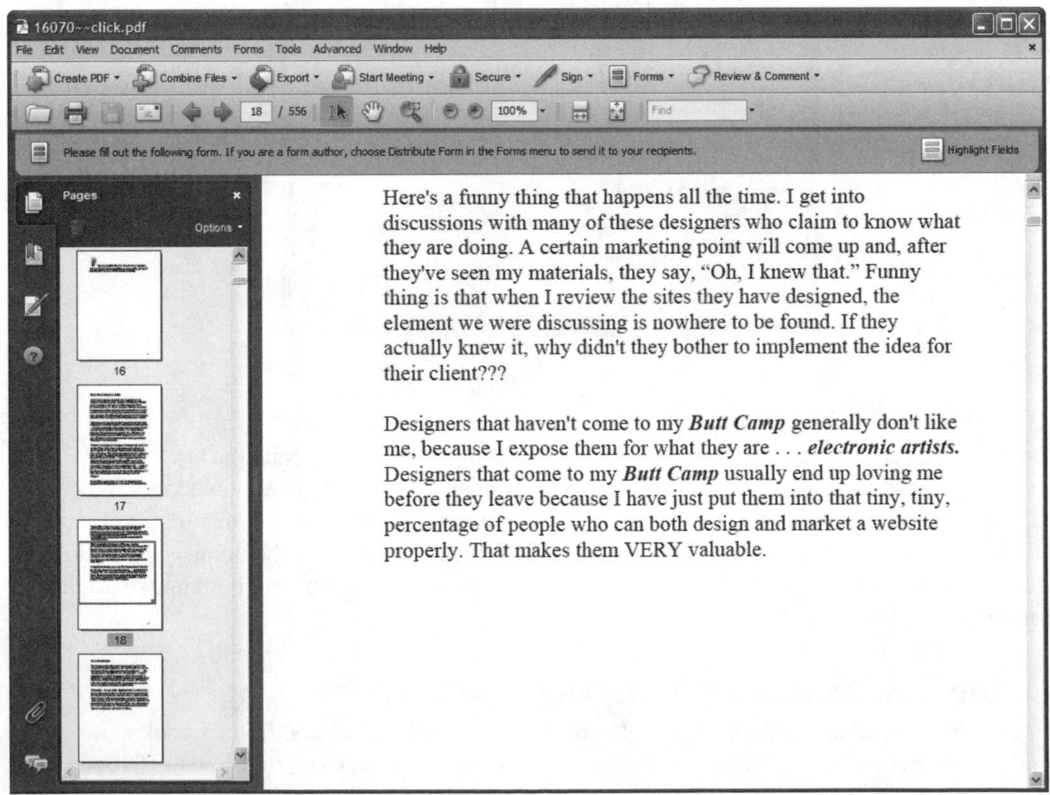

FIGURE 3-2 You can use thumbnails to navigate to a specific page in the document.

and dragging. At the bottom-right corner of the border is a red square. You can click-and-drag this to resize the view in the Document pane.

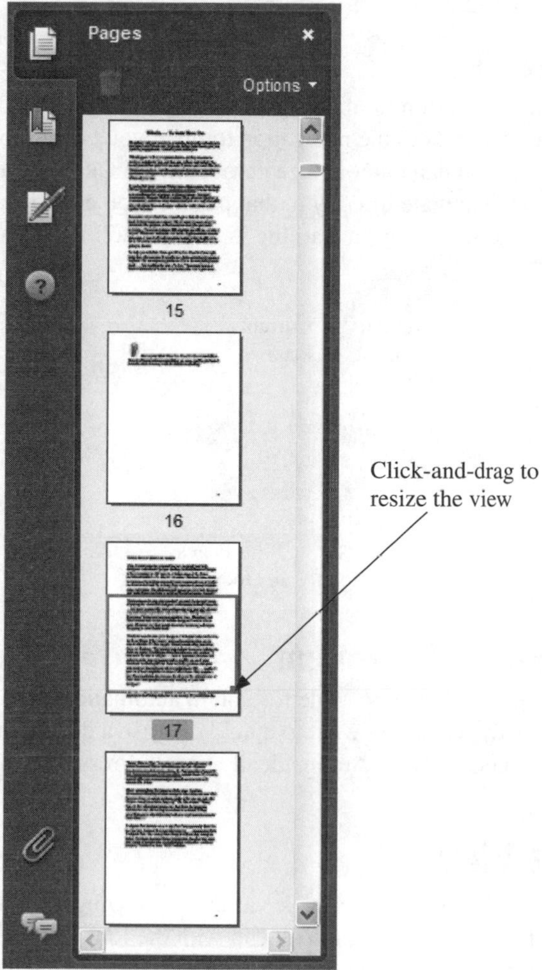

When you initially open the Pages panel, Acrobat displays the thumbnails in a neat column. You can display additional thumbnails by clicking-and-dragging the border between the Navigation pane and the Document pane. However, this may not be feasible if you are working on a monitor with a desktop smaller than 1024 × 768. If you work with a monitor resolution of 800 × 600 or less, you can shrink the size of the thumbnails. To shrink the thumbnails to the desired size, click the Options icon in the top-right corner of the Navigation pane, and then choose Reduce Page Thumbnails from the Pages Options menu. Or, you can right-click (Windows) or CTRL-click (Macintosh) and choose Reduce Page Thumbnails from the context menu.

You can apply this command several times to shrink page thumbnails to the desired size. To increase the size of page thumbnails, choose Enlarge Page Thumbnails from either the Pages Options menu or the context menu.

Navigate to a Page

You can use the tools in the Navigation toolbar, shown next, to navigate a PDF file in linear fashion or if you add additional tools to the navigation toolbar, you can jump to and from previous views you specified. You can enter a page number in the Current Page window, and then press ENTER or RETURN to navigate directly to that page. If you enter a value larger than the last page of the document, Adobe displays a warning dialog box telling you the page is not in the document.

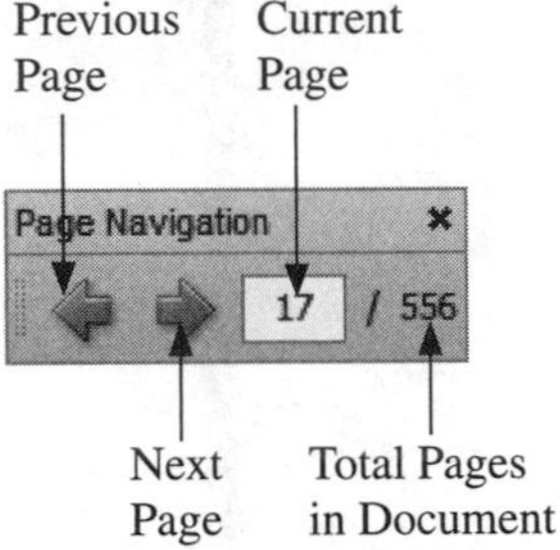

Automatically Scroll a Document

Acrobat includes a feature that makes it possible for you to automatically scroll through a document. This option is handy when you want to quickly peruse a document. To automatically scroll through a document, choose View | Automatically Scroll. Press ESC to stop scrolling.

Change Document View

When you view a PDF document, you have a wide variety of viewing options available to you. Unlike a printed document, where you have to contend with the font size and page size chosen by the author, you can modify the magnification of the PDF document, change how much of the document is displayed in the Document pane, change the number of pages displayed in the Document pane, and rotate the document. You can use tools, menu commands, or context menus to change the way Acrobat displays a document.

Change View Options

On the Page Display toolbar, you find two tools, as shown in the next illustration. You use these tools to change the way you view the document.

- **Single Page** Displays a single page of the document. You can use the Hand tool to scroll through the page, but not to advance to another page.
- **Single Page Continuous** In this mode, you can use the Hand tool to scroll through the document a page at a time.

You have additional viewing options available through menu commands you access from the Page Display submenu of the View menu commands, or by adding extra tools to the Page Navigation toolbar. The commands are:

- **Two-Up** Displays the pages in a multipage document side-by-side. But in Two-Up mode, you can use the Hand tool to scroll through the currently displayed pages, but not to scroll to the next spread in the document.
- **Two-Up Continuous** Displays the pages in a multipage document side-by-side. In Two-Up Continuous mode, you can use the Hand tool to scroll through the entire document two pages at a time.
- **Show Gaps Between Pages** This is the default display mode and displays a gap between pages. Deselect this command and Acrobat displays a dashed line between pages.
- **Show Cover Page During Two-Up** Displays the first page of the document as a single page and subsequent pages as a two-up spread when you select either of the Two-Up options.

Change Your View

You can use Acrobat to view a wide variety of documents of different layouts and sizes. Even though Acrobat is cross-platform and the document you view is identical to what authors create on their computers, you may find it necessary to make modifications to comfortably view the document on your monitor. When you view a PDF document with small font sizes or tiny graphics, you can magnify the document. You can choose from preset levels of magnification or choose to zoom in on a specific portion of a document. When you finish viewing the magnified document, you can zoom out. You can use tools from the Select & Zoom toolbar, as shown in the following illustration, or menu commands to change the magnification of a document you're viewing. The Acrobat Select & Zoom toolbar is identical.

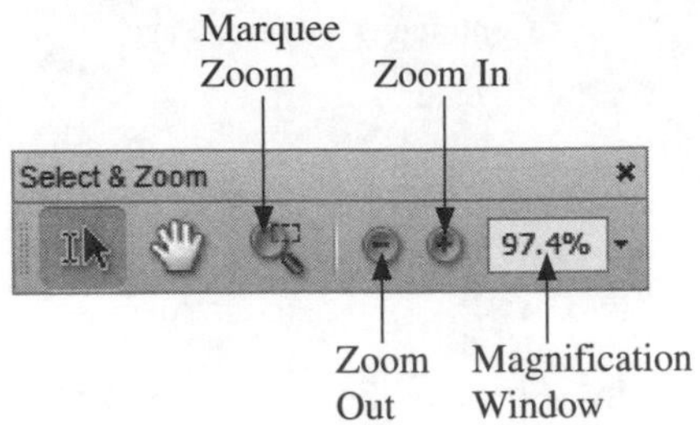

Zoom In or Out on a Document

You have many different ways to change the magnification of a document you view. Your first set of magnification tools is in the Select & Zoom tool group, which is as follows:

- Click the Marquee Zoom tool and drag diagonally within the document to zoom to that area. As you drag, a bounding box appears, showing you the currently selected area. Release the mouse button when the bounding box surrounds the area to which you want to zoom.
- Click the Zoom Out tool, which looks like a minus sign (–), to zoom out to the next lowest level of magnification.
- Click the Zoom In tool, which looks like a plus sign (+), to zoom in to the next highest level of magnification.
- Click the drop-down arrow to the right of the Magnification window and choose a preset magnification value from the drop-down menu. At the bottom of the menu, you also find page display options.
- Enter a value in the Magnification window, and then press ENTER or RETURN. You can enter any value between 1 percent and 6400 percent (the magnification drop-down menu only shows values between 10 percent and 6400 percent). These values are percentages of the original size of the document. If you enter a value out of this range, Acrobat selects the appropriate default value.

You can find an additional tool to change magnification on the Select & Zoom submenu of the Tools menu. Navigate to the submenu and select the following:

- **Dynamic Zoom** Select this tool, click inside the document, and drag up or left to zoom in, or down or right to zoom out. If your mouse has a scroll wheel, scroll forward to zoom in, or backward to zoom out.

Use the Acrobat Professional Zoom Tools

In addition to the zoom tools mentioned in the previous section, Acrobat Professional has two additional tools: the Loupe tool and the Pan & Zoom window, which you can find on the Select & Zoom submenu of the Tools menu.

To change magnification using the Loupe tool, follow these steps:

1. Choose Tools | Zoom & Select | Loupe Tool.
2. Click inside the document to define the area you want to examine more closely. The selected area appears in the Loupe Tool window. The selected area is also highlighted inside the document.
3. Click-and-drag the slider, shown in the following illustration, to set the magnification level:

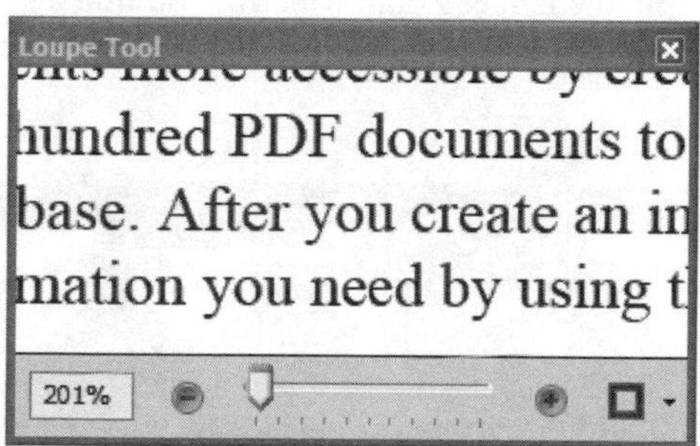

4. To examine a different area of the document, click-and-drag the tool to a different position in the Document pane. Release the mouse button when the bounding box is over the desired area.
5. To dynamically change the magnification, click-and-drag a handle at the corner of the selected area inside the document, as shown next:

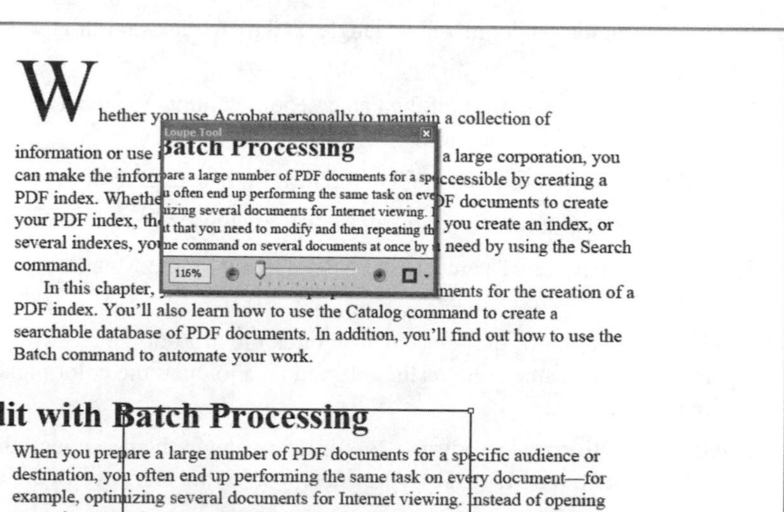

6. To change the color of the selected area, click the drop-down arrow to the right of the square that is the same color as the selected area to open the color picker. Click the desired color. The new color takes effect when next you move the selected area.
7. Click Close to exit the Loupe Tool window.

To change document magnification using the Pan & Zoom window, follow these steps:

1. Choose Tools | Zoom & Select | Pan & Zoom Window to open the Pan & Zoom window, shown in the following illustration. Or, you can click the Pan & Zoom tool from the Zoom toolbar. Within the Pan & Zoom window, you find a smaller view of the current page surrounded by a red bounding box that designates the section of the document being viewed.

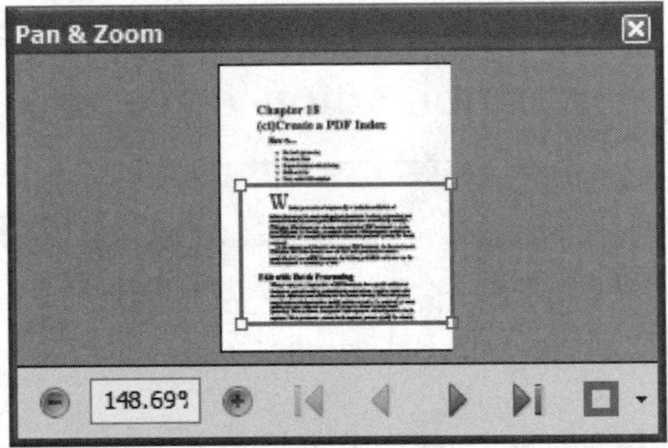

2. Drag one of the corner handles diagonally to zoom in or out on the document.
3. Place your cursor inside the red rectangle, and then click-and-drag to pan to a different view.
4. Click a button at the bottom of the Pan & Zoom window to advance to another page while preserving the same view.
5. Click the Zoom In tool to zoom in to the next highest degree of magnification.
6. Click the Zoom Out tool to zoom out to the next lowest degree of magnification.
7. Enter a value between 1 percent and 6400 percent in the Magnification window to zoom in or out to the desired value.
8. To change the color of the selected area, click the drop-down arrow to the right of the square that is the same color as the selected area to open the color picker. Click the desired color.
9. Click a navigation tool to advance to: the next page in the document, the previous page in the document, the first page in the document, or the last page in the document.
10. Click Close to exit the Pan & Zoom window.

View Document at Actual Size

After viewing a document at a different magnification, you can return it to its original size by choosing View | Zoom | Actual Size.

Fit Document in Window

You can change your view of a document, so an entire page of the document is sized to the window. You accomplish this choosing View | Zoom | Fit Page.

Fit Document to Width or Height

Many of the PDF files you open are narrow, formatted for destinations like Internet web sites. Narrow documents with small fonts present a reading challenge even to people with perfect vision. Fortunately, you can choose View | Zoom | Fit Width to expand the documents to fit the current width of the Document pane, making the document easier to read.

Another option you have available is to fit the document to fit the current height of the Document pane by choosing View | Zoom | Fit Height.

Fit Text and Graphics to Document Pane Width

Another useful option is to resize the document, so the width of the text and graphics expands to fit the current size of the Document pane. You can accomplish this task by choosing View | Zoom | Fit Visible.

View Document at Full Screen

If you prefer to read a document without Acrobat toolbars, choose Window | Full Screen Mode. Or, you can choose View | Full Screen Mode. However, it is difficult to navigate a document viewed in Full Screen mode if the author has not provided navigation devices, such as buttons or text links. To return to normal viewing mode, press ESC.

If you choose Continuous or Continuous Facing page display mode, and then switch to Full Screen, Acrobat sets the viewing mode to the default Single Page mode and you won't be able to scroll pages with the Hand tool.

If you're reading a PDF document, and you don't need access to any of the Acrobat menu commands or tools, choose View | Reading Mode.

Zoom to a Specific Magnification

You can also zoom to the desired degree of magnification by choosing from a drop-down list or by manually entering the desired degree of magnification. You can choose or enter a value from 8.33 percent to 6400 percent. Choose View | Zoom | Zoom To, which opens the Zoom To dialog box, shown here.

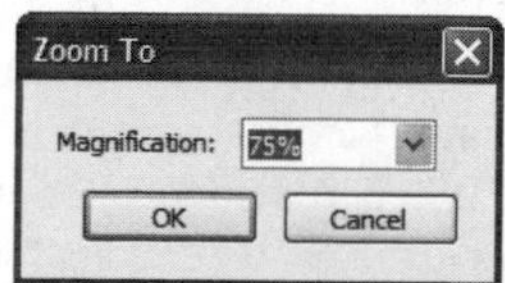

1. Click the Magnification drop-down arrow and choose an option from the drop-down list. Or, you can enter a value between 8.33 percent and 6400 percent.
2. Click OK to zoom to the desired degree of magnification, and close the dialog box.

You can zoom in on the document by pressing CTRL*+(+) (Windows) or Command+(+) (Macintosh). You can zoom out by pressing* CTRL*+(–) ((Window), or Command+(–) (Macintosh).*

Rotate the View of a PDF Document

Adobe also provides you with the necessary menu commands to rotate pages in a document. To rotate the view of a document, choose View | Rotate View to display the Rotate View submenu, and then choose one of the following self-explanatory commands: Clockwise or Counterclockwise.

NOTE

This rotates only the "view" of the document and not the actual page.

View a Document in Two Windows

If you're viewing a complex document and you need to zoom in on certain parts of the document while still seeing the big picture, you can view the document in split window mode. When you view a document in *split window mode,* you can change magnification or navigate to a different page in one window without affecting the document view in the other window. To view a document in two windows, choose Window | Split. Click a window to make it the active window. You can change the size of each window by clicking-and-dragging the divider. When you finish viewing the document in two windows, invoke the command again to return to single window mode, whereupon Acrobat uses the magnification settings of the previously active window.

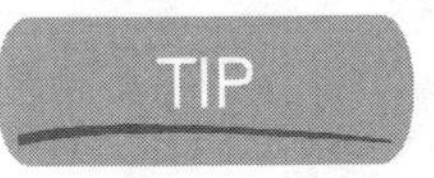

If you need to work with more than two windows, choose View | Spreadsheet Split to view the document in four windows. Click-and-drag the vertical or horizontal split bar to change the layout of the split windows.

View Multiple Documents

When you do research or create a PDF file that will include several existing PDF documents, it's convenient to work with all the documents open—or as many as your system resources allow—at the same time. When you have multiple documents open, you can switch from one document to another by choosing the Window menu, and then selecting another document from the list at the bottom of the menu. This menu also enables you to choose to have Acrobat arrange the documents in a cascading or tiling fashion.

Cascade Documents

When you work with multiple documents, you can speed your workflow considerably if you have easy access to each document. You can have Acrobat arrange multiple documents in cascading fashion by choosing Window | Cascade. When you choose this viewing option, Acrobat overlaps each PDF file. You can see each document title, as well as its Navigation pane. To switch to

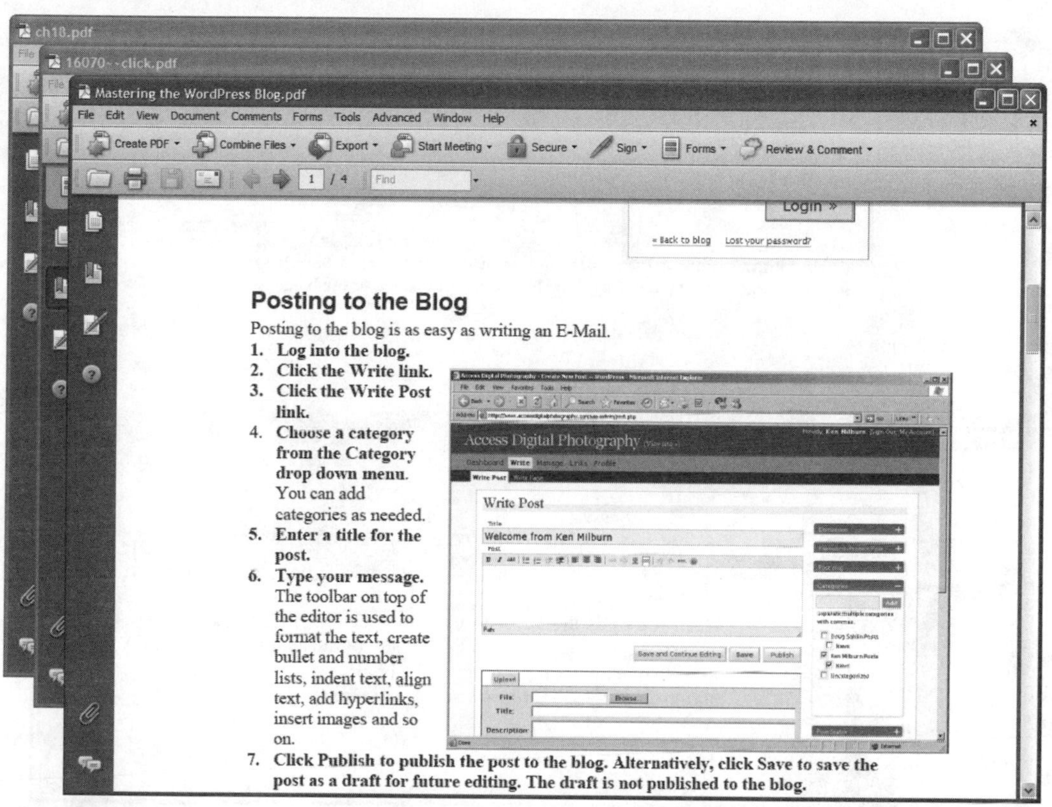

FIGURE 3-3 You have access to multiple documents when you use the Cascade command.

a document while in cascading mode, click its title bar. After you select a document, you can expand it by clicking Maximize. Click Minimize, and Acrobat returns the document to its position in the cascade. In Figure 3-3, you see several documents arranged in cascading format.

Tile Documents

If you prefer to view multiple documents neatly arranged in checkerboard fashion, choose Window | Tile. This command gives you the following two tiling options: Vertical and Horizontal. When you view tiled documents, you can see the document title bar and part of the document's contents. To select a document, click its title bar. Click Maximize to expand the document; click Minimize to return it to its tiled position. After you select a document from the tile, you can use Acrobat tools to navigate within the document. Experiment with both options to find which option best suits your working preference. Figure 3-4 shows two documents tiled horizontally.

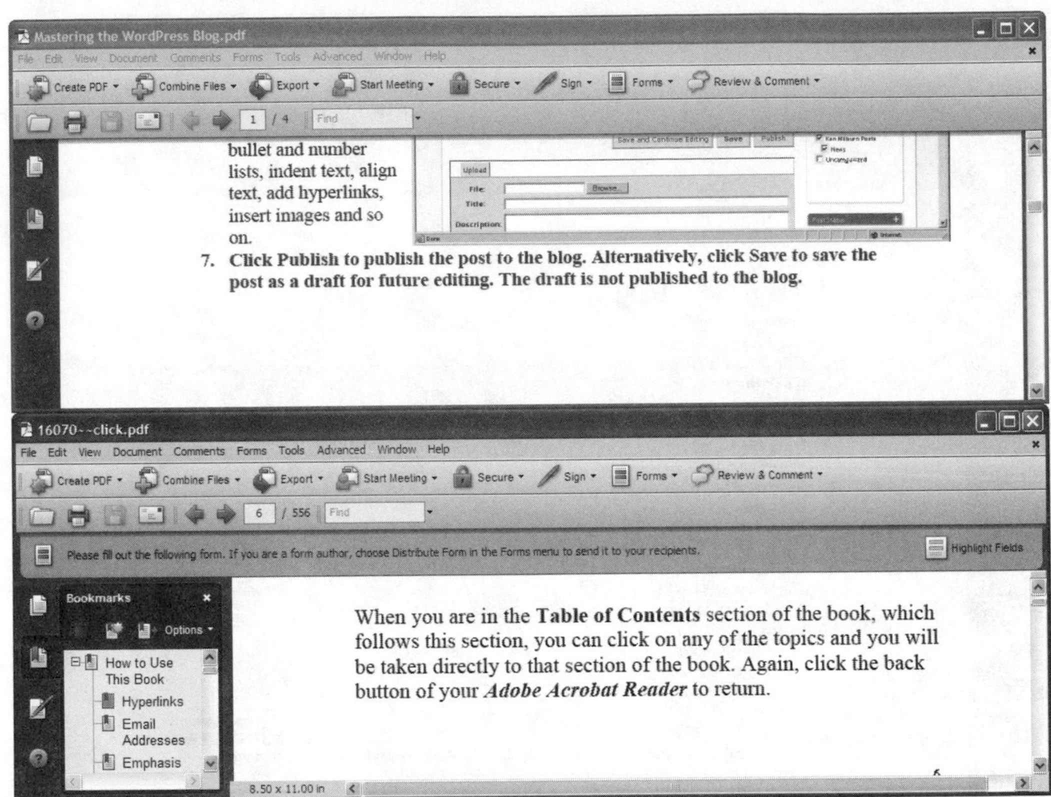

FIGURE 3-4 You can view multiple documents tiled horizontally or vertically.

Search for a Word or Phrase

When you're viewing a multipage PDF document, you can use bookmarks to navigate to parts of the document that appear to have the information you seek, or you can cut right to the chase and find instances of a specific keyword or phrase within the document by using the Search command. This powerful Acrobat feature can help streamline your work. What could be easier than typing a keyword or phrase and letting Acrobat take care of the grunt work? You can search the current document, search PDF files in a folder on your computer or network, and search for files on the Internet. To search for information:

1. Choose Edit | Search to open the Search pane. By default, the Search pane is displayed floating on the left side of the Acrobat workspace. The current document is resized and displayed to the right of the Search pane.

2. Enter the keyword or phrase you want to find. Choose from the following options to indicate where you want to search:
   - **In The Current PDF Document** Choose this option, and Acrobat searches for the keyword or phrase in the current document.
   - **All PDF Documents In** Choose this option, and then use the drop-down list to navigate to a folder in your computer or network that contains the PDF document(s) you want to search.
3. Check any of the following boxes to refine your search further:
   - **Whole Words Only** Acrobat returns only matches for the exact word or phrase you enter.
   - **Case-Sensitive** Acrobat returns only words or phrases that match the case you enter. For example, when you choose this option and search for the word Query, Acrobat returns instances of Query, not query.
   - **Include Bookmarks** Acrobat returns any instances of your keyword or phrase that appear within the document's bookmarks.
   - **Include Comments** Acrobat returns any instances of your keyword or phrase that appear in comments that have been added to the document.
4. Click Search to begin the search.

When you use the Search command, Acrobat highlights the first instance in the document of the keyword or phrase you enter in the Search dialog box. If the keyword or phrase doesn't exist in the document, Acrobat displays that information in the Search pane.

Acrobat finds the first instance of the keyword or phrase, as well as all other instances of the keyword or phrase. Each instance is displayed in the Search pane. You can navigate through the list of returned keywords using the scroll bar on the right side of the Search pane. To view an instance of the keyword, click it. The Document pane refreshes to the point in the document where the keyword appears. The keyword is highlighted, as well. You can initiate a new search at any time by clicking New Search.

Search an Index of Documents

Many authors of PDF documents use the Acrobat Professional Catalog command to launch Acrobat Catalog and create an index of PDF documents. (Creating indexes with the Catalog command is covered in Chapter 18.) Acrobat has a sophisticated search function that lets you search for a specific word or phrase in one or more indexed catalogs. To take advantage of this powerful feature, you use the Search command's advanced search options, and then specify which indexes you want included in the search.

To search an index of documents, you must first specify the list of indexes to search, as outlined in the next section. If you own Acrobat Professional and create your own indexes, you can add the indexes that may contain the information you seek.

Add an Index

To search other indexes, you add the files to the Available Indexes list. To display the indexes currently available for searching, follow these steps:

1. Choose Edit | Search. The Search pane appears on the left side of the interface.
2. Click the Use Advanced Search Options link at the bottom of the Search PDF pane.
3. Click the Look In drop-down arrow and choose Select Index. The Index Selection dialog box appears, as shown here:

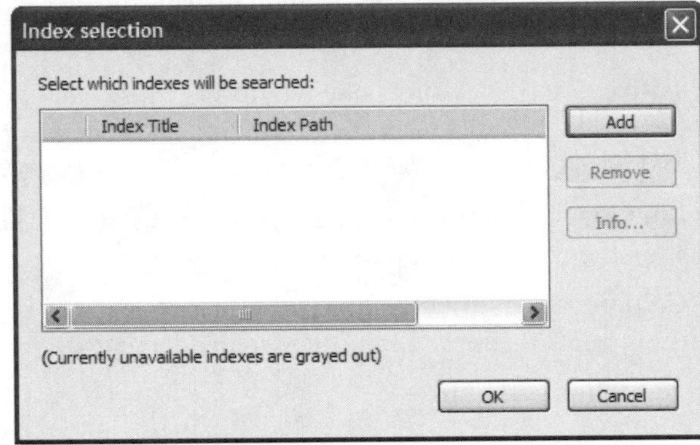

4. Click Add to display the Open Index File dialog box.
5. Navigate to the folder that contains the index you want to add to the list. Acrobat indexes have the .pdx file extension.
6. Select the desired index, and then click Open to add the index to the list. After you click Open, the Open Index dialog box closes, and the newly selected index appears in the Index Selection dialog box.
7. Repeat Steps 4 through 6 to add additional indexes to the list.

Only Acrobat 6, 7, and 8 indexes can be used. Version 5 indexes must be re-created to work under versions 6, 7, or 8.

Remove an Index

You can enable or disable an index from a search by clicking the check box to the left of the index name in the Index Selection dialog box. Using the check box is the preferred method of enabling or disabling an index in a search. If you are no longer using an index or have moved it to a different location on your hard drive, however, you can remove the index from the list by opening the Index Selection dialog box, selecting the index, and then clicking Remove to delete the index from the list. When you click Remove, Acrobat displays no warning, and the index is removed from the list. If you inadvertently remove an index, you can use the Add button to restore it to the list.

TIP *The best way to limit a search of indexes is by enabling only the indexes you want Acrobat to use for the search you're performing. For example, if you have added ten PDF indexes for advanced searches, but feel only five of them contain information pertinent to your current search, disable the ones you don't want Acrobat to search.*

Display Index Information

When an indexed PDF catalog is created, certain information is recorded with the file. If you have several indexes to choose from, or you're sharing indexes with coworkers on a network, this information can be valuable when deciding whether the PDF files included in the index contain the information you require. If the author of the index accepted the Acrobat default name of Untitled, using the Info option is the only way to know what's contained in the index. To access information about an index, open the Index Selection dialog box, shown previously, select an index, and then click the Info button to display the Index Information dialog box, shown here:

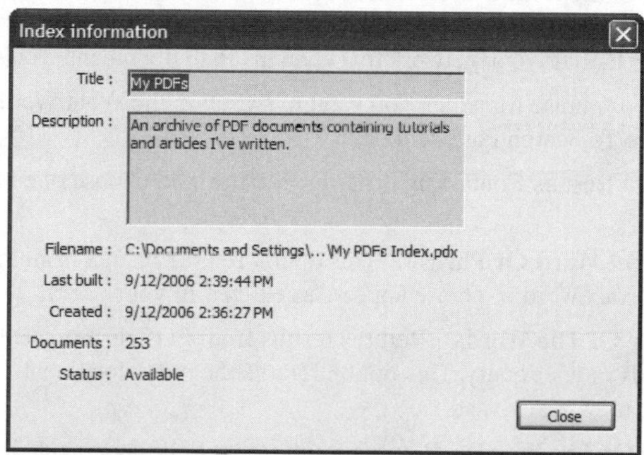

After you open the Index Information dialog box, you have the following information available:

- **Title** Shows the title entered by the creator of the index. When you build your own indexes, it's advisable to specify a title that describes the contents of the PDF files being indexed. Refer to Chapter 18 for information on naming an index.
- **Description** Describes the contents of the PDF index as entered by the author of the index.
- **Filename** Displays the path to the index and the full filename of the index.
- **Last Built** Shows you when the index was last updated. If the index hasn't been updated, the date is the same as when the index was created.
- **Created** Shows you the time and date the index was originally created.

- **Documents** Displays the number of PDF files in the index.
- **Status** If Acrobat successfully identified the index file when you added it, it is Available. Unavailable indexes are listed as such and are shown dimmed out in the list.

Create a Query

When you search an index of PDF files or multiple files, you create a *query*. Your query tells Acrobat exactly what information to retrieve. You can specify which indexes to search and which keyword or phrase you want Acrobat to find. You can fine-tune the search by specifying whether you want Acrobat to return exact matches or similar matches. To create a query:

1. Choose Edit | Search to open the Search pane.
2. Click the Use Advanced Search Options link near the bottom of the Search pane.
3. Click the Look In drop-down arrow and choose Currently Selected Indexes. To add an index to the list, follow the steps in the earlier section, "Add an Index." You can also select a folder on your hard drive or network that contains PDF documents you want to search.
4. Enter the word or phrase for which you want to search in the What Word Or Phrase Would You Like To Search For? field.
5. Click the Return Results Containing drop-down arrow and choose one of the following options:
   - **Match Exact Word Or Phrase** This option returns results from PDF documents where the exact word or phrase appears as entered in your query.
   - **Match Any Of The Words** Returns results from PDF documents that contain any of the words in your query. This option returns the most documents, but not all the documents may be relevant.
   - **Match All Of The Words** Returns results from PDF documents in which all the words in your query appear. The words don't have to be in the order as entered in your query.
   - **Boolean Query** Enables you to fine-tune a search by telling Acrobat exactly the information for which you're searching. You can combine words and phrases, and omit certain words from your query. This option is available only in multiple-document searches.
6. In the Use These Additional Criteria section, choose from the following options:
   - **Whole Words Only** Acrobat returns only whole words that match your query exactly, not words that contain your query. For example, if your query is the word "text," then Acrobat returns all instances of the word "text" in the documents you're searching, but not the words "texts" , "texture" , or "context."

- **Case-Sensitive** Acrobat finds only the words that match the case of your query. For example, if you enter "Adobe," the search returns instances of the word "Adobe," but not "adobe."
- **Proximity** When searching for results that match all the words in your query, using the AND Boolean operator, Acrobat returns one pair of matches per file for the words you enter. The match Acrobat returns will be within the first three pages of the document. If several matches exist for the pair of words you're searching for, Acrobat ranks the relevancy of the match based on the proximity of the words. For example, enter the query **Adobe AND Portable**, and Acrobat looks for the words "Adobe" and "Portable" in a document and highlights the first instance of each word, provided both words appear within the first three pages of the document. If further instances of either word occur in the document, they aren't selected or highlighted because Acrobat is returning instances of the keywords with the closest proximity to each other.
- **Stemming** Acrobat finds words that stem from the word you enter. For example, if you enter the word "index," Acrobat returns instances of the words "indexed," "indexes," and "indexing" (if these words appear in the files you're searching, of course).
- **Include Bookmarks** Acrobat returns instances of your query when it appears in the bookmarks of documents you're searching.
- **Include Comments** Acrobat returns instances of your query when it appears in the comments of documents you're searching.
- **Include Attachments** Acrobat returns instances of your query when it appears in files attached to the PDF documents you're searching.

NOTE *The Search command can only search inside PDF attachments.*

7. Click Search.

Your search results are displayed in the Search PDF pane, which displays a list of documents that contain instances of your query. The New Search button also becomes available. After perusing the search results, you can click New Search to create a search with different parameters or click Done. When you click Done, the Search PDF pane disappears.

TIP *You can also use the advanced search options on a single document if you want to include proximity and stemming in your search criteria.*

About Search Results

After you click Search, Acrobat searches for occurrences of your query in the selected documents or indexes. The results Acrobat returns depend on the keyword or phrase you entered and the parameters you selected. Results are displayed in the Search pane, as shown here:

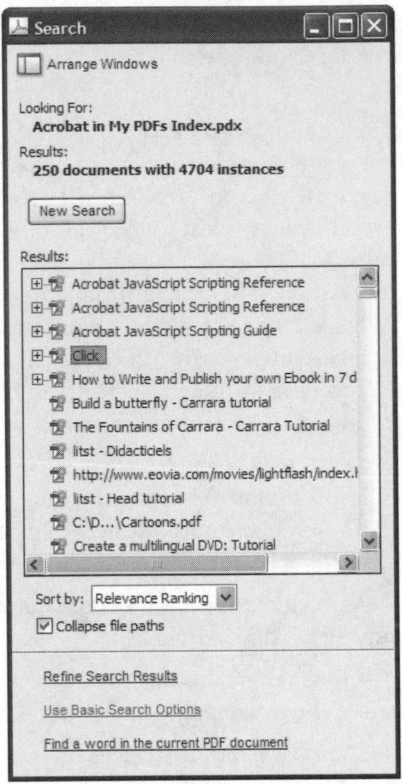

Your search results are displayed in descending order, according to relevancy or score. The documents at the top of the list are more relevant to the parameters of your query. In other words, these documents contain a higher percentage of instances of the keyword or phrase in your query.

View Query Results

After Acrobat finishes the search, you can select a result from the list by clicking its name. After viewing the result, you can view additional results by clicking another name in the Search pane.

If you decide to hide the Search pane to get a better view of the document, you can advance to the next occurrence of your query by choosing Edit | Search Results | Next Result. After viewing a few results, you may want to jump back to a previous result, a task you accomplish by choosing Edit | Search Results | Previous Result. If the Previous Result command is dimmed out, you're at the first occurrence of your query in the document. When you reach the last occurrence in a document of the keyword or phrase you searched for, choosing the Next Result command opens the next document Acrobat returned for your search. You can also view the first result of a query in the next document by choosing Edit | Search Results | Next Document. To view the first result in a previous document, choose View | Search Results | Previous Document.

Conduct an Advanced Search

When you conduct an advanced search by clicking the Use Advanced Search Options link, you can refine a search by searching for documents by keywords or phrases. In addition, you can choose an option from the Use These Additional Criteria section of the Search PDF pane's Advanced Search Options to search for documents by title, subject, author, keywords, or date info. You can add up to three search parameters, as shown in Figure 3-5.

To conduct an advanced search, follow these steps:

1. Choose Edit | Search to open the Search pane, and then click the Use Advanced Search Options link. The Search pane is reconfigured, as shown in Figure 3-5.
2. Enter the word or phrase for which you want to search and enter your other search parameters as outlined in the "Create a Query" section earlier in this chapter.

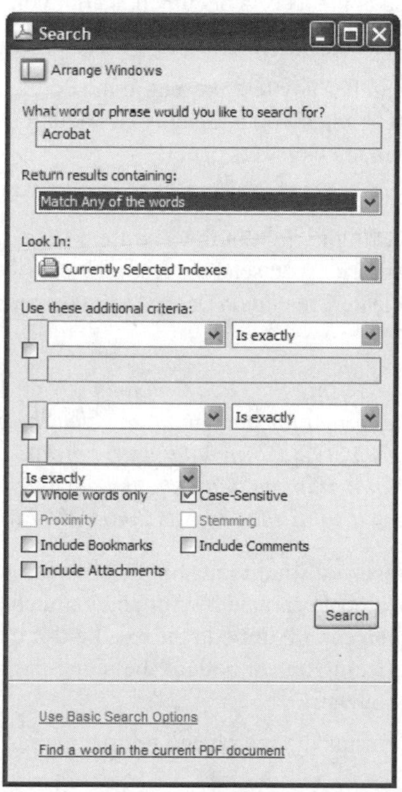

FIGURE 3-5 You can refine a search by using all available fields in the Search pane.

3. Click the first check box in the Use These Additional Criteria section.
4. Click the drop-down arrow to the right of the first blank field, and then choose one of the following criteria options:
   - **Date Created** Searches for documents using the date created as a search criterion.
   - **Date Modified** Searches for documents using the date modified as a search criterion.
   - **Author** Searches for documents created by a particular author.
   - **Title** Searches for documents by their titles.
   - **Subject** Searches for documents pertaining to a specific subject.
   - **Filename** Uses a document filename as a search criterion.
   - **Keywords** Searches for documents containing specific keywords.
   - **Bookmarks** Uses the contents of a document's bookmarks as a search criterion.
   - **Comments** Uses the contents of a document's comments as a search criterion.
   - **JPEG Images** Searches any text added to artifacts that are added to JPEG images.
   - **XMP Metadata** Searches any text present in the document's XMP metadata. This metadata is present when you add tags to a document It is also present with the various tags you find in the Contents panel.
   - **Object Data** Searches for keywords present in an object's metadata.
5. Click the drop-down arrow to the right of the next field to reveal a drop-down menu with factors that apply to the criterion you selected from the previous field. For example, the applicable factors for the Date Created or Date Modified criteria are Is Exactly, Is Before, Is After, and Is Not.

NOTE *When you conduct a search using the Date Created or Date Modified criterion, you must enter the date in the format for the region in which the document was created. For example, if you enter 03/20/2007 (mm/dd/yyyy) for date criteria in a search for a document created in Great Britain on that date, the document will not be returned in the search because the British display that date as 20/03/2007 (dd/mm/yyyy).*

6. Enter the keyword or phrase you want to match the criterion you selected. For example, if you want to find all documents created by Adobe, you'd choose Author in Step 4, Contains in Step 5, and then enter **Adobe** in the text field if desired, add additional criteria to the search by clicking one or both of the remaining criteria check boxes, and then following Steps 4 through 6.
7. Click Search. Acrobat performs the search and returns the results of your query in the Search pane.

After performing your search, you can select from the results. If desired, you can sort the results of your search as outlined in the next section.

Sort Your Search

After you perform a search using the advanced options, Acrobat uses the default method of sorting and returns the results according to relevance ranking. However, you can sort the search results according to different criteria by clicking the Sort By drop-down arrow, and then choosing one of the following options:

- **Relevance Ranking** The default option sorts search results in descending order, starting with the most relevant.
- **Date Modified** Sorts search results according to the date the document was modified, starting with the most recent date.
- **Filename** Sorts search results in alphabetical order according to the document's filename.
- **Location** Sorts search results according to the folder where the document is stored. If you search for documents across a network or multiple hard drives, the path to the folder is also factored into the sort.

By default, Acrobat collapses the path of a search result to the directory and document filename. If desired, you can display the full path by deselecting the Collapse File Paths option at the bottom of the Search PDF pane.

Refine Your Search with Boolean Operators

When you search for information in an index that contains a large number of documents, Acrobat finds every document that matches your query. If the sheer volume of documents is overwhelming, you can fine-tune your search by conducting a Boolean query. When you conduct a Boolean query, you can limit your search by using Boolean operators. To conduct a search using a Boolean query to filter your search results, follow these steps:

1. Choose Edit | Search to open the Search pane.
2. Click the Use Advanced Search Options link.
3. Click the Look In drop-down arrow and choose the location where you want to search.
4. Click the Return Results Containing drop-down arrow and choose Boolean Query.
5. In the What Word Or Phrase Would You Like To Search For? field, enter your query using one of the following Boolean operators:
   - **AND** Use this Boolean operator between two words to find all instances of both words in the PDF documents you're searching. For example, entering **Adobe AND Acrobat** would return documents that contain the words "Adobe" and "Acrobat."
   - **NOT** Use this operator between two words to find all documents that contain the first word, but not the second. For example, enter **cat NOT dog** to find all PDF documents that contain the word "cat," but not the word "dog."
   - **OR** Use this Boolean operator between two words to locate PDF documents that contain either word. For example, enter **Adobe OR Acrobat** and your search yields documents that contain either word.

- **Quotation marks** Quotation marks have two uses. The first is to search for documents with words that appear in the exact order you enter them between quotation marks. For example, enter **"Boolean query"** to find all documents that contain the phrase "Boolean query." The second use of quotation marks is to search for documents that contain phrases with Boolean operators. For example, enter **"John or Jane"** to find PDF documents that contain the phrase "John or Jane," as opposed to a Boolean search phrased **John OR Jane**, which would return PDF documents that contain the names "John" or "Jane."

*Acrobat's advanced search options also support the use of Boolean operator symbols, such as =, ~, +, <, and so on (except for the * and ? wildcards). Use quotes on your query words and use the desired Boolean operator to refine your search. For example, "Adobe"+"Acrobat" to return documents containing the words "Adobe" and "Acrobat."*

Using the Find Command

The Find command is like a mini-Search command or Search lite. You use the *Find command* to search for a specific word or phrase within a document. You can specify parameters to limit your search or, if you need to call out the heavy artillery, you can access the Search pane from within the Find dialog box to conduct a full search. To quickly find a word or phrase in a PDF document:

1. Choose Edit | Find to open the Find dialog box shown next. For the purpose of this demonstration, the dialog box is floating in the workspace. Enter the word or phrase for which you want to search in the text box:

2. To limit your search, click the Find drop-down arrow and choose one of the following:
   - **Whole Words Only** Acrobat returns only whole words that match your query and not words that contain your query.
   - **Case-Sensitive** Acrobat finds only the words that match the case of your query.
   - **Include Bookmarks** Acrobat returns any instances of your query that appear in the bookmarks of document you're searching.
   - **Include Comments** Acrobat returns any instances of your query that appear in the comments of document you're searching.
   - **Open Full Acrobat Search** The Search pane appears, enabling you to conduct a full Acrobat search.
3. Press ENTER or RETURN. Acrobat finds the first instance of your query in the document and two icons appear next to the Find dialog box. Click the icon that looks like a document with a right-pointing arrow to find the next instance of your query in the document, or click the icon that looks like a document with a left-pointing arrow to find the previous instance of your query in the document.

Get Document Properties

When you search for PDF documents from an index, the document's title in the list of search results generally gives you a good idea of what's contained in the document. You can find more information about documents Acrobat finds in a search by clicking the document title, which opens the file in Acrobat, and then choosing File | Properties. When you open a PDF file received via e-mail, or one that's part of a multimedia presentation, you can find out more about the document by choosing File | Properties, and then clicking a tab from the Document Properties dialog box, as shown in Figure 3-6.

Many of the options in this dialog box are applicable to creating a PDF document and are covered in Chapter 4. If you choose this command while using Adobe Reader 8.0, you have only four tabs: Description, Security, Summary, and Fonts. When you choose one of these options in Adobe Reader 8.0, all the fields are dimmed out, with the exception of Fonts, which cannot be modified. You cannot modify the information in the other tabs either. In Acrobat, however, unless security has been applied to the document, all the fields are available. You can modify the properties and save them with the document. The previous illustration is a typical Acrobat Document Properties dialog box. Notice some of the fields are the same ones you specify when conducting a search.

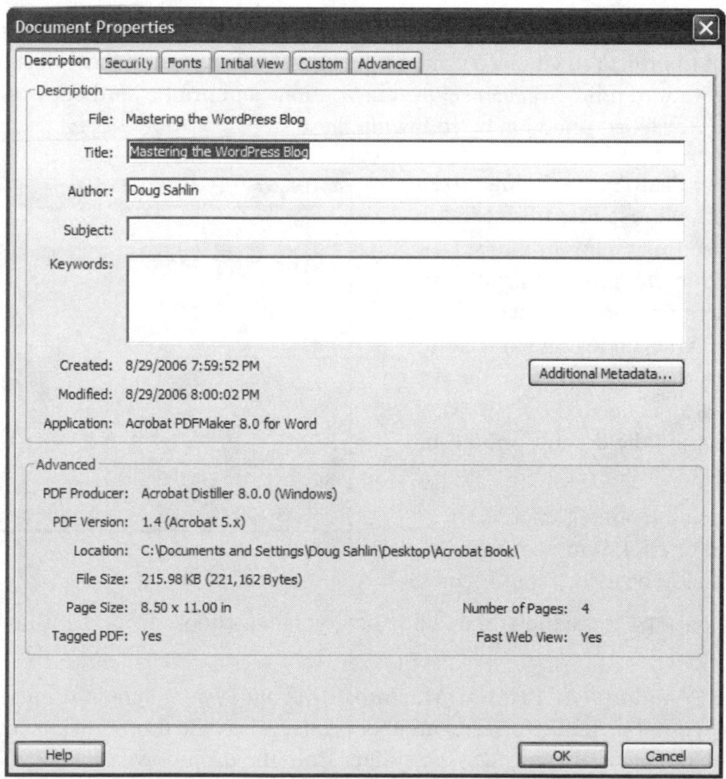

FIGURE 3-6 You can view and modify the properties of a document.

Print PDF Documents from Acrobat Standard

After you view a document onscreen, you have the option to print a hard copy of the document. Herein lies another strong suit of Acrobat: the document prints exactly as it was created on the author's computer. Printing a document from Acrobat is pretty straightforward. You have the same options available as you find in most word-processing software, such as Microsoft Word. You can print the document using the Adobe PDF printer, which is the Acrobat Distiller with a different name. (Printing a document using the Adobe PDF printer is covered in Chapter 4.) You can also choose a network printer or a printer attached to your computer. Your options vary, depending on the type of printer used to print the document. If you own Acrobat Professional, you have a wide variety of printing options, which are covered in the next section. To print a document from Acrobat Standard, choose File | Print. After the Print dialog box appears, select a printer, and then follow the prompts to print the document.

You can print comments attached to a document along with the document by choosing Documents | Print With Comments Summary.

Print PDF Documents from Acrobat Professional

When you print a document, you can print the entire document or select thumbnails to specify the pages you want to print. You can also print a selection of text by using the Select tool to select the text you want to print. You can set printing options and print a hard copy of a PDF file, a selection of pages, or a text selection by following these steps:

1. To open the Print Setup dialog box, shown next, choose File | Print Setup. You can use this dialog box to set general parameters for the print job, such as page orientation, size, printer, and so on. After choosing Print Setup parameters, click OK to close the dialog box. This step is needed only if you want to change the default printer and page size.

2. After selecting a printer, choose File | Print, or click Print to open the Print dialog box, shown in Figure 3-7.
3. In the Printer area at the top of the dialog box, you can choose from the following options:
   - **Name (Windows) or Printer (Macintosh)** Your system default printer is displayed in this field. To select another printer, click the drop-down arrow to the right of the text field and choose a printer from the drop-down menu.

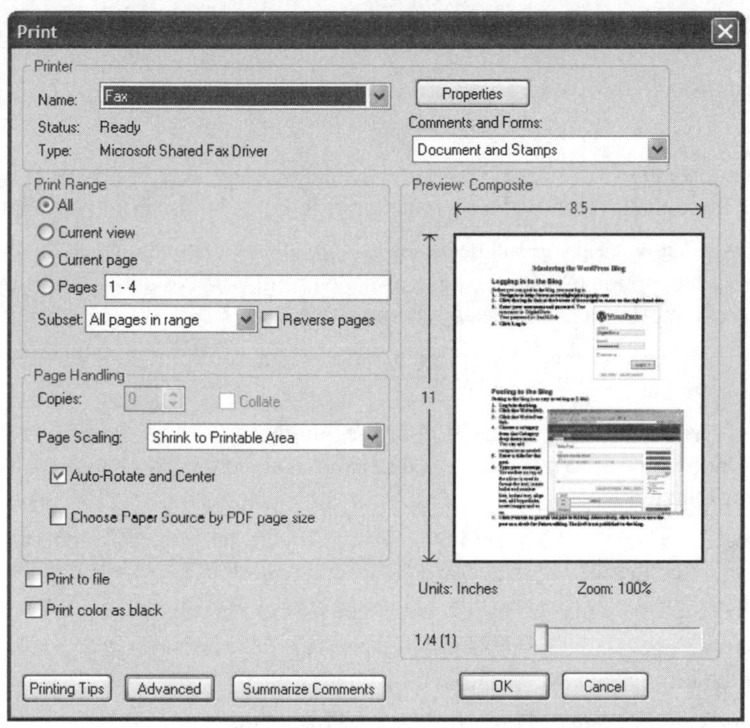

FIGURE 3-7 You specify options for printing in the Print dialog box.

- **Properties (Windows)** Click this button to set parameters for the currently selected printer. After you click this button, a dialog box appears that is specific for the selected printer.
- **Destination (Macintosh)** Your choice is either Printer or File.

4. Also in the Printer area, click the Comments And Forms drop-down arrow and choose one of the following options:
   - **Document** Prints the selected pages from the document as well as form fields.
   - **Document And Markups** Prints the selected pages from the document, comments, and form fields.
   - **Document And Stamps** Prints the selected pages, as well as any stamps that have been added to the pages.
   - **Form Fields Only** Prints only the form fields from the specified pages or selected area.

Form fields won't print if the document author selected the Visible But Doesn't Print option when creating the field.

5. In the Print Range area, you can choose from the following options:
   - **All** Choose this option to print all pages in the document.
   - **Selected Pages** This option becomes available and is selected if you select two or more thumbnails from the Pages pane, prior to invoking the Print command.
   - **Current View** This option becomes available if you zoomed in on the document. Choose this option to print the page as it's currently visible in the Document pane. This option prints any visible comments as well.
   - **Current Page** Choose this option to print the page currently visible in the Document pane.
   - **Pages From [ ] To [ ]** By default, the beginning and ending pages are entered. To print a range of pages, enter the beginning and ending page numbers in the appropriate fields.
   - **Subset** By default, all pages in the selected range are printed. To choose a different option, click the Subset drop-down arrow and choose one of the following options: All Pages In Range (the default), Odd Pages Only, or Even Pages Only.
   - **Reverse Pages** Choose this option to print the pages in reverse order, beginning with the last page in the specified range.
6. In the Page Handling area, choose from the following options:
   - **Copies** Enter a value for the number of copies you want to print. Or, you can click the arrows to the right of the field to increase or decrease the value in the text field. If you're working on a Macintosh, you specify this option in the General dialog box.
   - **Collate** Choose this option if you're using double-sided printing or are printing more than one copy of the document, to properly collate the pages in print order. If you work on a Macintosh, this option appears in the General dialog box. This option is unavailable if the selected printer doesn't support collating pages prior to printing.
   - **Page Scaling** Click the drop-down arrow and choose one of the following options:
     - **None** Prints the document at its current size beginning at the upper-left corner or center (if the Auto-Rotate And Center check box is selected). If the document dimensions exceed the paper size, the document is cropped.
     - **Fit To Printable Area** Increases the document width to fit the printer margins for the currently selected paper size. Choose this option if the document you're printing is narrower than the width of the selected paper.
     - **Shrink to Printable Area** Shrinks oversized pages to fit the selected paper size. This option comes in handy if the PDF file you're printing has different page sizes within the document. If you choose this option and the document has pages smaller than the currently selected paper size, the small pages aren't enlarged.

- **Tile Large Pages** Divides pages or selections larger than the currently selected paper size into tiles. Small pages aren't upsized when you use this option.
- **Tile All Pages** Divides all pages or selected areas into tiles.
- **Multiple Pages Per Sheet** Prints multiple pages on a single sheet. When you choose this option, the Pages Per Sheet field becomes available, enabling you to choose from 2 to 16 pages per sheet. This option also opens the Page Order field, which gives you four options: Horizontal, Horizontal Reversed, Vertical, or Vertical Reversed.
- **Booklet Printing** Prints a booklet of the selected pages. Pages are displayed side by side. You can choose whether to print on both sides of the page, the front, or back. You fold the resulting booklet in half.

- **Print Page Border** Inserts a border around each page when printed. This option is unavailable for certain print scaling options.
- **Auto-Rotate And Center** Choose this option if the PDF file you're printing contains pages in both landscape and portrait format. While printing is in progress, Acrobat changes page orientation as needed.
- **Choose Paper Source by PDF Page Size** Choose this option if your paper source has multiple feeders with different paper sizes. The paper size that's closest to the PDF size is selected.

7. Choose the Print to File (Windows) option to print the document to file in PRN (Printer Files) format. This is redundant, however, as you already have the file in PDF form.
8. Choose Print Color As Black option to have all non-white areas of the document printed as black. This option is useful if you're printing an AutoCAD file converted to PDF that has thin colored lines.
9. Click the Advanced button to open the Advanced Print Setup dialog box. Use this option if your printer, or the printer on which the document will be printed, supports marks and bleeds, transparency, and so on. Refer to your printer manual to select the proper settings for your device.
10. Click the Summarize Comments button to open the Summarize Options dialog box. This dialog box gives you options for printing the document with comments, comments only, or the document and comments on separate pages.
11. Click OK to print the document.

Use Text and Graphics from PDFs in Other Applications

You can capture text and graphic elements from a PDF document you want to use in another application. You can select text or graphic elements from a document, and then copy them to the system clipboard for use in another PDF document or a document in a different application that supports the elements you've captured from the PDF document.

You may be unable to capture text or graphic elements if Acrobat Security is applied to the document.

Capture Text from a PDF Document

You can easily select any text elements in a PDF document with the Acrobat Select tool. With the *Select tool,* you can select a single letter, a word, a sentence, an entire paragraph, or more. If graphic elements are dispersed in the text you're selecting, Acrobat ignores them and selects only text. To capture text from a PDF document:

1. Launch Acrobat and open the desired PDF file.
2. Choose the Select tool from the Select & Zoom toolbar.

Select

3. After you choose the Select tool, drag it into the Document pane toward the text you want to capture. Note, your cursor is now in the shape of an I-beam.

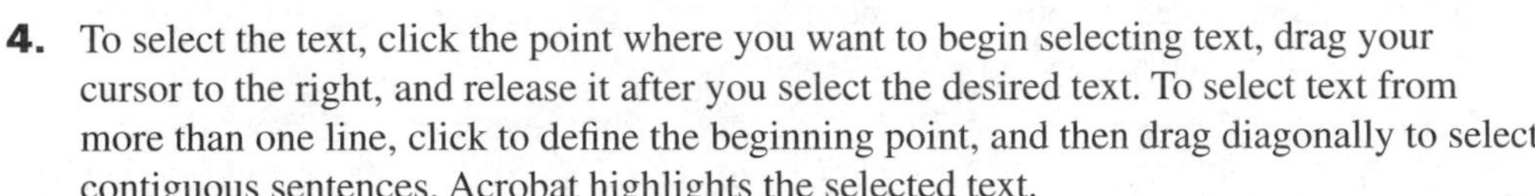

4. To select the text, click the point where you want to begin selecting text, drag your cursor to the right, and release it after you select the desired text. To select text from more than one line, click to define the beginning point, and then drag diagonally to select contiguous sentences. Acrobat highlights the selected text.
5. Choose Edit | Copy, and Acrobat copies the selected text to your system clipboard. Or, you can right-click (Windows) or CTRL-click (Macintosh) and choose Copy To Clipboard from the context menu.

If the text contains formatting you want to preserve, choose Copy with Formatting from the context menu.

6. Open a document in your favorite word processing program, place the cursor where you want to insert the text, and choose the Paste command. You can now edit the pasted text and save it for future reference.

Capture Graphic Elements from PDF Documents

When you open a PDF document with embedded graphics, the PDF retains the look and feel of the graphics as they were originally created. If the PDF document has a relatively low level of compression applied, the graphic elements will be crisp and clear. You can use the Acrobat Select tool to select a graphic element, such as a photograph or logo, from a PDF document as follows:

1. Launch Acrobat and open the PDF file that contains the graphic element(s) you want to select.
2. Choose the Select tool from the Select & Zoom toolbar. Or choose Tools | Select & Zoom | Select Tool.
3. Within the PDF document, navigate to the page that contains the graphic you want to select. Note, your cursor becomes a cross-hair when you move it over an image.

4. Click to the above-left (or above-right) of the graphic you want to select, and then drag diagonally to select the graphic. As you drag, a dotted rectangular bounding box appears, giving you a preview of the area you're selecting.
5. When the bounding box surrounds the graphic, release the mouse button. The selected graphic is surrounded by a rectangular blue overlay.
6. To use the graphic in another application, do one of the following:
   - Choose Edit | Copy, and Acrobat copies the graphic to the system clipboard.
   - Right-click (Windows) or CTRL-click (Macintosh) and choose Copy Image.
   - Right-click (Windows) or CTRL-click (Macintosh) and choose Save Image As to open the Save Image As dialog box. Then save the selection to a folder on your system or network.
   - Drag the selection into an open document in an application that supports graphic elements, such as Microsoft Word or Adobe Photoshop.

If you copied the graphic to the system clipboard, you can paste it into another application. Or, you can create a new PDF document by choosing File | Create PDF | From Clipboard Image, or paste it into an existing Acrobat document by choosing Edit | Paste.

You can select a portion of a graphic (known in photo-editing circles as cropping*) by releasing the mouse button when the rectangle surrounds the desired portion of the graphic.*

You can also create a bookmark or link after selecting a graphic. Choose the applicable command from the context menu to open the associated dialog box.

Using the Snapshot Tool

You can use the *Snapshot tool* to copy a combination of text and graphics to the clipboard. You can select an entire page, a portion of a page, or a portion of a graphic. After copying the selection to the clipboard, you can paste it into another application. To select text and graphics with the Snapshot tool, follow these steps:

1. Choose Tools | Select & Zoom | Snapshot Tool.
2. Copy a selection to the clipboard by clicking to define the corner of a selection, and then drag diagonally. As you drag, Acrobat displays a dashed bounding box that indicates the area of the current selection. Release the mouse button when the bounding box encompasses the area you want to copy to the clipboard.

After doing this, Acrobat displays a dialog box informing you the selection was copied to the clipboard. You can paste the selection into another application or create a new Acrobat document by choosing File | Create PDF | New From Clipboard.

TIP

Although you can use the Snapshot tool to capture text, the text is captured as an image and, as such, is not editable. If you need to capture text you can edit in another application, use the Select tool.

Use the Organizer

You use the *Organizer* to open PDF documents you've previously opened in Acrobat. The documents are segregated, based on the date they were opened. To launch the Acrobat Organizer, shown in Figure 3-8, choose File | Organizer | Open Organizer.

The Organizer stores thumbnail images of every document you've opened, regardless of whether it's still present on your system. If you open a document that's no longer on your system, the Open, Print, Email, Create PDF From Multiple Files, and Send For Review Task icons are grayed out.

Open Documents with the Organizer

After you launch the Organizer, you can locate documents opened during a specific time frame by clicking one of the History icons in the left pane of the Organizer. Clicking an icon displays

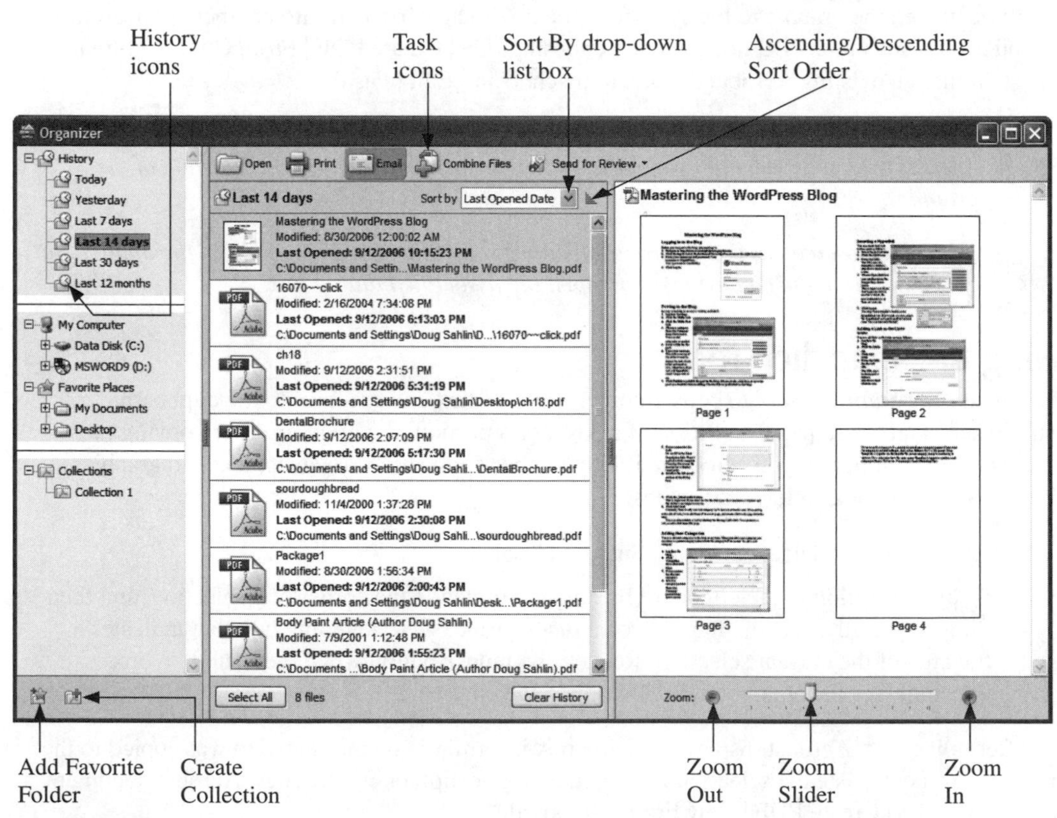

FIGURE 3-8 You can easily find previously viewed PDF documents using the Organizer.

descriptions of the documents opened during that period, as well as a thumbnail of the first page of the document. To view previously opened documents, follow these steps:

1. Open the Organizer as outlined previously.
2. Click the applicable History icon (see the previous Figure 3-8) in the left pane to display the documents opened during that period.
3. Click a document title to select the document. After selecting the document, a thumbnail version of the first document page appears in the right pane of the Organizer.

TIP *Click the Zoom Out icon to zoom out to the next lowest level of magnification. Click the Zoom In icon to zoom in to the next highest level of magnification. Or, you can drag the Zoom Slider to set the degree of magnification.*

4. After selecting a document, do one of the following:
   - Click the Open icon to open the document. Or, you can double-click the document title.
   - Click the Print icon to print the document.
   - Click the Email icon to attach the selected PDF file to an e-mail message.
   - Click the Combine Files icon to open the Combine Files dialog box. You can then click the Add Files or Add Folders button to select the files or folder of files you want to add to the document you just selected, and convert them to a new PDF document. For more information, see Chapter 4.
   - Click the Send For Review icon and choose one of the options from the drop-down menu to send the current document for review. A detailed discussion of the review process, and the options you'll find in this menu, is included in Chapter 10.

TIP *You can select multiple titles from within the Organizer and open, print, or create a PDF document from multiple files. You cannot, however, send multiple files for e-mail review. Click the Sort By drop-down arrow and choose a sorting option from the drop-down menu.*

5. Click the Sort Order icon to sort the titles by ascending or descending order. When the icon is an up-facing right triangle, the current sort is ascending order, and clicking the icon reverts the sort to descending order. When the icon is a down-facing right triangle, the current sort is descending order, and clicking the icon reverts the sort to ascending order.
6. Click the Favorite Folder icon to open the Browse For Folder dialog box. Select a folder and click OK to add it to your Favorite Places tree in the left pane of the Organizer.

TIP *Click a Favorite Places folder icon to display the titles of all PDF documents in that folder. You can then perform any of the tasks previously mentioned in this section.*

To quickly open a recently viewed document, choose File | History, and then choose the desired timeframe from the submenu. For example, to open a file that has been viewed within the past week choose File | History | Last 7 Days, and then choose the desired file from the submenu.

Create PDF Collections

You can also use the Acrobat Organizer to create a collection of PDF documents. The documents can be in any folder. After you create a collection, it appears as an icon in the Collections tree on the left side of the Organizer. This is a convenient method of organizing similar documents that appear in many different folders on your computer. To create a collection, follow these steps:

1. Click the Create A New Collection icon in the lower-left corner of the Organizer, shown previously in Figure 3-8. Or if the Organizer is not currently open choose File | Organizer | Create New Collection to create a new collection and open the Organizer in one fell swoop. The default name of the new collection is Untitled, followed by the next available number. The default title is selected indicating you can rename it by entering different text.
2. Enter the title of the new collection, and then press ENTER or RETURN.
3. Right-click (Windows) or CTRL-click (Macintosh) the collection and choose Add Files from the context menu to open the Select Files To Add To Your Collection dialog box.
4. Navigate to the folder that contains the desired files, and select the ones you want to add to the collection.
5. Click Add.
6. Repeat Steps 3 through 6 to add any files stored in different folders to the collection.

To open an existing collection, launch the Organizer as outlined previously and double-click the desired collection title.

To add the currently selected document to an existing collection, choose File | Organizer | Add To A Collection. Select the collection to which you want to add the documents from the Add To A Collection dialog box, and then click OK.

To delete a collection, open the Organizer, right-click (Windows) or CTRL-click (Macintosh) the title of the collection you want to delete, and then choose Delete Collection from the context menu. Note, deleting a collection doesn't delete the PDF files in the collection from your hard drive.

Summary

In this chapter, you learned how to use the Acrobat tools to navigate a document and how to use the Acrobat panels to navigate to specific elements in a document. You also learned how to use Acrobat's powerful Search command to search through a single document, a folder of documents, or an index of PDF documents. In the latter part of the chapter, you discovered how to use Acrobat tools to select elements from documents for use in other applications. In addition, you learned how to use the Organizer to view and organize PDF documents you opened in the past. In the next chapter, you discover how to create PDF documents.

Part II

Create PDF Documents

Chapter 4

Create a PDF Document

How to...

- Create a PDF file
- Use Acrobat Distiller
- Set conversion settings
- Set document properties
- Save PDF files
- Save PDF files in other formats

Acrobat enables you to create PDF documents from many sources. You can create a PDF file from within many authoring applications, use an application's Print command and choose Adobe PDF as the printer, or create documents directly in Acrobat. When you create a document within Acrobat, you have many options available. You can save a document using Acrobat defaults, or you can modify the document properties and add security to confidential documents. You can even use Acrobat to save documents in other formats. In this chapter, you learn the nuts and bolts of creating a bare-bones PDF file.

Create a PDF File

You can use Acrobat to quickly create PDFs from existing files. You can choose between two methods: the Create PDF command, or the drag-and-drop method. When you create a PDF file using one of these methods, Acrobat converts the original file into PDF format. After Acrobat converts the file, you can save it as a PDF file or export it using another supported format for use in another application. You can also create a PDF document from within an authoring application by exporting the file in PDF format (if supported), or by using the application's Print command and choosing Adobe PDF as the printing device. Creating a PDF file from within an authoring application is covered in Chapter 5.

Use the Create PDF Command

You use the *Create PDF command* or task button to open supported file formats as PDF documents. When you choose this command and select one or more files to open, Acrobat converts each file from its current format into PDF format. You can open the following formats as PDF files:

- **Autodesk AutoCAD (Professional only)** You can create technical drawings using the popular *Autodesk AutoCAD* software. You can create PDF documents from AutoCAD documents with DWG, DWF or DST file extensions.
- **BMP** You can export BMP files from the most popular photo-editing programs, such as Adobe Photoshop CS2, CorelDRAW Graphics Suite X, and Macromedia Fireworks 8. Image files saved in the *BMP format* can have color depth as high as 24-bit.

- **Compuserve GIF** Graphic Interchange Format (GIF) files have 8-bit (a maximum of 256 colors) color depth. You can open GIF files saved in the GIF 87 format or GIF 89a format as PDF files. You can also open an animated GIF, but only the first frame of the animation is converted to PDF format.
- **HTML** Hypertext Markup Language (HTML) files are created for use as web pages on the Internet. You can open HTML files as PDF documents. When you open an HTML file as a PDF file, Acrobat reads any image tags (<img src= "yourimage.jpg">) and converts the associated files as images in the PDF document in the exact position they appear when the HTML document is opened in a web browser. If the image is not available, Acrobat creates a bounding box that is the size of the image and displays the Alt text. Converting a web page to PDF format is a great way to create a client proof of a web site under construction. You can also use the Capture Web Page command to open a web page from your hard drive or download a web page from the Internet. Web capture is discussed in Chapter 6.
- **InDesign** New to Acrobat 8 is the capability to open Adobe InDesign documents, which have the .indd extension. *Adobe InDesign* is a popular page layout program.
- **JDF** Job Definition Format (JDF) files are created for PDF documents destined for output by a printing service. *JDF files* are instructions to the printing service center that contains information such as the client name, product name, number of copies to be printed, whether the job will have cover pages, the type of binding used, and so on. The command to create a PDF from JDF files doesn't create a PDF file, but instead, it opens the JDF file in the JDF Job Definitions dialog box.
- **JPEG** Joint Photographic Experts Group (JPEG) image files are used for web graphics and multimedia presentations. *JPEG files* are compressed for quick download from the Web or to save file space in a multimedia presentation.
- **JPEG 2000** *JPEG 2000* can be thought of as JPEG's big brother. The file format features advanced image compression, which results in high-quality images with smaller file sizes. The format also features progressive download and will be used by next-generation digital-imaging devices. JPEG 2000 files are designated with the .jpf, .jpx, .jp2, j2k, j2c, or .jpc file extension.
- **Microsoft Office Word** You use *Microsoft Office Word* to create documents with the .doc extension.
- **Microsoft Project (Professional only)** You use *Microsoft Project* to manage projects and communicate the status of a project, as well as manage project resources with colleagues in your organization.
- **Microsoft Visio (Professional only)** You use *Microsoft Visio* to create diagrams and flowcharts that enable you to document and share information and ideas with colleagues.
- **PCX** Image files in the Windows-only Picture Exchange format can be exported from most popular image-editing programs. The *.pcx format* is native to the Windows

Paintbrush program, but many applications, such as Photoshop CS2 and CorelDRAW Graphics Suite X3, offer full support of the .pcx format. The .pcx format supports 24-bit color depth and can be opened directly in Acrobat as PDF files.

- **PICT (Macintosh only)** Image files saved in the Macintosh PICT (Picture) format support 32-bit color depth. While PICT files can be created in Windows-based image-editing programs, only the Macintosh version of Acrobat can open PICT images as PDF files.
- **PNG** Portable Network Graphics (PNG) files use lossless compression, which ensures better image quality than JPEG and GIF files. The file format supports 8-bit color, 24-bit color, or 48-bit color.
- **PostScript/EPS** Encapsulated PostScript (EPS) files are used in illustration programs such as Adobe Illustrator, CorelDRAW, and Macromedia FreeHand MX. *EPS files* can be comprised of vector and bitmap graphics.
- **Text** You can open text documents saved in the TXT format as PDF documents. Text files can be created in programs as sophisticated as Microsoft Word, or as humble as the Notepad utility, which is included with versions of the Microsoft Windows operating system (OS).
- **TIFF** Tagged Image File Format (TIFF) files can be compressed or uncompressed and support 32-bit color. People who create images in both platforms for print favor this format because of the high-image resolution and clarity.
- **XPS** XPS (XML Paper Specification) is Microsoft's answer to the PDF. XPS will be part of the next Windows operating system: Vista. XPS is in its infancy so the impact on Adobe and the industry standard PDF will not be known for some time.

You have several options for creating PDF files. You can create a PDF from a single file or by combining multiple files. The upcoming sections cover both scenarios, and they show you how to choose compression and color management for images converted to PDF.

Use the Create PDF | From File Command

When you need to convert a single file into a PDF document, you use the Create PDF | From File command. To convert an existing file to a PDF document, do the following:

1. Choose File | Create PDF | From File to access the Open dialog box. Or, click the Create PDF task button and choose From File.
2. Choose an option from the Files Of Type drop-down menu, or accept the default All Files option. If you select a specific file type, only files of that type are visible for selection.
3. Select the file you want to open.
4. If you specify a file type, before you select a file, the Settings button may become available. The available settings options vary, depending on the selected file type.

For example, if you select TIFF from the Files Of Type drop-down menu and click the Settings button, you can specify compression and color management settings. These settings are covered in the next section.

5. Click Open, and Acrobat converts the file to PDF format. Figure 4-1 shows a JPEG image converted to PDF format.

After you convert a file to PDF format, you can modify the document using the Acrobat commands and toolset. You can then save the file in PDF format, or choose a supported file format. Saving files is covered in the section "Save PDF Files."

Choose Compression and Color Management Settings for Image Files

When you choose the Create PDF | From File command and choose an image format, the Settings button becomes available, which enables you to control how much compression is

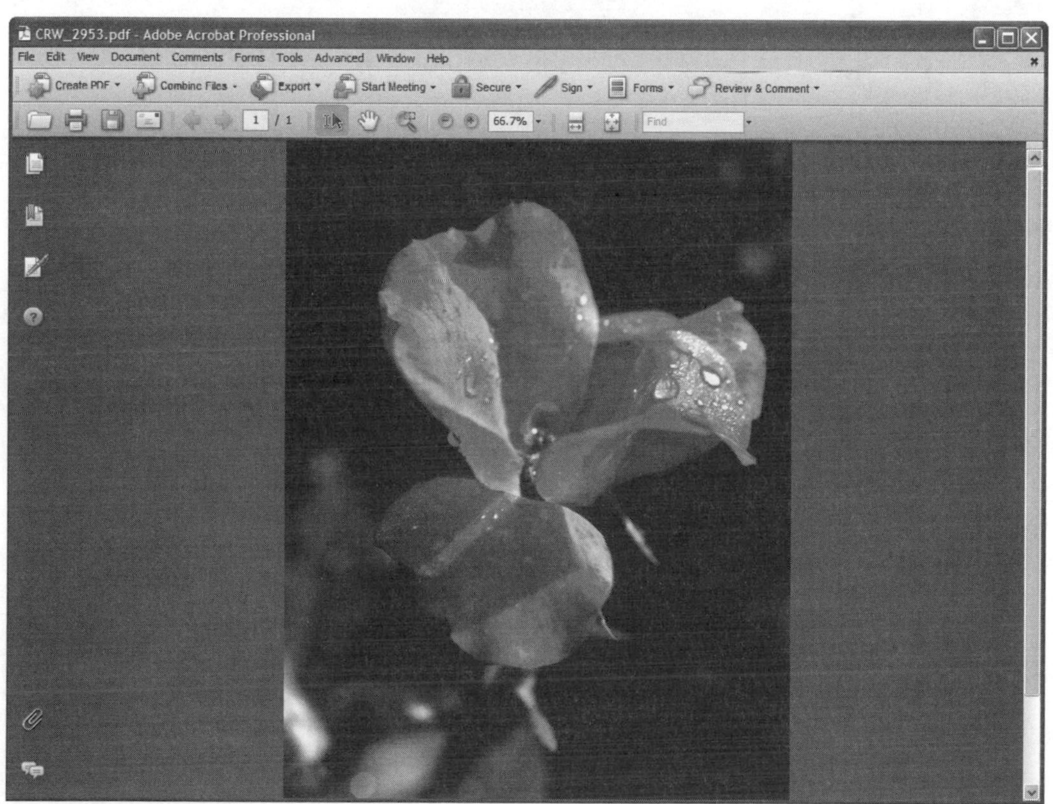

FIGURE 4-1 Use the Create PDF | From File command to convert supported files into PDF documents.

applied to the image and to specify color management options. The Settings option is not available when you convert Compuserve GIF or JPEG 2000 files to PDF documents and the Compression settings are dimmed out when you choose JPEG from the Files of Type drop-down menu. Click the Settings button to display the Adobe PDF Settings dialog box, shown in the following illustration.

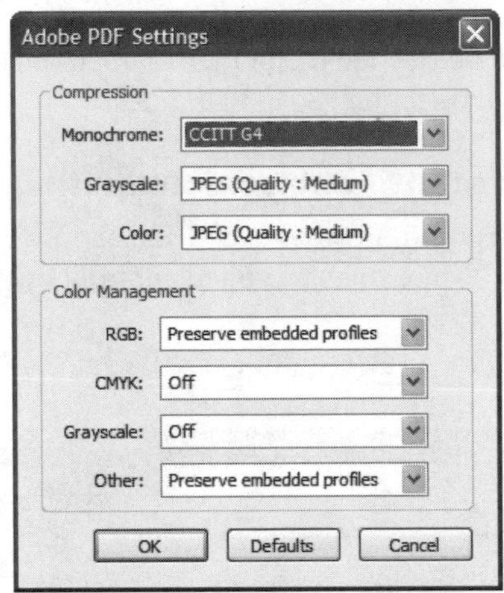

With all image formats except CompuserveGIF and JPEG 2000, you can specify the following compression settings from the Adobe PDF Settings dialog box:

- **Monochrome** For 1-bit monochrome images, choose CCITT G4 to achieve good image quality, JBIG2 (Lossy) for better image quality, and JBIG2 (Lossless) for the best image quality. When an image is compressed, data is lost, hence, the term "lossy."
- **Grayscale** For 8-bit grayscale images, choose ZIP to convert images or documents with images that have large areas of similar color or repeating patterns, choose JPEG quality for photorealistic images, or choose JPEG 2000 to take advantage of the format's superior compression and progressive download. When you choose JPEG, you have five quality options: from Minimum (high compression, small file size, and low image quality) to Maximum (minimal compression, largest file size, and best image quality). When you choose JPEG 2000, you have six options: from Minimum (high compression, small file size, and low image quality) to Lossless (little or no compression, largest file size, and best image quality).
- **Color** For images with thousands (16 bit) to millions (32 and 48 bit) of colors, you can specify ZIP, JPEG, or JPEG 2000 with the same compression settings as discussed in the previous bullet.

With all image formats except BMP, Compuserve GIF, JPEG2000 or PCX, you can specify color management settings. From within the Color Management section of the Adobe PDF Settings dialog box just shown, you can specify color management for RGB (image colors comprised of

Red, Green, and Blue hues), CMYK (image colors comprised of Cyan, Magenta, Yellow, and Black hues), Grayscale, and Other by choosing one of the following options for each format:

- **Preserve Embedded Profiles** Uses an ICC color profile that has been embedded with the image.
- **Off** Acrobat color profiles will be used in lieu of color profiles embedded with the image.
- **Ask When Opening** Acrobat displays color profiles embedded with the image, giving you the option to use them or not.

Use the Create PDF | From Multiple Files Command

You can use the Create PDF | From Multiple Files command to create a PDF document from multiple files in formats supported by Acrobat. When you create a PDF document from multiple files, you can mix files of different formats and specify the order in which the files appear in the converted PDF document. You can also use this command to append all currently open PDF documents. Yet another option is to create a PDF Package that creates a PDF document with a cover sheet. The other documents appear as bookmarks in the Bookmarks panel. Click a bookmark to open the associated document.

To convert multiple files into a PDF document:

1. Choose File | Create PDF | From Multiple Files to open the Combine files dialog box shown next. (Or, click the Create PDF task button and choose From Multiple Files, or click the Combine Files task button.)

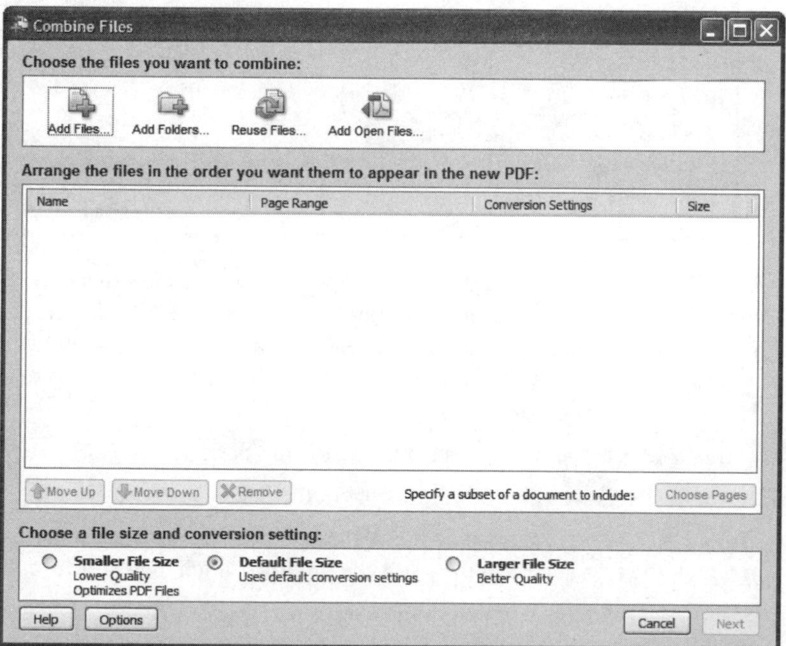

2. Choose one of the following options:
   - **Add Files** Click this button to open the Add Files dialog box. Navigate to, select the desired files, and then click OK to exit the dialog box.
   - **Add Folders** Click this button to open the Browse for Folder dialog box. Navigate to, select the desired files, and then click Add Files to exit the dialog box. All supported files from the selected folder are added to the list.
   - **Reuse Files** Click this button to open the Reuse Files dialog box shown next. The left pane of the dialog box displays a list of PDF documents created with the Combine Files command, while the right pane displays a list of the files used to create each PDF document. Click a PDF document to display the files used to create the document. You can elect to add all files used to create a PDF by selecting a title from the right pane, or select individual files in the right pane of the dialog box. Click Add Files to add the selected files to the list of files to combine.

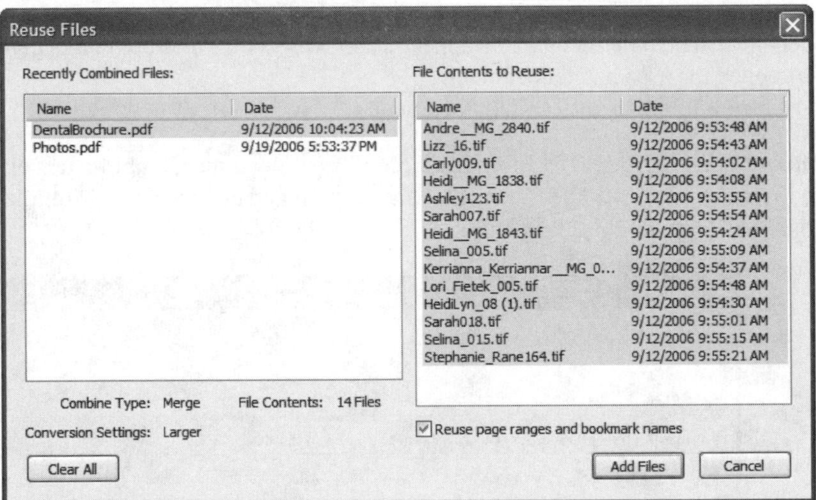

   - **Add Open Files** Click this button to open the Open PDF Files dialog box, which displays a list of all documents currently open in Acrobat. All files are selected by default. Click an individual file to select it, or CTRL-click (Windows)/CMD-click(Macintosh) to select multiple files. Click Add Files to add the selected files to the list of files to combine.

3. After adding files to the list, you have the following options:
   - **Remove** Removes the selected file from the list.
   - **Move Up** Moves the selected file to the next highest position in the list. The order in which the files appear in the list is the order in which they appear in the converted

PDF document. You can click this button as needed to move the file further up the list. This button is dimmed out when you select the first file or reach the top of the list.

- **Move Down** Moves the file to the next lowest position in the list. You can click this button as needed to move the file further down the list. This button is dimmed out when you move a file to the bottom of the list or select the last file.
- **Smaller File Size** Optimizes all files to achieve the smallest file size. This option produces a PDF suitable for monitor viewing and e-mail distribution.
- **Default File Size** Uses the default PDF conversion method. All PDF files retain their original settings. This option creates a PDF suitable for high-quality viewing and printing of business documents.
- **Larger File Size** Produces the highest quality PDF. If the original files are high quality, the resulting PDF is suitable for high-quality printing, or printing on an inkjet printer.
- **Options** Click this button to display the Options for Conversion Settings dialog box, which contains two options: Always Enable Accessibility and Reflow, which creates a document that is accessible for the impaired; and Always Add Bookmarks to Adobe PDF, which creates bookmarks in the resulting PDF.

NOTE *When selecting the Enable Accessibility option, Acrobat adds PDF structure/tags to the PDF. This increases the size of the resultant PDFs, regardless of the size option selected.*

4. Click Next to display the second Combine Files dialog box shown in the following illustration. Choose one of the following options:
   - **Merge files into single PDF** Combines the files into a single PDF. The resulting PDF has bookmarks for each file. If you choose this option, select a document from the list and the Edit Bookmark for File button appears, which, when clicked, opens the Edit Bookmark for File dialog box. Enter the desired bookmark name, and then click OK. The new bookmark name is displayed. Click the Reset Bookmark button to revert to the original bookmark name.
   - **Assemble files into a PDF Package** If you select this option, radio buttons appear that give you the option of using the Adobe template as a cover sheet, or using the first document as a cover sheet. If you choose the Adobe template option, the resulting PDF package consists of the cover sheet. When the package is opened, the first document is displayed. Readers can click the Cover Sheet icon to display the specified cover sheet. The documents in the PDF Package are displayed as PDF icons in the Bookmarks panel. Click on a bookmark to display the document. If you choose the first document cover sheet option, the PDF package uses the first document as the cover sheet, and displays the document when the package is opened. The other documents in the package appear as icons in the Bookmarks panel. Click the bookmark to display the associated document.

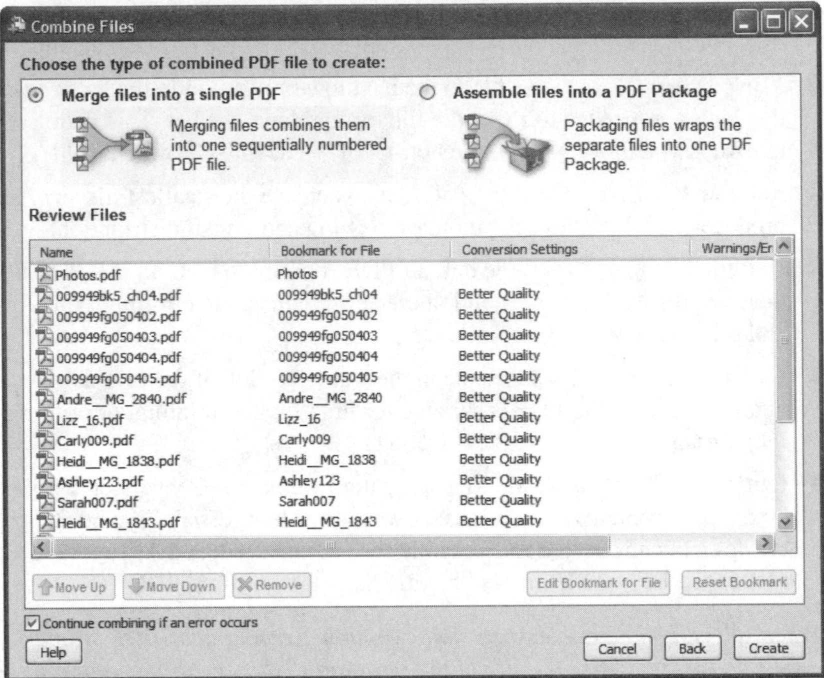

5. Click Create to combine the files. At this stage of the process, the dialog box reconfigures and displays a progress bar for each file being converted.
6. Click Save to open the Save As dialog box. Navigate to the folder in which you want to save the combined file, and then click Save.

Create a PDF File by Dragging-and-Dropping

You can quickly open one or more files as PDFs by dragging the file icon from your desktop or an open file folder, and then dropping it on the Acrobat icon. You can also drag-and-drop a file from a file folder directly into the Acrobat application. If you select several files to open as PDF documents using the drag-and-drop method, Acrobat creates a separate PDF file for each file you select.

If you have a project folder with several files you're converting to PDF documents, resize Acrobat and the open file folder, so both are visible on your desktop. Then, it's a simple matter of dragging files from the folder and dropping them into Acrobat.

To launch Acrobat and create a new PDF, drop a supported file format on your Acrobat desktop shortcut.

Dragging an Internet Shortcut into the Workspace of Acrobat automatically converts the web page found in the shortcut to a PDF document.

Capture HTML Documents as PDF Documents

If you're a web site designer, you can use the Create PDF | From Web Page command to create a PDF proof for client approval. This technique enables you to show your design to a customer before a web host is selected. Use this command to convert a single HTML document from your hard drive into a PDF document, or use it to convert the entire site into a PDF document, complete with links. To create a PDF document from HTML files, do the following:

1. Choose File | Create PDF | From Web Page to access the Create PDF From Web Page dialog box, shown next. If the command has been used before, the last site opened is listed in the URL field.

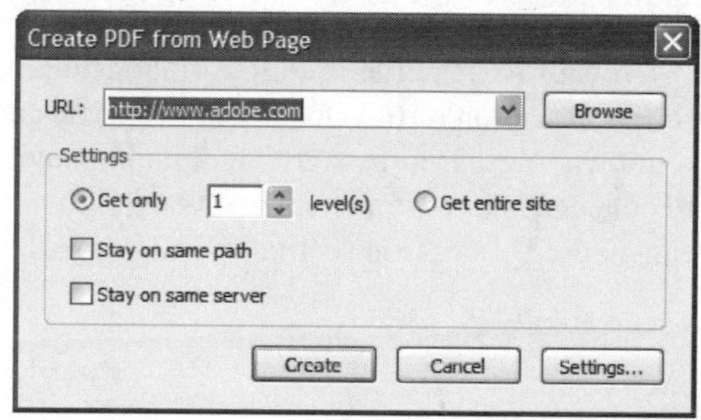

2. If you want to open a single HTML page, accept the default Settings options. If you want to open the entire site in PDF format, choose the Get Entire Site option.
3. Click Browse, and Acrobat opens the Select File To Open dialog box.
4. Navigate to the HTML file you want to convert to PDF format, and then click Open. If you chose the Get Entire Site option, select the home page of the site.

NOTE *The Get Only [ ] Level(s) option enables you to capture multiple levels of a web site, and is generally reserved for capturing web sites from the Web, not creating client proofs, as discussed here.*

5. Click Create. If you chose the Get Entire Site option, Acrobat displays a dialog box warning you of a potentially large download. Click Yes to begin the download; click No to abort. When you use this command to convert HTML documents stored in a folder on your hard drive, the conversion to PDF is relatively quick. However, when you download sites from the Web, the download time depends on the quality of your connection, your modem speed, your processor, and the size and complexity of the web site. (Capturing web pages from the Web is covered in detail in Chapter 6.)

After you click Download, Acrobat begins converting the HTML pages into PDF format. Acrobat downloads the entire site, including images and accompanying files.

Save PDF Files

After you convert a file to PDF format, you can save it for future reference. When you save a PDF file, you can accept the Acrobat defaults, name the file, and save it. Or, you can modify the document properties, name the file, and save it. The properties you modify determine how the document appears when opened, and what information is available for the Search command (if the document is included as part of a PDF index). To save a PDF file using the Acrobat defaults, do the following:

1. Choose File | Save, and Acrobat opens the Save As dialog box.
2. Navigate to the folder you want the file saved in and enter a name for the file. Accept the Save As Type default [Adobe PDF Files (*.pdf)] and click Save.

After you click Save, Acrobat saves the file in PDF format using the default information, which appears in the Description section of the Document Properties dialog box. If you're using the document for your own reference, the Acrobat defaults may be acceptable. If you distribute the document to colleagues or customers, however, it's to your advantage to modify the information that appears in the Description section of the Properties dialog box, as discussed in the next section.

Set Document Properties

When you convert a file to PDF format or open a PDF document and modify it, you can change the document properties before saving the document, except if security has been applied to the document. You can edit the document properties to include information you deem pertinent to your viewing audience. For example, you can set the document Initial View to change or specify what the viewer sees when the document is opened, and you can set the document security to limit access to the document while adding custom information.

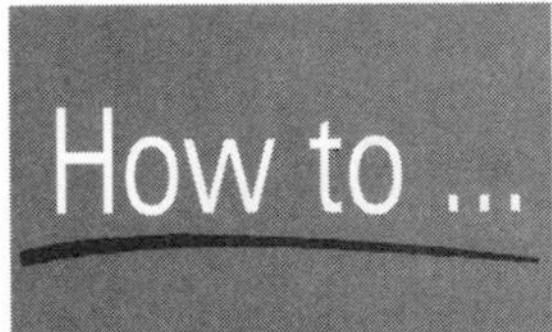

Add Headers and Footers to a PDF Document

To add headers and footers to a document, choose Document | Header And Footer | Add to open the Add Header And Footer dialog box. The dialog box has two windows that display the header and footer. Above the header and footer windows are six windows to which you can add the date, page number, or custom text for the header and footer you're creating. You can also specify the range of pages on which the header or footer appears, and how the margins are configured. There are also buttons to add the page number or date to the header or footer. In addition, you can use spinner buttons to create headers and footers a page at a time.

Edit Document Properties

When you convert a file to PDF format, Acrobat records the document's properties. This information is gleaned from the original file and displayed in the Document Properties dialog box, which is divided into six tabs: Description, Security, Fonts, Initial View, Custom, and Advanced. You can modify a document's properties summary by following these steps:

1. Choose File | Properties to open the Document Properties dialog box.
2. Click the Description tab, shown next, and modify the information in any or all of the following text fields: Title, Author, Subject, and Keywords. Remember, this information is often the first information your viewers see concerning your document, especially if they use the Search command to locate the information. Keep this information as relevant as possible.

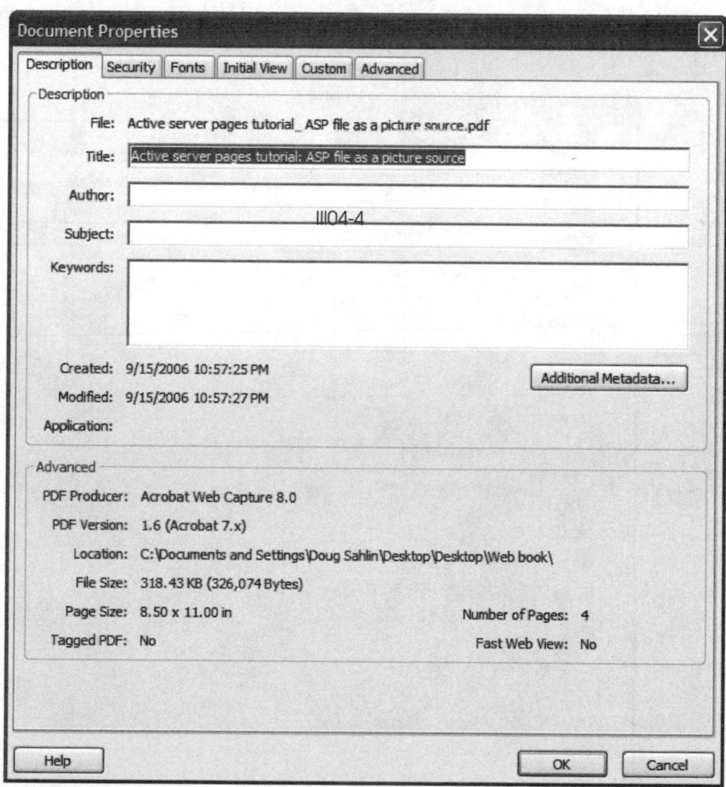

3. Click the Additional Metadata button to open a new window which is designated by the filename of the document. In this window you can add additional metadata in several categories. You can add copyright information, IPTC (International Press Telecommunications Council) contact information, IPTC Content information, and so on. This metadata can be used when searching a PDF index in which the document is included.

4. Click the Security tab to set document security options, as outlined in the upcoming section "Set Document Security."
5. Click the Fonts tab to display information about the fonts embedded and used in the document.
6. Click the Initial View tab to set viewing options when the document is opened, as discussed in the next section, "Set Document Initial View Options."
7. Click the Custom tab to define custom names and values for the document. Custom names and values can be specified as search options in PDF indexes. Creating indexes of PDF documents is covered in Chapter 18.
8. Click the Advanced tab, shown in the following illustration, to specify a base URL for the document, specify an index to be associated with the document, and set trapping options. When you specify an index and perform a search on the document, all documents in the index are searched as well. Base URLs are used when you create PDF documents for the Internet and are covered in Chapter 13.

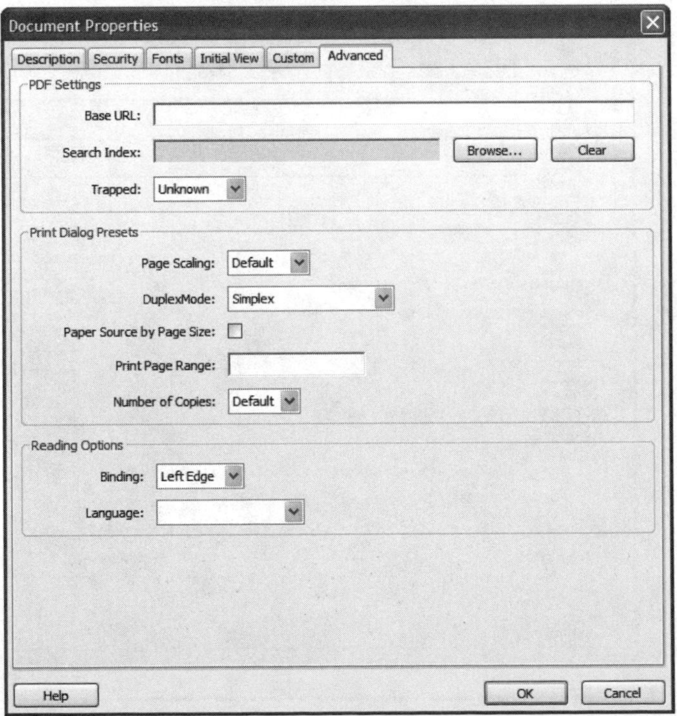

9. In the Reading Options area of the Advanced tab, click the Binding drop-down arrow and choose Left Edge or Right Edge. Binding is used when thumbnails are displayed or when a multipage document is displayed using the Continuous Facing mode.
10. Click the Language drop-down arrow and choose a language. This information is used when the document is viewed with a screen reader.

11. Click OK to exit the Document Properties dialog box. When you save the document as a PDF file, Acrobat updates the information you entered along with other Description information, such as the date modified.

Saving a document with pertinent information in the Description section of the Document Properties dialog box makes it easier for other people who view the document to understand the information contained within. Time is valuable. In today's hustle-bustle world, people don't have the time to sift through a document to see if the information meets their needs. In addition to changing the Document Properties Description tab information, you can specify what your viewers see when they open a PDF document. The information you include in the Description tab of the Document Properties dialog box can also be used in a search if the document is included in a PDF index. Creating a PDF index is covered in Chapter 18.

Set Document Initial View Options

If you save a PDF document with Acrobat defaults, when your viewers open the document, they see the first document page in the Document pane and all the Acrobat (or Adobe Reader) menus and tools. The Navigation pane is closed by default, but you can change a document's properties to have any of the tabs in the Navigation pane open when the document opens, which gives your viewers a way to navigate the document. The actual tabs available to viewers depend on the version of Acrobat or Adobe Reader they use to open the document. The default Initial View options work fine if you share the document with coworkers or work with a team of authors who will edit the document. When you create a document such as an e-book or multimedia presentation, however, you can change the default options by doing the following:

1. Choose File | Properties and click the Initial View tab:

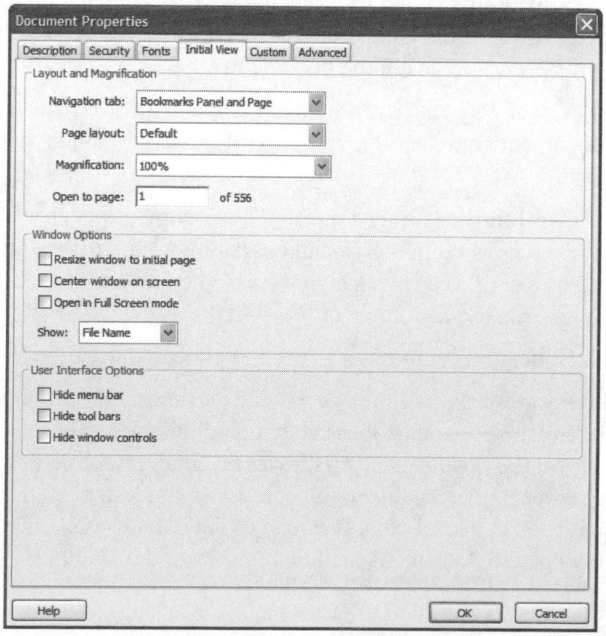

2. In the Layout and Magnification section, click the Navigation tab drop-down arrow and choose from the following options:
   - **Page Only** When the document opens, the viewer sees the full page with only the tab titles visible in the Navigation pane.
   - **Bookmarks Panel And Page** When the document opens, the viewer sees the full page with only the Bookmarks panel of the Navigation pane visible.
   - **Pages Panel And Page** When the document opens, the viewer sees the full page with only the Pages panel of the Navigation pane visible.
   - **Attachments Panel And Page** When the document opens, the viewer sees the full page with only the Attachments panel of the Navigation pane visible.
   - **Layers Panel And Page** When the document opens, the viewer sees the full page with only the Layers panel of the Navigation pane visible.
3. Click the Page Layout drop-down arrow and choose one of the following options:
   - **Default** Acrobat configures the document according to the user's viewing preference.
   - **Single Page** The document opens in single-page mode. Viewers will be able to use the Hand tool to navigate through a single page, but not to the next page.
   - **Single Page Continuous** The document opens in continuous mode. Viewers will be able to use the Hand tool to scroll from page-to-page in the document.
   - **Two Up (Facing)** The document opens with two pages arranged side-by-side in the Document pane.
   - **Two Up Continuous (Facing)** The document opens with two pages facing side-by-side displayed in the Document pane. Viewers will be able to use the Hand tool to scroll to different spreads in the document.
   - **Two Up (Cover Page)** The document opens with two pages arranged side-by-side in the Document pane, but the first page of the document is displayed as a single cover page.
   - **Two Up Continuous (Cover Page)** The document opens with two pages facing side-by-side displayed in the Document pane, but the first page of the document is displayed as a single cover page viewers will be able to use the hand tool to scroll to different spreads in the document.
4. Click the Magnification drop-down arrow and choose one of the following options:
   - **Magnification levels** Choose one of the preset magnification values (with the % symbol), and the document opens at that magnification. These values represent a percentage of the document size as it was originally published. You can also enter a value between 1 percent and 6400 percent in the Magnification field to have the document open at a level other than one of the defaults. Or, you can choose to have the document open to: Default, Actual Size, Fit Page, Fit Width, Fit Height, or Fit Visible.

- **Default** Acrobat sizes the document according to the general preferences of the user.
- **Actual Size** Acrobat sizes the document to its original dimensions.
- **Fit Page** Acrobat sizes the document to fill the entire Document pane when the file opens.
- **Fit Width** Acrobat sizes the document to fit the current width of the Document pane when the file opens.
- **Fit Height** Acrobat sizes the document to fit the current height of the Document pane when the file opens.
- **Fit Visible** Acrobat sizes the document so only visible elements fit the width of the Document pane. If you choose this option, no margins will be visible.

5. Enter the page number you want to be visible when the document opens.

NOTE *To have PDF documents reopen to the last page you viewed, choose Edit | Preferences, and then click Documents. Enable the Restore last view settings when reopening documents option.*

6. In the Window Options section, choose from the following options:
   - **Resize Window To Initial Page** Acrobat resizes the Document pane to fit around the first page of the document.
   - **Center Window On Screen** Acrobat opens the Document pane in the middle of the workspace.
   - **Open In Full Screen Mode** Viewers see the initial page in Full Screen mode, without any toolbars, menu bars, or navigation tabs. Viewers are unable to scroll a multipage document viewed in Full Screen mode, but they can use the Page Down, Page Up, and arrow keys to navigate the document. Or, pressing the Spacebar will display the next page. If you choose Open In Full Screen Mode and your document will be distributed to parties with limited Acrobat knowledge, then a good idea is to create an index or buttons your viewers can use for navigation.
7. Click the Show drop-down arrow and choose one of the following options:
   - **File Name** Acrobat displays the document filename in the application title bar.
   - **Document Title** Acrobat displays the document title in the application title bar. If you didn't specify a document title in the Description tab of the Document Properties dialog box, the document filename and extension are displayed.

NOTE *You can select every option in the Window Options section, but when options conflict, Acrobat applies the overriding option. For example, if you choose both Open In Full Screen Mode and Document Title, the document title isn't visible because the application title bar is hidden in Full Screen mode.*

8. In the User Interface Options section, choose any or all of the following options:
   - **Hide Menu Bar** Acrobat opens the document with the menu bar hidden. Press F9 to unhide the menu bar.
   - **Hide Tool Bars** Acrobat hides the toolbar when the document opens. If you don't choose the Hide Menu Bar option in conjunction with this option, the user can press F8 or choose Window | Hide Tool Bars to unhide the toolbars.
   - **Hide Window Controls** Acrobat opens the document with the Navigation pane hidden.

Even though it's possible for your viewers to reveal a hidden menu bar or tool bars using keyboard shortcuts, many of your viewers may not know this. Therefore, you may want to consider including some navigation aids for your viewers if you hide either the menu or toolbars. Or, you can annotate the first page of the document with a note instructing viewers on how to reveal the menu and tool bars when they're hidden. Click OK to apply the options and close the dialog box.

9. Choose File | Save.

When you save the document, the new Initial View options are saved with it and will be applied the next time the document opens. Of course, a viewer with the full version of Acrobat can modify any of the changes you make to the document. To prevent viewers from tampering with your handiwork, change the security level of the document, as described in the following section.

Set Document Security

You can add security to limit access to the document or prevent viewers from editing your document with the full version of Acrobat. You can use Acrobat Password Security to password-protect confidential documents. When you password-protect a document, you set document permissions; for example, you can prevent users from printing the document. Or, you can choose to use Acrobat Certificate Security, or Adobe Policy Server, both of which require a user to log in. When you use Acrobat Certificate Security, you specify which users can access the document. Acrobat security is covered in detail in Chapter 11.

Use the Save As Command

You use the Acrobat Save As command to save the same PDF document with different settings under another filename. Use this technique when you need to create different versions of the same document for different destinations—for example, to save a document optimized for print or to save a document optimized for a web page. To save the current PDF with a different filename, choose File | Save As to open the Save As Settings dialog box. Enter the new name for the document and click Save. When you use the Save As command, you also enable fast web viewing, which is discussed in Chapter 13.

You can also use the Save As command to save the document in another format. This is known as *repurposing content.* After you save the file in another format, you can edit the resulting file in a program that supports that format.

Save PDF Files in Other Formats

When you open a document in Acrobat, you can save the file in PDF format, or you can repurpose the document into another format. After you repurpose a document, you can edit the contents in another program. For example, if you repurpose all the text in a document by saving in Rich Text Format (RTF), you can edit the text in any word processing program that supports the RTF file format.

TIP *You can choose File | Save As, and then choose one of the HTML or XML formats to save a PDF document as an HTML or XML file for use on your web site. For additional information, refer to Chapter 13.*

Save Text from a PDF File

Although Acrobat enables you to select and edit text with the Select tool, this is a tedious process because Acrobat isn't set up as a word processing application. However, you can repurpose the document by saving all the text in RTF format, as a Text file, or as a Microsoft Word file, and then edit it in your favorite word processing program. If you use Microsoft Word for your word processing tasks, you can click one of the Adobe PDF buttons to export the edited text in PDF format. You can repurpose a PDF document as editable text by following these steps:

1. To save the text from a PDF file, choose File | Save As. Acrobat opens the Save As dialog box.
2. Name the document, click the Save As Type drop-down arrow, and choose Microsoft Word Document (*.doc), Rich Text Format (*.rtf), Text (Accessible) (*.txt), or Text (Plain) (*.txt).
3. Click the Settings button to define parameters for the text option you chose. The settings vary depending on the file type you chose. The default options for each file type work well in most cases, but you can modify the settings to suit the application in which you'll be using the file. For example, you can choose whether to have Acrobat generate images when the PDF document is repurposed.
4. Click Save to save the document to a file.

Save PDF Files as Images

You can also repurpose PDF documents by saving them in image formats. You can save PDF documents in the following image formats: EPS (Encapsulated PostScript), JPEG, JPEG 2000, PNG, PS (PostScript), and TIFF. When you save a document in one of these image formats, you can modify the settings, which differ depending on the image format you use to save the file. The settings you choose determine parameters such as image compression, colorspace, and the resolution of the saved image. Most file formats have a Settings button that enables you to modify the default settings to suit the application in which you'll be using the file. The settings are self-explanatory for those who are familiar with the file format.

Create PDF Files with Acrobat Distiller

In previous sections of this chapter, you learned how to create PDF documents by converting supported file formats into PDF documents, and then saving the files from within Acrobat. Acrobat Distiller is a separate program, but you can launch it from within Acrobat. When you install Acrobat, Acrobat Distiller is also added as a system printer under the moniker of Adobe PDF, which gives you the capability of printing a PDF file directly from within any application that supports printing. Printing from an authoring application is covered in Chapter 5.

Use Acrobat Distiller

Acrobat Distiller is a separate program that you use to convert EPS (Encapsulated Postscript) and PS (Postscript) files into PDF documents. With Acrobat Distiller, you have preset options available to optimize the file for an intended destination. Optimize a PDF document for a destination by choosing a specific setting. The Acrobat Distiller interface is shown next.

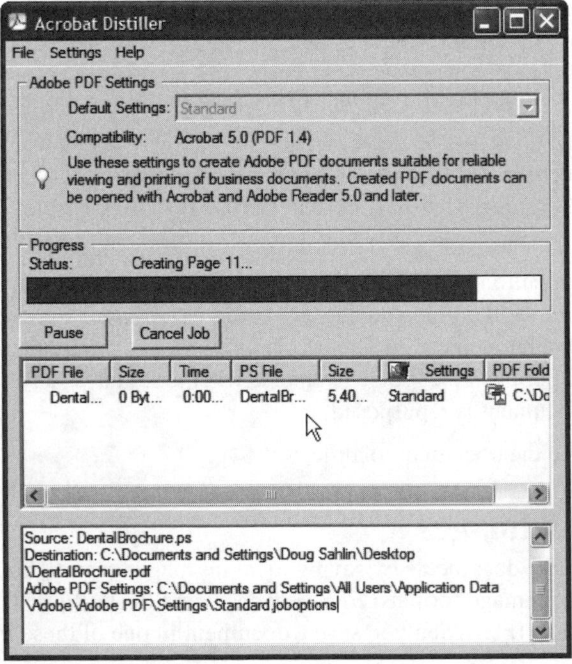

As you can see, there isn't much of an interface at all—just a few menu options, an information section, and a progress section. To create a PDF file using Acrobat Distiller, follow these steps:

1. Launch the program by choosing Acrobat Distiller from your OS program menu. Or, you can launch Acrobat Distiller from within Acrobat by choosing Advanced | Print Production | Acrobat Distiller, or by double-clicking the Acrobat Distiller desktop shortcut, if available.
2. Click the Default Settings drop-down arrow and choose the option that best suits the intended destination of the document. Choose from the following:
   - **High Quality Print** Choose this option when creating files that require higher image quality and will be printed.
   - **Oversized Pages** Choose this option when creating files that will be used to view and print engineering drawings larger than 200 × 200 inches. The resulting file can be opened with Acrobat and Adobe Reader 7.0 and later.
   - **PDFA/1b 2005 (CMYK) (Professional Only)** Choose this option when creating documents using the CMYK color model that must be compliant with PDFA/1b, and ISO standard for long-term archiving of electronic documents. The resulting file can be opened and viewed with Acrobat and Adobe Reader 5.0 and later.
   - **PDFA/1b 2005 (RGB) (Professional Only)** Choose this option when creating documents using the RGB color model that must be compliant with PDFA/1b, and ISO standard for long-term archiving of electronic documents. The resulting file can be opened and viewed with Acrobat and Adobe Reader 5.0 and later.
   - **PDF/X-1a: 2001 (Professional only)** Choose this option when creating files that must conform to PDF/X-1a 2001 standards, which are compatible with Acrobat 4.0 (PDF 1.3).
   - **PDF/X-3: 2002 (Professional only)** Choose this option when creating files that must conform to PDF/X-3 2002 standards, which are compatible with Acrobat 4.0 (PDF 1.3).
   - **Press Quality** Choose this option when you need the highest quality images in your files. This option is the way to go if you print your files on a high-end printer with PS capabilities. When you choose this format, minimum compression is applied to images.
   - **Smallest File Size** Choose this option to create the smallest possible file size at the expense of image quality when the resulting PDF document will be distributed via e-mail or viewed on the Internet.
   - **Standard** Choose this option when you create a PDF file for distribution across your corporate intranet or via CD-ROM for colleagues.

TIP

You can modify a PDF setting to suit the intended destination for the document you distill. Modifying settings is discussed in detail in Chapter 12.

3. To apply security to the distilled PDF file, choose Settings | Security. For more information about Acrobat security settings, refer to the previous section, "Set Document Security, or more details in Chapter 11."
4. Choose File | Open to access the Open PostScript File dialog box.
5. Navigate to the PS file you want to convert to PDF format, create a name for the file, and click Open.

After you click Open, Acrobat Distiller takes the reins and creates the PDF file. The Acrobat Distiller icon, which looks like a propeller, spins as the file is created. You can view information about the document in the PDF File window. If you distill a large multipage PS file, the distilling process may take some time. You can monitor the progress by viewing the Status bar in the Progress section. As the file is created, Acrobat Distiller shows you which page is being printed, the percentage of the job completed, and a visual reference in the form of a blue bar that moves across the window as the file is created.

By default, after completion of the distilling job, Acrobat Distiller creates a report that appears in the window at the bottom of the program interface. You can preview the PDF file in Acrobat by double-clicking its title in Acrobat Distiller.

Set Acrobat Distiller Preferences

Using Acrobat Distiller is a straightforward process: choose a setting, load an EPS or PS file, and Distiller does the rest for you. The real power of Distiller is in the number of settings you can modify, which you learn how to do in Chapter 12. You can also modify Distiller to suit your working preference by doing the following:

1. Launch Acrobat Distiller.
2. Choose File | Preferences to open the Preferences dialog box:

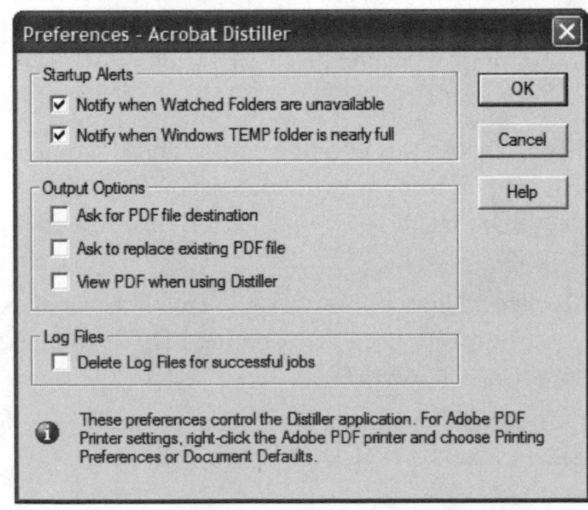

In the Startup Alerts section, you can modify the following options:

- **Notify When Watched Folders Are Unavailable** When you choose this option (the default), Acrobat Distiller has the capability of monitoring a folder or directory on your computer. Distiller automatically distills PS files placed in watched folders. You learn how to create watched folders in the following section, "Create Watched Folders."
- **Notify When Windows TEMP Folder Is Nearly Full** Distiller needs to write temporary files to disk when creating a PDF file. Choose this option, and Distiller warns you when the startup volume is less than 1 MB.

3. In the Output Options section, you can modify the following settings, all of which apply to Windows only:
   - **Ask For PDF File Destination** When you enable this option, Distiller prompts you for a folder in which to save the converted PDF file. When this option is disabled (the default), the converted PDF file is stored in the same location as the PS file.
   - **Ask To Replace Existing PDF File** This option is enabled by default and causes Distiller to prompt you when you try to overwrite an existing PDF file. If you enable the Ask For PDF File Destination check box, this option is unavailable.
   - **View PDF When Using Distiller** When you enable this option, on completion of the distilling job, the default Acrobat viewer launches and the converted PDF file is displayed.
4. In the Log Files section, check Delete Log Files For Successful Jobs if you want Distiller to delete the log file of the job if the file is successfully distilled. A *distiller log file* is a text file, created during the distilling process, which records any distilling errors, even if a PDF file is not created.

NOTE *Macintosh Acrobat users have an option unavailable to Windows users: Restart Distiller After PostScript Fatal Error. When this option is enabled, Distiller automatically relaunches after encountering a fatal PostScript error.*

Create Watched Folders (Professional Only)

If you regularly create PostScript files and save them to certain folders, you can configure Acrobat Distiller to watch these folders and automatically convert PostScript files to PDF files. You can also choose to move the original PostScript files to the Out folder or delete them. Each watched folder can have unique Distiller settings. Here's how to create a watched folder:

NOTE *You cannot save PostScript files to watched folders on a network server. Set up a watched folder on your workstation for converting your files. Other authors who need to convert PostScript files to PDFs must set up a watched folder on their own workstations using a licensed version of Acrobat.*

1. Launch Acrobat Distiller and choose Settings | Watched Folders to open the Watched Folders dialog box, shown here. (A folder to be watched has already been added.)

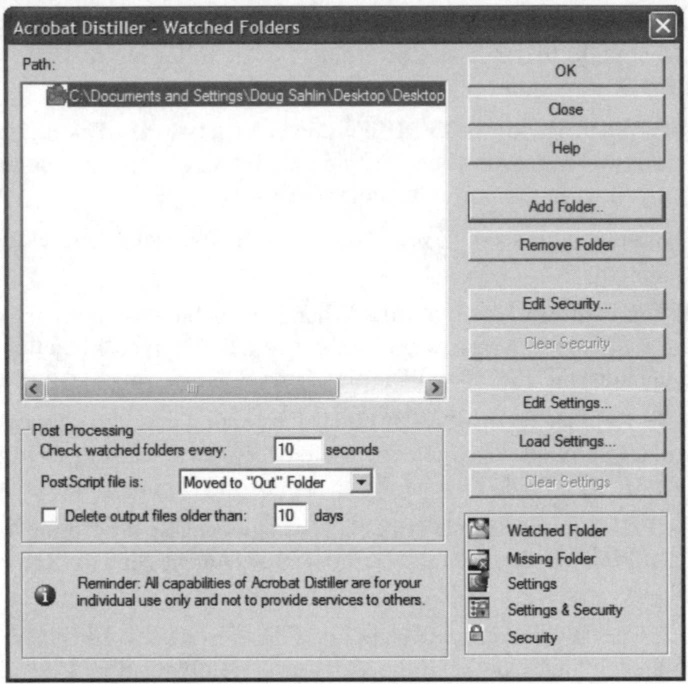

2. Click Add Folder to open the Browse For Folder dialog box.
3. Navigate to the folder you want Distiller to watch, select the folder, click OK, and the selected folder is added to the watched folders list. After you add the folder, Distiller automatically creates an In and an Out folder within the watched folder.
4. In the Check Watched Folders Every [ ] Seconds field, enter a value between 1 and 9,999 seconds. This value specifies how often Distiller checks a watched folder.
5. Click the PostScript File Is drop-down arrow and choose an option to determine whether the converted PostScript file is moved to the Out folder or deleted.
6. Click the Delete Output Files Older Than [ ] Days check box and enter a value between 1 and 999 in the text field. Distiller uses this value to determine when to delete PostScript files in the Out folder.
7. After you add a folder to the watched folders list, you can click OK to close the dialog box or click Add Folder to add additional folders to the list.

Set Watched Folder Options (Professional Only)

After you add one or several folders to the watched folders list, you can specify options for each folder, namely: Security Options, Job Options, Load Options, Add Additional Folders, or Remove Folders. To set options for a watched folder, do the following:

1. Launch Acrobat Distiller and choose Settings | Watched Folders.
2. Select the watched folder whose settings you want to modify. After you select a watched folder, additional buttons become available, as shown previously, for setting the following options:
   - **Remove Folder** Removes the selected folder from the watched folders list.
   - **Edit Security** After you click this button, the Security dialog box opens. You can apply Acrobat Standard Security to the PDF files that have been distilled. For information on individual security settings, refer to previous section "Set Document Security."
   - **Clear Security** Removes security for files distilled from the selected folder.
   - **Edit Settings** After you click this button, the Adobe PDF Settings dialog box opens. You can specify settings for all files distilled within the selected folder. You can find information for the options in this dialog box in Chapter 12.
   - **Load Settings** Click this button to open the Select Adobe PDF Settings dialog box. Navigate to the folder that contains the settings file you want to load and click Load. Adobe PDF settings files have the .joboptions extension. For more information on creating custom settings, refer to Chapter 12.
   - **Clear Settings** This button becomes available after you specify job options for files distilled from this folder. Click the button to clear Adobe PDF settings applied to the PostScript files being distilled from this folder.
3. Click OK to apply the new settings and close the Watched Folders dialog box.

4

Summary

In this chapter, you learned how to create PDF files from within Acrobat. You learned how to create PDF documents from single files and from multiple files. You also discovered how to save PDF documents in other file formats. In the latter part of the chapter, you saw how to use Acrobat Distiller to create PDF documents from PostScript files. In the next chapter, you learn how to create PDF documents from within authoring applications, such as Microsoft Word.

Chapter 5

Create PDF Documents in Authoring Applications

How to...

- Convert Microsoft Office documents to PDFs
- Set document conversion properties
- Convert documents to PDF files using the Print command
- Convert a document to PDF and then e-mail it

As discussed in Chapter 4, you can use Acrobat to convert supported file types into PDF documents from within Acrobat. You can also create PDF files from within authoring applications. When you create a file in any application that supports printing devices, you can create a PDF file using the application's Print command. Other software, such as CorelDRAW, supports PDF exporting. You can also create PDF files from within Adobe graphics applications such as Photoshop CS2, Photoshop Elements, and Photoshop Album. Adobe offers extensive PDF support with many of its image-editing, illustration, and page-layout applications. Adobe and a third-party associate created a plug-in that you use to create PDF files from within Microsoft Office applications. You can also create PDF documents from within Microsoft Outlook. This is a convenient way of archiving e-mail messages pertaining to a certain project. When you convert e-mail messages into PDF documents, the attached files are archived as well.

When you create a PDF file from within an authoring application, you gain many benefits. First, and primarily, you can save the original version of the file in its native format, which makes it available for future editing when needed. And, second, you can export the file in PDF format without leaving the host application. If you have several documents to create and convert to PDF format, this is a tremendous time saver. You can also export several PDF files from the original document, each optimized for a different destination.

Create PDF Files from Microsoft Office Software

When you install Acrobat, the install utility searches your machine for Microsoft Office applications. When a supported Microsoft Office application is found, Acrobat installs PDFMaker as a helper utility. With PDFMaker, you can create a PDF file that looks identical to the Microsoft Office file by clicking a Convert To Adobe PDF icon, which is added to your Microsoft Office application. If you prefer more control over the process, you can also modify the conversion settings to optimize a PDF file for its intended destination.

You can use PDFMaker to create PDF files from within the following Microsoft Office applications:

Install Microsoft Office beta and check functionality.

- **Word 97, 2000, 2003, and 2007** Use Adobe PDF to convert documents you create with Word to PDF files. The resulting PDF file retains font information, embedded graphics, and header and footer attributes.
- **Excel 97, 2000, 2003, and 2007** Use Adobe PDF to convert an Excel spreadsheet to PDF format. The converted PDF file retains column formatting, as well as column and row headers and embedded graphics.

- **PowerPoint 97, 2000, 2003, and 2007** Convert PowerPoint presentations to PDF files and add additional functionality to the presentation with many features of Acrobat.
- **Outlook** Convert Microsoft Outlook e-mail messages to PDF files. This is a wonderful way of archiving selected e-mail messages, or a folder of e-mail messages. File attachments are also archived with the PDF document.
- **Project (Professional only)** Convert Microsoft Project documents to PDF files. The converted file can be sent to other colleagues who don't have Microsoft Project, but who need to be privy to the information within the original document.
- **Visio (Professional only)** Convert Microsoft Visio documents to PDF files. You can share the converted file with other colleagues who don't have Microsoft Visio installed on their computers.

In all supported Microsoft Office applications, the Adobe PDF plug-in is, for all intents and purposes, identical, with the exception of the options available in each application when modifying conversion settings. The next section covers all the major features of Adobe PDF plug-in and shows you how to use it to convert documents to PDF format (with examples from Microsoft Word 2000).

Create PDF Files from Microsoft Word Files

When Adobe Acrobat finds a supported application, as previously mentioned, three icons are added to the application toolbar, and a menu group is added to the application menu bar. You use the icons shown in Figure 5-1 to convert a document to PDF format, to convert a document to PDF format and e-mail it, or to convert a document to PDF format and initialize a review. The Adobe PDF menu group contains commands that duplicate the button tasks and allow you to change PDF conversion settings.

Convert Word Files to PDF Files

When you create a document in Word, you can apply styles to the document. When you convert the Word document to PDF format, Acrobat uses these Word styles to create corresponding bookmarks in the PDF document. The Acrobat default setting uses Heading styles to create bookmarks. If you want, though, you can change the conversion settings to include other styles that exist in the Word document, such as numbered or bulleted lists. When you convert the Word file to a PDF file, the resulting file retains the formatting and font information, as well as any graphics you may have embedded in the Word file.

The easiest way to convert a Word file to a PDF file is by using the Convert To Adobe PDF button. You can also use a menu command to achieve the same result. To convert a Word file to a PDF file, do the following:

1. Click the Convert To Adobe PDF icon, shown in Figure 5-1. Or, choose Adobe PDF | Convert To Adobe PDF.
2. Adobe PDF displays a dialog box stating the file must be saved. If you click Yes, the Save PDF File As dialog box opens. If you click No, Adobe PDF stops the conversion process.

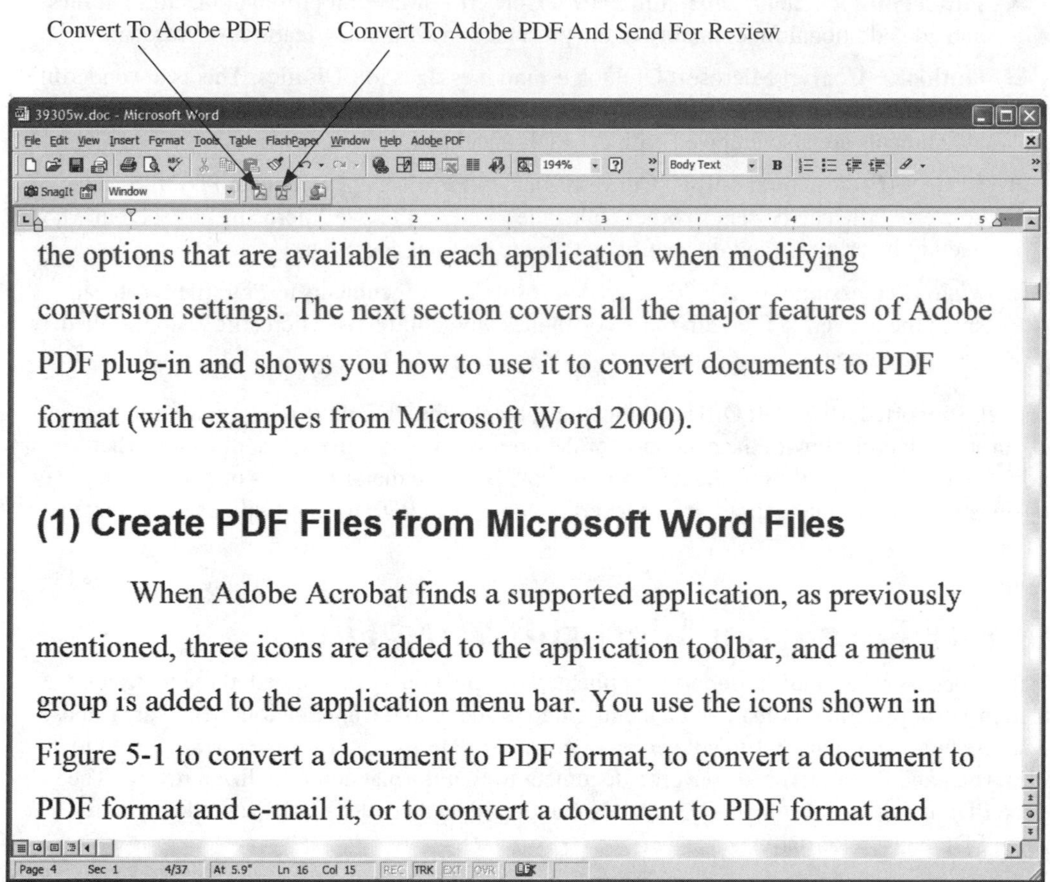

FIGURE 5-1 You can convert a Microsoft Office document into a PDF document by clicking an icon or choosing a menu command.

3. In the Save PDF File As dialog box, accept the default name (the Word filename) and location (the directory the Word file is saved in), or specify a document name and directory.
4. Click Save to complete the conversion.

After you convert the document to PDF format, you can modify it in Acrobat by adding interactive elements, such as links to navigate the document, or by adding comments, annotations, or multimedia elements. Figure 5-2 shows a PDF file in Acrobat converted from a Word document. Word documents converted to the PDF format have bookmarks that Adobe PDF creates using Word Heading styles. You can change the manner in which Adobe PDF creates bookmarks by changing conversion settings, which is covered in the upcoming section "Change Conversion Settings."

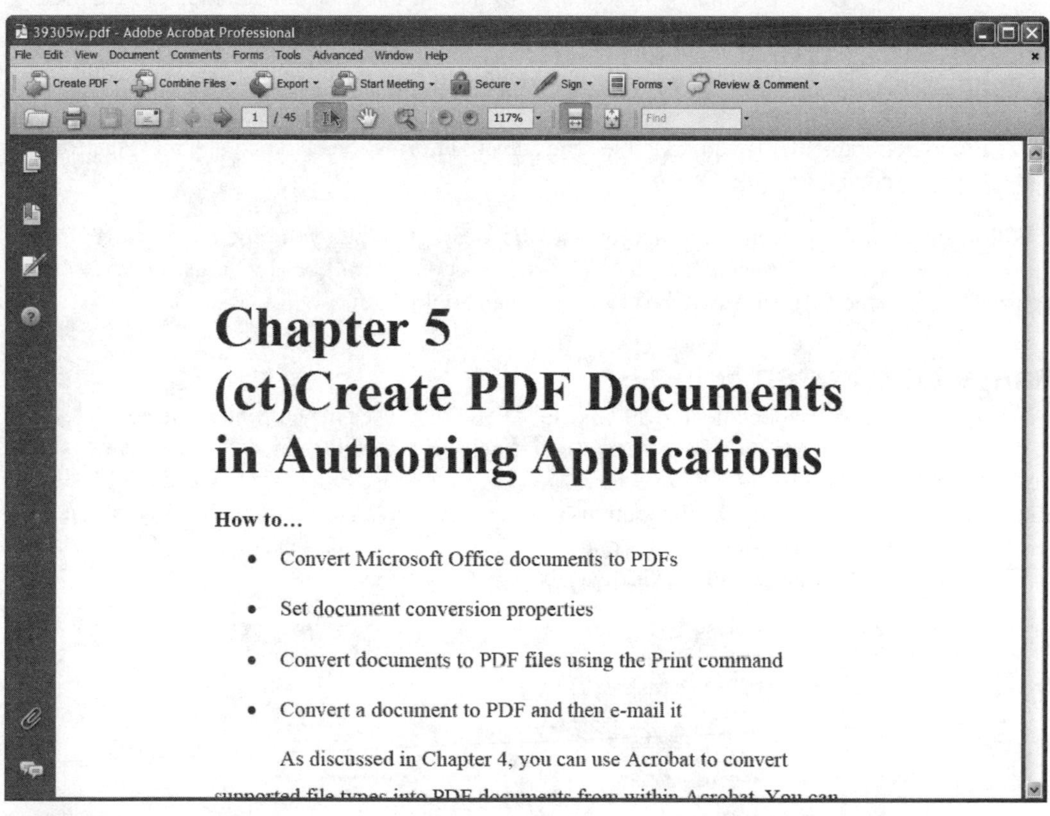

FIGURE 5-2 Use Adobe PDF to convert Microsoft Office files into PDF documents.

5

TIP *A command and a button can also convert a document to PDF format and send it for review. Chapter 10 covers reviewing PDF documents.*

Convert a Word Document to PDF, and Then E-Mail It

Thanks to the Internet and e-mail, it's now possible to efficiently conduct business with faraway clients. Whether you are a one-person entrepreneurship or work in a large organization, you can convert a Word document to a PDF file, and then e-mail it to a client or coworker. To convert a Word document to a PDF file and e-mail it, follow these steps:

1. Choose Adobe PDF | Convert To Adobe PDF And Email.
2. Adobe PDF displays a dialog box prompting you to save the file. Click Yes to open the Save PDF File As dialog box.

3. In the Save PDF File As dialog box, accept the default filename and location to save the file in, or specify your own parameters.
4. Click Save, and Adobe PDF converts the file to PDF format and launches your default e-mail application.
5. Enter the recipients' e-mail addresses and subject information, and add any message for your intended recipients.

Follow the e-mail application prompts to send the message. When you send the message, the PDF file is sent as an attachment. Until the message is sent, you won't be able to use any Acrobat menus or tools, as the focus has switched to your e-mail application.

Change Conversion Settings

When you convert a Word document to a PDF file, Adobe PDF uses the currently selected conversion settings. You can modify these conversion settings, as well as modify document security, specify how Microsoft Office features are converted to PDF, specify how Adobe PDF creates bookmarks, and specify display options. You change conversion settings by clicking the appropriate tab in the Conversion Settings dialog box. To open the Acrobat Adobe PDF dialog box, shown next, choose Adobe PDF | Change Conversion Settings:

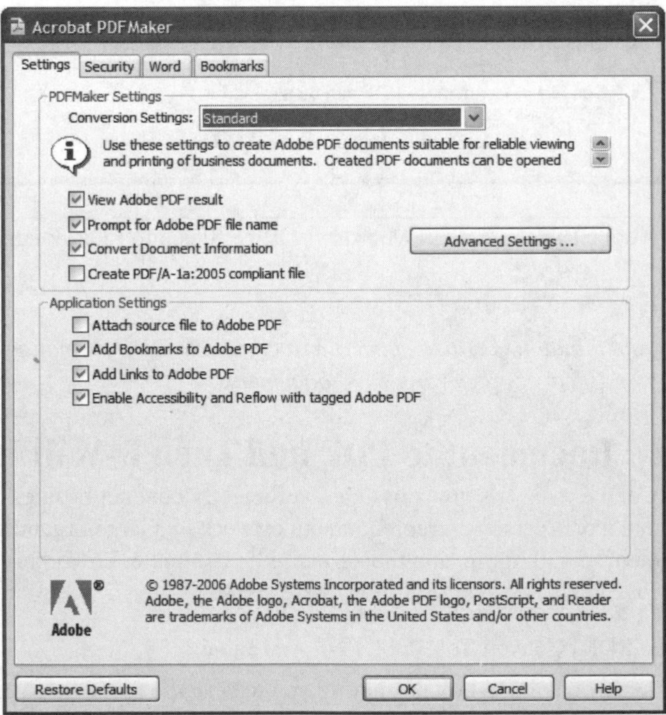

When you first open the Acrobat PDFMaker dialog box that modifies conversion settings, the Settings tab is active. Here you choose the setting that is the closest match for the intended destination of the PDF file, which you can then modify by following these steps:

1. Click the Conversion Settings drop-down arrow and choose one of the preset options (High Quality Print, Oversized Pages [Professional Only], PDF/A-1b 2005 (CMYK) [Professional Only], PDF/A-1b 2005 (RGB) [Professional Only], PDF/X-1a 2001 [Professional Only], PDF/X-3-2002, (Press Quality, Smallest File Size, Standard) or any custom conversion settings you have created. These options are the same as the Distiller Job Options discussed in Chapter 4. To apply the new settings, click OK. To modify additional conversion settings, click the appropriate tab and modify the parameters to suit the intended destination of your document, as outlined in Chapter 12.
2. In the Acrobat PDFMaker Settings area, the following options are selected by default:
   - **View Adobe PDF Result** Opens the document in Acrobat after the conversion process is completed.
   - **Prompt For Adobe PDF File Name** Prompts you for a filename before the document is converted to a PDF file. If you deselect this option, the resulting PDF file adopts the filename of the Microsoft Office document you're converting.
   - **Convert Document Information** Converts certain information (document title, author, keywords, and subject) from the Microsoft Office Properties dialog box into the PDF file's Document Properties, which can be displayed by opening the file's Document Properties dialog box.
   - **Create PDF/A-1a: 2005 compliant file** Creates a document that is compliant with PDF/A-1a: 2005 standards.
3. In the Application Settings area, you can choose the following options, the last three of which are selected by default:
   - **Attach Source File To Adobe PDF** Attaches the source file to the converted PDF document. Viewers can open the source file by opening the Attachments panel and double-clicking the file title.
   - **Add Bookmarks To Adobe PDF** Uses headings or styles from the Microsoft Office document to create bookmarks in the PDF document. You can specify which styles are converted to bookmarks on the Bookmarks tab of the Acrobat PDFMaker dialog box.
   - **Add Links To Adobe PDF** Preserves any links present in the Microsoft Office file. The links in the converted PDF file maintain a similar appearance to those found in the original file.
   - **Enable Accessibility And Reflow With Tagged PDF** Creates tags (objects that reference document structure objects, such as images and text objects) in the PDF document based on the structure of the source Microsoft Office file. This structure can be used to reflow a document when viewed on different devices.
4. Click OK to apply the settings. Or, click a different tab to modify additional settings.

You can create custom conversion settings by clicking Advanced Settings. After you click this button, Adobe PDF opens the Acrobat PDFMaker Settings dialog box. For more information on creating a custom conversion settings file, refer to Chapter 12.

Change Document Security Settings

When you convert a Word file to PDF format, you can specify document security from within Microsoft Word. You can assign a password to the converted file and limit permissions. The encryption level of the document (40-bit RC4, 128-bit RC4, or 128-bit AES) is determined by the conversion setting you choose in the Settings tab. Do the following to set document security:

1. Open the Acrobat PDFMaker dialog box, as outlined previously.
2. Click the Security tab to reveal the security settings options. The Encryption level is designated at the top of the dialog box, as shown here:

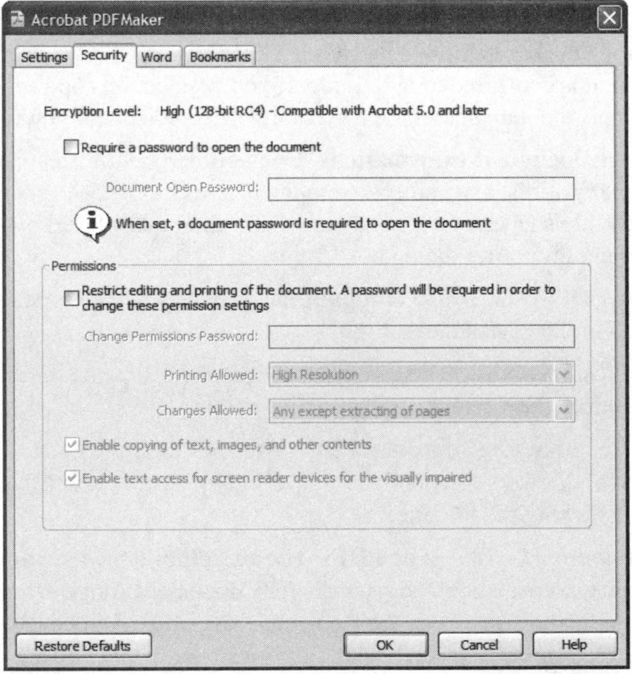

3. To assign a password to the PDF file, check the Require A Password To Open The Document check box. When you choose this option, the Document Open Password field becomes active. Enter the password in this field.
4. To assign a master password to the PDF file, which enables you to require entry of a password to change permissions, click the Restrict Printing And Editing Of The Document check box. When you choose this option, the Permissions Password field (and the two fields below it) becomes available. Enter the password in this field.

5. Click the Printing Allowed drop-down arrow and choose one of the following options:
   - **Not Allowed** Disables printing the document.
   - **Low Resolution (150 DPI)** Enables users to print only a low-resolution copy of the PDF document.
   - **High Resolution** Enables users to print the document at high resolution.
6. Click the Changes Allowed drop-down arrow and choose one of the following options:
   - **None** Disallows users with Acrobat 8.0 Standard or Professional to edit the document.
   - **Inserting, Deleting, And Rotating Of Pages** Enables viewers with Acrobat 8.0 Standard or Professional to insert, delete, and rotate pages.
   - **Filling In Of Form Fields And Signing** Enables viewers with Acrobat Standard or Professional to fill in form fields and digitally sign the document. Adobe Reader 8.0 users will only be able to fill in the form fields.
   - **Commenting, Filling In Of Form Fields, And Signing** Enables viewers with Acrobat Standard or Professional to add comments to the document, as well as fill in form fields and digitally sign the document.
   - **Any Except Extracting Of Pages** Enables viewers with Acrobat Standard or Professional to perform any editing with the exception of extracting pages from the PDF document.
7. When you require a permissions password to edit the document, the Enable Copying Of Text, Images, and Other Contents check box is disabled by default. This option is initially selected and grayed out until you choose the Use A Password To Restrict Printing And Editing Of The Document. Check this box to enable document viewers to copy text, images, or other contents of the document.
8. The Enable Text Access For Screen Reader Devices For The Visually Impaired check box is selected by default. If you deselect this option, visually impaired readers will be unable to access text with their screen readers.

TIP *When you add 128-bit security to a document, the document can be viewed only with Acrobat 5.0 (PDF 1.4) or newer. For earlier versions of Acrobat (Versions 3 and 4), you have to choose a conversion setting that supports 40-bit security. For more information on modifying document security settings, refer to Chapter 11.*

9. To apply the security settings, click OK. To modify additional settings, click the appropriate tab and modify the parameters as desired.

NOTE *Whether you assign a document password, a permissions password, or both, you will be prompted to verify the password(s) before the new settings are accepted.*

Change Word Settings

The settings you modify on the Word tab of the dialog box determine how Acrobat PDFMaker converts Word features. The actual wording of this tab varies, depending on the Microsoft Office program for which you're modifying conversion settings. For example, these settings have no tab in Microsoft Excel, Microsoft Outlook, or Microsoft PowerPoint. To change Microsoft Word settings, do the following:

1. Open the Acrobat PDFMaker dialog box as outlined previously.
2. Click the Word tab to reveal the settings illustrated here:

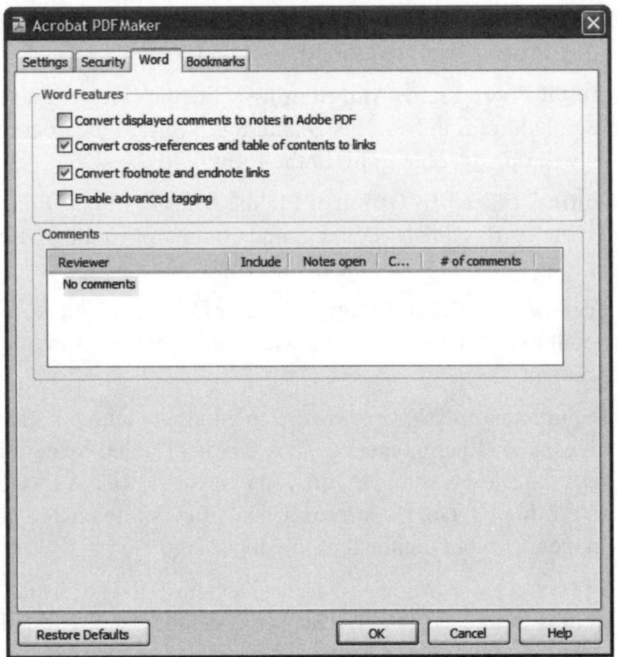

3. In the Word Features area, you can modify the following settings:
   - **Convert Displayed Comments To Notes In The PDF** Converts Word document comments to notes in the resulting PDF document. If you choose this option, any comments in the document appear in the Comments window. Comments are segregated by reviewer, and the number of comments entered by the reviewer is noted in the # Of Comments column.
   - **Convert Cross-References And Table Of Contents To Links (Default option)** Converts document cross-references and table of contents items into links to their destinations in the converted PDF document.
   - **Convert Footnote And Endnote Links (default option)** Preserves endnote and footnote links in the converted PDF document.
   - **Enable Advanced Tagging** Enables you to integrate advanced tagging in the PDF.

4. If you choose Convert Displayed Comments To Notes In The PDF, in the Comments window, you can perform the following tasks:
   - Click the check box in a reviewer's Include column to include his comments in the PDF file.
   - Click the check box in a reviewer's Notes Open column to have a note created by this reviewer open when the page on which the note appears opens.
   - Click the icon in a reviewer's Color column to select a color for the note. Each time you click the icon, it changes to a different color. You can choose different colors for other reviewers' comments in the document.
5. To apply the Word settings, click OK. To modify additional settings, click the appropriate tab and modify the parameters as desired.

Change Bookmark Settings

The settings you modify on the Bookmarks tab determine which Word text styles Acrobat PDFMaker converts to bookmarks. To change bookmark settings for the document conversion, do the following:

1. Open the Acrobat PDFMaker dialog box, as outlined in previous sections.
2. Click the Bookmarks tab and modify the settings, as shown here and as described in the following list:

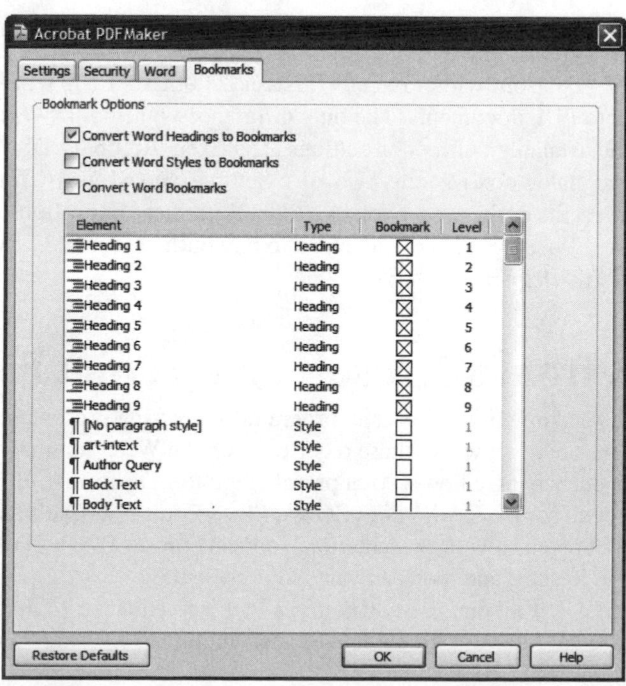

- **Convert Word Headings To Bookmarks (Default option)** Adobe PDF converts all Word headings in the document to PDF bookmarks. By default, Heading 1 through Heading 9 styles are converted to bookmarks. To modify which headings are converted to bookmarks, click a heading name in the Bookmark column to select or deselect it.
- **Convert Word Styles To Bookmarks** By default, no Word styles are converted to bookmarks. When you choose this option, all Word styles used in the document are converted to bookmarks when Acrobat PDFMaker converts the document. You can deselect any style you don't want converted to a bookmark by clicking its check box. Remember, if you decide to have bookmarks created for styles, the conversion process *may take a long time,* especially if you have a large number of styles in the document.
- **Convert Word Bookmarks** Converts any user created Word bookmarks to PDF bookmarks.

3. Click OK to apply the new settings, or click on another tab to make additional modifications to the document conversion settings.

After you modify conversion settings, they remain active until you modify them again. To restore the default settings, open the Acrobat PDFMaker dialog box, click the Restore Defaults button, and then click OK to complete the restoration. The next document you convert to PDF is converted with the default Adobe PDF conversion settings.

Create PDF Files from Microsoft Excel Files

You can also use Adobe PDF from within Excel 97, Excel 2000, Excel 2003, or Excel 2007 to convert spreadsheets to PDF documents. The only difference you find between Adobe PDF in Excel and Word is the available conversion settings. The Excel Acrobat PDFMaker dialog box for Microsoft Office dialog box has only two tabs: Settings and Security. You also have a menu command to convert the entire workbook to a PDF. With these exceptions, the process for converting an Excel spreadsheet to a PDF is identical to that outlined in the Convert Word Files to PDF Files section of this chapter.

Create PDF Files from Microsoft PowerPoint Files

If you use PowerPoint, you know it's a powerful program for creating presentations. It seems PowerPoint presentations are everywhere these days, even on the Web. You may not think any advantage exists to converting a PowerPoint presentation to PDF format. But if you want to share a presentation with someone who doesn't own PowerPoint or doesn't have a version of PowerPoint capable of opening your presentation, you can convert it to a PDF. All your recipients need is Adobe Reader, and they can view your presentation.

You can also convert a PowerPoint presentation to a PDF and enhance it with Acrobat features. For example, you can use the File Attachment tool to open another file during your presentation.

Did you know?

Creative Collaborations

If you work for a large corporation, computer-generated files are a fact of life. If these files need to be shared with or reviewed by other colleagues, they'll need the native application to open and edit these files. If the files need only to be reviewed, however, your corporation doesn't have to supply reviewers with the native software used to create these files. If the head of each department has Acrobat Professional, the files can be converted to PDF documents and sent via e-mail for review. The sender can choose Advanced | Enable Usage Rights in Adobe Reader, which makes the powerful Acrobat annotation features available to these reviewers. Using the free version of Adobe Reader, the reviewers can mark up the document with their comments and send it back to the creator, who can then use the native software to modify the document per reviewers' comments. When Adobe Reader 7.0 and later users open a document for which the author has enabled rights, a note to that effect appears at the top of the document. Users will also have Commenting and Drawing Markups submenus, which can be found under the Tools menu title. In addition, Adobe Reader 8.0 users can: save form data, use commenting and drawing markup tools, sign existing digital signature fields, and digitally sign the document. Sending PDF documents with usage rights enabled is also a convenient way to share information between creative entrepreneurs, such as graphic designers and web site designers, and their clients. The designer can convert the original artwork to PDF format and send it to the client for review.

The PowerPoint Acrobat PDFMaker dialog box has two tabs: Settings and Security. The process to convert a PowerPoint file to PDF is identical to that outlined in the Convert Word Files to PDF Files section of this chapter.

Create PDF Files from Microsoft Outlook

You can use Acrobat 8.0 to convert an e-mail message, a selection of e-mail messages, or a folder of e-mail messages in Microsoft Outlook into a PDF document. If you segregate e-mail messages in folders when you work on a project, or keep folders for important e-mail messages, you can archive the entire folder as a PDF document. When you archive e-mail messages, file attachments are saved as well.

New to Acrobat 8.0 is the capability to convert calendar items, contacts, and notes to PDF. In addition, you can migrate previous PDF Outlook archives to PDF Packages.

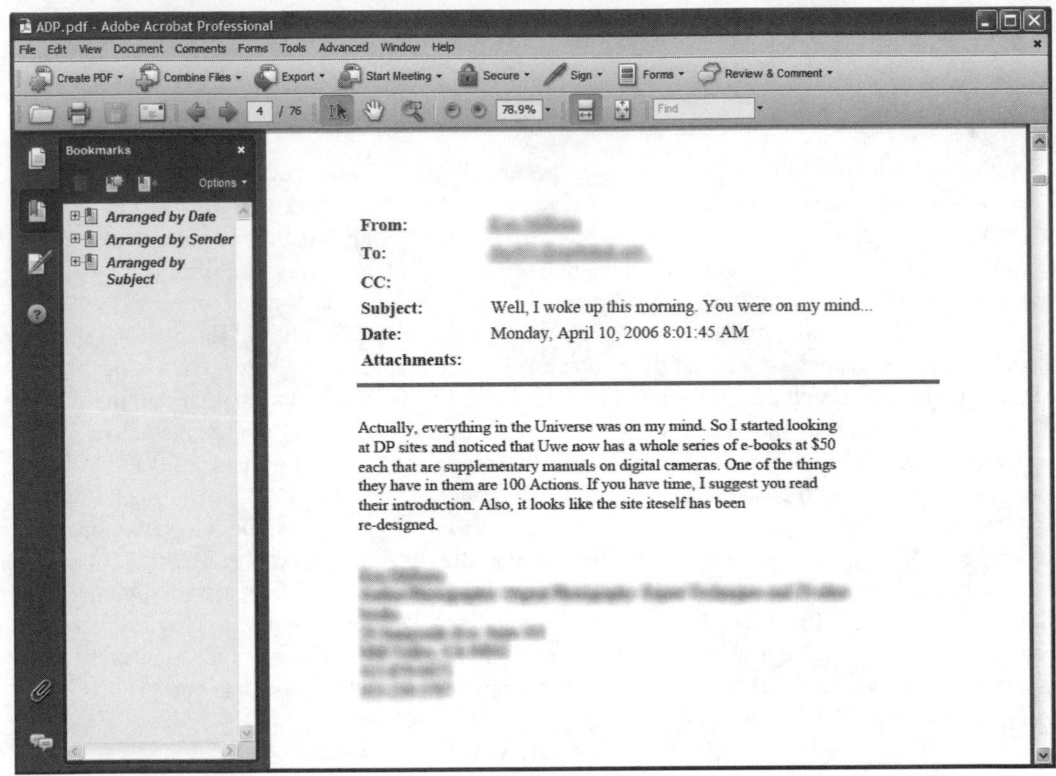

FIGURE 5-3 When you convert e-mail messages to a PDF document, bookmarks are created to help you easily locate specific messages.

When you create a PDF document from e-mail messages, bookmarks are created that arrange the messages by date, sender, subject, and personal folders, as shown in Figure 5-3, which is a PDF document created from Microsoft Outlook e-mail messages.

Convert Selected E-Mail Messages to a PDF Document

When you need to consolidate several e-mail messages pertaining to a certain subject, you can easily do so by converting them into a PDF document. You can select messages from within any folder or from your inbox. To convert Microsoft Outlook e-mail messages into a PDF document:

1. Navigate to the folder in which the messages you want to convert to a PDF document are located.
2. Select the desired messages.

3. Click the Create Adobe PDF from Selected Messages button.

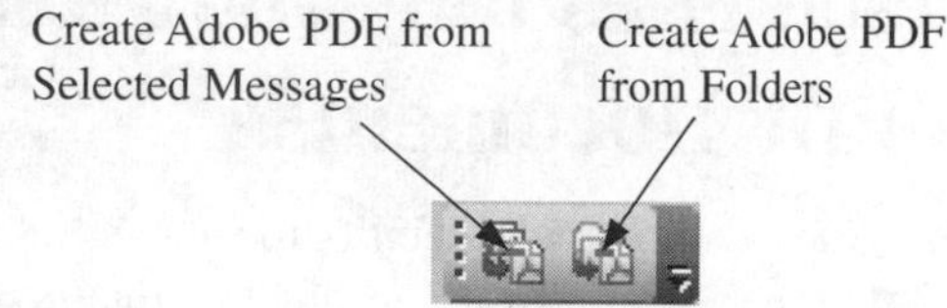

4. In the Save Adobe PDF File As dialog box, enter a name for the PDF document and navigate to the folder in which you want to save the document.
5. Click Save.

Convert a Selected Folder of E-Mail Messages to a PDF Document

When you work on a project, or receive a lot of e-mail from a particular individual or client, it makes good sense to store the messages in a folder. This is a task you can easily accomplish within Microsoft Outlook. You can also archive your Calendar, Contacts, and Notes folder to PDF. You can consolidate a Microsoft Outlook folder into a PDF document by following these steps:

1. Click the Create Adobe PDF from Folders button shown previously to display the Convert folder(s) to PDF dialog box shown next.

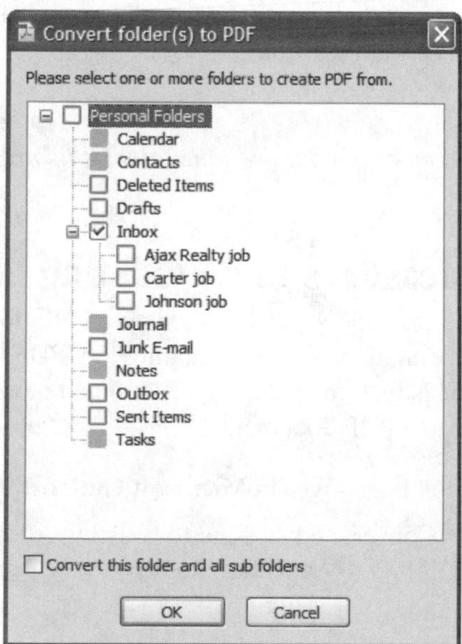

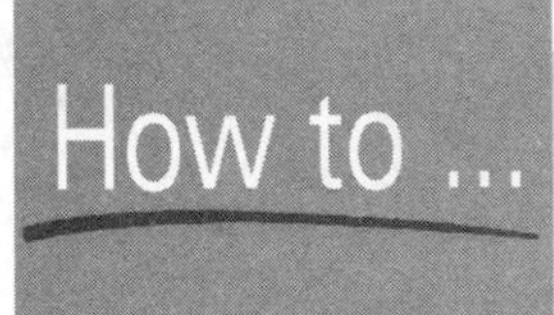

Attach Files to E-Mail Messages as PDF Documents

Acrobat's strong point has always been the capability to share a file with anybody who has the full version of Acrobat or the Adobe Reader installed on their system. In the past, you'd convert a file into PDF format, and then attach it to an e-mail. With Acrobat 8.0, Microsoft Outlook users can accomplish both tasks with one fell swoop. Supported file formats can be converted to PDF and attached to an e-mail message with the click of a button.

1. In Microsoft Outlook, click the New Mail Message button to open a blank e-mail message.
2. Click the Attach As Adobe PDF button to open the Choose File To Attach As Adobe PDF dialog box.
3. Select the desired file and click Open to display the Save PDF File As dialog box.
4. Enter a name for the PDF document, and then navigate to the folder in which you want to save the document.
5. Click Save. The file is converted to PDF and attached to the e-mail message.
6. Enter the desired title in the Subject field, type your message, and send the e-mail.

2. Select the folder(s) you want to covert to PDF.
3. Click OK

Depending on the number of e-mails in the folder, this process can take a considerable amount of time

Append Selected Messages to an Existing PDF

You can easily add selected e-mail messages to an existing PDF document. This feature is useful when you've received e-mail messages pertaining to a PDF document you're currently reviewing. You can also use this feature when you need to add new e-mail messages to those you've previously converted to a PDF document.

1. Select the desired e-mail messages in Microsoft Outlook.
2. Choose Adobe PDF | Convert and Append to Existing Adobe PDF | Selected Messages to display the Select PDF File to Append dialog box.
3. Select the desired PDF file.
4. Click Open to convert the selected messages to PDF and append them to the selected PDF document.

To convert a folder to PDF and append the resulting file to an existing PDF:

1. Choose Adobe PDF | Convert and Append to Existing Adobe PDF | Selected Folders to open the Convert folder(s) to PDF dialog box.
2. Select the folder(s) you want to append to an existing PDF.
3. Click OK to open the Select PDF File to Append dialog box.
4. Select the file, and then click Open.

Create PDF Files Using an Application's Print Command

When you install Acrobat software, Adobe PDF is automatically added as a system printer. You can use Adobe PDF to print from the authoring application file to disk in PDF format in the same manner as you use a printer to print a hard copy of a file. You can create a PDF file from any authoring application that supports printing, by following these steps:

1. Choose the application's Print command.
2. Choose Adobe PDF from the application's Printer menu. The actual Print dialog box varies, depending on your operating system (OS) and the software from which you are printing the file.
3. Click Properties to reveal the Adobe PDF Document Properties dialog box, which has three sections, separated by tabs. Click the Layout tab, as shown here:

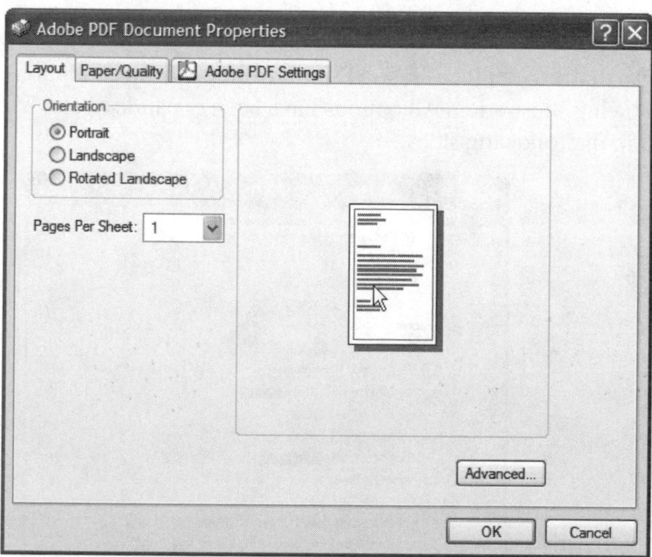

4. In the Orientation area, choose Portrait, Landscape, or Rotated Landscape.

5. Click the Pages Per Sheet drop-down arrow and choose an option from the drop-down menu. The default option of 1 displays one document page on one PDF page. If you choose one of the other options, multiple pages of the original document are displayed on a single PDF page. After selecting the number of pages per sheet, the Preview window updates to give you an idea of how the finished document will look.
6. Click the Paper/Quality tab, shown next, and then click the Paper Source drop-down arrow and choose an option from the drop-down menu.

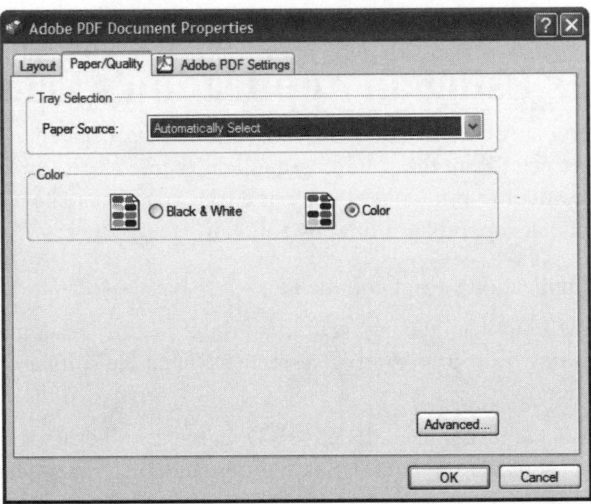

7. Click the corresponding icon to print the document in color or black-and-white.
8. Click Advanced to open the Adobe PDF Converter Advanced Options dialog box, shown in the following illustration. All options have been expanded here, because they are discussed in the following steps:

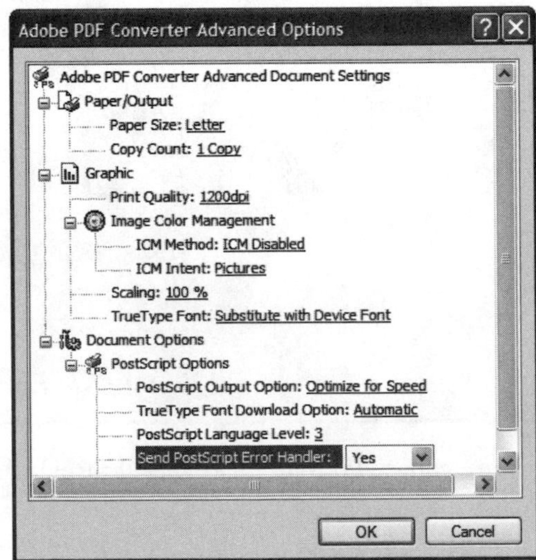

- In the Paper/**Output** section, choose the following options:
  - **Paper Size** Click the drop-down arrow and choose one of the presets from the drop-down menu.
  - **Copy Count** Click Copy Count and enter a value for the number of copies to print. When you choose this option, the Collate option is available. This option is enabled by default and causes Acrobat to collate the pages for each copy printed.

TIP *You can match the paper size to the file you're printing by choosing PostScript Custom Page Size from the Paper Size drop-down menu, and then entering the desired dimensions in the PostScript Custom Page Size Definition dialog box.*

9. Click the plus sign (+) to the left of the Graphic title to set the following parameters:
   - **Print Quality** Click Print Quality, click the drop-down arrow, and then choose an option from the drop-down menu. The default resolution, 1200 dpi (dots per inch), works well in most instances. If the document you're converting to PDF contains images and you will eventually print the file on a high-end printer, choose a resolution that closely matches the intended output device.
   - **Image Color Management** Click the plus sign to the left of the Image Color Management title to set the following parameters:
     - **ICM Method** Click ICM Method, click the drop-down arrow that appears, and then choose one of the following options: ICM Disabled, to disable color management; ICM Handled By Host System, to handle color management through the color management profile used by your computer; ICM Handled By Printer, to handle color management through the output device; or ICM Handled By Printer Using Printer Calibration. Refer to your printer operation manual to choose the right setting, or contact your service center if you are having the file printed professionally.
     - **ICM Intent** Click ICM Intent, click the drop-down arrow that appears, and then choose one of the following options: Graphics, if the document predominantly contains images with large areas of solid color; Pictures, if the document is largely made up of full-color photographs; Proof, to create a black-and-white proof for a customer; or Match, to match the document colors.
   - **Scaling** Click Scaling, and then enter a value to which you want the document scaled when distilled to PDF format. This value is a percentage of the document size as created in the authoring application. Or, you can click the spinner buttons to increase or decrease the scaling value.
   - **TrueType Font** Click Substitute With Device Font (the default), or click the drop-down arrow that appears, and choose Download As Softfont. This determines how Acrobat Distiller handles TrueType fonts used in the original document. In most cases, the default option works well.

10. Click the plus sign to the left of Document Options, and then click the plus sign to the left of PostScript Options to set the following parameters:
    - **PostScript Output Option** Click the PostScript Output Option, click the drop-down arrow that appears, and then choose one of the following options:
        - **Optimize For Speed** Choose this option to speed the distilling process. If you choose this option, though, you may be unable to take advantage of print spooling if you work on a network.
        - **Optimize For Portability** Choose this option to have the distilled file conform to Adobe Document Structuring Conventions (ADSC). When you choose this option, each PostScript page is independent of the other pages in the document. Choose this option if you're printing the file on a network spooler. When you use a network spooler, printing happens in the background, which frees up your workstation for other tasks. When you choose this option, the network spooler prints the PDF document one page at a time.
        - **Encapsulated PostScript (EPS)** Choose this option to create EPS files comprised of single pages in the authoring application you intend to use in documents of other applications. Use this option if you want to create a high-quality image and use it in a document that will be printed from another application.
        - **Archive Format** Choose this option to improve file portability. When you choose this option, printer settings that may prevent the distilled PDF file from printing on other output devices are suppressed.
    - **TrueType Font Download Option** Click TrueType Font Download Option, click the drop-down arrow that appears, and then choose one of the following options:
        - **Automatic** Choose this option to automatically embed any TrueType fonts from the source document to the resulting PDF file.
        - **Outline** Choose this option to embed any TrueType font in the source file as outlines in the resulting PDF file.
        - **Bitmap** Choose this option to convert TrueType fonts in the source file to bitmap images in the resulting PDF document. The resulting PDF document cannot be searched.
        - **Native TrueType** Choose this option, and TrueType fonts will not be embedded with the document. The resulting PDF file will download font information from the source computer from which the document is viewed.
    - **PostScript Language Level** Click this option, and then use the spinner buttons to select 1, 2, or 3. Or, you can enter the desired value.
    - **Send PostScript Error Handler** Click this option, and then choose Yes or No from the drop-down menu.

- **Mirrored Output** Click this option, and then, from the drop-down menu, choose No to print the PDF document the same as the source file, or click Yes to print the PDF document as a mirror image of the source document.

11. Click OK to close the Adobe PDF Converter Advanced Options dialog box.
12. Click the Adobe PDF Settings tab to set the parameters shown here.

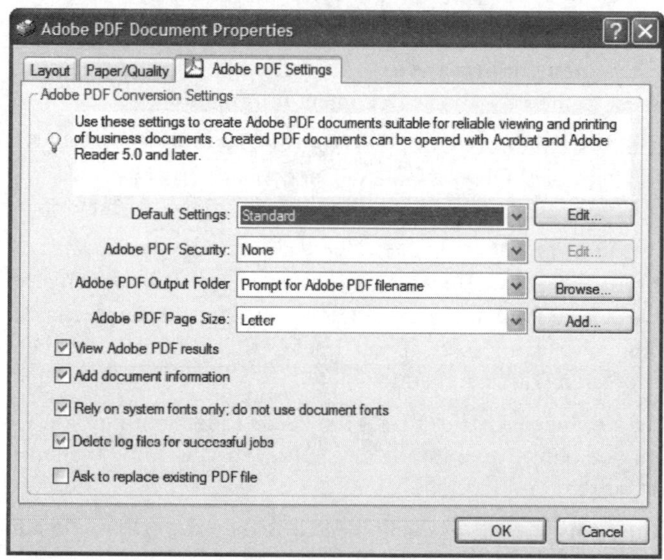

13. Click the Default Settings drop-down arrow, and then choose one of the presets from the drop-down menu. These are identical to the settings previously discussed in Chapter 4.
14. Click the Adobe PDF Security drop-down arrow and choose one of the following options:
    - **None** No security is applied to distilled documents.
    - **Reconfirm Security For Each Job** You will be prompted for security settings each time you use the Adobe PDF printer.
    - **Use Last Known Security Settings** On future printing jobs, Acrobat will use the last security settings you specified.
15. After you choose one of the preceding options, the Edit button to the right of the field becomes available. Click the Edit button to edit security settings. Acrobat security is discussed in detail in Chapter 11.
16. Leave the Adobe PDF Output Folder field at its default setting, Prompt For Adobe PDF Filename, which prompts you for a document name and a folder in which to save the document, or choose My Documents*PDF to save the file in your My Documents folder. Or, you can click the Browse button and navigate to the folder in which you want to save the document.

17. Click the Adobe PDF Page Size drop-down arrow and choose the desired size for the resulting PDF document.
18. At the bottom of the Adobe PDF Settings tab, check one or more of the following options, as appropriate to your needs:
    - **View Adobe PDF Results** This default option opens the resulting PDF document in Acrobat. Deselect this option to print the document without previewing the end result.
    - **Add Document Information** This default option adds information from the source document to the PDF file as Document Information.
    - **Rely on System Fonts Only: Do Not use Document Fonts** No fonts will be embedded in the PDF, if the document contains an embedded font, it will be unavailable in the PDF. Instead, the MM (Multiple Master) fonts will be used to reproduce; otherwise it'll be missing from the PDF.
    - **Delete Log Files For Successful Jobs** Acrobat Distiller creates a log file whenever you use Adobe PDF to create a PDF file. By default, the file is deleted when the distilling job is successful. If you deselect this option, Acrobat creates a log file that can be viewed with a text editor.
    - **Ask To Replace Existing PDF File** Select this option if you want Acrobat to prompt you before overwriting a PDF file with the same filename as the one selected for the current printing job.
19. Click OK to apply the settings, and then close the Adobe PDF Document Properties dialog box.
20. Click OK in the Application Print dialog box to print the document in PDF format.

If you are printing a multipage document with lots of embedded graphics, the printing process may take a while.

Create PDF Files in Adobe Programs

Adobe has gone to great lengths to enhance interactivity between Acrobat and its graphics software. You can create a PDF file using the following Adobe software:

- **FrameMaker** A page-layout program suitable for publishing long documents for viewing across multiple media. You can use the program to create content for the Web, CD-ROM, and print. FrameMaker offers extensive support for creating PDF documents. To create a PDF file in FrameMaker, you can use the application's Print command or the Save As PDF command.
- **Illustrator** A vector-based illustration program. Programs like Illustrator use mathematics to define a shape, which means the shape can be greatly enlarged without

loss of fidelity. You can convert Illustrator documents to PDF format using the Save command. Illustrator 9.0 and newer versions support transparency, which is preserved when you save an Illustrator document as a PDF file with Acrobat 7.0 (PDF 1.6) compatibility.

- **InDesign** The latest page-layout software from Adobe, featuring extensive PDF support. Use the Export command to convert documents you create in InDesign to PDF format. You can export a PDF for a commercial printer using one of the PDF/X settings. Check with your printer for this preferred setting.
- **Photoshop CS2** In the latest version of the award-winning image-editing application from Adobe, you use the Save As command, and then choose the PDF format to save a Photoshop file in PDF format. When you use the Save As command to convert a Photoshop file to PDF, you can specify image compression and the color model. When you save a file from Photoshop in PDF format, layers are flattened. But if you open the resulting PDF file in Photoshop, any layers and objects from the original file are preserved and available for editing. You can also use the Automate | PDF Presentation to save several images as a PDF presentation, or slideshow, complete with transitions. The option to create a PDF Presentation is also available from within the Adobe Bridge.
- **Photoshop Elements** The image-editing application has almost as much power as its big brother, Photoshop CS2. Photoshop Elements also enables you to save a single image file as a PDF.
- **Photoshop Album** This application is used to manage image files. From within Photoshop Album, you can select several images and make a creation known as a PDF Slideshow.
- **PageMaker 7.0** A page-layout program. To create a PDF file from a PageMaker document, use the Export PDF command.

Although the methods used to create PDF files differ between Adobe programs, many of the options are similar. Consult your software application manual for specific instructions on exporting the file as a PDF document. After you export the file, you can modify the file in Acrobat Standard or Acrobat Professional.

Create PDF Files from Vector-Drawing Software

If you create vector-based illustrations, you can convert them to PDF files by using one of the following methods:

- Save the file in either EPS or PS format, and then use Acrobat Distiller to print the file.
- Use the vector-drawing program's Print command and choose Adobe PDF for the printer.
- Export the file in PDF format if supported by the software.

Create Files from Adobe Illustrator

If you create illustrations with Adobe Illustrator, you can save documents in the PDF format. When you save an Illustrator document in PDF format, the Adobe PDF Format Options dialog box, which has seven sections, appears: General, Compression, Marks and Bleeds, Outputs, Advanced, Security, and Summary.

The settings you specify in each section determine the version of Acrobat with which the file is compatible, the amount of compression applied to images, which printer's marks are included with the document, whether the file is output with color conversion, whether to embed fonts, and whether to secure the document. Everything is neatly summed up in the Summary section.

Create PDF Files from CorelDRAW Documents

If you use CorelDRAW 10 or newer to create illustrations, you may be unaware that PDF documents you create in CorelDRAW or Corel PhotoPaint are produced with the Corel PDF engine. When you want to publish a CorelDRAW file as a PDF document, use the Publish to PDF command on the File menu. For more information on exporting a CorelDRAW illustration as a PDF document, consult your software owner's manual.

Summary

In this chapter, you learned to create PDF documents from within Microsoft Office applications that support Adobe PDF. You also saw how to create PDF files from within applications that support printing, and learned to configure Adobe PDF as a PostScript printing device. In the next chapter, you learn how to create PDF documents by capturing them from your scanner or from web pages.

Chapter 6

Capture PDF Documents

How to...

- Capture searchable PDF documents with your scanner
- Capture web pages
- Append web pages

You create most of your PDF documents in authoring applications, and then convert them to PDF files from within the authoring application (if supported) or by using Adobe PDF to print the document in PDF format. You can also create PDF files by using Acrobat Distiller to convert a PostScript file (*EPS or *PS) to PDF format. Both of these techniques are covered in Chapters 4 and 5. However, you can create PDF documents in other ways.

PDF documents can also be created with your scanner or by capturing pages from web sites. Either method is an excellent way to build an information library. You can scan magazine articles of interest, convert them to PDF format, and discard the original to avoid paper clutter. You can also capture single web pages or an entire web site. With the wealth of information available on the Internet, capturing web pages is a wonderful way to build a PDF library on your hard drive. If you own Acrobat Professional, you can use the Adobe Catalog plug-in to create a searchable index of PDF documents captured from the Web. Creating PDF indexes is covered in Chapter 18.

Capture PDF Documents from a Scanner

If you have a scanner attached to your computer, you can capture PDF documents directly from your scanner by using the Acrobat Scan plug-in. With the Acrobat Scan plug-in, it's possible to scan a document into Acrobat without leaving the program. After you scan the document, you can use Acrobat tools or menu commands to modify the document before saving it as a PDF file.

Your scanner probably has an interface or other software that makes the scanning process a relatively simple task. Most scanner applications let you crop the scanned image, select a color model, and adjust the image resolution before capturing the image into an application. If your scanner is equipped with similar software, you can adjust the image to suit its intended destination before returning the scanned image to Acrobat.

Capture Images and Text

After you have a scanner up and running on your system with a TWAIN device that Acrobat recognizes, you can scan any document into Acrobat and save it as a PDF file with searchable text. To capture a document into Acrobat with your scanner:

1. Insert the document you want to capture in your scanner.

To create a better-looking PDF document, make sure the document is square with the edge of your scanner. If the page is clipped from a magazine, trim and square the edges for better results.

2. Choose Create PDF | From Scanner to reveal the Acrobat Scan dialog box:

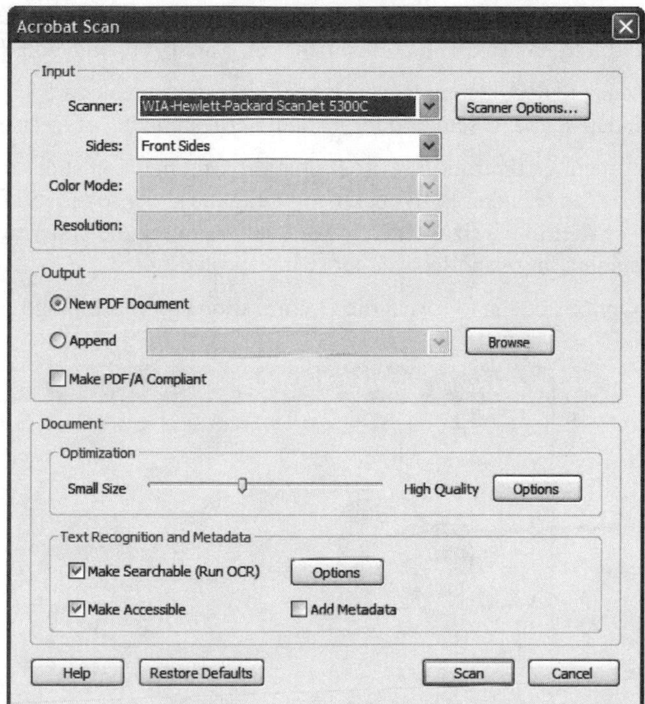

3. Click the Scanner drop-down arrow and choose the appropriate TWAIN device for your scanner.

TIP

The menu for TWAIN devices may show two listings for each item. For best results, choose the manufacturer's software for your scanner if it's listed. With some scanners, you may have to install special TWAIN drivers to make your scanner available as a TWAIN device in Acrobat.

4. Click the Scanner Options button to set options applicable to your scanner.
5. Click the Sides drop-down arrow and choose one of the following options: Front Sides (the default) and Both Sides. If your scanner supports double-sided scanning, choose Both Sides; otherwise, accept Front Sides.
6. Choose the desired options from the Color Mode and Resolution drop-down menus. These options are only available if you use the Acrobat scanning interface instead of the native scanner interface, and if you're using the Windows version of Acrobat. In a nutshell, these options enable you to choose a color mode (black-and-white, color, or grayscale) and resolution supported by your scanner.

7. In the Output section, accept the New PDF Document (the default if you don't currently have a PDF document open), or click the Append radio button. If you choose this option, you can choose a currently open document from the drop-down list. Or, you can click the Browse button to navigate to the document you want to append, and then open it.
8. Click the Make PDF/A-compliant check box. The option creates a document compliant with PDF/A standards, an ISO standard for the long-term archiving of electronic documents.
9. In the Document Optimization section, drag the Optimization slider to determine the quality of the resulting PDF document. Drag the slider to the left to create a PDF document smaller in file size with a lower quality or drag the slider to the right to create a PDF document larger in file size, but of higher quality.
10. Click the Options button to reveal the Optimization Options dialog box shown next.

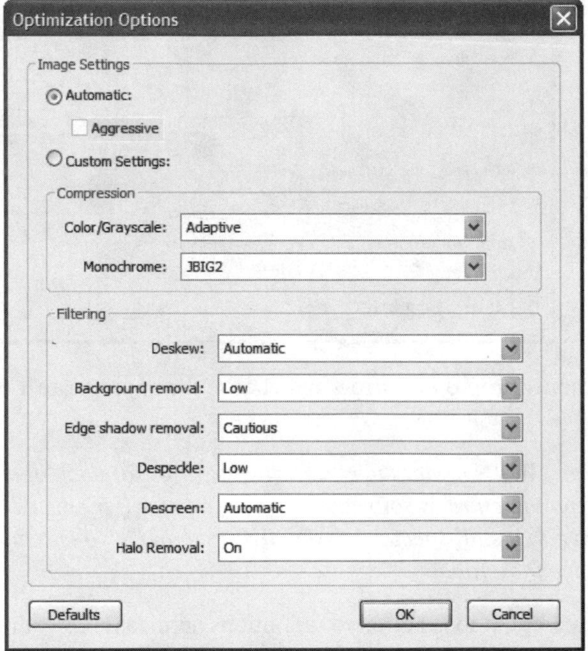

11. Accept the default Automatic, which uses the default settings and creates a document according to those specified with the Optimization slider. Or, you can click the Aggressive check box, which optimizes the image to minimize the file size of the resulting document. This option may noticeably degrade the PDF, especially if the original document contains photorealistic images.
12. Click the Custom Settings radio button to reveal the settings you can modify, as shown next.

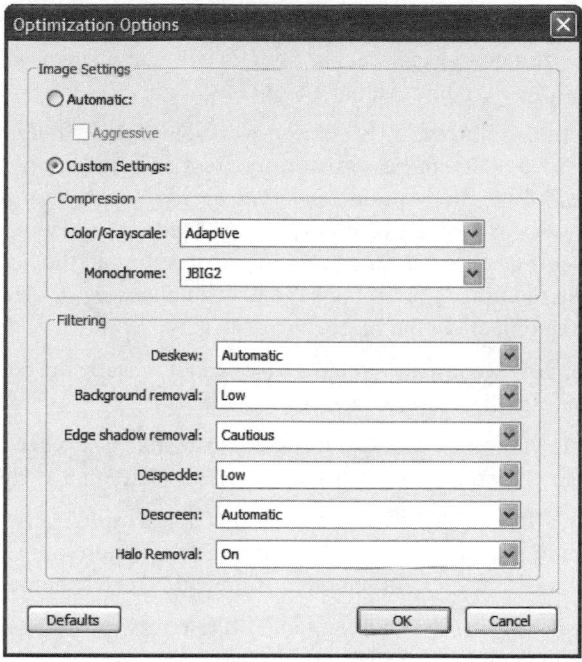

13. Click the Color/Grayscale drop-down arrow, and choose one of the following options:
    - **Lossless** Applies no compression and doesn't apply filters when converting the scanned image to PDF.
    - **Adaptive** Divides the image to be scanned into regions: black-and-white, grayscale, and color, and determines the optimum compression for each region, while preserving the original appearance of the document. Recommended resolution for this option is 300 PPI (pixels per inch) for grayscale and RGB color input, and 600 PPI for black-and-white input. Choose this option when you're scanning a document that contains both images and text.
    - **JPEG** Applies JPEG compression to grayscale or RGB input. Choose this option when you're scanning a document that contains predominantly RGB and/or grayscale images.
14. Click the Monochrome drop-down arrow, and then choose one of the following options:
    - **JBIG2** Applies the JBIG2 compression method to black-and-white input. This option is only compatible with Acrobat 5.0 (PDF 1.4) or later.
    - **Adaptive** Compresses the monochrome portions of the image, while preserving the original appearance of the document being scanned.
    - **CCIT Group 4** Applies CCIT Group 4 compression to black-and-white input. This compression method is lossless, compresses the page quickly, and is compatible with Acrobat 3.0 (PDF 1.2) and later.

6

15. In the Filtering section, choose the following options:
    - **Deskew** Rotates a page that isn't square with the scanner bed. Click the drop-down arrow and choose either Automatic or Off.
    - **Background Removal** This option works with color and grayscale portions of a scanned document, but has little or no effect on a document that is predominantly black-and-white. This option converts a background that is almost white to pure white. You have four options: None, Low, Medium, or High. In most instances, the default setting of Low does a good job of cleaning up the background. If something printed on the other side of the page is visible, however, Medium or High may remove the objectionable bleed-through.
    - **Edge Shadow Removal** Removes the shadow cast by the edge of the page. You have three options: Off, Cautious, and Aggressive.
    - **Despeckle** Removes random black marks that appear when you scan a black-and-white page. Low removes small spots, whereas Medium and High remove larger spots.
    - **Descreen** Removes the halftone dots that appear when certain images, such as newsprint or magazine pages, are scanned. Your options are Off and Automatic. In most instances, the default option of Automatic creates the best-looking PDF.
    - **Halo Removal** The default option (On) removes halos that appear at high-contrast edges, or images that have been over-sharpened.
16. Click OK to exit the Optimization Options dialog box.
17. Deselect the Make Searchable (Run OCR [optical character recognition]) option to create a PDF document without searchable text. If you accept the default option, click Options to reveal the Recognize Text—Settings dialog box shown next.

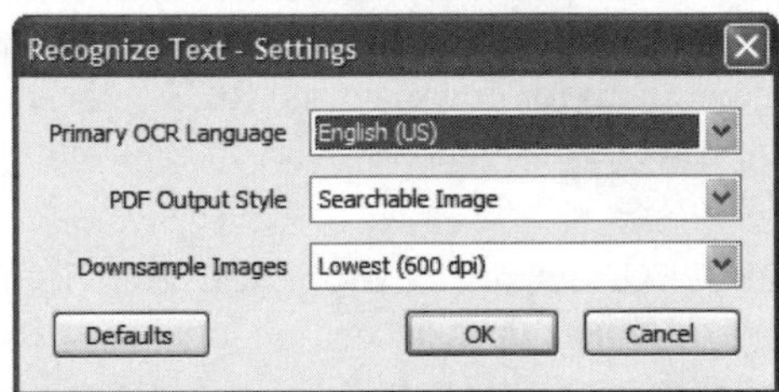

18. Accept the default Primary OCR Language option (the language specified when you installed Acrobat) or choose a different language from the drop-down menu.
19. Click the PDF Output drop-down arrow and choose one of the following options:
    - **Formatted Text and Graphics** Captures the scanned document as images and formatted text. The document can be searched and the text portions can be selected as text, while the graphics portions can be selected as images.

- **Searchable Image** Captures the scanned document as an image, but also recognizes the text in the document. The PDF document can be searched, and text can bc selected with the Select tool.
- **Searchable Image (Exact)** Captures the scanned document as an image, but also recognizes the text in the document. The PDF document can be searched, and text can be selected with the Select tool.

NOTE

If you deselect the Recognize Text Using OCR option in the Create PDF from Scanner dialog box, the PDF file created will be an image only and you can neither search the text from within Acrobat nor can you index the document using Adobe Catalog. The only real value in deselecting this option is the resulting unsearchable PDF has a smaller file size.

20. Click the Downsample Images drop down arrow, and choose an option. The default options, Lowest (600 DPI) is suitable for a document that will be printed. On the other end of the scale, High (72 DPI), creates a smaller file size and a document that is suitable for monitor viewing. Note that this option is unavailable if you choose Searchable Image (Exact) as the PDF Output Style.
21. Click OK to exit the Recognize Text—Settings dialog box and return to the Create PDF From Scanner dialog box.
22. Click the Make Accessible check box to create a PDF document with tags, which improves accessibility for disabled viewers. This option is only available when you choose the Make Searchable option. When you make a document accessible, you do increase the file size.
23. Click the Add Metadata check box to add information to the document, such as keywords. If you choose the option, the Document Properties dialog box appears after all pages of the document are scanned into Acrobat.

Did you know?

How TWAIN Got Its Name

When you install Acrobat, the install utility detects any TWAIN devices you have attached to your computer. As a note of interest, the name "TWAIN" was adopted from the phrase "and never the twain shall meet" in Rudyard Kipling's *The Ballad of East and West,* to reflect the fact that, when the technology was in its infancy, connecting a scanner to a personal computer was difficult. However, many people think TWAIN is an acronym for Technology Without An Interesting Name. A *TWAIN* device contains drivers that convert the optical input from a scanner or digital camera into a digital format that can be recognized by computer software. The TWAIN devices you have attached to your computer are listed on a drop-down menu in the Create PDF From Scanner dialog box.

24. Click Scan. After you click the Scan button, the interface for the TWAIN device you selected opens. Follow the prompts to preview the scan and return it to Acrobat. Refer to your scanner user guide for specific instructions.
25. After the image is scanned into Acrobat, modify the document as needed and save the file.

Capture PDF Documents from Web Sites

The Web is a treasure trove of information. You can find out almost anything about any subject by typing relevant keywords into one of the many online search engines. After you submit the search, the search engine usually returns several pages of links to web sites containing information that pertains to your search. The first three or four pages contain links to the sites with information that closely matches your query, but searching through 10 or 15 web sites can be time-consuming. If you have a slow Internet connection and the returned pages are filled with graphics, this exacerbates the problem. The solution is to use the Acrobat Web Capture command to download the page into Acrobat. You can download a single page or the entire site. After the download is complete, you can save the page(s) in PDF format for review at your leisure. Figure 6-1 shows a web page that has been downloaded into Acrobat.

Set Web Capture Preferences

Creating a PDF from a web page is a powerful option that can save you spending hours of time online. You can configure the Web Capture feature to suit your working style by changing Web Capture Preferences, as explained in the following steps.

1. Choose Edit | Preferences | Web Capture to open the Web Capture section of the Preferences dialog box:

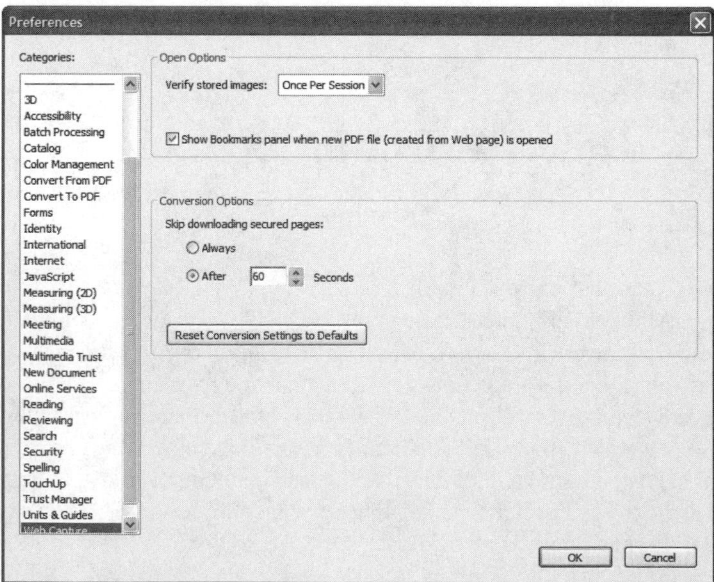

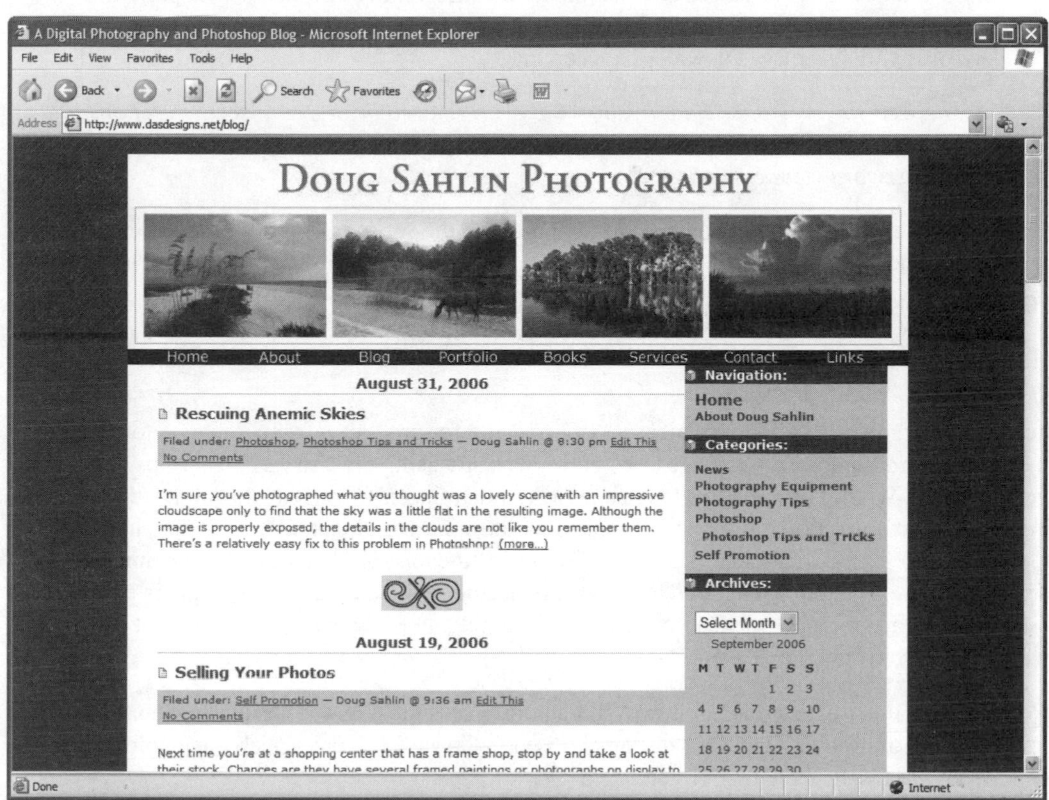

FIGURE 6-1 You can download web pages for future reference.

2. Click the Verify Stored Images drop-down arrow and choose Once Per Session, Always, or Never. The default option, Once Per Session, checks the web site you captured pages from to see if the images stored with the captured pages have changed at the site. If the images have changed, new images are downloaded.
3. Click the Show Bookmarks panel when new PDF file (created from Web page) is opened check box to display the Navigation pane open to the Bookmarks panel when the captured PDF is first opened. If you disable this option, when the download is complete, the document opens with the Navigation pane closed, but bookmarks have been created.
4. Choose a Skip Downloading Secured Pages option. The default option skips a secured page if it isn't downloaded within 60 seconds. Acrobat can download secured pages, but you generally need permission to access password-protected areas. When you attempt to download a secure page, a dialog box appears that you use to enter a login name and password. After you submit this information, Acrobat tries to download the page for the time interval specified in the Seconds field. You can enter a value between 1 and 9,999 seconds.

If the allotted time has passed and Acrobat hasn't successfully downloaded the page, a warning dialog box appears and the page is skipped. Or, you can choose Always, and Acrobat will never try to download a secure page.

TIP *If the web site server is set up to allow only certain web browsers in secure sections of the site, Acrobat may be unable to capture the page, even though the right user name and password were entered.*

5. Click Reset Conversion Settings To Default, and the settings in the Web Capture Preferences dialog box are restored to the default values Acrobat had when first installed.
6. Click OK to apply the settings and exit the dialog box.

Download Web Pages

Whether you're surfing the Web for pleasure or browsing for product information or tutorials, you can quickly download a web page or an entire web site using the Create PDF From Web Page command. When you capture a web page in Acrobat, the entire page is downloaded, complete with images. When Acrobat encounters an unsupported object, a rectangular shape the color of the web page background is displayed in lieu of the unsupported object. If an animated GIF is part of the page being captured, only the first frame of the animated GIF appears after Acrobat downloads the page. When you're on the Internet and find a web page you want to download, do the following:

1. Choose File | Create PDF | From Web Page to access the Create PDF From Web Page dialog box, shown next. Or, you can choose the Create PDF From Web Page command from the Create PDF task button.

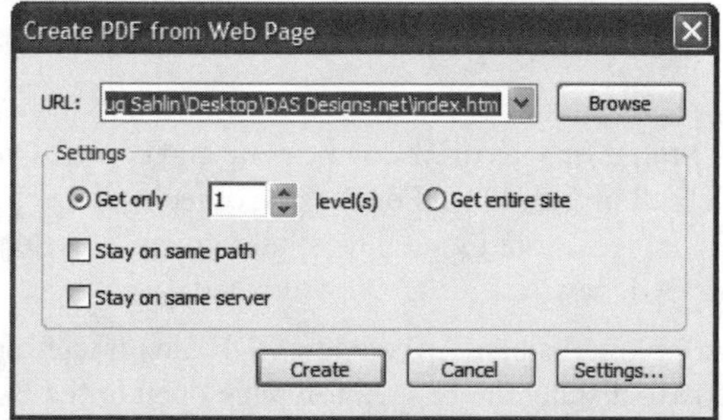

2. In the URL field, enter the URL for the page you want to capture.

TIP *Some URLs are long. Instead of manually entering the entire web address, you can select the web address in your web browser, and then press* CTRL-C *(Windows) or* COMMAND-C *(Macintosh) to copy the web address to your operating system (OS) clipboard. Switch to Acrobat, click inside the URL field, and then press* CTRL-V *(Windows) or* COMMAND-V *(Macintosh) to paste the URL into the field.*

3. In the Get Only [ ] Level(s) field, enter the number of levels to download, or use the spinner buttons to increase or decrease this value. Alternatively, you can choose the Get Entire Site radio button to download every level (and subsequently every page) in the site.

CAUTION *When you download a site that is several levels deep, you use a considerable amount of your system resources and run the risk of exceeding available system resources and perpetrating a system crash. If you're downloading a site with many levels, you're advised to download the first level, browse through the downloaded pages in Acrobat, and then click a link to download an additional page.*

4. If you specify the number of levels to download, you can specify the following options:
   - **Stay On Same Path** Acrobat downloads all pages along the path of the specified URL.
   - **Stay On Same Server** Acrobat downloads pages from the server of the specified URL only, disregarding links to URLs on other servers.
5. Click the Settings button to modify Acrobat web capture conversion settings. This feature is explained fully in the section "Specify Web Page Conversion Settings."
6. Click the Create button to begin capturing the page(s). As the site is downloading, Acrobat keeps you informed of the download progress by opening the Download Status dialog box.
7. To save the captured page in PDF format for future reference, choose File | Save to open the Save As dialog box. Enter a name for the file, specify the folder to save the file in, and then click Save.

When the download is complete, Acrobat displays the captured page in the Document pane according to the specified web capture preferences. At the top of the document you'll find the title of the captured page. This same title is displayed in your web browser when you view the page on the Web. You can change the name of document by choosing File | Properties, and then entering another name in the Title field of the Description tab of the Document Properties dialog box. This changes the title as it pertains to a PDF index, to which the file is added. When you reopen the document after assigning the new title, the filename you saved the PDF document with appears in the Document pane, not the title you specified in the Description section of the Document Properties dialog box. You can however, change whether the filename or title is displayed by changing the Show option in the Initial View tab of the Document Properties dialog box.

NOTE *Certain web page features won't download, such as pop-up menus, multistate JavaScript buttons, and JavaScript image swaps. Pop-up menus and similar web page features are created using JavaScript. You should also be aware that Acrobat won't convert certain CGI files, Java applets, or RealMedia to PDF. Although JavaScript is supported in bookmarks, links, and form fields that you create in Acrobat, JavaScript features aren't downloaded with a web page.*

Append Web Pages

After you successfully capture a web page, you may decide to add additional pages from the same site to the document, download the rest of the site, or append web pages from another site to the document. You can append the currently open PDF document that was captured from a web site by clicking document links or using menu commands.

Use Web Links

As you view a captured page in Acrobat, you may decide that another page from the same site, or a page from another site that is linked to the captured page, contains information you would like to archive in PDF format. To append a page to your current document by using a web link, follow these steps:

1. From within a PDF created from a web capture, move your cursor over the link to the page you want to capture. Your cursor becomes a pointing finger with a *W* in it. This signifies that the linked page will be viewed in your default web browser.
2. Right-click (Windows) or CTRL-click (Macintosh) the link, and choose one of the following from the context menu:
   - **Open Weblink in Browser** Opens the linked web page in your default web browser.
   - **Append to Document** Appends the linked web page to the PDF document.
   - **Open Weblink as New Document** Creates a new PDF document of the linked page.
   - **Copy Link Location** Copies the URL of the linked page to the clipboard.
3. Continue right-clicking (Windows) or CTRL-clicking links to add additional pages to the document. Or, choose one of the other options.
4. When you finish adding pages to the document, choose File | Save.

Use the View Web Links Command

To view all the web links within a captured page, you use the View Web Links command. You can use this command to add additional web pages to the document, as the following steps explain.

1. Choose Advanced | Web Capture | View Web Links, and Acrobat opens the Select Page Links To Download dialog box:

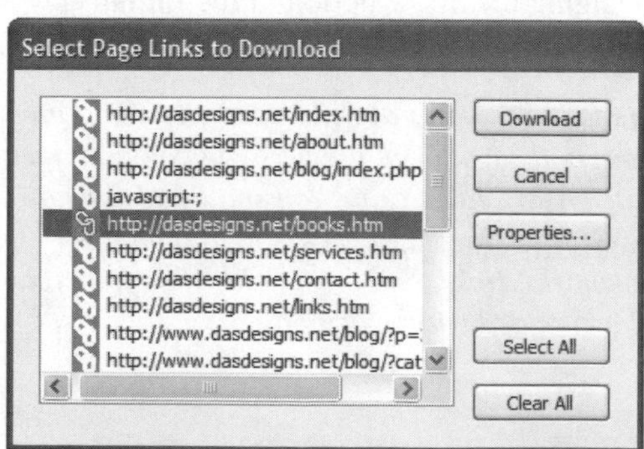

2. To add additional web pages to the current document, do one of the following:
   - To add contiguous links to the selection, click the first and last link you want to download while holding down SHIFT. To add noncontiguous links to the selection, click each link while holding down CTRL (Windows) or COMMAND (Macintosh).
   - To select all links, click Select All.
   - To clear the selection, click Clear All.
3. Click the Download button to begin the download. After you do so, Acrobat opens the Download Status dialog box and displays the progress of the operation. When the download is complete, Acrobat appends the downloaded pages to the document and adds additional bookmarks and thumbnails for the new pages.

TIP *If you download a web page with form fields, such as text boxes, check boxes, and submit buttons, these form fields are preserved in the PDF document. You can modify the properties of the fields, as outlined in Chapter 14.*

Use the Append Web Page Command

You can use the Append Web Page command to add additional pages to the current document. If you're appending links from within the same site to the current document, either click a link within the document, or use the View Web Links command to view the links within the document, and then select the links of the pages you want to add to the document. If, however, the page you want to add to the captured web page doesn't have a link on the page, do the following:

1. Choose Advanced | Web Capture | Create PDF From/Append Web Page to open the Add To PDF From Web Page dialog box:

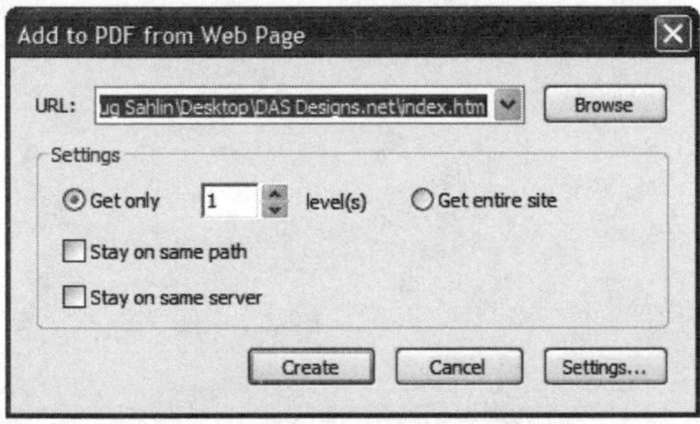

2. In the URL field, enter the address for the web page you want to add to the document.
3. In the Get Only [ ] Level(s) field, enter the number of levels to download, or use the spinner buttons to increase or decrease the value in the Levels field. Or, you can choose Get Entire Site to download every level (and subsequently every page) in the site.
4. Choose Stay On Same Path if you want Acrobat to download all pages along the path of the specified URL.

5. Choose Stay On Same Server if you want Acrobat to download only pages from the server of the specified URL and disregard links to URLs on another server.
6. Click the Create button to begin capturing the page(s). Acrobat opens the Download Status dialog box, which you can use to monitor download progress.
7. After the page downloads, you can invoke the command again to add additional pages to the document, or choose File | Save.

When you append a PDF document captured from a web page, you can modify the settings for the new pages by clicking the Settings button in the Add To PDF From Web Page dialog box. For more information on settings, refer to the upcoming section "Specify Web Page Conversion Settings."

When you append pages from another web site to a captured web page, Acrobat creates a bookmark for the URL of the site. Captured pages from each site are listed under the site's URL bookmark.

Right-click (Windows) or CTRL-click (Macintosh) a link to reveal a context menu with commands to open the link in a web browser, append the linked web page to the PDF, or open the link as a new PDF document.

Append All Links on a Page

After you download a web page, you can use any of the methods previously discussed to append other pages to the page, or you can download every page linked to the captured page by choosing Advanced | Web Capture | Append All Links On Page. After you choose this command, Acrobat downloads the linked pages one at a time and displays the download progress in the Download Status dialog box. This operation may take a considerable amount of time if the page has several links.

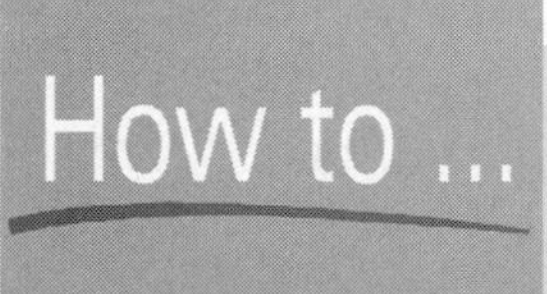

Save a Web Search

If you use a web search engine to find web pages you want to save for reference, after you enter your query, launch Acrobat and choose File | Create PDF | From Web Page, and then enter the URL for the search engine's results page. After Acrobat downloads the page, you can append the document with the web pages from the results of your search by clicking the links in the results page. Download additional web pages by clicking other links. After you download all the pages you want to save, you can delete the initial search page by clicking its thumbnail, and then choosing Document | Delete Pages. If your search returns pages of URLs, you can save the PDF document and open the document at a later date to peruse the desired URLs at your leisure.

After the linked pages are downloaded, you can view the downloaded pages by clicking a link in the main page or by opening the Bookmarks tab or Pages tab, and clicking a bookmark or thumbnail. You can apply the Append All Links On Page command on any of the newly downloaded pages to add additional pages to the document.

After you add all the desired pages to the document, you can disable web links by choosing Advanced | Document Processing | Remove All Links. This opens the Remove Web Links dialog box, with which you can specify how many pages of links to remove. After you apply this command, web links are visible in the document, but they will no longer function as links to URLs. Links to other downloaded web pages will still be functional, however, and open the proper document page when clicked. When you remove web links, you reduce the size of the PDF file.

TIP *You can also create links from URLs in a document by choosing Advanced | Document Processing | Create From URLs In The Document.*

Specify Web Page Conversion Settings

You can modify the conversion settings used to capture web pages and convert them to PDF format. When you modify these settings, this is a global action that applies to future web pages you capture until you modify the settings again. To modify web capture conversion settings, do the following:

1. Choose File | Create PDF | From Web Page to open the Create PDF From Web Page dialog box shown previously.
2. In the Create PDF From Web Page dialog box, click the Settings button to open the Web Page Conversion Settings dialog box, shown next. You can modify parameters for General options and Page Layout options, as detailed in the following sections.

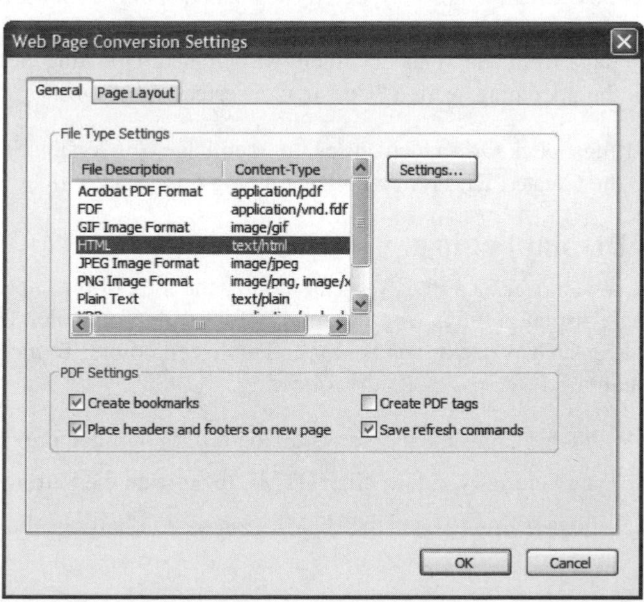

Modify General Conversion Settings

When you open the Web Page Conversion Settings dialog box, the General tab is selected by default, as shown previously. The supported file types Acrobat can convert to PDF are listed in the File Type Settings window. You can modify settings for two file types—HTML and Plain Text—as described in the next section, "Modify HTML Display Settings."

The following are the options you can modify in the PDF Settings area:

- **Create Bookmarks** Choose this option to have Acrobat generate a new bookmark for each additional page you capture. This option is checked by default.
- **Create PDF Tags** Choose this option to have Acrobat create a document structure that conforms to the layout of the HTML document. If you check this option, Acrobat adds bookmarks for HTML items, such as paragraphs, lists, tables, and so on. The tagged document can be reflowed for easier reading on devices with smaller viewing areas. For more information on tagged documents, refer to the section "About Tagged Documents" in Chapter 12.
- **Place Headers & Footers On New Page (Windows) or Put Headers And Footers On New Content (Macintosh)** Check this option to have Acrobat add a new header and footer to each captured web page. The header shows the web page title as it appears in the browser, and the footer displays the web page URL, plus the date and time the file was downloaded. If the URL is exceptionally long, the footer may be truncated to allow room for the page number.
- **Save Refresh Commands (Windows) or Save Update Commands (Macintosh)** Check this option to have Acrobat save a list of all URLs associated with the captured page, and remember the order in which they were downloaded. Choose this option, and you'll be able to update the content of the converted PDF document to match the current version of the web page from which the document was created. Updating captured web pages is covered in the upcoming section "Update Converted Web Pages."

To save the settings, click OK, which closes the Web Page Conversion Settings dialog box and returns you to the Create PDF From Web Page dialog box.

Modify HTML Display Settings

When you capture a web page as a PDF, you can modify the look of the captured page by changing the HTML display settings. You can modify font style, font color, and other parameters of the converted page, such as background color and table cell colors. To modify the display characteristics of captured web pages, do the following:

1. Open the Web Page Conversion Settings dialog box as outlined previously.
2. In the File Type Settings window, click HTML to activate the Settings button.
3. Click the Settings button to open the HTML Conversion Settings dialog box.

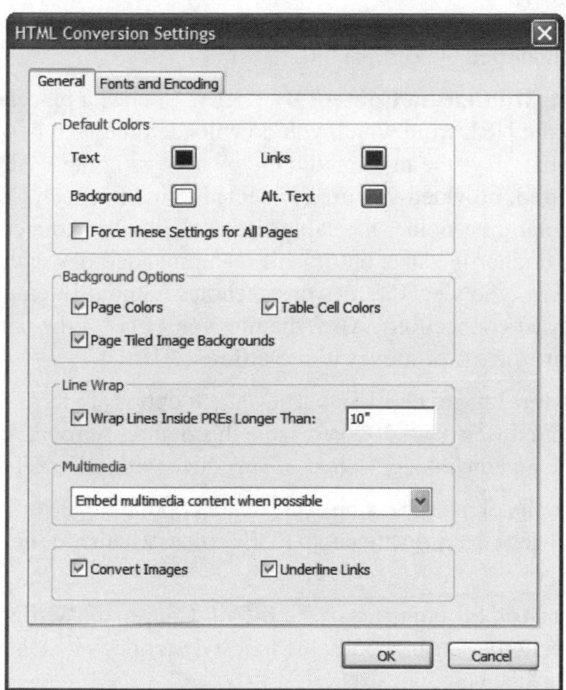

4. In the Default Colors section, you can modify the color of Text, Links, Background, and Alt Text by clicking the color button to the right of an item to open a color palette. Choose a color for the item, and then click OK to close the palette and apply the change. Repeat as needed to change the color of other items.
5. If you click the Force These Settings For All Pages check box, the colors you specify in the previous step are applied to all pages you capture, regardless of the colors specified in the actual HTML document. If you don't choose this option, Acrobat applies the colors you specified in the previous step only to HTML documents that don't have colors specified in the document HTML code.
6. In the Background Options area, Page Colors, Table Cell Colors, and Page Tiled Image Backgrounds are enabled by default. If you disable these options, the captured PDF document may look different from the actual web page, but may be more legible when printed.
7. In the Line Wrap area, check the Wrapped Lines Inside PREs Longer Than box and enter a value in the corresponding field. Acrobat wraps preformatted lines of HTML longer than the value you specify (10 inches is the default) to fit onscreen.
8. Click the Multimedia drop-down arrow and choose one of the following options:
    - **Disable Multimedia Capture** Captures HTML and images, but doesn't capture multimedia content such as Flash movies.

- **Embed Multimedia Content When Possible (Default)** Embeds multimedia formats supported by Acrobat 8.0.
- **Reference Multimedia Content By URL** Creates a placeholder for the media linked to the URL from which you downloaded the web page. When you open the file, Acrobat plays the multimedia file by accessing the URL from which the page was captured, provided you are connected to the Internet. Otherwise, you only see a rectangular placeholder the same size as the multimedia content. This option creates a smaller file size, but it isn't recommended if you distribute the document to recipients who view the files on machines without Internet connections or with slow Internet connections. Also, the file won't play if the parent web site removes the multimedia file or moves it to a different URL.

9. Click the Convert Images check box (the default option) to have Acrobat include images from the captured web page. If you disable this option, Acrobat replaces the image with a colored border and the image Alt text, if specified, within the HTML document.
10. Click the Underline Links check box (the default option) to have Acrobat underline all text links when converting the document to PDF format, whether or not they are underlined in the HTML page.
11. Click the Fonts And Encoding tab of the HTML Conversion Settings dialog box, shown next. In this section, you can modify the font style for body text, headings, or preformatted text, and change the base font size.

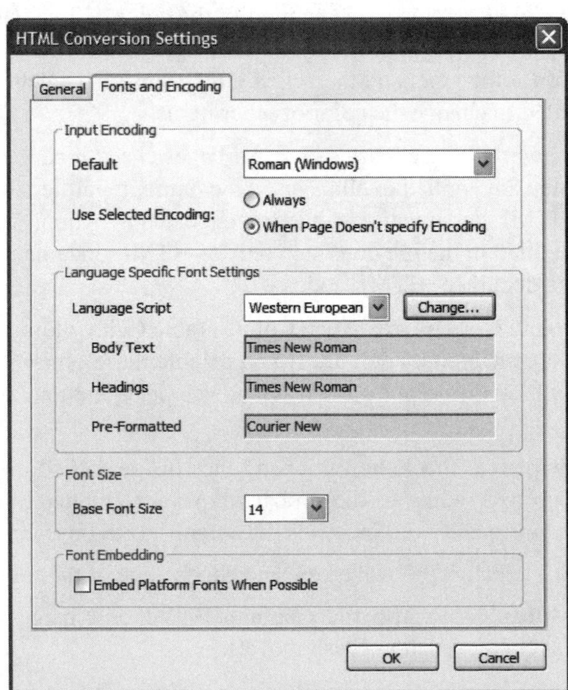

12. In the Input Encoding area, accept the default option or click the drop-down arrow and choose the appropriate encoding system from the drop-down menu.
13. Choose whether to use the encoding specified in Step 12 by clicking the desired radio button. Your options are Always, which always uses the encoding, regardless of the encoding specified in the web page HTML, or When Page Doesn't Specify Encoding, which uses the encoding when the web page HTML doesn't specify encoding.
14. In the Language Specific Font Settings area, accept the default or click the Language Script drop-down arrow and choose the desired encoding language from the list.
15. If desired, click the Change button to display the Select Fonts dialog box shown next. This dialog box enables you to specify the font used for body text, headings, and prefomatted text.

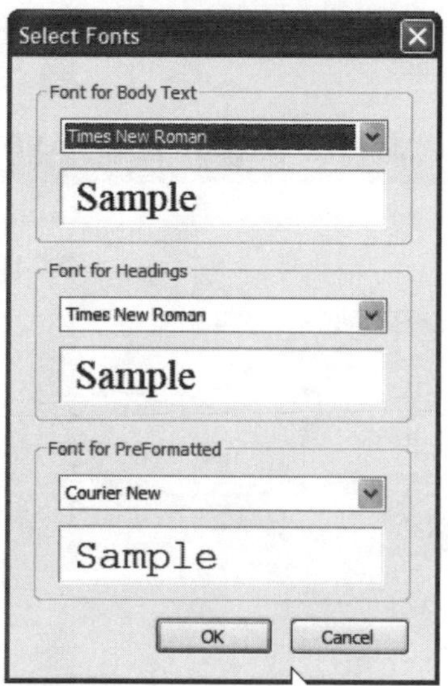

16. After selecting fonts for the encoding language, click OK to exit the Select Fonts dialog box.
17. In the Font Size area of the Fonts And Encoding tab, accept the default base font sizes or click the Base Font Size drop-down arrow and select the desired font size.
18. Check Embed Platform Fonts When Possible if you want the fonts you specify for the captured web pages embedded with the PDF document. Choose this option if the file will be viewed on other machines that may not have the same fonts you have on your machine. Note: embedding fonts increases the file size of the document. Also if you embed fonts, make sure you aren't violating a font-licensing agreement.
19. Click OK to close the HTML Conversion Settings dialog box.

Modify Page Layout Options

The Page Layout tab of the Web Page Conversion Setting dialog box enables you to modify the size, margins, orientation, and scaling of the converted web pages. These options come in handy if you want to maintain the dimensions of a captured web page. For example, if you know each page in a web site is configured to a certain size, say 760 × 420 pixels (a web browser maximized at an 800 × 600 desktop resolution), you can change the default Acrobat document size (8 ½ × 11 inches) to match. The following steps describe how to modify the page layout of a captured web page.

The default unit of measure for Acrobat is inches. When you capture web pages, you may find it helpful to convert the unit of measure to points by choosing Edit | Preferences, and in the Units and Guides section, choose Points.

1. Open the Web Page Conversion Settings dialog box as outlined previously.
2. Click the Page Layout tab:

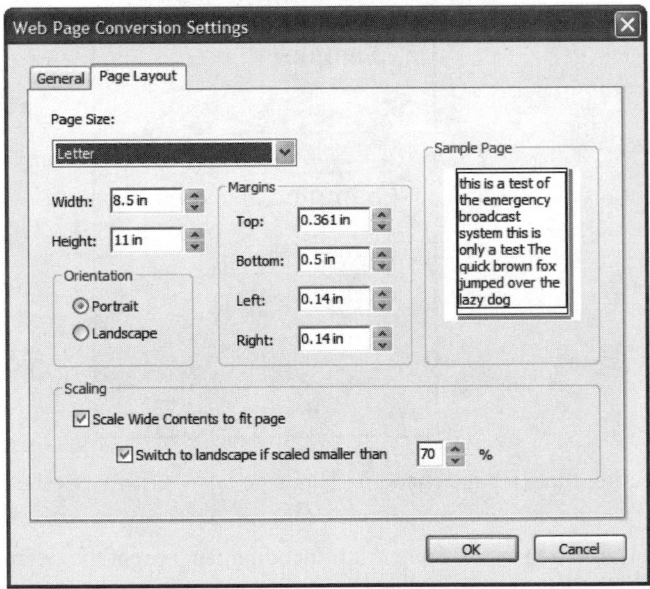

3. Click the Page Size drop-down arrow and choose an option. When you select a preset page size, the values in the Width and Height fields change to reflect your choice. Or, select Custom from the Page Size drop-down menu and specify the page size by entering values in the Width and Height fields, or by clicking the spinner buttons to change the values.

4. In the Margins area, accept the defaults or enter your own values in the Top, Bottom, Left, and Right fields.

TIP

If the web page you're capturing has no margins, you can duplicate this when you capture the page by entering 0 for each margin setting on the Page Layout tab of the Web Page Conversion Settings dialog box.

5. In the Orientation area, choose Portrait (the default) or Landscape.
6. In the Scaling area, you can modify the following options:
   - **Scale Wide Contents To Fit Page** Check this box to have Acrobat resize the contents of a web page that exceeds the width of the screen to fit the page.
   - **Switch To Landscape If Scaled Smaller Than [ ] %** Accept the default value (70 percent) or enter a value of your own in this field. Acrobat automatically switches the page layout from Portrait to Landscape if it's necessary to scale the page to a value lower than specified.
7. Click OK to apply the settings and close the Web Page Conversion Settings dialog box.

Using the Web Capture Feature

After you use the Web Capture feature a few times, you begin to see how useful it is. You can use the Create PDF From Web Page command to capture a web page with product specifications. If you're contemplating a major purchase, you can download the product specifications of every product you're considering, and then compare them at your leisure, without having to wait for the web pages to download or perhaps being bumped off the Internet during peak traffic.

If you use the Internet for research, capturing web pages is a great way to build a reference library. After you save several (or several hundred) web pages as PDF documents, you can use Acrobat Catalog (Professional only) to build a searchable index. Building a searchable index is covered in Chapter 18.

Update Converted Web Pages

If you surf the Web frequently, you know it's in a constant state of flux. New web sites open, old ones disappear, and web sites are frequently updated. If you specified the Save Refresh command (Windows) or the Save Update command (Macintosh) for your web page conversion settings (see the previous section, "Modify General Conversion Settings"), you can update a captured web page you saved as a PDF document by doing the following:

1. Launch Acrobat and log on to the Internet.
2. Open the PDF file you captured from a web page.

3. Choose Advanced | Web Capture | Refresh Pages to open the Refresh Pages dialog box, shown in the following illustration.

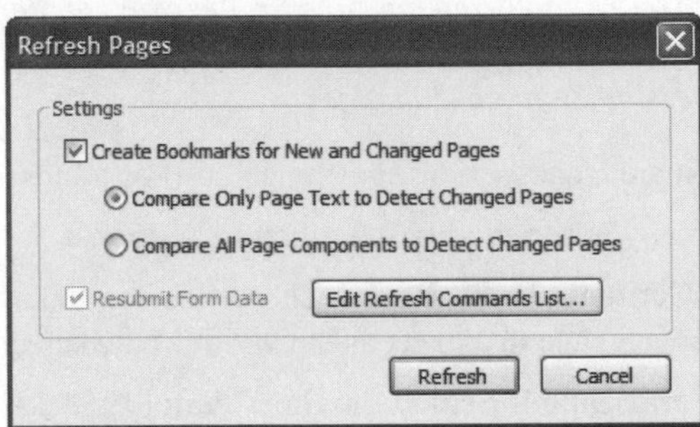

4. Click the Create Bookmarks For New And Changed Pages check box. When you choose this option, Acrobat creates bookmarks for downloaded pages added to the site or modified since you captured the web page.
5. Click the Compare Only Page Text To Detect Changed Pages radio button, and Acrobat compares the captured page to the web site page and downloads the page(s) if the page text has changed.
6. Click the Compare All Page Components To Detect Changed Pages radio button, and Acrobat compares all elements from the PDF document to the web site from which the document was captured. The document is updated if Acrobat detects any change, such as a new image or different text.
7. If the captured web page has a form in it, the Resubmit Form Data check box is active. This option is enabled by default. This option is grayed out if there is no form data on the captured page.

NOTE *When the Resubmit Form Data check box is selected, any data on the form is resubmitted. If you captured a web page with a form you used to purchase an item, a duplicate purchase may result if you enable this option.*

8. Click Edit Refresh Commands List to reveal the Refresh Commands List dialog box:

Capture Web Pages from Internet Explorer

If you have Internet Explorer (IE) installed on your computer, the Acrobat install utility adds a button to IE that enables you to capture a web page as a PDF document. After capturing a web page in this manner, you can append other web pages to the document or refresh it as outlined previously. To capture a web page from within IE, click the Convert Current Web Page To An Adobe PDF File button, as shown below. This feature is also a wonderful way to create a PDF of a transaction at a secure web site. The fact that the page is already open in the browser means the conversion is almost instantaneous. If you were to choose Create PDF | From Web Page and enter a secure link, the conversion would slow down to a crawl because the web site would require authentication before opening the secure page. You can also choose commands from a drop-down menu by clicking the drop-down arrow to the right of the icon. These options enable you to append the web page to an existing PDF, convert the web page to a PDF and send it via e-mail, and open the Adobe PDF Explorer Bar, which provides a list of PDF documents on your computer and their locations. This is similar to Windows Explorer.

Convert Current Web Page To An Adobe PDF File

6

9. To update all links in the list, click OK. Note, all links from the captured page are selected by default. If you want to update all captured pages, you don't need to click the Edit Refresh Commands List button. You need to choose this option only to update specific pages from the captured document by selecting the URLs you want to update from the list in this dialog box. Click a link to select it, or select multiple links while holding down SHIFT. Or, you can select all or clear all by clicking the corresponding button. After clicking OK, you exit the Refresh Commands List dialog box and are returned to the Refresh Pages dialog box.
10. Click Refresh to have Acrobat search for the changes as specified and download new or changed pages.

Summary

In this chapter, you learned how to create PDF documents by capturing them with your scanner, your digital camera, and from web pages. In the next chapter, you learn how to create navigation for your PDF documents.

Chapter 7

Create Navigation for PDF Documents

How to...

- Create bookmarks
- Edit bookmarks
- Use thumbnails
- Create links
- Create a navigation menu

When you create a PDF document within an authoring application, navigation devices are added to the document. PDF documents have two types of automatically created navigation devices: bookmarks and page thumbnails. Bookmarks and page thumbnails have their own panels in the Navigation pane.

When you create a PDF document, one thumbnail is created for each page. Viewers of your PDF documents can navigate to a specific page of the document by clicking its thumbnail or, for a single-page document, navigate to a specific part of the page, as you learn in this chapter. Bookmarks, on the other hand, may or may not be created, depending on how you created the PDF document. If, for example, you use Acrobat PDFMaker (the Adobe Acrobat plug-in for Microsoft Office applications) with its default settings to create a PDF file from a Microsoft Word document that contains Heading styles, a bookmark appears for each Heading style used in the document. If you use the Word Print command and choose Adobe PDF to create the PDF document, no bookmarks are created. To navigate to a bookmark within a document, viewers just click its name in the Bookmarks panel of the Navigation pane. For more information on the Navigation pane, refer to Chapter 3.

After you open a PDF file in Acrobat, you can modify bookmarks and thumbnails, as well as create other navigation devices, such as text links or buttons. After you create a link (also known as a *hotspot*), you can assign an action to it that determines what occurs when the link is activated with a mouse click. You can also add actions to bookmarks and links, and assign to an individual page one or more actions that occur when the page opens or closes.

Use the Bookmarks Panel

In Acrobat and Adobe Reader, you use the Bookmarks panel to navigate to bookmark destinations. In Acrobat, you also use the Bookmarks panel to navigate to a bookmark within the document, as well as to edit existing bookmarks and add new ones. The Bookmarks panel is part of the Navigation pane. To open the Bookmarks panel, click the Bookmarks icon. Figure 7-1 shows the Bookmarks panel for a PDF document.

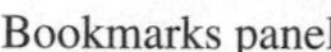

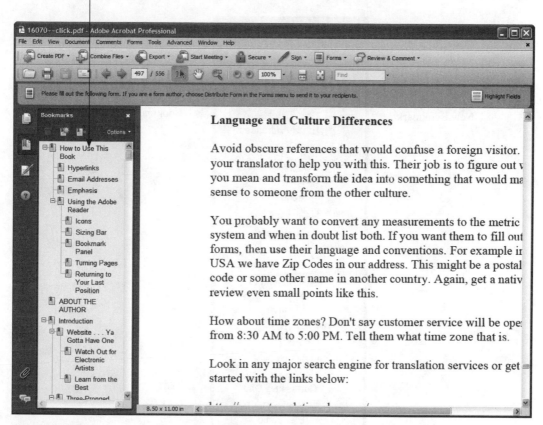

FIGURE 7-1 In Acrobat, you use the Bookmarks panel to navigate to, create, and edit bookmarks.

About the Bookmarks Panel Toolbar

Bookmarks are an important part of any multipage PDF document. Viewers of your PDF files would have a hard time navigating to the parts of the document they want to view without bookmarks. When you create bookmarks, edit bookmarks, or use bookmarks to navigate within a document, you can use the Bookmarks panel toolbar to streamline your work.

The Bookmarks panel toolbar contains three tool icons, an Options menu icon, and a Close icon, as shown here:

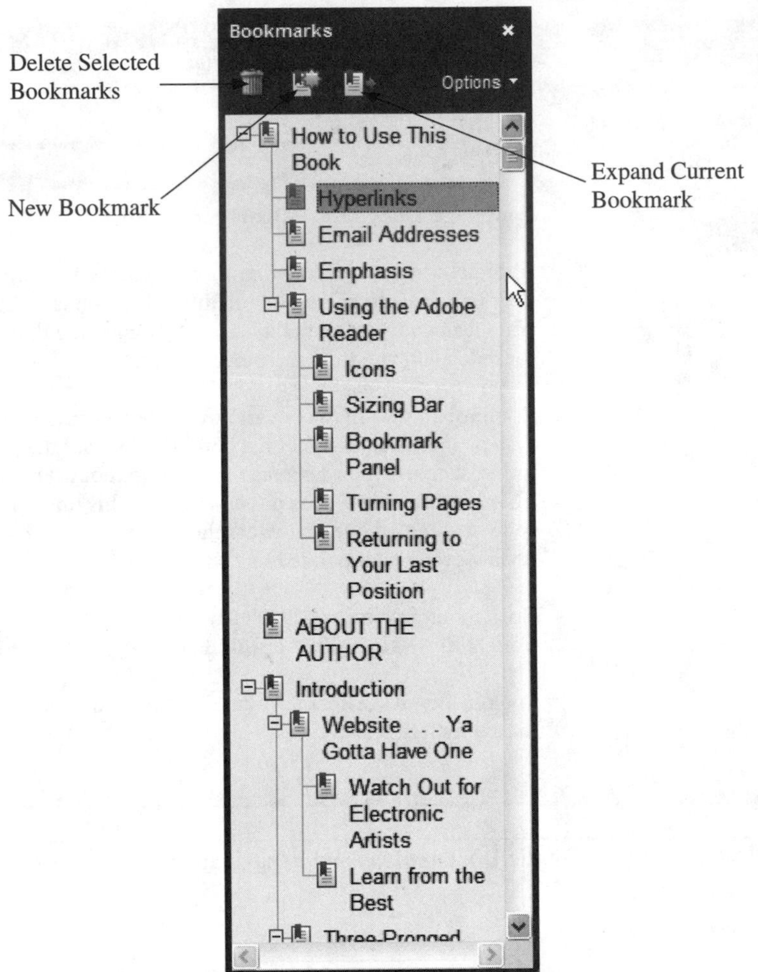

From left to right, you have the following at your disposal:

- **Delete Bookmarks** Click this icon to delete selected bookmarks.
- **New Bookmark** Click this icon to create a new bookmark. Specific instructions for creating bookmarks are presented in the upcoming section, "Create Bookmarks."
- **Expand Current Bookmark** Click this icon to expand the currently selected bookmark, which enables you to view bookmarks nested within a bookmark.

- **Options** Click the text icon to open the Bookmarks panel Options menu.
- **Close** Click this icon to close the Bookmarks panel.

Create Bookmarks

A *bookmark* is a text link in the Bookmarks panel of the Navigation pane that viewers of your PDF documents can use to navigate to a specific part of the document. If the bookmarks in the document are created from an authoring application plug-in, the bookmark is linked to a specific part of a document, such as a heading, or, in the case of a document comprised of captured web pages, to a specific web page. Bookmarks can also be configured to link to external PDF documents and other PDF files by modifying the action that occurs when the bookmark is clicked.

You can, however, create your own bookmarks to draw a viewer's attention to a specific place in the document. You can also use bookmarks to open other PDF documents or other files. To create a document bookmark, do the following:

1. Open the Navigation pane and click the Bookmarks icon to open the Bookmarks panel.
2. Click the bookmark above the place where you want the new bookmark to appear. If you don't specify a place for the new bookmark, it's added at the bottom of the list.
3. Use the Hand tool, Viewing tools, or menu commands to navigate to the part of the document where you want the bookmark to link. Note, you can also use existing bookmarks and thumbnails to navigate to desired parts of the document.

TIP *Remember, you can also link to a magnified view of a page to direct the reader's attention. You can magnify the page view by using the Zoom tool.*

4. Click the New Bookmark icon (introduced in the previous section). Or, click the Options icon and choose New Bookmark from the Bookmarks Options menu. Either way, the new bookmark appears below the bookmark you selected when you clicked the icon. Acrobat gives the new bookmark the default name of Untitled, and the bookmark name is highlighted, indicating you can edit the default title.
5. Enter the desired name for the new bookmark and press ENTER or RETURN. When choosing a name for a bookmark, remember to choose a name that accurately reflects the contents of the bookmark. Your viewers will rely on the bookmark title to get an idea of what they can expect to find when they click the bookmark.

NOTE *You will not be able to add a bookmark to a document that has security settings that prohibit editing of the document.*

Create Bookmarks from Document Structure

If the program used to create the PDF document didn't create bookmarks to your satisfaction, you can add additional bookmarks by using the method described in the preceding section, or you can automate the process by choosing certain elements from the document structure—such as headings—to create bookmarks. You can create bookmarks from the document structure only if you enabled the Enable Accessibility And Reflow With Tagged PDF option when choosing conversion settings in the authoring application from which you created the PDF. To create bookmarks from the document structure, do the following:

1. Open the document for which you want to create bookmarks.
2. In the Navigation pane, click the Bookmarks icon to open the Bookmarks panel.
3. Click the Options drop-down arrow and choose New Bookmarks From Structure to open the Structure Elements dialog box:

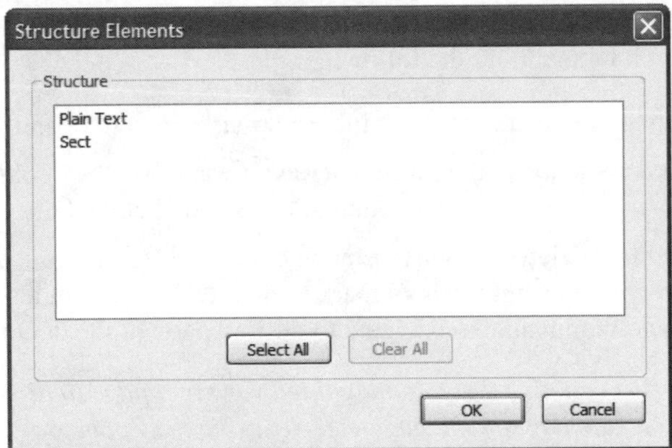

NOTE *The New Bookmarks From Structure command is dimmed out if the document doesn't have elements that Acrobat can use to create bookmarks.*

4. Click a structure element name to select it. To add additional structure elements, hold down SHIFT and click to add contiguous elements, or hold down CTRL (WINDOWS) or CMD (MACINTOSH), and then click to add noncontiguous elements. To select all structure elements, click the Select All button.
5. Click OK, and Acrobat scans the document and creates a bookmark for each selected structure element located. The bookmarks are untitled and nested in tree fashion. Click the plus sign (+) to the left of the top element to expand the first bookmark, as shown in the following illustration. The bookmarks in this illustration were created from a PDF file of this chapter, as created in Word, using the Caption structure element that notes where the figures and illustrations are inserted.

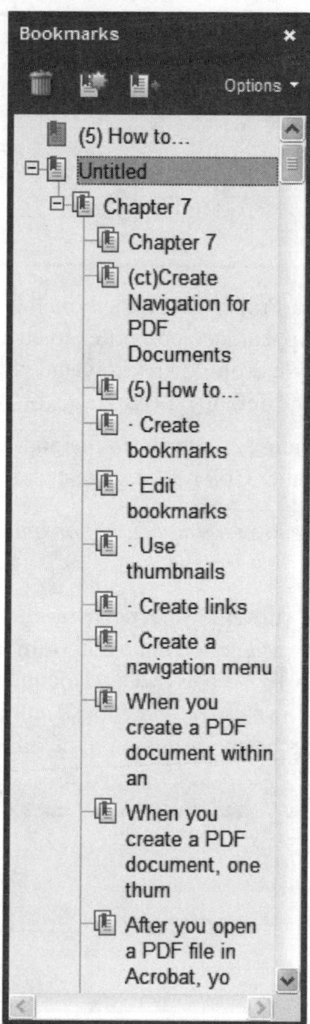

Modify Bookmark Properties

After you create a bookmark, you can modify it by changing its properties. You can modify the appearance of the bookmark, modify the view of the bookmark destination, and modify the action that occurs when a user clicks the bookmark. To change bookmark properties:

1. Click the bookmark whose properties you want to modify.
2. Click the Options drop-down arrow and choose Properties to open the Bookmark Properties dialog box, shown below. Or, you can right-click (Windows) or CTRL-click (Macintosh) a bookmark and choose Properties from the context menu.

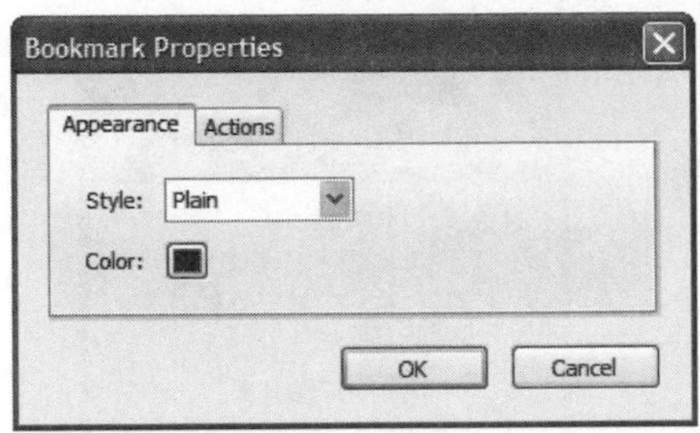

3. When you open the Bookmark Properties dialog box, the Appearance tab is selected by default. You can modify the Appearance properties to change the look of the selected bookmark's text. Click the Style drop-down arrow and choose one of the following from the drop-down menu: Plain (the default), Bold, Italic, or Bold & Italic.
4. Click the Color swatch and choose a color from the pop-up palette. You can choose one of the preset colors or click Other Color to create a custom color from the color picker.

TIP *You can direct a reader's attention to important bookmarks by changing the bookmark's text style and color.*

5. Click the Actions tab, and the currently selected action for the bookmark is displayed, as shown next. If the bookmark was created in an authoring application, the action shown in the Actions area is usually Go To A Page In This Document. To select a different action, click the Select Action drop-down arrow and choose an option from the drop-down menu. The other available actions are discussed in detail in Chapter 8.

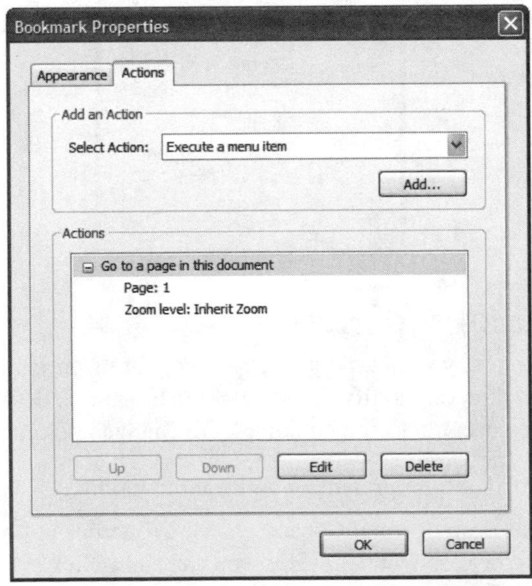

6. Click Edit to open the Go To A Page In This Document dialog box.
7. Enter the number of the page you want to open when the bookmark is clicked.

8. Click the Zoom drop-down arrow and choose an option from the drop-down menu. For more information on the magnification options, refer to the section "Change Bookmark Zoom Settings."
9. Click OK to close the Go To A Page In This Document dialog box, and then click Close to exit the Bookmark Properties dialog box and apply your changes.

TIP *You can change the size of bookmark text by selecting one or more bookmarks, and then choosing an option from the Text Size submenu of the Bookmark panels Options menu. Your options are Small, Medium (the default option), or Large.*

Use the Bookmarks Options Menu

You use the Bookmarks Options menu to perform functions associated with bookmarks. You can use commands from the Bookmarks Options menu to modify bookmarks, navigate to bookmarks, and maintain the Bookmarks panel.

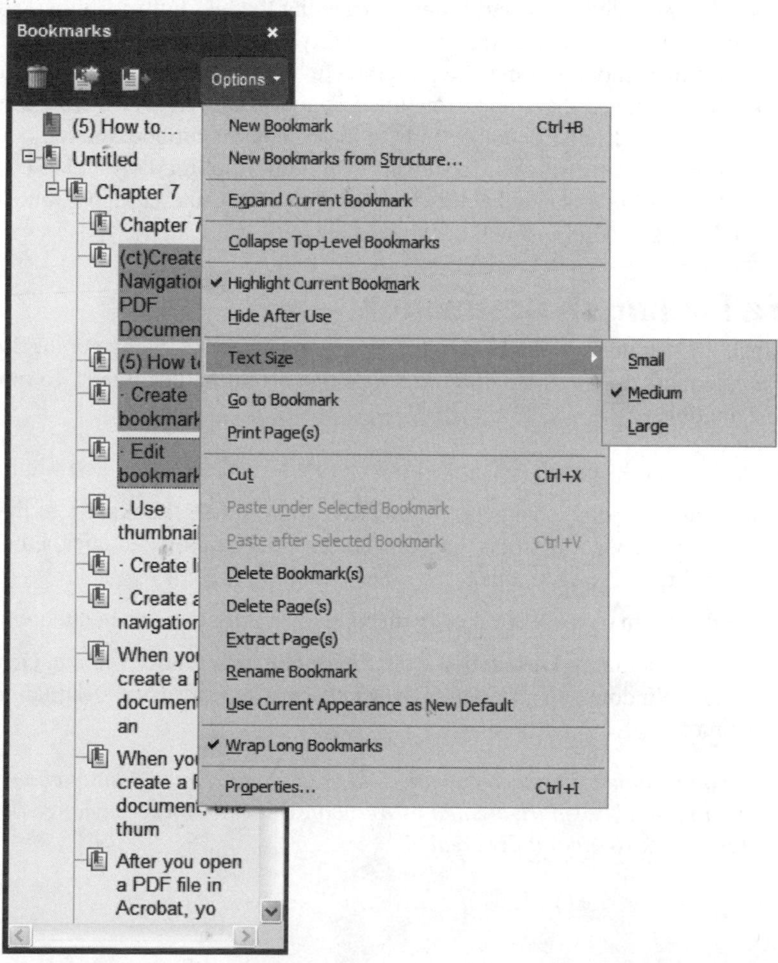

1. To open the Bookmarks Options menu, click Bookmarks in the Navigation pane to open the Bookmarks panel, and then click the Options icon.
2. After you open the Bookmarks Options menu, click the menu command you want Acrobat to perform. Some of the commands in this menu were already presented; others will do the same job as their toolbar counterparts. For example, to expand a bookmark, you can click the plus sign next to a collapsed bookmark, or choose the Expand Current Bookmark command from the Bookmarks Options menu. Detailed information about other relevant Bookmarks Options menu commands are discussed in upcoming sections.

TIP *If you're viewing a document with long bookmarks that aren't completely visible in the Bookmarks panel, choose Wrap Long Bookmarks from the Bookmarks Options menu.*

Edit Bookmarks

You can edit existing bookmarks by changing the bookmark destination, renaming the bookmarks, deleting selected bookmarks, and rearranging the hierarchy of bookmarks. When you add new bookmarks to a document, you can specify the bookmark destination and view magnification. At times, though, it may be preferable to lay out the document structure by creating bookmarks first, and then modifying the destination and view of the bookmarks later. You can use the Bookmarks panel toolbar and Options menu to edit bookmarks. You can also right-click (Windows) or CTRL-click (Macintosh) within the Bookmarks panel to choose a command from the Bookmarks panel context menu, which is a watered-down, but still useful, version of the Bookmarks Options menu.

Change a Bookmark Destination

You can change the destination of a bookmark, change its zoom, or change both. By modifying the view of a bookmark, you call attention to a specific part of the document. To modify a bookmark destination:

1. On the Bookmarks panel, select the bookmark whose destination you want to modify.
2. In the Document pane, change to the location you want the bookmark to link to by using the Hand tool, navigation tools, or menu commands. Or, you can click a thumbnail in the Pages panel to navigate to a page.
3. Change the zoom of the document by using the viewing tools or menu commands.
4. Choose Set Bookmark Destination from the Bookmarks Options menu. Or, you can right-click (Windows) or CTRL-click (Macintosh) and choose Set Destination from the context menu.

NOTE *When you combine files such as images to create a PDF, you cannot change the destination of a bookmark created by Acrobat. You can however change the destination of a bookmark you manually created.*

Rename a Bookmark

Another edit you may need to perform is to rename a bookmark. You have two methods available to change a bookmark name:

1. Select the bookmark, and then click inside the text box to select the bookmark text.
2. Enter a new name for the bookmark, and then press ENTER or RETURN.

   Or, you can

1. Select the bookmark, and then choose Rename Bookmark from the Bookmarks Options menu to select the bookmark text.
2. Enter a new name for the bookmark, and then press ENTER or RETURN.

Delete a Bookmark

You can delete any bookmark. When you delete a bookmark, you don't change the content of a document; you merely remove a link. If you created a PDF document that has several heading levels, you may want to consider deleting a few bookmarks to simplify navigation.

There is no warning before the bookmark is deleted. If you delete a bookmark in error, choose Edit | Undo Delete Bookmark or press CTRL-Z immediately after deleting the bookmark.

1. Select the bookmark. To add contiguous bookmarks to the selection, press SHIFT and click the bookmark(s) you want to add to the selection. To add noncontiguous bookmarks to the selection, press CTRL and click the bookmark(s) you want to add to the selection.
2. Choose Edit | Delete, press DELETE, or click the Delete Selected Bookmarks icon (looks like a trash can). Or, you can choose Delete Selected Bookmarks from the Options menu.

Arrange Bookmarks

When you create a PDF document, bookmarks are created in descending order from the first page of the document to the last. Acrobat nests bookmarks when you convert a document with multiple heading levels, or if you use the New Bookmarks From Structure command. You can create your own bookmark nests to organize a cluttered Bookmarks panel. To nest a bookmark or group of bookmarks under another bookmark:

1. Select the bookmark(s) you want to nest. You can select contiguous (SHIFT-click) or noncontiguous (CTRL-click) bookmarks.
2. Click-and-drag the bookmarks toward the bookmark under which you want to nest them. As you drag the bookmarks toward another bookmark, a left-pointing arrowhead with a dashed line appears.

3. Drag right so that the left pointing arrow appears to the right of the bookmark icon. If you don't do this, you're merely changing the order in which bookmarks appear rather than nesting a bookmark within another bookmark.
4. Release the mouse button when you reach the desired bookmark location. As soon as you release the mouse button, Acrobat nests the bookmark(s) in the new location. If the bookmark to which you're nesting is collapsed, Acrobat expands it. Collapse the bookmark by clicking the minus sign (–) to its left.

TIP *To create another level of bookmarks, follow the previous steps and drag the bookmark to the right to indent it another level.*

Remove a bookmark from a nested position by doing the following:

1. Expand the bookmark that contains the bookmark(s) you want to remove from a nested position.
2. Select the bookmark(s) you want to move.
3. Drag the bookmarks under the minus sign up and to the left of the parent bookmark.

NOTE *When you select and drag a branch that has children, the children of the parent are moved as well, maintaining the structure of the branch.*

4. Release the mouse button, and Acrobat moves the bookmark(s) out of a nested position.

Change Bookmark Zoom Settings

When you create or edit a bookmark, you can control the magnification setting of the bookmark destination. You can change magnification in the Zoom field of the Go To A Page In This Document dialog box, which can be accessed as follows:

1. Select the bookmark from within the Bookmarks panel whose zoom settings you want to modify.
2. Right-click (Windows) or CTRL-click (Macintosh) the bookmark and choose Properties from the context menu. After choosing this command, the applicable Properties dialog box appears with the previously used tab displayed. If it isn't already displayed, click the Actions tab.
3. Select the Go To A Page In This Document action from the list of actions assigned to the bookmark.
4. Click Edit to open the Go To A Page In This Document dialog box.

5. Click the Zoom drop-down arrow and choose one of the following options:
   - **Fit Page** Sizes the visible contents of the bookmark or link destination to fit the Document pane.
   - **Actual Size** Displays a selected link or bookmark destination at 100 percent magnification, the original size of the document.
   - **Fit Width** Zooms a selected link or bookmark destination to the current width of the Document pane. If you choose this option, images on the page may be pixelated. An image becomes pixelated when it is enlarged enough to make the individual pixels appear as square blocks of color. At normal magnification, pixels are blended so they aren't visible.
   - **Fit Visible** Zooms a selected link or bookmark destination so all visible elements on the page resize to the current width of the Document pane. Note, this view will differ at different monitor resolutions.
   - **Inherit Zoom** Displays a selected link or bookmark destination at the viewer-selected magnification level.
6. Click OK to close the Go To A Page In This Document dialog box, and then click Close to apply the zoom settings to the bookmark or link.

Use the Pages Panel

When you convert a file to PDF format and open the document in Acrobat, a thumbnail for each page is automatically generated. Thumbnails are neatly arranged by page order in the Pages panel, which resides in the Navigation pane. You can use thumbnails as navigation devices when reading a document, as well as to reorder pages, a technique discussed in Chapter 9. Thumbnails are also used to print and change the magnification of pages. To access the Pages panel, choose

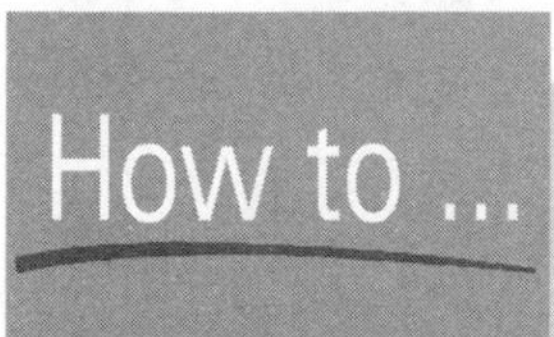

Change Page Magnification with Thumbnails

When you select a thumbnail, a red border appears, which signifies the current view of the page. You can change page magnification by clicking-and-dragging the red border's lower-right corner. After you change the page magnification, the shape and size of the red rectangle changes to reflect the current page view. Move your cursor toward any rectangle border. When your cursor becomes an open fist, click-and-drag to pan to a different view.

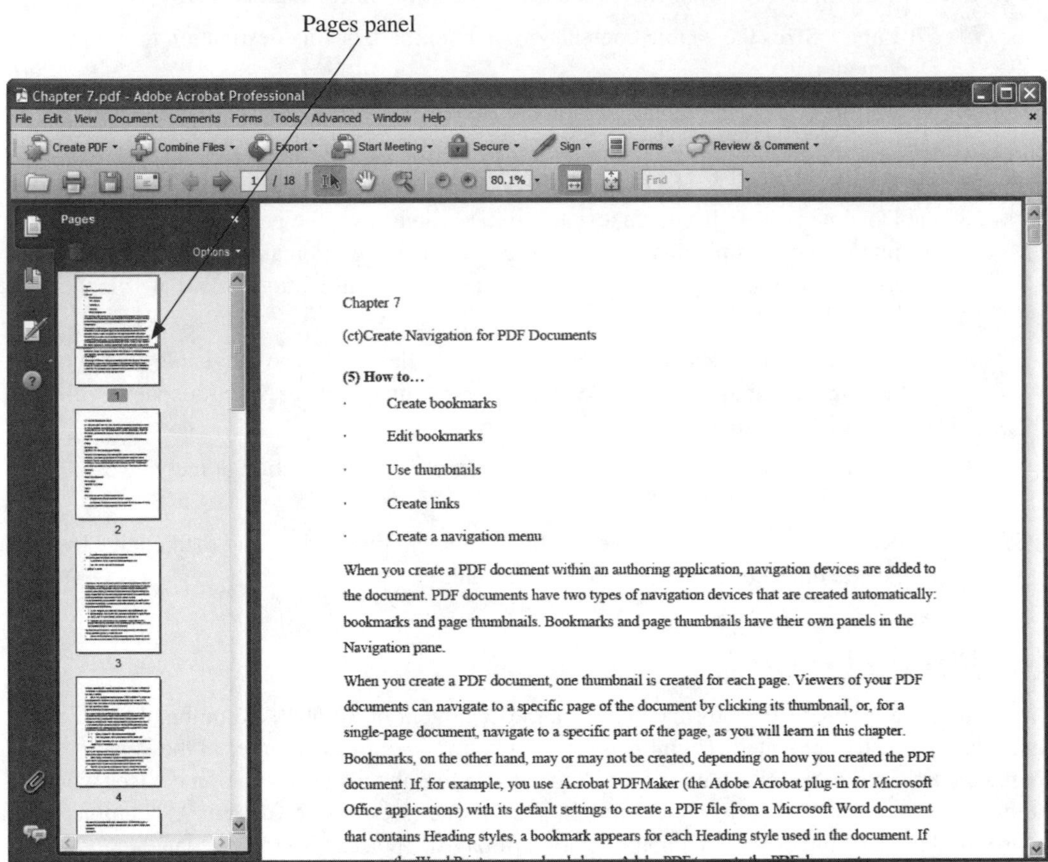

FIGURE 7-2 Use page thumbnails to navigate and edit a PDF document.

View | Navigation Panels | Pages. If the Navigation pane is open, but another pane is displayed, click the Pages icon to open the panel. Figure 7-2 shows the Pages panel with the default thumbnail size.

Use the Pages Panel Options Menu

The Pages panel has a menu you can use to perform tasks, such as edit pages, embed thumbnails or remove embedded thumbnails, and change the size of thumbnails. In upcoming sections, you learn how to use the commands that pertain to editing thumbnails. In Chapter 9, you learn how to use thumbnails to edit and reorder document pages.

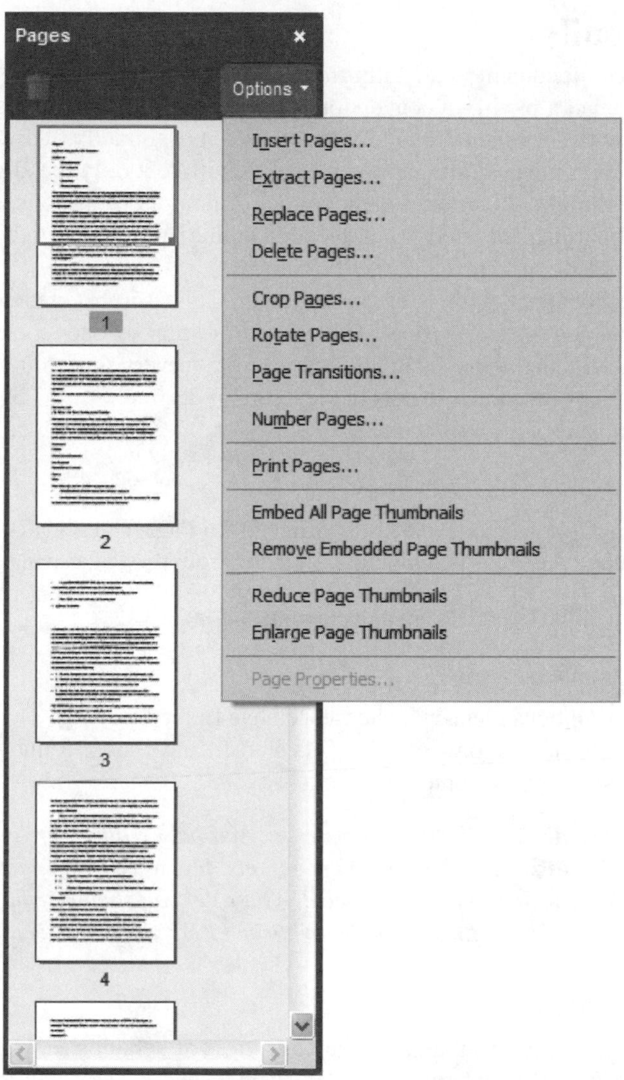

To open the Pages Options menu, open the Pages panel, and then click the Options icon.

Alternatively, with no thumbnail selected, you can right-click (Windows) or CTRL-click (Macintosh) within the Pages panel to open a Context menu. The Pages panel context menu is a watered-down version of the Pages Options menu. However, you may prefer to use the context menu when you need to access its commands quickly. You can access the complete version of the Pages Options menu by selecting a thumbnail, and then right-clicking (Windows) or CTRL-clicking (Macintosh).

Create Thumbnails

When you create a PDF document in an authoring application or by using the Adobe Acrobat PDFMaker plug-in, you can modify a conversion setting to embed thumbnails. Thumbnails increase the file size of the published PDF document by approximately 2KB or more per thumbnail for a page with images; thumbnails for pages with text only are slightly smaller. The actual size of the thumbnail varies, depending on the amount of graphics in the page from which the thumbnail is generated. An embedded thumbnail for a page with text only is about 0.5KB.

When you create a document without embedded thumbnails, Acrobat creates them dynamically when you open the Pages panel. This can take several seconds for a large document. You can choose to embed thumbnails to circumvent the redraw every time you open the panel. You can easily remove embedded thumbnails in the future, if desired.

To embed all thumbnails within a document:

1. Open the Pages panel as outlined previously.
2. Open the Pages Options menu and choose Embed All Page Thumbnails. Or, you can choose the Embed All Page Thumbnails command from the Pages panel context menu.

To remove embedded thumbnails from a document:

1. Open the Pages panel.
2. Open the Pages Options menu and choose Remove Embedded Page Thumbnails. Or, you can right-click (Windows) or CTRL-click (Macintosh) and choose Remove Embedded Page Thumbnails from the context menu.

After you remove thumbnails from a document, Acrobat creates them on the fly whenever the Pages panel is opened. As mentioned previously, this may take considerable time with a lengthy document. As a rule, you should remove embedded thumbnails only when the file size of the published PDF document is a factor.

Resize Thumbnails

When you open the Pages panel, all thumbnails are displayed at default size. Unless you resize the width of the Navigation pane, the thumbnails are displayed in a single column. If you prefer, you can display more thumbnails in the Navigation pane by choosing Reduce Page Thumbnails from the Pages Options menu. After you choose this command, thumbnails are displayed at reduced magnification. To return thumbnails to their original size, or to the next highest level of magnification in the case you've reduced the size several times, choose Enlarge Page Thumbnails from the Pages Options menu.

TIP

You can use the Reduce Page Thumbnails or Enlarge Page Thumbnails command more than once to arrive at the optimum thumbnail size for your working preference.

Create Links

As you already learned, when you convert a document into PDF format, navigation devices in the form of thumbnails and bookmarks are created for you. You can, however, exceed the limitations of these rudimentary navigation devices by creating links. When you create a *link,* you create an area in the document that, when a viewer pauses their cursor over the hotspot, the cursor icon becomes a hand with a pointing finger; the same thing that happens when you pause your cursor over a link on a web page. You can create links for text or images in a PDF document or create any other kind of link anywhere in the document. The links you create can be visible or invisible.

Links give you tremendous flexibility. You can create links that change the view of a document, load another document, open a web page, load a multimedia element, and more. You can specify the appearance of a link as a visible or invisible rectangle, as well as specify the type of highlight that appears when a user's cursor hovers over the link. The first step in creating a link is to define the active area of the link, also known as a hotspot.

Create a Hotspot

As it relates to PDF documents, a *hotspot* is an active area of the document that, when clicked by a user, causes an action to occur. You create a hotspot with the Link tool, found in the Advanced Editing submenu of the Tools menu group and on the Advanced Editing toolbar. The Link tool looks like two interconnecting links of a chain. Use the Link tool to define the boundary of the hotspot as follows:

1. Choose Tools | Advanced Editing | Link Tool. After you select the tool and move your cursor into the Document pane, it becomes a crosshair. As long as the Link tool is selected, any other links in the document, even invisible ones, are displayed.
2. In the Document pane, click a spot to define one of the hotspot corners, and then drag diagonally. As you drag, you see a bounding box, which displays the current area of the selection.
3. When the bounding box surrounds the area you want to define as a hotspot, release the mouse button. After you create the hotspot, the Create Link dialog box appears.

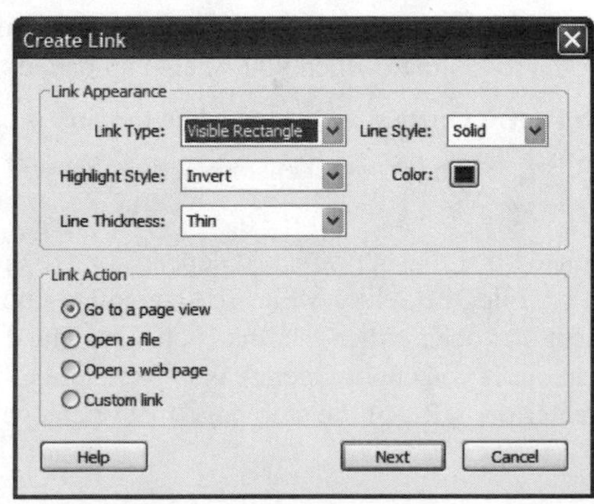

4. In the Link Appearance area of the Create Link dialog box, click the Link Type drop-down arrow and choose one of the following:
   - **Visible Rectangle** This option creates a hotspot with a visible rectangle at its perimeter.
   - **Invisible Rectangle** This option creates a hotspot that isn't visible. If you choose Invisible Rectangle, the Width, Color, and Style options aren't valid and are no longer displayed.
5. Click the Highlight Style drop-down arrow and choose one of the following options to determine how the link is highlighted when users click it:
   - **None** No highlight appears when the link is clicked.
   - **Invert** The link is highlighted in black when clicked.
   - **Outline** The link outline color changes when clicked.
   - **Inset** A shadow appears when the link is clicked. This effect is similar to a web page button that appears to recess into the page when clicked.
6. If you chose Visible Rectangle, click the Line Thickness drop-down arrow and choose Thin, Medium, or Thick. This option defines the thickness of the hotspot border.
7. Click the Line Style drop-down arrow and choose Solid, Dashed, or Underline. This option defines the line style for the hotspot border.
8. Click the Color swatch and choose the rectangle color from the pop-up palette. To choose a color other than the presets, click Other Color, and choose a color from the system color picker.
9. Choose one of the following from the Link Action area to specify what happens when the link is clicked:
   - **Go To A Page View** Enables you to specify which page will appear and at what zoom setting when the link is clicked.
   - **Open A File** Loads a file when the link is clicked. If you choose this option, Acrobat creates a link to the file, including the absolute path of the file. Use this option when the document will be viewed only on the computer where the document is created, or at a web site to which you've also uploaded the file to be opened.
   - **Open A Web Page** Opens a web page when the link is clicked.
   - **Custom Link** Lets you choose a custom action that will occur when the link is clicked.
10. Click Next. The dialog box that appears next depends on the option you selected in Step 9. If you chose Open A File, the Select A File To Open dialog box appears, enabling you to select the document that opens when the link is clicked. The document is opened in the associated application. If you chose Open A Web Page, the Edit URL dialog box appears, enabling you to enter the URL of the web page that opens when the link is clicked.

If you chose Custom Link, the Link Properties dialog box appears, enabling you to choose the action that executes when the link is clicked, as well as modify the appearance of the link. Custom links are discussed in detail in Chapter 8. If you chose the default, Go To A Page View, the Create Go To View dialog box appears, shown next. The remaining steps are based on this choice.

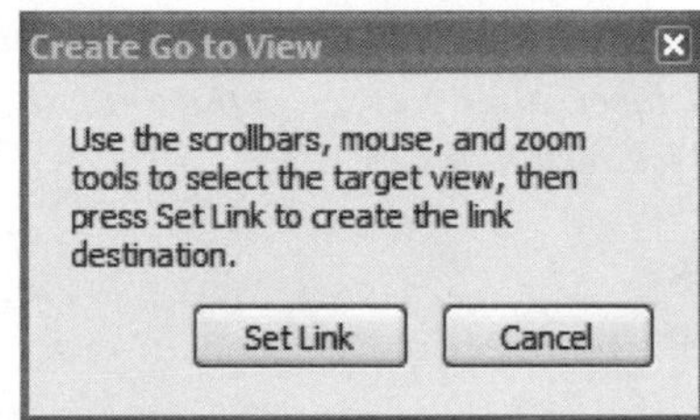

11. Navigate to the desired page by using the Hand tool, scrolling with the scroll bars, or clicking a page thumbnail.
12. Zoom to the desired magnification.
13. Click Set Link to close the Create Go To View dialog box.
14. Select the Hand tool and click the link to test it. If the link doesn't perform as you expected, you can edit the link by following the instructions in the upcoming section "Edit Links."

If you plan to add or edit extensive links in a document, you can save time by choosing Tools | Advanced Editing | Show Advanced Editing Toolbar. This command displays the Advanced Editing toolbar in the last position in which it appeared in the workspace, giving you easy access to the Link tool.

Did you know?

You Can Create Links with the Select Tool

You can quickly create a link by selecting text or a graphic element, such as a logo or photo, with the Select tool. After selecting text or a graphic element with the tool, right-click (Windows) or CTRL-click (Macintosh), and then choose Create Link from the context menu. After the Create Link From Selection dialog box appears, follow the instructions starting at Step 4 in the section "Create a Hotspot" to finish the process.

Edit Links

When the need arises, you can edit any property of a link. You can resize the link, change its destination, change the level of magnification, or change the appearance of the link. When you edit a link, the changes apply only to the selected link.

If you're editing multiple objects in a document, such as links, graphic objects, text objects, and so on you can use the Select Object tool from the Advanced Editing toolbar to select and edit an object. After you select the tool, all objects in the document are highlighted with a black rectangle.

Change Link Properties

To change link properties, do the following:

1. Choose Tools | Advanced Editing | Link Tool, or select the Link tool from the Advanced Editing toolbar if it's available in the workspace.
2. Double-click the link you want to edit, which opens the Link Properties dialog box. Or, you can right-click (Windows) or CTRL-click (Macintosh) the link, and then choose Properties from the context menu.
3. Modify the Link Properties as described in the previous section "Create a Hotspot."

After you edit a link and it's performing as you want it to, you can prevent inadvertently moving the link or otherwise editing it by right-clicking (Windows) or CTRL-clicking (Macintosh) the link with the Link tool, choosing Properties from the context menu, and then clicking the Locked check box in the Link Properties dialog box.

Resize a Hotspot

When you use the Link tool to create a hotspot, the resulting hotspot may not be sized properly. It's better to make the hotspot a tad larger than needed, unless you have several hotspots in close proximity. You can change the size of a hotspot at any time, but you cannot resize a locked link.

1. Choose Tools | Advanced Editing | Link Tool, or select the Link tool from the Advanced Editing toolbar if it's available in the workspace.
2. Click the hotspot you want to resize. After you click the hotspot, eight handles in the form of solid red rectangles appear on the hotspot perimeter. Click-and-drag any of the corner hotspots. Pressing SHIFT while you drag resizes the hotspot proportionately. Click the handle in the middle of the side of the hotspot and drag to resize the width of the hotspot. Click the handle in the middle of the top or bottom of the hotspot, and then drag to make the hotspot taller or shorter.

Delete a Link

If you decide a link is no longer needed, you can delete it from the document by doing the following:

1. Choose Tools | Advanced Editing | Link Tool, or select the Link Tool from the Advanced Editing toolbar if it's available in the workspace.
2. Select the link you want to delete, and then choose Edit | Delete. Or, select the link, right-click (Windows) or CTRL-click (Macintosh), and choose Edit | Delete from the context menu or simply press DELETE.

TIP

After you press DELETE, Acrobat does not display a warning dialog box asking you to confirm the action. If you delete a link in error, choose Edit | Undo or press CTRL-Z before performing another task.

Create a Menu Using Links

When you create a PDF document, you can, of course, rely on the Acrobat built-in navigation devices: bookmarks and thumbnails. If your intended audience is unfamiliar with Adobe Reader, though, your document will be easier to navigate if you create a menu.

If you create a document in a word processing program, you can create a menu page as the first page of the document. On the menu page, list the major parts of the document you want your readers to be able to select by clicking links. Create the rest of the document, convert it to PDF by using the application's Print command, and then choose Adobe PDF as the printing device. Or, if the application supports it, convert the document to PDF by using the application's Save As or Export command. If you're creating the document in Microsoft Word, you can click the Convert To Adobe PDF button. Open the document in Acrobat and use the Link tool to create a link for each menu item. After you create the links for the menu page, choose File | Document Properties. In the Initial View section of the Document Open Options dialog box, choose Page Only for the Show option. Click OK to close the dialog box, and then save the document. When your viewers open the document, the first thing they see is your menu page with the Navigation pane closed.

Summary

In this chapter, you learned how to work with bookmarks and page thumbnails, as well as how to create links. You learned how to use these objects as navigation devices and assign actions to these items to turn them into interactive devices. In the next chapter, you learn how to work with other navigation elements and specify document Open options.

Chapter 8

Create Interactive PDF Navigation

How to...

- Use actions
- Add JavaScript to documents
- Create articles
- Use named destinations
- Modify Open options

In Chapter 7, you learned how to add navigation to your documents by using bookmarks, page thumbnails, and links. You can take PDF navigation to the next level when you use actions. Adding actions to a PDF document lets you open files, play media, navigate to web sites, and more when a link or bookmark is clicked. You can assign multiple actions to a link or bookmark. You can also assign actions to page thumbnails to trigger an action when a page is opened or closed.

In this chapter, you find out how to work with actions. You learn how to add them to links, bookmarks, and page thumbnails. You also learn how to work with JavaScript. Acrobat features extensive JavaScript support. Another topic of discussion is the *Article tool,* which you use to create linked threads of text and graphics in different parts of the document. *Article threads* are much like magazine articles, where the topic of discussion begins on one page and is continued many pages later. You also learn how to add named destinations to your documents, which are also navigation devices. Toward the end of the chapter, you find out how to modify the view of a PDF document when it's opened.

Work with Actions

When you create a link or bookmark, the default action is Go To A Page View. However, Acrobat supplies you with a plethora of actions from which to choose that enable you to assign different actions to a link or bookmark, as well as add additional actions to these navigation items. You can also apply actions to form fields (Professional only) and individual pages. When you apply an action to a page, the action determines what the viewer sees or what happens when the page is opened or exited.

You set actions for bookmarks and links in their respective Properties dialog boxes within the Select Action field of the Actions tab. You can also add actions to individual pages of the document. For more information on page actions, refer to the upcoming section "Set a Page Action." To learn more about assigning actions to form fields, see Chapter 14. To add interactivity to a link, bookmark, form field, or page, choose from the following actions:

- **Execute A Menu Item** Use this action to execute a menu command. Even though you can choose any Acrobat command to execute as an action, the most logical choices would be to open another file, choose one of the navigation options from the Document menu, or choose one of the magnification options from the View menu.

NOTE *If you distribute your document to users with Adobe Reader, make sure the menu command you choose is also an Adobe Reader menu command.*

- **Go To A 3D View** Go To A 3D View switches to a view of a 3D file in the *.U3D format*, which is a 3D file you've embedded in the document. You can select which one of the 3D views are displayed when the action executes.
- **Go To A Page View** In most applicable dialog boxes, this is the default action. Use this action to advance to another page or view in the current document or another PDF file.
- **Import Form Data** Use this action to specify a file from which to import form data. The imported data is inserted in the active form. For more information on working with forms, see Chapter 14.
- **Open A File** Use this action to open a file when the action is triggered. The opened file is viewed in its native application. Use this action only when the PDF file is viewed on the same machine on which the file was created, from a CD disk to which the file has been added, or from a web site to which the file to be opened has been uploaded.
- **Open A Web Link** Use this action when you want to open a web page from a web site. When you choose this action, you are prompted for the URL of the web link you want to open when the action executes.
- **Play A Sound** Use this action to play a sound file. If you add this action to a document, the document must be viewed on the machine used to create the PDF file, or from a web site from which the PDF file is to be opened and to which the sound file have both been uploaded.
- **Play Media (Acrobat 5 Compatible)** Use this action to execute a QuickTime or AVI movie. To use this action, you must have a QuickTime or AVI movie within the document. For more information on adding movies to your PDF documents, see Chapter 17.
- **Play Media (Acrobat 6 And Later Compatible)** Use this action to play any Acrobat 6 and later-compatible media. To use this action, you must have the media within the document. For more information on adding Acrobat 6 and later-compatible media to your PDF documents, see Chapter 17.
- **Read An Article** Use this action to read an article when the action is executed. After choosing this action, a dialog box appears with a list of articles in the document. For more information on creating articles, refer to the section "Create a Thread of Linked Articles."
- **Reset A Form** Use this action to clear all previously entered data in a form.
- **Run A JavaScript** Use this action to run a JavaScript. When you choose this option, you can create or edit a JavaScript from within the JavaScript Editor.
- **Set Layer Visibility** Use this action to set the visibility for a layer in the document.
- **Show/Hide A Field** Use this action to toggle the visibility of a form field in the document when the link is clicked.
- **Submit A Form** Use this action with a button to submit data from a form to a URL.

Use Page Actions

You can make your PDF documents more interactive by specifying an action to occur when a page opens or closes. For example, you can use an action to play a movie when a page opens and play a sound when a page closes.

Set a Page Action

You use the Page Properties dialog box to specify one or more actions that occur when a page opens or closes. If you choose multiple actions, you can edit the order in which the actions execute. To set a page action, follow these steps:

1. Choose the page to which you want to assign the action by selecting its thumbnail in the Pages panel of the Navigation pane.
2. Choose Page Properties from the Pages Options menu to open the Page Properties dialog box, and then click the Actions tab to reconfigure the Page Properties dialog box to add page actions, shown in the following illustration. Or, you can right-click (Windows) or CTRL-click (Macintosh) and choose Page Properties from the context menu, and then click the Actions tab if it's not already open.

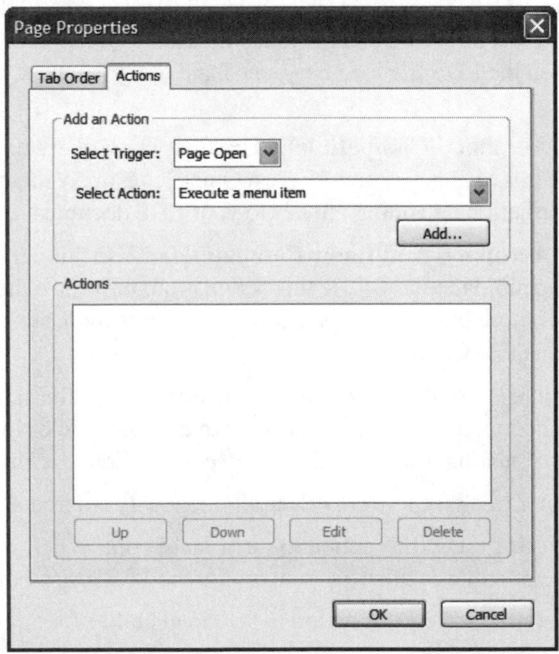

3. Click the Select Trigger drop-down arrow and choose one of the following:

- **Page Open** Executes an action when a page loads.
- **Page Close** Executes an action when a page closes.

4. Click the Select Action drop-down arrow and select an action from the drop-down menu, as shown here:

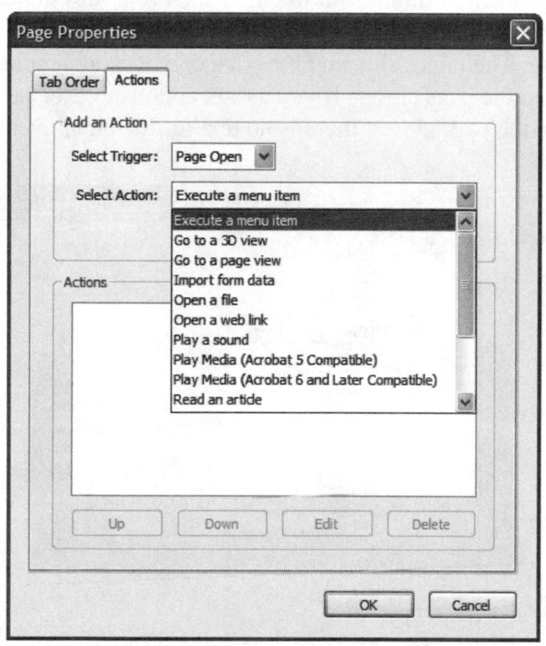

5. Click Add to add the action to the events that occur when the page opens or closes. This opens a dialog box for the selected action, in which you set the action's parameters.
6. After setting an action's parameters, click OK to apply the changes and exit the action's dialog box.
7. Repeat Steps 4-6 to add additional actions to the list.
8. Click Close to exit the Page Properties dialog box.
9. Save the document.

The next time you open the document and select the page to which you applied the actions, they execute.

Edit Actions

The majority of time, when you assign actions to a bookmark, link, or page, they perform without a hitch. However, sometimes the actions don't execute in proper order, or you may

8

decide to delete or add an action. When this occurs, you can easily edit actions by doing the following:

1. Select the bookmark, link, or page thumbnail to which you applied the actions.
2. Right-click (Windows) or CTRL-click (Macintosh) and choose Properties from the context menu. The following illustration shows the Page Properties dialog box, as it appears when actions have been applied to a page. Notice the minus sign (–) next to Page Open and Page Close. The minus sign signifies that one or more actions occur when the page opens and when the page closes. If you assign actions to execute only when the page opens or when the page closes, there is no text for the other event.

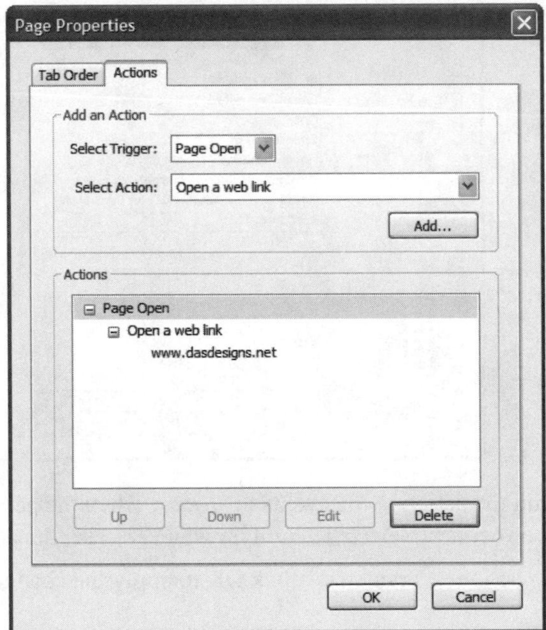

3. In the Actions window, select the event you want to modify.
4. To add an action, select it from the Select Action drop-down menu, and then click Add. This opens the selected action's dialog box. Set any parameters for the action as outlined earlier in this chapter.
5. To delete an action, select it, and then click Delete.
6. To edit an action, select the desired action, and then click Edit. This opens the dialog box for the action, which enables you to modify the action to suit your document.
7. To rearrange the order in which actions execute, select an action and click Up or Down. If the action is at the top of the list, only the Down button will be available, and vice

versa if the action is at the bottom of the list. If the action is in the middle of the list, both buttons are available. If only one action exists for a trigger, both buttons are dimmed out.

8. When you finish editing the actions for the bookmark, link, or page, click OK.

Use JavaScript Actions

You can add functionality and interactivity to your PDF document by creating JavaScript code to access database information, control document navigation, access information from the Internet, and more. In Acrobat 8.0, you have more JavaScript Actions to work with than ever before.

JavaScript is an object-oriented programming language. If you have designed web pages, you may be familiar with JavaScript. Each JavaScript object has associated methods and properties. Acrobat JavaScript uses standard JavaScript objects and has its own set of unique objects, such as the Bookmark object. Unfortunately, a detailed discussion of using JavaScript with Acrobat is beyond the scope of this book.

Create a JavaScript Action

You can use the JavaScript Action with form fields (Professional only), bookmarks, and links; or you can create global JavaScript that can be used for an entire document. When you choose the JavaScript Action, you create the actual script in a text editor known as the *JavaScript Editor.* As previously mentioned, there are myriad uses for JavaScript with PDF documents. The following steps show how to create a link and use JavaScript to navigate to a specific page when a link is clicked:

1. Choose Tools | Advanced Editing | Link Tool, or select the Link tool from the Advanced Editing toolbar if you have it floating in the workspace.
2. Create a link around the text or image that will trigger the JavaScript. This opens the Link Properties dialog box.
3. Click the Custom Link radio button, and then click Next to open the Link Properties dialog box.
4. Click the Actions tab.
5. Click the Select Action drop-down arrow, choose Run A JavaScript from the drop-down menu, and then click Add. The JavaScript Editor opens.
6. Enter the following JavaScript: `this.pageNum = x`, where *x* is the page number you want displayed when the JavaScript executes. When you enter the page number for a document, always subtract one from the page number you want to open when the

JavaScript executes. You need to do this because the JavaScript language, like most other computer languages, begins indexing with the number 0, so Page 1 is recognized as 0 in JavaScript. The following illustration shows JavaScript code to display Page 4 when the link is clicked:

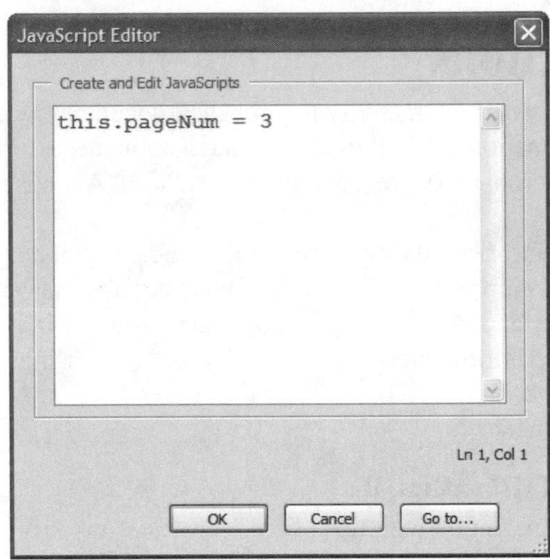

7. Click OK to exit the JavaScript Editor, and then click OK to exit the Link Properties dialog box. When the link is clicked, the desired page is displayed.

Edit a JavaScript Action

When you create complex, multiline JavaScript code, it's easy to make a mistake. If you have Acrobat Professional, you can put the JavaScript Debugger on the case, but if you own Acrobat Standard, you have to unravel your own JavaScript errors. If you mistype a variable name or choose the wrong method for a JavaScript object, your script will fall flatter than a cake without enough baking powder. When this happens, you need to put on your thinking cap, or perhaps deerstalker cap, as you may have to do a bit of Sherlock Holmes-style deducting to figure out where your script went wrong.

To edit a JavaScript Action, select the object to which the JavaScript is assigned and open the Actions tab of the object's Properties dialog box. Select the Run A JavaScript Action, click Edit to reopen the JavaScript Editor dialog box, and then examine the script. Make sure you have chosen the proper JavaScript object and the proper method of the object for the action you want to occur when the script executes. Note, many failed scripts are the result of typographical errors and not choosing the proper case for a JavaScript object. For example, if you refer to pageNum (proper syntax) as pagenum, your script will fail.

How to ...

Master JavaScript

JavaScript is a wonderful tool that you can use to make your PDF documents more interactive, but it does have a learning curve. You can find additional JavaScript information at *http://partners.adobe.com/public/developer/pdf/topic_js.html.* Here, you can download the Acrobat JavaScript Scripting Reference and the Acrobat JavaScript Scripting Guide. If you want to master JavaScript, consider investing in a good book to learn the proper syntax of this programming language. Two books to try are *How To Do Everything with JavaScript,* by Scott Duffy, and *JavaScript: The Complete Reference,* by Thomas Powell and Fritz Schneider, both published by McGraw-Hill/Osborne.

TIP

If you prefer working in a text editor when creating JavaScript, choose Edit | Preferences, and then choose JavaScript. In the JavaScript Editor section, choose Use External JavaScript Editor, and then enter the path to the external editor executable (.exe extension) file, or click the Browse button and navigate to the .exe file that launches the desired text editor. After changing the preference, whenever you edit JavaScript, Acrobat launches the external editor. After you enter the JavaScript, choose the external editor Save command before closing the Properties dialog box for the object to which you applied the JavaScript.

Create a Thread of Linked Articles

You create articles to link blocks of text within a PDF file. If you're creating an e-book in magazine format (an e-magazine, if you will), an article that begins on Page 23, for example, may be divided into sections and the next section may begin on Page 54. To make it easy for the reader to navigate from one part of the article to the next, define the block of the document that is the start of the article, and then define the additional blocks of content that cover the rest of the article.

If you create an e-book for educational purposes, you can use articles to link chapter summaries together, thus, making it easy for a student to skim through the book and locate desired information. An employee manual is another application that can benefit from articles. You create articles for pertinent information located in different parts of the document.

Create an Article

You define articles in a PDF document by using the Article tool to define the boundary of each block of content in the article. Note, an individual article can be a combination of text and graphics. The content area for different parts of the article are linked, and the viewer uses the Articles panel to easily navigate to each thread of the article. To create an article in a PDF document, do the following:

1. Choose Tools | Advanced Editing | Article Tool, or select the Article tool (shown here) from the Advanced Editing tool group if you have it floating in the workspace.

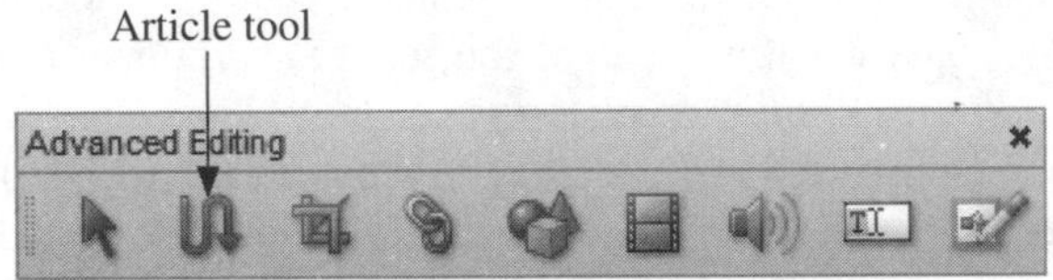

2. Click-and-drag the Article tool around the area you want to define as the first thread of the article. As you drag the tool, a rectangular bounding box gives you a preview of the area you're selecting. When the bounding box surrounds the desired content, release the mouse button to have Acrobat define the first block of the article, as shown in the following illustration. Notice the article numbering system at the top of the article box. The 1-1 designates that article 1, block 1 has been created.

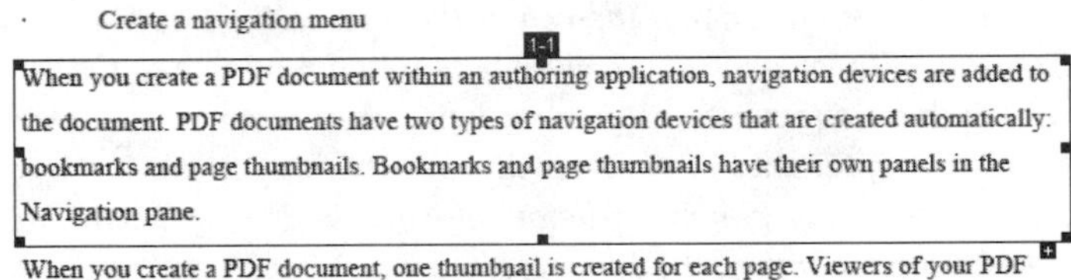

Create a navigation menu
1-1
When you create a PDF document within an authoring application, navigation devices are added to the document. PDF documents have two types of navigation devices that are created automatically: bookmarks and page thumbnails. Bookmarks and page thumbnails have their own panels in the Navigation pane.
When you create a PDF document, one thumbnail is created for each page. Viewers of your PDF

3. After you create the first block of an article, your cursor changes to two lines forming a right angle around the Article tool icon, which means Acrobat is ready for you to define the next content area in the article. Navigate to the section of the document that contains the next portion of the article.
4. Click-and-drag the Article tool until it encompasses the next area of the article.
5. Continue in this manner until you define all blocks of content in the article, and then press ENTER or RETURN to open the Article Properties dialog box:

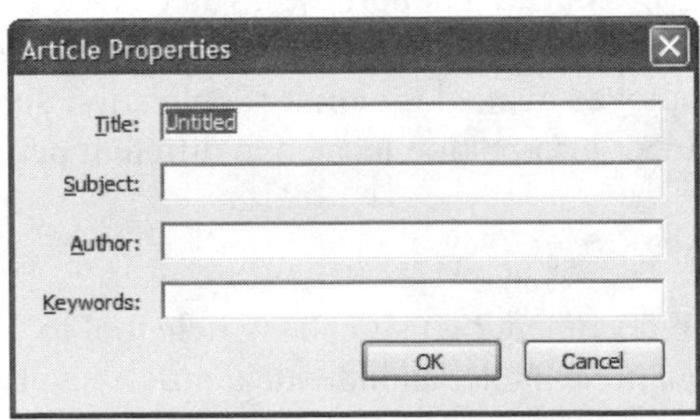

6. Enter the title, subject, and author of the article, plus any other keywords you want associated with the article, and then click OK to close the dialog box.

Use the Articles Panel

After you create one or more articles, you can use the Articles panel to test your handiwork. Readers of your document also use the Articles panel to select an individual article to read. To open the Articles panel, shown here, choose View | Navigation Panels | Articles:

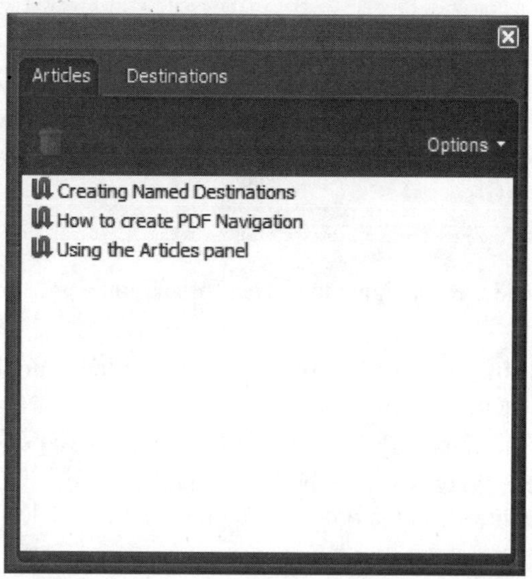

To read an article, double-click its title and Acrobat displays the first block of text in the article. After the first block of text is opened, your cursor becomes a hand with a down-pointing arrow in its palm. Click to navigate to the next thread in the article.

If you enable text selection for the Hand tool in Preferences, when reading an article, your cursor may fluctuate between an I-beam (which indicates you can select text) and the applicable icon for the article. To continue reading the article, wait until the article icon appears, and then click to advance to the next thread in the article.

When you reach the last text block of the article, a line appears underneath the arrow, which signifies you reached the end of the article. Click within the current article thread to return to the start of the article.

Add a Thread to an Article

After you review the article, you may find it necessary to add additional text blocks to the article. You can easily do this by following these steps:

1. Choose Tools | Advanced Editing | Article Tool. After you select the Article tool, Acrobat displays the bounding box of the first text block for each article in the PDF document.

2. Click the text block after which you want the new text block to appear. After you select the text block, a plus sign (+) appears at the lower-right corner of the box, as shown in the following illustration.

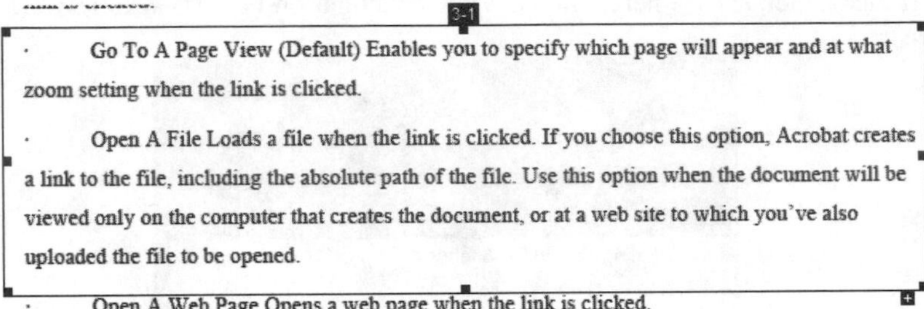

3. Click the plus sign and then navigate to the text block you want added to the article thread.
4. Click-and-drag to define the boundary of the box. When the bounding box encompasses the text, release the mouse button.
5. Add additional threads to the article, or deselect the Article tool to finish editing the contents of the article. When you add threads to an article, Acrobat automatically renumbers the other threads in the order they appear in the article.
6. Press ENTER or RETURN when you finish modifying the article.

Delete an Article

After previewing the document, you may decide certain parts of an article thread aren't needed. You can easily delete an entire article or article thread by doing the following:

1. Choose Tools | Advanced Editing | Article Tool to select the Article tool.
2. Click the article thread you want to delete. If you want to delete an entire article, click any thread in the article.
3. Right-click (Windows) or CTRL-click (Macintosh) to open the Article context menu.
4. Choose DELETE and Acrobat displays a dialog box asking if you want to delete the box or the entire article. Click Box to delete the article thread, or click Article to delete the article. When you delete a thread, Acrobat renumbers the remaining threads in the article in their proper order.

Move or Resize an Article Box

When your article thread is viewed, Acrobat magnifies the view to fit the confines of the article box. If, after reviewing the document, you decide the position or size of an article box isn't right, you can move or resize it.

To move the article box, do the following:

1. Choose Tools | Advanced Editing | Article Tool to select the Article tool.
2. Click the article box you want to move or resize.
3. Click inside the article box, or click a corner or side and drag to move or resize the box. After you move or begin resizing the box, Acrobat displays eight handles and the plus sign.
4. After displaying the handles, you can move the article thread by clicking inside the bounding box and dragging. When you click, your cursor becomes a filled arrowhead. As you drag the article box, a dashed bounding box gives you a preview of the current position of the box. When the article bounding box is in the desired location, release the mouse button.

To resize the article box, do one of the following:

1. Click one of the corner handles and drag to resize the entire article box. Hold down SHIFT to resize the box proportionately. Release the mouse button when the box is the desired size.
2. Click the handle in the middle on either side of the box and drag away from the box to make it wider or drag toward the center of the box to make it narrower. Release the mouse button when the box is the desired width.
3. Click the handle in the middle of either the top or bottom of the article box, and then drag up or down to change the height of the box.

NOTE *When you grab a handle to change the width or height of the box, only the handle you select is changed. The opposite side is unaffected.*

Edit Article Properties

After you create an article, you can change the title or any other article properties by doing the following:

1. Choose Tools | Advanced Editing | Article Tool to select the Article tool.
2. Click any thread of the article whose properties you want to modify.
3. Right-click (Windows) or CTRL-click (Macintosh) and choose Properties from the context menu to display the Article Properties dialog box.
4. Modify the article properties as needed, and then click OK.

TIP *When you create a document with Articles, add an action on the first page of the document that invokes the View | Navigation Panels | Articles command when the page opens. This displays the Articles panel in either Acrobat or the Adobe Reader, giving your document viewers a method to find the articles you added to the document.*

Work with the Destinations Panel

When you create a complex PDF document, you may find it helpful to work with named destinations. A *named destination* links to a specific point in a document. When you work with multiple documents, as is often the case when creating a multimedia presentation, you can simplify cross-document navigation by adding a JavaScript action that links to a named destination. When you link to a named destination, the link remains active, even when pages are added or deleted from the target document.

You use the Destinations panel to create, display, and sort named destinations within a document. You also use the panel to rename destinations. To create the named destinations within a document, do the following:

1. Navigate to the document page you want added to the named destination list, and set the magnification of the page.
2. Choose View | Navigation Panels | Destinations to open the Destinations panel.
3. Click the Create New Destination icon. Or, you can right-click (Windows), or CTRL-click (Macintosh) and choose New Destination from the context menu. After you create a new destination, it appears in the Destinations panel as Untitled.
4. Enter a name for the new destination. Give your destinations meaningful names that reflect the content of the destination. The following image shows two destinations after being renamed.

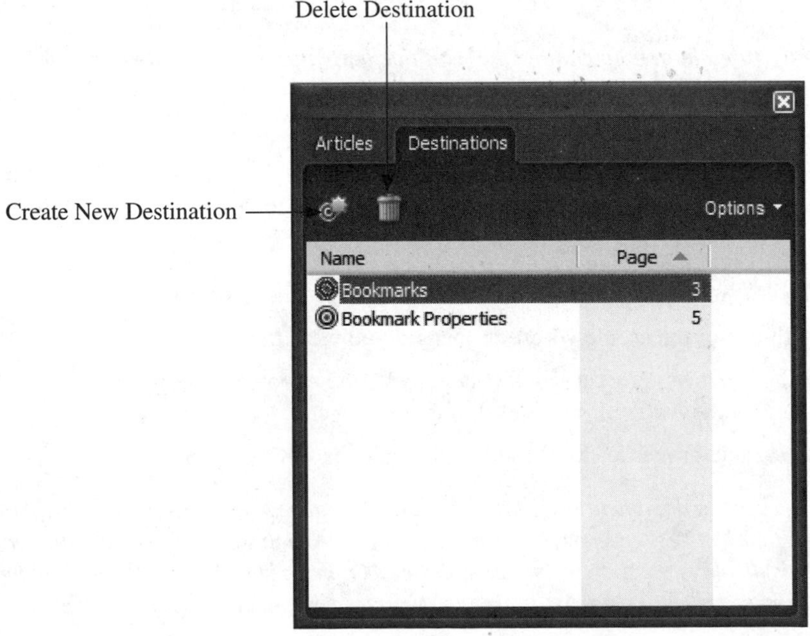

5. After creating several destinations, you can do the following:
   - To sort the destinations alphabetically, click the Name column title near the top of the panel.
   - To sort the destinations by page number, click the Page column title near the top of the panel.
   - To go to a named destination, double-click its name. Or, you can right-click (Windows) or CTRL-click (Macintosh) and choose Go To Destination from the context menu.
   - To delete named destinations, select them and press DELETE. Or, you can click the Delete Selected Destinations icon (which looks like a garbage can), or choose Delete from the context menu.
   - To rename a destination, select it and right-click (Windows) or CTRL-click (Macintosh), choose Rename from the context menu, and enter a new name for the destination.
   - To change the magnification of a destination, navigate to the destination, and then within the document, use the Zoom tool to set the desired magnification. In the Destinations panel, right-click (Windows) or CTRL-click (Macintosh) the destination title and choose Set Destination from the context menu.
6. Close the Destinations panel.

Summary

In this chapter, you learned how to enhance your navigation by assigning one or more actions to a link or bookmark. You discovered how to assign actions to a page that determine what occurs when a page opens or closes. You also learned how to create a thread of articles and how to work with named destinations. In the next chapter, you find out how to edit your PDF documents.

Part III

Edit PDF Documents

Chapter 9

The Basics of Editing PDF Documents

How to...

- Edit visually with thumbnails
- Edit with menu commands
- Append PDF documents
- Add page transitions
- Touch up a PDF document

After you create a PDF document, you can easily edit it. Within Acrobat, you can add, delete, reorder, and renumber pages. You can also edit individual objects within the PDF document.

You edit PDF documents by using panels, tools, and menu commands. Many of the edits you perform with Acrobat tools can also be accomplished using menu commands or by selecting commands from the appropriate panel Options menu or context menu. In this chapter, you learn how to edit PDF documents, as well as add pages to PDF documents. When you're editing a PDF document that's used for a presentation, you can create some interesting effects by applying page transitions, which are also discussed in this chapter.

Edit Visually with Page Thumbnails

Pages thumbnails (also referred to as thumbnails) are miniature images of each page in a PDF document. Each thumbnail is displayed with a page number beneath it. In previous chapters, you have seen thumbnails used as navigation devices. You can also use them to edit your documents. You can use thumbnails to insert pages, delete pages, and change the order of pages. Thumbnails are located on the Pages panel, as shown in Figure 9-1.

The Pages panel is part of the Navigation pane and can be opened by clicking the Pages icon or by choosing View | Navigation Panels | Pages. The Pages panel has its own Options menu, a context menu, and the Delete Selected Pages tool.

Use the Pages Panel Options Menu

You use the Pages panel Options menu to access certain menu commands that enable you to edit a document and work with thumbnails. To open the Pages panel Options menu, as shown here, click the Options icon near the upper-right corner of the panel.

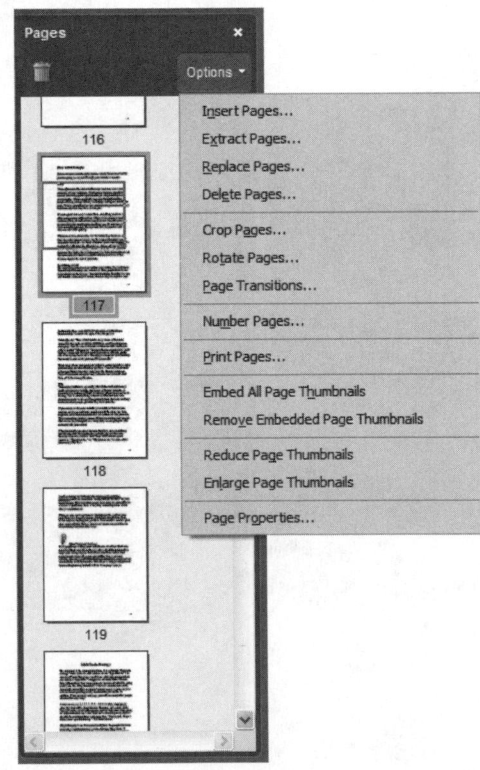

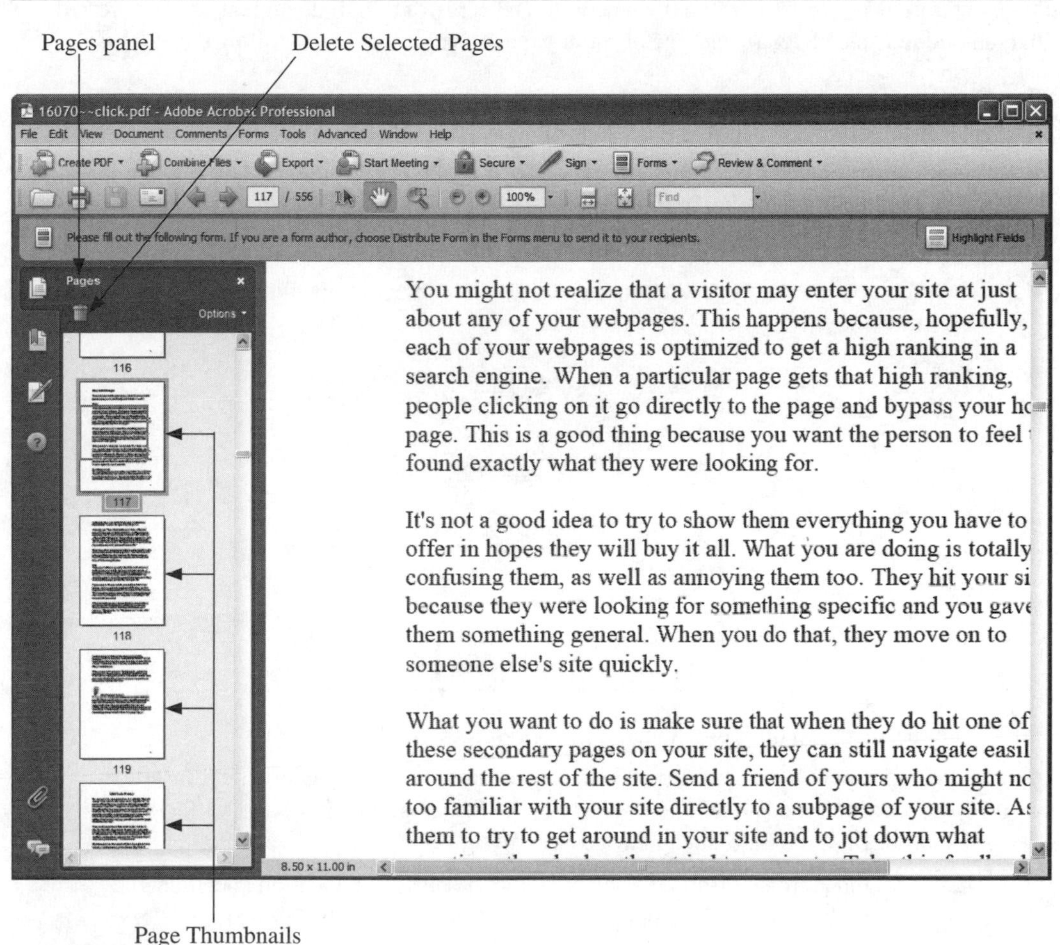

FIGURE 9-1 You can visually edit a document with page thumbnails.

Use the Pages Panel Context Menu

Many of the commands you use to edit PDF documents can be found on the Pages panel context menu. To access the Pages panel context menu, select a thumbnail and right-click (Windows) or CTRL-click (Macintosh). To access a context menu that contains menu commands to embed or change the size of thumbnails, place your cursor in the Pages panel, without selecting a thumbnail, and then right-click (Windows) or CTRL-click (Macintosh).

Insert Pages

You can insert pages from within the Pages panel. From within the panel, you click a thumbnail to navigate to a page, and then insert pages before or after the selected page. You can insert any file type supported by Acrobat. If the document you select isn't a PDF document, it is converted to PDF and added as a page. To add one or more pages to your document, follow these steps:

1. Open the Pages panel and click a thumbnail to navigate to the page before or after the place where the new pages will be inserted.
2. Choose Insert Pages from the Pages panel Options menu or context menu to open the Select File To Insert dialog box.
3. Click the Files Of Type drop-down arrow and select the type of document to insert.
4. Select the document(s) you want to insert and click Select to open the Insert Pages dialog box, shown next:

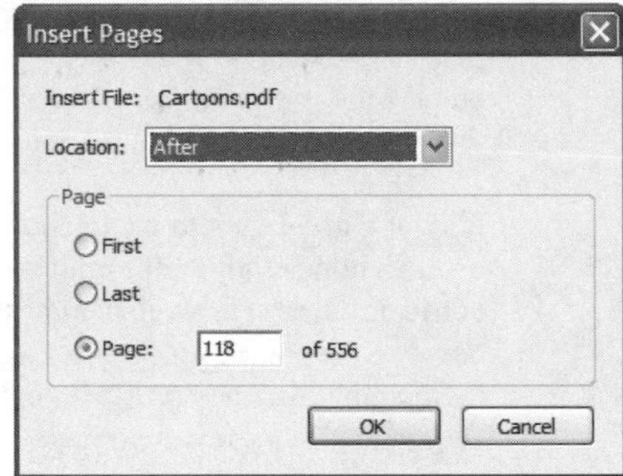

5. From the Location drop-down menu, choose Before or After.
6. In the Page section, select the page where you want the selected document inserted. You can insert the document before or after the first page, the last page, or the currently selected page in the PDF document you're editing.
7. Click OK, and Acrobat inserts the selected documents in the location specified and creates a thumbnail for each new page.

Delete Pages

You can also use page thumbnails to delete one or more pages. To delete pages from within the Pages panel, do one of the following:

- To delete a single page, click its thumbnail, and then click the Delete Selected Pages button. Acrobat displays a warning dialog box. Click OK to delete the page or click Cancel to stop the operation.
- To delete contiguous pages, click a thumbnail that corresponds to a page you want to delete, and then, while pressing SHIFT, click contiguous thumbnails to add them to the selection. When you finish selecting thumbnails, click the Delete Selected Pages button. Click OK to close the warning dialog box and delete the pages.

- To delete noncontiguous pages, click a thumbnail that corresponds to a page you want to delete, and then, while pressing CTRL (Windows), or COMMAND (Macintosh), click additional thumbnails to add them to the selection. Click the Delete Selected Pages button to delete the pages from the document. Click OK to accept the deletion of the pages.

You can also delete pages by selecting contiguous thumbnails and choosing Delete Pages from the Pages panel Options menu or context menu. When you choose this command, Acrobat displays the following dialog box, which gives you the opportunity to change the pages that will be deleted when you execute the action by clicking the From radio button, and then entering the first and last page you want to delete. Click OK to complete the deletion.

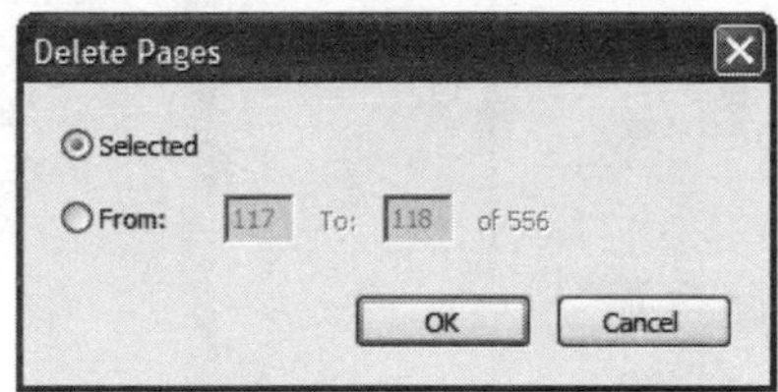

You can also delete pages by selecting them, and then pressing DELETE. This alternative circumvents the Delete Pages dialog box, but it displays a dialog box asking you to confirm delction.

Drag-and-Drop Editing

The Pages panel not only gives you a visual representation of each page in your document, but it also enables you to edit the document by dragging-and-dropping page thumbnails. You can use the Pages panel to change the order in which document pages display and to import pages from other documents.

Reorder Document Pages

You can use thumbnails to change the order in which pages appear in a PDF document. To move a single page or a selection of pages to a new position in the document, select them, and then drag-and-drop them to a new location. To change the order of document pages, follow these steps:

1. Open the Pages panel and select the page thumbnail that corresponds to the page you want to move. You can move more than one page at a time by selecting contiguous or noncontiguous thumbnails, as discussed previously.

TIP *To view several thumbnails at once, choose Reduce Page Thumbnails from the Pages panel Options menu or context menu. You can also display more thumbnails by clicking-and-dragging to the right the vertical border between the Navigation pane and the Document pane.*

2. Drag the selected thumbnails up or down. As you drag the thumbnails, your cursor becomes a filled arrow attached to a document, and a solid blue line appears to indicate the current position of the thumbnail(s) you are moving, as shown in the following illustration. If the Navigation pane is sized so that more than one column of thumbnails is visible, the blue line appears to the side of the thumbnail where the selection would be placed.

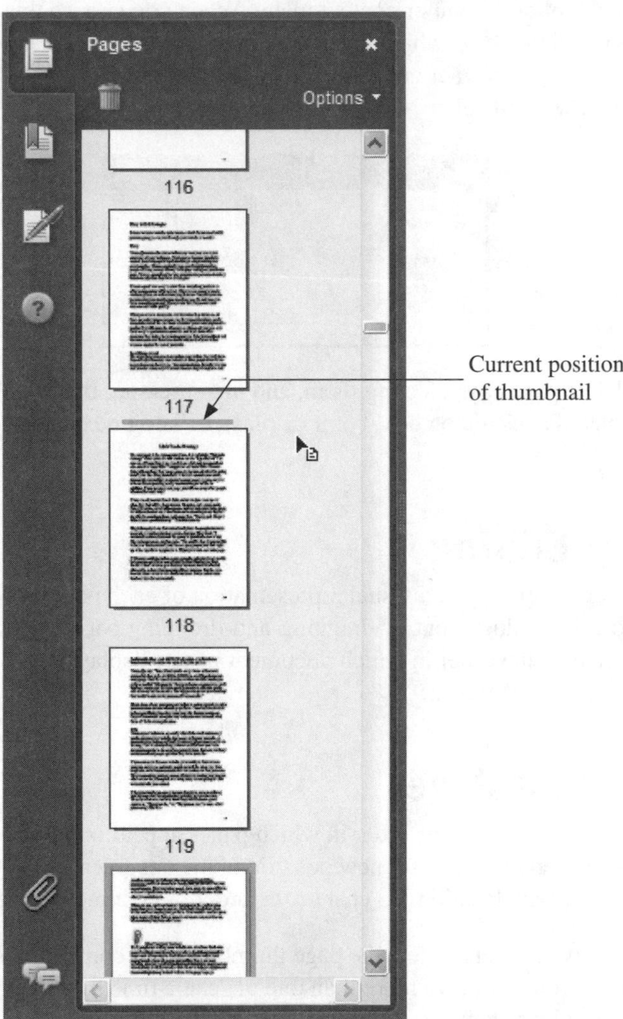

3. Release the mouse button when the selected thumbnails are where you want them. Acrobat moves the selected pages to their new location and renumbers the thumbnails.

Copy Pages from Other Documents

If you have more than one document open, you can use the Pages panel to copy pages from one document to another. Copying pages is an excellent way to build a document when working with a team of PDF authors. To copy pages from one document to another, follow these steps:

1. Open the source and target document(s).
2. Choose Window | Tile, and then choose Vertically or Horizontally. Or, you can choose Cascading, but you will have to rearrange the documents, so each document's Pages panel is visible.
3. If they aren't already visible, open the Pages panel of each document by choosing View | Navigation Panels | Pages while the respective document is selected.
4. On the Pages panel of the source document, select the thumbnail for the page you want to copy. You can select more than one thumbnail if necessary.
5. Drag the selected thumbnails from the Pages panel of the source document to the Pages panel of the target document.
6. As your cursor moves into the Pages panel of the target document, the cursor becomes an angled arrow attached to a document with a plus sign (+) in it.
7. On the Pages panel of the target document, drag the thumbnails to the desired position and release the mouse button. After you release the mouse button, Acrobat copies the selected pages to the target document, and then creates numbered thumbnails for the copied pages.

9

TIP *Hold the CTRL (Windows) or COMMAND (Macintosh) key while dragging the thumbnail to permanently move the page from the source document to the target document.*

Edit with Menu Commands

Many of the menu commands discussed in the following sections are exact copies of Pages panel Options menu commands and Pages panel context menu commands. When you use these commands in the Pages panel, you work with a single thumbnail or selection of thumbnails. When you use a menu command, you can specify any page in the document. The previous sections dealt with using editing commands in a specific manner within the Pages panel. The following sections show you how to use menu commands to edit selected pages within your documents.

Insert Pages

You can add existing documents to any PDF document by using the Insert Pages command. With the *Insert Pages command,* you specify the exact location within the document where the pages are to be added. You can insert an existing PDF document or any file type supported by Acrobat. To append an existing PDF document by using the Insert Pages command, follow these steps:

1. Open the PDF document to which you want to add pages.
2. Navigate to the document page before or after the place where you want to insert the pages. This step is optional—you can specify the exact location to add the pages in the Insert Pages dialog box.
3. Choose Document | Insert Pages to open the Select File To Insert dialog box.
4. Choose the file(s) you want to insert, and then click Select to open the Insert Pages dialog box.
5. From the Location drop-down menu, choose After or Before.
6. In the Page section, the Page radio button is selected by default with the page currently being viewed listed in the Page field. You can change this by choosing First or Last, or by entering a different page number in the Page field.
7. Click OK, and Acrobat inserts the selected pages at the specified location and creates a thumbnail for each added page.

Delete Pages

You can modify a PDF document by deleting unwanted pages. To do this, you use the Delete Pages command. This command enables you to delete a single page, a range of pages, or selected pages. To remove pages from a PDF document, follow these steps:

1. Open the document from which you want to remove pages.
2. Select the pages you want to delete by clicking their thumbnails in the Pages panel. This step is optional unless you want to delete noncontiguous pages. You can specify a range of pages you want to delete after invoking the command.
3. Choose Document | Delete Pages to open the Delete Pages dialog box, shown previously.
4. If you selected the pages to delete, click OK. Otherwise, enter the range of pages to delete, and then click OK. After you click OK, Acrobat displays a warning dialog box, asking you to confirm that you want the pages deleted.
5. Click OK, and Acrobat deletes the specified pages and their thumbnails, and then renumbers the remaining thumbnails.

Replace Pages

You can update a document by replacing a page or a selection of pages. This option is useful when you have a multipage PDF document that needs only minor revisions. Create the pages you need to replace in an authoring application, save them, and then choose Document | Replace Pages. You can replace pages with any existing file of a type supported by Acrobat. You can also replace a specific number of pages in one document with the same number of pages from another document. To replace pages in a PDF document, follow these steps:

1. Open the document that contains the pages you want to replace.
2. Open the Pages panel by clicking Pages in the Navigation pane or by choosing View | Navigation Panels | Pages.
3. Click the thumbnails that correspond to the pages you want to replace. Note, you can only select contiguous thumbnails. If you select noncontiguous thumbnails, Acrobat will replace a range of pages from the first selected thumbnail to the last.
4. Choose Document | Replace Pages to open the Select File With New Pages dialog box.
5. Locate the file with the pages that will replace the selected ones and click Select to open the Replace Pages dialog box:

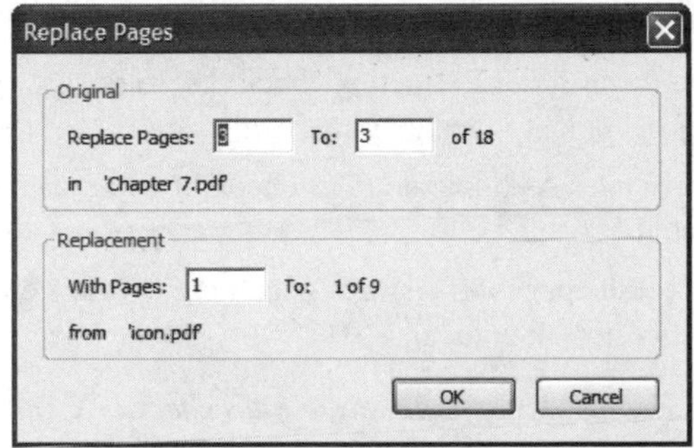

6. If you already selected the pages you want to replace, go to Step 7. Otherwise, in the Replace Pages field of the Original section, enter the number of the first page you want replaced, and then, in the To field, enter the number of the last page you want replaced.
7. In the With Pages field of the Replacement section, enter the number of the first replacement page of the file you selected. Acrobat automatically calculates the ending page, based on the number of pages selected in the original document. If you don't specify a page number, Acrobat will replace the first specified page in the target document with the first page of the replacement document.
8. Click OK, and Acrobat replaces the pages and generates thumbnails for the new pages.

Extract Pages

You can extract pages from an existing PDF document and use them as the basis for a new PDF document. When you extract pages, you can preserve the extracted pages in the original document or delete them. To extract pages from a PDF document, follow these steps:

1. Open the PDF document that contains the pages you want to extract.
2. Open the Pages panel by clicking the Pages icon in the Navigation pane or by choosing View | Navigation Panels | Pages.

3. Click the thumbnails that correspond to the pages you want to extract. Or, you can enter the range of pages to extract in the Extract Pages dialog box. Note, if you select noncontiguous pages, Acrobat extracts a range of pages from the first selected page to the last.
4. Choose Document | Extract Pages to open the Extract Pages dialog box:

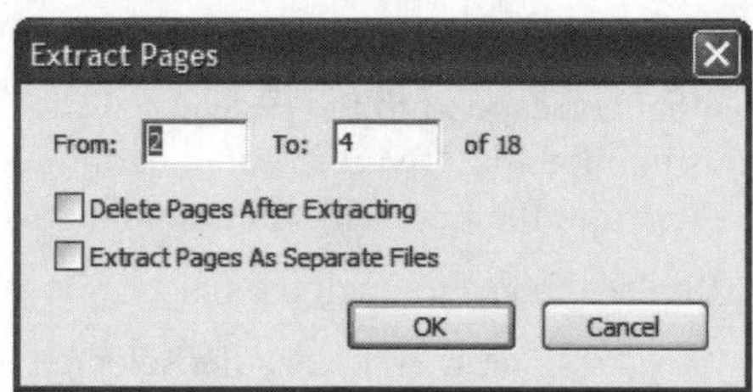

5. If you already selected thumbnails, go to Step 6. Otherwise, specify a range of pages by entering page numbers in the From and To fields.
6. Check the Delete Pages After Extracting check box to have Acrobat delete the pages from the original document when they're extracted.
7. Check the Extract Pages As Separate Files check box to create one PDF document for each page extracted.
8. Click OK to extract the pages. If a single document is being created, Acrobat opens the extracted pages as a new document.

If you check the Extract Pages As Separate Files check box, the Browse For Folder dialog box appears, prompting you for a folder in which to save the extracted pages. After you select the desired folder, click OK, and Acrobat creates a PDF file for each extracted page, but it doesn't open the new documents in Acrobat. The extracted pages inherit the filename of the document from which they were extracted, followed by the page number.

9. Choose File | Save As, and then specify a filename and location where you want the extracted pages saved.

Crop Pages

If you create a PDF document and you find one or more of the document pages have excessive margins, you can trim (*crop*) the pages. You can also use this command to crop extraneous material from a PDF document, such as a banner in a PDF document created from a web page. You crop pages by using a menu command or a tool.

Use the Crop Menu Command

To crop pages using the menu command, follow these steps:

1. Open the document whose pages you want to crop. Select a range of pages to crop by clicking thumbnails in the Pages panel. (Or, you can select the range of pages to crop after you open the Crop Pages dialog box.)

2. Choose Document | Crop Pages to open the Crop Pages dialog box, as shown in Figure 9-2.
3. Select the area you want to crop:
   - **CropBox** Choose this option, the default parameter, to crop the page(s) to the dimensions you specify.
   - **TrimBox** Choose this option to specify the size of the page(s) after applying the command.
   - **ArtBox** Choose this option to specify the relevant content of the page(s), including white space you want included in the finished document.
   - **BleedBox** Choose this option to specify the clipping path when the page is printed by a service center. This option allows for paper trimming and folding. Note, printer marks may fall outside the specified bleed area.

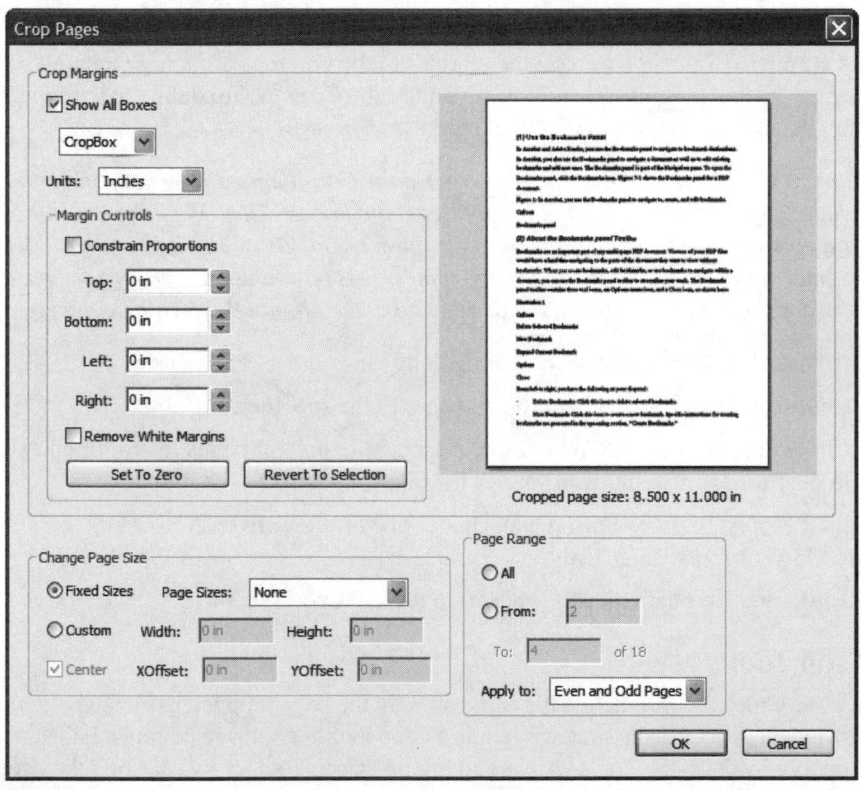

FIGURE 9-2 The Crop Pages dialog box holds all the options you need to define the crop you want.

4. Select a unit of measure from the Units drop-down menu. In most instances, the default unit of measure is the same as the unit of measure for the document.
5. In the Margin Controls area, enter a value to crop in any or all of the following fields: Top, Bottom, Left, and Right. For example, to crop one inch from the top margin, enter **1** in the Top field. Or, you can click the spinner buttons to select a value. Press SHIFT while clicking a spinner button to make the values change in greater increments. As you modify the margin values, a black rectangle around the thumbnail in the center of the Crop Margins section changes to reflect the size of the page with the modified margin settings.
6. Check Constrain Proportions to crop the document page proportionately. When you check this box and enter a value in a margin field, Acrobat updates the other fields, so the document will be cropped with its original aspect ratio.
7. Click the Remove White Margins check box to crop the side margins to the document contents, thus eliminating a white border.
8. Click Set To Zero to reset the margin values to zero.
9. Click Revert To Selection to reset the margins to the previous cropping rectangle. This button resets the margins to zero unless you use the Crop tool to define the cropping rectangle, and then modify one of the margins.

To crop a document to a given page size, open the Crop Pages dialog box, and in the Change Page Size area, click the Fixed Sizes radio button. Then, click the Page Sizes arrow, and choose an option from the drop-down menu. Or, click the Custom radio button, and enter values in the Width and Height fields. This option doesn't change the physical dimensions of the page content, but adds white space around the existing content.

10. In the Page Range area, choose one of the following:
    - Choose All to have Acrobat crop all pages to the specified size.
    - Choose From to have Acrobat crop to specify a range of pages to crop. Enter a value in the From and To fields to specify the first and last pages to crop.
11. From the Apply To drop-down menu, choose one of these: Even And Odd Pages, Odd Pages Only, or Even Pages Only.
12. Click OK, and Acrobat crops the page(s) to the sizes you specified.

Use the Crop Tool

When you use the Crop tool, you define the area you want the page cropped to by dragging the tool within the Document pane. This is similar to using a Crop tool in an image editing application. You select the Crop tool by choosing Tools | Advanced Editing, Crop Tool, or by selecting the Crop tool from the Advanced Editing toolbar (shown next), if available in the workspace. You use the *Crop*

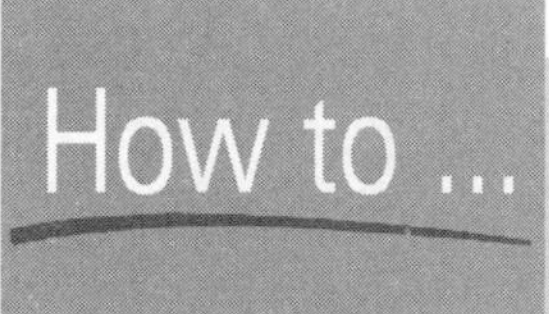

Restore Keyboard Shortcuts

If you're an Acrobat veteran, you've probably noticed the absence of keyboard shortcuts. For example, in Acrobat 5.0, you could select the Hand tool by pressing H, the Crop tool by pressing C, the Links tool by pressing L, and so on. With the release of Acrobat 6.0, Adobe decided to remove the keyboard shortcuts, a tradition that continues with Acrobat 8.0. However, if you like the convenience of keyboard shortcuts, you can restore them by choosing Edit | Preferences to open the Preferences dialog box. Click General in the left-hand window to open the General section of the dialog box, and then enable the Use Single-Key Accelerators To Access Tools option. Click OK to exit the dialog box. After enabling this option, each tool's keyboard shortcut is displayed in a ToolTip when your cursor is over the tool. After a while, the shortcuts for the tools you commonly use will become second nature and you'll be able to quickly access a tool by pressing the proper key.

tool to define the area to which the page is to be cropped. You can resize or move the area before cropping. After double-clicking inside the crop area, or pressing ENTER or RETURN, the Crop Pages dialog box, previously seen in Figure 9-2 appears.

Rotate Pages

When you create a PDF document by combining several documents, you often end up with different page sizes and orientations. For example, when you combine files to create a multiage PDF document, you may end up combining documents with both landscape and portrait orientation. When this happens, you can rotate pages as needed by following these steps:

1. Open the document whose pages you want to rotate.
2. To select specific pages, open the Pages panel and select the thumbnails for the pages you want to rotate. You can select noncontiguous pages to rotate. Or, you can navigate to a specific page or specify a range of pages in the Rotate Pages dialog box.

3. Choose Document | Rotate Pages to open the Rotate Pages dialog box:

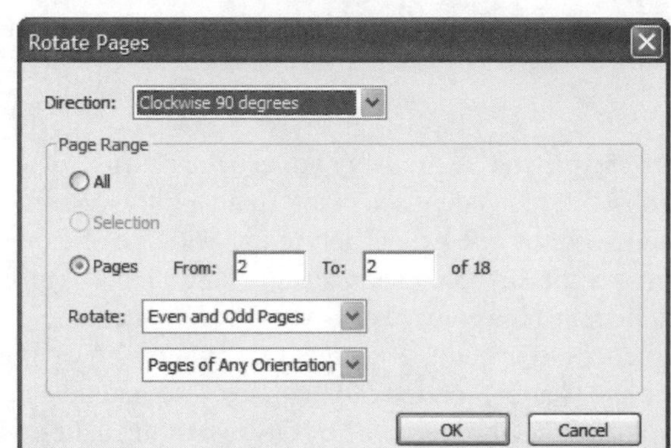

4. Choose one of the following options from the Direction drop-down menu: Counterclockwise 90 Degrees, Clockwise 90 Degrees, or 180 Degrees.
5. In the Page Range section, choose one of the following options:
   - **All** Choose this option, and Acrobat rotates all pages in the direction specified.
   - **Selection** This option is available if you selected pages by clicking their thumbnails. Otherwise, it's dimmed out.
   - **Pages** This option is available if you navigate to a specific page before invoking the Rotate Pages command. You can accept the page range (the page you navigated to) or modify the range by entering page numbers in the From and To fields.
6. Click the top Rotate drop-down arrow and choose one of the following: Even And Odd Pages, Even Pages Only, or Odd Pages Only.
7. Click the bottom Rotate drop-down arrow and choose one of these options: Landscape Pages, Portrait Pages, or Pages Of Any Orientation.
8. Click OK, and Acrobat rotates the specified pages to the desired orientation.

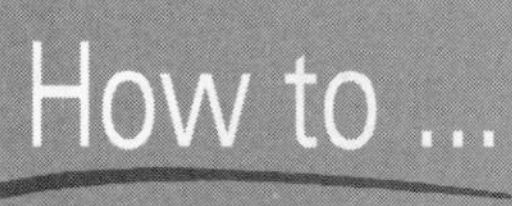

Combine Two PDF Documents

You can combine two PDF documents by opening one PDF document, and then navigating to the page where you want to add another document. Choose Document | Insert Pages, select the PDF file, and then choose the proper option to insert the new PDF file before or after the first, last, or current page of the currently open PDF document.

Number Pages

When you create a PDF document, Acrobat automatically numbers the pages. When you add pages, move pages, or delete pages, Acrobat updates the page numbers to reflect the order in which the pages appear. Acrobat uses a default integer-numbering system, starting with 1 for the first page of the document, and so on. If the document you create has a title page, copyright pages, or similar front matter pages, you can modify the numbering style by following these steps:

1. On the Pages panel, select the thumbnails of the pages you want to renumber. Or, you can specify a range of pages to renumber in the Page Numbering dialog box.
2. Click Options to open the Pages panel Options menu, and then choose Number Pages to display the Page Numbering dialog box:

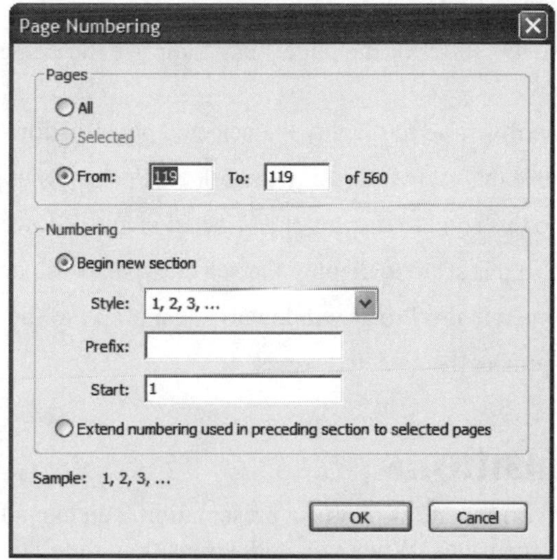

3. In the Pages area, choose one of the following options:
   - **All** Choose this option to have all pages renumbered.
   - **Selected** This option is available and selected by default when you create a selection of pages by clicking their thumbnails.
   - **From [ ] To [ ]** Choose this option to renumber a range of pages. To specify the range of pages you want to renumber, enter the desired page numbers in the From and To fields.
4. In the Numbering area, choose one of the following options:
   - **Begin New Section** Choose this option to begin a new numbering sequence. Click the Style drop-down arrow and choose an option. To add a prefix to the page

numbers, enter the desired prefix in the Prefix field. In the Start field, enter the beginning value for the new page sequence.

- **Extend Numbering Used In Preceding Section To Selected Pages** Choose this option to have Acrobat renumber the selected pages using the same sequence as the preceding pages, numbering the first selected page with the next page number in the sequence.

5. Click the Style drop-down arrow and choose an option. After you choose a style, a preview appears in the Sample section at the bottom of the dialog box. You can renumber selected pages using any of these styles:
   - **None** No page numbers appear below the thumbnails you selected for renumbering. However, the document page number information is still displayed in the Page Navigation toolbar.
   - **1, 2, 3** Use this style for the pages that comprise the content of a document or e-book.
   - **i, ii, iii** Use this style to display the selected pages as lowercase Roman numerals.
   - **I, II, III** Use this style to display the selected pages as uppercase Roman numerals.
   - **a, b, c** Use this style to display the selected pages as lowercase letters.
   - **A, B, C** Use this style to display the selected pages as capital letters.
6. If desired, enter text in the Prefix window to add a prefix to the page number.
7. Click OK to renumber the selected pages.

Adding Page Transitions

If you're creating a PDF document as part of a presentation, you can add a bit of panache by adding a transition between pages. When you add a transition, the PDF document looks similar to a PowerPoint presentation or a slideshow. Transitions are only displayed when the document is viewed in Full Screen mode. You can set a document to display in Full Screen mode by setting Window Options in the Initial view section of the Document Properties dialog box. To add transitions between pages, follow these steps:

Some of the more complex PowerPoint animation effects aren't supported in Acrobat and, therefore, won't be rendered as animations when a PowerPoint presentation is converted to PDF. Unsupported animation appears as a static image in the converted PDF.

1. Choose Advance | Document Processing | Page Transitions to open the Set Transitions dialog box:

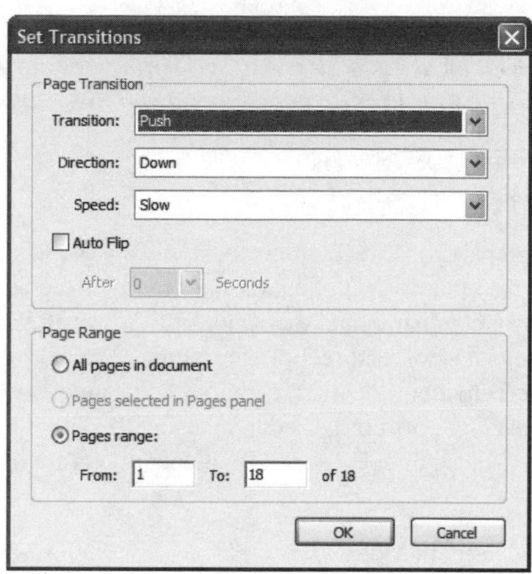

2. Click the Transition drop-down arrow and choose one of the presets from the drop-down menu. The effects are similar to those found in PowerPoint and other presentation programs.

TIP *If you choose Random Transition from the Transition drop-down menu, Acrobat randomly chooses a different effect every time the viewer navigates to a different page.*

3. If available for the selected transition, click the Direction drop-down arrow and choose the direction from which the transition begins.
4. Click the Speed drop-down arrow and choose one of the following: Slow, Medium, or Fast.
5. Click the Auto Flip check box to turn the pages automatically. When you choose this option, the After [ ] Seconds field becomes available. Enter a value for the number of seconds you'd like each page displayed, or choose a preset from the drop-down menu.
6. In the Page Range area, choose one of the following options:
   - **All Pages In Document** Applies the selected transition to all pages in the document.
   - **Pages Selected In Pages Panel** Applies the selected transition to the pages corresponding to the thumbnails you selected from the Pages panel. This option is dimmed out if no thumbnails are selected.
   - **Pages Range** Applies the selected transition to a range of pages. When you choose this option, enter values in the From and To fields to specify the page range.
7. Click OK to apply the transition to the selected pages.
8. Save the document.

Even though Acrobat provides an option for a random selection of transitions, when creating a presentation, a good idea is to stick with one transition type for the entire presentation. Mixing transitions can be jarring and looks unprofessional.

Touch Up a PDF Document

As you know, PDF documents originate in authoring applications, where you convert them to the PDF format by using the authoring application plug-in, by using an Export command, or by using the application's Print command, and then choosing Adobe PDF as the printing device. The converted document retains the look and feel of the original. When you open the document in Acrobat, you can add interactivity to the document, but you cannot perform wholesale edits to the document. You can, however, perform minor edits by using the TouchUp tools. You can also touch up the order of a tagged PDF document. Tagged PDF documents are discussed in Chapter 12.

Use the TouchUp Text Tool

You use the *TouchUp Text tool* to perform minor edits to text within a PDF document. You can use the tool to change a word or letter, to copy a line of text to the clipboard, to fit text within an existing selection, and more.

Edit Text

When you select the TouchUp Text tool, you can select text within a PDF document and delete or replace the text. To edit text with the TouchUp Text tool, follow these steps:

1. Choose Tools | Advanced Editing | TouchUp Text Tool. If you will be editing text and other elements in the document, you can choose Tools | Advanced Editing | Show Advanced Editing Toolbar. After you select the tool, Acrobat loads systems fonts. This may take a few seconds, depending on the number of fonts you have installed on your system.

When you attempt to edit a document with a font type that isn't loaded on your machine and not embedded in the document, Acrobat attempts to re-create the font using the built-in Multiple Master fonts. If the font cannot be re-created, it's displayed as your system's default serif or sans serif font.

2. Click a block of text to select it. Click the sentence or paragraph you want to edit, and Acrobat selects all text on the page. After you select the text, Acrobat highlights the selected text in blue, places a bounding box around the text block, as shown here, and your cursor becomes an I-beam:

You can delete any bookmark. When you delete a bookmark, you do not change the content of a document; you merely remove a link. If you created a PDF document that has several heading levels, you may want to consider deleting a few bookmarks to simplify navigation.

Caution: There is no warning before the bookmark is deleted. If you delete a bookmark in error, choose Edit | Undo Delete Bookmark or press CTRL-Z immediately after deleting the bookmark.

3. To change a letter or a word in a text selection, use the TouchUp Text tool to select the letter or word you want to change. As you drag the tool, your selection is highlighted. Release the mouse button after you select the characters you want to change.
4. Enter new text, and Acrobat applies the edit to the selected text. If the embedded font isn't installed on your system, Acrobat displays a warning dialog box to this effect. Click Yes to remove font embedding. If the unembedded single-byte font isn't present in your system encoding, you receive an error message saying you cannot edit the font.

Even though a font may be present in your system, legally you must own a licensed version of the actual font or have it installed on your system to change the text.

Change Text Appearance

After you select a block of text with the TouchUp Text tool, you can change the font style, font size, font color, and more. To change text appearance, follow these steps:

1. Select the TouchUp Text tool, as outlined previously.
2. Click a block of text to select it.
3. Click-and-drag to select a single character, word, or the entire line of text.
4. Right-click (Windows) or CTRL-click (Macintosh) and choose Properties from the context menu to open the TouchUp Properties dialog box, shown next. (Note, the Content and Tag tabs are available in Acrobat Professional only.) The dialog box gives you information about the original font, the editing font (if the original font isn't installed on the system), and permissions as to whether or not the font can be embedded.

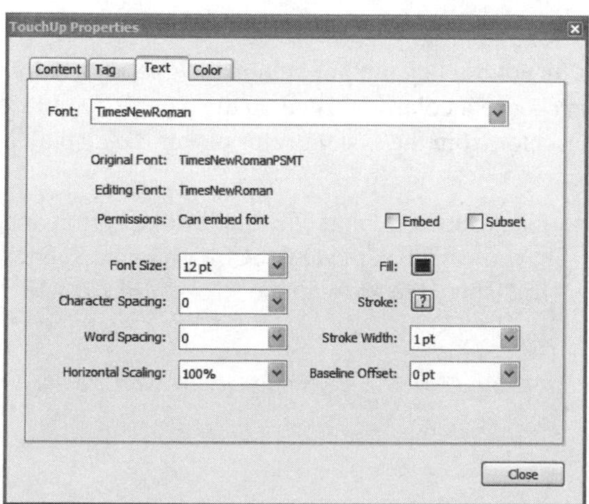

NOTE *As you change text parameters in the dialog box, the text updates in real time. If the dialog box covers the text, click-and-drag the dialog box title bar to move the dialog box to a new location.*

5. To change the font face, click the Font drop-down arrow and choose a font face from the drop-down menu.
6. If a licensed version of the font you chose is present on your system, you will see Can Embed Font to the right of the Permissions field. If you choose to embed the font, you have two options:
   - **Embed Font** Embeds the entire font set, even characters not used in the selected text.
   - **Subset** Embeds a subset of the font type to cover all characters used in the text selection. If another party attempts to edit the document, they won't be able to access characters that aren't part of the subset.
7. To change the font size, click the Font Size drop-down arrow and choose a size from the drop-down menu.

NOTE *If you use Acrobat on a computer with limited processing power, Acrobat may take a while to render your font changes, especially when you significantly enlarge the font size or make changes within large blocks of text.*

8. To change spacing between the characters of the selected text, click the Character Spacing drop-down arrow and choose a value from the drop-down menu. Or, you can enter a value between –0.5 and 2 points.
9. To change spacing between selected words, click the Word Spacing drop-down arrow and choose a value from the drop-down menu. Or, you can enter a value between –0.5 and 2 points.
10. To change the horizontal scale of the selected text, click the Horizontal Scaling drop-down arrow and choose a value (percentage) from the drop-down menu. This option changes the proportion between the width and height of the selected text.
11. To change the font fill color, click the Fill button and choose a color from the pop-up palette. Or, you can choose a color not listed on the palette by clicking the Other Color icon and choosing a color from the system color picker. To display only an outline around the selected text, click the No Color icon.
12. To change the font stroke (outline) color, click the Stroke button and choose a color from the pop-up palette. Or, you can click the Other Color icon and choose a color from the system color picker. To display the text with no stroke, click the No Stroke icon.

NOTE *If you choose No Stroke and No Fill, the selected text won't be visible.*

How to ... Look Up the Meaning of a Word

If you're connected to the Internet while working in Acrobat, you can look up the meaning of any word in a text object. Acrobat 8.0 has a powerful option that's equivalent to having a dictionary on demand. To look up the meaning of a word, access the Select tool and select the word for which you want to find the meaning. Right-click (Windows) or CTRL-click (Macintosh), and then choose Look Up *selected word,* where *selected word* is the word you highlighted with the Select tool. After selecting the command, Acrobat launches your web browser and the meaning for your selected word is displayed.

13. Accept the default Stroke Width, or choose a different value from the drop-down menu. This option determines the width of the outline around the selected letters.
14. To change the baseline shift of the selected text, click the Baseline Offset drop-down arrow and choose a value from the drop-down menu. Or, you can increase or decrease the baseline shift by clicking the spinner buttons or by entering a value between –4 points and 14 points. This option determines where the text appears in relation to the baseline. For example, if you select one word from a sentence and increase the baseline shift, the word appears above the other words in the sentence.
15. Click Close to exit the dialog box.

TIP *If you do extensive modifications to a document and it isn't turning out as you planned, you can eliminate all your modifications by choosing File | Revert. When you choose this command, Acrobat reverts to the last saved version of the document.*

TIP *The Color tab of the TouchUp Properties dialog box enables you to convert the current color space to a different color space.*

Use the TouchUp Reading Order Tool (Professional Only)

You use the TouchUp Reading Order tool to view and modify the reading order of a tagged document. When you choose this tool, a dialog box appears that shows all tags within the document as highlighted regions. You use this tool to modify the order of existing tags or to add tags to a document that has none.

1. Choose Tools | Advanced Editing | TouchUp Reading Order Tool. After you open the TouchUp Reading Order dialog box, each block of text in the document is selected and numbered. Your cursor becomes a cross-hair.

2. To specify a tag within a document, click-and-drag around the area you want to tag. The option buttons for tagging selections become available, as shown next.

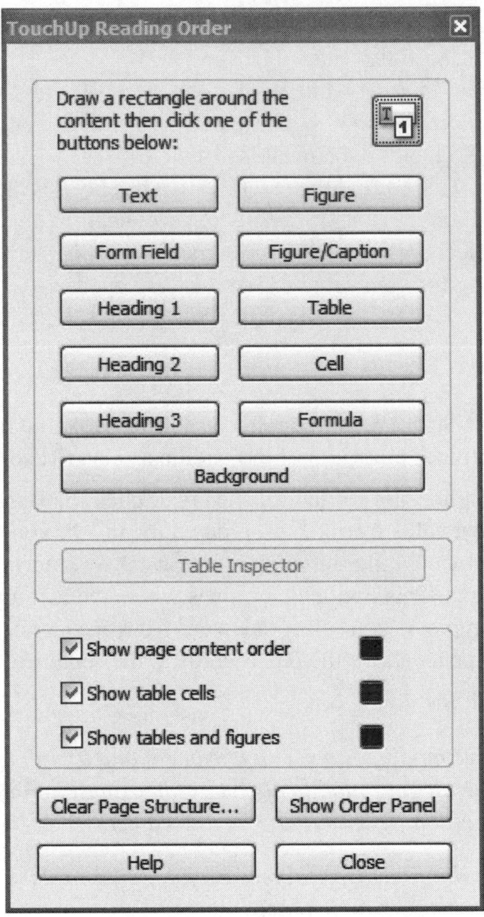

3. Click the appropriate button within the dialog box to tag the selection. You have the following buttons from which to choose:
   - **Text** Tags a selection as text.
   - **Figure** Tags an image within the document as a figure. Note, if you include text within the selection, it may not be accessible to a screen reader.
   - **Form Field** Tags the selection as a form field.
   - **Figure/Caption** Tags a figure and associated caption as a single tag. The text within the tag is defined as a caption. Use this option when you don't want a figure caption misread as text by a screen reader or added to an adjacent block of text.
   - **Heading 1, Heading 2, Heading 3** Tags a selection as a level 1, level 2, or level 3 heading.

- **Table** Tags a selection as a table.
- **Cell** Tags a selection as a table or a header cell. You can also use this button to merge cells that were incorrectly split.
- **Formula** Tags the current selection as a formula. Adding a description using alternate text is advisable because screen readers and speech recognition software often handle formula tags differently than normal text.
- **Background** Tags the current selection as a background element or artifact, which prevents the selection from being displayed on the tag tree.
- **Table Inspector** This button becomes available after you tag content as a table. Click the table, and then click the Table Inspector button to identify table headings, rows, and columns.

4. Check the Show Page Content Order check box (selected by default) to highlight tagged elements within the document. Each tagged element is numbered to reflect its reading order within the page. If desired, click the color swatch to choose a different highlight color from the color picker.
5. Check the Show Table Cells check box (selected by default) to highlight table cells within the document. If desired, click the color swatch to choose a different highlight color from the color picker.
6. Check the Show Tables And Figures check box (selected by default) to display a crossed-out box around each table and figure. If desired, click the color swatch to choose a different highlight color from the color picker.
7. Click the Clear Page Structure button to remove all tags from the current page.
8. Click the Show Order Panel button to display the Order panel, as shown next.

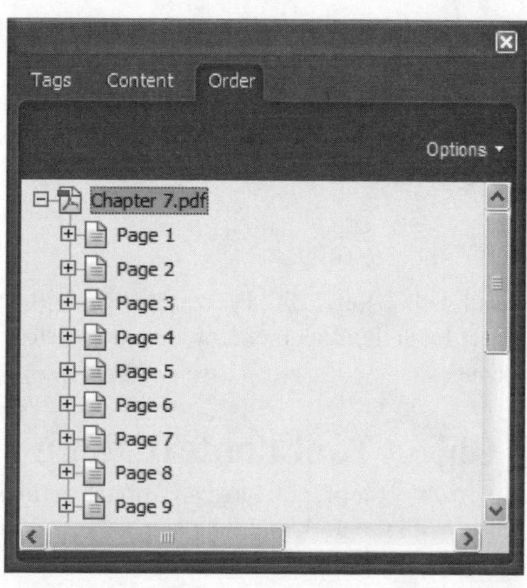

9. Click the plus sign to the left of a page to show the tagged elements on that page of the document.
10. Drag a tagged object to a different position in the Order panel to change the page reading order.
11. To exit the Order panel, click the Close (**X**) button in the upper-right corner of the panel.
12. Click Close to exit the TouchUp Reading Order dialog box.

To edit alternate text associated with a figure element, right-click (Windows) or CTRL-*click (Macintosh), and then choose Edit Alternate Text from the context menu to display the Alternate Text dialog box. Enter the desired text and click Close. Or, you can click Don't Add Alt-Text to exit the dialog box without adding alternate text.*

Use the TouchUp Object Tool (Professional Only)

You use the TouchUp Object tool to perform minor edits to an image, or to edit the image in a supported external image editor. The TouchUp Object tool context menu (described in the next section) has several commands that let you perform other tasks with embedded graphics. You can use the TouchUp Object tool to delete, move, or remove an object by performing the following steps:

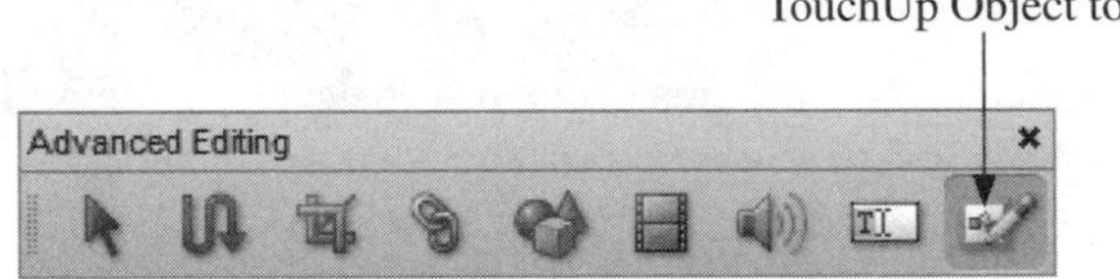

1. Choose Tools | Advanced Editing | TouchUp Object Tool. If you're going to touch up several objects in a document, choose Tools | Advanced Editing | Show Advanced Editing toolbar to display the toolbar in the workspace. Then, you have ready access to the TouchUp Object tool.
2. Click the object you want to edit. You can select graphic images or entire blocks of text with the TouchUp Object tool. To select more than one object, select the first object, and then click additional objects while pressing SHIFT. After selecting the object(s), do one of the following:
   - Drag the object to a new location.
   - Delete the object by choosing Edit | Delete. You can either press DELETE to remove the selected object from the document, or choose Delete from the TouchUp Object tool context menu.

Use the TouchUp Object Tool Context Menu

When you select the TouchUp Object tool, you have additional options available through its context menu. Select an object with the tool, and then right-click (Windows) or CTRL-click (Macintosh) to open the TouchUp tool context menu.

The available context menu commands vary, depending on previous actions you performed with the tool. The following list includes all the tasks you can perform from the TouchUp Object tool context menu, shown next. Most of the commands are similar to those found in many image-editing and word processing applications. The following explains the commands specific to Acrobat:

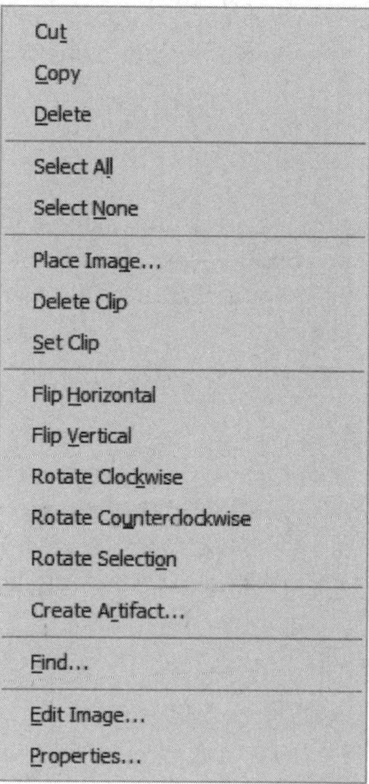

- **Place Image** Displays the Open dialog box, which enables you to select an image and place it in the document.
- **Delete Clip** Deletes any objects clipping the selected objects. For example, if you modify the size of a text object and some of the characters are clipped, choosing this command reveals the clipped text.
- **Set Clip** Sets the clipping region for the selected objects.
- **Create Artifact** Adds an artifact to the selected object. *Artifacts* are used as elements in tagged documents.
- **Remove Artifact** Removes an unwanted artifact from a PDF file.
- **Find** Launches the Find Element dialog box, enabling you to search for a document element such as an artifact, unmarked link, and so on.

- **Edit Image** Launches the supported image-editing application. To specify an external editor, choose Edit | Preferences | General and click the TouchUp title. You can then choose Photoshop or Photoshop Elements as the application to use for editing images or illustrations from within Acrobat.

NOTE

Although you can choose another image editor from within the Preferences dialog box, at press time, only Photoshop and Photoshop Elements have the capability to edit an image within a PDF document. If you attempt to do this after specifying a different image editor in Preferences, the image-editing application displays a warning dialog box stating the file type isn't supported.

- **Edit Object** Launches the supported illustration-editing application. To specify an external editor, choose Edit | Preferences | General and click the TouchUp title. You can then choose Adobe Illustrator as the application you will use to edit graphic objects selected with the TouchUp Object tool.
- **Properties** Opens the Properties dialog box, which supplies information about the selected object.

TIP

You can use the TouchUp tool to copy objects from one document to another. Open two documents, and then choose Window | Tile (or, if you prefer, Window | Cascade). Use the TouchUp tool to select an object, and then choose Copy from the context menu. Click anywhere in the second document, and then choose one of the Paste options from the context menu.

Summary

In this chapter, you learned how to edit your PDF documents by adding pages, deleting pages, and extracting pages. You discovered how to accomplish these tasks using the Pages panel, menu commands, and tools. And, you learned how to remove unwanted elements from pages with the Crop tool and the Crop Pages menu commands. If you create PDF documents for presentations, you now know how to add a touch of professionalism by using page transitions. In the next chapter, you learn how to review and add comments to PDF documents.

Chapter 10

Review PDF Documents

How to…

- Use the Comments panel
- Add comments
- Use the Sticky Note tool
- Add audio comments
- Use the File Attachment tool
- Use the Attachments panel

When you use Acrobat in a corporate environment, you can share information with colleagues in faraway locales. You can send documents via e-mail or a corporate intranet for review and approval. Team members or clients can mark up the PDF document with audio comments, notes, highlighted phrases, shapes to highlight items, text boxes, and more. Have you ever sent out an original document for review and had a team member alter the original by adding comments to the text or modifying the formulas of a spreadsheet? If so, you will appreciate how easy it is to create a PDF document from the original, and to use the copy to share and receive comments with colleagues using the Acrobat annotation tools.

When you mark up a document, you often need to identify the object you want modified, and then create a note or other annotation to reflect the desired change. You can use shapes to identify the object, highlight the object, or point to the object with an arrow, a straight line, a callout, or a squiggly line drawn with the Pencil tool. In this chapter, you learn how to use the annotation tools to mark up a document, add comments to a document, and more.

Initiate an E-Mail Review

If you created a PDF document that you want other colleagues to review, you can easily seek their input by initiating an e-mail review. When you start an e-mail review and send the document to selected reviewers, Acrobat sends a Forms Data Format (FDF) file that contains setup and configuration information, as well as a copy of the PDF document you want reviewed. Your reviewers can open the e-mail file attachment—which opens the document in Acrobat Standard or Professional, or the Adobe Reader 7.0 or later, if the review initiator chooses the option to include Adobe Reader users in the review—add their own comments to the document, and then send the comments back to you. As an added bonus, when Acrobat 8.0 Professional users initiate a review, they can invite Adobe Reader users to participate in a review, and display Drawing Markup tools for the review. To initiate an e-mail review, follow these steps:

1. Open the document you want to send for review.
2. Choose Comments | Attach for Email Review. Acrobat displays the Identity Setup dialog box.

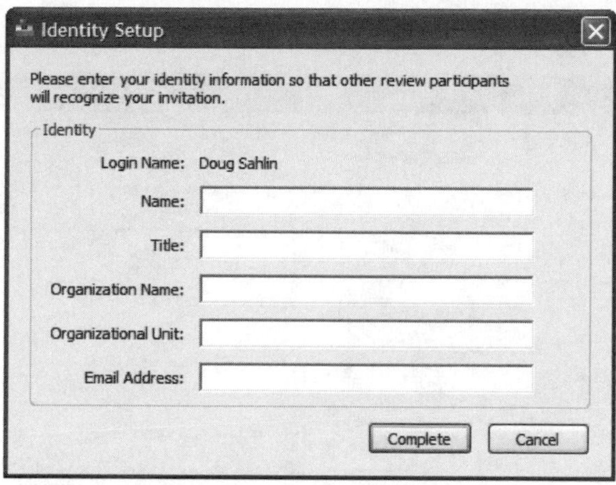
Identity Setup
Please enter your identity information so that other review participants will recognize your invitation.
Identity
Login Name: Doug Sahlin
Name:
Title:
Organization Name:
Organizational Unit:
Email Address:
Complete
Cancel

NOTE *The Identity Setup dialog box appears the first time you send any PDF document for an e-mail review. The information you enter is stored and automatically sent for each additional e-mail review you initiate.*

3. Enter your information in the Identity Setup dialog box, and then click Complete to display the first page, Getting Started, of the Send By Email For Review Wizard. If you currently have a document open, its filename is displayed in the Specify A PDF File To Send By Email For Review field, as shown next. You can send a different PDF document for review by clicking the Browse button, which displays the Open dialog box and enables you to navigate to the file you want to send.

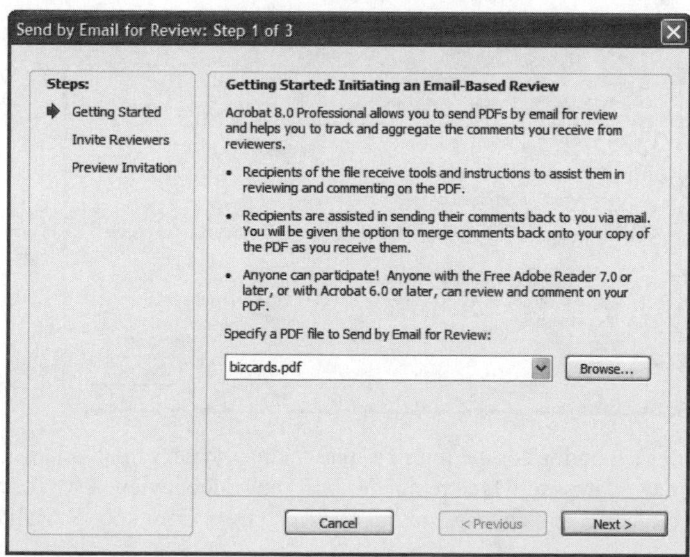
Send by Email for Review: Step 1 of 3
Steps:
Getting Started
Invite Reviewers
Preview Invitation
Getting Started: Initiating an Email-Based Review
Acrobat 8.0 Professional allows you to send PDFs by email for review and helps you to track and aggregate the comments you receive from reviewers.
• Recipients of the file receive tools and instructions to assist them in reviewing and commenting on the PDF.
• Recipients are assisted in sending their comments back to you via email. You will be given the option to merge comments back onto your copy of the PDF as you receive them.
• Anyone can participate! Anyone with the Free Adobe Reader 7.0 or later, or with Acrobat 6.0 or later, can review and comment on your PDF.
Specify a PDF file to Send by Email for Review:
bizcards.pdf
Browse...
Cancel
< Previous
Next >

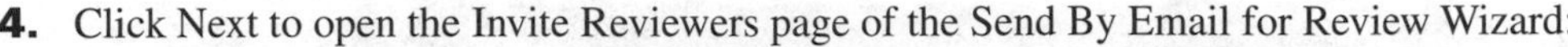

4. Click Next to open the Invite Reviewers page of the Send By Email for Review Wizard:

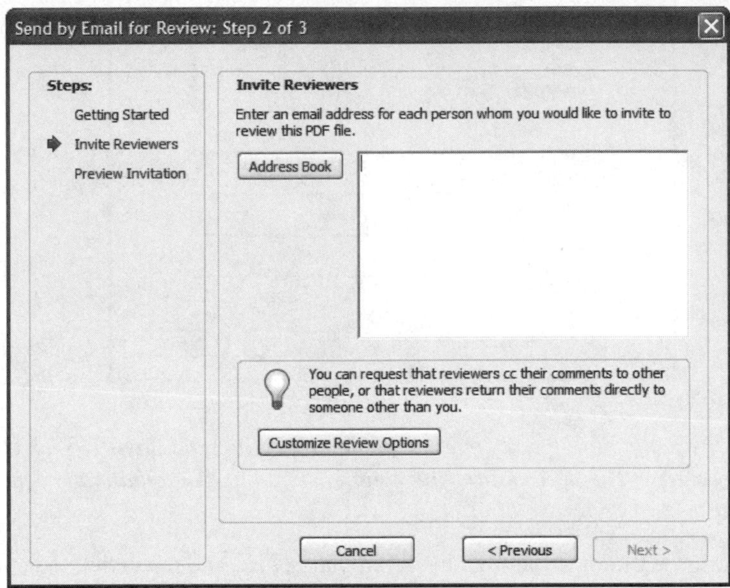

5. Enter the e-mail addresses of your reviewers in the Invite Reviewers field. Separate each e-mail address with a comma. Or, you can click the Address Book button and choose recipient e-mail addresses from your E-Mail address book.
6. Click the Customize Review Options button to display the Review Options dialog box:

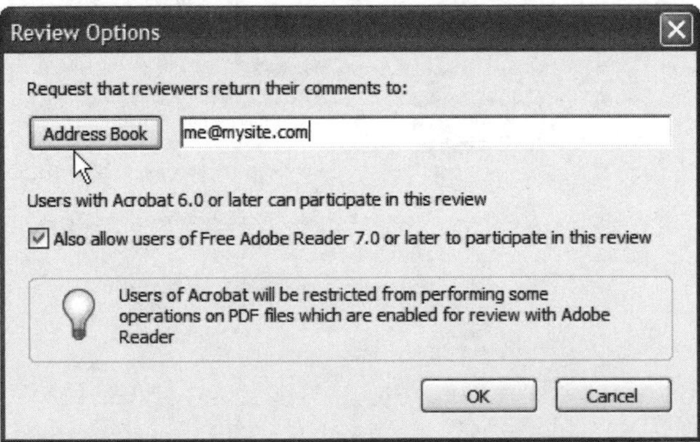

7. Accept the default option for the return e-mail address (your e-mail address), or enter a different e-mail address to which recipients will return the review. Or, you can click the Address Book button and choose a return e-mail address from your E-Mail address book.

8. By default, the Also Allow Users Of Free Adobe Reader 7.0 or Later To Participate In This Review check box is selected, which enables users of Adobe Reader 7.0 or later to review and mark up the document.
9. Click OK to exit the Review Options dialog box, and then click Next to display the Preview Invitation page of the Send By Email For Review Wizard:

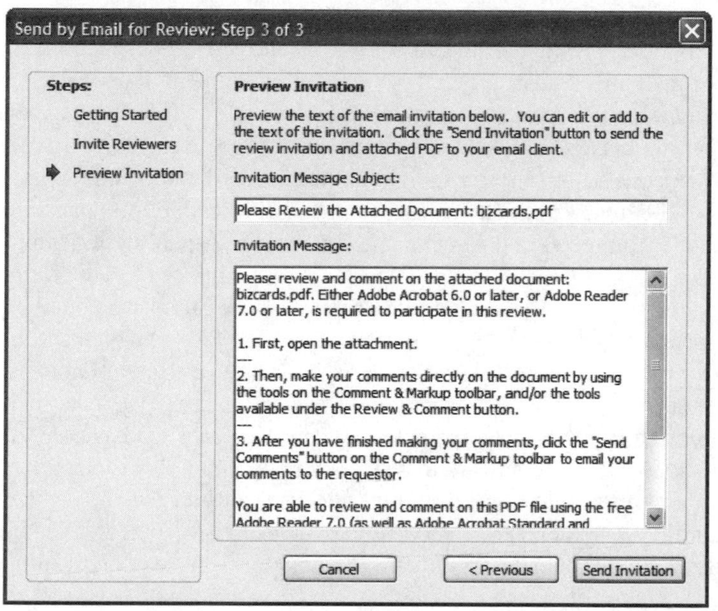

10. Accept the default Invitation Message Subject title or enter a different title.
11. Accept the default Invitation Message or modify it with additional information. The default message gives reviewers detailed instructions on how to conduct the review and return their comments to you.
12. Click Send Invitation. Acrobat sends the document for review and displays a message to that effect. If your e-mail application isn't set up to automatically send messages, Acrobat puts the e-mail message and attachment in the out box of your e-mail application. You will then have to manually send the review invitation from your e-mail application.

When you try to send a PDF document for review, certain e-mail applications may generate an error message saying the temporary file for the document isn't available. If this occurs, refer to your e-mail application's Help menu, or select another e-mail application, such as Microsoft Outlook Express, which should send the document with no errors.

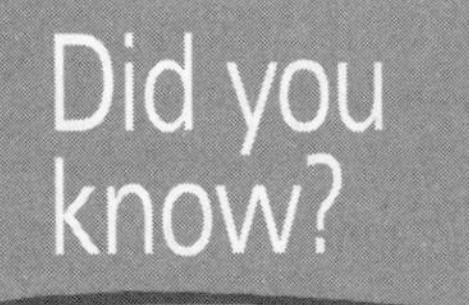

Using Adobe 7.0 and Later Reader in a Review

If you own Acrobat Professional, when you initiate an e-mail review, you can make it possible for users of the free Adobe 7.0 or 8.0 Reader to participate in a review. After enabling this option and sending the review, Adobe 7.0 and 8.0 Reader recipients receive the document as an e-mail attachment. When they open the attachment, it appears in Adobe 7.0 or 8.0 Reader, complete with a Comment & Markup toolbar. The Comment & Markup tools are identical to what's in Acrobat Professional, enabling Adobe Reader 7.0 and 8.0 users to add notes, indicate text edits, add stamps, highlight text, record audio comments, and add file attachments to the review document. Adobe 7.0 and 8.0 Reader users participating in a review also have the Comments and Attachments Panels. The capability to include Adobe 7.0 and 8.0 Reader users in a review makes it possible for you to send PDFs for review to clients and colleagues who don't own Acrobat Professional or Standard. Your Adobe 7.0 and 8.0 Reader reviewers can access help from the How To window, which automatically opens to the *Participate in an email-based review* section after the invitation to review the e-mail attachment is opened. There, they can find steps on how to participate in the review and links with information on how to add notes and comments, as well as how to indicate text edits and mark up a document. Certain restrictions apply to a PDF document enabled for Adobe Reader. These restrictions appear in the Adobe Reader interface below the toolbar. You can also enable Adobe Reader users to add comments to a document, even if it isn't sent out in an e-mail review by choosing Comments | Enable for Commenting in Adobe Reader.

You receive comments from your reviewers as FDF files attached to e-mail messages (reviewers won't be able to see the original document with comments from all reviewers unless you send the document with comments for another review). When you open the file, Acrobat opens the original file you sent for review and adds the reviewers' comments. You can keep track of your reviews by using the Tracker, as discussed in the upcoming section "Use the Tracker."

In addition to e-mail-based reviews, you can also launch shared reviews and browser-based reviews. For more information, see Chapter 13.

To add comments from other versions of a document to the document you're currently reviewing, choose Comment | Migrate Comments.

Use the Tracker

You use the Tracker to keep tabs on the documents you send out for review. When you use the Tracker, it appears in a floating window that you can maximize. To use the Tracker, follow these steps:

1. Choose Comments | Review Tracker. The Tracker opens, as shown in Figure 10-1. In the left pane, you see a list of the documents you've sent for review. When you click a document title, information about the review appears in the right pane of the dialog box.

NOTE *If you're participating in e-mail reviews instituted by other parties, they appear in the Reviews I've Joined section of the Tracker.*

2. Select a review in the left pane to display the following information in the right pane:
   - **Document** Displays the filename of the selected document. Click the link to open the document in the Document pane.
   - **Location** Displays the path to the document and also acts as a link to the document.
   - **Sent** Displays the date and time you initiated the review.
   - **Reviewers** Displays the e-mail address of each reviewer. Click the e-mail address to open your default e-mail application and send a message to the reviewer.

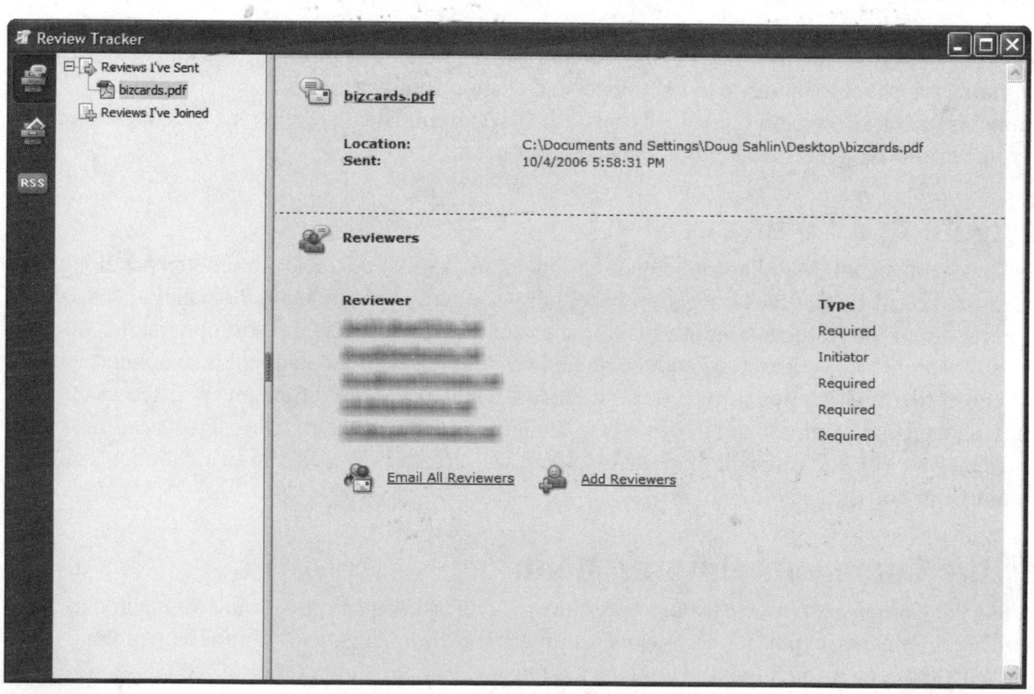

FIGURE 10-1 You use the Tracker to manage e-mail and browser-based reviews.

3. You can manage a review by clicking one of the following buttons beneath the reviewers' e-mail addresses:
   - **Email All Reviewers** Launches your e-mail application with the subject and the e-mail addresses of your reviewers already entered. Fill in the Subject field and, if desired, modify the default message, which reads, "Reminder: Please review and comment on," followed by the filename of the document you sent for review.
   - **Add Reviewers** Launches the Send By Email For Review Wizard. Follow the prompts to add additional reviewers, as outlined previously in the section "Initiate an E-Mail Review."

NOTE *If you select a document that is part of a browser-based review, the Manage button becomes the Go Back Online button, which, when clicked, opens the document in a web browser.*

Use the Comments Panel

When you open a document with comments, each comment is noted in the Comments panel. The *Comments panel* lists the title of each comment and the page number on which the comment can be found. You can configure the Comments panel to display comments by type, reviewer, or status. The Comments panel has several tools and an Options menu you can use to import comments, export selected comments, find comments, and delete comments. You can also use the Comments panel to navigate to comments and change comment properties. To open the Comments panel, shown in Figure 10-2, open the Navigation pane and click the Comments icon. Or, you can choose View | Navigation Panels | Comments.

Navigate to a Comment

The Comments panel is similar to the one introduced in Acrobat 6.0. The Comments panel icon resides on the left side of the Navigation pane, but when you click the icon, the panel opens at the bottom of the Acrobat window, making it easier for you to track and sort comments. A comment is noted by its icon type and the name of the reviewer. If a document is annotated with an attached file, it is referred to by a paper-clip icon. The attachment's filename is listed in the Attachments panel. A plus sign (+) appears to the left of each comment. Click it to reveal the comment type, plus the date and time the comment was created. To navigate to a comment, click the comment icon or the comment title.

Use the Comments Options Menu

You use the *Comments Options menu* to perform various tasks related to comments, such as importing comments, exporting comments, summarizing comments, and so on. To open the Comments Options menu, click the Options icon near the upper-right corner of the panel.

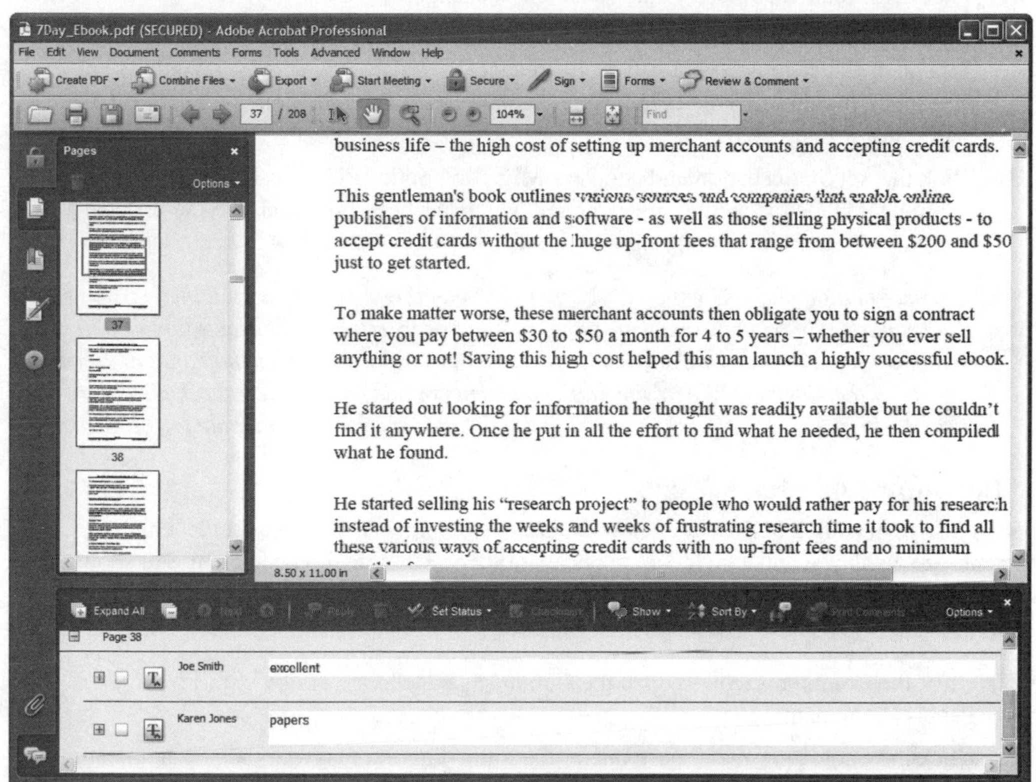

FIGURE 10-2 You use the Comments panel to navigate to and manage comments.

Use the Comments Panel Context Menu

Many Acrobat users prefer the convenience of a context menu to streamline workflow. When you select a comment in the Comments panel, you can access a context menu for that comment by right-clicking (Windows) or CTRL-clicking (Macintosh). Within the context menu, you can find commands to expand the comment, set the status of the comment, reply to the comment, delete the comment, or view its properties.

Set Comment Status

When you receive a document with comments from several reviewers, you can set the status of the comment to indicate your disposition to other reviewers regarding a particular comment. The default comment status is None, which changes as soon as a reviewer responds to a comment by setting its status. To set the status of a comment, follow these steps:

1. Select the comment whose status you want to change.
2. Click the Set Status button and choose one of the following Review options: None, Accepted, Cancelled, Completed, or Rejected . Or, you can right-click (Windows) or CTRL-click (Macintosh) the comment and choose one of the previous options from the Set Status drop-down menu.
3. Click the Set Status button and choose a Migration option. This enables you to verify a comment made by another reviewer and which has been migrated into the original document by marking it as None, Not Confirmed, or Confirmed.

You can mark comments with a check mark by selecting a comment, and then clicking the Checkmark icon on the Comments panel toolbar, or by clicking the check box next to a comment icon. Marking a comment in this manner is your reminder that you've already reviewed the comment. When you mark comments in this manner, the check marks are saved with your copy of the document, but other reviewers won't be able to see them.

Use the Show Comments Menu

When you're reviewing a PDF document with multiple comments, you can decide which comments are displayed and which comments are not. For example, you can choose to show only comments created by a certain reviewer, or show only comments created with the Sticky Note tool. To specify which comments are displayed, follow these steps:

1. Click the Comments icon to open the Comments panel. Or, choose View | Navigation Panels | Comments.
2. Click the Show icon and choose one of the following options from the pop-up menu:
   - **Comment & Markup Toolbar** Displays or hides the Comment & Markup toolbar.
   - **Hide Comments List** Closes the Comments panel.
   - **Hide All Comments** Hides all comments in the document and in the Comments panel. After invoking this command, the Show All Comments command appears on the pop-up menu. Choose the Show All Comments command to display comments again.
   - **Show By Type** Displays a drop-down menu with a list of all comment types. Select a comment type, and only comments of that type are displayed in the documents and Comments panel. You can select more than one comment type.
   - **Show By Reviewer** Displays a drop-down menu listing all reviewers. Select one or more reviewers whose comments you want to display, or select All Reviewers.
   - **Show By Status** Displays status types with individual drop-down menus for Migration and Review. Select one or more comment status types you want to display, or select All Status.
   - **Show By Checked State** Displays a drop-down menu from which you can choose to display checked comments, unchecked comments, or both.

- **Open All Pop-Ups** Opens all pop-up notes in the document.
- **Minimize All Pop-Ups** Minimizes all pop-up notes to their icons.
- **Show Connector Lines** Displays a connector line between an open pop-up note and its icon in the document when your mouse hovers over the icon.
- **Align New Pop Ups By Default** Aligns a pop-up note with the right border of the document, no matter where you click the Sticky Note or other annotation tool inside the document.

Sort Comments

By default, Acrobat sorts all comments by the number of the page on which they appear. You can, however, change the way Acrobat sorts comments. For example, if you work with a team of authors on a document, you can sort comments by author. To change the way in which comments in the document are sorted, follow these steps:

1. In the Navigation pane, click the Comment icon. Or, you can choose View | Navigation Panels | Comments.
2. Click the Sort By icon and, from the drop-down menu, choose one of the following:
   - **Type** Acrobat sorts the comments by type. When you choose this option, Acrobat creates one heading in the Comment panel for each type of comment used in the document.
   - **Page (Default)** Acrobat creates a heading for each page with comments.
   - **Author** Acrobat creates a heading for each author who added comments to the document.
   - **Date** Acrobat sorts comments by date, creating a heading for each date on which a comment was created. Acrobat displays the earliest date at the top of the panel. Dates are displayed numerically in the default format specified by your operating system (OS).
   - **Color** Acrobat creates headings that are square color chips. This option sorts the comments by the icon color of the tool used to create them. For example, if you click a yellow color chip, you see comments created with the Sticky Note tool, Text Box tool, and Highlight tool, all of which have yellow as the primary color for their tool icon.
   - **Checkmark Status** Acrobat creates two headings: Unmarked and Marked. If you have no Unmarked comments, Acrobat doesn't create an Unmarked heading. Likewise, if you have no Marked comments, Acrobat doesn't create a Marked heading. Note, the check marks created by other authors aren't saved with the document. This feature enables the current viewer of the document to check a comment after reading it.
   - **Status By Person** Acrobat creates headings for each status you assign a comment. As an example, you see separate headings for comments you have accepted, rejected, cancelled, and so on.

When multiple comments occur for a Sort By Type, a plus sign appears to the left of the heading. Click the plus sign to display all comments. Click the minus sign (−) to collapse all comments in a heading group.

Search Comments

When you're reviewing a document with multiple comments, you can search for specific information by entering a word or phrase in a field. To search comments, follow these steps:

1. Click the Comments icon in the Navigation pane to open the Comments panel. Or, choose View | Navigation Panels | Comments.
2. Click the Search Comments icon. The Search pane appears as a floating window to the left of the Document pane. This is a watered-down version of the pane that appears when you choose the Search command.
3. Enter the word or phrase you want to find within the document's comments. You can fine-tune your search by selecting the Whole Words Only option and/or the Case-Sensitive option.
4. Click the Search Comments button. Acrobat displays a list of all instances of the word or phrase you entered in the text field. Each keyword is a link to the comment.
5. Click a keyword to navigate within the document to the comment.

To print a copy of all comments in a document, click the Print Comments icon and choose to print a comments summary on a device printer or create a PDF comments summary.

Delete Comments

When a comment has outlived its usefulness, you can delete it. When you delete comments, you decrease the file size of the document and eliminate having to deal with comments that are no longer relevant. To delete a comment:

1. In the Navigation pane, click the Comments icon.
2. Select the comment you want to delete and press DELETE, choose Edit | Delete, or right-click (Windows) or CTRL-click (Macintosh), and then choose Delete from the context menu.

Modify Comments

You can modify the appearance of comments, such as the color, and change the author and subject information. You can also change the default icon used to display a comment created with the Sticky Note tool. However, the icons for many of the other annotation methods are set by default. To modify a comment, follow these steps:

1. In the Navigation pane, click the Comments icon.
2. Select the comment you want to modify.

3. Right-click (Windows) or CTRL-click (Macintosh), and then choose Properties from the context menu to open the Properties dialog box. Note, the dialog box name varies to reflect the comment type you select. The following illustration shows the Sticky Note Properties dialog box.

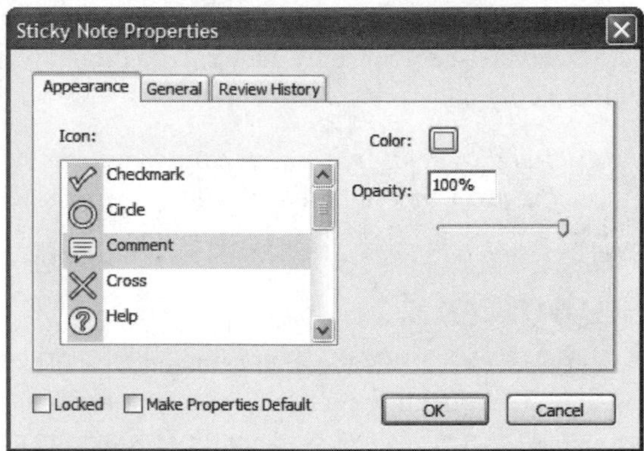

4. Modify the comment as desired. From within the Appearance tab, you can change the icon displayed with the comment. The General tab enables you to change the author of the comment and the subject. And, the Review History tab displays the Migration and Review History of the comment. In addition, you can choose from two check boxes: the first enables you to lock a comment, which prevents it from being moved; and the second makes the properties of the comment you're modifying the default properties for all other comments created with the corresponding tool.
5. Click OK to close the dialog box.

If Acrobat Password Security has been applied to the document and commenting is not allowed, you won't be able to edit comments unless the settings are changed. If Acrobat Certificate Security has been assigned to the document, you will be able to edit comments if the document author grants you permission to edit comments. For more information on Acrobat security, see Chapter 11.

Reply to Comments

When you receive documents for review, you can reply to comments other reviewers have added to the document. If you set the status for a comment, you can add a reply to let the reviewer know why you chose a particular status, or just add a general reply to add your two cents' worth to the review. To reply to a comment, follow these steps:

1. Open the Comments panel, as outlined previously in the section "Navigate to a Comment."
2. Select the comment to which you want to respond.
3. Click the Reply button at the top of the Comments panel. Acrobat displays a new title nested within the original comment with a Reply icon and a text field to the right of the comment title. Or, you can right-click (Windows) or CTRL-click (Macintosh) and choose Reply from the context menu.
4. Enter your reply, and then click outside of the reply window. Note, if you enter a lengthy comment, Acrobat wraps the text to a new line and displays a minus sign to the left of the comment title. You can also press ENTER or RETURN to continue the comment on a new line. Click the minus sign to collapse the reply to a single line.

Replies are nested within the original note and are also displayed in the Comments panel. When other reviewers see your reply, they can continue the thread by clicking your comment, and then clicking Reply.

To edit a reply, move your cursor over the reply until it becomes an I-beam, click to open the text window, and then apply your edits. To delete a reply, select it and press DELETE.

Add Comments

When you receive a PDF document or send a PDF document, you can add comments to the document. Comments are a handy way to communicate among team members or clients. Comments are readily accessible in the Comments panel and can easily be added with the click of a mouse. You can add sticky notes or audio comments, or create comments in text boxes.

If the document you're viewing is part of a review, you can display any changes made to an annotation created with a commenting tool. To do so, select the comment, right-click (Windows) or CTRL*-click (Macintosh), and choose Properties from the context menu. After the comment's Properties dialog box appears, click the Review History panel to view a list of any changes to the document.*

Use the Sticky Note Tool

Use the *Sticky Note tool* (known as the Note tool in previous versions of Acrobat) when you want to add a quick comment that's pertinent to a certain part of the document. When you use the Sticky Note tool to create a comment, you can accept the default option and leave the note open, so a reviewer can read it when the page opens, or collapse the note to an icon that, when clicked, opens the note in a window. When you create a comment with the Sticky Note tool, you can define the size of the note window, and the type and color of the note icon, as well as enter your comments. To add a comment to a PDF document with the Sticky Note tool, follow these steps:

1. Navigate to the point in the document where you want to add the note.
2. Choose Tools | Comment & Markup | Sticky Note. Or, you can choose Tools | Comment & Markup | Show Comment & Markup toolbar to display the toolbar shown here, and then select the Sticky Note tool:

3. Click the point in the document where you want the note to appear. When you create a note in this manner, Acrobat opens a blank note window of the default size. When you use the default window size, scroll bars are provided for use when reading lengthy notes. After you create the window, a blinking cursor appears in the window, signifying Acrobat is ready for you to enter some text.

TIP

To size the note window while creating it, click a point in the document where you want the note to appear, and then drag diagonally. As you drag, a bounding box appears and defines the size of the window you're creating. Release the mouse button when the window is the desired size. To constrain the window to a square, press shift while dragging. Acrobat sizes the note window as you specify when the document is next opened.

4. Enter the text you want to appear in the comment window. Click outside the note window when you finish entering text.
5. If desired, close the note window. Or, you can leave the note open.

If you opt to close each sticky note you've added to a PDF document, viewers of your document can read each closed sticky note by double-clicking its icon. After you create a note, you can modify the appearance of the sticky note icon and its colors by changing its properties.

About the Sticky Note Options Menu

When you add a note to a menu, an Options icon appears in the upper-right corner of the note. You can use the commands from this menu to modify note properties, set note status, and more. To display the Sticky Note Options menu, click the Options icon.

Set Sticky Note Properties

The default icon for a sticky note looks like a Post-it® note and, in keeping with that paradigm, the Acrobat designers gave the icon a default color of bright yellow. If you don't like bright yellow for your virtual sticky notes, you can change the characteristics of the icon by following these steps:

1. To select the sticky note you want to modify, click its name in the Comments panel, as discussed previously, or click the actual note in the document. You can select the sticky note with the Hand tool, Sticky Note tool, or Select tool.
2. Right-click (Windows) or CTRL-click (Macintosh) and choose Properties from the context menu. The Sticky Note Properties dialog box appears.
3. On the Appearance panel, choose an icon from the list in the Icon window:
4. Click the Color button and choose a color from the color picker. Or, click the Other Color icon and choose a color from the system color picker. When you choose colors from the system color picker, they may not look the same when viewed cross-platform.

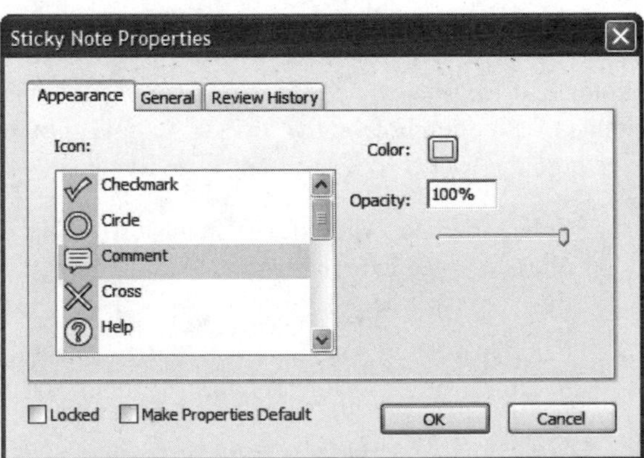

5. Enter a value in the Opacity field or drag the slider to specify note opacity. This determines how much of the document is visible through the note icon. The note icon is totally opaque (nontransparent) at the default setting of 100 percent. Note, note opacity isn't supported in Acrobat 5.0 and older.

6. Click the General tab, shown in the following illustration, which will enable you to enter text to change the authors' name or the note subject. For the Author field, Acrobat's default is to use the comment author's name (as given when the application owner registered the product with Adobe). Notice the time stamp at the bottom of this section. After you modify the note properties, the time stamp updates to reflect the time the properties were changed.

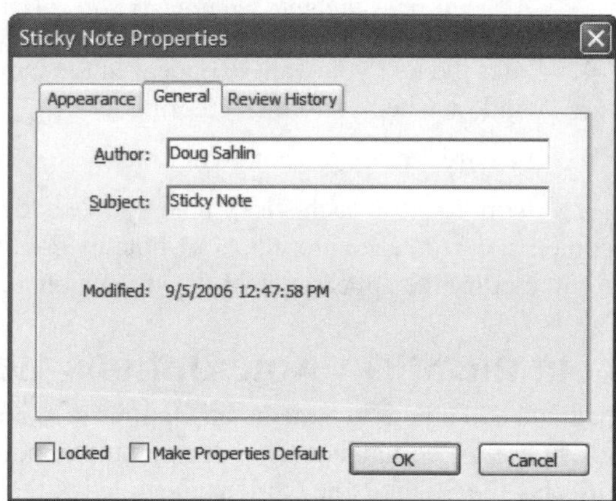

7. Click the Locked check box at the lower-left corner of the dialog box to lock the position of the note in the document and prevent any property changes until the note is unlocked by once again clicking the check box.

TIP *Even though you have locked a comment, another reviewer can unlock and modify it unless you add security to the document and disallow commenting.*

8. Click OK to exit the Sticky Note Properties dialog box and have Acrobat apply the changes to the note.

Modify Sticky Note Text

In addition to modifying a note's properties, you can also modify the text in a pop-up note. As mentioned earlier, you can display pop-up notes or hide them. Users can double-click a sticky note icon or an annotation made with any of the other commenting tools to reveal a hidden pop-up note. Text for pop-up notes is displayed in the Comments panel as well. You can also see the contents of a hidden note in the form of a ToolTip by holding your cursor over the note icon. You can change the font color, size, and style. To change text in a pop-up note:

1. Select the note whose text you want to modify. The easiest way to do this is to double-click the note icon in the document to open the pop-up note. If the note is already open, this step isn't necessary.
2. Click inside the note, and then drag to select the text you want to modify. You can modify a single character, word, sentence, or the entire text.

TIP *To select all text in a pop-up note, place your cursor inside the note, and then press ctrl-a (Windows) or command-a (Macintosh).*

3. Choose View | Toolbars | Properties Bar to open the Properties bar:

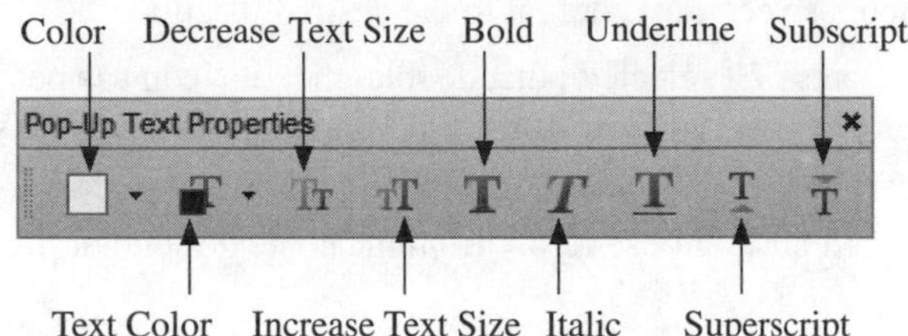

4. Click the drop-down arrow to the right of the Color icon and choose a color from the color picker. This determines the color displayed for the note's icon in the document, as well as the color of the title bar of the note when it's popped up.
5. To change the color of the pop-up note text, select the text in the note, click the drop-down arrow to the right of the Text Color icon in the Properties bar, and choose a color from the color picker. Or, you can click Other Color and choose a color from the system color picker.
6. To decrease the size of selected note text, click the Decrease Text Size icon. You can click the icon repeatedly, but Acrobat stops decreasing the text size when it reaches 6 points.
7. To increase the size of selected note text, click the Increase Text Size icon. You can click the icon repeatedly, but Acrobat stops increasing text size when it reaches 18 points.
8. Click the applicable icon to boldface, italicize, underline, superscript, or subscript the selected text.

10

Edit Notes

In addition to changing the properties of a note, you can change the position of a note, edit its contents, or delete it. In a previous section, you learned how to delete a note from within the Comments panel. In this section, you learn how to edit a note from within the document. To edit a note within the document, select it with the Hand tool, Sticky Note tool, or Select tool and perform one of the following tasks:

1. To delete a selected note, choose Edit | Delete. Or, press DELETE or choose Delete from the context menu. You can also click Options to open the Sticky Note Options menu, which contains commands to delete notes, reply to a note, change note properties, and more.

NOTE

When you position your cursor over a sticky note icon, your cursor icon becomes a diagonal arrowhead, which is the indication you can double-click and drag the note icon. When you move your cursor inside the note body, it becomes an I-beam, indicating you can edit text. When you move your cursor to the lower-right corner of the note, it becomes a diagonal line with an arrowhead on each end, indicating you can resize the note window.

2. To delete a reply to a note, right-click the reply within the note, and then choose Delete This Reply from the context menu.

3. To move a selected note, click the title bar of the note, and then drag it to a new location.
4. To move a note icon, select it and drag it to the desired location.
5. To change the contents of a selected note, double-click its icon to open the note, edit the contents, and then close the window. If the note is already open, place your cursor inside the note and perform your edits.
6. To reply to a selected note, choose Reply from the context menu or the Sticky Note Option menu.
7. To reply to a reply, select the reply from within the note, and choose Reply To This Reply from the context menu, or Reply from the Sticky Note Option menu.
8. To resize the window of a selected note, double-click its icon (if the note pop-up is closed), and then click-and-drag the lower-right handle of the pop-up note window. To resize the window proportionately, press SHIFT while dragging.

Add Audio Comments

If you prefer the spoken word to a written comment, you can record a comment and add it to a document. Audio comments can often be more effective than written comments. You can convey excitement and enthusiasm with a recorded comment.

You record the audio comments through a microphone attached to your computer, or you can choose an audio file stored on your system. Whichever method you use, the sound is embedded with the document. To record comments with your PDF documents, your computer must have a sound card and software capable of recording from a microphone. Acrobat relies on your system recording software to create the comment embedded with the PDF document. To record an audio comment for a PDF document:

1. Choose Tools | Comment & Markup | Record Audio Comment.
2. Click the spot in the document where you want to add the audio comment, and the Sound Recorder dialog box appears, as shown here. This is the Windows version of the recorder. The Macintosh version looks slightly different.

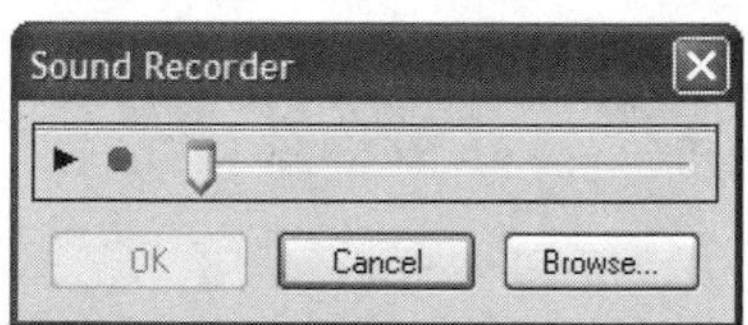

3. Click the Record button (a red circle) and speak into the microphone. When you begin recording, the Play button (a black triangle) changes to the Stop button (a solid black square). Or, click the Browse button to navigate to a folder on your computer that contains a prerecorded sound you want to attach to the document.
4. Click the Stop button to stop the recording. The button changes to Play again, which you can use to review the message you just recorded.
5. Click OK. Acrobat displays the Sound Attachment Properties dialog box.

6. On the Appearance panel, accept the default icon type (Sound), as shown here, or choose a different one from the list:
7. Accept the default sound attachment icon color (blue) or click the Color button to choose a different color from the color picker. Click the Other Color icon to choose a color from the system color picker.
8. Click the General panel and either accept the default information for the Author, Subject, and Description fields or enter different information.
9. Click OK to embed the sound in the document.

After you finish the recording, Acrobat designates the audio comment with the default speaker icon or the icon specified in the Appearance panel of the Sound Attachment Properties dialog box. To play the recording or sound file, double-click the icon. Or, right-click (Windows) or CTRL-click (Macintosh) the icon and choose Play File from the context menu.

You can modify the properties of an audio comment by right-clicking (Windows) or ctrl-clicking (Macintosh) the comment icon and choosing Properties from the context menu.

Create Text Annotations

You have another Acrobat tool at your disposal for adding comments to a document: the Text Box tool. When you use the *Text Box tool,* you can add text notes with borders and, if you desire, a solid-color background. When you annotate a document with the Text Box tool, you create a static note that occupies space in the document, whereas a Sticky Note tool annotation can be collapsed to an icon and popped up when needed. You can specify the font type, size, and style of text annotations.

Use the Text Box Tool

You can create a comment using the Text Box tool at any location in the document. When you create a comment with the Text Box tool, the comment appears on top of the actual elements in the PDF document; whereas a comment made with the Sticky Note tool appears as an icon in the document, with the actual comment appearing in a pop-up note.

To add a comment with the Text Box tool:

1. Choose Tools | Comment & Markup | Text Box Tool.
2. Click the point in the document where you want to add the comment, and Acrobat creates a rectangular text box (with default dimensions). A blinking cursor positions itself in the upper-left corner of the text box, prompting you to enter text.

If you find the default size of the Text Box tool text box isn't to your liking, you can size the box while creating it by clicking in the document, and then dragging diagonally. As you drag the tool, a rectangular bounding box gives you a preview of the text box size. Release the mouse button when the box is sized to your preference.

3. Enter the text for the comment. If you enter enough text, it will wrap to a new line.
4. After you write the comment, click outside the text box to stop entering text. You can now use the Text Box tool to create another text box.

You can modify the properties of an annotation created with the Text Box tool by choosing View | Toolbars | Properties Bar. After displaying the Properties bar, click inside the text box, and then you can change the background color. Select the text, and then change font type, text color, text size, text justification, and text style.

Edit Text Box Annotations

When you create a comment with the Text Box tool, you can edit the contents of the comment, move the location of the comment, and, when the comment has outlived its usefulness, delete the comment.

To modify text created with the Text Box tool, select the Hand tool, the Text Box tool, or the Select tool, double-click the comment you want to edit, and do one of the following:

- To select text, click-and-drag your cursor over the text characters you want to select.
- To select all text in the box, choose Edit | Select All. Or, you can choose Select All from the context menu or press CTRL + A (Windows) or COMMAND + A (Macintosh).
- To modify the selected text, enter new text from your keyboard.
- To delete selected text, press DELETE, choose Edit | Delete, or choose Delete from the context menu.
- To copy selected text to the clipboard, choose Edit | Copy. Or, you can choose Copy from the context menu.
- To cut selected text, choose Edit | Cut. Or, you can choose Cut from the context menu or press BACKSPACE.
- To paste text from the clipboard into a selected comment, place your cursor at the point you want to display the text, and then choose Edit | Paste. Or, you can choose Paste from the context menu. Note, some of the formatting you apply to the text in another application may be lost when it's pasted into a text box comment.

You can also change the position and size of a comment created with the Text Box tool. To move a comment, select the comment with the Hand tool, the Text Box tool, or the Select tool, and then drag it to a new location.

When you use the Text Box tool to edit a text box annotation, make sure you click or double-click the actual annotation. Otherwise, you create a new annotation with the tool.

To resize the text box, follow these steps:

1. Select the text box with the Hand tool, the Text Box tool, or the Select tool. Eight handles appear enabling you to change the width, height, or width and height.
2. Click-and-drag a corner handle to resize the box. To resize the box proportionately, press SHIFT while dragging. As you drag, Acrobat draws a rectangular bounding box, which gives you a preview of the current size of the box. Drag a handle in the middle of the right or left side to change the width, a handle at the top or bottom to change the height. Note, this doesn't change the size of the text.
3. Release the mouse button when the box is the desired size.
4. To move a selected text box comment, position your cursor over the comment. When you see a vertical and horizontal line with two arrowheads, click-and-drag the comment to the desired position.

TIP *You can spell check your comments before saving the document by choosing Edit | Check Spelling | In Comments, Fields & Editable Text.*

Use the Text Edits Tool

When you mark up a document with text, you can select text with the Text Edits tool and tell other reviewers how you'd like to modify the text. You can instruct reviewers to delete, change, or insert text in a document. The *Text Edits tool* is a great way to mark up a document created from a word-processing or page-making application. To use the Text Edit tool, follow these steps:

1. Choose Comment & Markup | Text Edits | Text Edits Tool. Acrobat displays the Indicating Text Edits dialog box, which gives you instructions on the use of the tool. Click OK to exit the dialog box and activate the Text Edits tool.

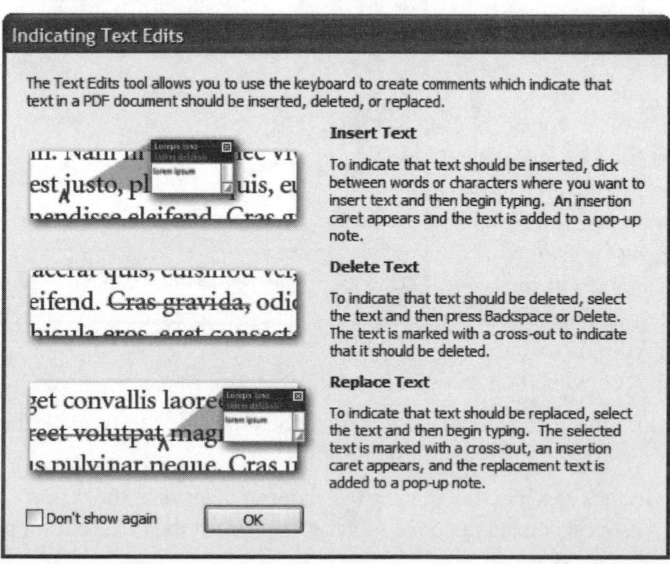

TIP *After you know how to use the Text Edits tool, you can prevent the Indicating Text Edits dialog box from appearing by clicking the Don't Show Again check box.*

2. To mark text for editing, do one of the following:
   - To insert text, click the point where you want the text inserted and begin typing the desired text. Acrobat places an insertion caret at the point where you clicked, and the text is displayed in a pop-up note.
   - To delete text, select the desired text, and then press BACKSPACE or DELETE. The text is marked with a red strikethrough.
   - To highlight, underline, or cross out text, select the desired text, right-click (Windows) or CTRL-click (Macintosh), and select the desired option from the context menu.

Attach Files to a Document

You can attach any file to a document for use by another reviewer or colleague. When you use the Attach File As A Comment tool to attach a file to a document, it becomes embedded in the document. Reviewers will need the software associated with the file installed on their computer to be able to view the file. To attach a file to a document:

1. Choose Tools | Comment & Markup | Attach File As A Comment.
2. Click the spot in the document where you want the File Attachment icon (a paperclip) to appear, and Acrobat opens the Add Attachment dialog box.
3. Navigate to the file you want to attach, click Select, and Acrobat opens the File Attachment Properties dialog box.

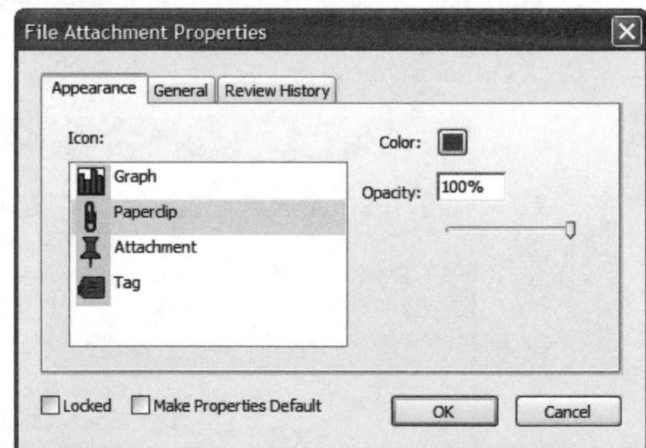

4. In the Icon list of the Appearance panel, select the icon you want to appear in the document. By default, the file attachment icon is a paper clip. You can choose a different icon, though, if you feel it's a better representation of the type of document you want to attach. For example, you may want to use the graph icon when attaching a spreadsheet.
5. Click the Color button and select a color from the color picker, or click the Other Color icon to choose a color from the system color picker.
6. Enter a value in the Opacity field, or drag the slider to determine the opacity of the text box background. The icon is totally opaque (nontransparent) at the default setting of 100 percent.

7. Click the General tab and accept the default information, or enter new information in the Author, Subject, and Description fields. If desired, click the Locked check box at the bottom of the panel to lock the position of the file attachment icon.
8. Click OK to exit the dialog box and attach the file to the document.

Attaching a file to a document may considerably increase the document file size. Because Acrobat stores additional information with the embedded (attached) file, the final document file size will be above and beyond the file size of the original document, combined with the file size of the attached file.

To add a file to the document without including a commenting icon, choose Document | Attach a File. When you attach a file in this manner, it's accessed from the Attachments panel.

Open a File Attachment

When you receive a PDF document with a file attachment, you open the file by double-clicking the file attachment icon. After you double-click the icon, Acrobat displays a warning dialog box saying the attached file may contain programs or macros with viruses. If you received the document from a trusted source, click Open This File to view the file. If you don't know the author of the PDF document, or you have reason to believe the attachment may have a virus, click Do Not Open, close the document, exit Acrobat, and then check the PDF document with your virus scanning software. If you decide to open the file, Acrobat launches the application on your computer associated with the file type of the attachment. When you open an attached file, your OS creates temporary files, the location of which will vary depending on the OS you use. Note, you can also open a file using the Attachments panel, as described in the upcoming section "Use The Attachments Panel."

If your antivirus software cannot scan an attachment to a PDF document, right-click (Windows) or CTRL*-click (Macintosh) the file attachment icon and choose Save Embedded File To Disk from the context menu. Close the PDF document to which the file was attached, and then, prior to opening the suspect file, use your antivirus software to scan the file you saved to disk.*

Edit File Attachment Properties

When you use the File Attachment tool to embed a file within a document, you cannot change the embedded file with the File Attachment Properties dialog box. Instead, you must make and save changes to the file before attaching it to a document. To delete the previous version of an attached file and embed a different one, select the file attachment icon with the Hand or Attach File tool and delete it by choosing Edit | Delete, pressing DELETE, or by choosing Delete from the context menu. After you delete the outdated file attachment, attach an up-to-date version of the file by using the steps outlined in the previous section.

As indicated, you can't change the file attached to a document by editing its properties in the File Attachment Properties dialog box. If it's unlocked, though, you can change the position of the file attachment icon by clicking it with either the Hand tool or the File Attachment tool, and then dragging it to a different location. You can also edit the properties of the file attachment icon by clicking the attachment icon, and then choosing Properties from the context menu to open the File Attachment Properties dialog box (shown previously). Modify the properties, as outlined in the previous section, and then click OK to exit the dialog box.

You can save an embedded file to your hard drive by clicking the file attachment icon, and then choosing Save Embedded File To Disk from the context menu. Or, you can click the Save button in the Attachments panel. Even if you know the author of the file, a good idea is to run a virus scan on the file before you open it, especially if it's a Word or Excel file that may contain macros, which can harbor viruses that can be harmful to your system.

Use the Attachments Panel

When you open a PDF file with attachments, the icon for the attachment appears on the page to which the attachment was added. You can view the attachment by double-clicking the icon as outlined previously. This is fine when you're perusing a PDF document page by page. However, when you want to cut to the chase and look at the document attachments, you can easily do so by using the Attachments panel, as shown in Figure 10-3.

To manage attachments within the Attachments panel:

1. Choose View | Navigation Panels | Attachments. Or, you can click the Attachments icon in the Navigation pane. After you open the Attachments panel, all file attachments are listed. Each attachment is divided into the following columns: Name, Description, Modified, Location In Document, and Size.
2. Click a column title to sort file attachments by that parameter. For example, if you click the Name column, attachments are sorted alphabetically in ascending order. Click the title again to sort the column in descending order.
3. Select a file attachment and do one of the following:
   - Click the Open button to open the attachment in the associated application. When you do this, Acrobat displays the Launch Attachment dialog box, which cautions you against opening the file as it may contain a virus. Click OK to open the document.

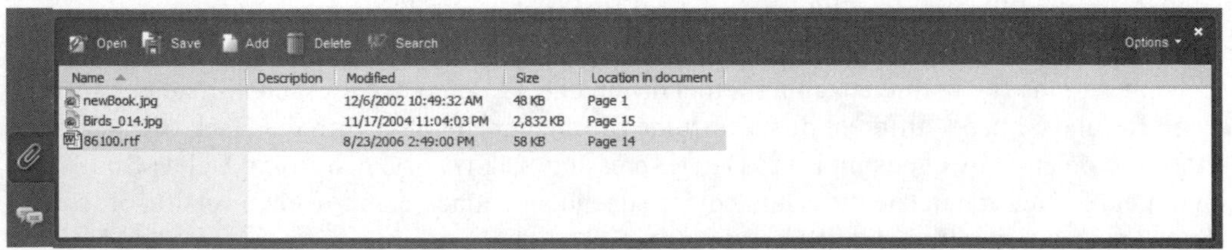

FIGURE 10-3 You use the Attachments panel to manage attachments to a PDF document.

- Double-click the document title to display the Launch Attachment dialog box. Click OK to open the document.
- Click the Save button to display the Save Attachment dialog box, which enables you to save the attachment to a folder on your hard drive.
- Click the Add button to open the Add Attachment dialog box. This enables you to add a new file attachment to the document. The attachment location is listed in the Attachments panel, regardless of the page you're viewing when adding the comment.
- Click the Delete button, which looks like a trashcan, to delete the attachment from the document.

4. Click the Options icon to reveal the Options menu. The commands on this menu match the buttons on the Attachments panel, with the additional option of editing the description of the attachment that appears in the Description column of the Attachments panel. If the attachment has no description, you can use the Edit Description command to add one. The description is only relevant in Acrobat and doesn't alter the original document in any shape or form.

Apply a Stamp

When you receive a PDF document for review, you can literally apply a stamp of approval to the document. You apply a stamp to a PDF document by using the *Stamp tool,* the virtual equivalent of a rubber stamp, minus the messy inkpad. You can use one of the Acrobat preset stamps on a document or create your own custom stamp. An Acrobat stamp, as it appears when applied to a document, is shown here.

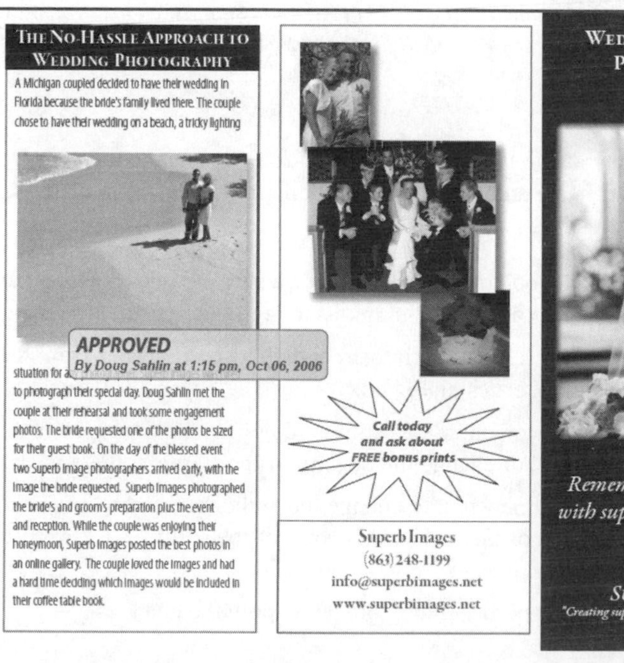

Use the Stamp Tool

You use the Stamp tool to apply a stamp to a PDF document. You can choose from a large selection of preset stamps. After you stamp a document, you can change the color, size, and location of the stamp. You can even attach a note to a stamp. To annotate a document using the Stamp tool, follow these steps:

1. Choose Tools | Comment & Markup | Stamps, and then choose a preset from one of these categories: Dynamic, Sign Here, Standard Business, and Favorites. Move your cursor over the category title to display a fly-out menu with a preview of the category stamps. Or, you can click the Stamp tool from the Comment & Markup toolbar (if present in the workspace), and then choose a preset.
2. Click the preview of the desired stamp to select it.
3. Click the location inside the document where you want the stamp to appear.
4. To move the stamp, select it with the Hand tool and drag it to another location. To resize the stamp, select it, and then move your cursor toward one of the rectangular handles at each corner of the stamp. Click the handle and drag in or out to resize the stamp. Press SHIFT while dragging to constrain the stamp to its original proportions. Click the round handle at the top of the annotation to rotate the stamp.

You can attach a pop-up note to a stamp. For more information, refer to the section "Attach a Pop-Up Note."

If you're reviewing several documents to which you'll apply stamps, choose Tools | Comment & Markup | Stamps | Show Stamps Palette to display the Stamps palette in the workspace.

Edit Stamp Properties

You can edit the properties of any stamp in a PDF document. You can change the appearance of the stamp, as well as the authors' name and subject description. To edit stamp properties, follow these steps:

1. In the document, use the Hand tool to select the stamp whose properties you want to change. Or, you can select a stamp annotation by clicking its icon in the Comments panel.
2. Right-click (Windows) or CTRL-click (Macintosh) and choose Properties from the context menu to display the Stamp Properties dialog box.
3. On the Appearance panel, you can choose a different color for the Stamp icon as it appears in the Comments panel or change the opacity of the stamp in the document.
4. Click the General tab and enter new text to change the author or subject information. By default, Acrobat uses the name of the registered owner of the software for Author and the name of the stamp for Subject.
5. Click OK to exit the Stamp Properties dialog box and apply the changes.

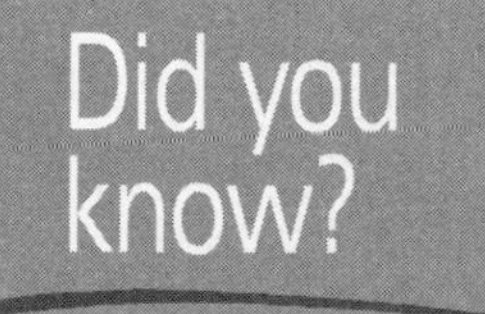

You Can Create Custom Stamps

If your organization has a need for stamps other than the robust set of presets that comes with Acrobat, you can create your own. In your favorite image-editing program, create a graphic approximately 2 × 1.5 inches. In Acrobat, choose Tools | Comment & Markup | Stamps | Create Custom Stamp. Follow the prompts in the dialog box to locate the graphic you created in your image-editing program. You'll be prompted for a category name and a stamp name. When you close the dialog box, your custom stamp is available for immediate use.

TIP *Another alternative for creating a custom stamp is copying an image to the clipboard and then choosing Tools | Comment & Markup | Stamps | Paste Clipboard Image as Stamp Tool. After you invoke the command, click inside the document where you want the stamp to appear.*

Delete a Stamp

To delete a stamp, select it with the Hand tool, and then choose Edit | Delete. Or, you can press DELETE or choose Delete from the context menu.

TIP *To mark a stamp as a favorite, select the desired stamp and choose Tools | Comment & Markup | Stamps | Favorites | Add To Favorites. Previews of favorite stamps are conveniently located at the top of the Stamps menu for easy access.*

Mark Up a Document

In addition to annotating your documents with notes, stamps, text boxes, and attached files, you can also highlight, strikethrough, and underline text to create annotations. You can also use graphic elements to mark up a document. You can create a circle, a rectangle, a line, or use a pencil tool to highlight areas of the document.

Use the Highlight Tools

When you want to draw attention to a block of text that needs to be changed in a paper document, you use a highlighter. Acrobat gives you similar tools that you can use to draw attention to text: the highlight tools. You have three from which to choose: Highlighter tool, Cross-Out Text tool, and Underline Text tool. The steps involved in using each tool are the same, as presented in the following steps:

1. Choose Tools | Comment & Markup and select the desired highlight tool from the menu.

2. Move the tool into the Document pane and highlight the desired text by clicking-and-dragging. After you select a single word with the tool, it automatically snaps to the end of the next word over which you position your cursor, and so on.

TIP *Double-click a word with any highlight tool to select the word.*

Reviewers of the document can access a pop-up note attached to the highlighted text by double-clicking it. By default, the pop-up note contains the highlighted text, word for word. You can edit the contents of the pop-up note as described in the section, "Attach a Pop-Up Note."

You can also edit properties of comments created with a highlight tool by following the steps in the next section.

Edit Comment Properties

Comments created with the Highlighter, Cross-Out Text, or Underline Text tool share the same properties: color, opacity, author, and subject. To modify comment properties:

1. In the document, use the Hand tool to select the comment whose properties you want to modify. You can select the actual comment in the document or click its title in the Comments panel.
2. Right-click (Windows) or CTRL-click (Macintosh) and choose Properties from the context menu to display the Highlight Properties dialog box.

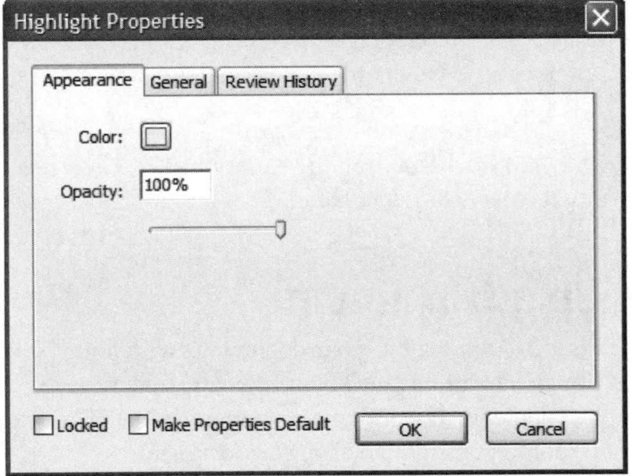

3. On the Appearance tab, click the Color button to choose a color from the color picker. This changes the color of the annotation in the document and the Comments panel. Or, you can click Other Color and choose a color from the system color picker.
4. Enter a value in the Opacity field. Or, drag the Opacity slider to specify the level of opacity for the comment as it appears in the document.
5. Click the General tab and you can modify the author and subject information by entering new text or editing the existing text. By default, Acrobat lists the registered owner of the application as the author and the tool name as the subject.
6. Click OK to exit the dialog box and apply the property changes.

NOTE

When you change a comment's properties, this doesn't automatically change the default properties for the tool, as it did in Acrobat 6.0 and earlier. When you next use a tool, it reverts to its default settings. You can, however, make the current properties of any modified comment the tool's default by right-clicking (Windows) or CTRL*-clicking (Macintosh) the comment icon and choosing Make Current Properties Default from the context menu.*

Use Graphic Elements

Some reviewers prefer to use graphic elements to mark up a document. You can create graphic elements to mark up a document with one of the tools on the Comment & Markup toolbar, or by using a command from the Comment & Markup menu group. When you mark up a document with one of these tools, you can attach a pop-up note, as outlined in the section "Attach a Pop-Up Note."

Some PDF reviewers prefer to mark up a document with a combination of graphic elements and text created with the Text Box tool. For example, you can use the *Circle tool* to highlight a graphic element that needs to be modified, and then use the *Arrow tool* or the *Line tool* to point to text created with the Text Box tool. In Figure 10-4, the Callout tool is used to draw attention to an image in a PDF document. This tool combines a text box with a line and callout arrow. The default Callout annotation can be modified to suit the document.

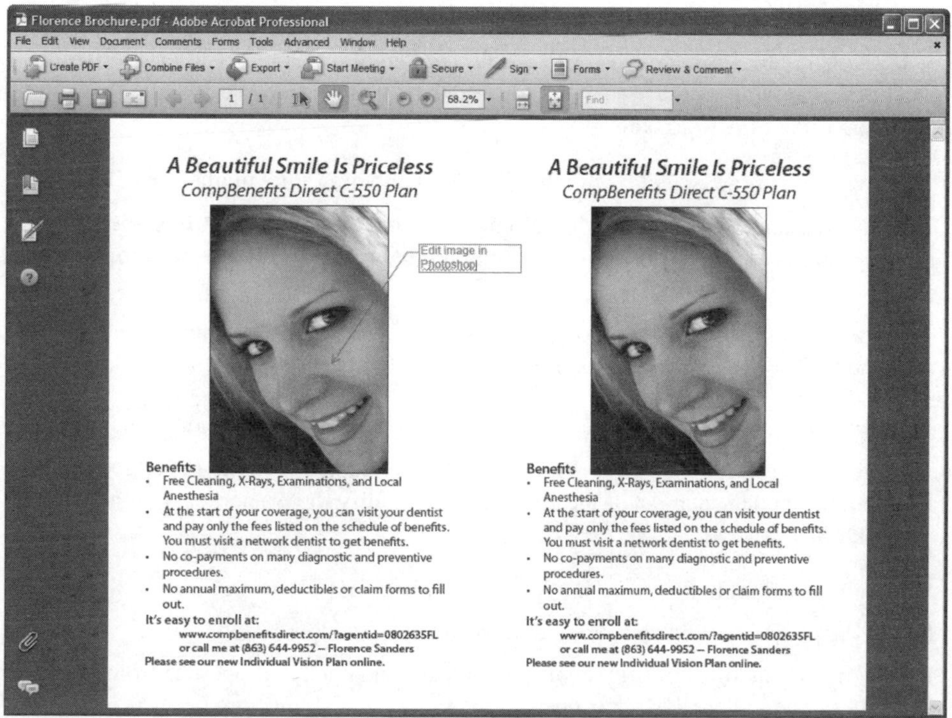

FIGURE 10-4 You can use the Callout tool to annotate objects with a text callout.

Use the Pencil Tool

If you're a card-carrying member of Pocket Pals Anonymous, the Pencil tool is right up your alley. You can use the *Pencil tool* to create expressive squiggles to direct another reviewer's attention to an element you feel needs correcting. When you mark up a document with the Pencil tool, Acrobat smoothes out the rough spots, but it isn't possible to constrain the tool to a perfectly straight line—for that you use the Line tool. To mark up a document with the Pencil tool:

1. Choose Tools | Comment & Markup | Pencil Tool. Or, you can select the Pencil tool from the Comment & Markup toolbar if you've previously displayed it.

Pencil Tool

2. Click anywhere inside the Document pane and drag to create a line.
3. Release the mouse button to finish drawing with the Pencil tool.

Edit a Pencil Tool Markup

After you create a markup with the Pencil tool, you can move or resize it. You edit a Pencil tool markup with the Hand tool. You can also edit it with the Pencil tool, but if you inadvertently click outside of the markup you want to edit, you create another line. You can edit a Pencil tool markup by doing one of the following:

1. To move the markup, select it with the Hand tool and drag it to another location.
2. To resize the markup, click it with the Hand tool, and then click-and-drag one of the rectangular handles at the corners of the markup bounding box. To resize proportionately, press SHIFT while dragging.
3. To erase part of the markup, choose Tools | Comment & Markup | Pencil Eraser Tool and drag the tool across the markup to erase the unwanted portion.

Modify Pencil Properties

You can change the color, opacity, and thicknesses of a line created with the Pencil tool, as well as change the author and the subject of the comment. To modify the properties of a line drawn with the Pencil tool:

1. Select the Hand tool.
2. Select the pencil mark whose properties you want to change.
3. Right-click (Windows) or CTRL-click (Macintosh) and choose Properties from the context menu to open the Pencil Mark Properties dialog box.
4. On the General tab, you can modify the default listing for the Author and Subject fields by entering new text.

5. Click the Appearance tab to display the appearance parameters for the comment, as shown next:

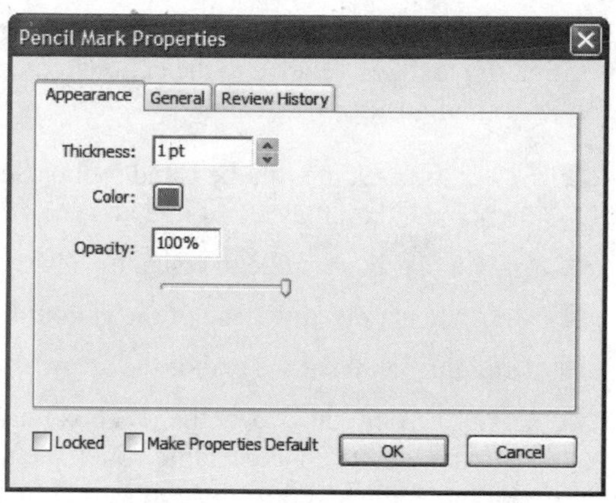

6. Click the spinner buttons to the left of the Thickness field to increase or decrease the thickness of the line. Or, you can enter a value between 0 and 12 points.
7. To change the color of the line, click the Color button and choose a color from the color picker or click the Other Color icon to choose a color from the system color picker.
8. To change the opacity of the line, enter a new value in the Opacity field. Or, you can drag the Opacity slider to set the value.
9. Click OK to exit the dialog box and apply the changes.

TIP *After changing the properties of a comment made with any tool, you can apply the new properties (except author and subject) to all future comments created with the associated tool. Before deselecting the comment, open the context menu again, and then choose Make Current Properties Default.*

10

Use the Callout Tool

If you're an author who submits illustrations to accompany your document text, you'll appreciate the Callout tool. The *Callout tool* enables you to create a text box with a connecting line and arrow that points to an object in the PDF document, as follows:

1. Choose Tools | Comment & Markup | Callout Tool. Or, you can select the Callout tool from the Comment & Markup toolbar if you've previously displayed it.

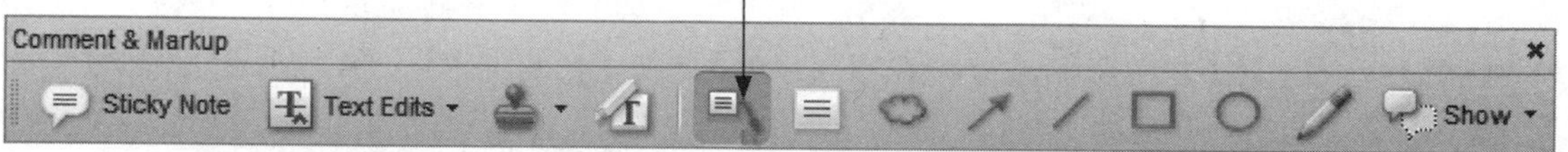

2. Click the object in the PDF to which you want the callout to point and then drag to position the callout text box.
3. Enter the desired text in the text box. If the text exceeds the default width of the callout, it wraps to a new line.
4. Click anywhere in the document to finish entering text. Your completed callout is the default size and position.

When you have multiple callouts in a document, you may need to size the text box, or reposition the text box relative to the callout to accommodate other callouts. To change the default size and position of a callout:

- Select the callout with the Hand tool or Select tool. Acrobat displays handles around the text box and on the callout line and arrow.
- Drag a text box handle to resize the text box.
- Drag the handle at the end of the callout line to resize the line.
- Drag the handle at the end of the arrowhead to reposition it.
- Position your cursor over the text box until the cursor becomes a diagonal arrowhead with the letter *T* in a rectangle. Click the text box and drag it to the desired position. As you move the text box, the connecting lines are also resized and repositioned.
- Double-click inside the text box and your cursor becomes an I-beam, signifying you can edit the text.

NOTE

You can edit the properties of a callout by right-clicking (Windows) or CTRL*-clicking (Macintosh), and then choosing Properties from the context menu. On the Appearance tab, you can modify the shape of the line-ending arrowhead, line thickness, line style, color of the text box, and color of the text box border. On the General tab, you can modify the author and subject information. To apply edited callout properties to other annotations created with the Callout tool, access the context menu again and choose Make Current Properties Default.*

Use the Drawing Tools

You can use shapes to draw attention to certain parts of a document. When you annotate a PDF document with drawing tools, you can select the tools by using menu commands or from the Comment & Markup toolbar. If you're annotating a large document with shapes from the Acrobat Professional Comment & Markup toolbar, shown next, it's more convenient to display the toolbar by choosing Tools | Comment & Markup | Show Comment & Markup Toolbar:

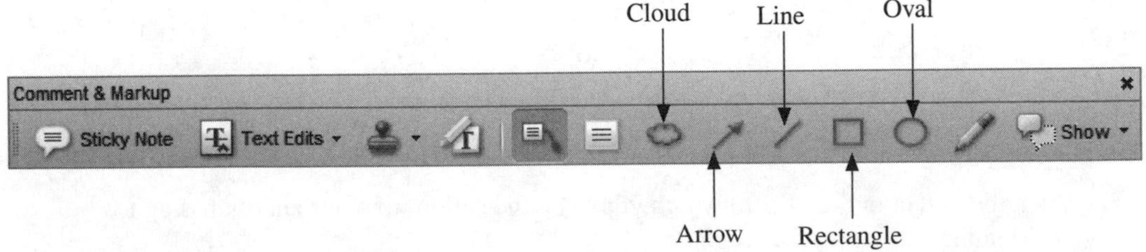

All the tools function in a similar manner. The following steps describe the process of commenting with one of the drawing tools:

1. Select a drawing tool from the Comment & Markup toolbar or by choosing Tools | Comment & Markup, and then selecting the desired tool from the drop-down menu.
2. Click the spot in the document where you want the comment to appear and do one of the following:

   - **Cloud tool (Professional Only)** Click to create the first point, and then click to create the additional points that define the cloud's shape. Double-click to close the shape.
   - **Arrow tool** Click-and-drag to create a line with arrowheads. Press SHIFT while dragging to constrain the line to 90-degree increments while dragging vertically or horizontally or to 45-degree increments while dragging diagonally.
   - **Line tool** Click the spot where you want the line to begin, and then drag. Press SHIFT while dragging vertically or horizontally to create a vertical or horizontal line. Press SHIFT while dragging diagonally to constrain the line to 45 degrees.
   - **Rectangle tool** Click-and-drag diagonally to create the shape. Press SHIFT while using the tool to create a square.
   - **Oval tool** Click-and-drag diagonally to create the oval. Press SHIFT while dragging to create a circle.
   - **Polygon Line tool** Click to create the first point, and then click to add additional points to the line.
   - **Polygon tool** Click to create the first point, and then click to add additional points to the shape. Double-click to close the shape.

Editing a Drawing Tool Comment's Properties

As you know from reading previous sections of this chapter, comments have properties you can modify. Comments created with the drawing tools are no exception. The following steps show how to modify the properties of a comment created with the Rectangle tool. These steps also follow suit for comments created with the other closed-shaped commenting tools (Cloud [Professional Only], Oval, and Polygon).

1. Select the comment whose properties you want to modify, right-click (Windows) or CTRL-click (Macintosh), and choose Properties from the context menu. The Rectangle Properties dialog box appears, shown next.
2. Click the Style drop-down arrow and choose an option from the drop-down menu. This option determines the appearance of the shape's border (or line).

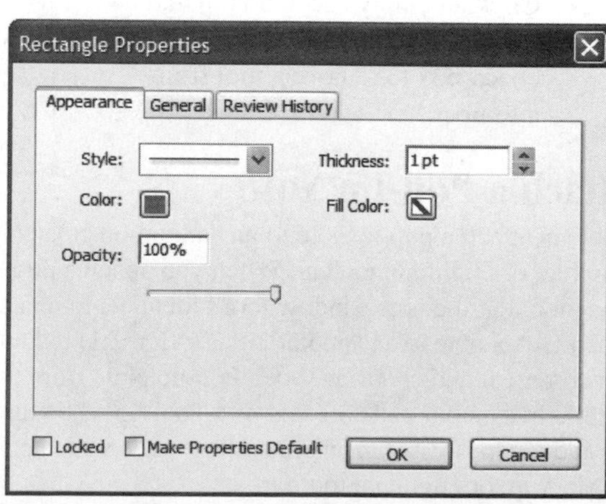

3. Click the spinner buttons to the right of the Thickness field to specify line thickness. Or, you can enter a value between 0 and 12 points.
4. Click the Color button, and then choose a color from the color picker. The selected color determines the color of the shape's border. Or, click Other Color to select a color from the system color picker.
5. Click the Fill Color button, and then choose a color from the color picker. This determines the color of the inside of the shape. Accept the default no-color option to create an outline of a shape.
6. Enter a value in the Opacity field to determine the comment's opacity. Or, you can click-and-drag the Opacity slider to set this value.
7. Click the General tab to modify the author and subject information by entering new information in each field.
8. Click OK to exit the dialog box and apply the changes.

Customize the Toolbars

If you've used earlier versions of Acrobat, you know each toolbar was jam-packed with tools. In fact, nearly every available tool had a spot on some toolbar. To simplify matters, the Acrobat design team put the toolbars on a diet, displaying only the most popular tools. You can however, modify the toolbars by adding and/or removing tools. To customize a toolbar:

1. Choose Tools | Customize Toolbars to display the More Tools dialog box, shown next.
2. Click an empty check box to add a tool to a toolbar, or click a filled check box to remove a tool from a toolbar.

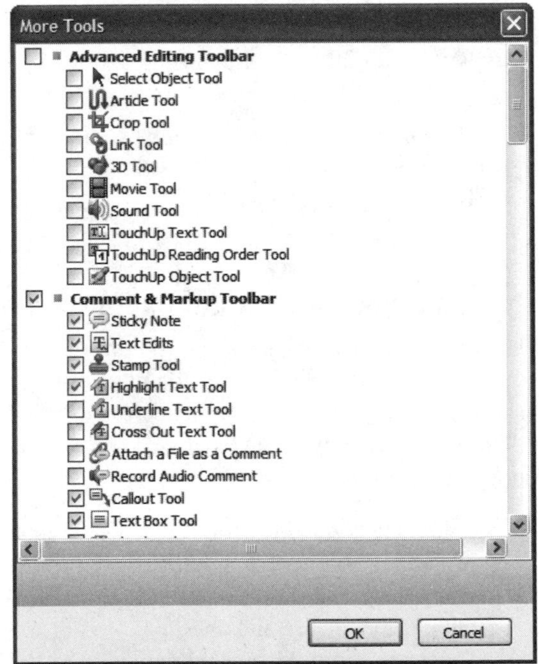

Attach a Pop-Up Note

You can attach a pop-up note to an annotation created with a tool from the Drawing, Comment & Markup, or Highlight toolbar. When you attach a pop-up note, with the exception of the default pop-up color, the note window looks identical to one created with the Sticky Note tool. When you attach a note to an annotation, it's viewable by double-clicking the comment or by selecting the comment and choosing Open Pop-up Note from the context menu. Viewers will also see the comment's author and note text as a ToolTip when they hover a mouse over the pop-up note icon. To add a pop-up note to an annotation made with a commenting tool from the Drawing, Comment & Markup, or Highlight toolbar:

1. Select the Hand tool, and then double-click an annotation created with a tool from the Comment & Markup toolbar or with a command from the Comment & Markup menu group. Acrobat opens a pop-up note with a flashing cursor inside the body of the note.
2. Enter the text for the note and, if desired, close the note. Or, you can leave the pop-up note open.

As with other pop-up notes, you can click the Options icon to open a menu from which you can choose commands applicable to the pop-up note.

Edit a Pop-Up Note

You can edit a pop-up note attached to an annotation by moving it to a new position or by changing the text of the pop-up note. You can also reset a pop-up note to its default position. To edit a pop-up note, double-click the comment the note is attached to and do one of the following:

1. Click the note title bar and drag it to a new location.
2. Select text to edit and enter new text.
3. Select text to delete, and then press DELETE or choose Edit | Delete.

To reset a pop-up note window to its default position, right-click (Windows) or ctrl-click (Macintosh) it and choose Reset Pop Up Note Location from the context menu.

Export Comments

You can export comments from one document and use them in another version of the same document. Exported comments are saved as an FDF file. The comment file contains all the comments exported from the document in their original positions, but not the actual document elements. You can export all comments from a document or export selected comments.

To export all comments from a document:

1. Choose Comments | Export Comments to Data File to open the Export Comments dialog box.
2. Choose the desired file type from the Save as Type drop-down menu. You can save comments as an FDF (Form Data Format) or XFDF (XML Forms Data Format).
3. Accept the default name for the comments (the document filename with the .fdf or .xfdf extension) or enter a different name.
4. Navigate to the folder where you want the comment file saved, and then click Save.

You can also export selected comments from a document—for example, all comments created by a particular reviewer. To export selected comments:

1. In the Navigation pane, click the Comments icon to open the Comments panel.
2. Select the comments you want to export.

3. Click the Options icon and, from the Comments Options menu, choose Export Selected Comments.
4. In the Export Comments dialog box, enter a name for the comment file, navigate to the folder you want to save the file in, and then click Save.

You can also export comments as a Word document by choosing Comments | Export Comments | To Word. Note, you must have Word 2002 or newer installed on your system to use this feature. You can also export comments to AutoCAD by choosing Comments | Export Comments | To AutoCAD.

Import Comments

You can import a comment file into a different version of a document. The imported comments appear in their original positions. If you receive several versions of the same document marked up by different reviewers, you can collate each reviewer's comments in a single document. First, export the comments from each document, as outlined in the previous section. Second, open the master copy of the document into which you want to collate the comments. Third, follow these steps:

1. Choose Comments | Import Comments to open the Import Comments dialog box. You can now import comments by having Acrobat strip comments from a PDF file or by importing an FDF or XFDF file.
2. Click the Files Of Type drop-down arrow and choose Acrobat FDF Files, Adobe PDF Files, or Acrobat XFDF files to view only files from the selected format. Or, you can select the desired file from the folder as only supported file types appear in the dialog box.
3. Choose the file, and then click Select.

After you invoke the command, Acrobat imports the comments and places them in the exact location they appeared in the document from which they were extracted. If you choose to import comments from a PDF file, this may take a while if the document is large and contains many comments.

If you own Acrobat Professional, you can compare two versions of the same document by choosing Advanced | Compare Documents. After you choose the documents to compare, you can choose to compare visual differences and textual differences and have Acrobat generate a report that annotates the differences with a side-by-side comparison.

Summary

In this chapter, you learned how to generate an e-mail review. You discovered how to keep tabs on the review with the Tracker. Other chapter topics showed you how to annotate a PDF document with notes, shapes, and text, as well as display comments from other reviewers by using the Comments panel. And, you learned how to reply to a comment. You also discovered how to manage file attachments with the new Attachments panel. In the next chapter, you learn how to add security to the PDF documents you create.

Chapter 11 Add Digital Signatures and Document Security

How to...

- Remove sensitive content
- Use digital signatures
- Modify signature appearance
- Use the Signatures Panel
- Use Acrobat Password Security
- Use Acrobat Certificate Security

When you create a document for use with several team members in a corporate environment, you can keep track of who did what to a document with digital signatures. When a reviewer or team member digitally signs a document, Acrobat acknowledges the reviewer and creates a time stamp. All changes to the document are noted as being performed by the digital signer. When more than one person digitally signs a document, you can compare different versions of the document.

Documents created in a corporate environment are often confidential. When this is the case, you can assign security to a document. Before applying security to a document, however, you might want to remove sensitive information from the document, such as passwords, credit card information, addresses, and similar details. You can easily do so using the new redaction feature available only in Acrobat Professional. After removing sensitive content, you can apply security to the document. When you add security to a document, you limit a viewer's access to the document. When you use Acrobat Password Security, you can assign a password to the document. Before a document can be viewed, the user must enter the proper password. You can also assign a permissions password to the document, which limits the viewer's ability to edit a document, print it, and so on. If a permissions password is assigned to a document, the user must enter it to modify any of the security settings. When you use Acrobat Certificate Security, you limit access to the document to certain team members, and you can create different user permissions for each team member. For example, you can disallow editing and printing for certain team members, while giving other team members carte blanche access to the document. Another option is to create a custom policy using the Adobe LiveCycle Policy Server, a service to which you can subscribe. After your company subscribes to this service, policies can be created that are stored on your company's server, which means you change security settings dynamically.

Remove Sensitive Content (Professional Only)

When you have a PDF document that contains sensitive information, you can permanently remove sensitive content, such as personal information. You remove sensitive content with the Redaction tool. When you redact a document, you can replace the removed content with colored boxes or leave the area blank. You can also specify that custom text or redaction codes appear over the redaction marks.

Marking Objects for Redaction

If you've ever seen television documentaries that show FBI documents with sensitive information removed, you know the document is a photocopy and the sensitive content is obliterated with black ink. The document is then photocopied, which is what the public sees. This is known as *redaction.* The Acrobat Redaction tool performs the same function with equal efficiency on a PDF document. Redaction of sensitive content is a two-step process. First, you mark text for redaction. After you mark text and graphics for redaction, you can still make changes. When you apply redaction, the marked text and graphics are permanently removed from the document. To redact content in a document:

1. Choose Advanced | Redaction | Mark for Redaction. If you're redacting several objects from a document, you might find it's beneficial to display the Redaction toolbar (shown next) by choosing Advanced | Redaction | Show Redaction toolbar.

TIP *When you choose the Mark For Redaction command, Acrobat displays a dialog box explaining the redaction process. You can prevent this dialog box from appearing again by clicking the Don't Show Again check box.*

2. Mark objects for redaction by doing one of the following:
   - To mark text for redaction, move the tool toward text you want to mark. When your cursor becomes an I-beam inside a square, click-and-drag across the text you want to mark for redaction. You can also double-click a word to mark it for redaction.
   - To mark a graphic object for redaction, move the tool toward the object you want to mark. When your cursor becomes a cross-hair, click-and-drag diagonally to select the object. As you drag the tool, a bounding box shows the area you selected. Release the mouse button when the bounding box surrounds the graphic you want to mark for redaction.

An object marked for redaction is surrounded by a red rectangle. To preview what the redacted content will look like when you apply redaction, pause your cursor over the content marked for redaction. If you're satisfied with the appearance of the redacted content, you can apply redaction. If not, you can modify redaction properties.

Searching for Text to Redact

If you're working with a multipage object that needs to be marked for redaction, you can speed the process by searching for the text you want to redact. This is similar to searching a document with the exception that you can mark results from the search from within the Search dialog box. The search and redact feature only works for searchable text, not for graphic objects that have text. To search for text you want to mark for redaction:

1. Choose Advanced | Redaction | Search and Redact to display the Search dialog box. Or, you can select the Search and Redact tool from the Redaction toolbar.
2. Enter the text in the What word or phrase would you like to search for? text field.
3. Choose an option for the location in which you would like to search. Your choices are: In the current PDF document, or All PDF Documents in. If you choose the latter, choose the desired folder from the drop-down list.
4. Click Search and Redact. Acrobat displays all instances of the search word or phrase. You can locate individual search results in the document by clicking the text in the Search panel.
5. To select search results you want to mark for redaction, do one of the following:
   - Click a search result instance's check box to select this instance of the search word or phrase for redaction.
   - Click Check All to select all instances of the search word or phrase for redaction.
6. Click Mark Checked Results for Redaction.

Modify Redaction Properties

Redaction is an ongoing process. After you make an initial pass over the document, you may find that you need to mark other objects for redaction, or change the properties of objects you've marked for redaction. By default, a black rectangle replaces redacted content. You can modify the appearance of the redacted objects in the document by changing redaction properties.

To modify redaction properties:

1. Choose Advanced | Redaction | Redaction Properties to display the Redaction Tool Properties dialog box shown in the following illustration. Or, you can choose the Redaction Properties tool from the Redaction toolbar, if it's available in the workspace.

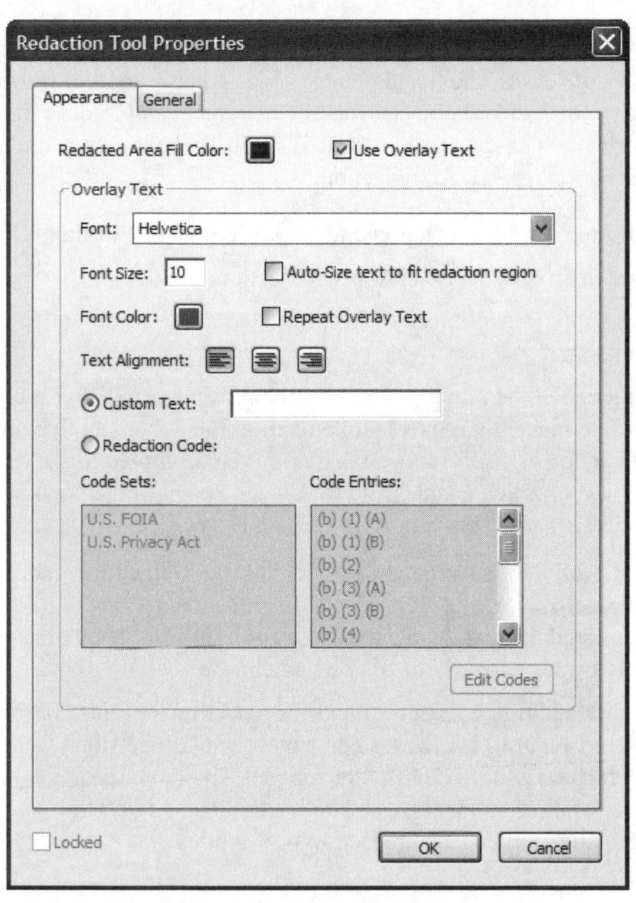

2. Accept the default black fill color for redacted areas, or click the color swatch and choose the desired color from the Color Picker.
3. Click the Use Overlay Text check box if you want to display text over areas where content has been redacted. If you choose this option, specify the text attributes, such as font type, color, size, and so on in the Overlay Text area.
4. Enter text in the Custom Text field. Or, click the Redaction Code radio button, and choose the desired code set and code entries from the Code Sets area.

TIP *If you're familiar with redaction codes, click the Edit Codes button to display the Redaction Code Editor dialog box, which enables you to add or remove code sets, import or export code sets, and add, remove, or rename individual code entries.*

5. Click OK to apply the properties to the Redaction tool.

Applying Redaction to Marked Objects

After marking instances of sensitive text and graphic objects you want to remove, the next step is to permanently remove the marked objects from the document and replace them with filled rectangles, and/or overlay text as specified in the Redaction Tool Properties dialog box. To remove sensitive information marked for redaction:

1. To permanently remove objects marked for redaction, do one of the following:
   - Choose Advanced | Redaction | Apply Redactions.
   - Select the Apply Redactions tool from the Redactions toolbar, if it's available in the workspace.

   After doing one of the previous steps, Acrobat displays a dialog box warning you you're about to permanently remove all items from the document that are marked for redaction. The dialog also informs you that you'll be prompted to rename the document when next it's saved, which enables you to have one copy of the document with redaction applied and one without.
2. Click OK to exit the Adobe Acrobat warning dialog box and apply redaction. Acrobat displays a dialog box, which enables you to examine the document for additional objects to redact, such as hidden text, metadata, and so on. This dialog box has an option which tells Acrobat to always perform the option you choose.
3. Click Yes to mark additional objects or text for redaction, or click No to apply redaction to marked objects. Figure 11-1 shows a document with objects that were permanently removed and replaced with filled black rectangles. The large rectangle in the upper left-hand corner of the document was a graphic that had a hyperlink to a web site. The hyperlink was also removed when redaction was applied.

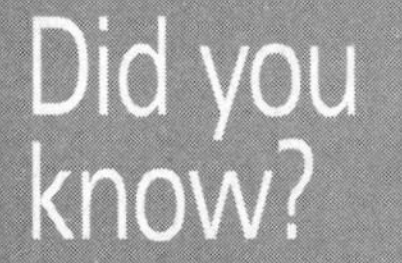

Add Bates Numbering Header or Footer

Bates numbering is a method of indexing legal documents which makes it easy to identify and retrieve them. Bates numbering is used by legal firms. When Bates numbering is applied to a document, each page of the document receives a unique number that also indicates its relationship to other Bates-numbered documents. Bates numbers appear in headers or footers on the pages of each PDF to which Bates numbering has been applied.

You apply Bates numbering by choosing Advanced | Document Processing | Bates Numbering | Add. The Bates Numbering dialog box prompts you for the documents to which you'll apply Bates numbering. You can also modify the order in which documents are arranged. The next step is to choose the Bates numbering options and decide whether the numbering will be added to the header or footer. At this stage, you can add additional text to the header and/or footer.

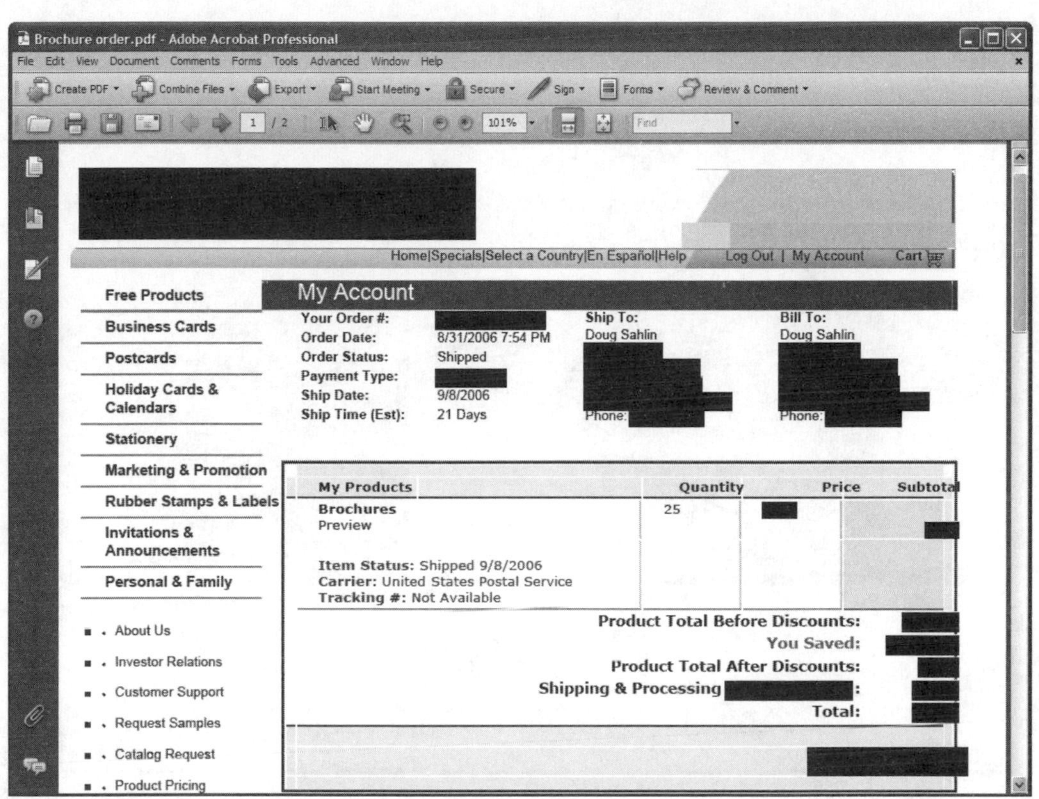

FIGURE 11-1 You can permanently remove sensitive content from a document.

About Digital Signatures

With Acrobat, documents can be digitally signed. A *digital signature* is like an electronic thumbprint; it identifies the signer of the document. A digital signature also records any changes made by the signer and stores information about the signer with the document.

When you add Acrobat Certificate Security to a document, only a team member with an authorized digital signature can view the document. Acrobat users with digital signatures can select their digital ID and log in prior to working on secure documents. Secure documents open without requesting the user for a password if an authorized user has selected their digital ID and logged in prior to opening the document.

If you use Acrobat to send contracts to clients, digital signatures can be used to approve contracts. If both parties accept a digital signature as an electronic facsimile of a handwritten signature, a digitally signed contract may be legally binding. Before you accept a digital signature as legally binding authorization to proceed with a contract, it's best to seek the advice of legal counsel. Figure 11-2 shows a digitally signed document.

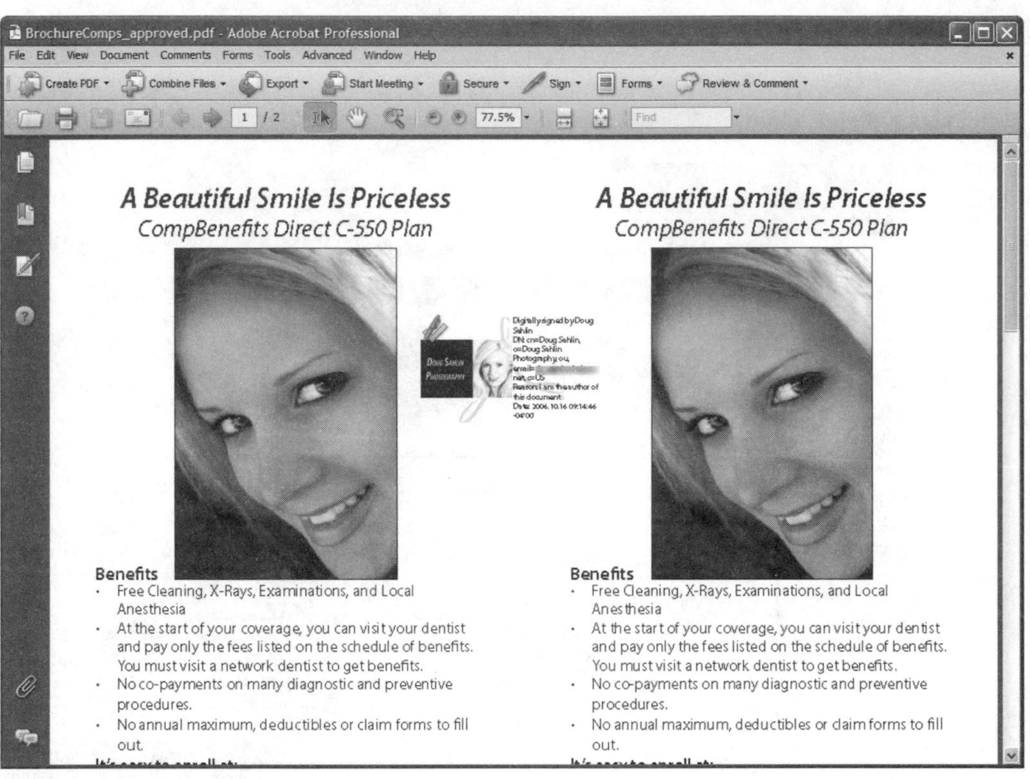

FIGURE 11-2 A digital signature can be legally binding.

Use Digital Signatures

When you decide to use digital signatures to verify the identities of users modifying your documents, you can use the default Acrobat Certificate Security or the Adobe LiveCycle Policy Server, or you can specify a third-party service to handle digital signatures. After you decide on a signature handler, you need to create a digital ID. Your *digital ID* stores information about you. You can use the default Acrobat graphic for a digital signature or customize the digital signature with a photo or other graphic, such as a logo. When you work with colleagues with whom you'll exchange secure documents, you can create a list of trusted identities. Trusted identities are digital signature certificates you have imported, which are files in FDF, P7C, P7B, CER, CRT, or APF format used to verify digital signatures. You can request digital IDs of colleagues via e-mail, and share your certificate with other colleagues so your digital signature can be verified.

Documents can be signed multiple times by multiple authors. Whenever a document is digitally signed, Acrobat records the changes made since the document was last digitally signed. When you open a document with multiple signatures, you view the most current version of the document.

You can view earlier versions of a digitally signed document and compare different versions. When you compare different versions of a document, you can also view the changes made by each signer.

NOTE *You can create a digital ID from within Acrobat and send your certificate to other parties to verify your signature. If you intend to distribute the document widely, this can be tedious. You can, however, secure a digital ID from a trusted Adobe party, which enables any user of Adobe Reader 7.0 or later, Acrobat Standard, or Acrobat Professional to verify your digital signature.*

Create a User Profile

You create a *user profile* to create identification and a password that links to your digital signature. You can create more than one user profile if you sign documents in different capacities. To create your first user profile, follow these steps:

1. Choose Advanced | Security Settings to open the Security Settings dialog box.

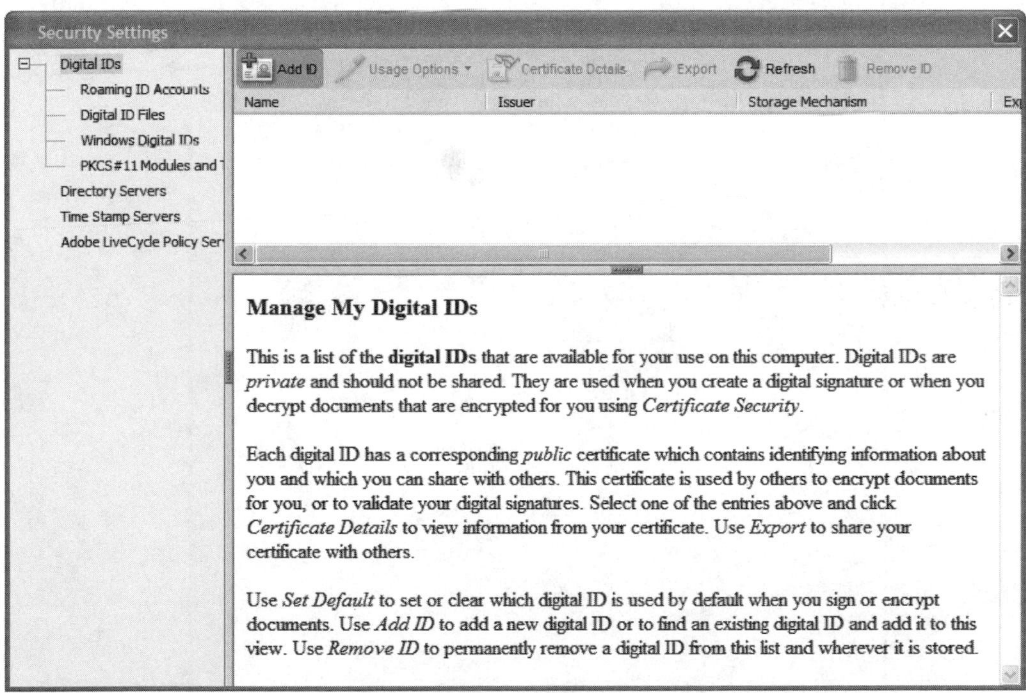

2. Click the Add ID button to open the Add Digital ID Wizard. On the first page, select one of the options: Browse For An Existing Digital ID File, Configure a Roaming ID for Use on This Computer, Create A Self-Signed Digital ID for Use with Acrobat, or Look For Newly Inserted Hardware Tokens.

11

3. Click Next. The following steps assume you selected Create A Self-Signed Digital ID for Use With Acrobat.

If you already have an existing digital ID, such as a Windows certificate, on your computer, click the Import An Existing Digital ID radio button, and then click Next. The next wizard page prompts you to locate the ID file and enter your password. After following these steps, you can use the digital ID from within Acrobat to certify documents and apply security settings.

The second Add Digital ID wizard page enables you to choose one of the following options to specify where you want to store your Self-Signed Digital ID:

- **New PKCS#12 Digital ID File** Creates a digital ID file using the PKCS#12 standard. Digital IDs created with this standard have a PFX or P12 file extension, and they can be used with most applications that require secure digital IDs, including certain browsers.
- **Windows Certificate Store** Creates a digital ID file that can be used with most applications supported by Windows.

4. Click Next to open the next page of the Add Digital ID Wizard:

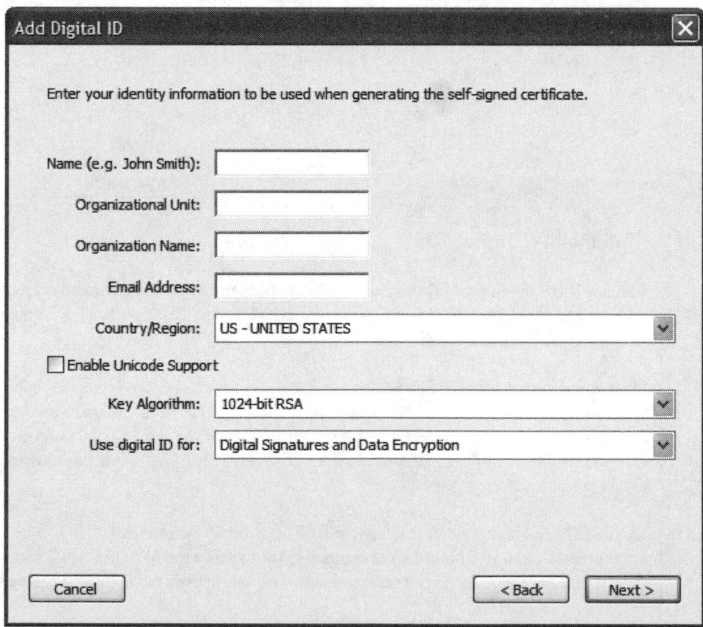

5. Enter your name in the Name field. If desired, supply additional contact information in the Organizational Unit and Organizational Name fields.
6. Enter your e-mail address in the Email Address field.

7. Click the Enable Unicode Support check box if you want to include Unicode information with the certificate. The *Unicode standard* provides a unique number for every character. Each number is cross-platform. The Unicode standard for most English documents is UTF-8. If you choose this option, Unicode fields appear to the right of your contact information. Enter the appropriate Unicode information in the desired fields.
8. Click the Key Algorithm drop-down arrow and choose 1024-bit RSA or 2048-bit RSA. The latter choice offers better security, but it may not be available to all users.
9. Click the Use Digital ID For drop-down arrow and choose an option from the drop-down menu. The default option, Digital Signatures And Data Encryption, enables you to use the digital ID for signing documents and encrypting. Or, you can choose Digital Signatures Or Data Encryption to limit your use of the digital ID.
10. Click Next to open the password page of the Add Digital ID Wizard.

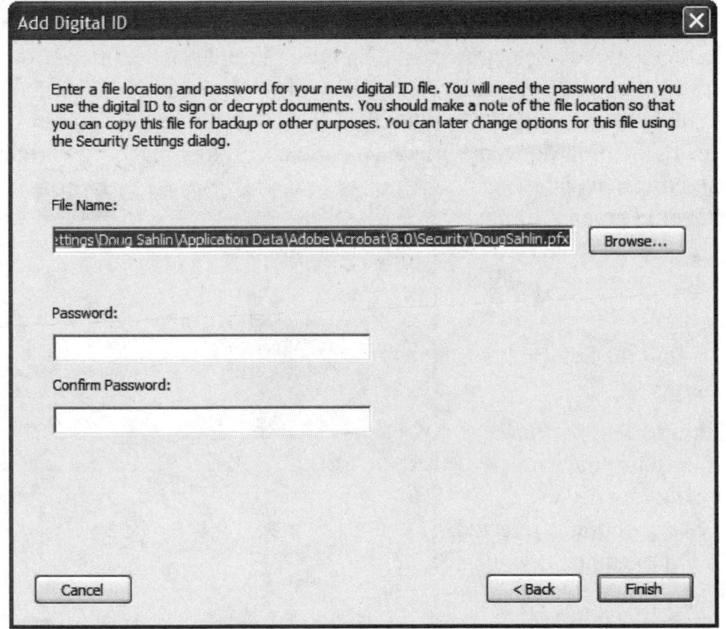

11. Accept the default location and filename for your digital ID, or enter a different path and filename. Or, you can click Browse to open the Save Digital ID dialog box, which enables you to navigate to the desired folder and enter the desired filename.
12. Enter and confirm your password. Your password must be at least six characters and cannot contain any of the following symbols: !@#$%^&*,|\<>_ or double quotation marks.
13. Click Finish to complete the process and exit the wizard.
14. Close the Security Settings dialog box.

Create Signature Appearance

When you digitally sign a document, Acrobat uses a default text-only signature with the Acrobat logo in the background. You can create an alternate of your digital signature by creating a file in a graphics program and converting it to PDF format. For that matter, you can choose File | Import | Scan, and then scan a copy of your actual signature and save it as a PDF file. After you create a PDF file with the graphic you want to use for your digital signature, follow these steps:

1. Choose Edit | Preferences to open the Preferences dialog box.
2. Click Security, and then in the Appearance section, click New to open the Configure Signature Appearance dialog box.
3. In the Title field, enter a name for the signature configuration.
4. In the Configure Graphic section, choose No Graphic, Imported Graphic, or Name. If you choose Imported Graphic, click the File button to open the Select Picture dialog box. Click the Browse button, navigate to the PDF file that contains the image for your digital signature, and then click Select. Acrobat displays a sample of the image in the Preview window. If the image is acceptable, click OK to close the Select Picture dialog box. If the desired image is not a PDF file, click the Files Of Type drop-down arrow and select an option from the drop-down menu, which contains all the image file formats supported by Acrobat. Next, navigate to and select the desired graphic format to display all files of that type. Select the desired image, and then click OK.
5. Click OK to exit the Select Picture dialog box.
6. In the Configure Text section, choose the options you want displayed with your digital signature. Every option is selected by default. For example, if you deselect Logo, the Acrobat logo won't be displayed with your new digital signature.
7. In the Text Properties section, choose the desired option to determine how the text and graphic are displayed. As you change the options, Acrobat updates the preview in real time, as shown here:

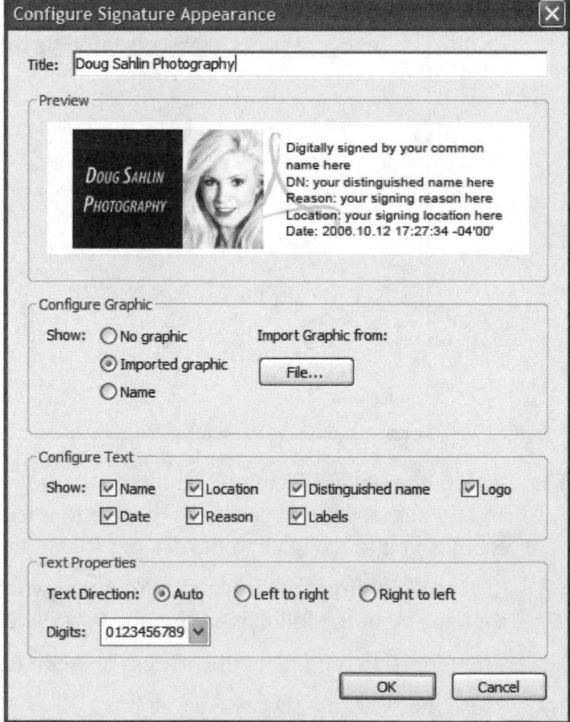

How to ... Create a Secure Password

When creating a password, many people create one that's easy to remember, such as their birthday, a relative's birthday, or a combination of initials from their name and their spouse's name. Passwords such as these are easy to decipher. When you need to create a secure password, create one with at least eight characters. Create a combination of alphabetic characters interspersed with numeric characters, such as *j87ty91w*. After creating the password, make sure you archive a hard copy of the password in a safe and remote location. You may also want to consider saving a digital copy of your password to your PDA (personal digital assistant) if it is secure.

8. Click OK to close the dialog box, and Acrobat adds your custom signature to the list, as shown in the following illustration. Notice when you select the signature, you have options to edit, duplicate, and delete the custom signature.

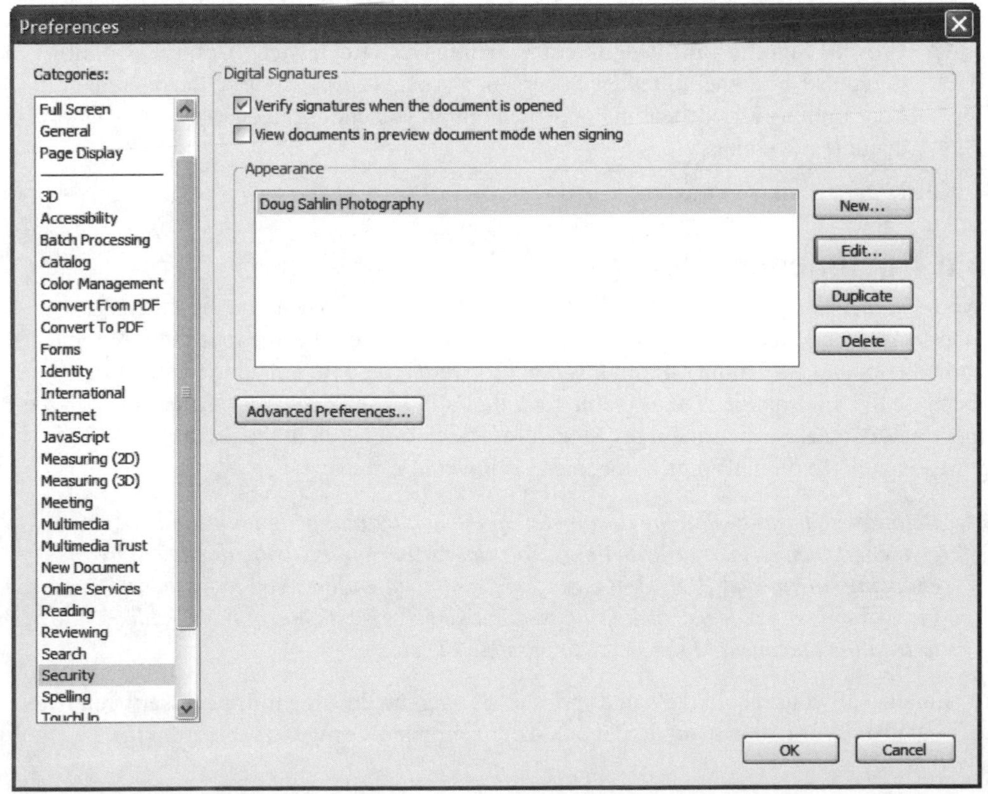

9. Click Advanced Preferences, and then click the Creation tab. Choose the desired preferences from the following:
   - **Include Signature's Revocation Status When Signing** Choose this option to embed information about your certificate's validity. Choosing this option expedites the validation process quicker as your recipient won't have to go online to determine whether the certificate has been revoked.
   - **Show Reasons When Signing** Choose this option, and a field with a drop-down menu arrow appears when you sign a document enabling you to specify a reason for signing the document.
   - **Show Location and Contact Information When Signing** Choose this option to have your location information added to the digital signature. Your contact information appears in the Signer tab of the Signature Properties dialog box. When you add a digital signature to a PDF, text boxes appear in the Sign Document dialog box where you enter the desired location and contact information.
   - **Enable Reviewing of Document Warnings** Choose an option from the drop-down menu, which, when you apply your digital signature, analyzes a document for content that might change the document appearance. Your options are Always, Never, or When Certifying a Document.Then, provide the option in the Sign Document dialog box to review this content.
   - **Prevent Signing Until Document Warnings Are Reviewed** Choose an option to require the signer to review document warnings before signing the document. Your options vary depending on which option you choose to enable reviewing of document warnings.
10. Click OK to exit the Preferences dialog box.

Sign a Document

After you create a user profile, you can digitally sign documents. When you digitally sign a document, you're required to save it. When you save the document for the first time, Acrobat saves it in an *append only* format. From this point forward, you won't be able to do a full save, because the Save option is unavailable for a digitally signed document. After you sign a document, your signature appears in the Signatures Panel, discussed in the section "Use The Signatures Panel." To digitally sign a document, follow these steps:

Before you digitally sign the document, optimize it by removing unneeded document elements, such as unused form fields. You can further optimize the document by choosing Advanced | PDF Optimizer. This command enables you to further optimize the file by removing objects, such as unused bookmarks. Next choose File | Reduce File Size to trim the document to the smallest possible file size.

1. Finalize all your required changes prior to signing the document. If necessary, remove sensitive information using Redaction menu commands or using tools from the

Redaction toolbar. If you digitally sign the document and then make additional changes, the document will be marked as modified since your digital signature was applied.

2. Choose Advanced | Sign & Certify | Place Signature. Or, you can click the Sign task button on the toolbar, and then choose Place Signature from the drop-down menu. After choosing one of the above, a dialog box appears with instructions on how to place the signature within the document. You can prevent this dialog box from appearing again by clicking the Do Not Show This Message Again check box.
3. Click-and-drag diagonally to define the area in which your digital signature will appear.
4. After you release the mouse button, the Sign Document dialog box appears.
5. Choose the desired digital ID from the Digital ID drop-down list.
6. Enter the password associated with the digital ID you selected.
7. In the Appearance field, accept the default Standard Text signature, or click the drop-down arrow and choose a signature you created.
8. Click the Reason drop-down arrow and choose a reason for signing the document. This option is unavailable if you didn't choose the Show Reasons When Signing option in the Security Preferences dialog box.
9. In the Other Information section, enter the desired text in the Location and Contact Info fields. This option is unavailable if you didn't choose the Show Location and Contact Information When Signing option in the Security Preferences dialog box.
10. Click the Review button if you see the Document Content May Impact Signing warning. This warning is unavailable unless you choose the option to always enable reviewing of document warnings in the Security Preferences dialog box.
11. Click the Sign button. The Save As dialog box appears.

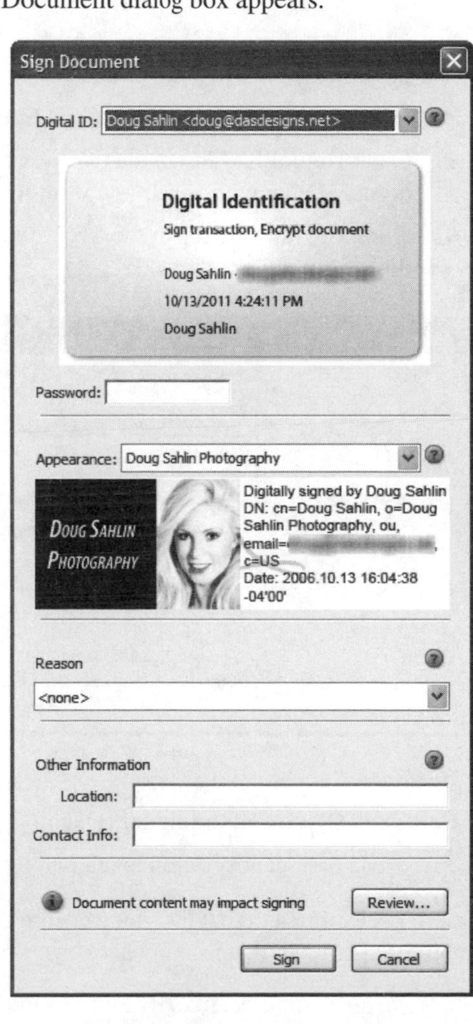

12. Enter a filename for the document and click Save. After you save the document, your digital signature appears on the document as noted in the Signatures panel.

To display a document in Preview Document mode prior to signing a document, choose Edit | Preferences, choose the Security category, and then click the View documents in preview mode when signing check box.

Choose a Digital ID

If you launch Acrobat for the purpose of reviewing documents with digital signatures, you need to choose the digital ID with which you'll be reviewing and signing the documents. When you choose a digital ID, you can validate digital signatures from your list of trusted identities as soon as you open a document. To choose a digital ID, follow these steps:

1. Choose Advanced | Security Settings. The Security Settings dialog box appears with a list of all digital IDs you created or that already exist on your system.
2. In the left pane, expand Digital ID Files to display all digital IDs you've created.
3. Click Digital ID Files in the expanded tree, and then from the right pane, select the digital ID file with which you want to work.
4. Click Login at the top of the Security Settings dialog box (shown next) to open the dialog box for the digital ID.

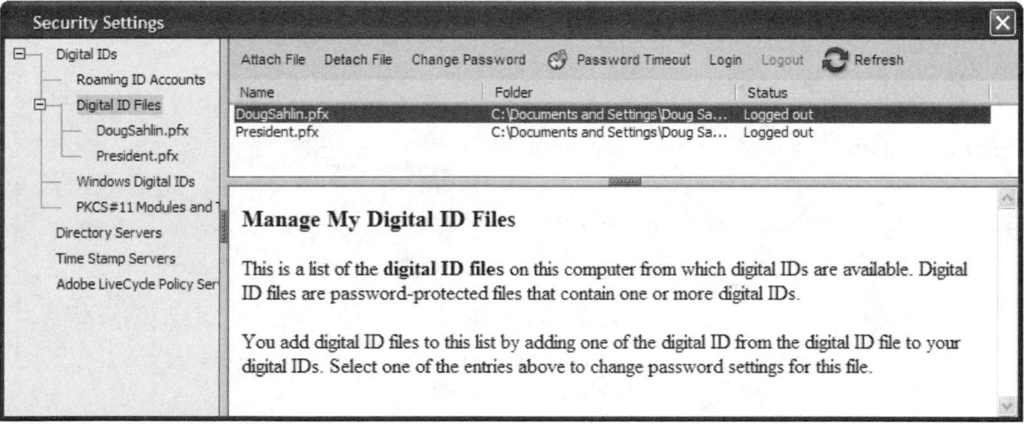

5. Enter the correct password.
6. Click OK to exit the digital ID dialog box.
7. Close the Security Settings dialog box.

After selecting a digital ID, you can sign documents with the digital ID and validate signatures, as shown in upcoming sections.

From within the Security Settings dialog box, you can add additional IDs and remove selected IDs, as well as view the settings for selected digital IDs. You can also export a copy of your digital ID to a folder on your hard drive. The exported digital ID serves as a backup if you ever have to reinstall Acrobat.

Change Digital ID Password

If you feel security has been breached, you can change the password for your digital ID. To change your digital ID password, follow these steps:

1. Choose Advanced | Security Settings to access the Security Settings dialog box, shown previously.
2. Click the plus sign (+) to the left of Digital ID Files, and then in the right pane, select the file you want to modify.
3. Click Change Password to open the Change Digital ID File Password dialog box.
4. Enter your current password in the Old Password field.
5. Enter your new password in the New Password field, and then confirm your new password.
6. Click OK to close the Change Digital ID File Password dialog box.
7. Click Close to exit the Security Settings dialog box.

Change Password Timeout Settings

By default, you're required to enter your password every time you sign a document. This feature prevents other people from using your digital signature on a document when you temporarily vacate your workstation while using Acrobat. You can, however, change password settings to avoid having to enter your password every time you digitally sign a document. The following steps explain how to change password settings.

1. Choose Advanced | Security Settings to access the Security Settings dialog box, shown previously.
2. Expand the Digital IDs listing in the left pane of the dialog box, and then click Digital ID Files
3. In the right pane of the dialog box, select the file you want to modify. The Security Settings dialog box reconfigures, as shown previously.
4. Click Password Timeout. Acrobat prompts you to enter the password for the digital signature.
5. Enter the correct password, and then click OK to open the Password Timeout Policy dialog box:

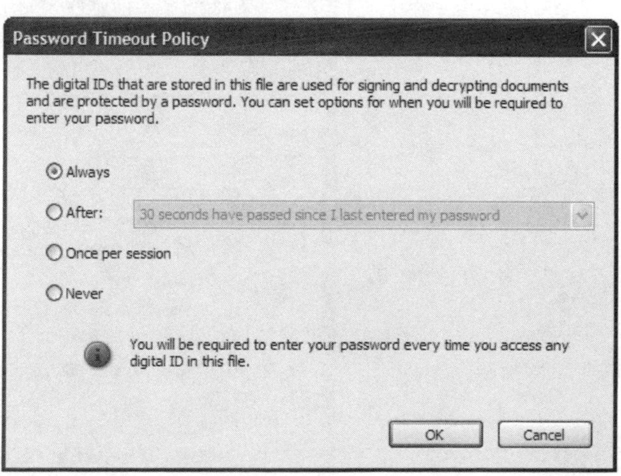

Here are your options:

- **Always** This option is selected by default and requires a password every time you digitally sign a document. You can deselect this option if you're a sole entrepreneur or you secure your computer when you're not at your workstation.
- **After** Click this button, and then click the drop-down arrow to choose a time interval after which you will be required to enter your password when digitally signing a document.
- **Once Per Session** Choose this option and you'll be prompted to enter your password the first time you digitally sign a document. You won't have to enter your password again until you close and launch Acrobat again.
- **Never** Choose this option and you never have to enter your password while working in Acrobat.

6. Click OK to apply the new settings.

Use the Signatures Panel

After you or another author digitally signs a document, information concerning the signature appears in the Signatures panel. You can select a signature in the panel and find out when the document was signed, who the author was, the validity of the signature, and the reason for signing the document. You use the Signatures panel to manage the signatures in the document, as well as perform other functions. To open the Signatures panel, shown next, open the Navigation pane and click the Signatures icon. Or, you can choose View | Navigation Panels | Signatures. For the purpose of this illustration, the Signatures panel is displayed as a floating panel.

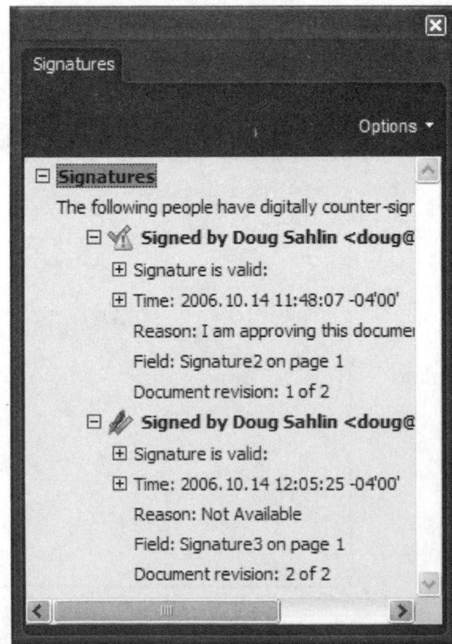

The Signatures panel has an extensive Options menu with commands pertaining to digital signatures. To open the Signatures panel Options menu, shown here, click the Options icon in the Signatures panel.

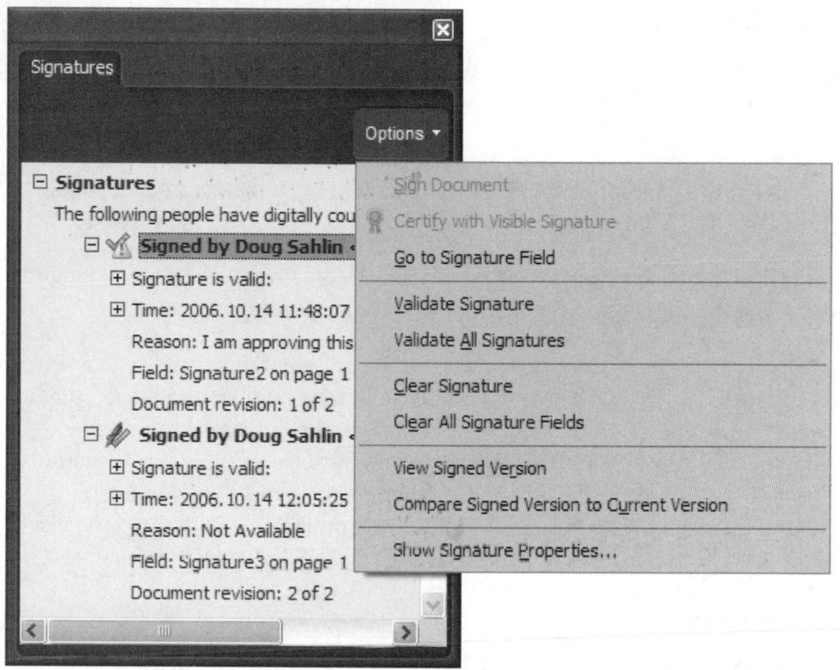

In the following sections, you learn how to use commands from this menu to sign signature fields, clear and delete signature fields, verify signatures, view different versions of the document, and more.

View Digital Signatures

After you open the Signatures panel, you see a single listing for each signature in the document. The listing notes the author's name, e-mail address, the verification status of the signature, and the date the signature was added to the document. Verifying signatures is discussed in the upcoming section "Validate Signatures."

To the left of the signature is a minus sign (–), as shown previously. Click the minus sign to collapse the signature. A collapsed signature is designated by a plus sign. Click the plus sign to expand the signature.

Sign Signature Fields

When you create a document with a blank digital signature field, you can sign the field in one of two ways: click the field with the Hand tool within the document, or select the signature field in the Signatures panel, and then choose Sign Signature Field from the Options menu. After you choose to sign the field using one of these methods, follow the previously discussed steps to sign the signature field. For more information on creating signature fields, refer to the upcoming section "Create a Blank Signature Field."

Clear Signature Fields

When you or another author digitally signs a document, you create a field that contains a digital signature. You can also clear a digital signature field for use by another reviewer by following these steps:

1. In the Navigation pane, click the Signatures icon to open the Signatures panel.
2. Click the name of the digital signature whose field you want to clear.
3. Choose Clear Signature from the Options menu. If you want to clear all signature fields, choose Clear All Signature Fields from the Options menu.

After you clear a signature field, it's represented in the Signatures panel with a signature icon followed by a title that designates the signature field by a number and the document page on which the signature appears. In the document, the cleared signature is represented by the signature field icon. You can sign a blank signature field by selecting it in the Signatures Panel, and then choosing Sign Signature Field from the Options menu or by clicking the field in the document with the Hand tool. Either method opens the Sign Document dialog box, discussed previously in the section "Sign a Document."

Validate Signatures

When you open a document with digital signatures, they are verified by default, unless you deselect the Verify signatures when the document is opened check box in the Security category of the Preferences dialog box. Acrobat checks the authenticity of the signature to see if the document or signature has been changed since the signing. If you select a digital ID prior to opening a document, Acrobat checks all signers' digital IDs against the list of trusted identities in your user profile. If the signature matches one of the certificates, Acrobat verifies the signature. If the document has been modified after the signature was placed, Acrobat displays a warning icon. You can verify selected signatures or all signatures.

To verify signatures, do one of the following:

- Click a signature in the document with the Hand tool.
- Open the Signatures panel, select the signature you want to verify, and then choose Validate Signature from the Options menu.
- Open the Signatures panel, and then choose Validate All Signatures from the Options menu.

Acrobat verifies the signature of a member of your trusted identities list by replacing the question mark icon with a green check mark. When you validate one signature in the Signatures panel or within the document, Acrobat displays the Signature Validation Status dialog box. If the document has been modified after being digitally signed, Acrobat displays a yellow exclamation mark in the Signature Validation Status dialog box:

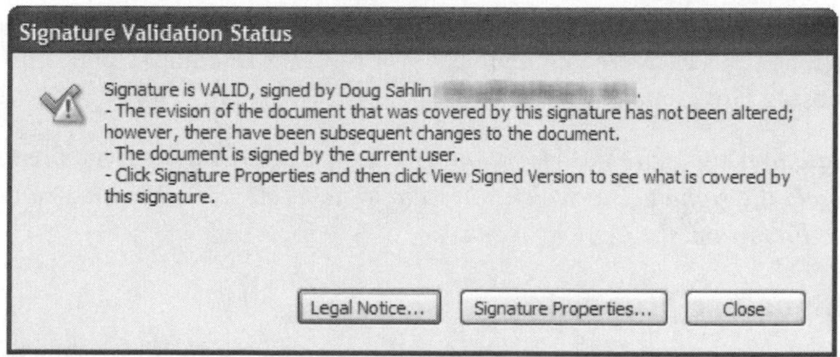

To accept the verification and continue working, click the Close button.

View Document Version

When a document is digitally signed, Acrobat remembers the exact contents of the document at that stage of the revision process. You can use the Signatures Panel or menu commands to view any version of the document. To view a signed version of the document:

1. In the Navigation pane, click the Signatures icon.
2. Click the digital signature that corresponds to the version of the document you want to view.
3. Choose View Signed Version from the Options menu. Or, you can choose Advanced | Sign & Certify | View Signed Version.

After you invoke this command, Acrobat re-creates a version of the document as it appeared at that stage of the revision process, and displays it in another window. You can view as many

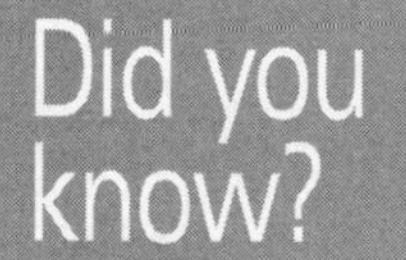

You Can Compare Signed Versions of Documents

If you own Acrobat Professional, choose Advanced | Compare Documents. This opens a dialog box that enables you to choose which signed versions of the document you want to compare. After selecting two versions, click OK, and Acrobat Professional creates a side-by-side comparison (or a detailed report if you choose that option) of each page of the document. You can see differences between versions by scrolling through the pages. By default, differences are highlighted in pink rectangles.

You can also compare a signed version to the current version by selecting a digital signature in the document, and then choosing Advanced | Sign & Certify | Compared Signed Version to Current Version. Acrobat displays the signed version beside the current version of the document and displays a pink rectangle for each difference.

signed versions of the document as needed. You can compare signed versions to the original by following the previous steps to re-create previous versions of the document, choosing Window | Tile, and then choosing Horizontally or Vertical.

To navigate to a signature field location within the document, open the Signatures panel, select the signature to which you want to navigate, and then choose Go To Signature Field from the Options menu.

View Digital Signature Properties

You can learn everything you want to know about a digital signature by viewing its properties. When you view a digital signature's properties, you can verify the signature and get information about the author of the digital signature. To view the properties of a digital signature, follow these steps:

1. In the Navigation pane, click the Signatures icon to open the Signatures panel.
2. Click a digital signature to select it.
3. Choose Show Signature Properties from the Options menu to open the Signature Properties dialog box:

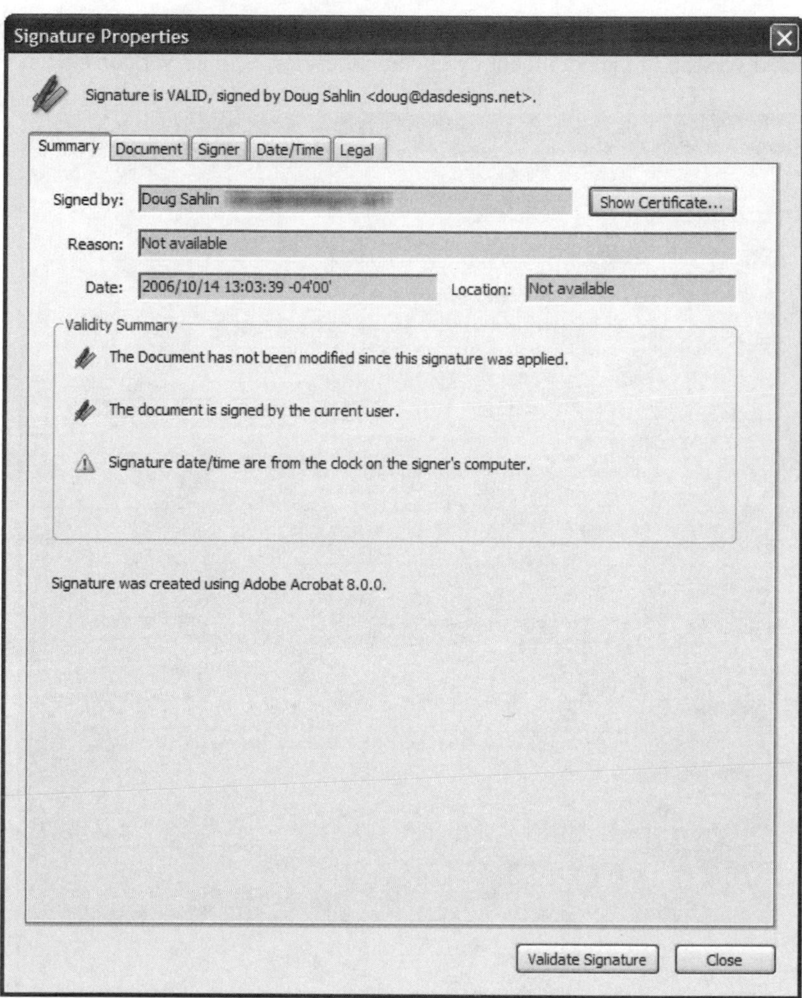

4. On the Summary tab of the dialog box, you can perform the following operations:
   - Click the Validate Signature button at the bottom of the tab to verify the digital signature.
   - Click the Show Certificate button to display the Certificate Viewer dialog box, which is divided into the following tabs: Summary, Details, Revocation, Trust, Policies, and Legal Notice. If the creator of the certificate isn't on your trusted identities list, you can add the certificate owner to the list by clicking the Add To Trusted Identities button on the Trust tab of the dialog box. After viewing information about the certificate, click Close to exit the Certificate Viewer dialog box.
5. Click the Document tab, shown next, to reveal information about the version of the document associated with the digital signature. From within this tab, you can verify

whether the document was altered after the digital signature was applied and view the associated version of the document by clicking the View Signed Version button.

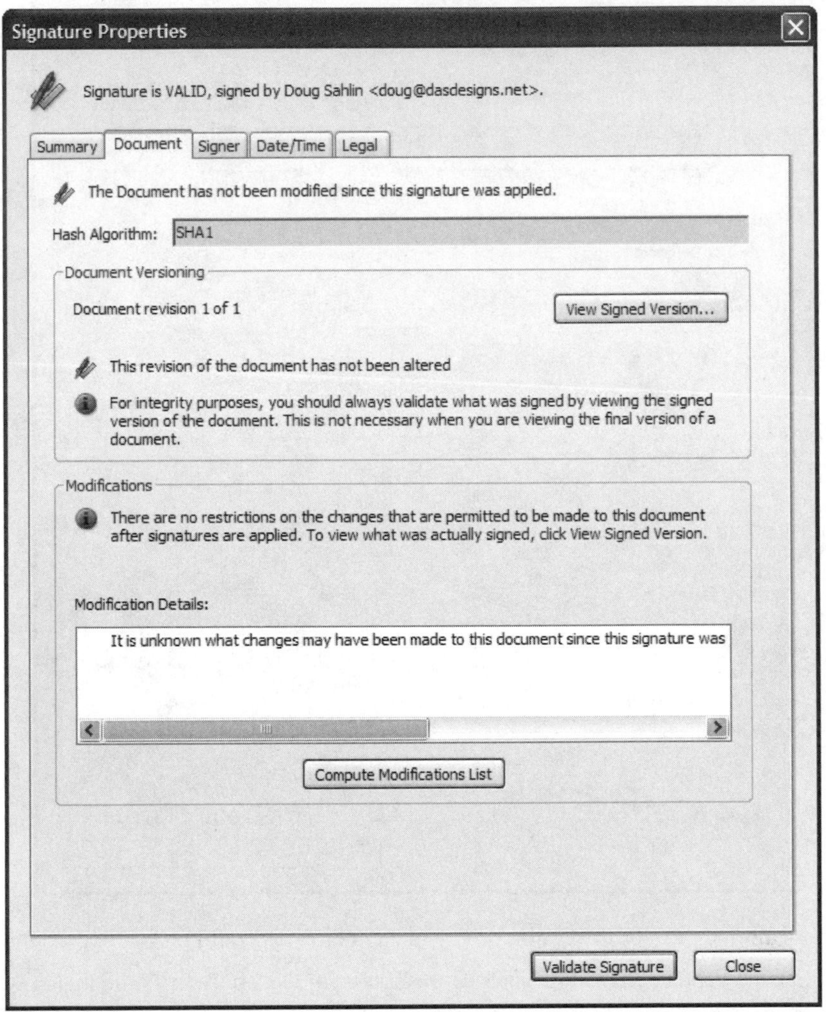

6. Click the Compute Modifications List button to reveal a detailed list of the changes made to the version of the document associated with the selected digital signature.
7. Click the Signer tab to reveal information about the signer associated with the selected signature. From within this tab, you can click the Show Certificate button to view the signer's certificate.
8. Click the Date/Time tab to view the date and time the selected digital signature was applied to the document. If the date and time stamp are from the signer's computer, Acrobat displays a yellow exclamation point and warning text.

9. Click the Legal tab to view the Legal Notice, which contains additional information about the digital ID and a disclaimer. From within this tab, you can click the Signer Legal Notice button to view the Legal Notice tab of the Certificate Viewer dialog box.

NOTE

You have another option on the Legal tab of the Signature Properties dialog box. This option is to click the View Document Integrity Properties button to display the Certified Document Warnings dialog box, which contains warnings about potential problems with the document, such as links that open URLs in web browsers. If the document doesn't contain any problems, Acrobat displays a dialog box to that effect.

10. Click Close to exit the Signature Properties dialog box.

Create a Blank Signature Field

When you create a document to be sent to other colleagues for review, you can request their digital signature after they review and comment on the document. When the document is returned to you, the digital signature can be validated. Any alterations to the document after the field is signed are readily apparent on the Signatures panel, as well as at the location of the digital signature within the document. To create a blank signature field, follow these steps:

1. Choose Tools | Forms | Digital Signature tool.
2. Click-and-drag the field diagonally to define the shape of the digital signature field. As you drag the Digital Signature tool, Acrobat displays a bounding box, showing you the current size of the signature field. Release the mouse button when the field is the desired size. The Digital Signature Properties dialog box appears.
3. Click the General tab, shown here.

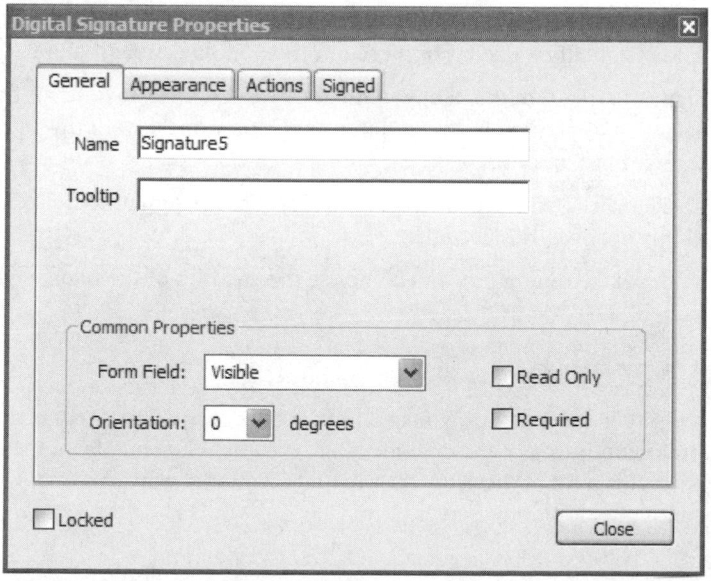

4. Accept the default Name (Signature followed by the next available signature number) or enter a different name.
5. If desired, enter instructions or other information in the Tooltip field. This information is displayed when a user's mouse hovers over the signature field.
6. Click the Form Field drop-down arrow and choose one of the following: Visible, Hidden, Visible But Doesn't Print, or Hidden But Printable.

If you choose a Hidden option, make sure you enter information in the Tooltip field or leave other instructions for reviewers, as they will be unable to see the signature field in the document. An alternative is to create JavaScript that displays the field when a member of your trusted identities list views the document.

7. Click the Orientation drop-down arrow and choose an option from the drop-down menu. This option determines how the field is oriented to the document.
8. Click the Required check box, and the field is marked as Required. If you distribute the document with a Submit button and the Submit button is clicked when the field is still blank, Acrobat displays a warning to that effect.

You also have an option to make signature fields read only. If a signature field is read only, it cannot be signed unless a JavaScript is created to change the field status when an authorized user accesses the document. Unfortunately, the JavaScript involved is beyond the scope of this book.

9. Click the Appearance tab. Within this tab, you can set the color and line type of the signature field border and fill color, as well as the font type used to display the digital signature.
10. Click the Actions tab. Within this tab, you can assign one or more actions that occur when the field is digitally signed. For more information on actions, refer to Chapter 8.
11. Click the Signed tab. Within this tab, you find options to create JavaScript that executes when the document is signed. For more information on using JavaScript in PDF documents, refer to Chapter 8.
12. Click the Locked check box if you want to specify that the signature field cannot be moved until this option is deselected.
13. Click Close to exit the dialog box and complete the creation of the blank signature field.

About Acrobat Security

When you assign security to a document, you can limit user access to the document. For example, you can prohibit printing of the document and copying elements from the document. You have three versions of Acrobat Security: Acrobat Password Security, Acrobat Certificate Security, and Adobe LiveCycle Policy Server.

With *Acrobat Password Security,* you can password-protect a document and require a permissions password to change the document password or security settings. When you use Acrobat Password Security, the same permissions level is granted to all recipients of the document. Acrobat Password Security is available with 40-bit encryption for Acrobat 3.*x* or Acrobat 4.*x,* and is available with 128-bit encryption for Acrobat 5.*x* and 6.0. Acrobat 7.0 and later have a different version of 128-bit encryption, which is compatible with Acrobat 7.0 and later, as well as Adobe Reader 7.0 and later.

If you need to assign different levels of permission for different recipients of your document, use *Acrobat Certificate Security*. When you secure a document with Acrobat Certificate Security, a user can open the document only if you selected that user from your list of trusted certificates and they are logged in with the corresponding digital signature. You can assign differing levels of permission for each user on your trusted identities list, as discussed in the upcoming section "Use Acrobat Certificate Security."

If your organization has decided to subscribe to the *Adobe LiveCycle Policy Server* service, you can tailor security policies for the documents you create. For example, you can create a policy that disables opening a document after a certain date. When you choose Adobe LiveCycle Policy Server, you're prompted to log in with the credentials assigned by your system administrator. You can then create security policies online, which, after completed, are stored online on the Adobe LiveCycle Policy Server. For further information on the Adobe LiveCycle Policy Server as it pertains to securing documents, visit *http://www.adobe.com/products/server/securityserver/main.html.*

General information on the Adobe LiveCycle Server can be found here: *http://www.adobe.com/products/server/policy/.*

Certify a Document

When you certify a document, you digitally sign it to verify its contents. Other reviewers will be able to fill in form fields and digitally sign the document, but if they attempt to change any of the other document attributes—such as links, text, and so on—the document is no longer listed as certified. To certify a document, follow these steps:

1. Choose the digital ID with which you want to certify the document, as discussed previously in the section "Choose a Digital ID."
2. Choose File | Save As Certified Document. Acrobat displays a dialog box with information about certifying documents. You also have the option of clicking the Get Digital ID From Adobe Partner button, which transports you to a web page on the Adobe web site where you can procure a third-party digital ID. Third-party digital IDs may be easier for recipients to validate if you widely distribute the document. Or, you can choose Advanced | Sign & Certify | Certify with Visible Signature.
3. Click OK. Acrobat displays a dialog box with instructions on how to create a signature field. After you certify a few documents, you may find this dialog box is intrusive. You can prevent the dialog box from appearing again by clicking the Do not show this message again check box.

4. Click OK, and then create a digital signature, as outlined previously. After creating the digital signature, the Certify Document dialog box appears.

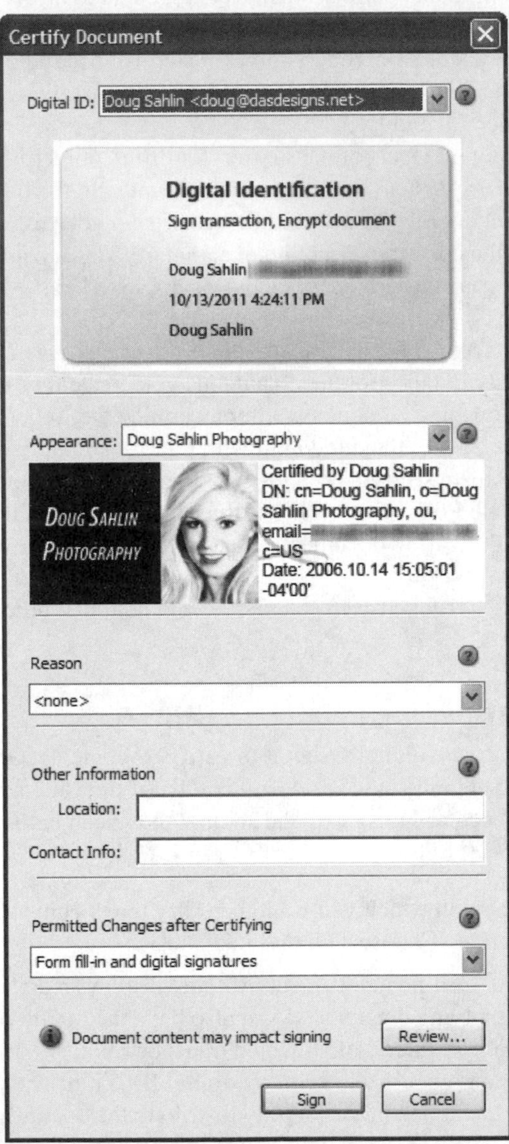

5. Choose a signature appearance, a reason for signing the document, and enter location and contact info, as outlined previously.

6. Click the Permitted Changes after Certifying drop-down arrow and choose one of the following options:
   - **No Changes Allowed** Prevents any document changes by future viewers.
   - **Form fill-in and digital signatures** Enables future viewers of the document to fill in form fields and apply a digital signature.
   - **Annotations, form fill-in and digital signatures** Allows future viewers of the document to create annotations with any of the commenting tools, fill in form fields, and digitally sign the document.
7. Click the Review button to display information about document content that may impact certifying the document. This option is unavailable if you don't choose the Show Review option in the Security category of the Preferences dialog box.
8. Click Sign. Acrobat displays the Save As dialog box.
9. Enter a name for the document and click Save.

When the document is opened again, a blue ribbon appears in a purple field at the top of the document. The name of the certifier is listed along with the validity of the digital signature. The reader of the document can click the Signature Properties icon to display the Signature Properties dialog box.

Use Acrobat Password Security

In today's economy, corporations often have branches in different counties, states, and countries. Before the advent of e-mail, corporations had to send documents via courier, an expensive way to communicate. With e-mail, corporate documents can be sent as e-mail attachments. However, anyone with a bit of computer savvy can access an e-mail message and, with the proper software, view sensitive communications. When you use Acrobat Password Security, you can assign to a document a password that must be entered to open the document. When a user tries to open a password-protected document, Acrobat prompts the user for a password. The document can only be opened with the proper password. When you password-protect a document, you can assign permissions to the document to restrict what changes the user can perform to the document after accessing it with the correct password. For example, you can specify whether a viewer with Acrobat can edit the document. To limit access to a document by using Acrobat Password Security, follow these steps:

1. Choose Advanced | Security | Password Encrypt. Or, you can click the Secure task button and choose Password Encrypt from the drop-down menu. After choosing the command, Acrobat displays the Applying New Security Settings dialog box, which asks you if you're sure you want to change the security of the document.

TIP *Click the Do not show this message again check box to prevent the Applying New Security Settings dialog box from appearing in the future.*

2. Click Yes to display the Password Security-Settings dialog box.

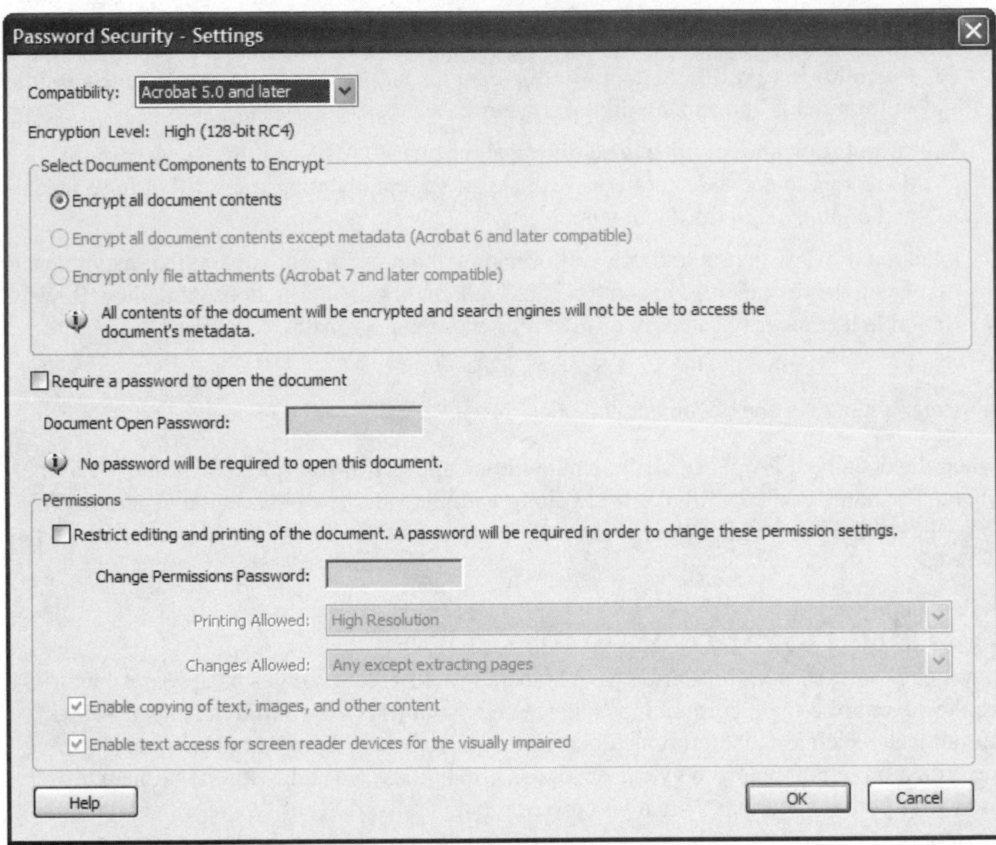

3. Click the Compatibility drop-down arrow and choose one of the following: Acrobat 3.0 And Later, Acrobat 5.0 And Later, Acrobat 6.0 And Later, or Acrobat 7.0 And Later. Choosing 6.0 or 7.0 gives you the best security, but the document will be available only to users with Adobe Reader 6.0 and later, or Adobe Reader 7.0 and later.
4. Select the desired option in the Select Document Components to encrypt section.

NOTE *If you choose compatibility for Acrobat 5.0 and later, or an earlier version, your only option is to encrypt all document components, which means the document metadata will be unavailable to search engines. If you choose compatibility for Acrobat 6.0 and later, you can encrypt all document components except metadata. If you choose compatibility for Acrobat 7.0 and later, you have the additional option to encrypt only file attachments to the document.*

5. To assign a password to the document, check the Require A Password To Open The Document box. The Document Open Password field then becomes available.

NOTE *If you encrypt document attachments, Require A Password To Open File Attachments is selected by default.*

6. In the Document Open Password field, enter the password that will be required to open the document. If you choose to encrypt file attachments, this field is listed as: File Attachment Open Password. As you type each letter of the password, an asterisk appears to prevent prying eyes from seeing the password you enter.
7. To restrict document printing and editing, click the Restrict Printing And Editing Of The Document check box. The Change Permissions Password field then becomes active. When you assign a permissions password to a document, a user who enters the proper document-open password can view the document, but cannot change the document-open password, and can only perform the tasks allowed by the permissions settings. If the viewer enters the proper password in the Change Permissions Password field, they can change the document password, as well as the permissions allowed to future viewers of the document.
8. In the Change Permissions Password field, enter the password that must be entered to change document passwords or permissions. As you enter text in the Permissions Password field, each letter appears as an asterisk. The document-open password and permissions password must be unique. For security reasons, a good idea is to use dissimilar passwords.

TIP *To prevent being locked out of a document you created, consider copying your document passwords in a safe place—for example, your PDA, if you use one. If you frequently secure documents, consider creating a spreadsheet that lists documents with fields for date, title, and password. Refer to the spreadsheet to quickly locate the password of a document based on its title, or the date it was created.*

9. Click the Printing Allowed drop-down arrow and choose an option. Your choices vary depending on the compatibility option you choose in Step 4. If you choose Acrobat 5.0 And Later, your options are None, Low Resolution (150 DPI), and High Resolution (300 DPI). If you choose Low Resolution and a document viewer chooses Acrobat Distiller as the printing device, the resulting PDF file is also printed at low resolution, which prevents the user from pirating a high-resolution copy of the document.
10. Click the Changes Allowed drop-down arrow and choose an option. If you chose Acrobat 5.0 And Later, choose one of the following options:
    - **None** Viewers cannot make any changes to the document.
    - **Inserting, Deleting, and Rotating Pages** Viewers can only insert, delete, and rotate pages.
    - **Filling In Form Fields and Signing Existing Signature Fields** Viewers can fill in form fields and sign signature fields, but they cannot create them.
    - **Commenting, Filling In Form Fields, And Signing Existing Signature Fields** Viewers can add comments to the document and fill in and sign the document, but they cannot create or otherwise alter form fields.

- **Any Except Extracting Of Pages** Viewers have full access to the document with the exception of extracting pages, within the limits of the version of Acrobat or Adobe Reader being used to view the document.

11. Click the Enable Copying Of Text, Images, And Other Content check box to allow Acrobat users to use the applicable tools to copy content to the clipboard for use in other PDF documents, or applications.
12. Check the Enable Text Access For Screen Reader Devices For The Visually Impaired box to allow the visually impaired to read the document with their screen readers. They will be unable to copy or extract objects from the document.
13. Click OK to set document security. If you password-protected the opening of the document, the Confirm Document Open Password dialog box appears.
14. Confirm the document password and click OK. Acrobat displays a warning dialog box, telling you the viewers using third-party products to view the document may be able to circumvent the security you apply.

TIP

To prevent this warning about third-party security products from appearing in the future, click the Do Not Show This Message Again check box.

15. Click OK to exit the warning dialog box. If you assigned a permissions password to the document as well, the Confirm Permissions Password dialog box appears again, prompting you to confirm the permissions password.
16. Confirm the permissions password and click OK. Acrobat displays a warning dialog telling you security won't be applied until you save the document.

TIP

To prevent this warning from appearing in the future, click the Do Not Show This Message Again check box.

17. Choose File | Save. When the document opens again, the security measures you selected are assigned to the document.

If changes in your organization prompt a change in document security permissions settings, you can easily change them by opening the document whose security permissions settings you need to change and then choosing Advanced | Security | Show Security Settings. Click the Change Settings button. After correctly entering the document permissions password, you can change the security settings, as outlined in this section.

Use Acrobat Certificate Security

When you use *Acrobat Certificate Security,* you have complete control over who is permitted to open the document and who is permitted to edit the document. You can assign varying degrees of permission as well, which is useful if you create a document to be distributed in a corporate environment.

You can allow some team members to have complete access to the document and allow other team members to have varying degrees of access. For example, if the document needs to be available to a recent hire, you can disable that person's access to edit, print, and extract elements from the document. When you assign Acrobat Certificate Security, you choose the users who can have access to the document from your list of trusted identities.

Build a List of Trusted Identities

Before you can assign Acrobat Certificate Security to a document, you need to build a list of trusted identities. *Trusted identities* are Acrobat users who have sent you their certificates. When users create a digital ID, they have the option to export to a file the certificate associated with their digital ID. You can exchange certificates with other members of your team via e-mail, as discussed in the following section.

Exchange Certificates The first step in building a list of trusted identities is to exchange certificates. You can import certificates received from other team members, or you can request a certificate from a recipient via e-mail. To exchange certificates via e-mail, follow these steps:

1. Choose Advanced | Manage Trusted Identities to access the Manage Trusted Identities dialog box.
2. Click the Display drop-down arrow and choose Certificates to display a list of your trusted identities, as shown here:

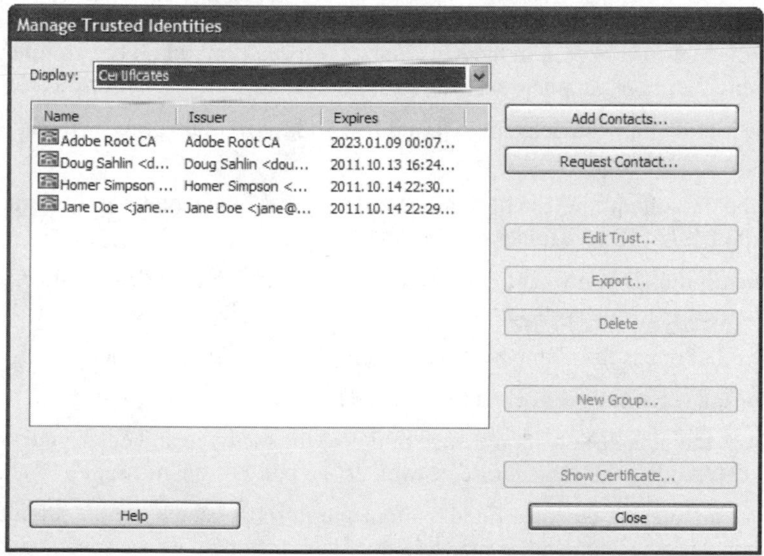

3. Click Request Contact to display the Email A Request dialog box.

4. Enter your name in the My Name field, and your e-mail address in My Email Address field, similar to what is shown here:

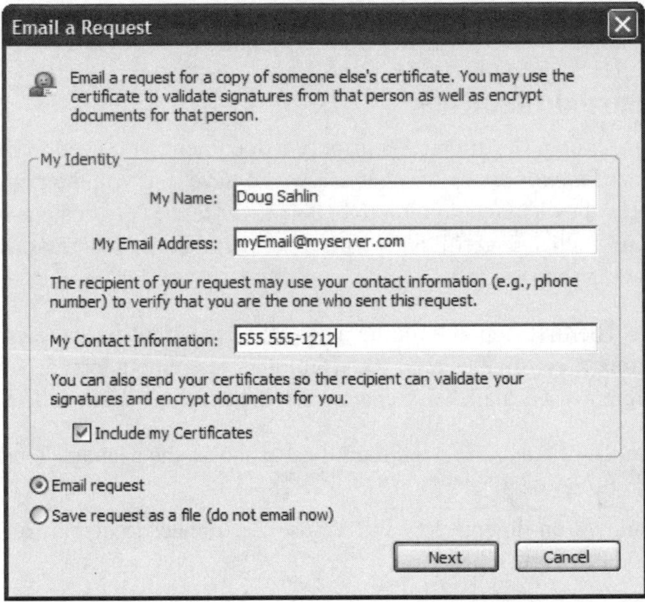

5. If desired, enter information in the My Contact Information field. For example, you may want to enter a phone number that recipients can use to verify your certificate.
6. Click Next to display the Selecting Digital IDs To Export dialog box, which contains a list of your digital IDs.
7. Accept the default option (Email request), or click the Save request as a file radio button to save the Digital ID to a folder on your hard drive.
8. Select the digital ID you want to export, and then click Select to display the Compose Email dialog box. Note, you can select only one digital ID to export.
9. After Acrobat opens the Compose Email dialog box, do the following:
   - Enter the recipient's e-mail address in the To field.
   - Accept the default Subject message or delete the message and enter your own. Note, you can modify the subject title, as well as the body of the message.
10. Log on to the Internet, click the Email button, and Acrobat launches your default e-mail application with the recipient's e-mail address filled in along with the subject and message. Use your e-mail application's Send command to send the message and certificate. When the recipient opens your e-mail, the certificate appears as an attachment.

After you click the Email button, your certificate is sent to the recipient as an e-mail attachment. Your e-mail recipient can add your certificate by clicking the file attachment.

After clicking the attachment, Acrobat launches and displays the Data Exchange File - Request And Contact dialog box, shown next. Note, a certificate comprises two components: a public key and a private key. The *public key* can be viewed by someone who intercepts a certificate you send via e-mail, but the *private key* is invisible and cannot be reverse engineered (RE).

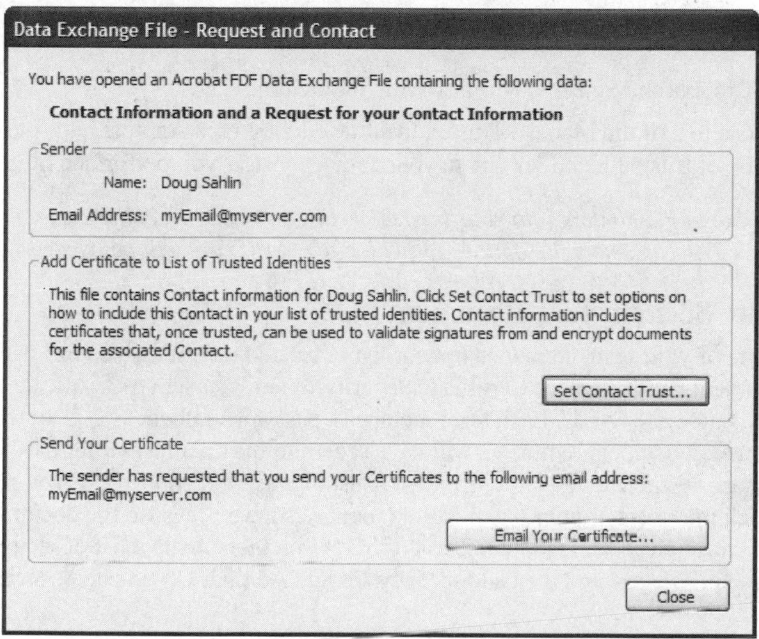

Recipients can add your certificate to their trusted identities list by clicking the Set Contact Trust button, which opens the Import Contact Settings dialog box. Recipients can select the options for which the certificate will be trusted, and then click OK to add the certificate to your trusted identities list. If you requested a return certificate, the user can send it by clicking the Email Your Certificate button.

When you receive a return certificate, open the e-mail attachment, double-click the file extension as described previously, and follow the prompts. Make sure you select the digital ID to which you want the certificate saved.

Import a Certificate After exchanging certificates, your next step in building your list of trusted identities is importing the certificate. E-mail is an efficient way to exchange certificates. The files are small and can be sent quickly with even the slowest Internet connection. However, you may receive certificates on floppy disk or other media. When you receive a certificate in this manner, you can import it. To import a certificate into your list of trusted identities, follow these steps:

1. Choose Advanced | Manage Trusted Identities to open the Manage Trusted Identities dialog box.
2. Click the Display drop-down arrow and choose Certificates.

3. Click Add Contacts to open the Choose Contacts to Import dialog box.
4. Click Browse to open the Locate Certificate File dialog box, navigate to the folder where the certificate you want to add to the list is stored, select it, and then click Open.
5. Click Import to add the issuer of the digital ID to your list of contacts. Note, you can only import one certificate at a time. Repeat Steps 3 through 5 to import additional contacts.
6. Click OK to exit the Select Contacts To Add dialog box.
7. Click Close to exit the Manage Trusted Identities dialog box. Acrobat adds the certificate to your list of trusted identities and to your contacts list, if you performed Step 6.

After importing a contact into your trusted certificates list, select the contact, and then click Edit Trust to select the options for which the certificate will be trusted.

Add Certificate Security to a Document

After the members of your team are added to your list of trusted identities, you can begin to secure your documents with Acrobat Certificate Security. When you set up Certificate Security, you don't have to enter passwords. Each team member's password information is stored with their own certificate. Document recipients will have access to the document after they log in with the digital ID whose certificate you chose from your list of trusted identities. All you need to do is determine which members of your list of trusted identities have access to the document and which level of permissions each team member will have. You then create a list of recipients that will have the same privileges, and then add security. To add Acrobat Certificate Security to a document:

1. Choose Advanced | Security | Certificate Encrypt. Acrobat displays a warning dialog asking if you want to change security on the document.

Click the Do not show this message again check box to prevent this dialog box from being displayed in the future.

2. Click Yes to exit the warning dialog box. Acrobat displays the Certificate Security Settings dialog box, shown next.

If you have more than one digital ID, the Document Security-Digital ID Selection dialog box appears, which enables you to select the digital ID with which you want to certify the document.

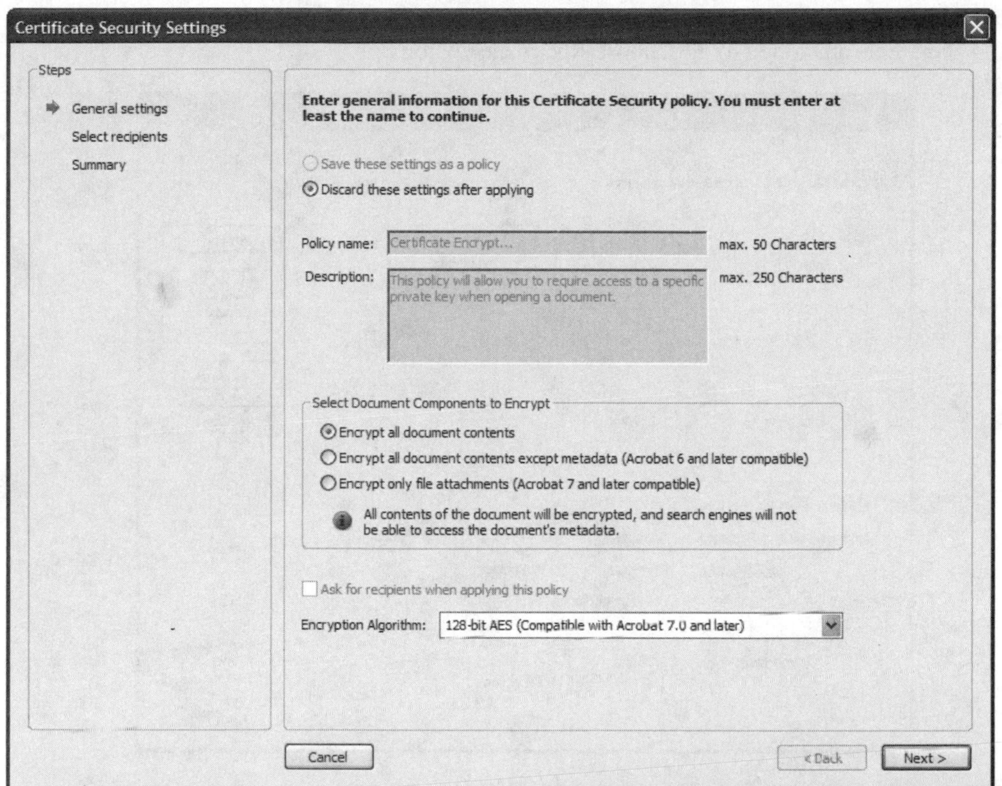

3. Click Search to open the Search for Recipients dialog box. From within this dialog box, you can search for recipients by entering contact information in the Search area, and then clicking the Search button. This method returns recipients from your e-mail address book and other locations that have valid digital IDs. You can choose recipients from the Search Results field. However, if you've already gone to the trouble of importing certificates as Trusted Identities, go to Step 4.
4. Deselect the Search All Directories check box, click the Directories drop-down arrow, and then choose Trusted Identities from the drop-down list, as shown next.

5. Choose the desired recipients from the Search Results field, and then click OK. The recipients are added to the Choose Recipients dialog box.

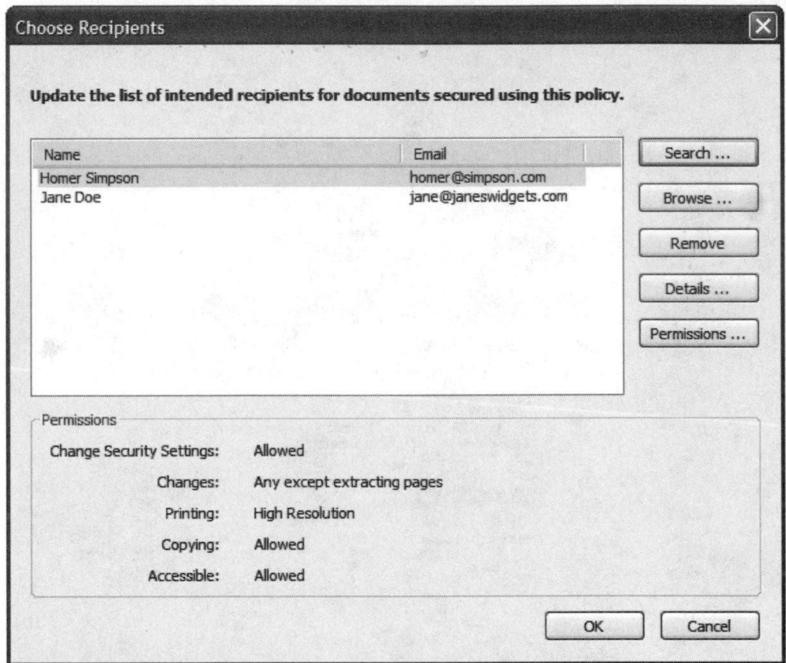

6. Select one or more recipients, and then click Permissions. Acrobat displays the Acrobat Security dialog box, informing you that viewers using third-party products to view the document may be able to bypass the security.

Click the Do Not Show This Message Again check box to prevent the dialog box from appearing in the future.

7. Click OK to reveal the Permissions Settings dialog box. By default, no restrictions are applied.
8. Click the Restrict printing and editing of the document and its security settings check box, and then choose the level of permissions you'll grant to the selected recipient(s). These are the same options discussed previously in the section "Use Acrobat Security."
9. Click OK to apply the permissions to the selected recipient(s). The Permissions section of the dialog box updates to show the permissions you granted to the selected recipient(s)
10. Repeat Steps 6 through 9 for the other recipients on your list. Remember, you can assign different permissions for each user, which is what makes Acrobat Certificate Security such a powerful tool.
11. Click OK. Acrobat displays a dialog box telling you security settings won't be updated until you save the document.

Create a Security Envelope

If you have confidential files, such as Word documents or Excel spreadsheets, that you want to send as editable documents to colleagues, you can send them via e- mail. But if a third party intercepts the e-mail, they'll be able to open the documents using the associated application. To prevent this, you can employ the new Secure Envelope feature in Acrobat. When you create a Secure Envelope, you use a secure PDF document as the envelope for the editable documents, which you also encrypt. To create a security envelope:

1. Choose Advanced | Security | Create Security Envelope to display the Create Security Envelope dialog box. Any documents currently open appear in the dialog box, as shown next.

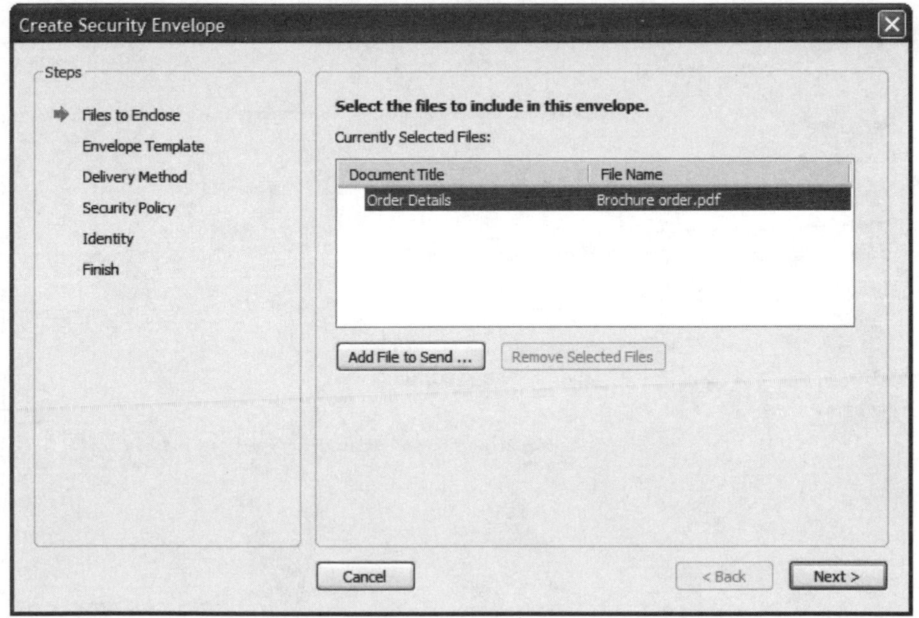

   To add additional files to the security envelope, click the Add File to Send button, which reveals the Files to Enclose dialog box.

2. Select the files you want to enclose in the security envelope, and then click Open.
3. Click Next to reveal the Envelope Template section of the Create Security Envelope dialog box. This section lists the default Acrobat security envelope templates. You can substitute an envelope of your own design, which has been saved as a PDF document by clicking the Browse button, and then selecting the desired PDF document.
4. After choosing a template, click Next to reveal the Delivery Method section of the Create Security Envelope dialog box.

5. Choose the method of delivery. Your options are to send the envelope later, in which case the completed envelope is saved to your hard drive, or to send the envelope now, in which case you're prompted for a list of recipients to whom you'll e-mail the envelope.
6. Click Next to display the Security Policy section of the dialog box. At this stage of the process, you can click the New Policy button to create a new policy, or click the Show all policies check box to show all security policies associated with Acrobat, as shown next. The default Certificate Encrypt and Password Encrypt methods of security aren't recommended for PDF documents with attached files, however. If you don't have a security policy that encrypts document attachments, your best bet is to create a new policy. If you already have a security policy that encrypts file attachments, go to Step 16.

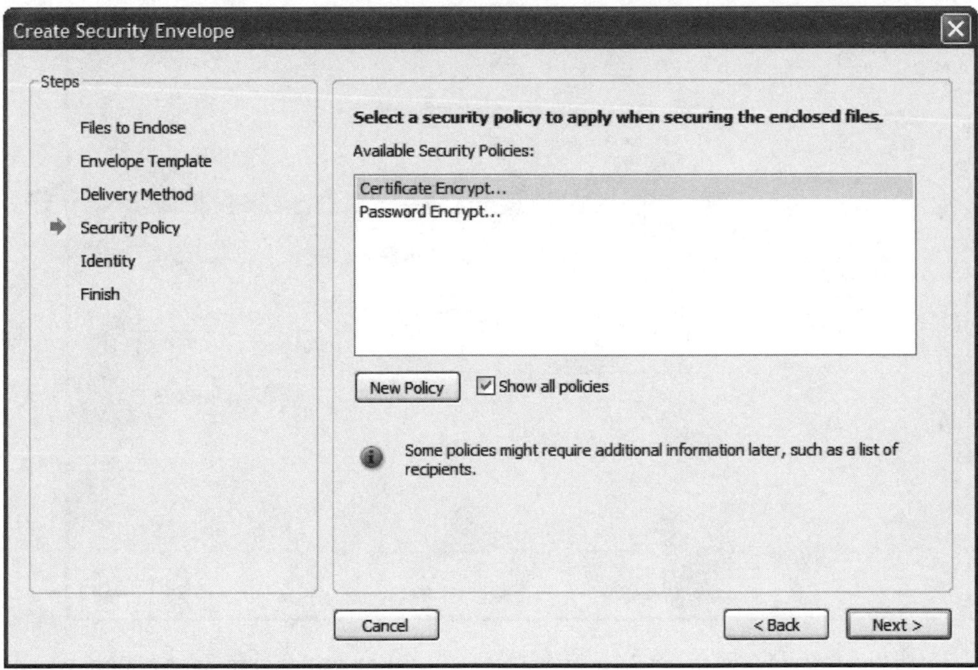

7. Click the New Policy button to reveal the first page of the New Security Policy dialog box, shown next.

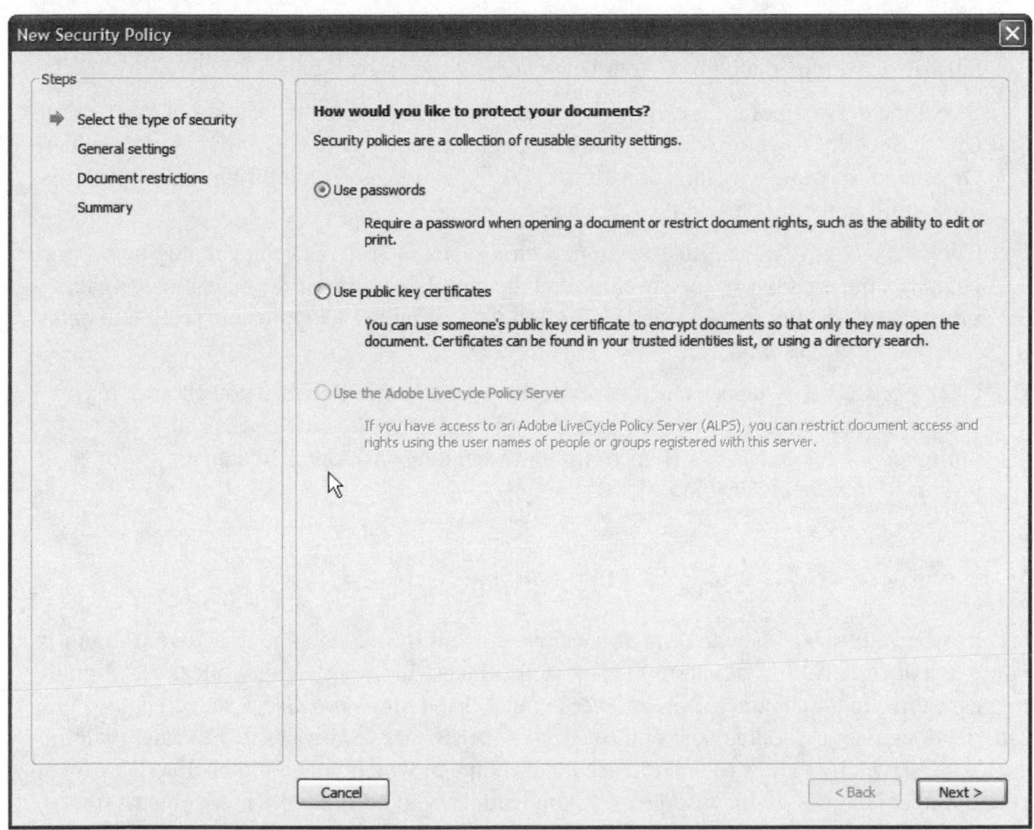

8. Choose the Use Passwords option. The reason for choosing this option for the new policy is because file attachments can be encrypted when specifying Acrobat 7.0 and later compatibility.
9. Click Next to reveal the General Settings section of the dialog box.
10. Enter the desired information in the Policy Name and Description fields.
11. Click Next to reveal the Document Restrictions section of the dialog box. The options in this dialog box are identical to those found in the Password Security - Settings dialog box, previously discussed in the section "Use Acrobat Password Security." When you're choosing settings, make sure you choose Acrobat 7.0 and later compatibility, which encrypts the document, as well as the attachments.
12. After completing the Document Restrictions section of the dialog box, click Next. At this stage, you're prompted to confirm your passwords.

13. Confirm the password(s), and then click OK to reveal the Summary section of the New Security Policy dialog box, which lists the details of the new policy. At this stage, you can click the Back button to navigate to a previous section and change settings.
14. If the details on the Summary page are acceptable, click Finish to return to the Create Security Envelope dialog box. Your new policy is shown on the list.

    Select the desired policy, and then click Next to reveal the Identity section of the Create Security Envelope dialog box. This page enables you to enter your Name, Title, Organization Name, Organization Unit, and Email address. The information you enter is used to fill in form fields on the template.
15. Click Next to reveal the Finish section of the Create Security Envelope dialog box. This page lists the contents of the envelope and the template to be used. You can modify this information by clicking the Back button and navigating to the applicable section to enter different information.
16. Click Finish. What happens next depends on the method of delivery you choose. If you choose to send the envelope now, your default E-Mail application opens and you're prompted for recipients to whom you want to send the envelope. Otherwise, you're prompted to save the envelope.

Summary

In this chapter, you learned how to remove sensitive content from a document, add your digital signature to a document, add signature fields to a document, and verify other colleagues' digital signatures. Certifying a document was another topic of discussion. You also discovered how to restrict a document by adding password security or certificate security to it. The final topic of discussion showed you how to create a secure envelope in which you could enclose files for distribution to colleagues. In the next chapter, you learn how to optimize PDF documents for specific destinations.

Chapter 12

Optimize PDF Documents

How to...

- Optimize documents for the visually impaired
- Optimize documents for print
- Optimize documents for CD/DVD applications
- Optimize documents for the Web
- Customize Distiller conversion settings

When you create a PDF document using Acrobat Distiller or PDFMaker, you can optimize it for a specific destination or for several destinations by choosing the proper conversion settings. If you create a document in an authoring application and (if available) use the PDF export feature of the application, or use Adobe PDF to print the file as a PDF document, you can modify the output settings for an intended destination by changing Adobe PDF Settings in the Adobe PDF Document Properties dialog box. When you change Adobe PDF Settings, you can specify how Adobe PDF compresses the images in your document and how it adjusts color settings for the intended destination of the document. You can also specify whether fonts are embedded.

Previous chapters covered how to use preset Adobe PDF Settings when converting documents into PDF format. In this chapter, you find out how to fine-tune Adobe PDF Settings to suit the intended destination of the document. Fonts are an important consideration when you create a PDF document, so this chapter discusses font issues, as well as when it's necessary to embed fonts. You learn specific strategies for optimizing your documents for an intended destination. You also see how to create a document that can be reflowed for easier reading in devices with different monitor sizes, and how to modify a document for the visually impaired. Finally, you find out how to fine-tune document graphics for the intended destination of the PDF.

About Tagged Documents

When you create a document that will be distributed to users who view the document on devices with a limited viewing area, you can create a tagged document that can be reflowed to any window or screen size. When a user *reflows* a tagged document, the font size remains unchanged, so it's legible even on a smaller viewing device. Images, however, are reduced in size to accommodate the reduced viewing area. If your tagged PDF document will be viewed on devices, such as a handheld PDA (Personal Digital Assistant) or some of the smaller e-book readers, viewers with Adobe Reader or Acrobat can reflow the document to fit the smaller viewing area.

You can create a tagged PDF in several key ways:

1. Create using PDFMaker
2. Create manually
3. Create by converting already structured content, such as html or xml

Creating tagged PDFs has been covered in previous chapters.

Create a Tagged Document

You can create a tagged document by converting web pages to PDF format or by creating a document within a Microsoft Office application, and then using Acrobat PDFMaker to convert the document to PDF. To create a tagged document from a Microsoft Office application, you modify the Application Settings option in the Settings section of the Acrobat PDFMaker dialog box, as detailed in the upcoming section "Customize Acrobat Distiller Conversion Settings."

To create a tagged document from web pages and HTML documents, follow these steps:

1. Choose File | Create PDF | From Web Page.
2. In the URL field, enter the URL of the page you want to convert to a tagged document. Remember, you can also capture an HTML document located on your computer by entering the relative path to the file.
3. Click the Settings button to open the Web Page Conversion Settings dialog box.
4. Click the Create PDF Tags check box, and then click OK to close the dialog box.
5. Click Create, and Acrobat captures the web page with PDF tags. For more information on converting web pages to PDF documents, refer to Chapter 6.

Reflow a Tagged Document

The recipients of a tagged document can reflow the document to fit the viewing area of the device they use to view the document. Tagged PDF files are optimized for accessibility, making them available to viewers using screen-reader devices. To reflow a document with Acrobat or Adobe Reader, choose View | Zoom | Reflow.

Optimize Documents for the Visually Impaired (Professional Only)

When you create a document that will be viewed by visually impaired people using onscreen readers, a different challenge presents itself to you—the document will be viewed at varying degrees of magnification. Creating a tagged document eliminates the problem of reflowing the document, but the issue of images in the document still exists. When a document is greatly magnified, only a portion of the image will be rendered. To offset this difficulty, you must provide a way for visually impaired readers to identify what the image is. To accomplish this, provide alternate text for tagged, nontext elements in the document by using the Tags panel.

TIP *You can optimize a document for the visually impaired in Acrobat Standard or Acrobat Professional by choosing Advanced | Accessibility | Quick Check, or perform a thorough check in Acrobat Professional by choosing Advanced | Accessibility | Full Check. A Quick Check is automated, while a Full Check gives you options from which to choose.*

Use the Tags Panel (Professional Only)

You use the *Tags panel* to view the logical order of a tagged document. When you open the Tags panel, you see the logical structure of the document, which is a visual representation of the organization of the document elements. Elements are objects, such as a block of text, an image, a document page, and so on. You can use the Tags panel to modify tags in a document. For example, many onscreen readers can take advantage of alternate text for a tagged element. The alternate text gives the visually impaired person a description of the element. You can also use tag information to specify the text language of the document. To open the Tags panel, shown next, choose View | Navigation Panels | Tags. In this illustration, each tag has been expanded. When you initially open the Tags panel, tags have a plus sign (+) to their left, indicating other tags are nested within. Click each plus sign to expand the tag. If the document isn't tagged, No Tags Available displays at the top of the panel.

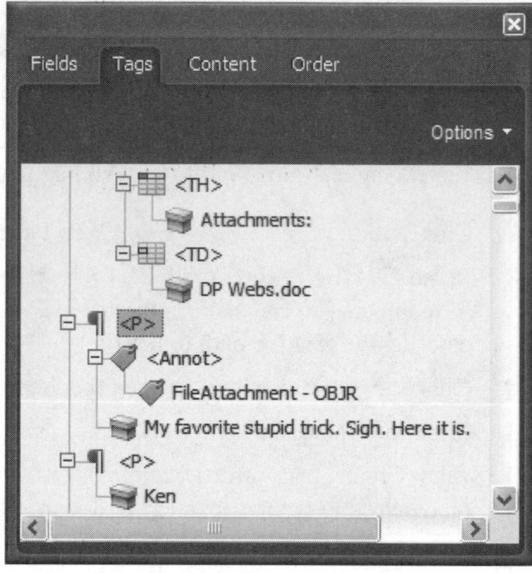

TIP *If you open the Tags panel and see No Tags Available, you can add tags in Acrobat Professional by choosing Advanced | Accessibility | Add Tags To Document.*

If you create a tagged document with images to be viewed with onscreen reading devices that have limited graphics capabilities, you can add an alternate tag that describes what the image shows. To add an alternate text tag to a nontext element, follow these steps:

1. Open the Tags panel (View | Navigation Panels | Tags).
2. Select the tag that denotes the image in the PDF document. If you have a hard time determining which tag is associated with which element in the text, click the Options icon in the upper-right corner of the panel and choose Highlight Content. When you enable this option, Acrobat highlights the element in the document when you select the corresponding tag. Also, note, graphic elements have different icons in the Tags panel.
3. Click the Options icon and choose Properties to open the TouchUp Properties dialog box. Or, you can right-click (Windows) or CTRL-click (Macintosh) the desired tag in the Tags panel, and then choose Properties from the context menu.
4. In the Alternate Text field, enter a description of the image. For example, if the image depicts El Capitan in Yosemite National Park, you might enter the following: **This image is a photograph of El Capitan in Yosemite National Park.**
5. Click Close to assign the alternate text to the tag. Alternate text is displayed in a screen reader.

Optimize Documents for Your Local Printer

When you create a PDF document for print, you modify the Press Quality or High Quality Print Adobe PDF conversion settings (in either Acrobat Distiller or when using the PDFMaker in a Microsoft Office application) to match the intended output device. If the document is to be printed by a service center, check with the service center technicians to get the necessary information about the printing device with which your documents will be printed. This is the information you need to modify conversion settings—in particular, when modifying the Color and Advanced settings of either the Press Quality conversion settings or, if the document contains high-resolution images, the High Quality Print conversion settings. You should also pay careful attention to image resolution. If the document is for print only and file size isn't a concern, you can choose Maximum for the Image Quality settings in the Images section of the Adobe PDF Settings dialog box to maintain maximum image quality. If you create documents that will be printed by a service center or on a printer attached to a different computer, embed all fonts to ensure the document prints properly.

The default resolution of 2400 dpi is fine for most commercial printing devices, however, it's higher than needed for most laser printers. You can change the resolution setting to match your laser or InkJet-type printer in the General section of the Press Quality – Adobe PDF Settings dialog box or the High Quality Print – Adobe PDF Settings dialog box. Modifying conversion settings is discussed in detail in the section "Customize Acrobat Distiller Conversion Settings." Or, you can also choose the Press Quality conversion settings as the basis for documents you print in-house on laser or InkJet-type printers. If you're optimizing documents for a commercial printer, you use one of the PDF-X conversion settings. Optimizing PDF documents for commercial printers is covered in detail in Chapter 16.

Optimize Documents for CD/DVD Applications

When you optimize a document for a CD/DVD application, use the Standard conversion settings as a starting point. This option has compression settings with higher resolutions than those generally needed for screen viewing, but when you create a CD/DVD, file size is generally not an issue. If you choose the High option in the Image Quality drop-down list boxes in the Image section of the Adobe PDF Settings dialog box, the document images will have low compression and your viewers will be able to zoom in on document images with little or no loss in quality. In fact, you may want to use the Maximum Image Quality setting and disable downsampling if your CD/DVD presentation has many intricate images, such as maps that will be examined at higher magnification settings, and the required files will fit on the CD/DVD with high-image resolution settings.

Optimize Documents for the Web

When you optimize documents for viewing on the Web, begin with the Smallest File Size conversion settings. The default settings resample document images to 100 pixels per inch (PPI). The resulting file is a compromise between file size and image quality. Experiment with the Low and Minimum settings in the Image Quality drop-down list box. These settings will result in images of lower quality because of the higher compression applied. If the images in the original document were high quality, you may be able to produce an acceptable document using the Low or Minimum image-quality settings.

You can create a document using the default Smallest File Size conversion settings, and then create another document using the Smallest File Size conversion settings with Medium image quality settings. Compare the two documents in Acrobat, arranged in tile format, and you will be able to see the difference in image quality between the different compression settings.

By default, documents created with the Smallest File Size conversion settings are optimized for *byteserving* (sending a document to a web browser a page at a time) over the Web if the web-hosting service supports byteserving.

Customize Acrobat Distiller Conversion Settings

When you create a document for a specific destination using Acrobat Distiller or Adobe PDFMaker, you can use one of the preset Adobe PDF conversion settings to convert the file. You can also customize any of the preset conversion settings by modifying the parameters to suit your needs. To modify an Adobe PDF conversion setting, you begin with a preset that closely suits your needs, apply the needed changes, and then save the Adobe PDF conversion setting with a different filename. After you save a modified Adobe PDF setting, the new setting appears on the Default Settings drop-down menu in Acrobat Distiller, and on the Conversion Settings menu of the Acrobat PDFMaker dialog box, which you access from the Adobe PDF menu in Microsoft Office applications.

Each Adobe PDF Settings dialog box is comprised of five sections in Acrobat Standard, and six in Acrobat Professional. You can modify as many or as few sections as needed to create the optimal conversion for your document(s). To create a custom-conversion setting in Acrobat Distiller, follow these steps:

1. In the Adobe PDF Settings area, click the Default Settings drop-down arrow and choose a conversion setting from the drop-down menu. Choose a conversion setting that closely matches the intended destination of the document. For example, if you're customizing settings for documents that will be viewed on a web site, choose Smallest File Size.
2. Choose Settings | Edit Adobe PDF Settings to open the Adobe PDF Settings dialog box, shown in Figure 12-1. Note, the dialog box shown in Figure 12-1 is for the Standard - Adobe PDF Settings as viewed in Acrobat Distiller. The title of the dialog box changes, depending on the conversion setting you're modifying. For example, if you modify Press Quality Adobe PDF Settings, the dialog box title reads Press Quality - Adobe PDF Settings.

You can also modify Adobe PDF settings from within a Microsoft Office application. When you modify a conversion setting from within a Microsoft Office application, you're modifying an Adobe PDF Settings job option. Adobe PDF Settings created in Acrobat Distiller can be used to convert a document to PDF in a Microsoft Office application. You have access to the same settings in Acrobat Distiller. To modify an Adobe PDF Settings option from within a Microsoft Office application, follow these steps:

1. Choose Adobe PDF | Change Conversion Settings to open the Adobe PDFMaker dialog box.
2. Click the Conversion Settings drop-down arrow and choose a conversion setting to modify.
3. Click the Advanced Settings button to open the Adobe PDF Settings dialog box, shown in Figure 12-1.

After you open the Adobe PDF Settings dialog box, modify the conversion settings by making changes in each section. To access the settings in each section, click the section folder. The following sections of this chapter discuss the conversion settings you can modify in each section of the Adobe PDF Settings dialog box.

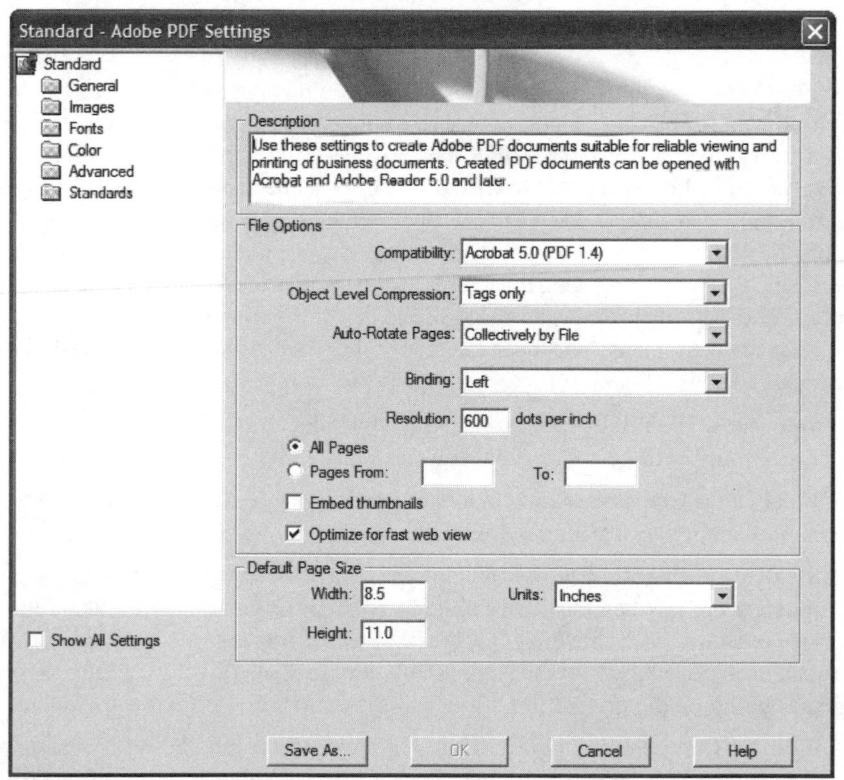

FIGURE 12-1 You can customize Adobe PDF Settings to suit the documents you convert to PDF.

Acrobat Distiller defaults to the last conversion setting used. Before converting a document to PDF with Acrobat Distiller, using Adobe PDF as a printing device, or using PDFMaker in a Microsoft Office application, choose the desired PDF Setting from the Change Conversion Settings menu (PDFMaker), the Default Settings drop-down list (Acrobat Distiller), or the Default Setting drop-down list in the Adobe PDF Document Properties dialog box when using Adobe PDF as a printer. Your document will be created with the new conversion settings.

Set General Options

In the General section of the Adobe PDF Settings dialog box, you determine which version of Acrobat is compatible with the published document. Also, you can optimize the file for fast Web viewing, set the document resolution for printing, and set the page size of the published document. To set General job options, follow these steps:

1. Choose a conversion setting to modify and open the Adobe PDF Settings dialog box, as discussed previously. By default, the dialog box opens to the General section, as shown in Figure 12-1.
2. In the File Options section, click the Compatibility drop-down arrow and choose the version of Acrobat with which you want the published document to be compatible. You can choose Acrobat 3.0 (PDF 1.2), Acrobat 4.0 (PDF 1.3), Acrobat 5.0 (PDF 1.4), Acrobat 6.0 (PDF 1.5), Acrobat 7.0 (PDF 1.6), or Acrobat 8.0 (PDF 1.7). Choose the version of Acrobat that supports the features in the document you created. Remember, take into account which version of Acrobat, Acrobat Reader, or Adobe Reader the majority of your target audience is likely to have installed on their computers. If a PDF is opened with a version higher than a viewer's Acrobat Reader or Adobe Reader, a dialog box to that effect appears. When a PDF version higher than the viewer's reader is opened, some of the features authored into the document might not work.
3. After you choose the version of Acrobat with which documents created with this conversion setting will be compatible, you can modify the following settings:
   - **Object Level Compression** Choose Off or Tags Only if you want to apply compression to the structure of a PDF document.
   - **Auto-Rotate Pages** Choose this option to have Acrobat automatically rotate document pages when the page should be rotated for viewing without scrolling. You can choose Off, in which case Acrobat won't rotate pages; Individually, to rotate each page based on the page orientation; or Collectively By File, to rotate all pages based on the orientation of the majority of pages within the document.
   - **Binding** Choose either Left or Right binding to determine how Acrobat displays the document in Continuous-Facing viewing mode, and how thumbnails are displayed when the thumbnails are resized so they can be viewed side-by-side. Thumbnails are arranged from left-to-right when you choose Left binding, and right-to-left when you choose Right binding.

- **Resolution** Enter a value that matches the resolution of the device on which the document will be printed. When you create a PDF file with Acrobat Distiller or Acrobat Distiller in the guise of Adobe PDF, the device is printing a PostScript file for display in PDF format. The value you enter for Resolution emulates the resolution setting of a printing device. If you specify a higher resolution, recipients of your document can print the file on a high-resolution device, but the file size will be larger.
- **All Pages** This default option converts all pages in the document to PDF.
- **Pages From [ ] To [ ]** Choose this option to specify a range of pages to convert to PDF by entering the first page to convert in the Pages From field and the last page to convert in the To field.
- **Embed Thumbnails** Choose this option to have Acrobat Distiller embed a thumbnail for each page of documents converted to PDF with this conversion setting. Remember, this increases the file size of the published document. If you choose not to select this option, Acrobat automatically generates thumbnails on the fly when the document viewer opens the Thumbnails panel. If, however, you're creating large PDF documents with hundreds of pages, you may want to consider embedding thumbnails, as generating hundreds of thumbnails every time the Pages panel is open can severely tax the system resources of the computer used to view the document.
- **Optimize For Fast Web View** Choose this option if you create a document to view on the Web. When you choose this option, Acrobat converts documents created with this job option for page-at-a-time downloading (byteserving) from the host web server.

4. In the Default Page Size section, enter values in the Width and Height fields, and then choose a unit of measure from the Units drop-down menu. The settings you enter here determine the dimensions of the files Acrobat creates with this conversion setting. Enter dimensions that match those of documents you create in the authoring application, which you use as the basis for PDF files created with this conversion setting. Remember, if you use Adobe PDF as a printing device to convert a Microsoft Office file to PDF format, you must configure Adobe PDF to match the page dimensions specified in the Conversion Settings setting. Otherwise, Adobe PDF (which is using Acrobat Distiller to print the PDF file) reverts to the default dimensions for Acrobat Distiller. For more information on configuring Acrobat Distiller page size, refer to Chapter 5.

After you modify the General settings of an Adobe PDF conversion setting, you can click a folder to modify other settings or save the modified conversion setting, as described in the upcoming section "Save Conversion Settings."

Set Conversion Settings Images Options

When you choose a specific conversion settings option to create a PDF document, Acrobat compresses the document text, line art, and images using settings deemed optimal for the conversion setting. You can, however, modify the compression settings to suit documents you create for specific applications. You can modify the settings to reduce file size by applying more compression to images, or enhance the quality of the published document by specifying a higher quality for document images. With a bit of experimentation, you can modify compression settings for optimal file size while still maintaining a high level of detail in the published document.

Acrobat Distiller Compression Methods

The compression method you choose greatly affects the overall quality of the images in your published document. When you modify compression settings, you can have Acrobat Distiller automatically choose the compression method deemed right for the images in the document, or you can choose one of the following Acrobat Distiller compression methods:

- **ZIP** Use the ZIP (Adobe's variation of the ZIP filter as derived from the zlib package of Jean-loup Gailly and Mark Adler) method of compression for images with large areas of solid color, such as GIF images. This method of compression works well with simple images created in painting applications, such as Windows Paintbrush or Corel Painter. It also works quite well with artwork created in vector-based drawing programs, such as Adobe Illustrator, Macromedia FreeHand, or CorelDRAW. You can use ZIP compression with 4-bit and 8-bit color depth. If you choose 4-bit color depth on an 8-bit image, you end up with a smaller file size, but degraded image quality because you lose data when the image is compressed.
- **JPEG** Use the Joint Photographic Experts Group (JPEG) method of compression on full-color or grayscale images, such as photographs. When you use JPEG compression, you can control the size of the file by telling Acrobat how much compression to apply to the images. You can modify the settings to create a PDF document with high-quality images at the expense of a larger file size, or you can apply a higher level of compression and your published PDF file will be smaller, but the images won't be as detailed due to the data lost during compression. JPEG compression is also known as *lossy* compression, because data is lost when the document images are compressed. Acrobat Distiller has five JPEG compression options. JPEG compression is best suited for photographs. If you have images with large areas of solid color, such as GIF images, in your document, use ZIP compression.
- **Automatic JPEG** When you choose this option, Acrobat determines the best settings to achieve the highest image quality.
- **JPEG 2000** This option is available if you choose Acrobat 6.0 (PDF 1.5) or later for compatibility. *JPEG 2000* is the new international standard for attaining high-quality images through superior compression and packaging.
- **Automatic JPEG 2000** This option is available if you choose Acrobat 6.0 (PDF 1.5) or later for compatibility. When you choose this option, Acrobat determines the optimum compression settings using the JPEG 2000 image format for image compression.

- **CCITT** Use the International Consultative Committee for International Telephone & Telegraph (CCITT) method of compression for 1-bit black-and-white images, such as faxes. When you use the CCITT method of compression, no data is lost. Use the CCITT Group 4 method for general-purpose compression of monochrome images. Use the CCITT Group 3 method for faxed documents.
- **Run Length** Use this option when your document contains images with large areas of solid black or white. *Run Length* is a lossless compression method.

Acrobat Distiller Resampling

When Acrobat Distiller compresses images, it also resamples them. When you use software to *resample* an image, pixels are either added or removed from the image to change the resolution PPI at which the image is displayed. When pixels are added to an image to increase resolution, image degradation generally occurs because you're asking the software to interpolate between neighboring pixels to create new pixels. Starting with a high-resolution image is always best, and then downsample it to the desired resolution when converting it to PDF. You can specify one of the following interpolation methods to resample images. These settings are found in the Downsample drop-down lists in the Color Images, Grayscale Images, and Monochrome Images sections of the Images section of the conversion setting you're modifying:

- **Off** Acrobat Distiller doesn't interpolate when the image is downsampled. This option is applicable only when the document contains high-resolution images and you've selected High or Maximum for the Image Quality setting.
- **Average Downsampling** Acrobat Distiller creates new pixels at the specified resolution using the average color of neighboring pixels within a given area.
- **Bicubic Downsampling** Acrobat Distiller creates new pixels at the specified resolution using a weighted average to determine pixel color. In other words, the resulting color is weighted toward the dominant color in each area Acrobat Distiller samples. This is the slowest method, but it gives you the highest-quality images.
- **Subsampling** Acrobat Distiller creates new pixels at the specified resolution using the color of a pixel in the center of the sampled area. Because this method of interpolation uses a single pixel to create new pixels, this is the quickest interpolation method, but it can lead to images with harsh transitions between adjacent pixels.

Set Image Compression Settings

Each Adobe PDF Settings option has a specific set of compression options that you can modify for documents you create. You modify compression settings to determine the quality of the text, line art, and images in the published PDF document. To modify image compression settings for an Adobe PDF conversion setting, follow these steps:

1. Choose a Conversion Settings option to modify and open the Adobe PDF Settings dialog box, as discussed previously.

2. Click the Images folder to open the Images section of the Adobe PDF Settings dialog box, shown here:

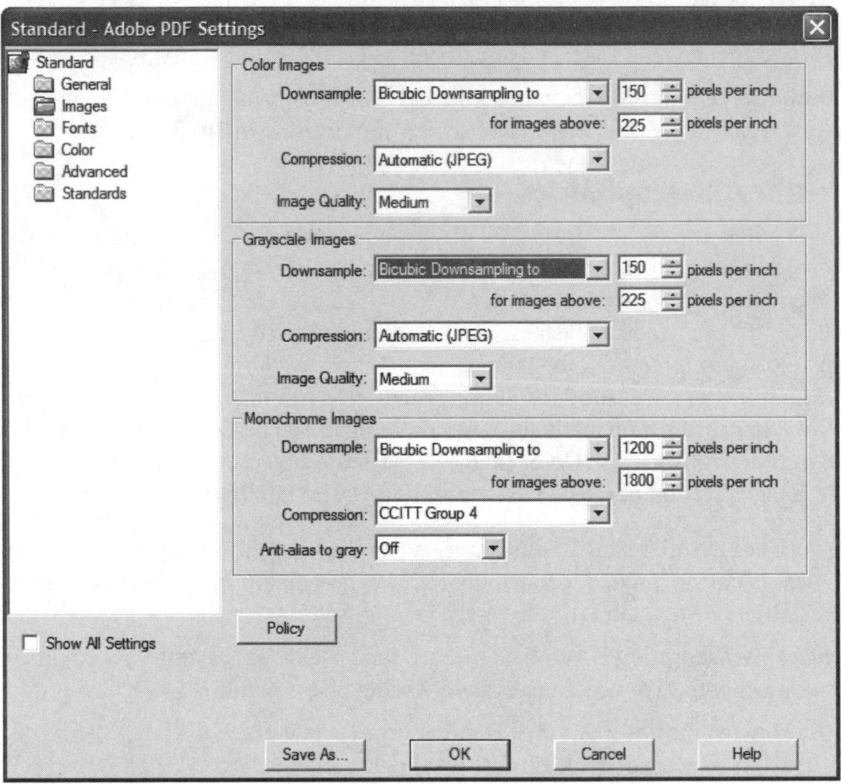

3. In the Color Images and Grayscale Images sections, click the Downsample drop-down arrow and choose an option.

4. In the Color Images and Grayscale Images sections, click the Compression drop-down arrow and choose a compression method. By default, Acrobat Distiller compresses images and, based on the selected Adobe PDF job option, automatically chooses the compression option it deems best for the color and grayscale images in the document. You can choose Off to have Acrobat Distiller convert the file to PDF without compressing it.

5. In the Color Images and Grayscale Images sections, to the right of the Downsample field, enter the PPI value to which you want Acrobat Distiller to downsample color and grayscale images. Or, click the spinner buttons to specify the desired resolution.

6. In the Color Images and Grayscale Images sections, enter a value (in PPI) in the For Images Above fields. Or, click the spinner buttons to specify the desired resolution.

When you convert a document to PDF using the conversion setting you're editing, Acrobat Distiller downsamples all images above the resolution you enter in this field to the lower output resolution you entered in Step 5.

7. In the Color Images and Grayscale Images sections, click the Image Quality drop-down arrow and choose an option. This setting varies, depending on the Adobe PDF Settings job option you're modifying. Choose High or Maximum to create a better-looking document with a larger file size, or choose Minimum or Low to create a PDF document with a smaller file size and less-detailed images.
8. In the Monochrome Images section, click the Downsample drop-down arrow and choose an option.
9. In the field to the right of the Downsample field, enter the PPI value to which you want Acrobat Distiller to downsample monochrome images. Or, click the spinner buttons to specify the desired resolution.
10. In the For Images Above field, enter the value above which you want Acrobat Distiller to downsample images to the value entered in Step 9. Or, click the spinner buttons to specify the desired resolution.

TIP *If a PDF document converted with applied downsampling doesn't properly display black-and-white images, modify the Adobe PDF Settings option and choose Off for the Monochrome Images Downsample option.*

11. In the Monochrome Images section, click the Compression drop-down arrow and choose an option.
12. Click the Anti-Alias To Gray drop-down arrow (*anti-aliasing blends neighboring pixels of different colors to avoid jagged edges*) and choose Off (the default option), 2-bit, 4-bit, or 8-bit. This option determines how many levels of gray are used to smooth edges in the image. Choose 8-bit (256 levels of gray) for the best results. 12
13. Click the Policy button to reveal the Image Policy dialog box. In this box, you specify processing options for images that are less than the specified resolutions. For each color setting, you have the following choices: Ignore, Warn and Continue, Cancel Job.

After you modify the Images settings of an Adobe PDF conversion setting, you can click a panel to modify other settings or save the modified conversion setting, as described in the section "Save Conversion Settings."

Set Fonts Options

When you want to ensure that a document appears exactly as you created it, you embed the font set with the document. When you embed fonts with a document, the document displays and prints correctly, even if the user's computer doesn't have the document fonts installed. Acrobat Distiller can embed most modern fonts, but certain fonts cannot be embedded due to licensing issues.

Specify which fonts to embed when you convert documents to PDFs by modifying the settings in the Fonts section of the Adobe PDF Settings dialog box as follows:

1. Choose a conversion settings option to modify and open the Adobe PDF Settings dialog box, as discussed previously in the section "Customize Acrobat Distiller Conversion Settings."
2. Click the Fonts folder to reveal the Fonts section of the Adobe PDF Settings dialog box, shown here:

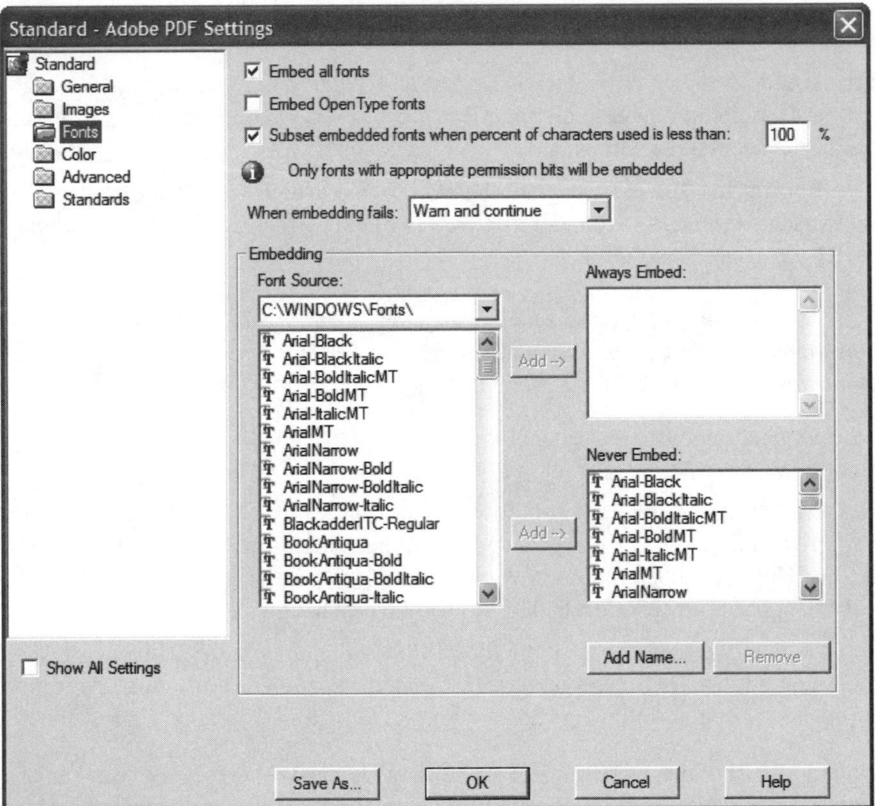

3. Enable the Embed All Fonts option to embed all fonts used in the document.
4. Enable the Embed All Open Type fonts to embed Open Type fonts that were used in the document.
5. Enable the Subset Embedded Fonts When Percent Of Characters Used Is Less Than [ ] % option and enter a percentage value. When you choose this option, Acrobat Distiller embeds only the characters used to create the document when the percentage of characters used from the font set falls below the value you specify. For example, if you

enter a value of 60, Acrobat Distiller embeds only characters used to create the document when less than 60 percent of the font set is used.

6. Click the When Embedding Fails drop-down arrow and choose one of the following: Ignore, Warn And Continue, or Cancel Job.
7. To select a different font list, click the Font Source drop-down arrow and select the desired font folder from the drop-down menu.
8. If you always want to embed a certain font set with documents created using this Conversion Settings option, select the font family or families from the left pane and click the Add button to the left of the Always Embed pane to add the fonts to the Always Embed list.
9. To add a font to the Never Embed list, select the font family from the left pane and click the Add button to the left of the Never Embed pane. To remove a font from the Never Embed List, select the font from the Never Embed list and click the Remove button.

NOTE *Licensing issues prohibit you from embedding certain fonts in a document. If you select a font with licensing issues, Acrobat Distiller displays a key icon before the font name and a warning at the bottom of the dialog box saying the font cannot be embedded because of licensing issues.*

After you change the Fonts folder conversion settings parameters, click another folder to modify different settings, or save the job option by following the steps in the section "Save Conversion Settings."

NOTE *When you install Acrobat, the install utility locates every folder in your system that contains fonts. If you add a new font folder to your system after installing Acrobat, launch Acrobat Distiller and choose Settings | Font Locations to open the Acrobat Distiller – Font Locations dialog box. Click the Add button, navigate to the folder that contains the fonts you want to use with Acrobat Distiller, select the folder, click OK, and then close the Font Locations dialog box. The next time you launch Acrobat Distiller, the font folder will be available.*

12

Set Color Options

When you convert a document to PDF format using Acrobat Distiller or PDFMaker you can modify the color options. You can choose a color-management settings file and let Acrobat Distiller manage the color of the images during conversion, or you can modify the color settings to suit a specific output device. To set color options, follow these steps:

1. Choose a Conversion Settings option to modify and open the Adobe PDF Settings dialog box, as discussed previously.

2. Click the Color folder to open the Color section of the Adobe PDF Settings dialog box, shown here:

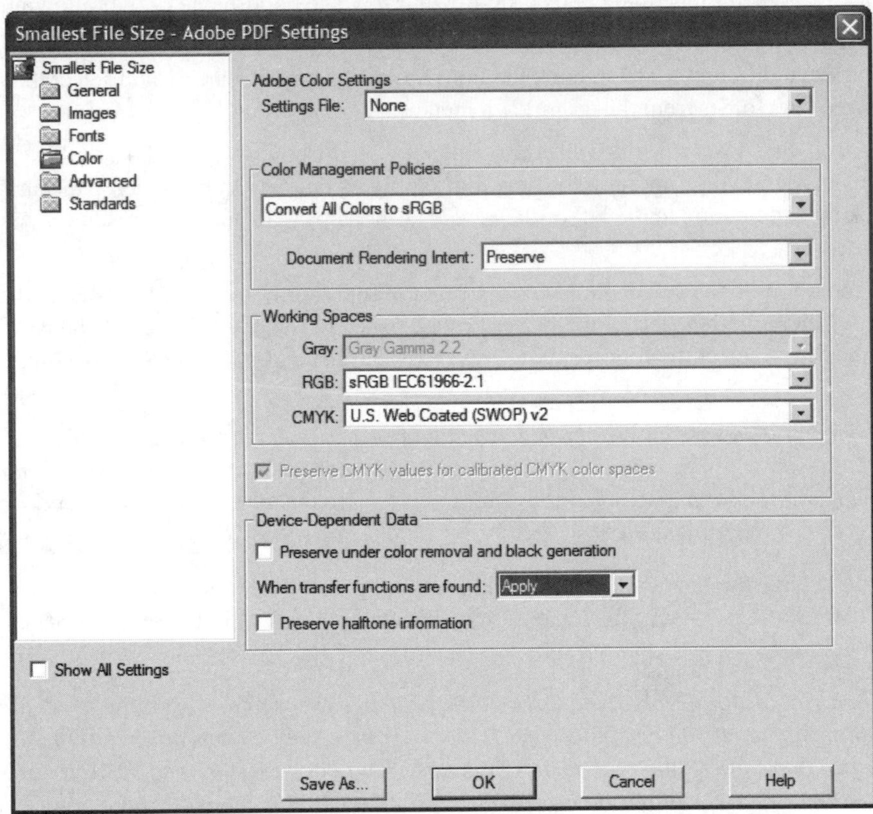

3. To use a preset color settings file, click the Settings File drop-down arrow and choose an option. When you choose one of the color-management setting files, all the color options are dimmed out. You can choose None (the default) for no color management, Color Management Off for documents that will be displayed on a monitor, or one of the Prepress defaults.

4. Accept the default settings option (None), or click the Color Management Policies drop-down arrow and choose one of the following:

   - **Leave Color Unchanged** Choose this option, and Acrobat Distiller doesn't modify device-dependent colors. Instead, Distiller processes device-independent colors to the nearest match in the resulting PDF. Use this option if the file will be printed by a color-calibrated device that specifies all color management.
   - **Tag Everything For Color Management** When you choose this option and specify Acrobat 4.0, 5.0, 6.0, 7.0, or 8.0 compatibility in the General section of Adobe PDF

Settings dialog box, Acrobat Distiller embeds an International Color Consortium (ICC) color profile with the document. The ICC color profile calibrates image color and makes the colors in the converted PDF document device-independent. *Device-dependent colors* in the original files (RGB, Grayscale, and CMYK) are converted to *device-independent color spaces* (CalRGB, CalGrayscale, and LAB) in the resulting PDF file. (*Cal,* in these examples, stands for calibrated.)

- **Tag Only Images For Color Management** Choose this option, so that when Acrobat Distiller converts a document to PDF format, it embeds ICC color profiles with document images, but not with text or line art.
- **Convert All Colors To sRGB** When you choose this option, all images with RGB and CMYK colors are converted to standard RGB (sRGB).
- **Convert All Colors To CMYK** When you choose this option, all images with RGB and CMYK colors are converted to DeviceGray or DeviceCMYK.

5. Click the Document Rendering Intent drop-down arrow and specify how Acrobat Distiller maps color between the color spaces. Choose from the following options:
   - **Preserve** Preserves color spaces in the original document.
   - **Perceptual** The original color values of the document images are mapped to the gamut of the output device. This method preserves the visual relationship between different colors, but color values may change.
   - **Saturation** The file that Acrobat Distiller produces maintains the same relative color saturation as the original image pixels. Choose this method when document color saturation is more important than maintaining the visual relationship between colors of the original document.
   - **Absolute Colormetric** Acrobat Distiller disables the black-and-white point matching when converting colors in the document. This option isn't recommended unless your intent is to preserve specific colors used in a trademark or logo.
   - **Relative Colormetric** Acrobat Distiller preserves all colors within the output device gamut range. Colors in the original document that are out of the printing-device gamut range convert to brightness values within the printer gamut.
6. If you choose any Color Management Policies option other than Leave Color Unchanged, in the Working Spaces section you will be able to choose an ICC profile for managing grayscale, RGB, and CMYK color conversion, as described here:
   - **Gray (Grayscale)** Choose None from the drop-down menu, and Acrobat Distiller doesn't convert grayscale colors. The default option is determined by your operating system (OS): Gray Gamma 2.2 for Windows or Gray Gamma 1.8 for Macintosh. Or, you can choose one of the Dot Gain options (10 percent to 30 percent). Choose a lower Dot Gain value to lighten document images or a higher value to darken document images. Your other options are Black and White or Gray.

- **RGB** Choose a color-management profile from the drop-down menu. The available options are the color profiles installed on your computer. If you're uncertain about which profile to choose, the default option (sRGB IEC61966-2.1) yields good results. Choose None, and Acrobat Distiller doesn't convert colors in RGB images when distilling them to PDF.
- **CMYK** Choose one of the options from the drop-down menu to specify how Acrobat Distiller handles colors in CMYK images when converting them to PDF format. If in doubt, choose U.S. Web Coated (SWOP) v2 or the default CMYK color profile for the country in which you live. If you choose None, Acrobat Distiller doesn't convert colors in CMYK images when distilling them to PDF.

7. If you click the Preserve CMYK Values For Calibrated CMYK Color Spaces checkbox, device-independent color values will be treated as device-dependent (DeviceCMYK) color values, and device-independent color spaces will be ignored and discarded.
8. In the Device-Dependent Data section, choose from the following options that pertain to the device with which the converted documents will be printed (these options have no effect on screen viewing):
   - **Preserve Under Color Removal And Black Generation** Choose this option if the documents you want to convert with this job option are PostScript files that contain Color Removal and Black Generation settings.
   - **When Transfer Functions Are Found** Click the drop-down arrow and choose one of the following options:
     - **Remove** Acrobat Distiller removes all applied transfer functions when converting the file to PDF. You should choose this option unless the resulting PDF file will be printed on the same device for which the PostScript file was created.
     - **Preserve** Acrobat Distiller preserves transfer functions if they're present in the original file. Transfer functions are traditionally used to compensate for dot gain or dot loss when an image transfers to film.
     - **Apply** Acrobat Distiller applies the transfer functions to the file. This option changes the colors in the file.
   - **Preserve Halftone Information** The resulting file that Acrobat Distiller produces preserves halftone information embedded in the original PostScript document. Halftone screens control the amount of ink deposited in specific locations when the file prints. By varying the dot size, halftone screens simulate the illusion of flowing color and varying shades of gray. CMYK images have four halftone screens, one for each color (cyan, magenta, yellow, and black).

After you modify the Conversion Settings Color folder settings, click another tab to modify another setting or save the job option, as outlined in the section "Save Conversion Settings."

TIP *If you're modifying multiple settings, click the Show All Settings check box to display all conversion settings in the Adobe PDF settings dialog box. Click a setting title to display the parameters in each settings folder.*

Set Advanced Options

The Advanced section in the Adobe PDF Settings dialog box enables you to modify Document Structuring Convention (DSC) comments that appear in the original PostScript file, as well as other options that affect the conversion from PostScript to PDF. To modify Advanced Options for a conversion setting, follow these steps:

1. Choose a Conversion Settings option to modify and open the Adobe PDF Settings dialog box, following the steps presented earlier in this chapter.
2. Click the Advanced folder to reveal the Advanced section of the Adobe PDF Settings dialog box. In the Options section, choose from the following:
   - **Allow PostScript File To Override Adobe PDF Settings** Choose this option if you're reasonably certain the PostScript files you convert with this job option contain the necessary information for the intended output device. Deselect this option if you want conversion settings to take precedence over any settings embedded in the PostScript files that you intend to convert with this job option.
   - **Allow PostScript XObjects** Choose this option to have Acrobat Distiller create XObjects (eXternal Objects) that store information that appears on multiple pages of the same file. This can result in faster printing, but it requires more printer memory because the XObjects are stored in printer memory and called when needed.
   - **Convert Gradients To Smooth Shades** When you choose this option, Acrobat Distiller smoothes gradients from the original files, creating a seamless blend. This option has no effect on how the document appears onscreen. If you print the converted file to a PostScript 3 device, however, you will notice a marked improvement in quality. Note, if you choose this option, it may take longer for Acrobat to render the gradient onscreen.
   - **Convert Smooth Lines To Curves** Choose this option if the files you're converting are CAD drawings. When you choose this option, Acrobat Distiller reduces the number of points used to define gentle curves, which results in a smaller PDF file.
   - **Preserve Level 2 Copypage Semantics** Choose this option to have Acrobat Distiller use the copypage editor defined in LanguageLevel 2 PostScript, instead of the one defined in LanguageLevel 3 PostScript. Don't choose this option if you're printing to LanguageLevel 3 PostScript devices. If the converted file will be sent to a service center, check with the technicians to see which PostScript level its devices support.
   - **Preserve Overprint Settings** Choose this option if the PDFs you intend to create with this job option originally had overprint information. An *overprint* is when two or more colors are printed on top of each other to produce another color.

  - **Overprinting Default Is Nonzero Overprinting** If you choose this option, files with overprints that contain zero CMYK information won't prevent underlying colors from printing.
- **Save Adobe PDF Settings Inside PDF File** Choose this option, and Acrobat Distiller includes the settings used to create the file as a file attachment within the PDF document. This document can be accessed by other applications to duplicate the settings.
- **Save Original JPEG Images In PDF If Possible** Choose this option to have Acrobat Distiller save JPEG images from the original file in the resulting PDF file with the compression settings from the original file.
- **Save Portable Job Ticket Inside PDF File** Choose this option to have Acrobat Distiller create a job ticket that contains information about the PostScript file used to create the PDF document. The *job ticket* includes information, such as page size and orientation, resolution, halftone information, and so on. Disable this option if the PDF documents you create with this job option are strictly for screen viewing.
- **Use Prologue.ps And Epilogue.ps** Choose this option to send a prologue and epilogue file with each document Acrobat Distiller converts with this job option. *Epilogue files* can be edited to append information to the PDF file. *Prologue files* can be edited to resolve procedure problems with PostScript files. Sample Prologue.ps and Epilogue.ps files are located in the Distiller folder. Neither file contains data, but you can use them as templates. Unless you're familiar with creating PostScript code, you should disable this option.

3. In the Document Structuring Conventions (DSC) section, enable the Process DSC Comments option to have Acrobat Distiller preserve DSC information from the original PostScript file. With this default option, you can include any of the following:

- **Log DSC Warnings** Choose this option, and Acrobat Distiller displays warning messages about troublesome DSC comments in the original PostScript file and creates a text file log of these errors. Choose this option if the files you process with this job option contain DSC comments.
- **Preserve EPS Information From DSC** Choose this option when processing EPS files with DSC comments, and the DSC comments will be preserved when the file converts to PDF.
- **Preserve OPI Comments** Choose this option, and when Acrobat Distiller processes files with For Placement Only (FPO) images or comments, they are replaced with the high-resolution image located on servers supporting Open Press Interface (OPI) versions 1.3 and 2.0.
- **Preserve Document Information From DSC** Choose this option, and Acrobat Distiller includes the title, creation date, and time information when you use this job option to convert files to PDF. When the PDF file opens, this information appears in the Document Summary and can be accessed by choosing File | Document Summary.

- **Resize Page And Center Artwork For EPS Files** Choose this option when processing EPS files, and Acrobat Distiller resizes the page to the document artwork and centers the artwork.

After modifying the settings for a conversion settings' Advanced folder, you can click another tab to modify different settings or save the job option file, as covered in the upcoming section "Save Conversion Settings."

Set Standards Options (Professional Only)

If you own Acrobat Professional, you have an additional section from which you can modify PDF/A and PDF/X settings. PDF/A (Portable Document Format/Archive) is an ISO standard used for long-time archiving of electronic files. PDF/X (Portable Document Format Exchange) is an ISO standard used for print production. The *PDF/X* format combines all print and workflow settings for the PDF document in a single file. To set PDF/X options for a conversion setting, follow these steps:

1. Choose a Conversion Settings option to modify and open the Adobe PDF Settings dialog box, following the steps presented earlier in this chapter.
2. Click the Standards folder to open the Standards section of the Adobe PDF Settings dialog box, shown here:

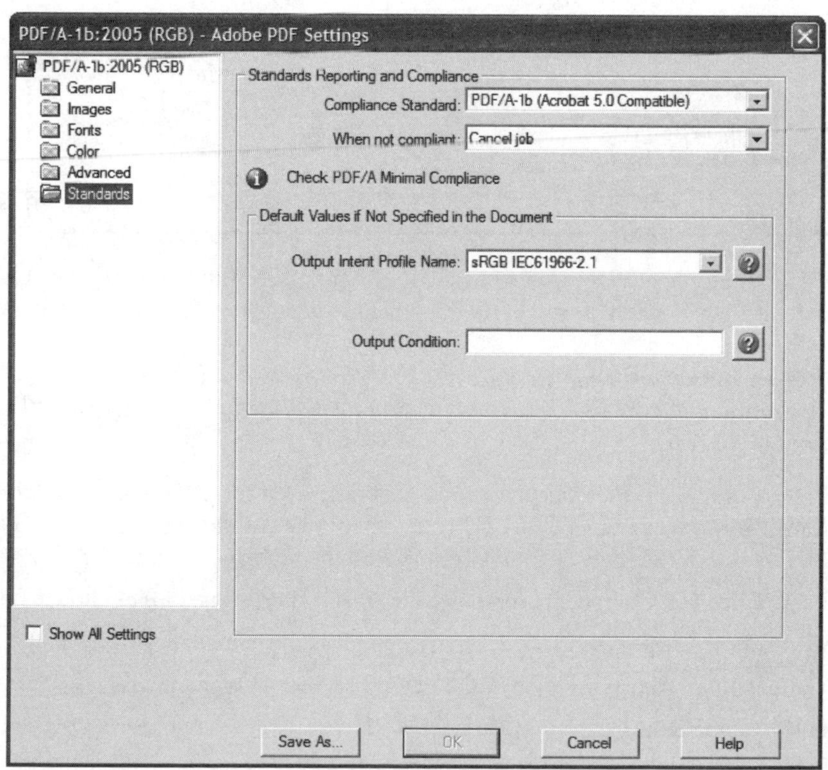

3. Click the Compliance Standard drop-down arrow and choose a compliance option from the drop-down menu, shown here:

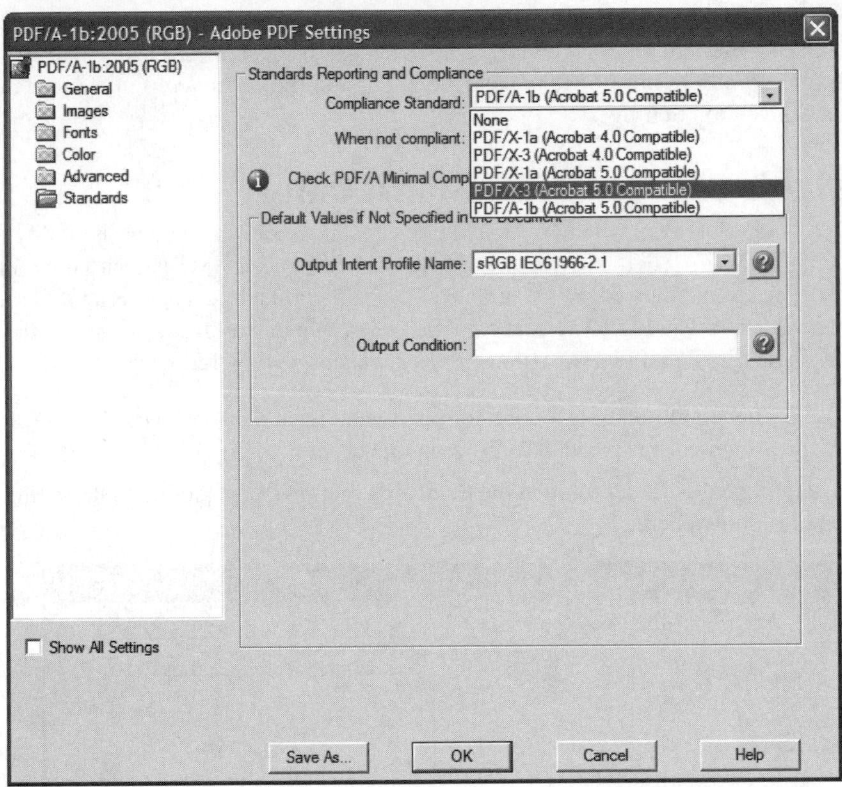

- PDF/X-compliant PDF documents are used for high-resolution print jobs. Accept the default PDF/X settings, unless the document is being used for print production.

PDF/X-1A (Acrobat 4.0 Compatible) and PDF/X-3A are available only when you choose Acrobat 4.0 (PDF 1.5) compatibility in the General tab of the Adobe PDF Settings dialog box.

- PDF/A-compliant PDF documents are generally used for archiving of electronic files. PDF/A files can contain only text, raster images (bitmaps), and vector graphics. PDF/A doesn't support including scripts with the archived document.

4. Click the When Not Compliant drop-down arrow and choose one of the following options:
   - **Continue** Creates the PDF file anyway and lists the compliancy issues in the report.
   - **Cancel Job** Aborts creation of the PDF file when compliancy issues occur.
5. In the If Neither TrimBox Nor ArtBox Are Specified section, choose from the following options:

- **Report As Error** If neither option is specified in the PostScript document, this is reported as an error.
- **Set TrimBox To MediaBox With Offset (Points)** Choose this option and enter values in four fields: Left, Right, Top, and Bottom. The TrimBox is always the same size, or smaller than the MediaBox.

6. In the If BleedBox Is Not Specified section, choose one of the following options:
   - **Set BleedBox To MediaBox** Sets the BleedBox dimension equal to the MediaBox dimensions.
   - **Set BleedBox To TrimBox With Offsets (Points)** Choose this option and enter values in four fields that let you set the offset from BleedBox size to TrimBox size. The BleedBox is always the same size or larger than the TrimBox.
7. Click the Output Intent Profile Name drop-down arrow and choose an option. This option indicates the printing profile with which the document will be printed if this option isn't included with the PostScript file from which the PDF document is being created.
8. An entry is automatically made in the Output Condition Identifier field if you choose an Output Intent Profile with a known Output Condition Identifier. The option also becomes available if you choose Use Output Condition Identifier from the Output Intent Profile drop-down list, whereupon you enter the output condition identifier manually.
9. Enter text in the Output Condition field (optional) to describe the intended printing condition. This parameter isn't required, but when used, it provides useful information to recipients of the PDF document.
10. An entry is automatically made in the RegistryName (URL) field when you choose an Output Intent Profile with a known URL. If no entry is provided, enter a URL for the web site associated with the ICC profile associated with the document. A URL is provided by default for the ICC registry names associated with the document. More information about the ICC registry can be found at the URL provided.
11. Click the Trapped drop-down arrow and choose an option for color trapped state, which determines whether colors in the document are trappedt. This is required for PDF/X compliance. Choose from Leave Undefined (when the PostScript document specifies this option), Insert True, or Insert False.

Save Conversion Settings

After you modify an Adobe PDF Settings option, you can save it for future use. To save a conversion setting and close the Adobe PDF Settings dialog box, follow these steps:

1. Click the Save As button to open the Save Adobe PDF Settings As dialog box. By default, the Adobe PDF Settings option you use to create the new setting is appended by the next available number—for example, Standard(1).

2. Accept the default filename or enter a different name. Choose a name that reflects the intended source of documents you create with this conversion setting. For example, if the documents you create with this job option will be included on a CD/DVD-ROM, enter **CD/DVD-ROM**.
3. Click Save.

After you save the new job option, it appears on the Acrobat Distiller Default Settings drop-down menu. If you use Microsoft Office applications, the job option appears on the Adobe PDF Conversion Settings menu.

PDF Font Considerations

When you create a document in an authoring application, a little time spent choosing fonts can produce a better-looking document. Try to avoid highly stylized fonts with long swooping curves. They may look great printed, but they often don't display properly on monitors. If you choose a large bold font, the center of characters such as *a, o,* and *p* fill in and are hard to read, unless the user greatly magnifies the PDF document. When you're in doubt about whether a particular font style will display well in Acrobat, create a test document in the authoring application using every character from the font set in both uppercase and lowercase. Convert the document to PDF format and view the document in Acrobat at 100 percent magnification. One look and you'll know whether to use the font.

You should also be cautious about mixing fonts. If you create a document with multiple fonts, make sure the finished document is aesthetically pleasing. A document with multiple fonts can be hard to read. The actual number of fonts you can safely include in a document is a matter of personal taste and document size. For example, creating a single-page document with more than two fonts wouldn't be a good idea. Also, when you create a document with multiple fonts and embed those fonts, the file size of the document increases dramatically.

When you create a PDF document and view the output on your computer, everything may look as you planned, with crystal clear images and sharp and stylish text. If your intended audience doesn't have the fonts used in the document installed on their computer, though, the document will look quite different, especially if you selected highly stylized fonts. If you don't embed fonts and a viewer doesn't have the document fonts installed on their system, Acrobat substitutes either the AdobeSansMM font or the AdobeSerifMM font. (MM is the acronym for Multiple Master.) Through the use of these fonts, Acrobat tries to create a reasonable facsimile of the original font, while maintaining the width of the original font to preserve line breaks from the original document.

Embed Fonts

When you embed fonts, you can rest assured that viewers of your document will see the document as you intended. Embedding several fonts, however, can dramatically increase the file size of the document. You can embed fonts when you set Adobe PDF Settings for Acrobat Distiller, but make sure you don't violate any font-licensing agreement when you decide to embed a specific font.

For more information on embedding fonts when setting Adobe PDF Settings, refer to the section "Set Fonts Options."

You should embed fonts whenever you need the published document to look identical to the original. If, for example, your clients use a font as part of their corporation identity package, embed the font. If you use a stylized font that's difficult for Acrobat to re-create with an MM font, then embed the font.

Subset a Font

When you embed a font, you can reduce the file size of the resulting PDF document by subsetting the font. When you *subset* a font, you embed only the characters used in the document being converted to PDF format. You can have Acrobat subset a font when the percentage of characters used drops below a certain value. By default, Acrobat subsets a font when the percentage of characters used drops below 100 percent. To subset a font, click the Fonts tab in the Adobe PDF setting you're modifying, choose the option to subset fonts, and then specify the value Acrobat uses as its signal to embed the entire font set or subset the font set.

The only disadvantage to subsetting a font is when you (or a third party) edit a document with subset fonts. If you don't have the font set installed on your computer, you can only edit the document with the subset characters and you cannot add other characters from the font set.

Preview an Unembedded Font in Acrobat

If you have any question as to whether you should embed a font, create a test document in an authoring application and view it in Acrobat without using local fonts. When you view a PDF document in Acrobat without using *local fonts,* fonts installed on your system are disregarded and Acrobat goes into font substitution mode. To preview an unembedded font in Acrobat, follow these steps:

1. Create a document in a word-processing application using every character of the font set in both uppercase and lowercase.
2. Choose Adobe PDF from the application's Print command, or, if you're in a Microsoft Office application, choose Adobe PDF | Convert To Adobe PDF to convert the document to PDF format.
3. Edit the Adobe PDF Settings you're using to convert the document and, in the Fonts section, deselect the Embed All Fonts option, as outlined previously in the section "Set Fonts Options."
4. Convert the document to PDF format.
5. Launch Acrobat.
6. Choose Edit | Preferences and select the Page Display category.
7. Deselect the Use local fonts, and then click OK.
8. Open the document with unembedded fonts. If a font cannot be substituted, Acrobat displays the text as bullets and an error message appears.

When this preferences option is deselected (unchecked), Acrobat substitutes document fonts with MM fonts. You see what the document looks like on a viewer's system without the document fonts installed. When you deselect Use Local Fonts, you can also print a copy of the document using the Adobe substituted fonts. If the test document isn't satisfactory, embed the fonts when you create the final document.

Summary

In this chapter, you learned about tagged PDF documents and how to optimize documents for intended destinations. You also learned how to modify default Adobe PDF settings to suit the documents you create and save the new settings. The topic of fonts and whether to embed them was also presented. In the next chapter, you learn how to create PDF documents for the Web.

Chapter 13 Acrobat Online

How to...

- View PDF documents in a web browser
- Use the Acrobat plug-in
- Prepare PDF documents for the Internet
- Create links to web sites
- Initiate a Shared Review
- Use PDF forms on the Internet

In this chapter, you learn how to view PDF documents within a web browser and prepare PDF documents for use on the Internet. Also covered are web-browser considerations and information about the Acrobat plug-in. In addition, you learn how to initiate a shared review, work with PDF forms, and conduct a meeting.

View PDF Documents in a Web Browser

When you view non-HTML documents from a web site, your web browser detects the document type and loads the necessary helper application so you can view the document in the web browser. Depending on the type of document you view, the helper application (or *plug-in,* as it's known to web developers) may load within the browser or externally. Some applications give web designers the freedom to embed a document and call up the plug-in interface within the HTML document or open the application in an external window. When you view PDF documents from web sites, your version of Adobe Acrobat appears in your web browser.

For viewers who don't own the full version of Acrobat, but who have Adobe Reader installed on their systems, Adobe Reader launches in the web browser when a PDF document is encountered. Or, in Acrobat or Adobe Reader, you can display a PDF from a web site without the web browser by choosing Edit | Preferences, and then disabling the Display PDF In Web Browser option in the Web Display Options section.

When you view documents online, Acrobat provides you with a slightly different set of tools. You can select objects from the document, review and comment on the document, and digitally sign the document. However, there are no menu commands—only the Acrobat tools, and the web browser menu commands and tools. With the stripped-down web-browser version of Acrobat, you only have tools to view the document, save a copy of the document, and annotate the document. The tools and menus in your web browser don't change, though. When you finish viewing a document, use the web browser controls to navigate to a different web site or back to the page called the PDF document.

After you open a PDF document within your web browser, you can save a copy of the document for future use. After you save a copy of the document, you can open the document in Acrobat and use the menu commands and tools to modify the document, provided security hasn't been applied to it.

You can also download PDF documents directly from the Internet to your hard drive by means of the hyperlink to the document. To download a PDF document using Netscape Navigator, right-click (Windows) or CTRL-click (Macintosh) the document link, and then choose Save Link As from the context menu. If you use Internet Explorer (IE), right-click (Windows) or CTRL-click (Macintosh) the link, and then choose Save Target As from the context menu to download a PDF document. Follow the prompts to download the document to the desired folder on your hard drive.

About PDF Web Browser Plug-ins

When you install Acrobat, the install utility automatically detects the Internet Explorer or Netscape web browsers installed on your system, and Acrobat is configured as the application for the following Multipurpose Internet Mail Extensions (MIME) types:

NOTE *If you have web browsers other than IE or Netscape installed on your system, you might have to manually configure the browser to use Acrobat as the application to read the following MIME types.*

- **PDF** When you click a web site link to a PDF file, it's displayed in your web browser using the Acrobat plug-in.
- **FDF** When you receive an FDF file as an e-mail attachment and open it, Acrobat launches. When you send your digital signature certificate via e-mail, it's an FDF attachment. When you initiate an e-mail review, reviewer's comments are returned as an FDF file attachment, which when clicked, opens the original PDF and imports the reviewer's comments.
- **XFDF** When you receive form data via e-mail in XFDF format, the Acrobat program handles the attachment.
- **PDX** When someone sends you an Acrobat index via e-mail, double-clicking the attachment launches the Acrobat program. The Acrobat program also launches if you open a PDX file from within the web browser.
- **RMF** When you purchase locked PDF documents, the seller sends RMF files, which contain the licensing information *Web Buy,* a plug-in used to authorize a computer to view a locked PDF, used to unlock the document.

NOTE *If you install Acrobat on a new system, be sure to install your web browser first. If you install Acrobat first, to view PDF documents in a web browser, you must manually configure each web browser on your system or reinstall Acrobat and perform a custom installation, choosing only the web browser plug-in.*

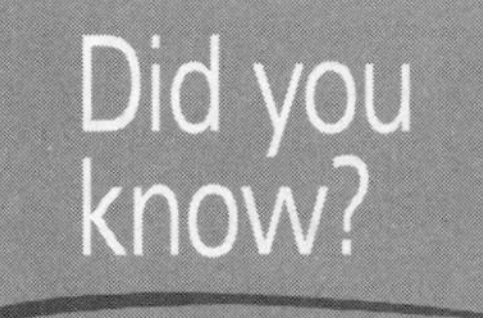

You Can Initiate a Browser Based Review

Acrobat makes it possible for you to conduct a browser-based review. You can upload a PDF document for review to a network folder or a server that supports Web Distributed Authoring and Versioning (WebDAV). After choosing the document for review, you send an e-mail message to your reviewers that includes an attached FDF setup file. Reviewers open the FDF attachment, which opens a copy of the PDF document in the reviewer's browser and configures the review settings. Reviewers can neither open the PDF document at the web server nor participate in the review. If you work on the Windows platform, browser-based reviews are conducted with the Internet Explorer web browser. If you work on the Macintosh operating system (OS), browser-based reviews are conducted with the Safari web browser.

Reviewers can annotate the document online or download the PDF for review offline. Comments can be modified only by the original author, but reviewers using Acrobat Standard, Acrobat Professional, or Adobe Reader 7.0 or later (provided the review initiator owns Acrobat Professional and has enabled review privileges to Adobe Reader users) can respond to comments or add their own.

Download Adobe Reader

A large majority of Internet users already have a version of Adobe Acrobat or Adobe Reader installed on their systems. If, however, you post a PDF document on your web site or on a client's web site and some visitors to that web site don't have Adobe Reader, they will be unable to view your document. To accommodate web site visitors who don't have a copy of Adobe Reader, you can include a link to the Adobe web page from which visitors can download a free copy of Adobe Reader. The following URL takes the viewer to the Adobe Reader download page: *http://www.adobe.com/products/acrobat/readstep2.html.*

Distribute Adobe Reader

You can post the Adobe Reader installer on a company intranet or a local network. You can also distribute the Adobe Reader installation software on a CD-ROM, provided you accept the conditions of the Acrobat electronic End User License Agreement (EULA) and the Supplement to Permit Distribution. When users install the Adobe Reader, they are also prompted to accept the conditions of the EULA.

You cannot distribute Adobe Reader from a web site. Adobe requires any third-party web site that wants to make the Adobe Reader available for visitors to include a link to the Adobe Reader download page at *http://www.adobe.com/products/acrobat/readstep2.html.* If you post a link to the web page from which Adobe Reader can be downloaded, include a Get Adobe Reader logo or an Adobe PDF logo as a link to the site. You can download both logos at *http://www.adobe.com/misc/linking.html#readerlogo* after you read the information contained in the section "Get Adobe Reader and Adobe PDF Web Logos" at *http://www.adobe.com/products/acrobat/distribute.html.* To distribute Adobe Reader from an internal web site (corporate intranet), you must fill out the online form at *http://www.adobe.com/products/acrobat/acrrdistribute.html.*

Conduct a Shared Review

A shared review is the ideal option if all users are on the same network behind a firewall, and if they all have read and write access to the folder where the comments are stored. After a shared review is initiated, reviewers receive notification they have been requested to review a document. Review participants are notified after new comments have been posted by other reviewers.

Initiate a Shared Review

You can initiate a shared review from within Acrobat. You select the document to review, specify where comments will be stored, and then invite reviewers. To initiate a shared review:

1. Choose Comments | Send for Shared Review to open the Send PDF for Share Review dialog box. The following illustration shows Step 1 of 4 dialog box. Or, you can click the Review and Comment task button, and then choose Send for Shared Review.

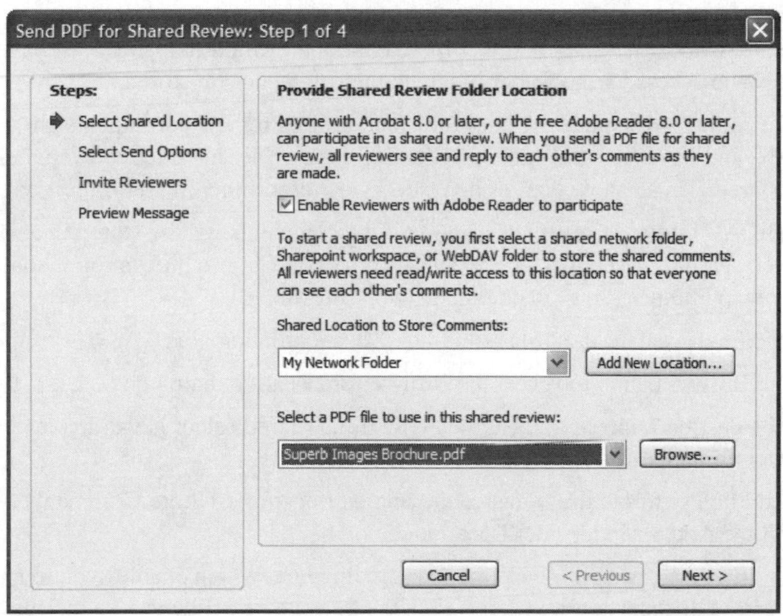

13

2. Click the Add New Location button to display the Add Shared Folder Location dialog box, shown next.

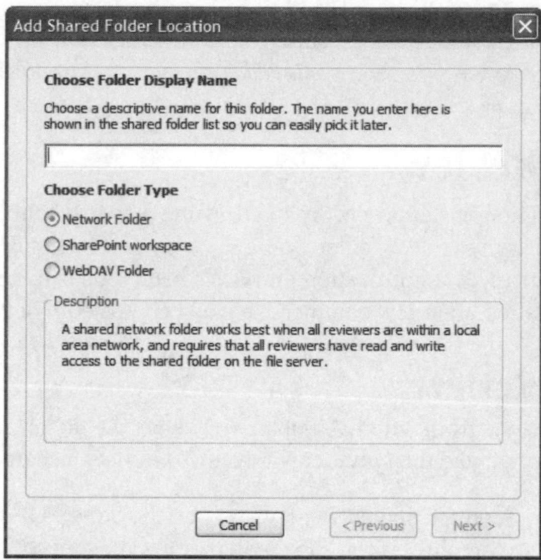

3. Choose the desired folder type from the following:
   - **Network Folder** Choose this option if all review participants have access to a local area network (LAN), such as a corporate intranet. All participants must have read and write access for the folder in which the comments are stored.
   - **Sharepoint workspace** Choose this option if all review participants are within a LAN, and have read and write privileges for the folder in which the comments will be stored. This option requires a Windows server running SharePoint Services.
   - **WebDAV folder** Choose this option if the comments will be stored in a folder on a web server that supports the WebDAV protocol. Choose this option if some of the review participants are outside the network firewall.
4. Click Next to reveal the Add Shared Folder Location dialog box.
5. Click the Browse button to reveal the Browse for Location dialog box.
6. Select the desired folder, and then click OK. If the shared folder is valid, a message to that effect will appear to the right of the Verify button.
7. Click Add Folder to add the folder to the Shared Location to Store Comments list, and then exit the Add Shared Folder Location dialog box.
8. Click the Browse button to reveal the Open dialog box, which enables you to navigate to the desired document. Or, you can click the Select a PDF File to Use in This Shared Review drop-down arrow and choose a currently open document from the list.
9. Click Next to open the Send PDF for Share Review: Step 2 of 4 dialog box.

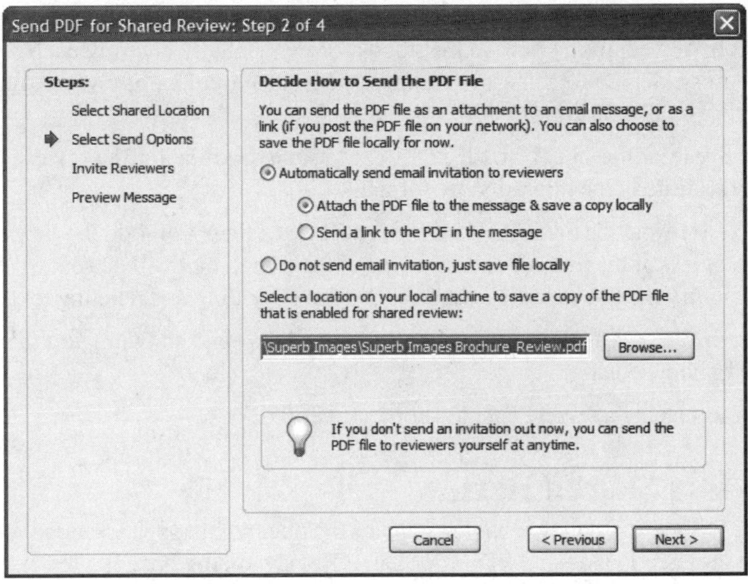

10. Choose the manner in which you're going to send the invitation. You can attach the PDF to an e-mail or send a link to the network folder in which the document is stored. By default, the path to the current location of the review document is displayed. Accept the default location, or click Browse to store the document in a different location.
11. Click Next to reveal the Send PDF for Shared Review: Step 3 of 4 dialog box.

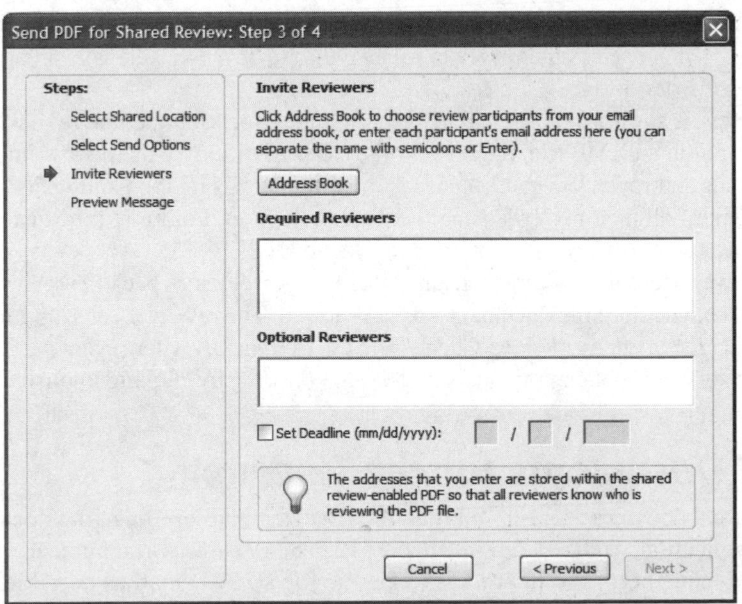

13

12. Specify the Required Reviewers and, if desired, add Optional Reviewers to the list. You can select reviewers from your Address book, or by manually entering each reviewer's e-mail address. Separate each e-mail address with a semi-colon, or press ENTER after entering an e-mail address.
13. Click the Set Deadline check box if you want to set a deadline for the review, and then enter the deadline in the mm/dd/yyyy format.
14. Click Next to reveal the Send PDF for Shared Review: Step 4 of 4 dialog box. This dialog box is a preview of the Subject and Message of the e-mail that will be sent to reviewers. You can modify the Subject or Message as desired by adding and deleting text.
15. Click Finish. The Create Shared Review dialog box appears, showing you the results of the shared review creation.
16. Click OK to display a review enabled copy of the PDF.

Participate in a Shared Review

When you initiate a review, a review-enabled copy of the document appears immediately after you complete the last step in the Send PDF for Shared Review dialog box. Reviewers are notified by e-mail with either a review-enabled version of the document attached, or the path to the network folder where the review document is stored.

Reviewers can participate in the review by double-clicking the e-mail attachment, which launches Acrobat and displays a welcome message, or by navigating to the network folder, and then opening the document. After reading the welcome message, reviewers can annotate the document using the Comment & Markup toolbar (see Figure 13-1) discussed in Chapter 10. After adding comments to the document, a reviewer can check for new comments, publish comments, or check server status. The reviewer can click the Server Status drop-down arrow to reveal a drop-down menu, which enables the reviewer to open the Review Tracker, save an archive copy of the document, or work offline.

A shared review is similar to an e-mail review, with the exception that the reviewer's comments are stored in an XML file in the network folder specified by the review initiator. The review initiator and reviewers can keep track of comments using the Comments panel, and they can keep track of all their reviews using the Review Tracker. For more information on the Comments panel and the Review Tracker, refer to Chapter 10.

When a reviewer opens the document again, a dialog box welcomes back the reviewer and displays a list of changes since the document was last viewed. The reviewer can add new comments to their copy of the document by clicking Check for New Comments. After reviewing and adding new comments, they can add their comments to the shared review by clicking Publish Comments.

Prepare PDF Documents for the Internet

When you prepare a document for the Internet, the first step is to optimize the document in the authoring application, as discussed in Chapter 12. The most important consideration in optimizing a document for the Internet is to get the file size as small as possible.

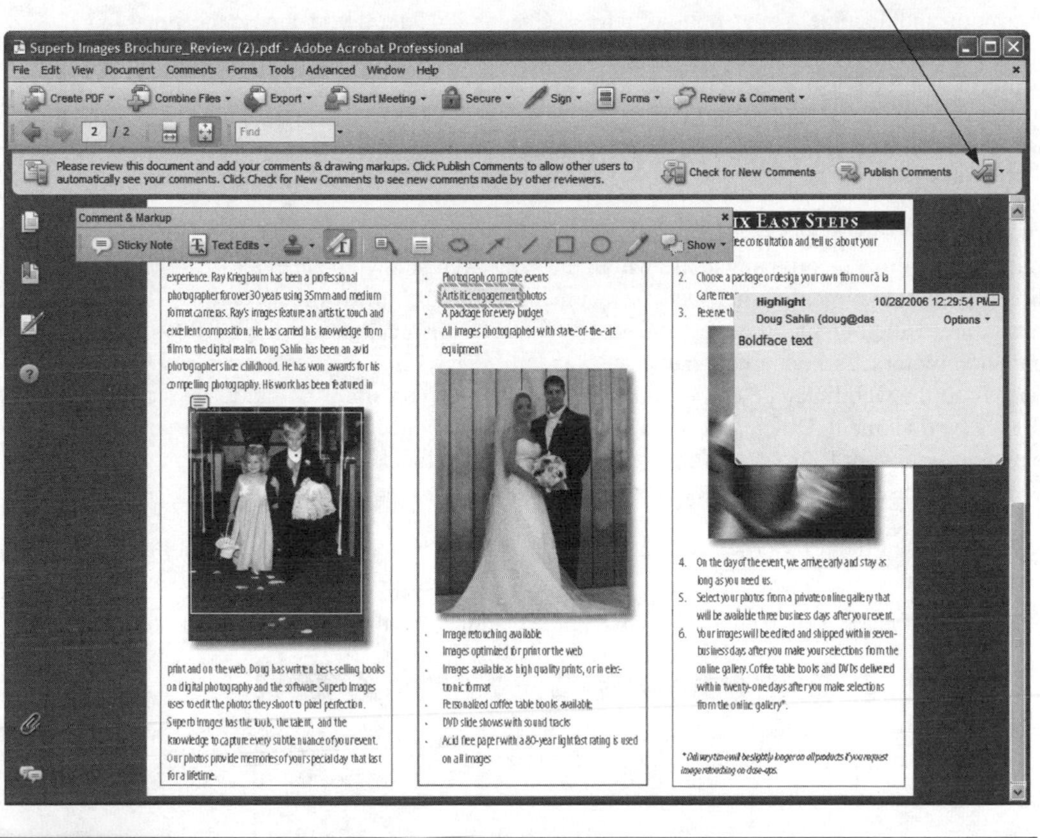

FIGURE 13-1 Reviewers can annotate the document, and then publish their comments.

Remember to resample all images to a resolution of 72 dots per inch (dpi) and enable Fast Web View (the default option with all conversion settings except PDF/A and PDF/X) when converting the document to PDF format. You can modify conversion settings in the Images section to change resample the images to 72 DPI. If you modify the converted document in Acrobat, you need to use the Save As command to enable Fast Web View, as outlined in the section "Save the Document for the Internet."

You should also consider document security issues, document description information, and the manner in which the first page of the document is displayed when a viewer downloads it. If you include document description information, the web site visitor can get an idea of the information included in the document. Add document security if you want to prevent web site visitors from extracting content from the document or printing the document. If you assign security to the document, be sure to include a permissions password, and be sure to use Acrobat 6.0 or greater compatibility, so the document metadata is available for search engines. For more information about Acrobat security, refer to Chapter 11. For more information on modifying the document description and document open options, refer to Chapter 4. Note, if you choose the Open In Full Screen Mode option in the Initial View section of the Document Properties dialog box, the document won't be displayed in full-screen mode when viewed in a web browser.

But that's only the beginning of your task. After you convert the original document to PDF format, you apply the finishing touches in Acrobat.

Add a Base URL to the Document

If all the web links in a document are within the same web site, you can enter the relative path (directory and document name, such as documents/pdfdocs.htm) for the web link. If all the links point to another site, though, you need to enter the absolute path to the URL (web site domain, directory, and document name, such as *http://www.othersite.com/documents/pdfdocs.htm*). If all the web links are to the same external site, you can simplify matters by adding a base URL to the document. When you add a base URL, you only need to enter the relative path to the document you want to open. Acrobat automatically links the relative path to the base URL. To specify a base URL for the document, follow these steps:

1. Choose File | Properties, and then click the Advanced tab of the Document Properties dialog box.
2. Enter the absolute path to base URL of the document in the Base URL field, as shown here:

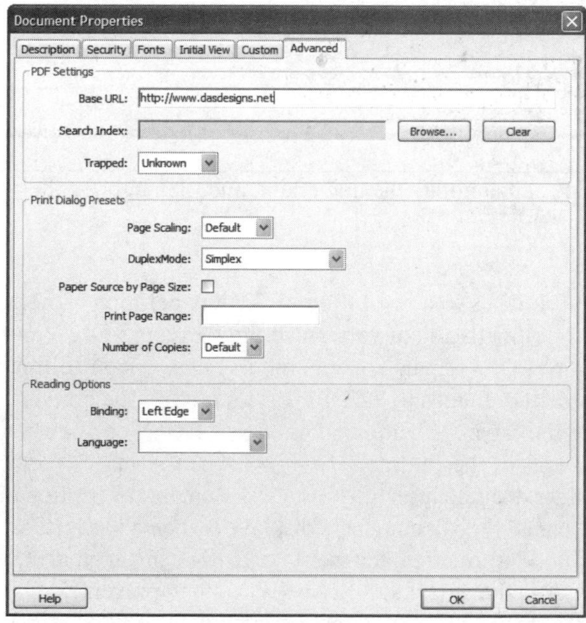

3. Click OK to close the dialog box.

Create Links to Web Sites

When you create PDF documents for viewing from a web site, you may need to create one or more links to other web pages. If you have several interlinked PDF documents, you also need to create some sort of link back to the HTML pages of the web site. You can ask visitors to rely on the Back button of the web browser. If a viewer has navigated through several documents, however, clicking the Back button several times to exit Acrobat and return to the HTML portion of the web site can be annoying. You can create a link to a web site by defining the area of the document that will link to an external web site with the Link tool, and for the link action, choose Open A Web Page. Enter the URL for the web page you want the link to launch and viewers can then get back to the HTML page with a single click.

Create Named Destinations and Links

When you create links from an HTML document to a PDF document, the link destination can be the document itself or a *named destination* (a named link to a specific location within a PDF document). When you create a destination, you can change the view to zoom in on a specific image or paragraph within a document.

You can link to a named destination from within an HTML document. In Acrobat, create a named destination for each part of the document you want to link to from within an HTML document. For example, if you post a PDF product manual on the Web, you can create a named destination for each product. Remember to use proper naming conventions for web browsers, because you will be using each destination name as part of a web link. With this in mind, the destination name should be eight characters or less with no spaces. For more information on

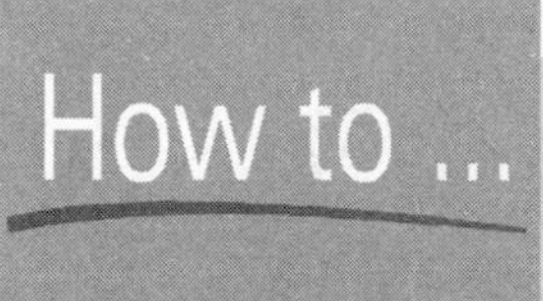

Create an E-Mail Link

When you create a PDF document for a web site, you can create an e-mail link within the PDF document. When viewers of your PDF document click the e-mail link, their default e-mail application opens with a blank message window addressed to the e-mail address of your choice. To create an e-mail link in a PDF document, select the Link tool and define the target for your e-mail link. In the Create Link dialog box, click the Open A Web Page radio button and, in the Address field, enter **mailto:** followed by the desired recipient's e-mail address, for example, mailto: JoeSmith64@Webserver.com.

creating named destinations, refer to Chapter 8. For more information on creating a link to a named destination, refer to the section "Create HTML Hyperlinks to Named Destinations."

You should also create a link within the document that takes viewers back to the HTML page after they have viewed the information. You may also need to create links from within the document to other web pages, and you can use text or images within the document as the basis for your links. If you own Acrobat Professional, you can also create a button in the PDF document that acts as a link. If you create several buttons within a document, however, you increase the file size, which isn't a desirable outcome when creating documents for the Web. For more information on creating links, refer to Chapter 7.

Create a Welcome Page

If you have a large collection of PDF documents at a web site, you can link the documents together using PDF navigation. When you do this, create a welcome page in PDF format that explains what the document collection is about. On the welcome page, you can create a text menu, and then use the Link tool to create links from menu titles to the other PDF documents. When you create a welcome page in this manner, as long as the other PDF documents are in the same folder, you can use the Open File action to open a specific document when the user clicks the link.

You can also create a welcome page by using HTML. Create hyperlinks on the welcome page for each document, as outlined in the section "Create HTML Hyperlinks to PDF Documents."

When you create navigation links for a large PDF document collection at a web site, after the viewers have followed several links within the document collection, they may have a hard time navigating back to the HTML section of the site. Therefore, you should include a link back to the web site home page in each PDF document or create a PDF navigation menu with links to the major areas of the web site.

Use PDF Forms on the Internet

You can use PDF forms to get feedback from visitors of a web site, to conduct an online opinion poll, to build a customer database, and much more. When you use Acrobat Professional to create a PDF form for the Internet, create a Submit button to forward the information to the site webmaster or site owner.

After filling in the form, the user clicks the Submit button to submit the information to the server. Some web-hosting services have preformatted CGI scripts that you can modify to forward form results. CGI scripts can be used to password-protect web sites, create guest books, and much more. In this case, you need a CGI script that collects the information from the PDF form and forwards it to a specified person. In Acrobat Professional, create a Submit button that links to the web server script.

With most web servers, CGI scripts are stored within a folder named cgi-bin. Check with the web-hosting service's technical support staff for the relative path to the mail-forwarding CGI script. For more information on creating PDF forms with Acrobat Professional, refer to Chapter 14. For information on creating forms with Adobe LiveCycle Designer 8.0 (Windows only), refer to Chapter 15.

TIP

In lieu of using a CGI script, you can forward the form results to an e-mail address. After you create the Submit button in Acrobat Professional, choose the Submit Form action. Click the Add button and, instead of entering the URL to a web page, enter **mailto:** *followed by the e-mail address of the recipient. When a visitor to the web site fills in the form and clicks the Submit button, the viewer's default e-mail application opens. The viewer can add a message or send the e-mail as is. When the recipient receives the e-mail, the form results are attached as an HTML, FDF, or XFDF file, or as the complete PDF document, depending on which option you selected with the Submit Form action.*

Save the Document for the Internet

Before you upload the document to a web site, double-check your work. Make sure all links function properly. If any of the document links are to a web site, make sure you have the correct URL. Nothing is more frustrating for a web visitor than trying to open a link and getting a Not Found error. Remember to test your links in a browser; otherwise, Acrobat will append the current document with the web page specified in the link.

If all the links are formatted properly, choose Advanced | PDF Optimizer (Professional only). With the PDF Optimizer, you can remove any bookmarks or links with invalid destinations, and reduce the file size by specifying compression settings for images in the document and removing unused objects. If you created any named destinations that you intend to use as link destinations from an HTML document or other PDF document, deselect the Remove Unreferenced Named Destinations check box in the Clean Up tab of the PDF Optimizer, shown here:

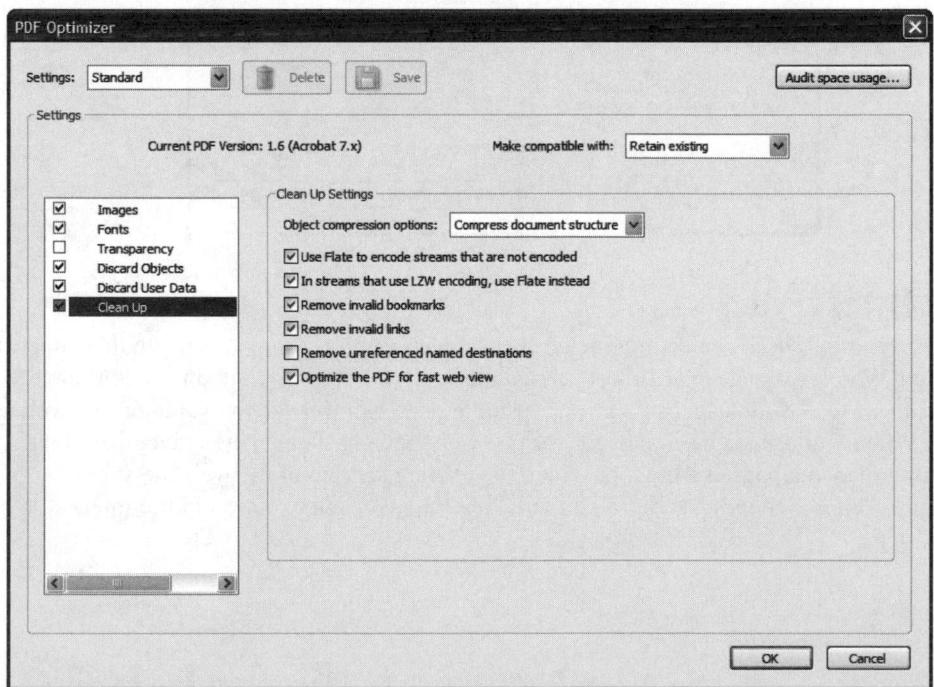

13

If you frequently use the same settings to optimize PDF documents, click the Preset drop-down arrow and choose Custom. After you select the desired optimize options and specify optimize parameters, click the Save button to open a dialog box that prompts you for a name for the custom settings. After you save the custom settings, the name you specify appears in the Preset drop-down list.

After using the PDF Optimizer, you can remove further nonessential data by choosing Document | Examine Document. This opens the Examine Document dialog box (shown next) and gives you the option of removing items the PDF Optimizer doesn't recognize. Make sure you don't remove document metadata if you want search engines to include the PDF document when indexing a web site.

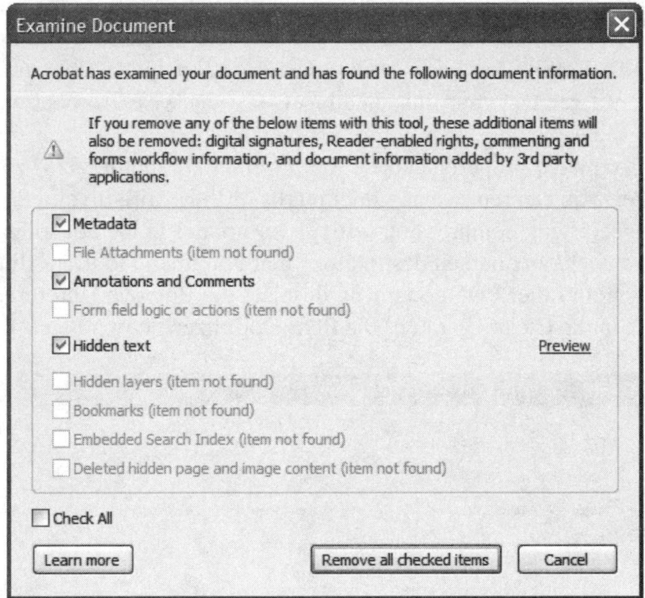

About Byteserving

When you view a PDF document optimized for fast web viewing from a web site that supports byteserving, you see a page load almost immediately. If you've ever waited for a 350-page PDF document to download before viewing a single page, you realize the value of fast web viewing. When you optimize a document for fast web viewing, you create a document that can be downloaded a page at a time, provided the hosting service of the web site supports byteserving. Unless the user has disabled the Allow Fast Web View option in the Internet section of Acrobat Preferences, Acrobat or Adobe Reader communicates directly with the web server. If, for example, a web site visitor opens a lengthy PDF document, it opens to the link specified in the HTML document or linking PDF document. If the viewer enters *50* in the Navigation window, the viewer doesn't have to wait for the preceding pages to load. Acrobat requests Page 50 and Acrobat downloads it from the web server.

NOTE *After the first page of a PDF file optimized for fast web viewing downloads, Acrobat continues downloading the rest of the document by default. To disable this option, choose Edit | Preferences | Internet and deselect Allow Speculative Downloading In The Background.*

Create Byteserving PDF Files

Even though you specify fast web viewing when optimizing the conversion of the document to PDF from within an authoring application, after you add navigation links and other interactive features in Acrobat, you must once again save the document in a manner that produces a file optimized for the Web. If you use the Save command to save the document to file, Acrobat doesn't create a file optimized for fast web viewing. To create a PDF document optimized for fast web viewing, choose File | Save As. By default, the Save As command optimizes a document for fast web viewing unless you disable this option by editing Acrobat Document Preferences.

Name the Document

When you name a document for distribution on the Internet, remember different web browsers react differently. Refrain from using spaces within a filename and always include the .pdf extension. Web browsers are configured to use Acrobat or Adobe Reader as the default application to view PDF files. Another good idea is to refrain from using long filenames. When in doubt, stick with DOS naming conventions by using filenames with eight characters or less and no spaces.

TIP *When you create a document for the Internet and you want the smallest possible file size, choose File | Document | Reduce File Size. This opens a dialog box in which you choose the version of Acrobat for which you want the file optimized. Choosing an earlier version of Acrobat results in a smaller file size. Don't choose an earlier version of Acrobat if you have added features, such as page transitions, which are supported only in Acrobat 6.0 or later.*

Combine HTML and PDF Files

When you create PDF documents that will be viewed from a web site, use HTML pages as the basis for the web site and create links from within the HTML pages to PDF documents. After you create the HTML pages for your web site, you need to create the links that will open the

PDF documents in the web site visitor's browser. You can link directly to a PDF document, or you can link to a named destination within a PDF document. You can also create links from within PDF documents to web sites.

Create HTML Hyperlinks to PDF Documents

After you create your web pages, you need to create hyperlinks to open the PDF documents within the web site visitor's browser. As long as the PDF documents are stored at the same web site as the HTML documents, you need to enter only the relative path to the document when creating the hyperlink. If the PDF documents are in the same folder as the HTML pages, your hyperlink is equal to the filename of the PDF document, followed by the .pdf extension. The following example shows a text link to a PDF document:

```
<a href="empMan.pdf"> Employee Manual </a>
```

Refer to your HTML editing software documentation for more information on creating hyperlinks.

Create HTML Hyperlinks to Named Destinations

If the PDF documents you create for Web viewing have named destinations, you can create links that open directly to the named destinations. When the viewer clicks a link to a named destination, Acrobat or the Adobe Reader launches in the viewer's web browser, and the document opens to the named destination rather than to the first page of the document. To create a link to a named destination, follow these steps:

1. Create the HTML page in your HTML editor.
2. Create a hyperlink to the named destination. You format a hyperlink to a named destination the same way you format a link to a bookmark within an HTML page. The hyperlink (href) is equal to the filename of the document, followed by the extension, which is then followed by the pound sign (#) and the name of the destination exactly as it appears in the PDF document. Refer to your HTML editing software user manual for more information on creating hyperlinks. The following example shows a text hyperlink to a named destination (Cat1) within a PDF document (myDoc.pdf). When you create the hyperlink, make sure you use the proper case for the named destination; otherwise, the document will open at the first page, rather than the named destination. Also refrain from using any spaces when entering a name for a named destination that will be used on the Web. For more information on named destinations, see Chapter 8.

   ```
   <a href="myDoc.pdf#Cat1"> Catalog Number 1 </a>
   ```

CAUTION

Linking to a named destination isn't supported by some browsers. If your viewing audience is likely to have older web browsers or web browsers tailored for an Internet service provider (ISP), such as AOL, add a note telling viewers which web browsers the document is optimized for, and provide a link where viewers can download the web browser. Also, tell your viewers they need Acrobat 4.0 and later, or Adobe Reader 7.0 and later to view the document properly, and then provide a link to download the proper version.

Create and Distribute PDF Documents via E-Mail

As you learned throughout the course of this book, Acrobat PDF documents can be shared with anyone who has Acrobat or Adobe Reader installed. PDF documents are often referred to as *ePaper,* or electronic paper. What better way to share an electronic document than to send it via e-mail? In Chapter 5, you learned to convert a document from a Microsoft Office application to PDF format and e-mail it to an associate. You can also e-mail any document you create or append within Acrobat. After you digitally sign a PDF file and add your comments or otherwise mark up the document, you can send it via e-mail without leaving Acrobat by following these steps:

1. Log on to your ISP.
2. From within Acrobat, choose File | Attach to Email. Acrobat launches your default system e-mail application.
3. Within the e-mail composition window, enter any message to accompany the file, and then send it. Acrobat automatically sends the PDF document as an e-mail attachment.

NOTE

A smart idea is to save the document before e-mailing it. Acrobat uses a good bit of your system resources. Adding the e-mail application to the tasks the system is already processing may exceed the limits of your processing power and lock up your computer.

Conduct an Online Meeting

13

A new feature to Acrobat 8.0 is the capability to launch an online meeting from within Acrobat. *Acrobat Connect* is technology created by Macromedia, a company Adobe acquired in December 2005. To use Acrobat Connect, you need to create an Acrobat Connect account, but you can sign up for a 30-day trial subscription to see if it's right for your business.

The Acrobat Connect meeting room is hosted by an Adobe server. To conduct an online meeting, click the Start Meeting task button to reveal the Start Meeting Log In dialog box. From this dialog box, you can create a trial account or log in if you have an existing account. After logging in, you enter the meeting room, which enables you to send e-mail invitations to those whom you want to participate in the meeting. After attendees arrive, you can share your desktop or any open application with them. This is a wonderful tool for reviewing documents or holding online classes. In addition, if you have a fast connection, you can share your web cam with participants. Other features include the capability to chat with meeting participants, pause the desktop and use Acrobat Connect annotation tools to highlight parts of the screen, add text, and so on. You can even elevate attendees to host status, which gives them access to your desktop. Figure 13-2 shows an online meeting in progress. Figure 13-3 shows the annotation tools being used to point out the Marquee select tool in Adobe Photoshop, which the host is sharing with meeting participants.

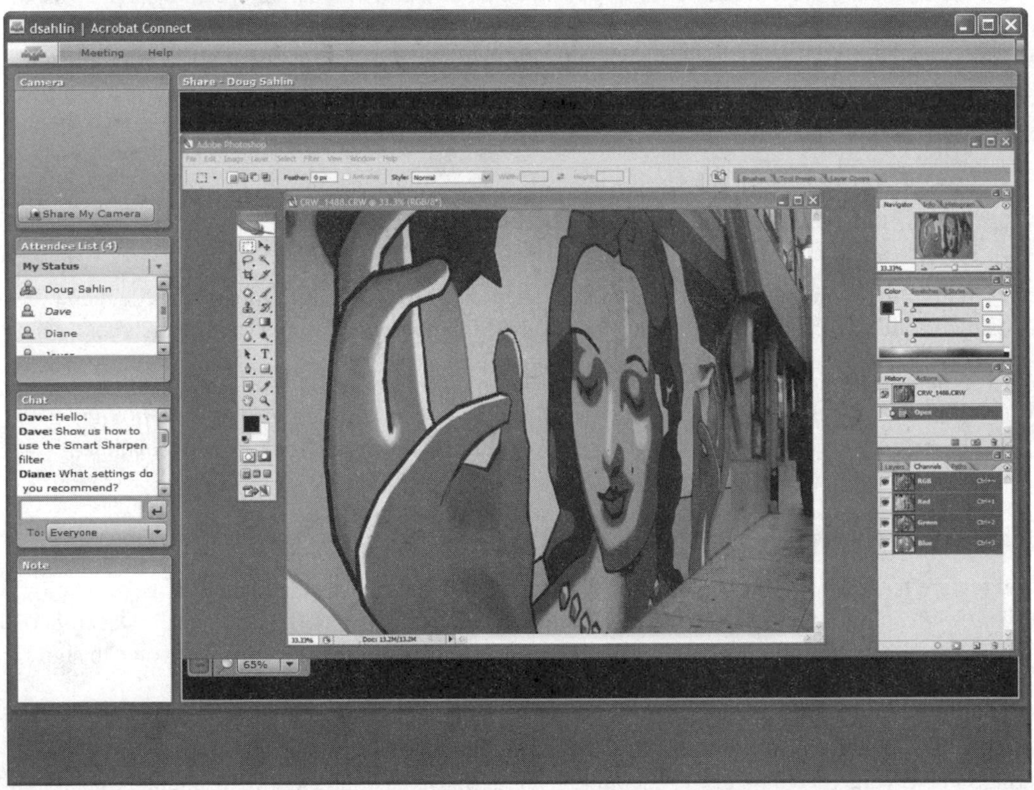

FIGURE 13-2 You can conduct an online meeting using Acrobat Connect.

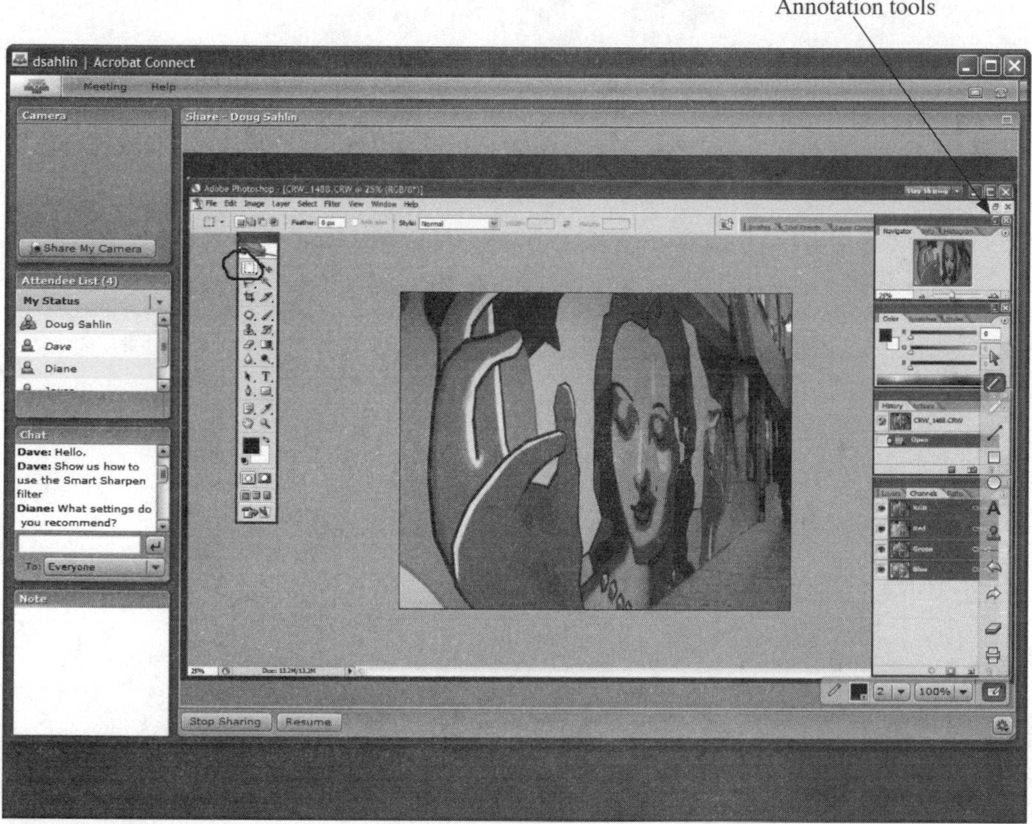

FIGURE 13-3 You can use Acrobat Connect to conduct online classes.

Summary

In this chapter, you learned how to work with PDF documents for posting to the Internet. You discovered how to initiate and participate in a shared review. You also learned how to prepare documents for the Internet, create links to named destinations, save documents for fast web viewing, and reduce the file size of PDF documents. And, you received an introduction to a powerful new feature called Acrobat Connect. In the next chapter, you learn how to create PDF forms with Acrobat Professional.

Part IV

Create Enhanced PDF Documents with Acrobat Professional

Chapter 14 Create Forms

How to...

- Add form fields
- Define form properties
- Validate form fields
- Create form buttons
- Submit forms

Acrobat Professional makes it possible for you to add form fields to your PDF documents. You use *form fields* to retrieve information from readers of your PDF documents. You can also create forms for orders, questionnaires, and for getting viewer feedback from a web site. You can create forms that tally the results of an online purchase, and then submit the order to the online seller.

In this chapter, you learn to use the basic Acrobat form elements to create your own forms. A *PDF form* is a compilation of form fields you use to accumulate data from users. The fields can be used to collect text and numeric data. You can specify field formatting to determine the type and look of the data entered. Your form can be a combination of text boxes, check boxes, combo boxes, list boxes, radio buttons, and signature fields. You can create buttons for the users to submit the data or reset the form. If you create a form for Web use and the web host server supports Common Gateway Interface (CGI) scripting, you can have the form results forwarded to a web site or entered into a database.

Create a PDF Form

When you create a PDF form, you can scan an existing paper form into Acrobat, and then use the tools from the Forms toolbar to create interactive form fields in the same position as the fields in the scanned document. You can use the new form-field recognition feature to convert items that have the appearance of form elements into actual form elements. When you create a form in this manner, you have the look and feel of the original form, along with the interactivity of the Acrobat form fields. You can also create a form from scratch by creating the textual and graphic elements in an authoring application, converting the document to PDF format, and then using the Forms tools to create interactive form fields and elements. Or, if you prefer to have total control of the form in Acrobat and you're on the Windows platform, you can use a menu command that launches a separate application, known as Adobe Designer, to create a form. Figure 14-1 shows an IRS form created by scanning the document into Acrobat, and then creating the individual form elements in Acrobat with the Forms tools.

Fill Out a PDF Form

When users decide to fill out a form, such as the one shown in Figure 14-1, they click inside a field with the Hand tool. In Adobe Reader 7.0 and later, and in Acrobat, users have the option to highlight fields. When users click inside the form field, the cursor becomes an I-beam, indicating

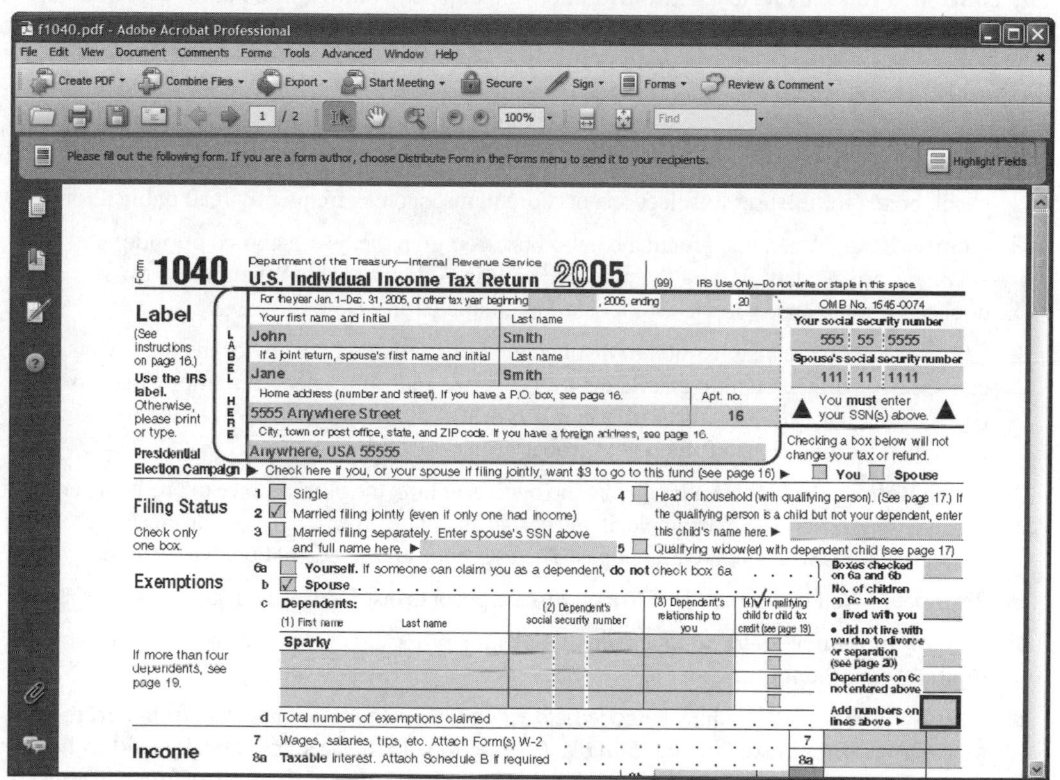

FIGURE 14-1 You can use a paper form as the basis for a PDF form.

that data can be entered from the users' keyboard. To navigate to another field, users can either click inside another field after selecting the Hand tool or press TAB to advance to the next field. Users can correct an entry error by clicking inside the field with the Hand tool, selecting a word or letter that needs to be changed, and then entering the new data. If the form is equipped with a properly programmed Reset button, users can start over by clicking the button.

About Acrobat Form Fields

To create fields in your PDF forms, you use a tool from the Forms toolbar or choose Tools | Forms, and then choose the desired tool. Your choice of tool specifies what the resulting field does or what type of data it accepts. You can assign actions to form fields to create a desired result when a user interacts with the form field. In Acrobat Professional, you have tools listed on the following page to create these types of form fields.

14

- **Button** You can create a text-only button, an icon-only button, or a button with both an icon and text. You can create an invisible button and place it over an existing graphic on a form you scanned and converted to PDF format, which gives the appearance that the graphic is executing the action instead of the form field.
- **Check Box** You create a group of check boxes when you want the user to choose from a set of options. For example, if you create a PDF questionnaire, you can create a series of check boxes for the user to select one or more items, such as frequently read publications.
- **Combo Box** When you create a combo box, you give the user a choice of options. A *combo box* is identified by the presence of a drop-down arrow. When the arrow is clicked, a menu drops down with a list of available choices.
- **List Box** You create a list box to display a list of available choices for the user. You can specify parameters that enable the user to make multiple selections from a list box (something that isn't possible with a combo box). If the number of items in the list box exceeds the dimensions of the box, Acrobat provides scroll bars.
- **Radio Button** You create a group of radio buttons to limit the user's choice to one item per group of radio buttons. For example, if you design an online order form, you can create a group of radio buttons with credit card options. The user chooses the one option that applies.
- **Text Field** You create a text field to accept user input or to display data, such as the current date.
- **Digital Signature Field** You create digital signature fields for authorized users to digitally sign the form.
- **Barcode Field** You create a barcode field when you want to translate data from a form that was printed or faxed to you. *Barcode fields* eliminate the need to manually read and record data from a form that hasn't been submitted electronically. To process printed forms with a barcode field requires you to purchase Adobe's Barcoded Paper Forms software.

Design a Form

You can use any existing PDF document as the basis for your form. You create the labels for all your fields by creating read-only text boxes, and then you create the fields for user input data. The easiest method of creating a form, though, is to lay out the basic design of the form in an authoring application and convert the file to PDF format. Then, open the PDF file in Acrobat to add and format the form fields, or use the Run Form Field Recognition command. Another alternative is to scan an existing form into Acrobat and create the necessary form fields or have Acrobat recognize existing form fields. Or, if you use Acrobat Professional on a Windows machine, you can quickly create a form using Adobe Designer, which Chapter 15 covers in detail.

Use the Layout Grid

Whether you decide to create your form from an existing document or lay out one from scratch, you can use the Layout Grid to provide a visual reference while creating and aligning form fields. To enable the Layout Grid, shown in Figure 14-2, choose View | Grid.

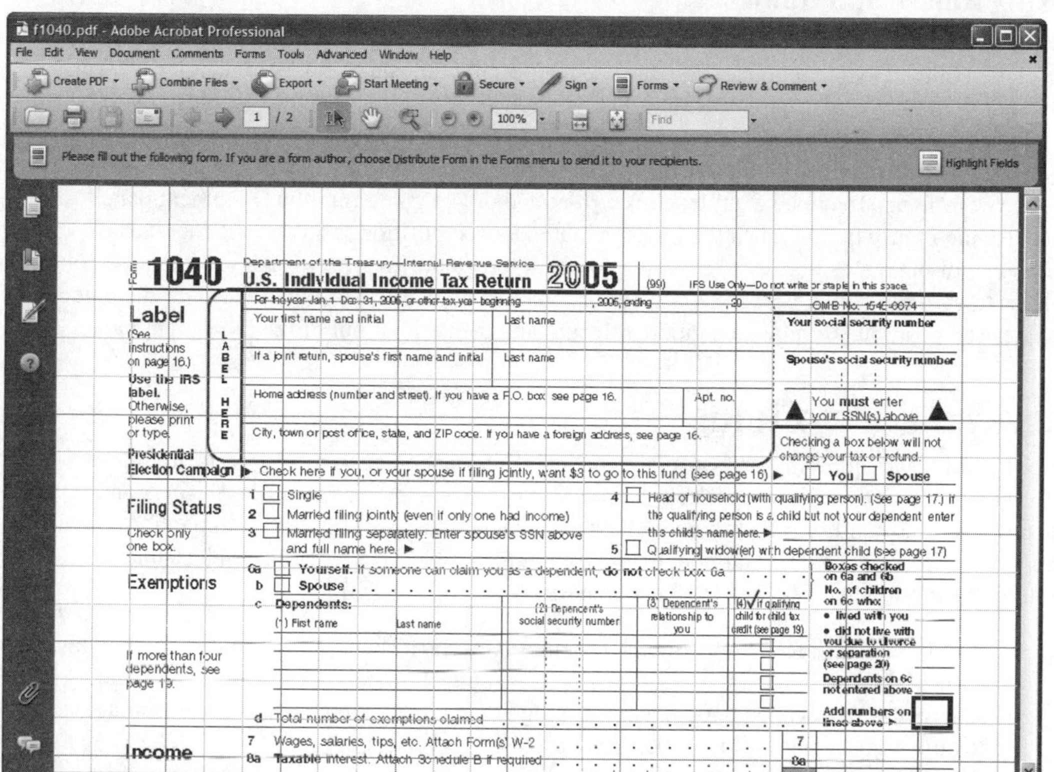

FIGURE 14-2 You can use the Layout Grid as a visual aid when designing your form.

Use the Snap To Grid Command

When you enable the Layout Grid, you can visually align and size items to intersecting grid points. Use any of the Viewing tools to zoom in on your work. For exact alignment and sizing, choose View | Snap To Grid. When you use this command, the Layout Grid develops a magnetic personality, and any object you create snaps to the grid points.

14

TIP

The default color and grid spacing work well in most instances, but you can modify the color and spacing if they're unsuited to your preferences or the document you're modifying. Choose Edit | Preferences, and then click Units And Guides. Within this section of the Preferences dialog box, you can modify grid spacing, color, width between lines, and so on. You can also change the guide color, which, by default, is the same light blue as the grid line color.

Using Rulers and Guides

When you're creating your form, you may find it helpful to have a vertical and horizontal ruler displayed in the Document pane. You can use the visual reference of rulers to position a form element with pin-point accuracy. Rulers also provide a visual reference that enables you to create a form element of a given size. To display rulers, choose View | Rulers.

After you display rulers in the workspace, you can create as many guides as you need to design your form. To create a guide, click a ruler and drag a guide into the Document pane. Release the mouse button when the guide is in the desired position. You can use the visual reference of the opposite ruler to precisely position the guide. To reposition a guide, move your cursor toward the guide. When your cursor becomes an angled arrow, click-and-drag the guide to the desired position. To remove a guide, select it, and then drag it out of the Document pane.

Recognize Form Fields

A powerful new feature in Acrobat 8 Professional is the capability to recognize form fields. This is a tremendous time saver. For example, you can scan a paper form into Acrobat, and then invoke the Run Form Field Recognition command. After invoking the command, Acrobat recognizes elements in the document that resemble form fields. To recognize objects that resemble form fields in an open PDF document:

1. Choose Forms | Run Form Field Recognition. Acrobat scans the document and displays detected form fields in the Recognition Report panel. The accuracy depends on the quality of the scanned document. Scanning at the highest optical resolution available from your scanner is always best.
2. Click on a form field with the applicable tool to change the properties for a recognized field. Or, you can click the Highlight Fields button and Acrobat highlights all fields with a light blue color.
3. After modifying recognized form field properties, save the document.

Create Form Fields

After you create the PDF document that's the basis for your form, you're ready to start creating interactive form fields. You create form fields by selecting the desired tool and defining the field area with the selected tool. After you define the field area, the Properties dialog box for the selected form tool appears. From within this dialog box, you name the field and define properties. Each field type has its own parameters, which you use to modify the field to suit the needs of the form you're creating. If the form fields contain text, you can also spell check the field. To create a form field, follow these steps:

1. Choose Tools | Forms, and then choose the desired form tool from the drop-down menu. An alternative is to choose Tools | Forms | Show Forms toolbar to display the Forms Toolbar (shown next) in the workspace.

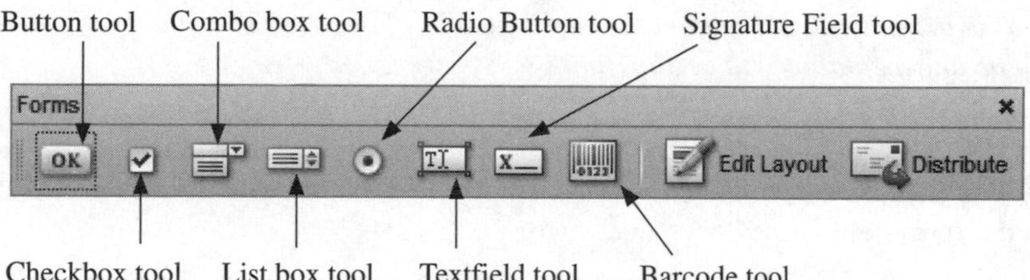

2. Click the point where you want the form field to begin, and then drag diagonally. When you use one of the form tools, your cursor becomes a crosshair. As you drag the tool to define a field, a bounding box gives you a preview of the form field area. When the form field is the desired size, release the mouse button to open the Properties dialog box for the selected tool. The dialog box has different tabs and options, depending on the tool you choose. The following illustration shows the Text Field Properties dialog box:

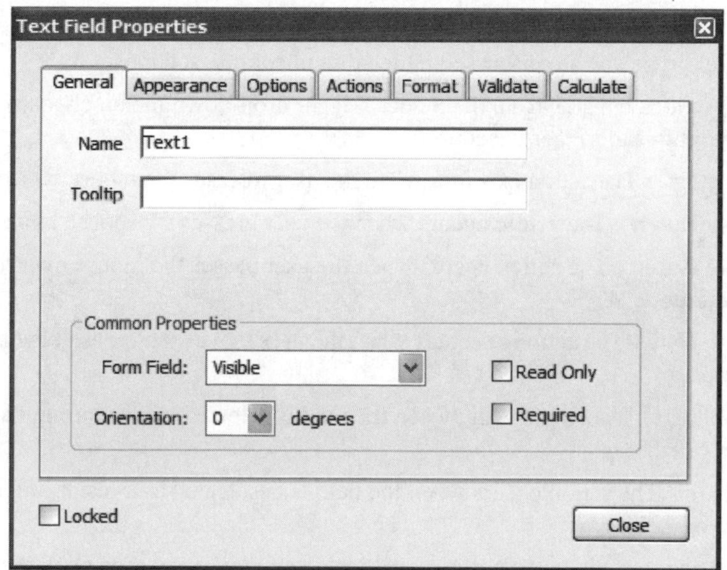

3. In the General tab Name field, enter a name for the field.
4. In the Tooltip field, enter any text you want displayed as a tooltip when a user holds his mouse over the form field. This step is optional.
5. In the Common Properties section, click the Form Field drop-down arrow and choose one of the following options: Visible, Hidden, Visible But Doesn't Print, or Hidden But Printable.
6. Click the Orientation drop-down arrow and choose one of the following options: 0, 90, 180, or 270 degrees. This determines how the field data is oriented to the document.

NOTE *If text is in the field, it's rotated the same number of degrees. The quality of rotated text may be unacceptable with certain fonts.*

7. Click the Read Only check box to make the field read only. When you choose this option, users will be able to see the content of the form field, but they won't be able to interact with the form field.
8. Click the Required check box if users are required to interact with the form field. For example, if you choose this option on a text field, users are required to enter information in the field. If the document in which the text field is included has a Submit button and the user attempts to submit the form without filling in a required field, a warning dialog box appears, telling the user the required field was found empty during export.
9. Click the Appearance tab and select appearance options for the field. For specific instructions on setting appearance parameters, refer to the upcoming section "Specify Field Appearance."
10. Click the Options tab and specify the options for the field. The choices in this tab differ for each field type and are discussed in detail in upcoming sections.
11. Click the Actions tab and, from the Select Trigger drop-down menu, choose one of the following options to trigger the action:
    - **Mouse Up** The action executes when the user releases the mouse button.
    - **Mouse Down** The action occurs when the user presses the mouse button.
    - **Mouse Enter** The action occurs when the user passes the mouse over the field boundaries.
    - **Mouse Exit** The action executes when the user moves the mouse beyond the field target area.
    - **On Focus** The action occurs when the field is selected, either through a mouse action or tabbing.
    - **On Blur** The action occurs when the field is deselected as a result of a mouse action or tabbing.
12. Choose an action from the Select Action drop-down menu, and then click the Add button. Actions were discussed in detail in Chapter 8 and are presented in this chapter as they apply to individual field types.
13. Click OK to complete the creation of the form field.

Specify Field Appearance

When you create a PDF form, you can change the appearance of a field to suit the document. You can choose whether to have a border and/or a background, and, if applicable, specify border and background colors. You can also control text attributes. To specify the appearance of a form field, do the following:

1. Create a form field, as outlined in the previous section.
2. Click the Appearance tab to reconfigure the dialog box, as the following illustration shows:

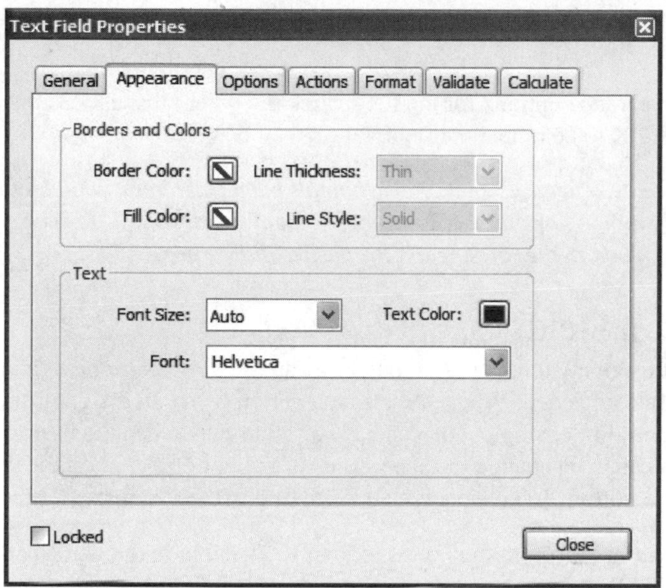

3. In the Borders And Colors section, click the Border Color swatch and choose a color for the field border, and then click the Fill Color swatch and choose a color for the field background. Some field objects have a diagonal red slash through both swatches, which means the default option for the element is no border color and no fill color. Click the applicable swatch to specify a color. You can choose a color for the border, and then choose a Fill Color or none.
4. If you specify a border color, the Line Thickness option becomes available. Click the Line Thickness drop-down arrow and choose Thin, Medium, or Thick to specify the width of the border.
5. Click the Line Style drop-down arrow and choose Solid, Dashed, Beveled, Inset, or Underlined.
6. If the field type you chose has text, click the Font Size drop-down arrow in the Text area and choose a size from the drop-down menu. Or, you can enter a value between 2 pts (points) and 300 pts (points). If you select Auto, Acrobat sizes the text to fit the field, with the exception of a text field set to display multiple lines, in which case the Auto option sizes the text to fit the field as the user enters it.
7. Click the Text Color button and choose a color from the pop-up palette. Or, you can click the Other Color button to create a custom color from the system color picker.

8. Click the Font drop-down arrow and choose a font. Note, if you select a font that isn't available on the user's system, the field font reverts to the user's default system font or, if possible, Acrobat renders a reasonable facsimile of the original font. You can always embed the font, but be aware that font licensing issues may be involved and embedding fonts bloat the file size.

After you set appearance options for the field, click the other tabs, choose the parameters that apply, and then click OK to complete the field.

After you create a field, align it, and set up all the parameters, you can prevent accidentally moving or otherwise editing the field by locking it. To lock a field, click the Locked check box in the form field's Properties dialog box.

Create a Button Field

You can use buttons for many things in Acrobat. You can use *buttons* for navigation devices, or to submit forms or initiate an action. When you create a button, you can assign different actions to each state of the button. For example, you can have a sound play when the user rolls the mouse over the button. You can even change the appearance of the button based on the interaction of the user's mouse with the button. To create a button field, follow these steps:

1. Select the Button tool from the Forms toolbar if available in the workspace. Or, choose Tools | Forms | Button tool.
2. Drag diagonally on the document to define the dimensions of the button. The Button Properties dialog appears.
3. In the General tab Name field, enter a name for the field, and then modify other parameters, as previously outlined in the section "Create Form Fields."
4. Click the Appearance tab and specify the applicable appearance options, as outlined previously in the section "Specify Field Appearance."
5. Click the Options tab.
6. Click the Layout drop-down arrow and, from the drop-down menu, choose one of the following options: Label Only; Icon Only; Icon Top, Label Bottom; Label Top, Icon Bottom; Icon Left, Label Right; Label Right, Icon left; or Label Over Icon.
7. Click the Behavior drop-down arrow and choose one of the following options:
    - **None** The button appearance doesn't change when clicked.
    - **Push** You can change the button face in the Up, Down, and Rollover states.
    - **Outline** The button outline is highlighted when clicked.
    - **Invert** The button colors invert when the button is clicked.

8. In the Icon And Label section, if you choose a layout with text, enter the button text in the Label field. If you choose a layout with an icon, click the Choose Icon button and select an image for the button face.
9. If you chose Push for the Behavior option, click one of the three states (Up, Down, or Rollover) and, in the Icon And Label section, specify the text and icon decoration for the button when it's in this state, and then repeat for the other button states.
10. Click the Actions tab and specify the actions you want to occur when the user interacts with the button. Remember, you can apply multiple actions to the button for each state. For example, on Mouse Enter, you can have a sound play and a tooltip appear; on Mouse Exit, you can hide the tooltip and mute the sound. When you specify different actions and use the Push Behavior option, you create highly interactive buttons that pique user interest. When you add a sound file to a button, use a sound of short duration. Otherwise, the timing may be off, as Acrobat has to load the sound and the necessary libraries to play it. For more information on mouse events, refer to the section "Create Form Fields."
11. Click Close to complete the creation of the button.

After creating the button, you can forge ahead to the next field you need to create for the form. A good idea, though, is to select the Hand tool and test the button to make sure it has the functionality you desire.

Rescale a Button Icon

After you test the button, you may find you need to fine-tune the size of the button icon. You can modify the size of the button icon by doing the following:

1. With the Button or Select Object tool, select the button you want to modify.
2. Right-click (Windows) or CTRL-click (Macintosh) and choose Properties from the context menu.
3. Click the Options tab, and then click the Advanced button to open the Icon Placement dialog box:

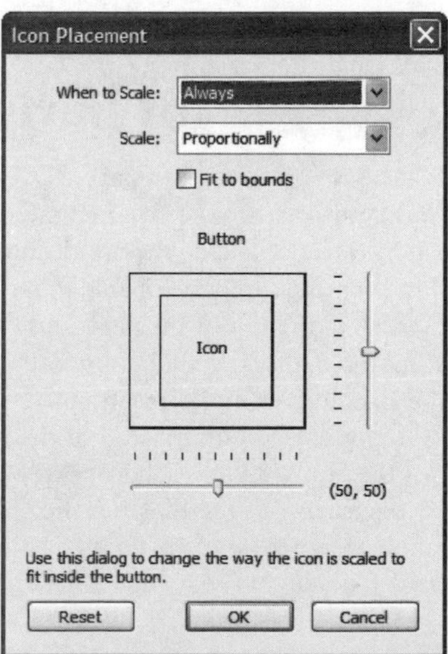

4. Click the When To Scale drop-down arrow and choose one of the following options:
   - **Always** Acrobat always scales the icon to fit, regardless of its size in relation to the form field.
   - **Never** Acrobat inserts the icon as originally sized. If the icon is too large for the field, it is clipped from top-left to bottom-right.

- **Icon Is Too Big** Acrobat resizes the icon to the form field if it's larger than the form field dimensions.
- **Icon Is Too Small** Acrobat resizes the icon to the form field if it's smaller than the form field dimensions. Note, if the icon is considerably smaller than the field size, the image will be pixelated.

5. Click the Scale drop-down arrow and choose one of the following options:
   - **Proportionally** Acrobat preserves the proportion of the original image when resizing it to fit the form field.
   - **Non-Proportionally** Acrobat resizes the icon to the proportions of the form field.
6. Drag the sliders in the Button area to determine icon placement in relation to the form field. By default, equal margins are preserved around the icon and the border of the button field. To modify the margin on the sides of the icon, drag the horizontal slider left or right. To modify the margin on the top and bottom of the icon, drag the vertical slider up or down.
7. Click the Fit to Bounds check box to constrain the icon image to the boundary of the button.

TIP *Click Reset to reset the icon placement to the default parameters.*

8. Click OK to apply the parameters to the button icon.

Did you know?

You Can Use Button Fields for Navigation

When you create a multipage PDF document, readers can use Acrobat navigation tools to find their way around the document. If you distribute the document to casual Acrobat or Adobe Reader users who aren't familiar with all the navigation tools and menu commands, however, they may be unable to navigate the document. To solve this problem, create three buttons at the top of the page and label them Back, Next, and Home. Remember to assign a unique name to each button in the General tab of the Button Properties dialog box. Assign the Execute Menu Item action to each button. For the Back button, choose the View | Go To | Previous Page command. For the Next button, choose View | Go To | Next Page command. For the Home button, choose View | Go To | First Page command. Duplicate the buttons on all pages, as outlined later in the chapter. On the first page of the document, delete the Back and Home buttons and, on the last page of the document, delete the Next button. You now have a document that can be navigated by anyone.

TIP

When you're creating a form in Acrobat, you can choose a tool by using a menu command. For example, when you need the Text Field tool, choose Forms | Text Field Tool. However, it's much easier to simply select the tool from the Forms toolbar, which you can display by choosing Tools | Forms | Show Forms Toolbar.

Create a Check Box

You use check boxes to give the user the opportunity to choose more than one option. For example, if you create a questionnaire, you can use check boxes to collect information about which magazines the user reads. The user selects each applicable magazine and the results are sent to the location you specify when the form is submitted. To create a check box, follow these steps:

1. Select the Check Box tool from the Forms toolbar and define the area and position of the field. Generally, you want to create a square form field for a check box. Remember, you can always enable the Layout Grid and choose the Snap To Grid option for assistance when creating form fields. After releasing the mouse button, the Check Box Properties dialog box appears.
2. In the General tab Name field, enter a name for the check box and modify the other parameters, as outlined previously in the section "Create Form Fields."
3. Click the Appearance tab and modify the parameters, as outlined previously in the section "Specify Field Appearance."
4. Click the Options tab.
5. Click the Check Box Style drop-down arrow and choose Check, Circle, Cross, Diamond, Square, or Star. This option determines what the check box looks like when selected. Note, some of these options may not render properly on different platforms. If possible, test the document on every platform your intended audience may use. When in doubt, Check is usually the best choice.
6. In the Export Value field, Yes is entered by default. This means the value of "Yes" will be exported when users select the check box. Enter different text to export a different value when users select the check box.
7. Select Check Box Is Checked By Default, and the check style you choose appears in the check box when the document loads. If you deselect this option, the check box is empty.
8. Click the Actions tab and specify the actions you want to occur when users interact with the check box.
9. Click Close to complete creation of the check box.

If you create a series of check boxes that are different options for a form element, such as a question, choose the same name for each check box, but specify a different export value. For example, if you're creating check boxes to gather a response for a simple question, you create two check boxes for each question and give one a Yes export value and the other a No export value.

Create a Combo Box

You can use a combo box to display a list of items when you want the user to select only one item from the list. If you desire, the combo box can be configured to accept text input from the user. A combo box functions like a drop-down menu, which can be accessed by clicking a down arrow. To create a combo box, follow these steps:

1. Select the Combo Box tool from the Forms toolbar and define the area of the field in the PDF document. After releasing the mouse button, the Combo Box Properties dialog box appears.
2. In the General tab Name field, enter a name for the field, and then modify other parameters, as outlined previously in the section "Create Form Fields."
3. Click the Appearance tab and adjust the parameters to suit the style of your form, as previously outlined in the section "Specify Field Appearance."
4. Click the Options tab.
5. In the Item field, enter the first item in your list.
6. In the Export Value field, enter the export value for the item. If no value is entered, the item is exported with the value listed in the Item field.
7. Click Add to add the item to the combo box.
8. Repeat Steps 4 through 7 to add additional items to the list.
9. After adding all the items to the list, you can select the following options:
   - **Sort Items** Acrobat sorts the items numerically, and then alphabetically.
   - **Allow User To Enter Custom Text** Users can enter their own value for the combo box.
   - **Check Spelling** Users can spell check the custom text they enter. This option is selected by default.
   - **Commit Selected Value Immediately** Users' selections are saved immediately. Otherwise, the value is saved when the form is submitted. This option is handy when another field in the form will use the combo box export value.
10. If you didn't choose the Sort Items option, you can manually reorder the list. Select a list item and click the Up button to move the item one position higher in the list. Click the Down button to move the item one position lower in the list. If the item is at either extremity of the list, the applicable button is dimmed out. Or, you can click the Delete buttonto remove a selected item from the Combo Box list.
11. Click the Actions tab and specify the actions you want to occur when users interact with an item in the combo box. This step is optional.
12. Click the Validate tab to restrict the range of data that can be entered in the combo box. For more information on this option, refer to the section "Validate Form Fields."

13. Click the Calculate tab if you want to use items from the combo box to perform a mathematical calculation. For more information on creating a calculating form field, refer to the section "Calculate Form Fields."
14. Click Close to complete the creation of the combo box.

Create a List Box

You create a list box when you want to enable users to select multiple items. When you create a list box, users can scroll through the list, as opposed to opening a drop-down menu with the combo box. Users cannot edit items in a list box, but they can select multiple items from the list, whereas they can select only one item from a combo box. You can use JavaScript to create a custom action when users change the list box selection. To create a list box:

1. Select the List Box tool from the Forms toolbar and drag diagonally in the document to define the area and position of the list box. When you release the mouse button, the List Box Properties dialog box appears.
2. In the General tab Name field, enter a name for the field, and then modify the other parameters as outlined previously in the section "Create Form Fields."
3. Click the Appearance tab and define the appearance parameters for the list box, as discussed previously in the section "Specify Field Appearance."
4. Click the Options tab.
5. In the Item field, enter a name for the first item in the list.
6. In the Export Value field, enter the export value of the item. If you leave this field blank, the item name becomes the export value.
7. Click the Add button to add the item to the list box.
8. Repeat Steps 5 through 7 to add additional items to the list box.
9. After you complete adding items to the list, you can choose the following options:
   - **Sort Items** Acrobat sorts the list items in numerical and alphabetical order.
   - **Multiple Items** Enables users to make multiple selections from the list.

NOTE *If you select Multiple Items, the Commit Selected Value Immediately option is no longer available.*

   - **Commit Selected Value Immediately** Users' selections are saved immediately; otherwise, the value is saved when the form is submitted.
10. If you didn't choose the Sort Items option, the Up and Down buttons are active. To move a selected item up one position in the list, click the Up button. To move a selected item down one position in the list, click the Down button. Or, you can click the Delete button to remove a selected item from the list.

11. Click the Actions tab and specify the actions you want to occur when users interact with an item in the list box. This step is optional.
12. Click the Selection Change tab and, in the When The List box Selection Changes section, choose one of the following options:
    - **Do Nothing** This is the default option and, true to its name, nothing other than the selection change happens when you change a selection.
    - **Execute This Script** Choose this option, and the Edit button becomes active. Click the Edit button to open the JavaScript Editor dialog box. Create the script that will execute when a list box item changes, and click OK to close the dialog box.
13. Click Close to complete the creation of your list box.

Create a Radio Button

When you create a *radio button,* you create a form device that enables users to make a selection. When you create a group of radio buttons from which users can choose an option, only one button can be selected from the group, thus limiting users to one selection from the group. When you create a group of related radio buttons, each button has the same name, but a different *export value.* If you're adept at JavaScript, your custom script can use the export value. To create a radio button:

1. Select the Radio Button tool from the Forms toolbar, and define the size and position of the form element in the document. After releasing the mouse button, the Radio Button Properties dialog box appears.
2. In the General tab Name field, enter a name for the field and modify additional parameters, as discussed previously in the section "Create Form Fields."
3. Click the Appearance tab and define the appearance parameters for the list box, as discussed previously in the section "Specify Field Appearance."
4. Click the Options tab.
5. Click the Button Style drop-down arrow and choose one of the following: Check, Circle, Cross, Diamond, Square, or Star. This option determines what the radio button looks like when selected.
6. In the Export Value field, Yes is entered by default. This means the value of Yes will be exported when users select the radio button. Enter different text to export a different value when users select the radio button.
7. Choose Button Is Checked By Default and, when the document loads, Acrobat will fill the field with the radio button style you selected in Step 5. If you create a group of radio buttons with the same name, only one button can be set up with the Default Is Checked option.
8. Click the Buttons With The Same Name And Value Are Selected In Unison option if you have more than one radio button with the same name and export value in the document. When you select this option, all buttons with the same name and export value are selected when the button you're creating is selected.

9. Click the Actions tab and specify the actions you want to occur when users interact with the button. This step is optional.
10. Click Close to complete the creation of the radio button.

TIP *To create an exact copy of any field, select the field with the form tool with which it was created, and then, while pressing CTRL (Windows) or COMMAND (Macintosh), drag the form field. After you begin dragging the form field, press SHIFT to constrain motion vertically or horizontally. Release the mouse button to complete copying the field. If the copied field is part of a group of radio buttons, choose Properties from the context menu and change the export value of the field, but don't change its name.*

Create a Text Field

You can create text fields to accept user input or to display text strings, such as the current date. You can also use text fields to display multiple lines of text. You can limit the number of characters users can enter in the field and determine whether the field is visible. To create a text field, follow these steps:

1. Select the Text Field tool from the Forms toolbar and drag in the document to define the area for the field. After releasing the mouse button, the Text Field Properties dialog box appears.
2. In the General tab Name field, enter a name for the field, and then modify other parameters, as outlined previously in the section "Create Form Fields."
3. Click the Appearance tab and set the appearance options for the field, as outlined previously in the section "Specify Field Appearance."
4. Click the Options tab to modify the following parameters:
   - Click the Alignment drop-down arrow and choose to align the field contents to the Left, Center, or Right.
   - In the Default Value field, enter the default value for the field. This value is submitted unless the user enters different data. Or, you can leave this field blank.

14

TIP *In the Default Value field, enter instructions on what information you want users to enter in the field.*

   - Enable the Multi-Line option to display the contents of the field on multiple lines. If this option is unchecked and the contents of the field exceed the width of the text box, the text is truncated.
   - Enable the Scroll Long Text option, so users can scroll through the contents of a multiline text box. This option is selected by default. Users of the form can scroll through the field and edit the contents. Furthermore, if you use the text box to display read-only text and the Scroll Long Text option is deselected, users will be unable to scroll the contents of the field because no scroll bars will be present. If you create

a read-only text box with multiple lines of text with this option deselected, be sure to properly size the box, so every line of text is visible.

- Enable the Allow Rich Text Formatting option to allow users to apply styles such as bold, italic, or underline to the text they enter in the field. Users with Acrobat Standard, or Acrobat Professional can format text by choosing View | Toolbars | Properties Bar, selecting the text, and then selecting a style from the toolbar.
- To limit the number of characters a user can enter in the field, enable the Limit Of [:] Characters option and enter a value in the field.
- Enable the Password option, and each character of text displays as an asterisk. This option is unavailable until you deselect the Check Spelling option.
- Enable the Field Is Used For File Selection option, and a path to a file can be entered as the value of the field, which enables a form to be submitted with the document.
- This option is dimmed out until you deselect the Scroll long text option. It is also unavailable if you enabled the Multi-Line, Limit Of Characters, or Password option. Likewise, this option is unavailable if you defined the field with formatting script.
- Enable the Check Spelling option (selected by default), and users can perform a spell check for the field.
- To spread a given number of characters evenly across the width in the field, enable the Comb Of [:] Characters option and enter a value in the field. This option is available only if you deselect all other choices in the Options tab.

5. Click the Actions tab and specify which actions occur when a user's mouse interacts with the field. This step is optional.
6. Click the Format tab to specify the type of data that will be accepted in the field. For more information on formatting a field, refer to the upcoming section "Format Form Fields."
7. Click the Validate tab if you want to restrict the range of data that can be entered in the field. For more information on this option, refer to the upcoming section "Validate Form Fields."
8. Click the Calculate tab if the field will be used to perform a mathematical calculation. For more information on creating a calculating form field, refer to the section "Calculate Form Fields."
9. Click Close to finish creating the text box.
10. Select the Hand tool and click the text box to test it.

Create a Digital Signature Field

You can create a digital signature field when you want the user to sign the form. When you create a digital signature field, you can specify what occurs after the field is signed. To create a digital signature field, follow these steps:

1. Select the Digital Signature tool from the Forms toolbar and drag inside the document to define the area for the field. Make sure you define an area large enough for the details of the signer's digital signature information to be readable. After releasing the mouse button, the Digital Signature Properties dialog box appears.
2. In the General tab Name field, enter a name for the field and set additional parameters, as outlined previously in the section "Create Form Fields."
3. Click the Appearance tab and set the appearance options for the field, as outlined previously in the section "Specify Field Appearance."
4. Click the Actions tab and select the actions that occur when a user's mouse interacts with the field. This step is optional.
5. Click the Signed tab and choose one of the following options:
   - **Nothing Happens When Signed** Choose this default option, and the signature transmits with the submitted form, but nothing else happens.
   - **Mark As Read Only** Choose this option, and you can limit certain fields on the form to read-only status after the document is signed. When you select this option, choose one of the following from the drop-down menu: All Fields, All Fields Except These, or Just These. When you choose either of the latter options, click the Pick button to select the fields to include or exclude.
   - **This Script Executes When The Signature Is Signed** Choose this option to create a JavaScript that executes when the field is signed. After you choose the option, click the Edit button and create the JavaScript in the JavaScript Editor dialog box.
6. Click Close to complete the creation of the Signature field. For more information on digital signatures, refer to Chapter 11.

Did you know?

Create a Barcode Field

If your organization distributes PDF forms that will be filled out in Acrobat or the Adobe Reader, printed and then returned, you can greatly reduce processing time using a barcode field. As the form is filled out, the barcode appearance changes. To process a completed form, you simply scan the barcode. To integrate the new Barcode Tool into your workflow, purchase Adobe LiveCycle Barcoded Forms software. For more information visit: http://www.adobe.com/products/server/barcodedpaperforms/.

Spell Check Form Fields

You can spell check form fields and comments you create in a PDF document. You can add words to the Acrobat Spell Check dictionary and edit the dictionary as needed. To spell check form fields and comments in a document:

1. Choose Edit | Check Spelling | In Comments, Fields & Editable Text to open the Check Spelling dialog box.
2. Click Start to begin the spell check. When Acrobat finds a word that isn't in its dictionary, the word is highlighted in the Word Not Found field, as the following illustration shows. Acrobat supplies a list of suggested replacements in the Suggestions field. You can then take one of the following actions:
   - Click Ignore to leave the highlighted word unchanged and continue with the spell check.
   - Click Ignore All to leave the highlighted word and all future instances of the highlighted word unchanged.
   - Edit the suspect word, and then click Change.
   - Edit the suspect word, and then click Change All to change all instances of the suspect word to your edited text.
   - Double-click a word from the Suggestions list to replace the highlighted word.
   - Click Add, and Acrobat adds the word to your personal dictionary.
   - Select one of the words from the Suggestions list, and then click Change to replace the highlighted word.
   - Select one of the words from the Suggestions list, and then click Change All to change all occurrences of the highlighted word to the selected correction.
3. Click Done to end the spell check.

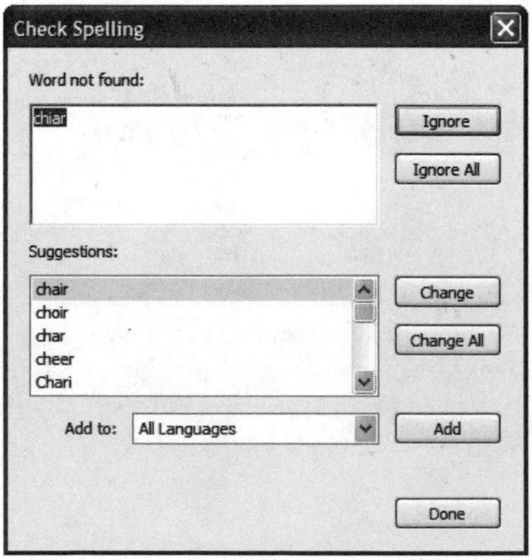

Specify Spell Check Preferences

Acrobat spell check is a powerful feature that you use to guard against typographical and spelling errors in your form fields and comments. You can configure the spell check feature to suit your preferences by following these steps:

1. Choose Edit | Preferences to open the Preferences dialog box.
2. Choose Spelling in the Categories list to open the dialog box, as shown here:

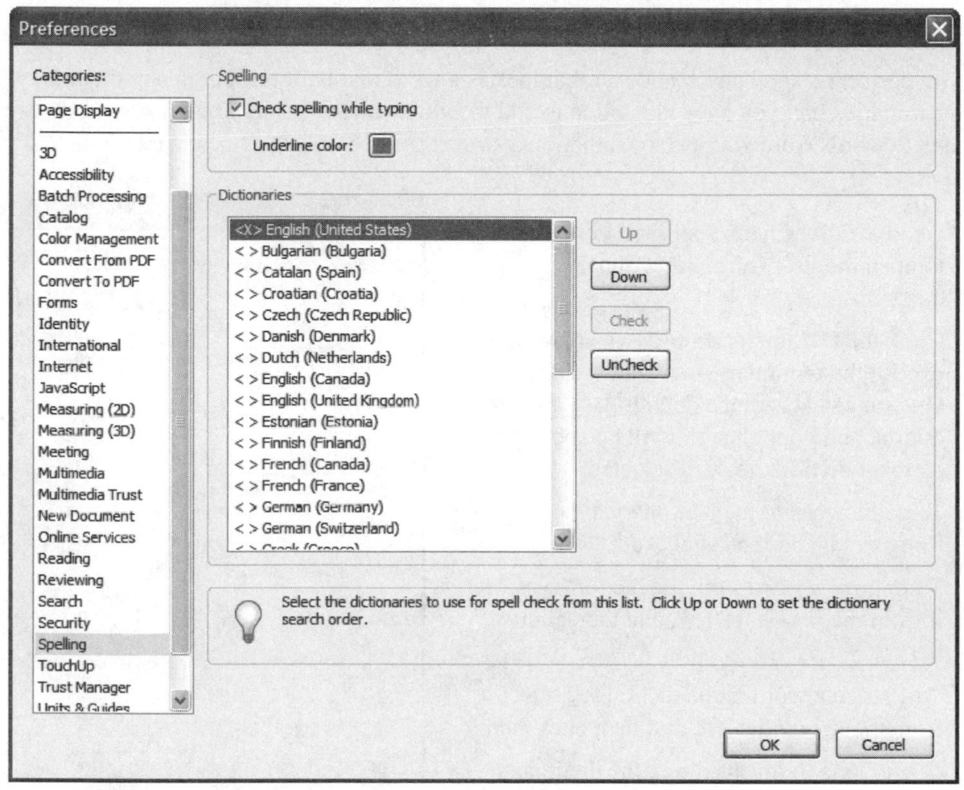

3. Choose the Check Spelling While Typing check box (the default option) to have Acrobat underline any words immediately after you misspell them.
4. To change the underline color (red is the default), click the Underline Color button and choose a color from the pop-up palette.
5. To add a dictionary to the list, select one from the Dictionaries list, and then click Check. The default dictionary is the language you selected when you installed Acrobat. When you have multiple dictionaries, Acrobat searches the dictionary at the top of the list first.

6. To change the order in which Acrobat searches the dictionaries, select a dictionary from the Dictionaries list, and then click the Up button to move the dictionary toward the top of the list. Click Down to move the dictionary toward the bottom of the list.
7. To remove a dictionary from the Dictionaries list, select it from the list (selected dictionaries are designated by an *X* between the < and > brackets), and then click UnCheck.
8. Click OK to apply the changes.

Edit the Dictionary

When you perform a spell check and Acrobat locates a word that isn't present in any dictionary in the Dictionaries list, you have the option to add the word to your personal dictionary. You can add or delete words from your personal dictionary when they're no longer needed, by following these steps:

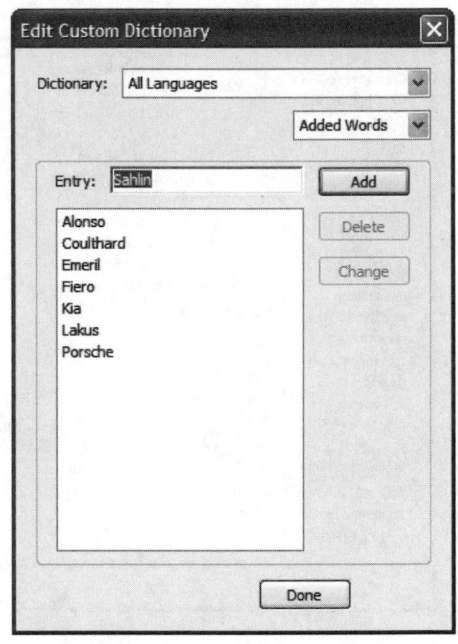

1. Choose Edit | Check Spelling | Edit Dictionary to open the Edit Custom Dictionary dialog box:
2. Click the Dictionary drop-down arrow and choose the dictionary you want to customize. Or, you can accept the default All Languages option, and your changes will be applied to all Acrobat dictionaries you selected.
3. To add a word to the dictionary, type it in the Entry field, and then click Add.
4. To remove a word from the dictionary, select it from the list on the left, and then click DELETE.
5. To change a word in the dictionary, select it from the list on the left, and then click Add.
6. Click Done to finish editing the dictionary.

Format Form Fields

When you create a form field that accepts data input, you can format the field for a specific type of data. For example, if the form field requests the user's fax number, format the field using the Phone Number option. If the user fills out the form and enters 5555551212, when the data is submitted, Acrobat reformats the entry to read (555) 555-1212. To format a form field, follow these steps:

1. Create a text field as outlined previously in the section "Create Form Fields."
2. Click the Format tab in the form field's Properties dialog box.

3. The options in the Select Format Category drop-down list are None, Number, Percentage, Date, Time, Special, or Custom. Each category has different formatting options. The following illustration shows the available options for the Number category:

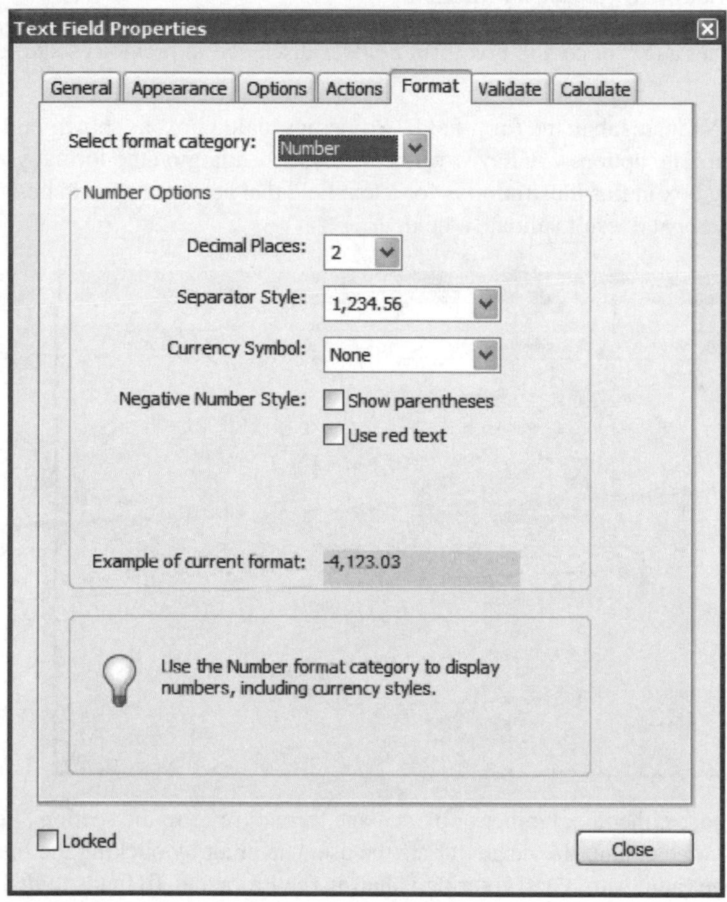

4. Choose the options that best suit the form you're creating.
5. If you chose the Custom category, click the Edit button beside Custom Format Script or click the Edit button beside Custom Keystroke Script to open the JavaScript Editor dialog box. Enter the script or paste an existing script into the dialog box, and then click OK.
6. Click Close to exit the form field's Properties dialog box.

Validate Form Fields

When you create a form field that accepts data, you can limit the amount of data the user enters by validating the form field. When you validate a form field, you specify a range of numerical data that can be entered, or you can create a custom JavaScript to limit the amount of data that can be entered. Validating a form field is useful when you put a form on the Internet. By limiting the amount of data you let the user enter, you eliminate a potential server bottleneck when a malicious user submits a form with copious amounts of data. You can only validate text and combo box form fields. To validate a form field:

1. Create either a text or combo box form field, as discussed in previous sections of this chapter.
2. Click the Validate tab in the form field's Properties dialog box, as shown in the following illustration. The options you have available vary, depending on the format you specify. The dialog box in this illustration is for a text field that accepts numeric input. By default, Acrobat doesn't validate a field.

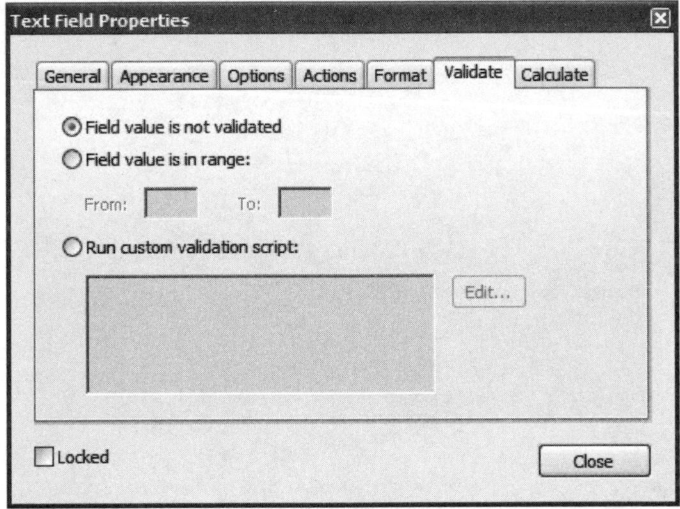

3. If you choose either the number or percentage format (refer to the section "Format Form Fields"), you can limit the range of data the user can enter by clicking the Field Value Is In Range radio button and entering values in the From and To fields to define the acceptable range of data.
4. To create a validation script using JavaScript, click the Run Custom Validation Script radio button, and then click the Edit button to open the JavaScript Editor dialog box. Enter the script you want to be used to validate the form field, and then click OK.
5. Click Close to exit the form field's Properties dialog box.

Calculate Form Fields

When you create form fields with numeric data, Acrobat can calculate the value of two or more fields. You can choose from common arithmetic functions or you can create a complex calculation using JavaScript. To calculate two or more form fields, follow these steps:

1. Create the form field that will display the result of the calculation, as outlined previously in this chapter.
2. Click the Format tab and choose Number from the Select Format Category drop-down menu.
3. Select the options that pertain to the calculation. For example, if you want to calculate a price, choose the appropriate style from the Currency Symbol drop-down menu.
4. Click the Calculate tab.
5. To use one of the present mathematical operations, choose the second option listed and, from the drop-down menu, choose the operation you want performed. You can choose from Sum (+), Product (×), Average, Minimum, or Maximum. Or, you can choose Simplified Field Notation, and then click Edit, which opens the JavaScript Editor dialog box, where you can enter a script to calculate the selected fields using simplified notation, such as `Sum: Sum = Field1 + Field2`, and then click OK to close the dialog box. Another option is to choose Custom Calculation Script, click the Edit button to open the JavaScript Editor dialog box, create the JavaScript to perform the calculation, and then click OK to close the dialog box and apply the custom calculation script.
6. Click the Pick button to display the Field Selection dialog box, which lists all the fields present in the document.
7. Click a field check box to use the field in the calculation.
8. Add the other fields necessary to perform the calculation, and then click OK to exit the Select A Field dialog box.
9. Click Close to exit the form field's Properties dialog box.

Set Field Calculation Order

When you create a complex form with multiple fields of data that you call on for calculation, the order in which the calculation is performed may differ from the tab order of the fields. To change the order of the calculated fields:

1. Choose Forms | Edit Fields | Set Field Calculation Order to open the Calculated Fields dialog box, which shows all the calculable fields in your form and the order in which the calculations are performed on them.

NOTE *If the Edit Fields menu option is dimmed out, choose Forms | Edit Form in Acrobat, or select the Select Object tool.*

2. To change a field's order in the list, select it, and then click the Up button to move the field one position higher in the list. Click the Down button to move the field one position lower in the list.
3. Click OK when you finish reordering the fields.

Create a Reset Form Button

If you create a form with multiple fields, you may want to consider creating a reset button. Adding a *reset button* gives the user the option of starting over by clicking the button. When you create a reset button, you can specify which form fields are cleared when the button is used. To create a reset button:

1. Select the Button tool from the Forms toolbar and drag inside the document to define the size and position of the field.
2. In the General tab Name field, enter a name for the field (Reset is a good choice).
3. Modify the button appearance and options to suit your form, as presented previously in the section "Create a Button Field."
4. Click the Actions tab and choose Mouse Up as the trigger.
5. Click the Select Action drop-down arrow and choose Reset A Form.
6. Click the Add button to open the Reset A Form dialog box:

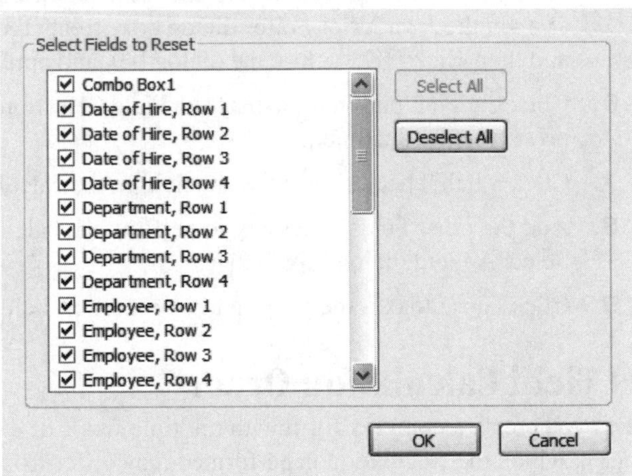

7. Click Deselect All, and then select the fields you want to reset. Or, you can accept the default Select All option to select all form fields in the document.
8. Click OK to exit the Reset A Form dialog box, and then click Close to assign the action to the button.

Create a Submit Form Button

When you create a form for use on the Internet or a local intranet, you can add a submit form button to transmit the results to a web server. You can specify the export format and specify which fields are submitted. To create a submit form button, follow these steps:

1. Select the Button tool from the Forms toolbar, and then drag inside the document to define the size and position of the field.
2. In the General tab Name field, enter a name for the field. Remember to choose an appropriate name for the button. Submit Form is a good choice.
3. Modify the button appearance and options to suit your form, as discussed previously in the section "Create a Button Field."

4. Click the Actions tab and choose Mouse Up for the trigger.
5. Click the Select Action drop-down arrow and choose Submit A Form.
6. Click the Add button to display the Submit Form Selections dialog box:

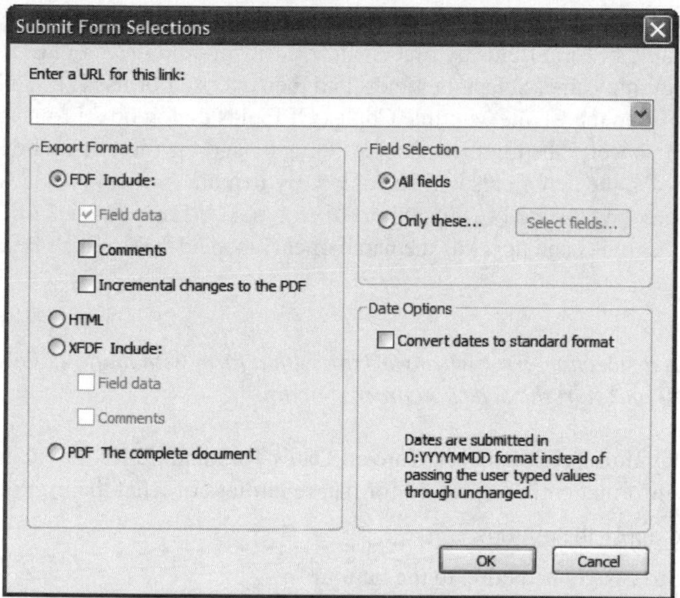

7. In the Enter a URL for this Link field, enter the destination URL for the form results.
8. In the Export Format section, choose one of the following options:
   - **FDF Include** Acrobat exports the data as a Forms Data Format (FDF) file. With this format, you can choose to export field data, comments, incremental changes to the PDF, or all the preceding. When you check the Incremental Changes To The PDF box, data from digital signature fields can be exported in a manner recognized by a web server.
   - **HTML** Acrobat exports the form data in HTML format.
   - **XFDF Include** Acrobat exports the form data as an XFDF file. This file format is similar to FDF, with the exception that the file structure is XML.
   - **PDF The Complete Document** Acrobat exports the entire PDF file that contains the form data.
9. In the Field Selection section, accept the default All Fields option or click Only These. If you select the Only These option, click the Select Fields button to open the Field Selection dialog box. Click Select All to select all fields or click the fields you want submitted when a user clicks the submit button. After selecting the fields, click the Include Selected radio button (the default) to include the selected fields when the form is submitted, or click the Exclude Selected radio button to exclude the selected fields when the form is submitted. If you choose the Empty Field option, fields with no data will be exported. Click OK to exit the Field Selection dialog box.

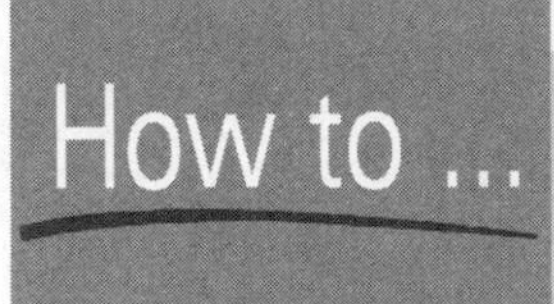

Create a Form Table

You can create a table of form fields by first creating a row or column of fields. Remember to give each field a unique name. Select the fields, and then choose Forms | Edit Fields | Place Multiple Fields to open the Create Multiple Copies Of Fields dialog box. From within the dialog box, you can specify the number of copies to make and the direction (above, below, left, or right) in which the new fields will be copied. By default, Acrobat provides a preview, so you can fine-tune the table before you exit the dialog box. When you click OK, Acrobat creates the multiple copies and appends the name of each copied field, so the field is unique.

If you make a selection error when working with a form with multiple fields, click Deselect All and start the selection process again.

10. In the Date Options section, check Convert Dates To Standard Format to have Acrobat export date information in a standard format, regardless of what the user entered.
11. Click OK to apply the options.
12. Click Close to assign the action to the button.

Edit a Form

After you create a form, you may find you need to edit the form to make it more aesthetically pleasing. You can resize, realign, reposition, and duplicate form fields to achieve this result. You may also find it necessary to edit the properties of individual fields if, for example, an action doesn't execute as planned or a calculation doesn't give the expected result. When you open a previously saved form, your first step in editing the form is to choose Forms | Edit Form in Acrobat.

Use the Form Context Menu

You can find many of the commands needed to modify forms by choosing the desired command from the Forms menu, or by using one of the Forms tools. You can also quickly access a command from the context menu. To modify a form field with a command from the context menu, select a form field with the form tool with which it was created or the Select Object tool, and then right-click (Windows). Or, CTRL-click (Macintosh) and choose a command from the context menu. Note, some of these commands are exclusive to the context menu.

Use the Fields Panel

You can use the Fields panel to edit the form fields within your document. The Fields panel lists every field in your document. You can use the Fields panel to delete fields, navigate to fields, change field properties, and more. Open the Fields panel, as the following illustration shows, by choosing View | Navigation Panels | Fields.

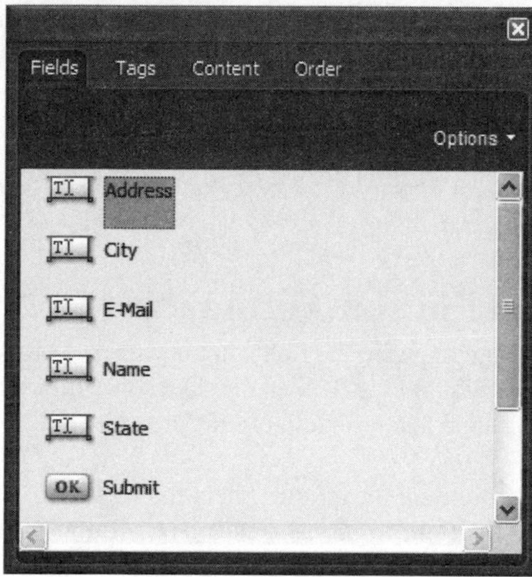

TIP *To delete a field, select the field and press DELETE.*

To edit any field from the list in the Fields panel, select the field, click the Options icon, and choose a command from the drop-down menu. Or, you can select a field in the panel, right-click (Windows) or CTRL-click (Macintosh), and then choose a command from the context menu. The Go To Field command at the top of the menu is unique to the context menu.

NOTE *If you use Acrobat on the Windows platform, commands are at the top of the Fields panel's Options menu to create a new form (which launches Adobe LiveCycle Designer 8.0), choose form tools, and more. Adobe LiveCycle Designer 8.0 is covered in detail in the next chapter.*

Edit Form Field Properties

When a form works exactly as planned, it's time to move on to the next task—or take a quick break and bask in the glow of your accomplishment. More often than not, though, you'll need to tweak one or more properties of a form field. To edit form field properties, select the field with the form tool with which it was created, right-click (Windows) or CTRL-click (Macintosh), and then choose Properties from the context menu to open the form field's properties dialog box.

TIP *When you're editing a document with multiple fields of different types, you can edit them by choosing the Select Object tool from the Advanced Editing toolbar. After you select the tool, every object in the document, including form fields, is highlighted. You can then use the tool to modify an object's properties by right-clicking (Windows) or CTRL-clicking (Macintosh), and then choosing Properties from the context menu.*

Delete a Form Field

When you revise a form and no longer need a particular form field, you can easily delete that form field. First, select it with the form tool with which the field was created or the Select Object tool, and then choose Edit | Delete. Or, you can right-click the field and choose Delete from the context menu or select the field and press DELETE.

When you're editing a form, you can use the Forms toolbar to preview the form as it will look when you save the document by clicking Preview. After you preview the document, click Edit Layout to return to editing mode.

Align, Reposition, and Resize Form Fields

If you use the Layout Grid to align and size the fields in your form, you generally end up with a neatly laid-out form. However, you may still need to make some minor adjustments to the location or size of a field. You can resize individual fields or select multiple fields, and then size and align them to each other.

To resize or reposition an individual form field, select the field with the form tool with which it was created. After you select the field, eight handles appear around the field perimeter. You can then modify the field by doing any of the following:

- To reposition the form field, click the center of the field with the tool used to create the field and drag the field to the desired location. As you drag the field, a bounding box gives you a preview of the current position of the field. When the field is in the desired position, release the mouse button.
- To resize the field, click any corner handle and drag. To resize the field proportionately, press SHIFT while dragging. As you resize the field, a bounding box appears that gives you a preview of the current size of the field. Release the mouse button when the field is the desired size.
- To modify the field width, click the center handle on either side of the form field, and then drag left or right to change the width of the field.
- To modify the field height, click the middle handle at the top or bottom of the field and drag up or down.

You can also modify the size and alignment of several fields. Select the form tool used to create the fields or use the Select Objects tool to select any form field in the document, and then click the desired field. To add fields to the selection, press SHIFT and click the fields you want to add to the selection. The last form field you click is highlighted in red. All fields will be modified to the applicable parameter of the last field selected. After selecting two or more fields, you can do any of the following:

- To change the alignment of the selected fields, right-click (Windows) or CTRL-click (Macintosh) and choose Align. Then, choose Left, Right, Bottom, Top, Vertically, or Horizontally.

- To center the selected fields to the current document, right-click (Windows) or CTRL-click (Macintosh) and choose Center. Then, choose Vertically, Horizontally, or Both.
- To equally distribute the selected fields, right-click (Windows) or CTRL-click (Macintosh) and choose Distribute. Then, choose Vertically or Horizontally. Note, the fields will be distributed relative to their center points.
- To change the size of the selected fields, right-click (Windows) or CTRL-click (Macintosh) and choose Size. Then, choose Height, Width, or Both. Note, selected fields are sized to the last selected field.

TIP *You can set the tab order of form fields by opening the Pages panel and clicking the thumbnail for the page on which the form is displayed. Right-click (Windows) or CTRL-click (Macintosh) and choose Page Properties. In the Tab Order section, choose Use Row Order to set the tab order from left to right, Use Column Order to tab order by columns from top to bottom, or Use Document Structure to tab in the order in which the fields appear on the structure tree.*

Or, you can select the form field for which you want to set the tab order, and then choose Forms | Edit Fields | Set Tab Order. This command gives you the option of allowing Acrobat to set the tab order automatically, or choosing to set the order manually by clicking the fields in the desired order.

Duplicate a Form Field

If the information or data entered in a form field needs to be in multiple locations of the document, you can duplicate the form field. You can duplicate a form field on the same page or across a range of pages. When you duplicate a form field, the field retains all the attributes you assigned to the original field. When you change a parameter in a field that was duplicated (in other words, a field with the same name that appears more than once in the document), the parameter changes in the duplicated fields as well. You can duplicate a single form field or a selection of form fields.

To duplicate form fields on a page, follow these steps:

1. Choose Tools | Advanced Editing | Select Object Tool, and then select the field(s) you want to duplicate. Press SHIFT and click additional fields to add them to the selection.
2. Press CTRL (Windows) or OPTION (Macintosh) and drag the selected fields. To constrain the motion of the fields vertically or horizontally, press SHIFT (along with CTRL or OPTION) after you begin to drag the fields.
3. Release the mouse button, and Acrobat duplicates the selected fields where you released the mouse button.

To duplicate fields across a range of pages:

1. Choose Tools | Advanced Editing | Select Object Tool, and then select the field(s) you want to duplicate.

2. Choose Forms | Edit Fields | Duplicate to open the Duplicate Field dialog box:

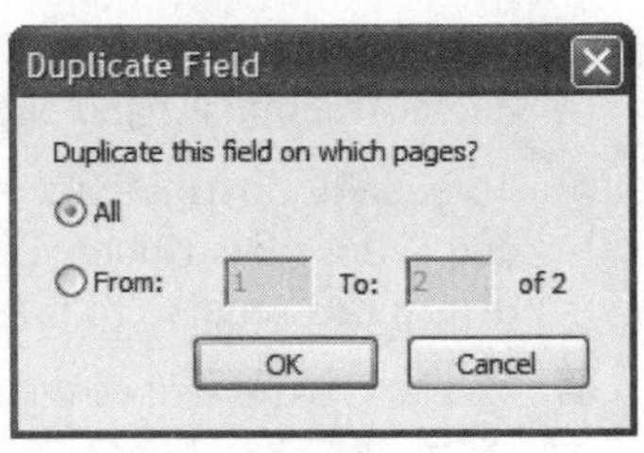

3. Accept the All option (the default) to duplicate the field on all document pages, or choose the From option and enter the range of pages on which to duplicate the field.
4. Click OK, and Acrobat creates the duplicates, per your specification.

When duplicating form fields, the name of the field remains the same, but a hash/pound sign is appended to the name, along with a sequential index number.

Export Form Data

You can export data from a form for use in other PDF forms with the same field names. When you export data, you create a smaller file with data only. You can export the data as an FDF file, an XFDF (an XML representation of the FDF data) file, an XML file, or a text file. To export form data, follow these steps:

1. Choose Forms | Manage Forms Data | Export Data to open the Export Form Data As dialog box.
2. Enter a name for the file and the folder where you want the data file stored. If you don't assign a name for the file, Acrobat uses the current name of the file by default.
3. Click the Save As Type drop-down arrow and select the desired file format.
4. Click Save.

Import Form Data

You can import form data in the following formats: Acrobat FDF files (*.fdf), Acrobat XFDF files (*xfdf), XML files (*.xml), FormFlow99 Data files (*.xfd), or Text files (*txt), to automatically fill in form fields. When you import form data, Acrobat automatically inserts the data in document form fields with the same names. To import data into a PDF document:

1. Choose Forms | Manage Form Data | Import Data to open the Select File Containing Form Data dialog box.
2. Navigate to the file containing the data you want to import and select the file.
3. Click Select to open the file.

You can also share form data with other users. For example, if you work in a corporate environment, you can post a form that contains fields pertaining to product information, such as current cost and list price. When the data needs to be updated, you can update the master version of the form and export the data. The version of the form posted on the corporate intranet can be programmed to automatically update using the Import Form Data action you program to execute when the page opens or when the user clicks a button. For more information on actions, refer to Chapter 8.

TIP

If you're working with multiple forms, you can merge multiple forms into a spreadsheet by choosing Forms | Manage Form Data | Merge Date Files into Spreadsheet. The command opens the Export Data From Multiple Forms dialog box, which prompts you to add the PDF forms you want exported as CSV data. This can be viewed in a spreadsheet application, such as Microsoft Excel.

Use JavaScript Actions

When you create a form field, you can use the Run a JavaScript Action to create a custom script for the field. You can use the JavaScript Action to create JavaScript code and assign it to a button for use as navigation. You can also use JavaScript to augment Acrobat mathematical functions.

Use JavaScript to Subtract and Divide

In the section "Calculate Form Fields," you may have noticed Acrobat doesn't provide the capability to subtract or divide form fields. To perform either operation, you must use the JavaScript Action to create JavaScript code. To subtract a text field named Field *B* from a text field named Field *A,* follow these steps:

1. Select the Text Field tool.
2. Create a form field where you want the results of the calculation to appear.
3. Click the General tab, enter a name for the form field, and specify other parameters for the text field, such as the border color, fill color, font type, font size, and so on.
4. Click the Appearance tab and set the parameters for the field text, background color, and border color.
5. Click the Format tab and choose a format option for the field. Choose the same format as Field *A* and Field *B*. For example, if Fields *A* and *B* work with currency values, choose Number, and then choose the currency symbol that applies.
6. Click the Calculate tab, choose Custom Calculation Script, click the Edit button, and then enter the following in the JavaScript Editor dialog box:

```
var a = this.getField("Field A");
var b = this.getField("Field B");
event.value = a.value - b.value
```

7. Click OK to exit the JavaScript Editor dialog box.

You can modify the script to perform division by entering the following JavaScript in Step 6:

```
var a = this.getField("Field A");
var b = this.getField("Field B");
event.value = a.value / b.value;
```

Division by a value of 0 isn't possible. If the user enters a value of 0 for the second field, an error message appears warning that the value doesn't match the format of the field. To guard against this, click the Validate tab and specify the number must be greater than or equal to 1. Validating the field in this manner also results in an error message if the user enters a value less than 1. This includes dividing by negative numbers.

You can use JavaScript to perform complex calculations involving multiple form fields in a document. Simply create a variable for each form field and use the `getField` method to get the value of the field. To calculate the result, set the value method of the event object equal to a mathematical calculation using the value of each variable and the applicable operands. For example:

```
var a = this.getField("Field A");
var b = this.getField("Field B");
var c = this.getField("Field C");
event.value = c.value * (a.value + b.value);
```

Add JavaScript Actions to Form Fields

You can use the Run A JavaScript Action with form fields (Professional only), bookmarks, and links, or you can create global JavaScript that can be used for an entire document. When you choose the Run A JavaScript Action, you create the actual script in the JavaScript Editor (or a text editor, if you so specified) by editing JavaScript preferences. As previously mentioned, there are myriad uses for JavaScript with PDF documents. The following steps show how to use JavaScript to display the current date when a page loads:

1. Select the Text Field tool from the Forms toolbar.
2. Click the spot on the document page where you want the field to appear and drag to define the shape of the field. When you release the mouse button, the Text Field Properties dialog box is displayed.
3. In the General tab Name field, enter ***todaysDate***. This is the name of the form field that will display the current date, which will be retrieved from the host computer using JavaScript you'll create in a future step.
4. Click the Read Only check box.
5. Define the appearance and other parameters of the text field, as outlined previously and then close the Text Field Properties dialog box.
6. On the Pages tab, select the thumbnail for the page to which you just added the text field.
7. Right-click (Windows) or CTRL-click (Macintosh) and choose Properties to open the Page Properties dialog box.
8. Click the Actions tab and choose Run A JavaScript from the Select Action drop-down menu.
9. Click the Add button to open the JavaScript Editor.
10. In the Create And Edit JavaScripts window of the JavaScript Editor, enter the following JavaScript code:

```
var today = util.printd("mmmm, d, yyyy", new Date());
this.getField('todaysDate').value = today;
```

11. The first line of code creates a variable called `today` and sets its value to the current date `(new Date())`. The first part of the printd method of the `util` object formats the date, where mmmm is the long form of the month, d is the day in numeric form, and `yyyy` is the four-digit representation of the year. The second line of code sets the value of the `todaysDate` field you created in Step 4 equal to the variable `today`. To display the day name before the date, modify the code to read as follows:

```
var today = util.printd("dddd, mmmm, d, yyyy" new Date());
this.getField('todaysDate').value = today ;
```

TIP *When you create JavaScript that uses variables, be aware that variables are case-sensitive. For example, if you refer to the variable as* `today` *in one line of code and* `Today` *in another, the JavaScript won't function as you desire because the second instance of the variable isn't lowercase.*

The addition of `dddd` adds the name of the day to the value of the variable `today`. The date is returned as text data (or *string data*, as it's known in the programming world). The code between the quotation marks is what returns the current date when the page opens. Notice the addition of commas and spaces. This tidies up the formatting. Without them, everything would run together and the result would be something like MondayAugust22010, instead of Monday, August 2, 2010.

TIP *The JavaScript programming language has formatting rules, as does the language with which this book was written. In programmer speak, formatting protocol is known as* syntax. *When your JavaScript has a syntax error, it's noted at the bottom of the JavaScript Editor dialog box.*

12. Click OK to close the JavaScript Editor dialog box.

13. Click Close to close the Page Properties dialog box, and then save the document.

The next time you open the document, the date will be displayed on the page where you created the form field. If the date doesn't appear or if the formatting is incorrect, you'll have to edit the JavaScript.

TIP *If you prefer working in a text editor when creating JavaScript, choose Edit | Preferences, and then choose JavaScript. In the JavaScript Editor section, choose external editor, and then enter the path of the external editor executable (.exe) file. After changing the preference, whenever you edit JavaScript, Acrobat launches the external editor. After you enter the JavaScript, choose the external editor, Save command before setting the JavaScript Action in Acrobat. If you prefer working with the Acrobat JavaScript Editor, you can use this dialog box to change the font type and size, as displayed in the JavaScript Editor.*

Distribute and Manage Forms

If you create a form for the purpose of gathering data, you can simplify the process of distributing a form and compiling data from returned forms. You manage forms with the new Forms Tracker, and you can export data from compiled forms as a spreadsheet.

Distribute Forms

When you have a form that needs to be distributed via e-mail to multiple recipients, you can easily do so within Acrobat. You can send the form immediately, or save the form for future distribution. To distribute a form in Acrobat:

1. Create a form in Acrobat.
2. Add a submit button to the document. Instead of entering a URL in the URL field, enter **mailto:***myEmail@myserver.com*.
3. Choose Forms | Distribute Form to display the Forms Distribution Options dialog box. Your choices for distribution are: Send Now Via Email or Save and Send Later.
4. Choose the method of distribution, and then click OK to display the first page of the Distribute Forms dialog box, shown next.

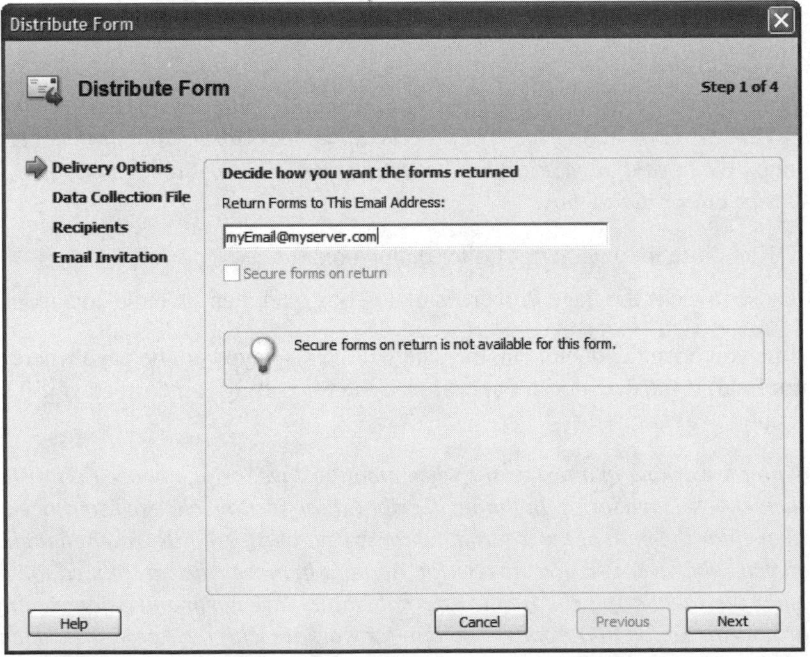

5. Verify the e-mail address, and then click Next to display the second page of the Distribute Forms dialog box, shown in the following illustration.

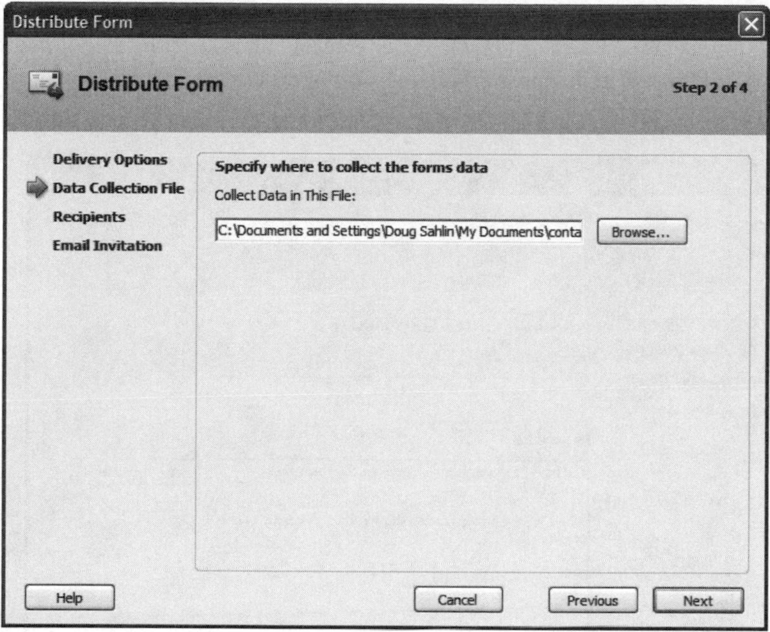

6. Accept the default path and filename for the document used to collect returned form data. Or, click the Browse button and specify a different filename and folder in which to save the file.
7. Click Next to reveal the third page of the Distribute Form dialog box, shown next.

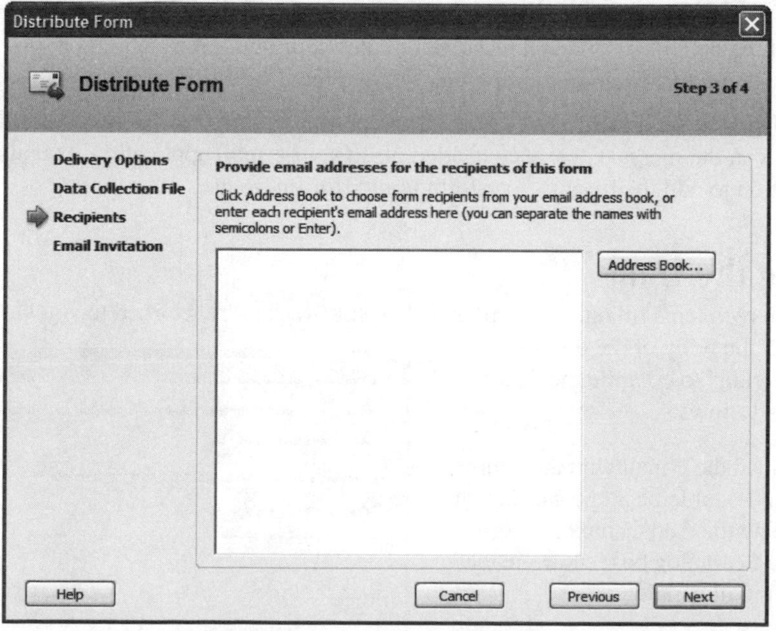

8. Enter the e-mail addresses of the intended recipients. Separate each e-mail address with a semi-colon, or press ENTER or RETURN after entering an e-mail address. Or, click the Address Book button and choose recipients from your e-mail address book.
9. Click Next to reveal the fourth page of the Distribute Form dialog box:

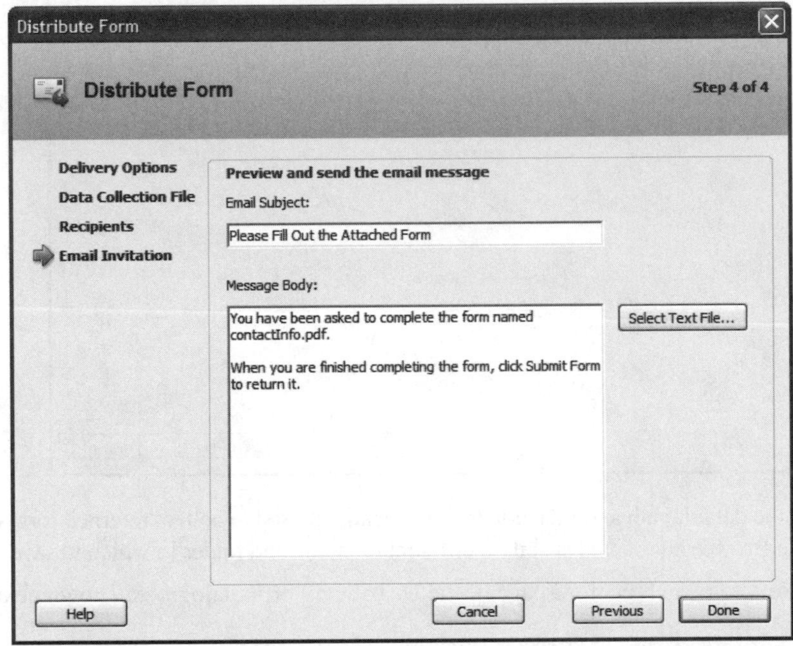

10. Accept the default subject and message or enter your own information. Or, you can click the Select Text File button to import an existing text (*txt) file for the e-mail message.
11. Click Done to send the message. Acrobat displays a different Distribute Form dialog box telling you the message has been handed off to your e-mail application. You also have the option to add the form to your form library for future use.

Compiling the Data

After your form recipients fill out the forms and click SUBMIT, they're returned to you via e-mail. The message in the body of the e-mail contains instructions to compile the data to a data set, as follows:

1. Download the e-mail with the returned form and double-click the attachment to display the Add Completed Form to Data Set dialog box, shown in the following illustration.

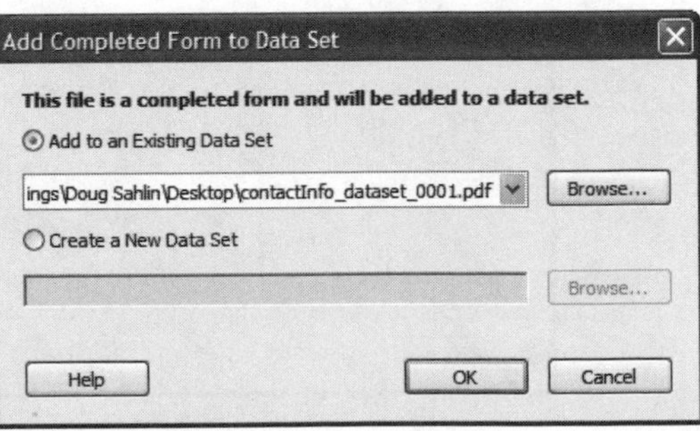

2. Accept the default option, which adds the data to the data set created when you distributed the form.
3. Complete Steps 1 and 2 for other returned forms.
4. Open the original form.
5. Choose Forms | Compile Returned Forms to open the Compile Data dialog box, shown next. Or, click the Forms task button and choose Compile Returned Forms.
6. Click the Browse button, navigate to and select the data set created when you distributed the form, and then click Open.
7. Click OK. Acrobat displays the data in tabular form above the original form.

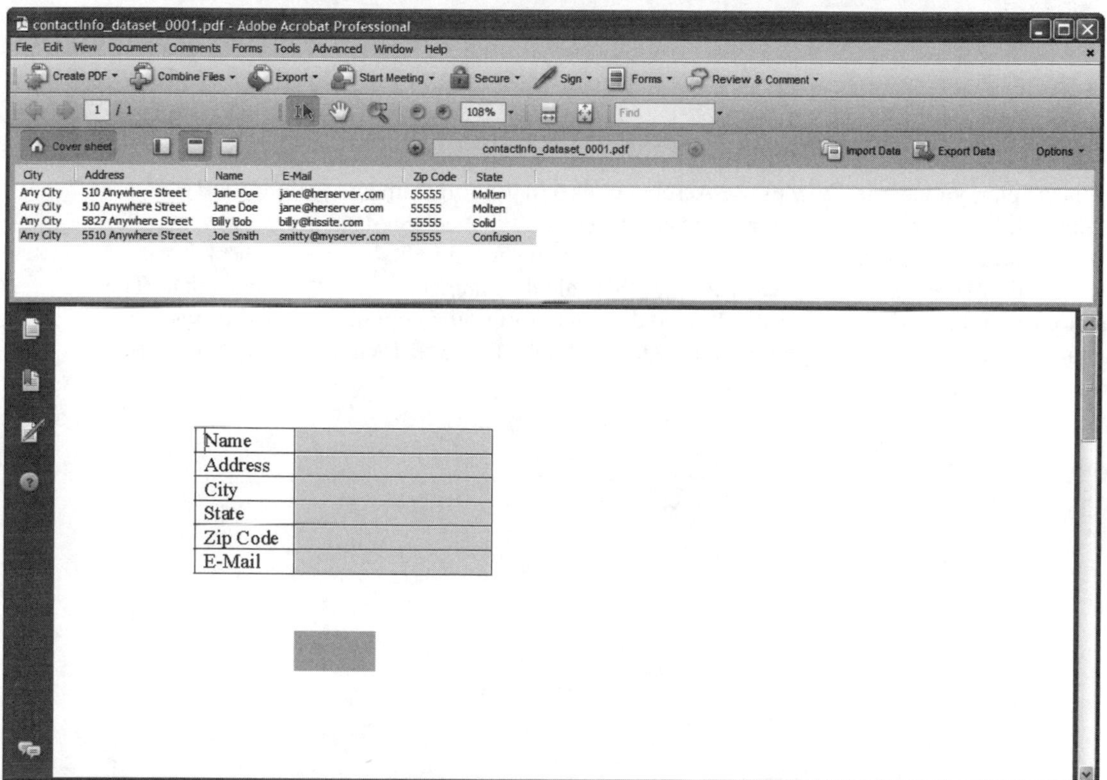

8. Click a block of data to see it inside the form.
9. Click the green right-pointing arrow to display each subsequent block of data in the original form.
10. Click Export Data to open the Select Folder To Save File dialog box.
11. Accept the default name or enter a different name, navigate to the desired folder, and then click Save. Acrobat saves the data as a Comma Separated Value (CSV) file, which you can open as a spreadsheet.

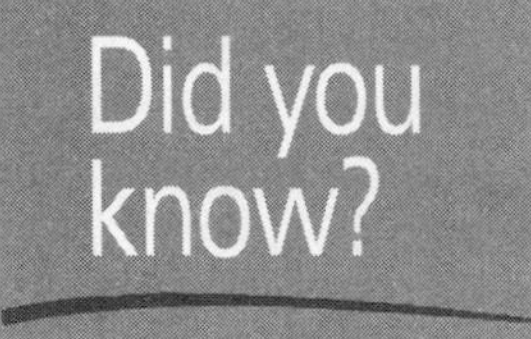

Manage Forms

When you distribute forms, you can easily manage them using the Forms Tracker. This is similar to the Review Tracker and contains the following categories: **To Do**, which displays forms you've received; **History**, which displays forms you've distributed; **Search Results**, which enables you to search for specific forms; and **Library**, which displays the forms you saved for future distribution. To display the Forms Tracker, choose Forms | Track Forms. Or, click the Forms task button and choose Track Forms.

Summary

In this chapter, you learned how to use Acrobat tools to add form elements to your PDF documents. You learned how to create and edit form fields that collect data, allow viewers to make a choice from a list or combo box, and choose items using radio buttons or check boxes. You also discovered how to create form fields that calculate numeric data and validate data. The final topics of discussion showed you how to distribute forms and compile returned forms into a data set. In the next chapter, you learn how to use Adobe Designer (Windows only) to create forms from scratch.

Chapter 15

Create Forms with Adobe LiveCycle Designer (Windows Only)

How to...

- Create a PDF form using a template
- Create a PDF form from scratch
- Add form fields
- Create calculation scripts
- Create copies of form fields
- Preview a form

Prior to Acrobat 7.0, the only way you could create a PDF form was to convert a document in an authoring application, such as Microsoft Word, into PDF format. Or, you could scan an existing paper document as the basis for your form. After you converted the document to a PDF file, you'd use the form tools to add form fields to your form. With the Windows version of Acrobat 7.0, Adobe offered another tool to create forms: Adobe LiveCycle Designer.

Adobe LiveCycle Designer 8.0 is an application that ships with the Windows version of Acrobat 8.0 Professional. The application enables you to create a sophisticated form by using one of the preset templates or by starting with a blank document, and then dropping form elements, such as text boxes, check boxes, list boxes, and submit buttons into the form. The application also enables you to add text objects and graphic objects to your form. You can then publish the form as a PDF document.

Create Forms with Adobe LiveCycle Designer 8.0

Adobe LiveCycle Designer 8.0 enables you to create a sophisticated form by dragging-and-dropping form elements into the workspace. You can use one of the preset templates to create a form, or add elements, such as images and text, to create a custom form from scratch.

The form you create in Adobe LiveCycle Designer has tremendous flexibility. You can use your own graphics in the form, create text as needed, and add the needed form elements to complete your form. You can also choose the manner in which the form results are returned: HTML submission to a URL, e-mail submission, or print. The electronic forms of submission send the form data to the URL or e-mail address specified when the form is created. The saved or submitted data can then be imported into the form in Acrobat Professional or Acrobat Standard.

When you create a form in Adobe LiveCycle Designer 8.0, the application writes XML code that places the elements within the form. If you're conversant with XML code, you can view and modify the XML source code, which changes the fields in the PDF form. The versatile application also features database and XML connectivity. Unfortunately, this feature is beyond the scope of this introduction to Adobe LiveCycle Designer 8.0.

Launch Adobe LiveCycle Designer 8.0

You can launch Adobe LiveCycle Designer 8.0 either from within Acrobat or by selecting Start | Programs | Adobe LiveCycle Designer 8.0 in Windows. After you launch the application, a wizard guides you through the process of creating a form from a template or creating a new blank form. The wizard also lets you specify the manner in which the form is submitted by end users. Here's how to get started:

1. In Acrobat, choose Forms | Create New Form. Acrobat Professional displays the Create New Form dialog box, shown next.

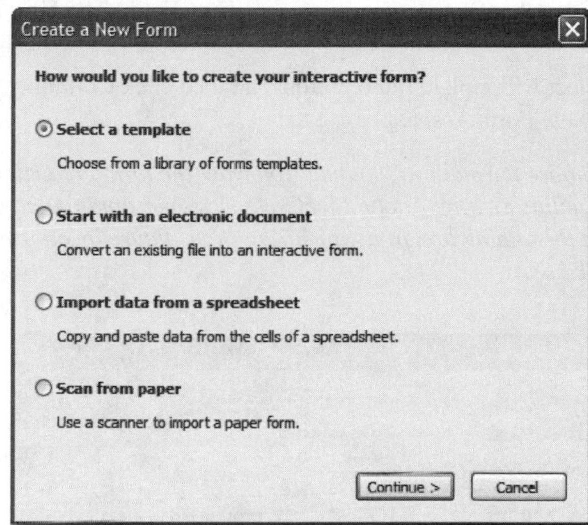

2. Click the applicable radio button to choose the manner in which you want to create the form.
3. Click Continue. What happens next depends on the method you selected. If you choose Select a Template, the New Form Assistant Wizard appears in Adobe LiveCycle Designer 8.0, whereupon you're prompted to select a template and the manner in which the data is submitted. If you choose Start with an Electronic Document, the Create a New Form Dialog box appears, which prompts you to import the file you want to convert into a form. If you choose Import Data from a Spreadsheet, the New Form Assistant Wizard appears, which prompts you to set up the document and copy the cells from the spreadsheet that will be the basis for the form. If you choose Scan from Paper, the Create a New Form dialog box appears, prompting you to begin the scanning process. After the paper form is scanned, Acrobat identifies the forms fields and hands off the form to the Adobe LifeCycle Designer 8.0.

Create Custom Forms with Adobe LiveCycle Designer 8.0

After you launch Adobe LiveCycle Designer 8.0, you can create all manner of forms with the application. You can use a template as the basis for your new form or create a form from scratch. The application affords you a tremendous amount of versatility because you can create text and import images into the application.

Create a New Form from a Template

The easiest way to create a form in Adobe LiveCycle Designer is to use a template. The application has a wide variety of templates for almost every imaginable business use. You can customize the forms by adding your company name and logo. To create a new form from a template:

1. From within Acrobat, choose Forms | Create New Form. The New Form Assistant appears.
2. Click the Select A Template radio button, and then click Continue. The Document Setup page of the New Form Assistant appears:

NOTE *After you choose the manner in which you want the form created, Acrobat displays a dialog box telling you the Adobe LiveCycle Designer application creates the form. You can prevent this dialog box from appearing in the future by clicking the Do Not Show Again check box.*

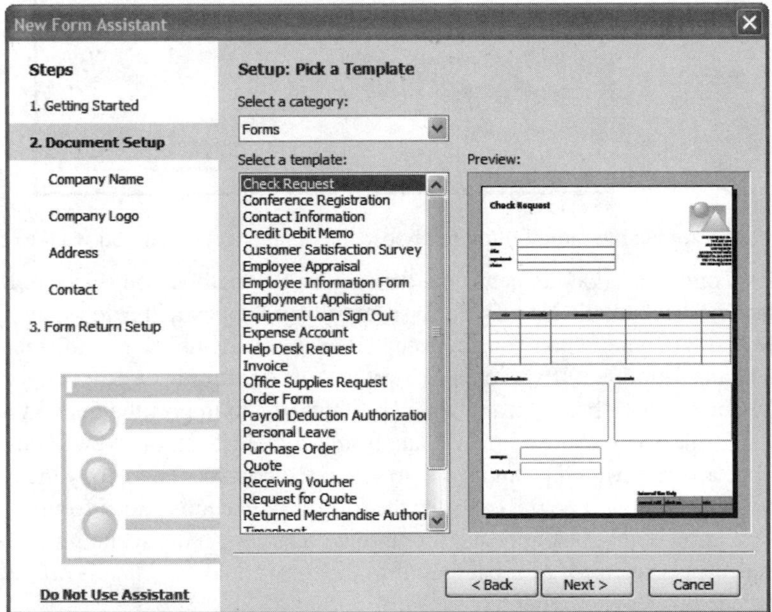

3. Click the Select a Category drop-down arrow and choose an option from the drop-down list. The list gives you the option of starting with a blank form, a form on a white background, or a form on a vanilla, beige, or blue background.
4. Click a template name to display a preview of the form in the Preview pane.
5. After you select the desired template, click Next. At this stage of the process, you're prompted for several items: company name, company logo, address, and contact information. After supplying the information, click Next.

6. The Form Return Setup page of the New Form Assistant appears. The options to add an e-mail button and a print button are selected by default.
7. Enter your e-mail address, and then click Finish.
8. The completed form appears in the Adobe LiveCycle Designer 8.0 workspace, as shown in Figure 15-1.

Create a Form from Scratch

You can also use Adobe LiveCycle Designer to create a custom form. To do this, you begin by creating a blank form, which, in essence, gives you a blank canvas with which to work. Then, you add form objects, such as text fields, check boxes, list boxes, and so on to the document. You can also add custom touches, such as a text header with your company name, and, if desired,

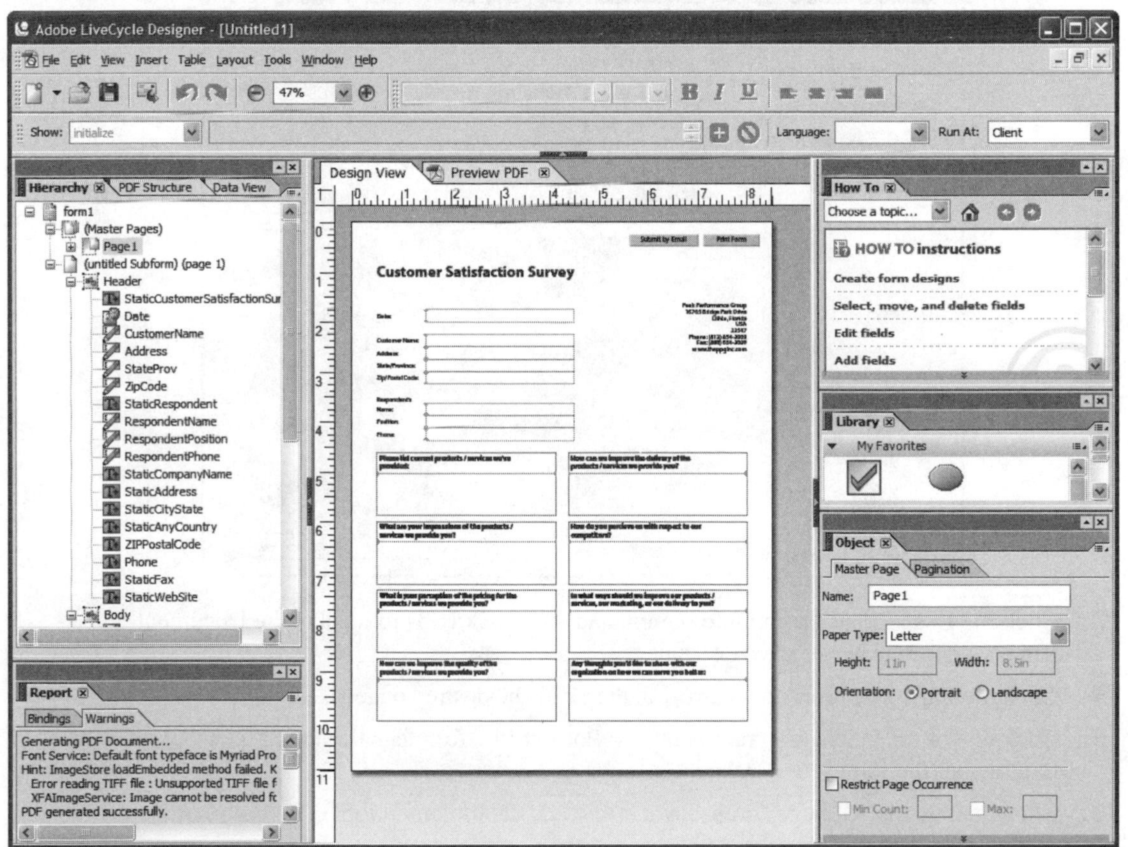

FIGURE 15-1 You can create an interactive form using an Adobe LiveCycle Designer template.

a graphic of your company logo. In the following sections, you learn how to create an invoice form that inserts the price of each object the customer orders and tallies the final cost of the sale, including sales tax.

Create a Blank Form

Creating a blank form is the first step in creating any custom form. After you create the blank form, you can begin adding form elements.

1. Launch Adobe LiveCycle Designer 8.0 from your Windows Start menu. With most installations the path is: Start | Programs | Adobe LiveCycle Designer 8.0.
2. Choose File | New to display the New Form Assistant, shown in the following illustration.

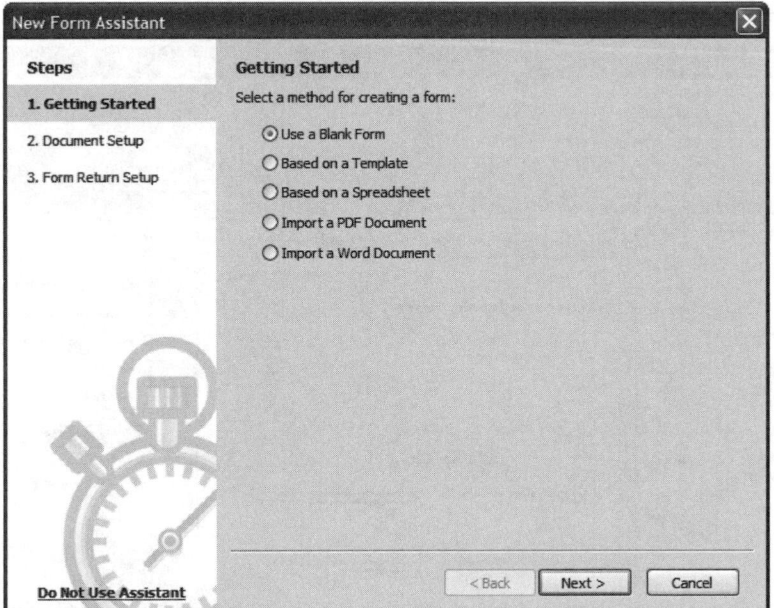

3. Click the Use a Blank Form radio button, and then click Next to display the Document Setup page of the New Form Assistant.
4. Click the Page Size drop-down arrow and choose the desired page size.
5. Click one of the Orientation radio buttons: Portrait (the form is taller than it is wide) or Landscape (the form is wider than it is tall).
6. Click the Number Of Pages drop-down arrow and choose an option.

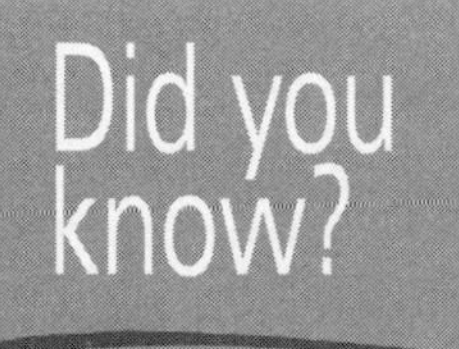

Create a Form from a PDF File or Word Document

You can easily create a form using an existing PDF file or a Word document as the basis for your form. Launch Adobe LiveCycle Designer, and then choose File | New. Within the first page of the New Form Assistant, click the Import A PDF Document or Import A Word Document radio button to import the document into Adobe LiveCycle Designer 8.0. You can then flesh out the form by adding form fields as outlined in the upcoming sections.

NOTE

When you use the wizard, you cannot create a form with more than ten pages. After the wizard creates the form, however, you can add pages to the form by choosing Insert | New Page.

7. Click Next to display the Form Return Setup page of the New Form Assistant. These are the same options discussed previously in the section "Create a New Form from a Template."
8. Enter the return information, and then click Finish. Adobe LiveCycle Designer 8.0 creates a new blank form.

After you create a blank form, you populate the form with elements from the application's Library palette. To add an element to your form, select it in the Library, click the location where you want the upper-left corner of the element to appear, and then drag diagonally to size the form element.

Create a Header Section

You can create a header section for your form that identifies your company. You use the Text object to add your company's contact information to the header. If desired, you can also use the Image object to insert a picture of your company's logo in the form. To create a header section, follow these steps:

1. Select the Text object from the Library.
2. Click where you want the upper-left corner of the header to appear, and then drag diagonally to size the element. If you move your cursor outside the margins of the form, a circle with a slash appears, indicating you cannot create a form element in this part of the document. As you create the object, it snaps to the grid, making it easy for you to accurately align the object to the margins or, if present, other objects in the form.

If you have two objects occupying the same space, the last placed object is at the top of the stacking order. You can rearrange the stacking order by choosing one of the following commands from the Layout menu: Bring To Front, Bring Forward, Send Backward, or Send To Back.

3. If desired, you can resize and reposition the Text object by entering values in the Layout palette (Window | Layout) shown next.

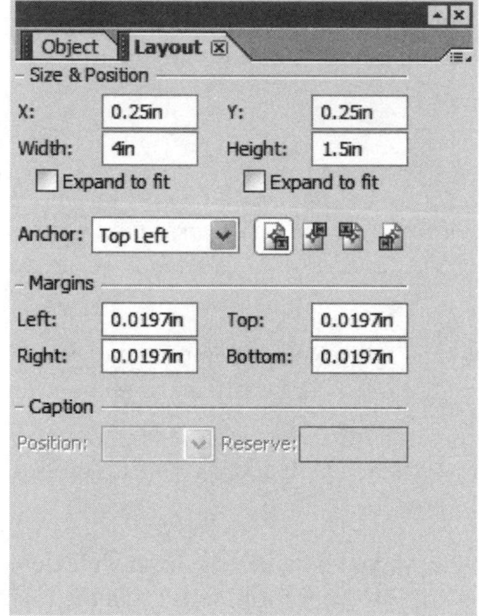

4. Select the default text of the Text object and enter the desired text.
5. Format the text as desired. From the toolbar at the top of the workspace, you can specify the font face, font size, style, and alignment. These are almost identical to the tools you find for formatting text in a word processing application.
6. If desired, you can flesh out the header by adding a logo, which you do by dragging the Image object from the Library into the desired position in your form.
7. From within the Object palette (Window | Object), click the folder icon to the right of the URL field and select the logo you want in the header. If you're sending the form for distribution, choose the Embed Image Data, which embeds the image in the form.
8. Click the PDF Preview tab. Your header should resemble Figure 15-2.

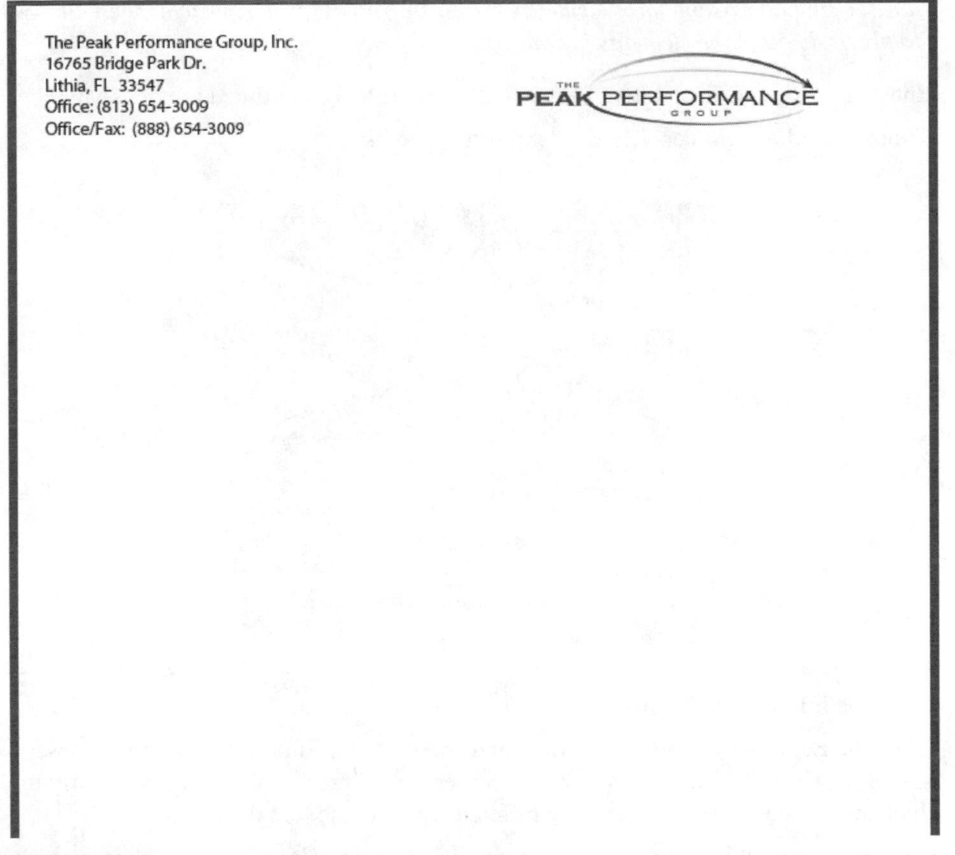
The Peak Performance Group, Inc.
16765 Bridge Park Dr.
Lithia, FL 33547
Office: (813) 654-3009
Office/Fax: (888) 654-3009

FIGURE 15-2 You can create a header for your form.

Creating Column Headers

If you create a rough sketch of your form before launching Adobe LiveCycle Designer 8.0, you'll have a good idea of how many fields you need in the document. When you're creating a form like an invoice, you often need column headers to display what each column in the form does. To create form column headers, follow these steps:

1. Select the Text object from the Library palette.
2. Click the lower-left corner of the header, and then drag diagonally to create the field.

Adobe LiveCycle Designer 8.0 will snap new form objects to existing elements in the form. Using an existing form element as a starting point for a new element enables you to precisely align the elements in your form.

3. Enter the desired text, and then format and align the text as outlined previously.
4. Choose Window | Border. The Border palette appears:

5. Click the Edges drop-down arrow and choose Edit Together.
6. Click the Edges style drop-down arrow and choose Solid. If desired, you can choose one of the Corners options to stylize the corners of the border. You can also modify the thickness of the border by entering a different value in the text field.
7. Accept the default border color (black), or click the Edge Color icon and choose a color from the pop-up palette.
8. Click the Background Fill Style drop-down arrow and choose an option from the drop-down list.
9. Click the color button and choose the desired background color from the pop-up palette. Note, if you choose one of the gradient (Linear or Radial) or Pattern options, two color buttons are available in LiveCycle Designer 8.0. However, gradient fills on buttons aren't supported in Acrobat 8.0.

Gradient fills on buttons isn't supported by Acrobat. The first color you select for the background color is the solid color used in Acrobat as the background fill.

10. Repeat Steps 1-8 to create the other column headers for your form. The following illustration shows a typical column header displayed below the document header:

NOTE

If you make use of rounded and otherwise stylized corners for buttons or other objects, the stylization won't come through in the resultant PDF.

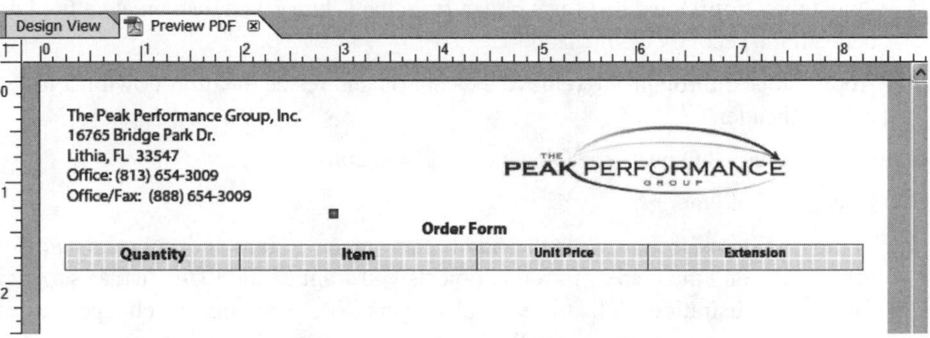

TIP

When you create additional headers for your form, they snap to the previously created headers, enabling you to create headers with no gaps and of equal height. You can resize a header by entering values in the Layout palette or by clicking the header, which causes eight handles to appear around the perimeter of the object. Click a corner handle to resize the object's width and height. Press SHIFT *to resize proportionately. Click the middle handle on either end of the object, and then drag left or right to change the width of the object. Click the center handle on the top or bottom of the object, and then drag up or down to change the height of the object.*

Add Form Fields

You can add form fields to flesh out your form. Form fields can be read-only, or fields in which users can enter data. The invoice form in this exercise uses several rows of fields that enable users to order several products. On each row, users specify the quantity and product they want to order. The final fields in each row display the unit price of the selected product and the extended price. Follow these steps to add form fields to your form:

1. Select the Numeric Field object from the Library, and then create a field directly under the first column header.
2. Choose Window | Layout. The Layout palette appears.
3. In the Caption section at the bottom, click the Position drop-down arrow and select None. This removes the caption from the form element, which isn't needed because this form has a row of column headings.
4. Select the Numeric form field you just created, and then select the first column header.
5. Choose Layout | Make Same Size | Both.

NOTE *When using the Make Same Size command, make sure the object you want other elements sized to is selected last.*

6. Select the Drop-Down List form object from the Library, and then create a field directly beneath the second column header.
7. Apply Steps 2 through 5 to remove the caption and resize the drop-down list to the column header.
8. Click Window | Object. The Object palette appears.
9. Click the Field tab.
10. In the List Items section, click the Add button (green + sign) and enter the name of the first object, and then repeat for other objects you want to add to the list, as shown in the following illustration. Note, there are also icons to delete items and change the order in which items are displayed in the list.

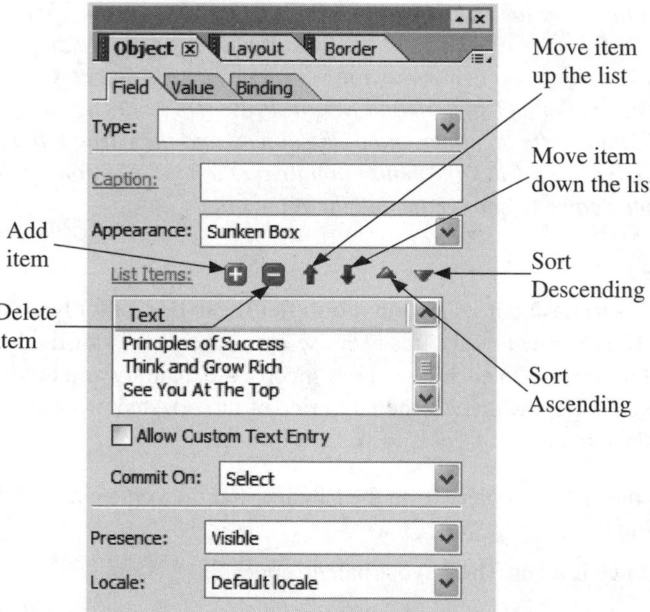

11. Click the Binding tab. Select the default name in the Name field and enter the desired name in its place. For in this example invoice, change the name to product, as shown here.

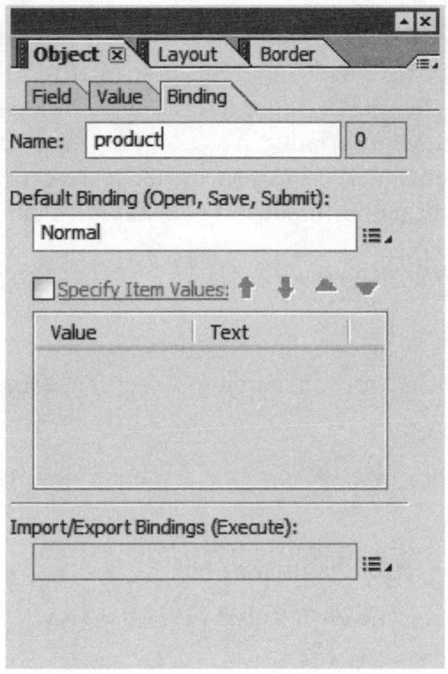

12. Click the Specify Item Values check box. The item names you entered in Step 10 are displayed and given default values. These values are changed to the actual price of each item, which is displayed in the Unit Price column after you create a simple script.
13. Double-click the value of the first item in the list, and then enter the desired value. Repeat for each item in the list.
14. Select the Numeric Field object from the Library and create a field underneath the third column header. Remove the caption and resize the object to its corresponding header, as outlined in Steps 2 through 5.
15. Select the Numeric Field object again and create a field underneath the fourth column header. Remove the caption and resize the object to its corresponding header, as outlined in Steps 2 through 5.
16. Select the third numeric field, and click the Align Right icon in the toolbar. Repeat for the fourth numeric field.

TIP *You can align fields to each other by selecting them, and then choosing Layout | Align, and then choosing the desired alignment option from the drop-down menu. Alignment is made to the last item selected. You can also evenly distribute selected form elements by choosing Layout | Distribute, and then choosing the desired option from the drop-down menu. Another option is to align selected form objects to the page by choosing Layout | Center in Page, and then choosing the desired option from the drop-down menu.*

Create Calculation Scripts

After creating the form fields, it's time to add the scripts that will display the unit price and calculate the extended price. Scripts in Adobe LiveCycle Designer can be created using the FormCalc or JavaScript method of scripting. You also have to give the fields in your document unique names, as they're used in the scripts you create. In the previous section, you already gave the Drop-Down List object the name "product." You still have three fields to name.

NOTE *Don't include spaces when creating a field name because a name with spaces cannot be used in a script.*

1. Select the first field and choose Window | Object. The Object palette appears.
2. Click the Binding tab.
3. Select the default name in the Name field and enter **quantity** in its place.
4. Select the third field.
5. On the Object palette, click the Binding tab.
6. Select the default name and enter **unitPrice** in its place.
7. In the Object palette, click the Field tab.
8. Click the Display Pattern drop-down arrow and choose $z,zz9.99. This formats the field, so the price is displayed in the currency format.
9. Choose Window | Script Editor, and then click the Show drop-down arrow in the Script Editor and choose calculate*.
10. Enter the following in the Script Editor text field: **(product)**. This simple script creates XML code that displays the value for the product selected from the *product* drop-down list.
11. Select the fourth field.
12. In the Object palette, click the Binding tab.
13. Select the default name and enter **extendedPrice** in its place.
14. In the Object palette, click the Field tab.
15. Click the Display Pattern drop-down arrow and choose $z,zz9.99, so the price is displayed in the currency format.
16. In the Script Editor, click the Show drop-down arrow and choose calculate*.
17. Enter the following in the Script Editor text field: **(quantity*product)**. This simple script creates XML code that multiplies the value entered in the *quantity* times the value of the item selected from the *product* drop-down list.

To flesh out a multirow form like an invoice, you can create multiple copies of the fields in the first row to create additional rows in your form. Before copying the fields, though, testing your form to make sure the first row is formatted correctly and the scripts perform as desired is a good idea.

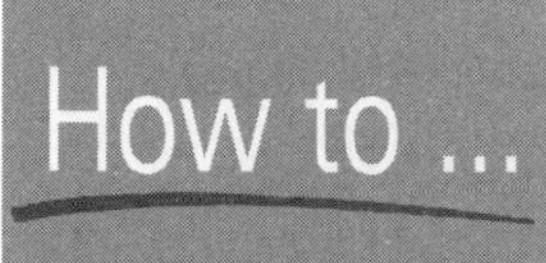

Preview a Form in Adobe LiveCycle Designer

After creating your form, you can preview and test the form prior to saving it. It's also a good idea to test a form while you're constructing it to make sure everything is functioning properly before copying fields. To preview a form, click the PDF Preview tab to display the form as it will appear in Adobe Acrobat or Adobe Reader. You can then test the form fields to make sure everything is working properly.

NOTE *You can view the hierarchy of all fields in your form by clicking the Hierarchy tab.*

Create Multiple Copies of Form Fields

After you test the first row of your form and know all the fields are formatted properly and are calculating correctly, you can create copies of each form field to create the additional rows for your form. When you copy fields to create multiple rows, you don't have to rename the fields. Adobe LiveCycle Designer takes care of this for you. To create copies of form fields:

1. Select the first form field in the first row.
2. Choose Edit | Copy Multiple. The Copy Multiple dialog box appears:

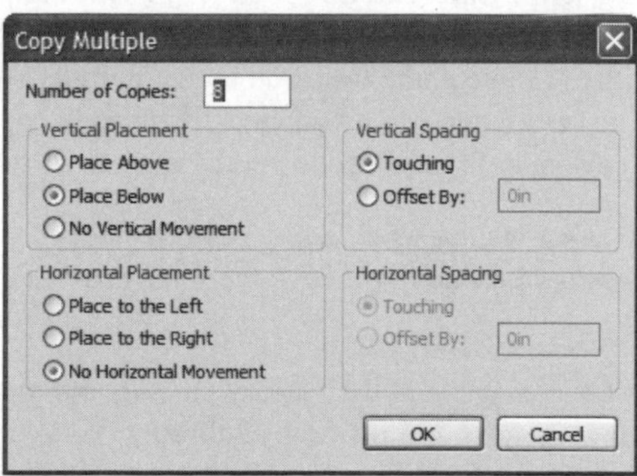

3. Enter the desired number of copies in the Number Of Copies field.
4. In the Vertical Placement section, click the applicable radio button to specify how you want the copies placed vertically. In the case of the product invoice form, the copies are placed below the selected field.

5. In the Horizontal Placement section, click the applicable radio button to specify how you want the copies placed horizontally. In the case of the product invoice form, the copied field won't be moved horizontally.
6. Repeat Steps 2 through 5 to create multiple copies of the last three fields in the first row.

Finalize the Form

After you create multiple copies of the first row of fields, you need to create fields to calculate the total of all items purchased, the sales tax, and the total invoice price. The final step is to create text fields that enable users to enter their personal information.

1. Select the Numeric Field object in the Library, and then create a field as wide as the last two fields in the last row of copied fields.
2. Select the object caption and enter **Subtotal**.
3. Select the Subtotal text, click the Bold icon in the toolbar, and then click the Align Left icon. This aligns the caption text to the left of the field.
4. Click inside the numeric field to the right of the caption.
5. Click the Paragraph tab. Click the Align Right icon. This aligns the subtotal to the right of the field.
6. Choose Window | Object. The Object palette appears.
7. Click the Field tab. Click the Display Pattern drop-down arrow and choose $z,zz9.99.
8. Click the Binding tab. Select the default text in the Name field and enter **subTotal** in its place.
9. In the Script Editor, click the Show drop-down arrow and choose calculate.
10. Enter the following script: **sum(extendedPrice[*])**. This script creates a sum by adding each value in the extendedPrice fields. The asterisk signifies the value comes from multiple fields with the same name followed by the number Adobe LiveCycle Designer 8.0 appended to the field name when you created multiple copies. For example, the name of the first field is extendedPrice[0], followed by extendedPrice[1], and so on.

NOTE *Field names are case-sensitive. If a script doesn't perform as expected, make sure the field names are spelled properly and have the same case as the field that accepts the data.*

11. Select the Numeric Field object in the Library palette, and then create an additional form field below the subTotal field. Follow Steps 2 through 10 to create a field with a caption that reads Sales Tax. In the Field tab of the Object palette, choose the $z,zz9.99 Display Pattern option, and in the Binding tab, enter **salesTax** in the Name field. Align the caption to the left and numbers to the right, as outlined previously.

12. In the Script Editor, click the Show drop-down arrow and choose calculate *.
13. Enter the following script: **(subTotal*0.075)**. This script calculates the sales tax by multiplying the subtotal by a value that represents the sales tax for the region in which the product is being sold. In this case, the sales tax is 7.5 percent. If you were creating the form for Internet sales, you would charge sales tax only to buyers who are in the same state in which the product is being sold. You could create a drop-down list with the abbreviation for each state. You would then set the value to zero for each state other than the state in which the product is being sold. You would choose the applicable value for sales tax in your state and modify the script to read something like *(subTotal*state),* where *state* is the drop-down list field from which users choose the state in which they live.
14. Select the Numeric Field object in the Library palette, and then create an additional form field below the salesTax field. Follow Steps 2 through 10 to create a field with a caption that reads Total Sale. In the Field tab of the Object palette, choose the $z,zz9.99 option from the Display Pattern drop-down menu. In the Binding tab, enter **total** in the Name field.
15. In the Script Editor, click the Show drop-down arrow and choose calculate*.
16. Enter the following script: **(subTotal+salesTax)**. This script adds the result of the subTotal field to the result of the salesTax field.
17. Select the Text Field object from the Library and create a field below and to the left of the Total field.
18. Select the default caption and enter **Customer Name**. Format the text as desired.
19. Choose Window | Object. After the Object palette opens, click the Binding tab.
20. Select the default name in the Name field and enter **custName** in its place.
21. Repeat Steps 18 through 21 to create the additional fields for customer information, such as street address, city, state, and ZIP code. Each field name should be unique, for example, streetAddress. Field names cannot contain spaces. Figure 15-3 shows the completed form with form fields filled out as previewed in Adobe Acrobat.
22. Choose File | Save. The Save dialog box appears.
23. Enter a name for the form, and then navigate to the folder in which you want to save the form.
24. Click Save. This saves the project as a PDF document.

TIP

After saving a form, you can distribute the form by choosing File | Distribute. This launches Acrobat and prompts you for the recipients to whom you want to distribute the form. This is identical to the Acrobat Distribute Form that was discussed in Chapter 14.

The Peak Performance Group, Inc.
16765 Bridge Park Dr.
Lithia, FL 33547
Office: (813) 654-3009
Office/Fax: (888) 654-3009

THE PEAK PERFORMANCE GROUP

Order Form

Quantity	Item	Unit Price	Extension
4	Dress For Success eBook	$9.95	$39.80
2	Principles of Success	$14.95	$29.90
		Subtotal	$69.70
		Sales Tax	$5.23
		Total Sale	$74.93

FIGURE 15-3 The completed invoice form is put to the test in Adobe Acrobat.

Summary

In this chapter, you received an introduction to Adobe LiveCycle Designer 8.0. You learned how to create a new form from an Adobe LiveCycle Designer 8.0 template, as well as how to create a form from scratch. You learned how to work with the application's form field elements, and how to create scripts to calculate results based on the content of other form fields in the document. In the next chapter, you discover how to harness Acrobat Professional's powerful print production prepress features.

Chapter 16

Optimize PDF Documents for Print

How to...

- Create PDF/X-compliant documents
- Perform a preflight check
- Preview print separations
- Preview transparency flattening
- Add information for the printer
- Use the Print Production toolbar

Acrobat 8.0 continues to provide robust tools for prepress print production. Document authors can create Portable Document Format Exchange (PDF/X)-compliant documents that are ideally suited for documents that will be printed commercially. The PDF/X format follows a set of rigid guidelines that ensures your printed document looks identical to the document you created in your authoring application. Before sending a document to a publisher or a printer, you can use the powerful set of prepress tools in Acrobat 8.0 to perform sophisticated tests to ensure your document is ready for print. In this chapter, you learn how to use these tools on your own documents before sending them to the printer.

Create PDF/X-Compliant Documents

PDF/X is now the standard for PDF documents destined for printers and publishers. The *PDF/X format* ensures the document will be printed correctly, while maintaining color and font integrity. The author creates the document using graphics and fonts in an illustration or publishing application, and then exports a PDF document that's PDF/X-compliant. You can export a PDF-X compliant PDF document from the authoring application, or convert a PDF document to PDF/X standards within Acrobat Professional.

Create a PDF/X-Compliant Document in an Authoring Application

You use an application's Print command to create a PDF/X-compliant document from within an authoring application using Adobe PDF as the printer. You can specify the version of PDF/X with which the document will be compliant in the Print Properties dialog box.

1. Choose your application's Print command, and then choose Adobe PDF as the printer.
2. Click the Properties button to display the Adobe PDF Document Properties dialog box.

3. Click the Adobe PDF tab.
4. Click the Default Settings drop-down arrow and choose one of the PDF/X conversion settings from the drop-down menu, shown here:
5. If necessary, click the Edit button to edit the conversion setting, as outlined in Chapter 12.
6. Exit the Adobe PDF Document Properties dialog box.
7. Print the document.

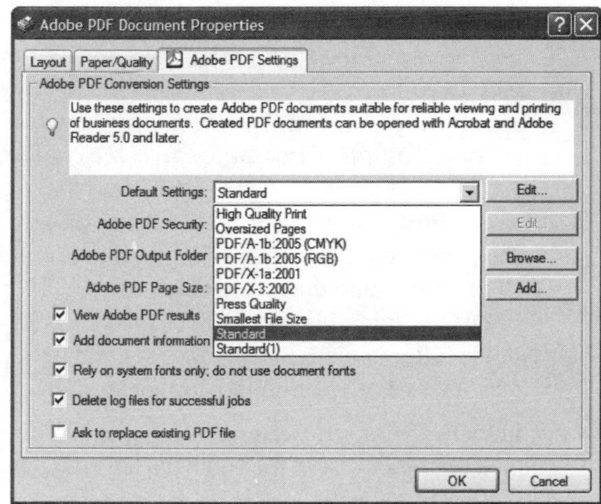

Perform a Preflight Check

Within Acrobat, you can check an existing document to make sure it's compliant with the PDF/X format by performing a preflight check. When you perform a preflight check, you choose the version of Acrobat with which the document will be compliant. To perform a preflight check, follow these steps:

1. Open the PDF document you want to check.
2. Choose Advanced | Print Production | Preflight. The Preflight dialog box appears and Acrobat begins loading profiles:

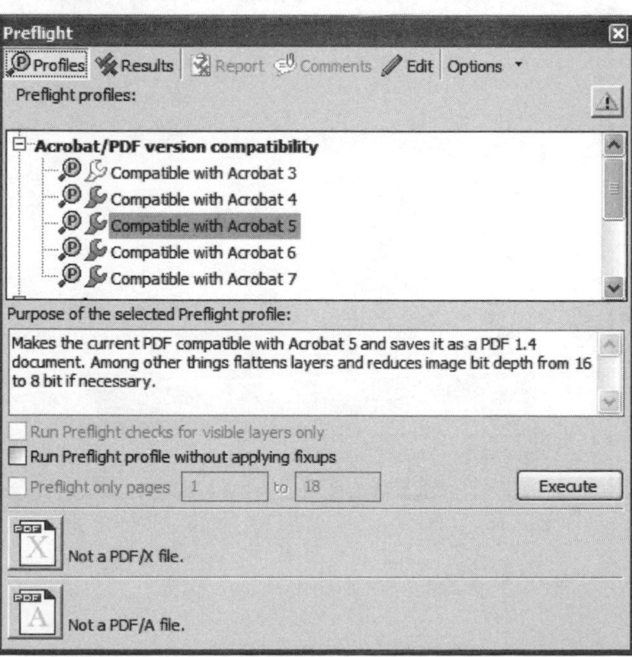

After the profiles load, you might see a yellow exclamation point in the upper right-hand corner of the Preflight dialog box. Click the icon to open the Preflight: Display Settings Alert dialog box that warns you of any potential problems in the PDF, such as overprinting elements or present color management that doesn't have a corresponding embedded profile. Click Adjust to fix the conflict.

3. Select a Profile from the list (the version of Acrobat with which you want the document to be compatible), and then click Execute. Acrobat displays a warning that the profile will fix errors, and then close the document. Or, you can click the Run Preflight Profile without Applying Fixups check box to check for items that aren't PDF-X compliant. Another alternative is to click the Preflight only pages [ ] to [ ], which enables you to check a range of pages in the document.
4. Click OK to exit the warning dialog box and run the preflight tests. After the tests are run, a report similar to the following appears, showing any problems that are preventing PDF/X compliance:

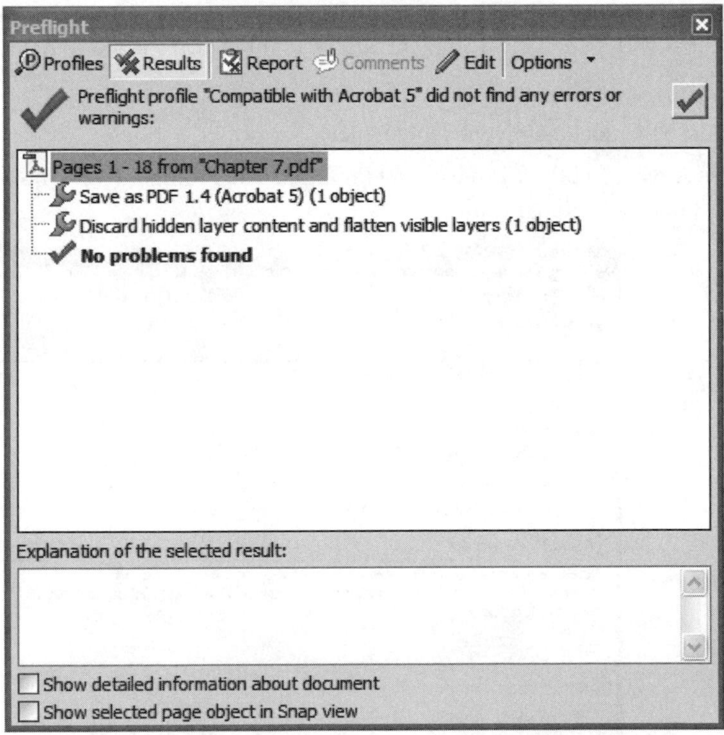

After you run the Preflight check, you have other options. Click the Show Detailed Information about Document check box, and Acrobat expands the list to show any problem areas in the document. Click an object, and then click the Show Select Page Object in Snap View check box to display the problem area in a small window, as shown next. If the problem area doesn't stand out, choose a different color from the Background Color drop-down menu.

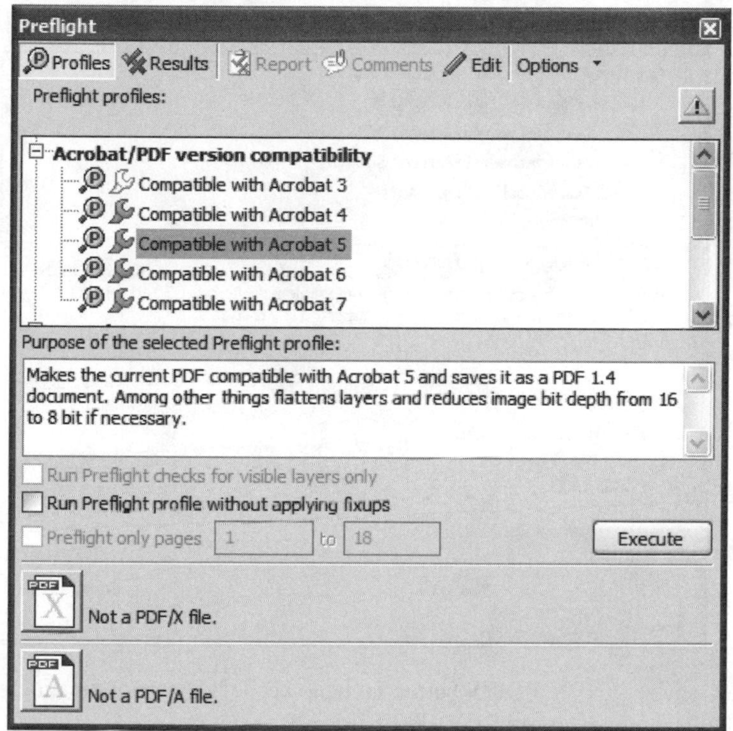

Convert an Existing PDF Document to PDF/X

After running a preflight check, if you find the PDF document isn't PDF/X compliant, you can attempt to convert it to PDF/X, using either the same profile against which you checked compliance or a different one:

1. Choose Advanced | Print Production | Preflight. The Preflight dialog box appears and Acrobat loads profiles.
2. Select the desired profile and click Execute. Acrobat runs a preflight check and displays the results, as outlined previously.

3. After reviewing the results, click the Profiles button. The Profiles section of the Preflight dialog box appears.

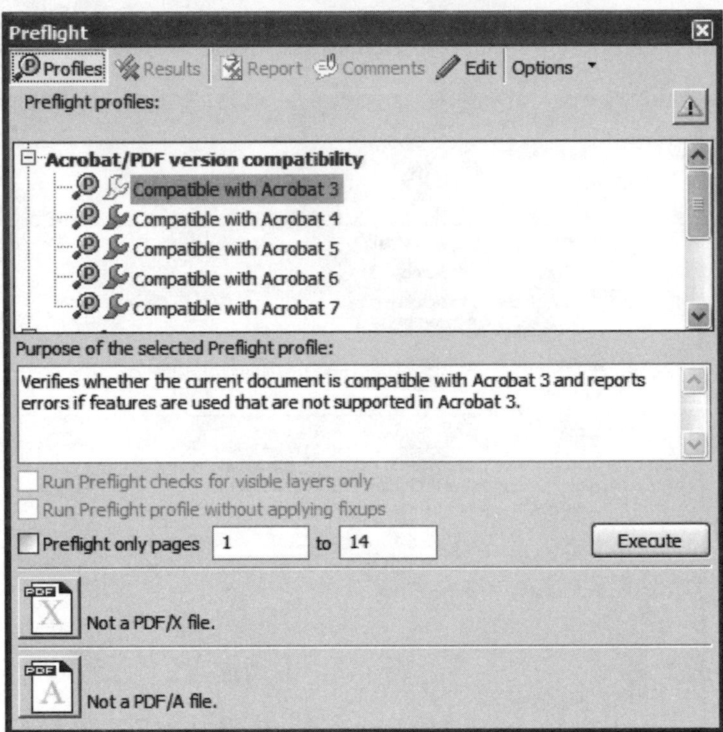

4. Click the Convert PDF To PDF/X button in the lower-left corner of the dialog box to display the Preflight: Convert To PDF/X dialog box:

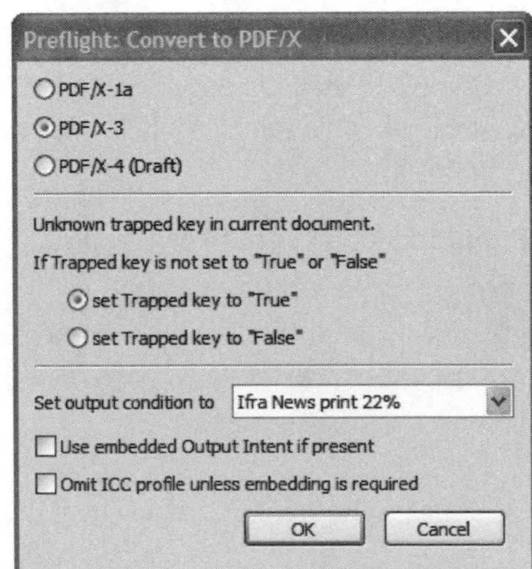

5. Click the applicable radio button to specify the version of PDF/X to which the document is to be converted.
6. Choose an option for setting the Trapped key. If the document contains color-trapping information, choose Set Trapped Key To True. Otherwise, choose Set Trapped Key To False.
7. Click the Set Output Condition To drop-down arrow and choose the desired option. This option is the printing condition for which you prepared the document.
8. Click the Use embedded Output Intent if present. This option embeds Output Intent from the original document, which maps out of gamut colors to the output device.
9. Click the Omit ICC Profile Unless Embedding Is Required check box to remove an ICC profile that has been embedded with the original document.
10. Click OK. Acrobat attempts to convert the PDF to PDF/X. If the conversion fails, the Results section shows the items not in compliance. To convert the file to PDF/X, you have to address these issues in the application you used to create the document, and then use the application's Print command to convert the document to PDF or PDF/X. The following illustration shows a Preflight report for a file that has successfully been converted to PDF/X:

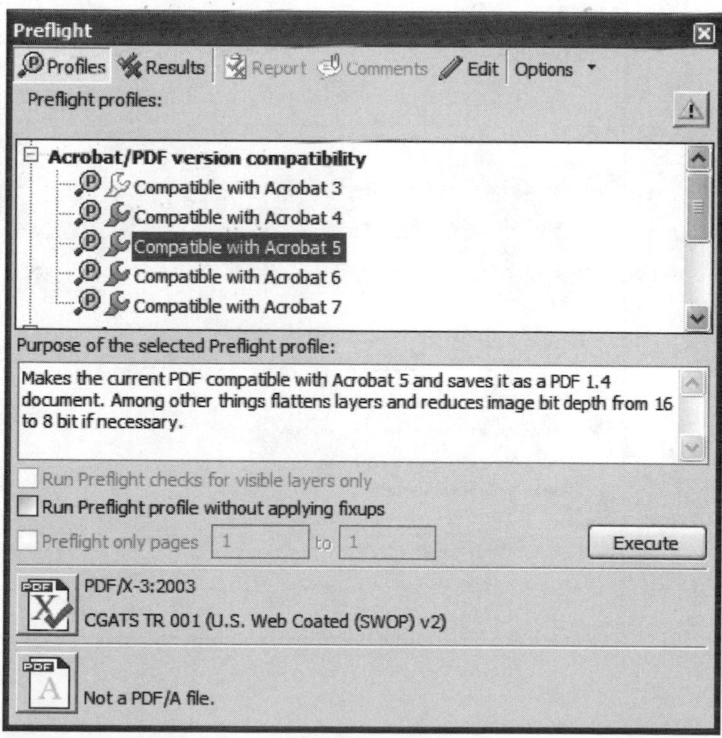

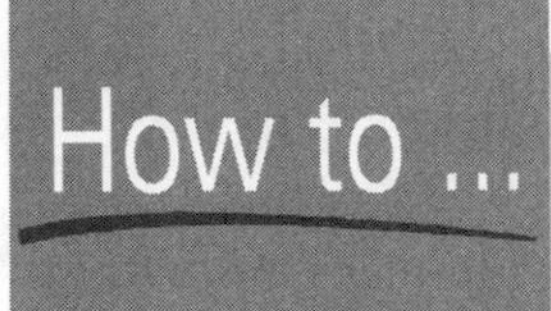

Convert Colors

Sometimes the only thing preventing a document from being PDF/X-compliant is the presence of RGB colors in the document. If this error appears on a Preflight report, or when you attempt to convert a PDF to PDF/X within Acrobat, you can convert the document colors to CMYK by choosing Advanced | Print Production | Convert Colors. This opens the Convert Colors dialog box, as shown here. Choose the applicable options, and then click OK. If you're unsure of which options to select, check with the service center or the publisher that will print the document.

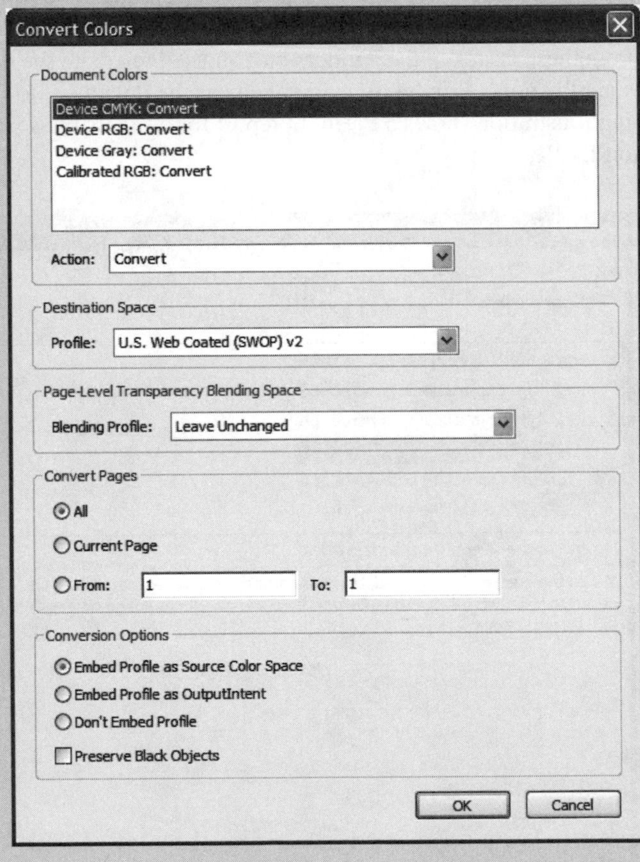

Perform Prepress Production Tests

When you prepare a PDF document for a printer, you can perform several tests to make sure the document is as desired. You can preview the color separations and transparent areas of the document, add information for the printer, and so on. You can also specify the sizes of the crop, trim, art, and bleed boxes—information the printer uses when setting up the printing device and trimming the printed pages.

Preview Print Separations

You can preview print separations before sending your work to the printer to ensure the separation plates and ink coverage meet your requirements. You get your best results when previewing separations if you're working with a calibrated monitor. To preview print separations:

1. Choose Advanced | Print Production | Output Preview. The Output Preview dialog box appears:

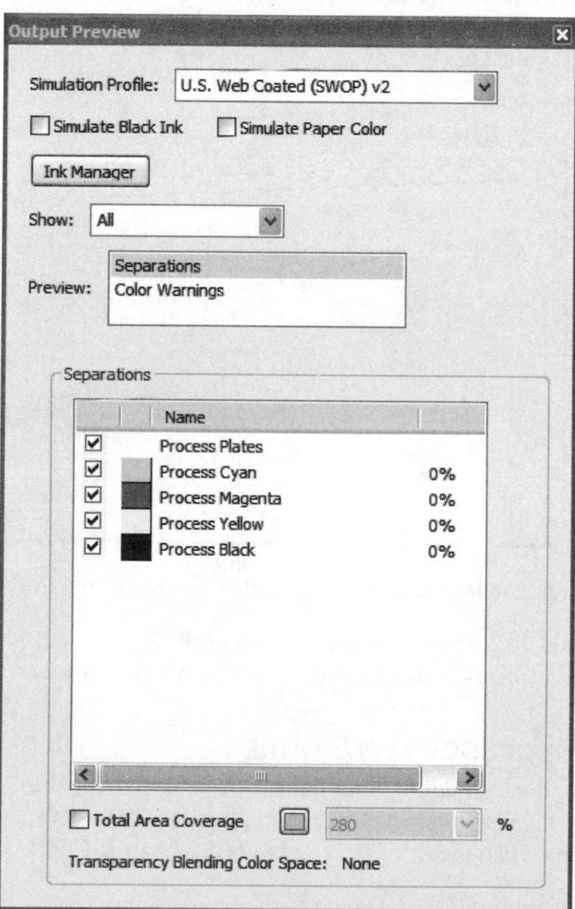

16

2. Check the Simulate Ink Black check box, and the document changes to show you how the black colors will appear when the document is printed.
3. Check the Simulate Paper White check box, and the document changes to show how the white of the paper will appear when the document is printed.
4. To preview an individual process plate or spot plate in the document, deselect the other colors by clicking their check boxes in the Separations section.
5. To view the percentages of ink in a specific area, hover your cursor over the area you want to check, and the percentage of each ink appears to the right of its name in the Output Preview dialog box.
6. Click the Ink Manager button to open the Ink Manager, shown next, which enables you to convert spot colors to process and modify the density of the inks used to print the document. The Ink Manager is primarily used by prepress service providers.

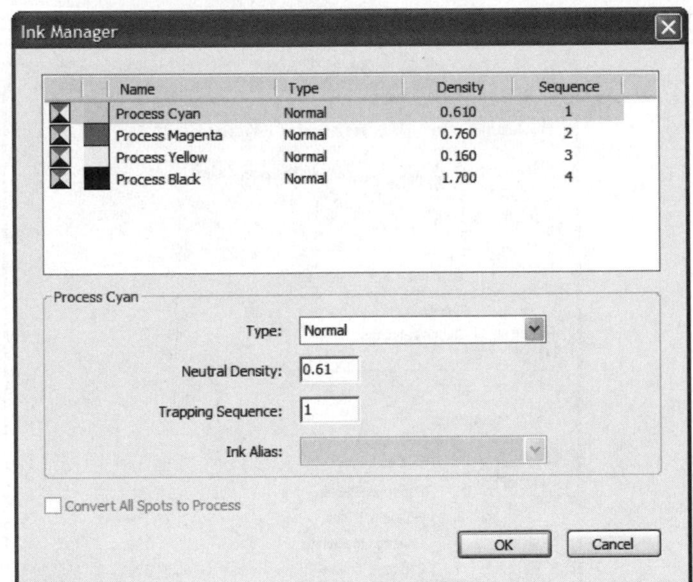

7. Click OK to exit the Ink Manager, and then close the Output Preview dialog box.

Choose Advanced | Print Production | Overprint Display and the display changes to approximate blending of colors and overprinting in color-separated output.

Preview Transparency Flattening

Today's illustration and image-editing programs make it easy to include transparency in a document. For transparency to print properly on some PostScript printers, though, the transparency needs to be flattened, or converted to raster images. Check with the service company handling your printing to see if transparency needs to be flattened. You can preview the way flattened transparency will appear and flatten transparency by doing the following:

1. Choose Advanced | Print Production | Flattener Preview. The Flattener Preview dialog box is displayed:

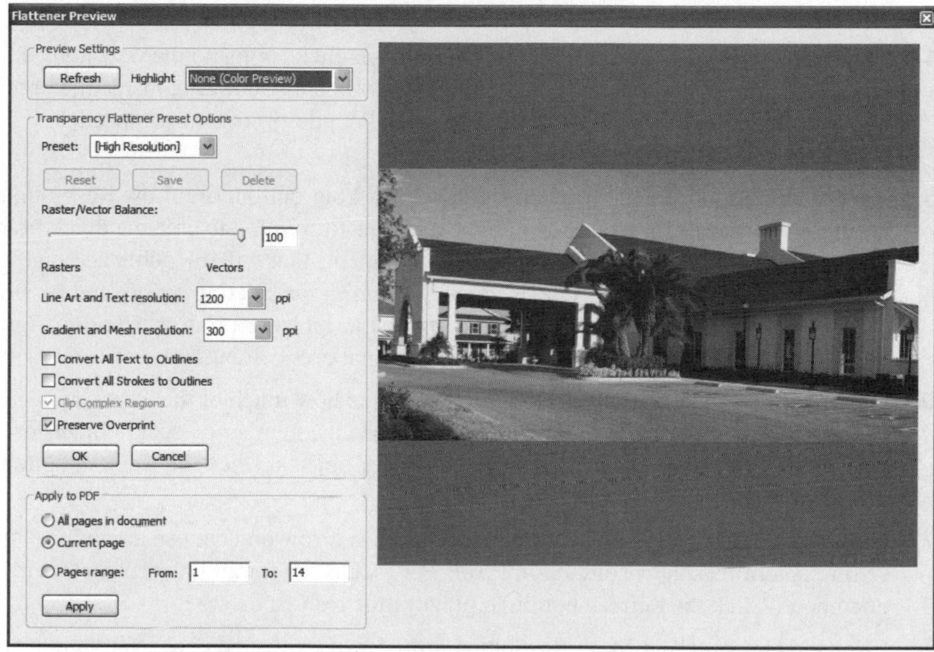

2. Click the Highlight drop-down arrow and choose the desired option to highlight. The options vary, depending on the artwork in the document and the Flattener setting specified in the Transparency Flattener section of the Acrobat Advanced Print Setup dialog box. The following is a list of all possible options:
   - **None (Color Preview)** The default option doesn't highlight transparent objects in the document and shows a color preview of the entire document.
   - **Rasterized/Complex Regions** Highlights the areas of the document that will be rasterized in accordance with the setting you specify with the Raster/Vector Balance slider in Step 5.
   - **Transparent Objects** Highlights objects in the document with transparency, objects with blending modes, and objects with opacity masks. In addition, objects with styles and effects that contain transparency are highlighted.
   - **All Effected Objects** Highlights all objects in the document that contain transparency, including objects that overlap transparent objects.

- **Expanded Patterns** Highlights all patterns that will be expanded if they contain transparency.
- **Outlined Strokes** Highlights all strokes that will be outlined if they contain transparency.

3. Click the Refresh button to refresh the preview and display the objects in accordance with the Highlight option you selected.
4. Click inside the preview window to zoom in. Each click zooms to the next highest level of magnification. While pressing the SPACEBAR, click-and-drag inside the preview window to pan within the document. CTRL-click (Windows) or COMMAND-click (Macintosh) to zoom out.
5. Choose an option from the Preset drop-down list. Your options are: Low Resolution, Medium Resolution, or High Resolution. Use *Low Resolution* to create a quick proof for output on a desktop printer, or for PDF documents that will be published on the web or converted to SVG format. Use *Medium Resolution* for creating proofs and for print on demand documents that will be output to PostScript color printers. Choose *High Resolution* for documents you're preparing for final press output.
6. Drag the Raster/Vector Balance slider to determine how much of the transparency will be converted to raster objects. Drag left to increase the number of raster objects or drag right to convert more transparent objects to vector objects. Click the Refresh button to preview the results.
7. Click the Line Art And Text Resolution drop-down arrow and choose an option. This setting determines the resolution in Pixels Per Inch (PPI) for all line art and text in the document. Click the Refresh button to preview the results.
8. Click the Gradient And Mesh Resolution drop-down arrow and choose an option. This setting determines the resolution in PPI for complex objects in the document.
9. Specify flattening options:
   - **Convert All Text To Outlines** Converts any text in the document to graphic objects. This renders the text unsearchable.
   - **Convert All Strokes To Outlines** Keeps all stroke widths constant. Fine details like thin lines and thin fonts may appear larger when this option is enabled.
   - **Clip Complex Regions** Preserves the boundaries between vector objects and raster objects along object paths. Choose this option to reduce artifacts when part of an object is rasterized and other parts are vectors.
   - **Preserve Overprint** Blends the color of transparent objects with the background color to produce an overprint effect.
10. In the Apply To PDF section, choose an option to determine whether flattening is applied to the entire document, the currently selected page, or a page range.
11. Click Apply to apply transparency flattening to the document.

Add Information for the Printer

When you have a document that contains artwork, such as the graphics for a business card, and you use an application's Print command to convert the document to PDF, it appears on an 8.5 × 11-inch page, unless you specify a different size. The additional white space around the graphic isn't wasted because you can add valuable information for the printer. But, before you can add the printer's information, you must specify the size for the trim box, the art box, and the bleed box.

Modify the Trim Box, the Art Box, and the Bleed Box

Before you can add printer marks to a document with art smaller than the page size, you must specify the size of the trim box (the size to which the printer will trim the printed document). At the same time, you can also specify the size of the art box (the actual size of the artwork) and bleed box (the extended area beyond the trim box to which content is clipped if a bleed area is present). You set the sizes for the trim box, art box, and bleed box as follows:

1. Choose Advanced | Print Production | Crop Pages to open the Crop Pages dialog box, shown in Figure 16-1.
2. Click the Units drop-down arrow and choose the document's unit of measure.
3. Choose ArtBox from the Boxes drop-down list.
4. In the Margin Controls area, enter the Top, Bottom, Left, and Right values. These values crop the art box from the document size to the actual artwork. To arrive at these values, subtract the size of the artwork from the size of the document, divide the difference in the width by 2 to determine the Left and Right values, and then divide the difference in the height by 2 to determine the Top and Bottom values. For example, if you're specifying trim values for a 2 × 3.5-inch business card on an 8.5 × 11 page, the values for Left and Right are 3.25 inches, and the values for Top and Bottom are 3.75 inches.
5. Choose TrimBox from the Boxes drop-down list and enter the Top, Bottom, Left, and Right values to specify the trim box size.
6. Choose BleedBox from the Boxes drop-down list and enter the Top, Bottom, Left, and Right values to specify the bleed box size.

NOTE *When you specify the values for cropping margins and deselect the Show All Boxes option, the color of the border surrounding the artwork changes when you select an option from the Boxes drop-down list. In the preview window, a blue rectangle shows the current bleed box size, a green rectangle shows the current trim box size, and a red rectangle shows the current art box size. The dimensions are noted beneath the artwork.*

7. In the Change Page Size section, you can change the page size by clicking the Page Sizes drop-down arrow and choosing the desired page size. Or, click the Custom radio button

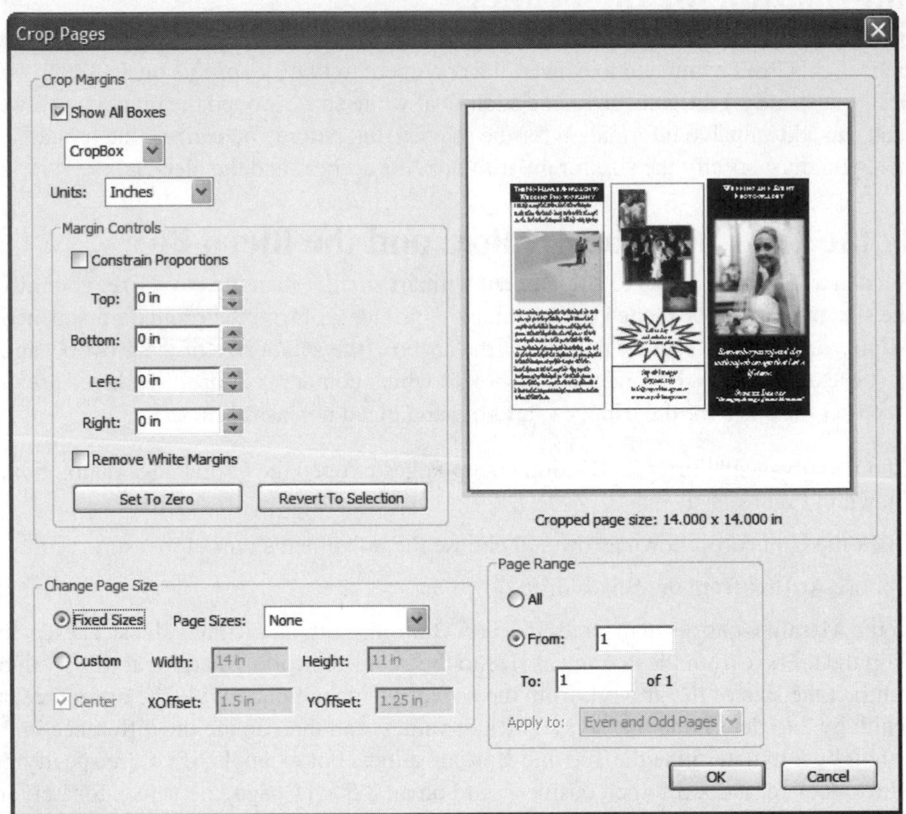

FIGURE 16-1 You can use the Crop Pages dialog box to specify the trim box size.

and enter values for Width and Height. This option is handy if the document is the same size as the artwork and you need additional white space to show printer marks.

8. In the Page Range section, specify the number of pages that will be cropped in the document. You can crop all pages, crop a range of pages, or crop only the pages you selected from the Pages tab. If you select a range of pages, you can specify whether to crop odd pages, even pages, or both.
9. Click OK to crop the margins to the specified sizes.

Add Printer Marks

Before finalizing your document for print, you can add printer marks such as trim, bleed, and registration marks as described on the next page. This information ensures the document is printed to your specifications.

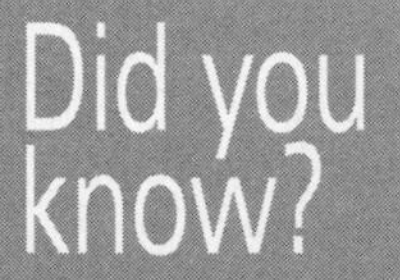

Printing Documents with Thin Lines

Commercial printers sometimes have difficulty when printing a document with thin lines. If you're preparing a PDF document for print production and it contains thin lines, they may not show up in the final print. You can fix this problem by using the Fix Hairlines tool or menu command, which identifies hairlines and assigns them a thicker line weight, which you can specify. The tool also fixes hairlines in Type 3 fonts and PostScript patterns.

1. Choose Advanced | Print Production | Add Printer Marks. The Add Printer Marks dialog box opens:

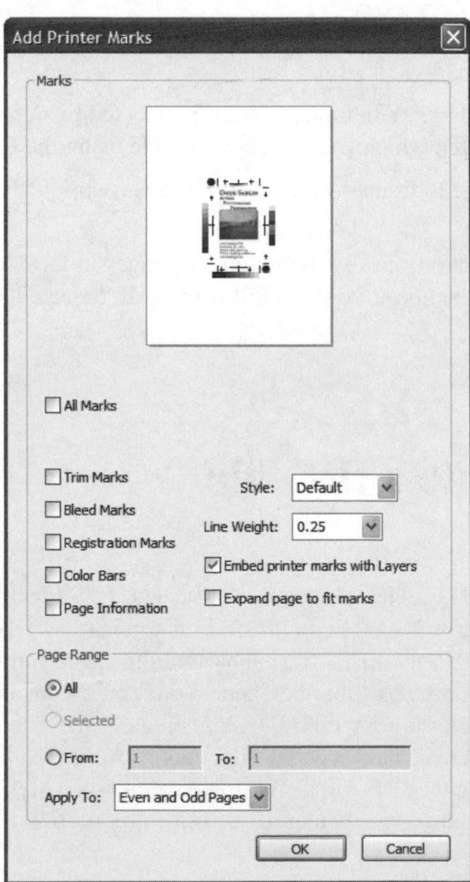

2. Choose from the following options:
   - **All Marks** Adds all printer marks to the document.
   - **Trim Marks** Adds a mark at each corner of the trim box.
   - **Bleed Marks** Adds a mark at each corner of the bleed box.
   - **Registration Marks** Adds marks outside of the trim box area, which are used by the printer when aligning separations for a color document.
   - **Color Bars** Adds a small bar for each spot or process color. Your printer uses these marks to adjust ink density when setting up the printer for your document.
   - **Page Information** Places information such as the filename, current date, and page number outside of the trim box.
3. Click the Style drop-down arrow and choose the desired mark style. Your choices are printer mark styles used by Adobe InDesign, Adobe Illustrator, or Adobe Quark. If you choose the Default style, Acrobat uses generic printer marks that are universally recognized by printers.
4. Click the Line Weight drop-down arrow and choose the desired weight for the lines used to create the printer marks.
5. The Embed Printer Marks With Layers option is selected by default. This option embeds printer marks on a layer, which you can show or hide using the Layers tab.
6. Click the Expand Page to fit marks check box if the artwork is the same size as the document.
7. In the Page Range section, specify the number of pages in the document that will have printer marks. You can choose from the following: All, Selected, or From, which enables

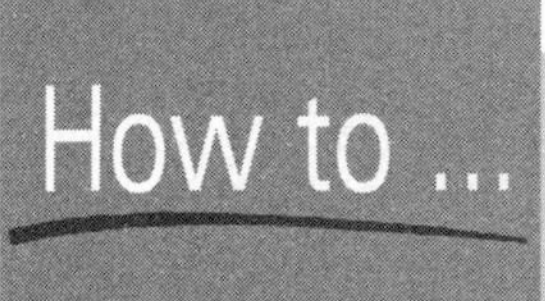

Create a JDF File

Job Definition Format (JDF) files are electronic job tickets. *JDF files* can be embedded in the file when the artwork is created in an illustration application, or you can create a file known as a JDF file in Acrobat. This file enables you to specify information such as the product name, job ID, job ID part number, and so on. You can also embed a Preflight profile and a PDF conversion setting with a JDF. You create a JDF file within the Edit JDF Definitions dialog box. To create or edit a JDF file, choose Advanced | Print Production | JDF Job Definitions to open the JDF Job Definitions dialog box. Click New, and then follow the prompts. Check with your service center to see if it supports JDF files.

you to specify a range of pages. Selected is dimmed out if you haven't selected page thumbnails from the Pages panel.

8. Choose an option from the Apply To drop-down menu to determine whether printer marks are added to odd pages, even pages, or odd and even pages.
9. Click OK to add printer marks to the document.

Use the Print Production Toolbar

The Print Production commands are duplicated on the Print Production toolbar. If you're doing a lot of print production work, you may find floating the toolbar in the workspace beneficial, as clicking a print production tool immediately opens the applicable dialog box. To float the Print Production toolbar (shown next), choose Advanced | Print Production | Show Print Production toolbar. You can also dock the Print Production toolbar with the other toolbars.

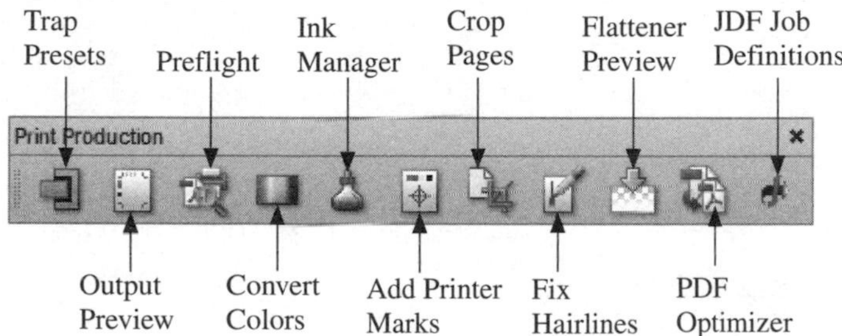

Summary

In this chapter, you learned how to prepare a document for a commercial printer. You saw how to perform a preflight check, convert a PDF file to a PDF/X file, and convert colors. You also learned how to flatten transparency, how to specify the size of the trim box, art box, and bleed box, as well as how to add printer marks to a document. In the next chapter, you learn how to add multimedia to your PDF documents.

Chapter 17

Add Multimedia Elements to PDF Documents

How to...

- Work with images
- Extract images from documents
- Add sound to documents
- Add movies to documents

When most people think of creating multimedia presentations, they think of programs such as Microsoft PowerPoint or Macromedia Director. Indeed, these are two of the most frequently used programs to create full-fledged multimedia presentations. However, with a bit of imagination, Acrobat Professional, and a smidgen of JavaScript, you can create impressive multimedia presentations.

When you create a multimedia presentation for CD-ROM, file size generally isn't an issue. A CD-ROM can hold 700 MB of data, which means you can fill your PDF documents with stunning full-color images, audio files, and full motion video. In this chapter, you learn how to integrate multimedia files into your PDF documents to create multimedia presentations that will impact your viewing audience.

Work with Images

When you create a multimedia PDF presentation, images are a must. Whether you're creating a corporate portfolio presentation, educational media, or a product catalog, images add visual spice that pique user interest and make the presentation a success. When you prepare images for multimedia PDF presentations, you can use high-resolution images and save them in file formats that aren't compressed, or if you use an image file format that compresses images, you can apply less compression to create a sharper image.

If you create documents with images and intend to use these as the basis for a multimedia PDF, consider investing in a page-layout program, such as Adobe InDesign. When you use a page-layout program, you have better control over image placement, especially when you want text to wrap around the image. In lieu of a page-layout program, many popular word processing applications support embedding images in documents. If the authoring program supports PDF export, you should export the document with little or no image compression. If PDF export isn't supported, choose Adobe PDF as the printing device to convert the document to PDF format, and use the High Quality conversion setting.

When you're working with a PDF document with images you want to use in another document, you can export the images by choosing Advanced | Document Processing | Export All Images. This opens a dialog box you use to specify the export format for the images and the folder in which you want to store the images.

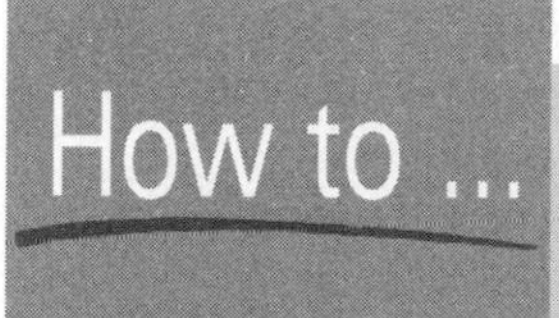

Optimize Images for Multimedia PDF Presentations

If you have image-editing software, such as Adobe Photoshop CS2 or Adobe Fireworks, scan your images into the program with a resolution 300 dpi (dots per inch). This is more than you need for monitor viewing, but it allows the image to be magnified in the resulting PDF with negligible loss of quality. If you're capturing images with a digital camera, shoot them at the highest resolution possible. Resample the image to the desired size for your presentation. Ultimately, your presentation will be viewed on a 72- or 96-dpi monitor, but you can leave the resolution at a higher value and the images will look better when your viewers magnify the document. Export the finished image as a BMP file (Windows) or an uncompressed TIFF file (Macintosh and Windows) for the best results.

Add Sound to Documents

No multimedia experience is complete without sound. When you add sound to a presentation, you involve another one of the viewer's senses, which makes the experience more complete. You can use sounds in a variety of ways, including with buttons, when a page opens, or when a page closes. Acrobat now supports sounds for all popular formats, including MP3.

When you add a sound file to an Acrobat document, you can choose to embed the file or not. When you embed a sound file in a document, it's saved with the document. When a sound file isn't embedded with a document, Acrobat records the path to the sound file and the file plays when the trigger you specify occurs. If you move a sound file that isn't embedded in a document to a different folder on your computer, it won't play. Adding a sound file to a document you plan to display on the Internet would result in an extremely long download for users with a dial-up connection, unless the sound file is extremely small. Or, you can include the path to a streaming audio file on a web site. When you create a PDF document and add sound files for a multimedia CD-ROM, Internet bandwidth is no longer a concern.

Add Sound to a PDF Document

You can use the Sound tool to add sound to a PDF document. When you use the Sound tool, you create an activation area that, when clicked, plays a sound. This is useful when you want to augment an image with a prerecorded narration or, perhaps, a song. When you use the Sound tool, you enable viewers to play a sound on demand.

You can also play a sound when a page opens or closes by using the Play Media (Acrobat 6 And Later Compatible) action. The *Play Media (Acrobat 6 and Later Compatible) action* gives you complete control over the sound file you want the user to hear when the page opens. Depending on the type of presentation you create, you can have a short musical piece play when a page opens or have a vocal introduction. You can also use a sound when the page closes. (For more information on actions, refer to Chapter 8.) When you use the Play Media (Acrobat 6 And Later Compatible) action and choose Page Close as the trigger, you can choose to play a sound that's been added to the page by using the Sound tool, as outlined in the next section.

TIP *Sound can enhance your presentation, but the blatant use of sound will have your viewer turning down the speaker volume or, worse yet, exiting your presentation before it's finished.*

Adding a button is another method you can use to add sound to your PDF presentation. Create a button, and then use an action to play the sound when the button is clicked or a user pauses their cursor over the button. You can use an action to play a sound during the Mouse Enter event to alert viewers that the button warrants their attention. Or, you can play the sound during the Mouse Down event, which alerts the viewers that the button has successfully been clicked. For more information on events, refer to Chapter 14.

If you use sounds for both events, and the sound assigned to the Mouse Enter event is longer than the sound you use for the Mouse Down event, the first sound plays until conclusion. This means the button action may execute before the second sound ever plays.

If you're creating a CD-ROM product catalog or an educational tool, you can have a product description or tutorial play when an image is clicked. To have a sound play when an image is clicked, select the Link tool and create a hotspot around the image, as outlined in Chapter 7. In the Create Link dialog box, choose Invisible Rectangle from the Link Type drop-down list, and choose the Custom Link option. In the Actions tab, choose Play A Sound from the Action Type drop-down menu, and then select the sound you want to play when the image is clicked. If you already have Acrobat 6.0 and later compatible media embedded in the document, you can choose the Play Media (Acrobat 6 And Later Compatible) action, and then select a sound file previously embedded in the document.

Use the Sound Tool

When you use the *Sound tool,* you define an active area of the document that viewers can click to play a sound file. You can choose to embed the file with the document or not. When you don't embed the sound file with the document, Acrobat plays the sound from the folder where it resides on your computer or from the web site where the sound file is stored. If you intend to send a PDF document with a nonembedded sound to someone, you have to send the sound file as well. Or, you can upload the sound to a web site and enter the URL to the sound file when you specify sound properties. As long as your recipient has a reasonably fast Internet connection, and is online when viewing the document, they'll be able to hear the sound file. The only times you should consider *not* embedding a sound file is when the document is for playback on your own computer or for a CD-ROM compilation where the sound file will be used by several documents, or if you've uploaded a streaming sound file to a web site. When you compile the assets for burning the CD-ROM and you have PDF documents with sounds that aren't embedded, be sure to include the folder with the audio clips. You also have to maintain the same relative path to the sound files. In other words, if the sound files are in a subfolder to the parent directory named Sounds, you must create a subfolder named Sounds at the web site or on the CD-ROM from which the PDF presentation will be viewed.

To add a sound to a document by using the Sound tool, follow these steps:

1. Navigate to the page to which you want to add the sound file.
2. Choose Tools | Advanced Editing | Sound Tool. Or, if the Advanced Editing toolbar is present in the workspace, click the Sound tool, whose icon looks like a speaker.
3. Drag diagonally inside the document to define the active area that will play the sound when clicked. This opens the Add Sound dialog box:

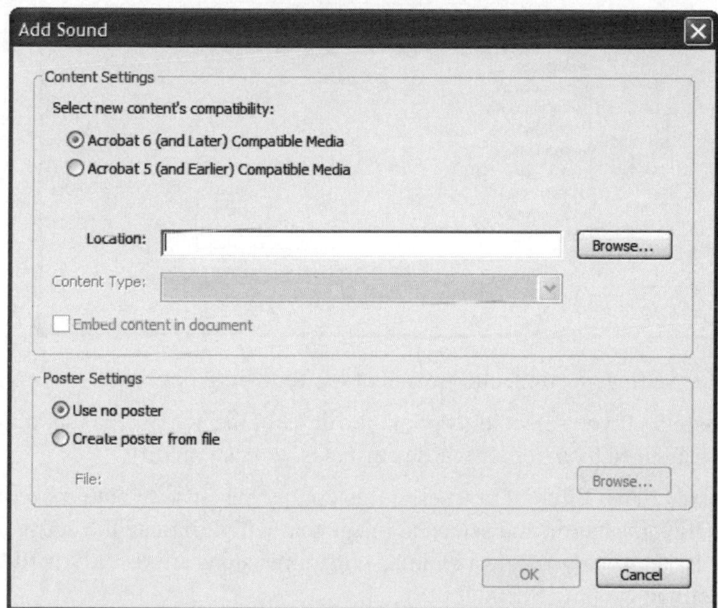

4. In the Content Settings section, click either of the compatibility radio buttons. Note, if you choose the Acrobat 5 option, you won't be able to embed the sound with the document.
5. Click the Browse button to open the Select Sound File dialog box. Next, select the desired sound file, and then click Select to exit the dialog box. Or, you can enter the path to the web site where the sound file is located, for example: http://www.mysite.com/mysong.mp3.
6. If you chose Acrobat 6 (And Later) Compatible Media in Step 4 and selected a file from your computer, the Embed Content In Document check box is selected by default. Deselect the check box if you don't want the sound embedded with the document.
7. If Acrobat didn't choose the correct content type, click the Content Type drop-down arrow and choose an option from the drop-down list, shown next. If you do change the content type,

make sure you choose the correct one. Otherwise, the file might not play. The Content Type drop-down list is only available when you choose the Acrobat 6 option.

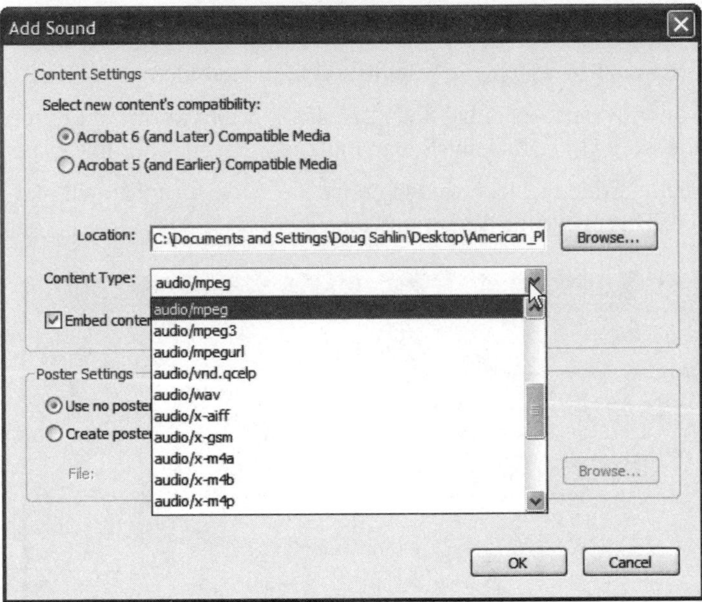

8. In the Poster Settings section, choose one of the following options:

- **Use No Poster** If you select this option, the default, the active area that plays the sound, is designated by a border whose attributes you can modify.
- **Create Poster From File** If you select this option, the Browse button becomes available. Click the button and select an image that will designate the active area for the sound file. Note, when you select an image, its dimensions are reconfigured to fit the area you defined with the Sound tool.

9. Click OK to finish adding the sound to the document and close the Add Sound dialog box.

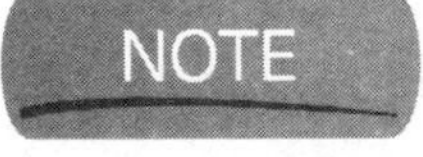

If you use an image as a poster for a sound object, you may have to resize the area to conform to the dimensions of the image by clicking the poster with the Sound tool or a Select Object tool, and then dragging the handles around the perimeter of the object until the image is no longer distorted.

Viewers can play the sound by clicking the active area with the Hand tool. Or, you can use the Play Media (Acrobat 6 And Later Compatible) page action to play the sound when the page opens or closes. (For more information on actions, refer to Chapter 8.) When you add a sound to a document, you can edit the properties of the sound to hide the annotation from view, and choose an alternate rendition for users who view the document in different situations, as outlined in the section "Edit Media Renditions."

Create Audio Tracks for Your PDF Documents

Acrobat doesn't have the capability to edit soundtracks. If you intend to use sound extensively when creating multimedia PDF presentations, you may want to consider investing in sound-editing software. You can use sound-editing software to record your own sound clips, and then edit them to fit your presentation. Most popular sound-editing software can be used to enhance a recording, remove noise from a recording, add special effects (such as echo or reverb) to a sound recording, and much more. Some sound-editing programs enable you to mix soundtracks with other recordings. Software is also available to create musical soundtracks. Sony Media Software sells both sound-editing and music-sampling software for Windows-based PCs. For more information, visit Sony's web site at *http://mediasoftware.sonypictures.com/*.

Add Video Clips to PDF Presentations

You can also add full motion video to your PDF documents, by using the *Movie tool.* When you add a movie to a PDF document and choose Acrobat 6 (And Later) Compatible Media, you can embed the movie with a document or not. You can also specify multiple versions of the movie that are tailored for playing from a CD-ROM or from an Internet web site.

Add Movies to Documents

You use the Movie tool to add movies to your document. When you specify Acrobat 6 (And Later) Compatible Media, you can embed the movie in the document. You can also specify different renditions of the file for users who view the document with different desktop sizes, or access the document via the Internet at different connection speeds. Finally, you can specify a rendition using a different format; for example, you may want to include one rendition of the movie in the WMV (Windows Media Viewer) format for viewers with the Windows Media Player installed, and another rendition in the MOV (Movie) format for viewers who have the QuickTime player installed on their systems. If you choose Acrobat 5.0 (And Earlier) Compatible Media, you won't be able to embed the media with the document and are limited to your choice of media. Of course, your viewing audience largely determines the compatibility you choose. If the majority of your audience doesn't have the Adobe Reader 6.0 or later, you have to include the installer with your CD-ROM presentation, or provide a link to the page at Adobe's site from which the software can be downloaded. Or, you can use the Acrobat 5.0 media option if your audience is unlikely to have the latest version of Adobe Reader.

By default, Acrobat Professional snaps the movie window to the size of the movie and uses the first frame of the movie as a poster in the document. To add a movie to a PDF file, do the following:

1. Choose Tools | Advanced Editing | Movie Tool or select the Movie tool from the Advanced Editing toolbar if present in the workspace.
2. Click-and-drag inside the document to specify the position in which the poster frame of the movie appears. You don't have to worry about sizing the area. By default, Acrobat

snaps the activation area to the dimensions of the movie. After releasing the mouse button, the Add Movie dialog box appears:

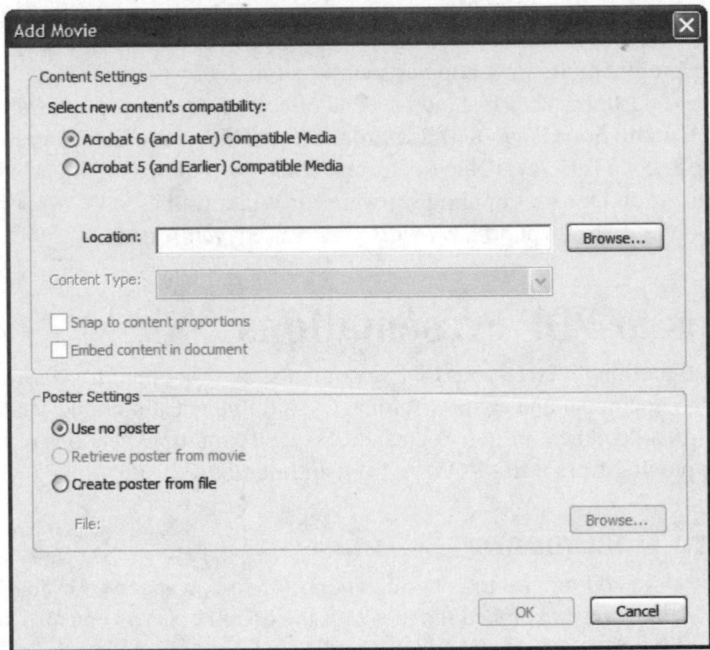

3. In the Content Settings section, choose Acrobat 6.0 (And Later) Compatible Media (the default) or Acrobat 5 (And Earlier) Compatible Media. If you choose Acrobat 5.0 compatibility, the options to embed the movie in the document and create a poster from the file are no longer available.
4. Click the Browse button to open the Select Movie File dialog box, and then select the file and click Select. Or, enter the path to the web site where the movie file is stored, as in http://www.mysite.com/mymovie.wmv.
5. Acrobat chooses the content type. If applicable, click the Content Type drop-down arrow and choose a different content type from the drop-down list, shown next.

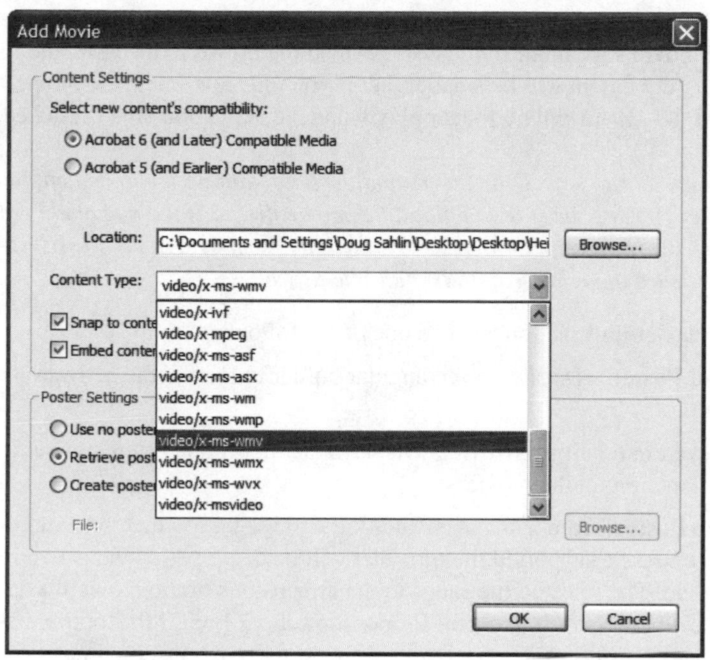

CAUTION *If you choose the wrong content type, the movie might not play.*

6. Deselect the default Snap To Content Proportions check box and the movie is sized to its default dimensions.

CAUTION *If you resize the movie to smaller dimensions manually, you may distort the moving images if you don't resize the movie proportionately. You will also distort the images if you resize the movie to larger dimensions. You can proportionately resize the movie by dragging a corner handle while pressing* SHIFT. *However, the recommendation is that you size the movie to standard dimensions (320×240, 160×120, and so on) in a video-editing application prior to adding the movie to a PDF document.*

7. Deselect the default Embed Content In Document check box to have Acrobat create a link to the movie's location. If you don't embed the movie in the PDF, the file size of the resulting document will be smaller, but if you move or delete the movie, the link is broken and the movie will no longer play when the activation area is clicked.

If you choose not to embed the movie and, instead, upload the document to a web server for Internet viewing, be sure to upload the movie file, or if the document will be included with a CD-ROM presentation, be sure to include the movie file in the assets you burn to disk. Make sure the relative path is the same as well.

8. In the Poster Settings section, choose one of the following options:
   - **Use No Poster** Displays a rectangular border to signify the activation area for the movie.
   - **Retrieve Poster From Movie** Displays the first frame of the movie to signify the activation area for the movie.
   - **Create Poster From File** Activates the Browse button that, when clicked, enables you to choose a supported file type that will be displayed as the activation area for the movie. The selected file snaps to the dimensions of the movie if you haven't deselected the Snap To Content Proportions check box. If this option is selected and the image isn't the same proportion as the movie contents, the image is distorted.
9. Click OK. Acrobat adds the movie to the document and displays a poster according to the options you selected.

Add Renditions to a Document

After you add a movie or sound to a document, you can add different versions of the media and specify the system requirements to determine which rendition Acrobat plays when the activation area is clicked. In Acrobat, different versions of a movie are known as *renditions*. To add a rendition to a document:

1. Right-click (Windows) or CTRL-click (Macintosh) the movie activation area with the Select Object tool or the Movie tool, and choose Properties from the context menu. Acrobat displays the Multimedia Properties dialog box.

2. Click the Settings tab to configure rendition settings, as shown here.

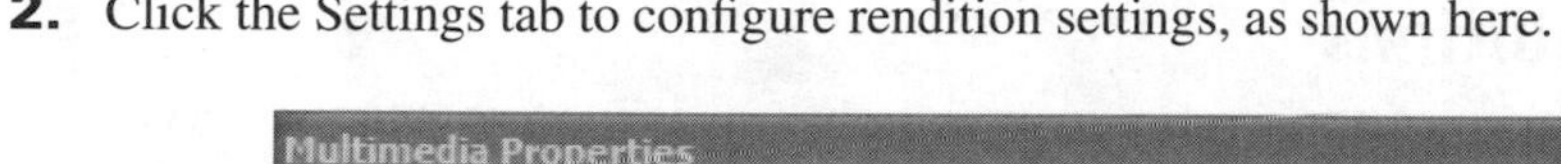

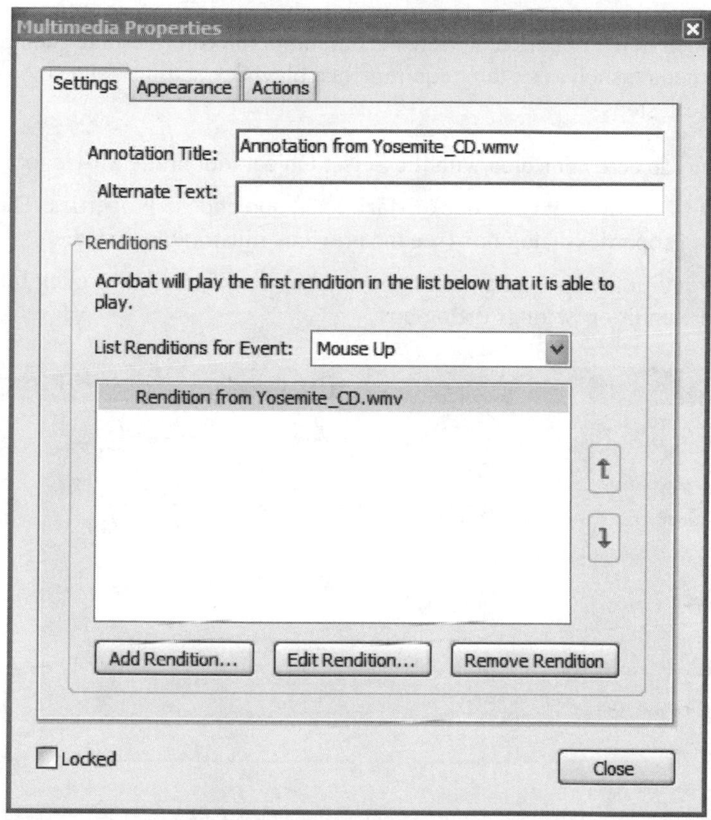

3. Click the Add Rendition button and, from the drop-down list, choose to add the rendition by specifying a URL, choosing a file, or copying an existing rendition. When you copy an existing rendition, you can choose different options, such as whether to display media player controls. After choosing an option, Acrobat displays the applicable dialog box. If you choose a rendition from a file, Acrobat gives you the option of embedding the file with the document or not.
4. After choosing a rendition, click OK.

You can add as many renditions as needed to cover the different viewers, processors, media players, connection speeds, and so on to compensate for the different scenarios you anticipate users will encounter when viewing the document. If you embed several renditions, the document will have a rather large file size, especially if you're embedding lengthy movies, movies with large dimensions, or both. You may want to consider embedding the rendition that the majority of your viewers will be using, and then linking the other files. After adding several renditions to a document, you can edit each rendition to compensate for situations under which the rendition will be viewed.

Edit Media Renditions

If you add several renditions of a movie to a document, chances are you've optimized each movie for the intended delivery device or viewing situation. You can fine-tune each rendition by modifying parameters, such as system requirements, playback settings, and so on. To edit a rendition, follow these steps.

1. Click the movie activation area with the Select Object tool or the Movie tool.
2. Right-click (Windows) or CTRL-click (Macintosh) and choose Properties. The Multimedia Properties dialog box (see the previous illustration) appears.
3. Select the rendition whose parameters you want to modify, and then click Edit Rendition to open the Rendition Settings dialog box:

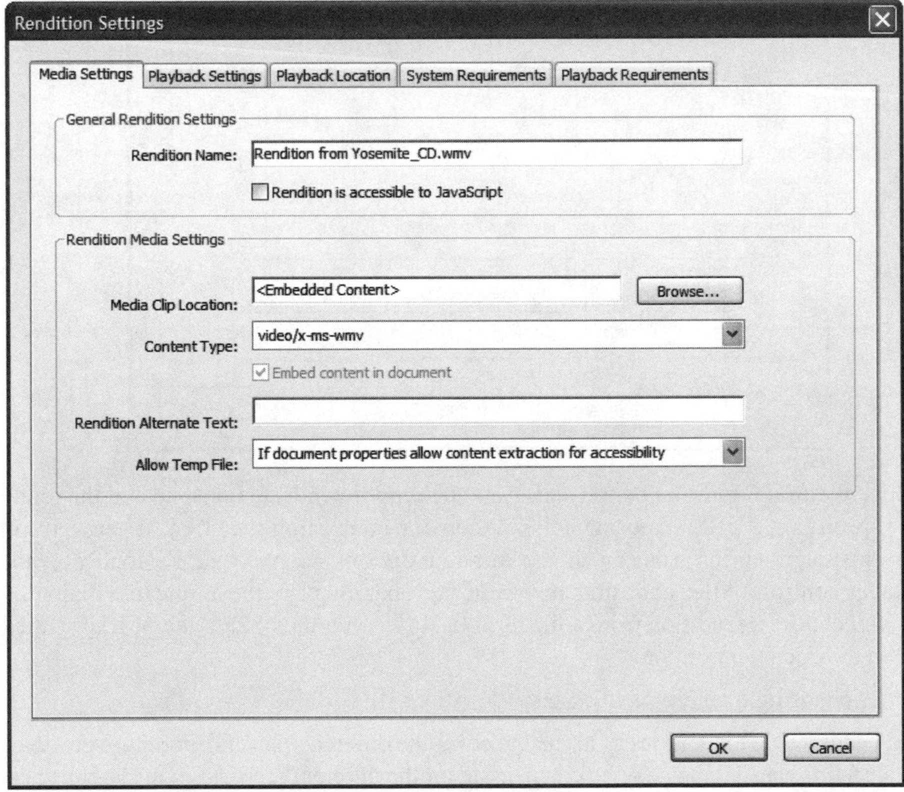

4. In the General Rendition Settings section of the Media Settings tab, you can specify the following settings:
   - **Rendition Name** Determines the name of the rendition as displayed in the Renditions list. The Rendition Name doesn't determine which file is played.

- **Rendition Is Accessible To JavaScript** Selecting this check box enables you to control the movie with JavaScript code.

5. In the Rendition Media Settings section of the Media Settings tab, you can specify the following settings:
    - **Media Clip Location** Enables you to specify the location from which Acrobat plays the file. You can accept the default option (which varies depending on the rendition option you chose), or specify a different clip location.
    - **Content Type** Enables you to specify a different content type for the media clips. In most instances, you want to stick with the default content type Acrobat chooses. If you choose the wrong content type, the clip might not play.
    - **Rendition Alternate Text** Enables you to enter alternate text for the movie clip, which is used by visually impaired viewers.
    - **Allow Temp File** Enables you to specify whether the user's system will be able to write a temporary file of the movie and which document properties must be present to allow the temporary file.
6. Click the Playback Settings tab to modify the following options:
    - **Keep Player Open** Click the drop-down arrow and choose one of the following options: For Normal Length Of Content, Forever Once Activated, or For A Number Of Seconds. If you choose the final option, the Seconds field becomes available. Enter the number of seconds for which you want the player to remain open, or click the spinner buttons to specify the duration. Note, if you specify a duration less than the length of the movie, the movie will stop prematurely and the player will close. If you choose Forever Once Activated, the player will remain onscreen after the movie plays. If you choose this option, be sure to specify the Show Player Controls option, so the viewer can play the movie again if desired.
    - **Volume** Enter a value to specify the percentage at which you want the volume of the clip to play. Or, you can click the spinner buttons to select a value. Note, you can play a clip at a higher percentage than its original volume, but this, most likely, will result in distortion or poor sound quality.
    - **Show Player Controls** Select this check box to display the controller associated with the media type. The controls displayed are the default controls used with the user's default system media player associated with the movie's file type.
    - **Repeat** Select this check box if you want the movie to play more than once. After selecting this option, click the Continuous radio button (the default) or Times radio button. If you choose the Times option, a text field becomes available. Enter the number of times you want the movie to play or click the spinner buttons to select a value.
7. In the Player List selection, click the Add button to display the Specify Player dialog box. From within this dialog box, you can select a player to associate with the rendition.

In addition, you can specify which version of the player is required to play the video content, as well as which players aren't allowed to play the video. You can also specify which operating system (OS) is associated with the player. The settings you choose determine which player on the viewer's computer is used to play the video.

8. Click the Playback Location tab to specify the following options:
   - **Playback Location** Gives you the option of choosing a different playback location other than the default Document location. You can choose Hidden, Floating Window, or Full Screen. When you embed a sound in a document and use an action to play the sound when the page opens or closes, your best choice is Hidden. If you choose Floating Window, the media plays in a window that users can move to a different location. If you choose this option in conjunction with Player Controls, viewers will be able to manipulate the volume, pause the media, and so on. The options vary depending on the default system player for the media type associated with the rendition you're editing, or the one you specify in the Specify Player dialog box.
   - **Background Color** Click the color swatch and select a background color for the media player. This option has no visible effect on a movie player, but you can see the background color if you choose to display player controls for an embedded sound.
9. If you choose Floating Window for the Playback Location in Step 8, the following options are available:
   - **Show Title Bar (selected by default)** Displays the title bar at the top of the floating window.
   - **Show Control For Closing Window (selected by default)** Displays a control that viewers can use to close the window prior to the movie finishing.
   - **Title Text** Enables you to enter text you want displayed in the title bar. This field is unavailable if you deselect the Show Title Bar option.

NOTE

If your document isn't on the viewer's list of trusted documents, the Manage Trust for Multimedia Content dialog box appears, which gives the viewer the choice of adding the document to their list of trusted documents, playing the media one time, or cancelling playback. Title text won't be displayed unless the viewer opts to add the document to their list of trusted documents.

10. The remaining options in this tab let you specify resizing options for the window. The recommendation is that you accept the default Acrobat options, because resizing the window may cause image distortion.
11. Click the System Requirements tab to specify which conditions cause the rendition you're editing to appear. For example, if you have two renditions of a movie, one sized at 160 × 120 pixels and another sized at 320 × 240 pixels, you can use this tab to specify the smaller clip plays if the user's desktop size is 800 × 600 pixels and the other clip plays for 1,024 × 68 screen resolution. You have other options in this tab to play a rendition based

on a user's connection speed to the Internet, and so on. Acrobat determines which system requirements are satisfied and serves up the rendition you specify.

12. Click the Playback Requirements tab to specify which requirements must be met by the user's hardware to play the clip. Note, users have to change permissions for nontrusted documents to allow the document to control the playback of the media.
13. Click OK to exit the Rendition Settings dialog box, and then click Close to exit the Multimedia Settings dialog box. Or, select another rendition whose settings you want to modify.

Create a Multimedia PDF Presentation

When you use Acrobat to create a multimedia PDF presentation, you can include documents with images you've created in other applications, and then use Adobe PDF as a printing device to convert the documents into PDF format. You can augment the images with text documents you converted to PDF files. But, the real power of Acrobat Professional comes when you add multimedia files, such as Flash SWF movies, video clips, and sound files.

You can create a single multimedia document or create a series of documents you link with interactive menus. When you create a multimedia presentation for CD-ROM distribution, you have considerable leeway. You can create a menu with multistate rollover buttons that play sounds, trigger movies, and much more. As long as you can fit the entire production on a CD-ROM, you're good to go. You can use the Button tool as the basis for your menu. For more information on using the Button tool, see Chapter 14.

Create an Introduction

You can create an effective introduction to your multimedia presentation by creating a series of pages that play one after the other, similar to a movie's opening credits. After Acrobat displays the last page, you use an action to open the main page of the presentation. The number of introduction pages varies, depending on your presentation. You could create an interesting introduction by gradually increasing the size and opacity of a corporate logo until it fills the entire page. Another visually stimulating introduction for a presentation is to have various images assemble into a splash screen, like the pieces of a jigsaw puzzle coming together.

If you have image-editing software, such as Adobe Photoshop, Corel Photo-Paint, or Adobe Fireworks, you can create the individual images for the introduction. Create the images with the same dimensions as your PDF presentation and convert each image to PDF format using the High Quality conversion setting. Name each file in the order it will appear in the introduction—for example, intro1.pdf, intro2.pdf, and so on. After you convert the images to PDF format, launch Acrobat and do the following:

1. Choose File | Create PDF | From Multiple Files to open the Combine Files dialog box. Click Add Files and then select the files created for your introduction.

2. In the Combine Files window, arrange the files in the order in which they'll appear, choose the option to combine the files into a single PDF, and then click Create to convert the files to a PDF document.
3. Open the Pages panel, select the first thumbnail, right-click (Windows) or CTRL-click (Macintosh), and then choose Page Properties from the context menu. When the Page Properties dialog box appears, click the Actions tab. The Page Open trigger is selected by default.
4. Click the Select Action drop-down arrow and choose Run A JavaScript.
5. Click the Add button to open the JavaScript Editor dialog box.
6. Enter the following code in the JavaScript editor:

```
var interval = app.setInterval("this.pageNum = this.pageNum + 1;",
3000);
```

7. Click OK to close the JavaScript Editor dialog box, and then click Close to exit the Page Properties dialog box and assign the action to the page. The JavaScript in this step causes the page to turn every three seconds. The code continues to execute every three seconds until you stop the code by clearing the interval.
8. In the Pages panel, select the thumbnail for the last page in the document, and then right-click (Windows) or CTRL-click (Macintosh) and choose Page Properties. When the Page Properties dialog box appears, click the Actions tab. The Page Open trigger is selected by default.
9. Click the Select Action drop-down arrow, choose Run A JavaScript from the drop-down menu, and then click the Add button to open the JavaScript Editor dialog box.
10. Enter the following JavaScript to stop the pages from turning:

```
app.clearInterval(interval);
```

11. Click OK to close the JavaScript Editor dialog box. Now you need to specify which document opens after the introduction plays.
12. Click the Select Action drop-down arrow, choose Open File, and then click the Add button to open the Select File To Open dialog box.
13. Select the file you want to open after the introduction plays, click Select to select the file and exit the Select File To Open dialog box, and then click Close to exit the Page Properties dialog box.

That's all you need to do to create an automated introduction. You could have created each page of the introduction as a separate PDF file and used the Open File action to advance to the next PDF document. But, on all but the slowest computer, the files would open too quickly for the viewer to get a good look at them. When you use JavaScript, you can control the amount of time each page of the introduction is displayed. To increase or decrease the interval time, enter a new value in Step 6. Remember, one second equals 1,000 milliseconds and you can precisely control the amount of time each page is displayed. If you attempted to do this with Acrobat's page transitions, the file you selected in Step 13 would open before the last page of the introduction displayed for the specified duration.

Create a Pop-Up Menu Using Named Destinations

You can create an effective pop-up menu for your multipage PDF documents by using named destinations and a bit of JavaScript. Pop-up menus are useful because they don't take up much space and you can cram several destinations into a single menu. To create a pop-up menu, do the following:

1. Choose View | Navigation Panels | Destinations to open the Destinations panel. Acrobat displays a list of destinations in the document. If the document contains no destinations, create the desired destinations. For information on creating named destinations, refer to Chapter 8.
2. Decide which destinations you want included as menu items.
3. Change the name of each menu item destination to the name you want to appear on the menu. For example, if the menu item will be called Chapter 1, change the name of the destination to Chapter 1. This technique is intended for desktop viewing. If you create a document for viewing in a web browser, spaces may cause inconsistent results.
4. Using the Button tool, create a button field where you want the pop-up menu to appear. Acrobat opens the Button Properties dialog box.
5. On the General tab, enter a name for the button.
6. Define the appearance and options for the button, as outlined in Chapter 14.
7. Click the Actions tab, click the Select Action drop-down arrow, and then choose Run A JavaScript from the drop-down menu. The JavaScript Editor dialog box appears.
8. Enter the following code, replacing the `Dest` designations with the destination names as they appear in the Destinations panel—named destinations are case-sensitive. Open the Destinations panel prior to creating your JavaScript for a handy visual reference.

   ```
   var c = app.popUpMenu ("Dest1","Dest2","Dest3","Dest4");
   this.gotoNamedDest(c);
   ```

9. Click OK to close the JavaScript Editor dialog box, and then click Close to close the Button Properties dialog box. When users click the button with the Hand tool, the JavaScript pop-up menu appears, listing each named destination. When the named destination is clicked, Acrobat displays the page view associated with the named destination.

Summary

In this chapter, you learned how to add multimedia elements to your PDF documents. You discovered how to embed multimedia elements with the Sound and Movie tools. You also learned how to add different renditions of multimedia objects to a document for users who view the document with different system configurations and Internet users who view the document at different connection speeds. Another topic of discussion showed you how to use JavaScript to create an automated introduction and pop-up menus. In the next chapter, you learn how to use the Acrobat Professional Catalog command to create PDF indexes and how to automate your work by using batch processing.

Chapter 18 Create a PDF Index

How to...

- Use batch processing
- Create an index
- Prepare documents for indexing
- Build an index
- Purge and rebuild an index
- Embed an index

Whether you use Acrobat personally to maintain a collection of information, or you use it to create and maintain documents in a large corporation, you can make the information in your PDF documents more accessible by creating a PDF index. Whether you use a few or several hundred PDF documents to create your PDF index, the result is a searchable index. After you create an index, or several indexes, you can quickly find the information you need by using the Search command.

In this chapter, you learn how to use the Batch command to automate your work. You discover how to prepare PDF documents for the creation of a PDF index and use the Catalog command to create a searchable database of PDF documents. In addition, you learn to embed an index in a PDF document to decrease the time needed to search the document.

Edit with Batch Processing

When you prepare a large number of PDF documents for a specific audience or destination, you often end up performing the same task on every document—for example, optimizing several documents for Internet viewing. Instead of opening every document you need to modify, and then repeating the same task, you can perform the same command on several documents at once by using batch processing. You can choose from preset batch sequences or create your own batch sequence. When you create a custom batch sequence, you can specify the order in which the commands execute. You can also use batch processing to perform a specific sequence of commands on a single document or multiple documents.

Use Preset Batch Sequences

When you choose a preset batch sequence, Acrobat prompts you for the files to process. If a command in the batch sequence requires user input, the applicable dialog box appears. To perform a batch sequence, follow these steps:

1. Choose Advanced | Document Processing | Batch Processing. The Batch Sequences dialog box appears:

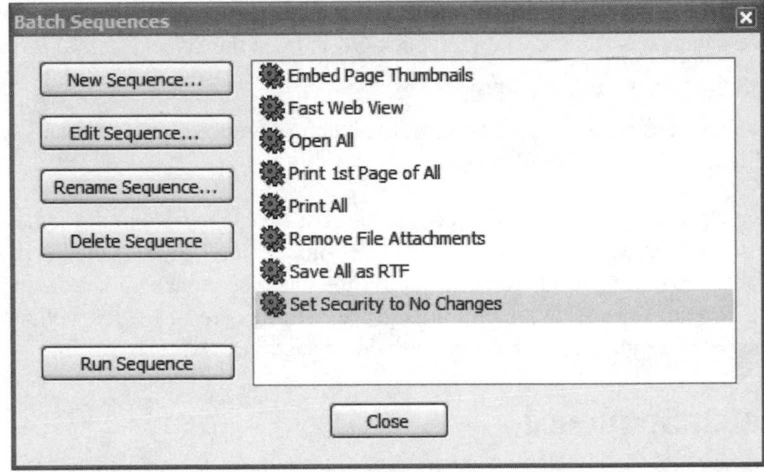

2. Choose a preset batch sequence from the menu. If, for example, you have several documents you want to prevent viewers from changing, you'd choose the Set Security To No Changes batch sequence.
3. Click Run Sequence after you select a batch sequence. The Run Sequence Confirmation dialog box appears, as the following illustration shows. This illustration shows the result of selecting, in Step 2, the Set Security To No Changes batch sequence, which sets security so users cannot change the document. The plus sign (+) to the left of the actual batch sequence command has been clicked to illustrate the settings that will be applied to each document on which the batch sequence is executed.

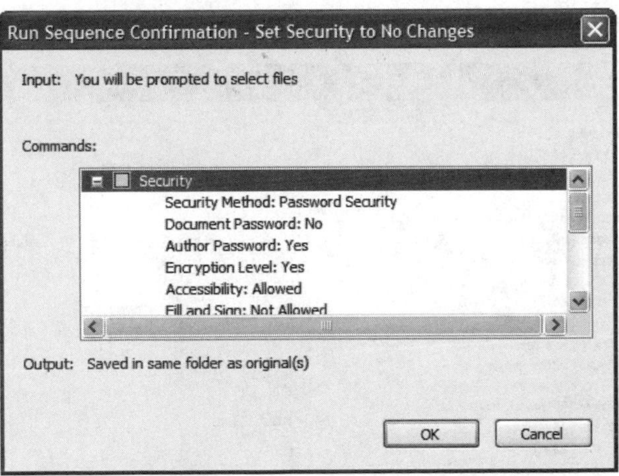

4. Verify that the commands in the Run Sequence Confirmation dialog box are the tasks you want to perform. If the batch sequence command has a plus sign to the left of the title, click

18

it to see the exact command or sequence of commands that Acrobat will perform. If the batch sequence is the one you want, click OK to open the Select Files To Process dialog box.

5. Select the files you want to process.
6. Click Select to have Acrobat perform the batch sequence commands and save the modified files in the original folder.

When you choose a preset batch sequence, Acrobat saves the files in the same folder by default. Storing processed documents in a separate folder is advisable. If the batch sequence doesn't perform as you expected, you can modify the batch sequence and perform it again on the original files. You can specify in which folder processed files are stored, as well as other options, by editing the batch sequence, as outlined in the next section.

Edit a Batch Sequence

When you edit a batch sequence, you can modify an existing batch sequence, create a new batch sequence, rename a batch sequence, or delete a batch sequence. When you modify an existing batch sequence, you can add or remove commands from the sequence, change the order in which the commands execute, change the files the commands run on, change the folder in which the files are saved, and modify the output options. To edit an existing batch sequence:

1. Choose Advanced | Document Processing | Batch Processing to open the Batch Sequences dialog box.
2. Select the sequence you want to edit, and then click Edit Sequence to open the Edit Batch Sequence dialog box.
3. To add additional commands to the sequence, click the Select Commands button to open the Edit Sequence dialog box:

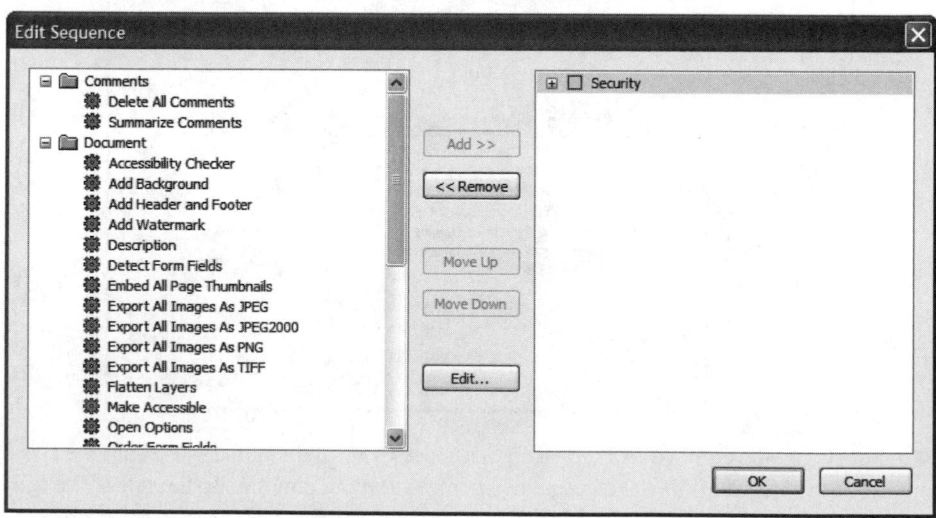

4. In the Edit Sequence dialog box, you can modify the sequence as follows:
   - To add a command to the sequence, in the left window, select the command, and then click the Add button.
   - To remove a command from the sequence, in the right window, select the command, and then click the Remove button.
   - To modify the order in which Acrobat executes multiple commands in the batch sequence, select a command in the right window and click the Move Up button or Move Down button to change the order in which the commands execute.
   - To edit a command, select the command, and then click the Edit button to open the applicable dialog box for the command. For example, if you add the Execute JavaScript command to a batch sequence, clicking the Edit button opens the JavaScript Editor dialog box, enabling you to write the script to be executed when the batch sequence runs.
5. Click OK to close the Edit Sequence dialog box and revert to the Edit Batch Sequence dialog box, which reflects the changes made when you edited the sequence:

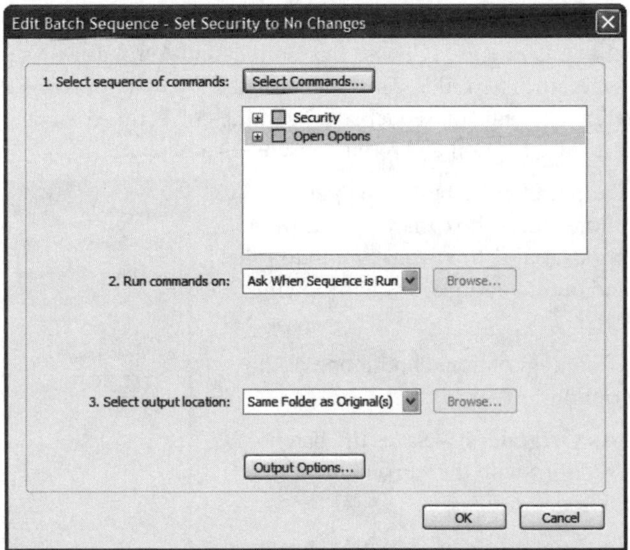

6. Click the Run Commands On drop-down arrow and choose one of the following:
   - **Selected Files** Choose this option, and the Browse button becomes active. Click the button and choose the files on which you want the sequence to be executed.
   - **Selected Folder** Choose this option, and the Browse button and Source File Options button become available. Click the Browse button and choose the folder on which you want the batch sequence commands executed, or click the Source File Options button to open the Source File Options dialog box, which is a list of file types supported by Acrobat. By default, all file types are selected and will be processed unless you deselect a file type by clicking its check box.

- **Ask When Sequence Is Run** Choose this option (the default), and a dialog box appears when the sequence runs, prompting you to select the files on which to execute the commands.
- **Files Open In Acrobat** Choose this option, and when this batch sequence is executed, it runs on files currently open in Acrobat.

7. Click the Select Output Location drop-down arrow and choose one of the following options:
   - **Specific Folder** Choose this option to specify the folder in which the modified documents are stored. After you choose this option, the Browse button becomes active. Click it and choose the folder in which to save the output files.
   - **Ask When Sequence Is Run** Choose this option, and Acrobat prompts you for a folder to save the files in when the sequence executes.
   - **Same Folder As Original(s)** Choose this option (the default), and Acrobat saves the processed files with the same name(s) as the original(s) in the same folder. Note, if you choose this option, and then choose the same output folder as the originals, Acrobat prompts you for a new filename as each file is processed, so as not to overwrite the original file(s).
   - **Don't Save Changes** Choose this option, and Acrobat won't save the changes or output the processed files. This option enables you to test the batch process. After you ascertain the batch sequence is working correctly, you can choose a different output location option and rerun the sequence.
8. Click the Output Options button to open the Output Options dialog box, shown next. In the Output Options dialog box, you can modify the filename and output options, as the following steps describe.

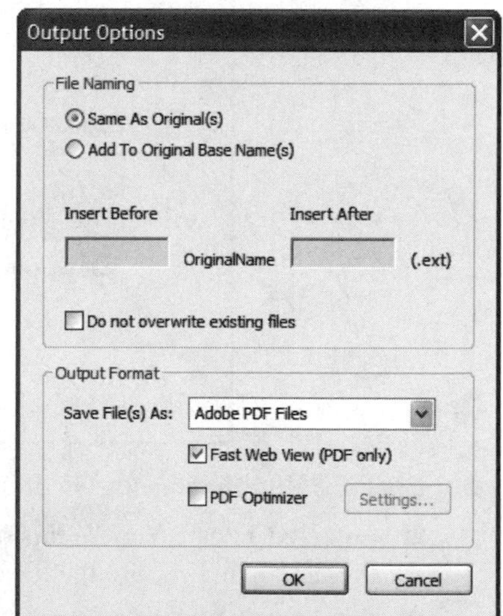

9. In the File Naming section, choose one of the following options:
   - **Same As Original(s)** Saves the batch processed files with the same name as the original document.
   - **Add To Original Base Name(s)** Changes the original base filename. When you select this option, the Insert Before and Insert After fields become available, which enables you to add a prefix or suffix to the filename of the processed files.
   - **Do Not Overwrite Existing Files** Prevents Acrobat from overwriting any files with the same name as those being processed.
10. In the Output Format section, click the Save File(s) As drop-down arrow and choose to save the processed files in one of the following formats: Adobe PDF Files, Encapsulated

PostScript, HTML 3.2, HTML 4.01 with CSS 1.0, JPEG, JPEG 2000, Microsoft Word Document, PDF/A, PDF/X, PNG, PostScript, Rich Text Format, Text (Accessible), Text (Plain), TIFF, or XML 1.0.

11. If you save the files in PDF format, accept the default Fast Web View (PDF Only) option to optimize the files for Internet viewing. This nets the same results as saving files using the Save As command.
12. Choose the PDF Optimizer option, and all files processed with this batch sequence run through the PDF Optimizer. If you choose the PDF Optimizer option, the Settings button becomes available. Click the button to configure the PDF Optimizer for the batch sequence you're editing.
13. Click OK to close the Output Options dialog box, click OK to close the Edit Sequence dialog box, and then click OK to exit the Edit Batch Sequence dialog box and return to the Batch Sequences dialog box.
14. Click Rename Sequence to open the Name dialog box. This step is optional, but if you're modifying a preset batch sequence, a good idea is to give the modified sequence a new name. Otherwise, you won't have access to the default preset.
15. Enter a new name for the sequence, and then click OK.
16. Click Close to exit the Batch Sequences dialog box and apply the changes.

Note, you can also use the Batch Sequences dialog box to delete a sequence, rename a sequence, run a sequence, or create a new sequence—the topic of discussion in the next section.

Create a New Sequence

You can create a new sequence and tailor it for operations you perform frequently on your PDF documents. When you create a new sequence, you specify the commands run when the sequence executes, the order they run in, and how the processed files are saved. To create a new batch sequence, follow these steps:

1. Choose Advanced | Document Processing | Batch Processing to display the Batch Sequences dialog box.
2. Click the New Sequence button. Acrobat opens the Name Sequence dialog box.
3. Enter a name for the sequence and click OK to open the Edit Batch Sequence dialog box.
4. Click the Select Commands button to open the Edit Sequence dialog box.
5. From the left window, select each command you want to execute when the sequence is run, and then click the Add button. If the command has options, such as the Crop Pages command, you can set the options either by selecting the command name in the right window and clicking the Edit button, or by double-clicking the command. Remember, when you create a sequence with multiple commands, you can use the Move Up and Move Down buttons to change the order in which the commands are executed.
6. Click OK to close the Edit Sequence dialog box, and then follow Steps 6 through 11 in the preceding section to specify how and where the files are saved.

After you create a new batch sequence, it's displayed in the list in the Batch Sequences dialog box. To run the new batch sequence, choose Advanced | Batch Processing, and then select the name of the custom batch sequence from the list.

Create an Index

To create an index of PDF documents, use the Catalog command. You can create an index of PDF files stored in one folder or several folders. When you create an index from a folder, Acrobat includes all PDF files located in the specified main folder, plus all PDF files located within subfolders of the main folder. You can specify which subfolders to add or remove from the catalog, as well as specify certain words you want to exclude from the index. Create as many indexes as you need to organize specific documents. For example, you can keep corporate documents in one index, personal documents in another, and research information downloaded from the Internet in yet another one. The long and the short of it is this: you can use this powerful tool to create custom PDF indexes to suit your specific needs.

Prepare the Documents

Before you can create the PDF index, you need to prepare the documents you want to include in the index. When you create an index, Acrobat creates a PDX (index definition) file and IDX files in the same folder as the documents. To prepare your documents for inclusion in a PDF index, follow these steps:

1. Create a folder in which to store the PDF documents you want to index. If you create an index to be shared cross-platform, choose a folder name with no more than eight characters and no spaces. Also, refrain from including any nonstandard characters, such as $, %, ^, &, *, £, $, ", or !.
2. Locate the PDF documents you want to index and move them into the folder that will become the index folder. If desired, break the index folder into subfolders to keep subgenres of the index separated. Be advised, though, that deeply nested folders may adversely affect the performance of the index. If you have deeply nested folders with pathnames longer than 256 characters, you'll also get unexpected results. Moving the PDF files to their own index folder is optional, but this is an excellent way to keep track of related PDF files. You can create an index using any folder as the root, and Acrobat will index all PDF files in the subfolders you specify.
3. After you add the PDF documents to the index folder, you can begin the preparation process. Examine the documents in the folder and pay special attention to the following:
   - If you have an exceptionally long document in the index, consider breaking it down into several documents. For example, if you have a manual in the index, break the manual down into individual chapters or sections. This speeds the search process after you index the documents.
   - Rename any documents with long filenames. Long filenames may adversely affect the performance of the index when truncated. This is especially true if you share the

index cross-platform. Stick with the old tried-and-true DOS naming convention of eight letters, followed by the three-letter .pdf extension.

- Rename any documents with spaces by using DOS naming conventions. For example, empbnfts.pdf would be an acceptable alternative for Employee Benefits.pdf, while emp bnfts.pdf would not. If desired, you can always use an underscore to separate words or capitalize the first letter of the second word. For example: emp_bnft.pdf or empBnfts.pdf.
- Rename any documents that use ASCII characters 133 through 159, as an Acrobat index doesn't support these characters. (You can see the ACSII character table at *http://www.lookuptables.com.*)

4. If any of the documents need structure editing, perform the edits before renaming and adding the files to the index. If you change the document filename after creating cross-document links and other document structure, the links may not be functional. If a file needs extensive editing and you don't have the time, move the file to another folder. You can always perform the necessary edits, add it to the folder, and then rebuild the index.
5. After you create the index folder and modify filenames, you can modify the documents for optimal search performance by following the steps in the upcoming section.

Optimize PDFs for the Index

When you create a PDF index, the resulting index will be more efficient if you pay a little attention to detail when preparing the documents that will be included in the index. Acrobat uses the contents of the Document Properties Description section when conducting a user query. For example, a user can search a document by author or keywords—metadata that you can add to the Description section of the Document Properties dialog box. Recipients of your PDF documents will be able to search more efficiently if you consider the following when preparing your files:

1. Optimize each document for space. This may seem like an arduous task if you have a large document collection to index. If you run a batch process on the documents and choose Fast Web View and PDF Optimizer in the Output Options dialog box, as outlined in the previous section "Edit A Batch Sequence," however, you can quickly optimize a large number of documents.
2. Audit the content of the Document Properties Description section of each document to be included in the index. This may prove to be a lengthy task with a large document collection. If Acrobat users have their search preferences configured to search by document information, they can search an index by Title, Subject, Author, or Keywords, the same information included in the Document Properties Description section. If you create documents with the intention of including them with an index, choose File | Document Properties to open the Document Properties dialog box. On the Description tab, in the Description section, include the necessary document

information, and then save the document. When adding this information, pay attention to the following:

- **Title** Make sure the document title accurately reflects the contents of the document.
- **Author** Include the author's name for each document. Remember, users of the document collection can specify a search by author. If you index a document for a large corporation, keep in mind that personnel frequently change. For this reason, use the department information in this field, rather than the author's actual name.
- **Subject** When you create an index with a variety of documents that contain different subject matter, be consistent with your naming conventions. For example, when indexing documents pertaining to employee benefits, don't use Employee Benefits for the subject of some documents and Benefit Package for others.
- **Keywords** Acrobat can also use keywords to select documents for a user's search query. Enter the keywords that pertain to each document you include in the collection. Again, be consistent with your naming conventions. If your organization uses a numbering system for memos and correspondence, you can include it in this field.

Build an Index

After preparing the documents, you're ready to build the document index by using the Catalog command. When you build the index, you specify a name for the index, as well as the folders and subfolders to include in the index. You can also add a description of the index, as well as modify the index options to exclude certain words from a search. To create a PDF index, do the following:

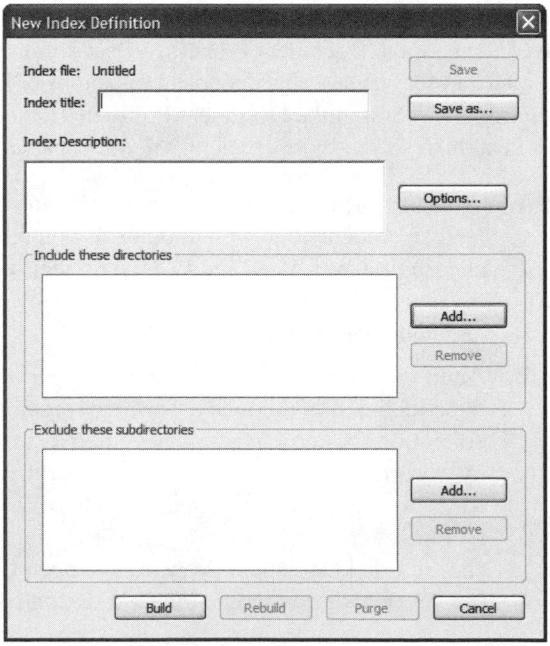

1. Choose Advanced | Document Processing | Full Text Index with Catalog to open the Catalog dialog box.
2. Click the New Index button to open the New Index Definition dialog box.
3. Enter a name in the Index Title field. People within your

organization use the index name when they decide whether to include the index in a search. Enter a descriptive name that accurately reflects the type of documents in the document collection (such as Human Resources). Remember, long names will be truncated on the list of available indexes. Stick with a short, two- or three-word index title that fits within the bounds of the Index Selection dialog box.

4. In the Index Description field, enter a description. This step is optional. However, adding a brief description of the type of documents in the index makes it easier for users to decide whether the index contains the information they're searching for before adding the index to the currently selected indexes. The information you enter in this field is available in the Index Information dialog box that appears after a user clicks the Info button from within the Index Selection dialog box.
5. Click the Options button to open the Options dialog box.

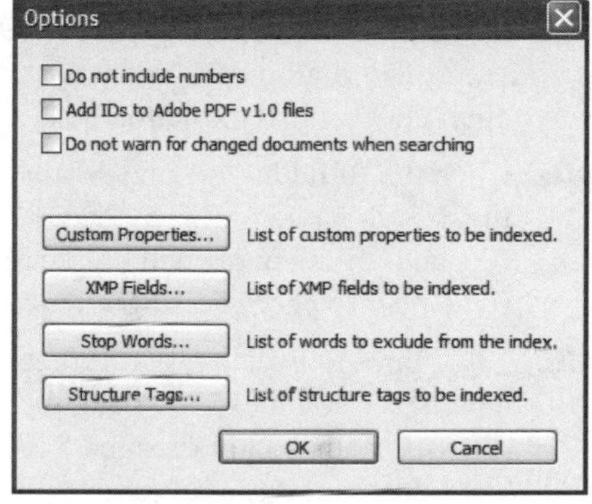

6. You can fine-tune your index by modifying the following parameters:
   - To exclude numbers from the search, click the Do Not Include Numbers check box.
   - Choose Add IDs to Adobe PDF v 1.0 files, if you have any.
   - Choose the Do Not Warn For Changed Documents When Searching check box to prevent Acrobat from displaying a warning dialog box when a document has been changed since being indexed.
   - Click the Custom Properties button to include custom properties relevant to the documents you're indexing. Custom properties are added to PDF documents by choosing File | Document Properties, and then adding the custom properties to the Custom section of the Document Properties dialog box. Custom properties are added to the Search These Additional Criteria list after the index is built. For example, if you want users to be able to search by document name, add the custom property Document_Name and choose String as the property type.
   - Click the XMP Fields button to open the XMP Fields dialog box. From within this dialog box, you can enter the names of the XMP fields you want to be searchable.

NOTE *You add information to a document's XMP fields by choosing File | Properties to open the Document Properties dialog box. In the Description section, click the Additional Metadata button to gain access to the XMP metadata fields. Never put sensitive or personal information into metadata fields or make them available to a search index.*

   - To exclude any words from a search, click the Stop Words button, enter your stop words one at a time in the Word field, and then click the Add button. To speed a search, eliminate articles, such as "a," "an," "the," and so on.

- To include tag names as searchable objects in an index, click the Structure Tags button, add the tag names one at a time in the Tag field, and then click the Add button. Remember, tags are elements used to define document structure.

7. After you modify the search index options, click OK to exit the Options dialog box and return to the New Index Definition dialog box.
8. In the Include These Directories section, click the Add button to open the Browse For Folder dialog box. Select the folder containing the documents you want to index, and then click OK to close the dialog box. Remember, you can add more than one folder of documents to an index as long as the additional folders are nested in the main index folder. Acrobat automatically indexes documents in each subfolder of the directory, unless you exclude certain subdirectories, as outlined in Step 9.
9. In the Exclude These Subdirectories section, click the Add button to open the Browse For Folder dialog box. Select the subfolders you want to exclude from the index, and click OK to close the dialog box. Repeat as needed to exclude additional subdirectories.
10. Click the Build button, and Acrobat displays the Save Index File dialog box. Accept the default name for the index you entered in the Index Title field or enter a different filename. If the index will be accessed from an intranet server or shared cross-platform, remember to choose an eight-letter filename with no spaces.
11. Click Save to have Acrobat Professional begin building the index. If you haven't entered a name in the Index Title field, the index is given the default name of untitled. Enter a different name, and then click Save to begin building the index. As Acrobat builds the index, the build progress and applicable comments are displayed in the Catalog dialog box. You can stop a build by clicking the Stop button. If you stop a build, you can still search the partial index, and then finish building it—just choose Advanced | Document Processing | Full Text Index with Catalog, and then choose Open Index. When the partially built index is open, click the Build button, and Acrobat scans the index to determine how many files were indexed, and then completes building the index.
12. Click Close to exit the Catalog dialog box. Your index is now ready for use.

After you create an index, you can add it to the list of indexes to search by following the steps outlined in Chapter 3.

Purge and Rebuild an Index

After you create an index, it becomes obsolete as you add and delete documents from the index folder. When you open an index with deleted documents, the indexed information about the original versions of modified documents and deleted documents remains in the index. When you try to select a moved or deleted document whose title still appears in the index, Acrobat displays a warning dialog box to that effect. You should periodically purge an index of modified documents and rebuild it to reflect the current content. To purge a PDF index, follow these steps:

1. Choose Advanced | Document Processing | Full Text Index with Catalog to open the Catalog dialog box, shown previously.
2. Click the Open Index button to display the Open Index File dialog box.
3. Select the index you want to purge. Remember, the index is in the index root folder with a .pdx extension.
4. Click Open. The Index Definition dialog box appears.
5. Click the Purge button. Note, if you purge an index in a network situation, it's advisable to notify coworkers in advance, just in case they're searching the index when you intend to purge it.
6. After Acrobat completes the purge, repeat Steps 1 and 2 to reload the index.
7. Click the Rebuild button.
8. Click Close after the index is rebuilt.

TIP *You can specify the default options for each catalog you create by choosing Edit | Preferences to open the Preferences dialog box, and then choosing Catalog from the window on the left. The options enable you to modify the defaults for every index you create.*

Move an Index

You can use your operating system (OS) utilities to move an index to another folder, another hard drive, or another network server. When you relocate a PDF index, you need to move the index root folder, which contains the PDF documents, the index *PDX file, and all associated subfolders containing PDF documents in the index. This maintains the necessary links for the index to function properly. After moving an index, you need to load it again, as the previous section outlines.

Create and Manage an Embedded Index

A new feature to Acrobat 8.0 Professional is the capability to embed an index with a PDF document. Embedding an index in a long PDF document can reduce the amount of time it takes to search an index. A document with an embedded index is searched in the same manner as a PDF document without an embedded index.

Embed an Index in a PDF

A document with hundreds of pages is a perfect candidate for an embedded index. You can easily create and embed an index in a PDF document by following these steps:

1. Open the document in which you want to embed an index.
2. Choose Advanced | Document Processing | Manage Embedded Index.
3. Click Embed Index. Acrobat displays a dialog box explaining the process and prompts you to confirm.
4. Click OK. Acrobat creates the index and displays a confirmation message.
5. Click OK to exit the Manage Embedded Index dialog box.

Manage the Embedded Index

When you create an embedded index, Acrobat uses every page in the document to create the index. If, though, you delete pages from the document, the index will still refer to those pages. Conversely, if you add pages to the document, the index won't have a record of the text that appears on those pages. You may also find it necessary to remove an index. To manage an embedded index:

1. Choose Advanced | Document Processing | Manage Embedded Index.
2. Click Update Index. Acrobat updates the index and displays a confirmation message. Or, click Remove Index to remove the embedded index from the document.
3. Click OK.

Summary

In this chapter, you learned how to automate your work by using batch processing. You learned how to use the preset Acrobat batch sequences, how to edit them to suit your working situation, and how to create new batch sequences. You also discovered how to create a searchable index of PDF documents by using the Acrobat Professional Catalog command. And, you learned how to maintain indexes by purging and rebuilding them. The final topic of discussion showed you how to embed an index in a lengthy PDF, which decreases the amount of time it takes to search a document.

Part V

Appendixes

Appendix A Acrobat 8.0 Keyboard Shortcuts

If you use Acrobat frequently and find yourself doing the same tasks repeatedly, you can streamline your workflow by memorizing the keyboard shortcuts for the commands you use most frequently. You don't have to memorize every keyboard shortcut in one sitting—begin memorizing the shortcuts for the commands you use most often. Soon the shortcuts will become second nature and you can memorize additional shortcuts to become more proficient with Acrobat.

Tool-selection keyboard shortcuts are disabled by default when you install Acrobat. To enable keyboard shortcuts for tools, choose Edit | Preferences to open the Preferences dialog box. Click the General tab, and then enable the Use Single Key Accelerators To Access Tools option. After closing the dialog box, you'll be able to use any of the keyboard shortcuts in this appendix. Where you see an asterisk (*) following a tool description, you can toggle to the next tool in the group by pressing SHIFT and the keyboard shortcut. For example, press U to select the last used highlighting tool; press SHIFT-U - to select the next highlighting tool in the group.

Tool Selection

Tool	Windows	Macintosh
Article	A	A
Distance tool	B	B
Crop	C	C
Drawing tool last selected*	D	D
Form tool last selected (Professional only)*	F	F
Snapshot	G	G
Hand	H	H
Stamp	K	K
Attach File	J	J
Link	L	L
Movie (Professional only)*	M	M
Callout	P	P
Sticky Note	S	S
TouchUp* (however, Standard has only the TouchUp Text tool)	T	T
Highlight Text*	U	U
Select Tool	V	V

Tool	Windows	Macintosh
Select Object	R	R
Text Box	X	X
Text Edits Tool	E	E
Zoom In	Z	Z
Zoom Out	CTRL-Z	COMMAND-Z
Zoom In while working with another tool	CTRL-SPACEBAR, and then click inside document	COMMAND-SPACEBAR, and then click inside document
Zoom Out while working with another tool	CTRL-SHIFT-SPACEBAR, and then click inside document	COMMAND-SHIFT-SPACEBAR, and then click inside document
Temporarily select Hand	SPACEBAR	SPACEBAR

Navigation

Desired Navigation	Windows	Macintosh
Previous Screen View	PAGE UP	PAGE UP
Next Screen View	PAGE DOWN	PAGE DOWN
First Document Page	HOME	HOME
Last Document Page	END	END
Previous Page	LEFT ARROW	LEFT ARROW
Next Page	RIGHT ARROW	RIGHT ARROW
Scroll up one line	UP ARROW	UP ARROW
Scroll down one line	DOWN ARROW	DOWN ARROW
Show/Hide Full Screen View	CTRL-L	COMMAND-L
Escape Full Screen Mode	ESC	ESC
Go to Page command	CTRL-SHIFT-N	COMMAND-SHIFT-N
Go to previous view	ALT-LEFT ARROW	COMMAND-LEFT ARROW
Go to next view	ALT-RIGHT ARROW	COMMAND-RIGHT ARROW
Go to Previous document	ALT-SHIFT-LEFT ARROW	OPTION-SHIFT-LEFT ARROW
Go to Next dcoument	ALT-SHIFT-RIGHT ARROW	OPTION-SHIFT-RIGHT ARROW

Function Key

Desired Action	Windows	Macintosh
Complete Acrobat Help	F1	F1
Show/Hide Navigation pane	F4	F4
Spell check comments or form fields	F7	F7
Show/Hide Toolbars	F8	F8
Show/Hide Menu Bar	F9	F9
Open Context Menu	SHIFT-F10	CTRL-click
Navigate to Next Window (in cascade or tile mode)	CTRL-F6	n/a
Rename Selected Bookmark	F2	n/a

Document Editing

Desired Action	Windows	Macintosh
Select All	CTRL-A	COMMAND-A
Copy	CTRL-C	COMMAND-C
Zoom To Command	CTRL-Y	COMMAND-Y
Open Document	CTRL-O	COMMAND-O
Print Command	CTRL-P	COMMAND-P
Exit Acrobat	CTRL-Q	COMMAND-Q
Show/Hide Rulers (Professional only)	CTRL-R	COMMAND-R
Save Document	CTRL-S	COMMAND-S
Paste	CTRL-V	COMMAND-V
Close Document	CTRL-W	COMMAND-W
Cut	CTRL-X	COMMAND-X
Undo	CTRL-Z	COMMAND-Z
Fit Page	CTRL-0	COMMAND-0
Actual Size	CTRL-1	COMMAND-1
Fit Width	CTRL-2	COMMAND-2
Fit Visible	CTRL-3	COMMAND-3
Zoom In	CTRL-+	COMMAND-+
Zoom Out	CTRL-–	COMMAND-–

Desired Action	Windows	Macintosh
Deselect All	SHIFT-CTRL-A	SHIFT-COMMAND-A
Delete Pages	SHIFT-CTRL-D	SHIFT-COMMAND-D
Insert Pages	SHIFT-CTRL-I	SHIFT-COMMAND-I
Page Setup (for printing)	SHIFT-CTRL-P	SHIFT-COMMAND-P
Save As	SHIFT-CTRL-S	SHIFT-COMMAND-S
Show/Hide Grid	CTRL-U	COMMAND-U
Snap to Grid	SHIFT-CTRL-U	SHIFT-COMMAND-U
Rotate Clockwise	SHIFT-CTRL++	SHIFT-COMMAND++
Rotate Counterclockwise	SHIFT-CTRL-–	SHIFT-COMMAND-–
Add New Bookmark	CTRL-B	COMMAND-B

Document Information and General Preferences

Desired Action	Windows	Macintosh
Open Document Properties dialog box	CTRL-D	COMMAND-D
Open Preferences dialog box	CTRL-K	COMMAND-K

Display Multiple Documents

Desired Action	Windows	Macintosh
Cascade documents	SHIFT-CTRL-J	SHIFT-COMMAND-J
Tile documents horizontally	SHIFT-CTRL-K	SHIFT-COMMAND-K
Tile documents vertically	SHIFT-CTRL-L	SHIFT-COMMAND-L

Miscellaneous

Desired Action	Windows	Macintosh
Create PDF From Web Page	SHIFT-CTRL-O	SHIFT-COMMAND-O
Automatically Scroll Document	SHIFT-CTRL-H	SHIFT-COMMAND-H
Read Out Loud Current Page	SHIFT-CTRL-V	SHIFT-COMMAND-V
Read Out Loud to End Of Document	SHIFT-CTRL-B	SHIFT-COMMAND-B
Pause Out Loud Reading	SHIFT-CTRL-C	SHIFT-COMMAND-C
Stop Out Loud Reading	SHIFT-CTRL-E	SHIFT-COMMAND-E

Appendix B Acrobat Resources

The Internet is a treasure trove of information. All you need to do is navigate to your favorite search engine and let your fingers do the walking. With the right keywords, you can find out almost anything about almost everything. Acrobat is no exception. In this section, you can find some Acrobat web resources. At press time, Acrobat 8.0 has just recently been released. As such, many of the sites listed may still have material pertaining to earlier versions of Acrobat. You can rest assured, though, that all the sites in this section are working with the latest release of Acrobat and are updating their resources for Acrobat 8.0. At press time, the information is accurate, the URLs have been verified, and the web sites are online. The Internet is in a constant state of flux, however, so some of the URLs may have changed or a resource may have gone by the wayside by the time you read this.

Adobe Resources

The Adobe web site features a wealth of information about Adobe Acrobat and the other products Adobe distributes. The following sections list individual pages in the Adobe web site that may be of interest to Acrobat users.

The Adobe Web Site (http://www.adobe.com)

This is the gateway to the Adobe web site. Here you can find links to all Adobe products, including Acrobat. You can use the Adobe search engine to find specific information about Acrobat and other products. The Adobe web site features technical support sections for all its products.

Acrobat Reader Download Web Site (http://www.adobe.com/products/acrobat/readstep2.html)

If you distribute PDF documents from a web site, you can include a link to this web page where web site visitors can download a free copy of Adobe Reader 8.0.

Distributing Adobe Reader (http://www.adobe.com/products/acrobat/distribute.html)

This section of the Adobe web site has all the information you need to distribute the Adobe Reader via an internal web site (intranet), CD-ROM, or other media.

Third-Party Resources

The PDF format is tremendously popular—so popular, in fact, that a number of web sites are devoted to Acrobat tutorials, tips, and plug-ins. The web sites listed in the following sections are home to information about Acrobat PDF and products you can use when creating your PDF documents.

Sony Media Software (http://mediasoftware.sonypictures.com/)

If sound is a staple element in your PDF documents and other multimedia projects, you can find some sophisticated sound-editing software at this web site. Sony's *Sound Forge application* enables you to manipulate a sound and apply effects to it. You can use the software to record sounds directly into your PC, and then edit and mix them with other sounds. Sony ACID Music Studio and ACID Pro are software products you can use to create sound loops for your PDF documents. You can also use the Sony software to create soundtracks for Flash movies and videos that you composite with Apple QuickTime Pro or other video-editing software. If you embed movies in your PDF documents, you may also want to check out the sophisticated video-editing tools at Sony Media Software's web site. Unfortunately, the software is only for the Windows platform.

Planet PDF (http://www.planetpdf.com/)

At this web site you can find all manner of resources for Acrobat. Peruse its many tutorials, check out the latest PDF news, and browse through its store, which is chock-full of useful third-party PDF plug-ins. Check out its forums at *forum.planetpdf.com,* where you can exchange information and ideas with other Acrobat users.

activePDF (http://www.activepdf.com/)

At this web site, you can find a collection of server-based PDF products. The web site purveyors promise no licensing hassle, no per-user costs, and no per-document costs, which you find with many other plug-in products. You pay one price for each server on which you use its products. activePDF also features developer tools.

ARTS PDF (http://www.artspdf.com)

This web site features plug-ins you can use to check document links, split large documents for the web site of CD-ROM catalogs, copy links, and more. The company claims all its products are compatible with Acrobat 8.0.

Enfocus (http://www.enfocus.com)

This web site features third-party plug-ins for PDF creation and editing. Enfocus's *PitStop* software makes it possible to edit large volumes of PDF documents. This web site also features software that enables you to perform enhanced editing of a PDF document without having to modify the original document in its native application.

PDFzone.com (http://www.pdfzone.com)

Here's another web site that features a plethora of PDF information. Browse through its Tips section for useful PDF tips and tricks. And, check out the Discussions section, which features Acrobat e-mail discussion lists.

AcroTips.com (http://www.acrotips.com)

This PDF guru's web site is the premier place on the Internet for free Acrobat tips, tricks, articles, and downloads. The web master, Dave Wraight, is a most talented fellow. In addition to doing a thorough job as the technical editor of this book, Dave is also the editor for Planet PDF's Developer Learning Centers, a site to which he has contributed many articles and tips, and he is CEO of Office2PDF.com (see the next entry).

Office2PDF.com (http://www.office2pdf.com/)

This web site features a number of useful applications for use with Microsoft Word applications. These applications enable you to add features to a Word document before it's converted to PDF. For example, *Office2PDF Destinations* enables Word authors to insert named destinations into a Word document that are automatically converted to named destinations in the converted PDF document.

John Deubert's Acumen Training (http://www.acumentraining.com/index.html)

John Deubert is an Adobe Certified Trainer who has been a PDF instructor since 1996. His web site features Acrobat resources and information about the classes he teaches.

MicroType.com (http://www.microtype.com)

Shlomo Peret's web site is an excellent resource for FrameMaker users who author PDF documents in the application. Of special interest is the *24 Easy Ways to Improve Your PDFs with TimeSavers/Assistants*.

Index

Symbol

A

B

C

D

E

G

H

I

J

N

O

P

Q

R

T

U

V

W

X

Z